Apps and Services w

Second Edition

Build practical projects with Blazor, .NET MAUI, gRPC, GraphQL, and other enterprise technologies

Mark J. Price

BIRMINGHAM—MUMBAI

Apps and Services with .NET 8
Second Edition

Senior Publishing Product Manager: Suman Sen

Acquisition Editor – Peer Reviews: Tejas Mhasvekar

Project Editor: Janice Gonsalves

Content Development Editor: Shazeen Iqbal

Copy Editor: Safis Editing

Technical Editor: Karan Sonawane

Proofreader: Safis Editing

Indexer: Rekha Nair

Presentation Designer: Pranit Padwal

Developer Relations Marketing Executive: Priyadarshini Sharma

First published: November 2022
Second edition: December 2023

Production reference: 1051223

Published by Packt Publishing Ltd.
Grosvenor House
11 St Paul's Square
Birmingham
B3 1RB, UK.

ISBN 978-1-83763-713-3

www.packt.com

Contributors

About the author

Mark J. Price is a Microsoft Specialist: Programming in C# and Architecting Microsoft Azure Solutions, with over 20 years of experience. Since 1993, he has passed more than 80 Microsoft programming exams and specializes in preparing others to pass them. Between 2001 and 2003, Mark was employed to write official courseware for Microsoft in Redmond, USA. His team wrote the first training courses for C# while it was still an early alpha version. While with Microsoft, he taught "train-the-trainer" classes to get Microsoft Certified Trainers up-to-speed on C# and .NET. Mark has spent most of his career training a wide variety of students from 16-year-old apprentices to 70-year-old retirees, with the majority being professional developers. Mark holds a Computer Science BSc. Hons. degree.

Thank you to all my readers. Your support means I get to write these books and celebrate your successes.

Special thanks to the readers who give me actionable feedback via my GitHub repository, email, and interact with me and the book communities on Discord. You help make my books even better with every edition.

Extra special thanks to Troy, a reader who became a colleague and more importantly, a good friend.

About the reviewers

Troy Martin is a self-taught developer of over 10 years, focusing mainly on C# for the last several of those years. Deeply passionate about programming, he has over 20 certifications in various languages and game development engines. He is currently engaged in developing his first solo game development project and strives to help others achieve their own programming goals.

> *I'd like to thank my wonderful girlfriend, Haley, who has stood by me even through the worst of times; I love you, Penne!*
>
> *Also, my deepest thanks to Mark J. Price, the author himself, who has been a wonderful and incredibly informative friend throughout this process.*

Kieran Foot is a self-taught C# developer with a deep passion for learning new technologies and techniques. He is constantly exploring the latest developments in C#, with a particular focus on web technologies. As the lead software developer at ConnX Business Solutions, a small software company based in the UK, he has the opportunity to apply his knowledge in practice and assist others in acquiring new skills. He enjoys helping others and is an active member of the Packt community.

Learn more on Discord

To join the Discord community for this book – where you can share feedback, ask questions to the author, and learn about new releases – follow the QR code below:

https://packt.link/apps_and_services_dotnet8

Table of Contents

Chapter 14: Building Web User Interfaces Using ASP.NET Core   621

Chapter 15: Building Web Components Using Blazor   663

Epilogue   743

Index   749

Preface

There are programming books that are thousands of pages long that aim to be comprehensive references to the C# language, the .NET libraries, and app models like websites, services, and desktop and mobile apps.

This book is different. It is a step-by-step guide to learning various technologies for building apps and services with .NET. It is concise and aims to be a brisk, fun read that is packed with practical, hands-on walkthroughs of each topic. The breadth of the overarching narrative comes at the cost of some depth, but you will find many signposts to explore further if you wish.

In my experience, that hardest part of learning a new technology is getting started. Once I have had the most important key concepts explained and seen some practical code in action, I then feel comfortable going deeper by exploring the official documentation on my own. You can feel confident in experimenting on your own once you have seen how the basics work correctly.

This book is best for those who already know the fundamentals of C# and .NET.

If you already have experience with older versions of the C# language and .NET libraries, then I have covered what is new in C# 8 and .NET Core 3.1 and later in an online-only section at the end of *Chapter 1*, *Introducing Apps and Services with .NET*.

I will call out the most important aspects of app models and frameworks for building modern user interfaces and implementing services, so you can participate in conversations with colleagues about technology and architectural choices and get productive with their implementation fast.

Where to find the code solutions

You can download or clone solutions for the step-by-step guided tasks and exercises from the GitHub repository at the following link: https://github.com/markjprice/apps-services-net8.

If you don't know how, then I have provided instructions on how to do this at the end of *Chapter 1*, *Introducing Apps and Services with .NET*.

What this book covers

Introduction

Chapter 1, Introducing Apps and Services with .NET, is about setting up your development environment and using Visual Studio 2022, Visual Studio Code, or JetBrains Rider. You will also learn about some good places to look for help, and ways to contact me (the author of this book) to get help with an issue or give me feedback to improve the book. The online-only sections review the new features added to the language and libraries in modern C# and .NET, how to benchmark the performance of your code, and how to work with types for reflection and attributes, expression trees, and dynamically generating source code during the compilation process.

Data

Chapter 2, Managing Relational Data Using SQL Server, is about setting up SQL Server on Windows or in the Azure cloud using SQL Database. (An online-only section shows how to set SQL Server up in a Docker container on Windows, macOS, or Linux.) You will then set up an example database for a fictional organization named Northwind. You will learn how to read and write at a low level using ADO.NET libraries (`Microsoft.Data.SqlClient`) for maximum performance, and then by using the object-to-data-store mapping technology named **Dapper** for ease of development.

Chapter 3, Building Entity Models for SQL Server Using EF Core, is about using the higher-level object-to-data-store mapping technology named **Entity Framework Core** (**EF Core**). You will create class libraries to define an EF Core model to work with the Northwind database that you created in *Chapter 2*. These class libraries are then used in many of the subsequent chapters.

Chapter 4, Managing NoSQL Data Using Azure Cosmos DB, is about the cloud-native non-SQL data store Azure Cosmos DB. You will learn how to read and write using its native API. An online-only section also covers the more specialized graph-based Gremlin API.

Libraries

Chapter 5, Multitasking and Concurrency, shows how to allow multiple actions to occur at the same time to improve performance, scalability, and user productivity by using threads and tasks.

Chapter 6, Implementing Popular Third-Party Libraries, discusses the types that allow your code to perform common practical tasks, like formatting text and numbers using Humanizer, manipulating images with ImageSharp, logging with Serilog, mapping objects to other objects with AutoMapper, making unit test assertions with FluentAssertions, validating data with FluentValidation, and generating PDFs with QuestPDF.

Chapter 7, Handling Dates, Times, and Internationalization, covers the types that allow your code to perform common tasks like handling dates and times, time zones, and globalizing and localizing data and the user interface of an app for internationalization. To supplement the built-in date and time types, we look at the benefits of using the much better Noda Time third-party library.

Services

Chapter 8, Building and Securing Web Services Using Minimal APIs, introduces the simplest way to build web services using ASP.NET Core Minimal APIs. This avoids the need for controller classes. You will learn how to improve startup time and resources using native AOT publish. You will then learn how to protect and secure a web service using rate limiting, CORS, and authentication and authorization. You will explore ways to test a web service using the new HTTP editor in Visual Studio 2022 and the REST Client extension for Visual Studio Code. An online-only section introduces building services that quickly expose data models using **Open Data Protocol (OData)**.

Chapter 9, Caching, Queuing, and Resilient Background Services, introduces service architecture design, adding features to services that improve scalability and reliability like caching and queuing, how to handle transient problems, and how to implement long-running services by implementing background services.

Chapter 10, Building Serverless Nanoservices Using Azure Functions, introduces you to Azure Functions, which can be configured to only require server-side resources while they execute. They execute when they are triggered by an activity like a message sent to a queue, a file uploaded to storage, or at a regularly scheduled interval.

Chapter 11, Broadcasting Real-Time Communication Using SignalR, introduces you to SignalR, a technology that enables a developer to create a service that can have multiple clients and broadcast messages to all of them or a subset of them live in real time, for example, notification systems and dashboards that need instantly up-to-date information like stock prices.

Chapter 12, Combining Data Sources Using GraphQL, introduces building services that provide a simple single endpoint for exposing data from multiple sources to appear as a single combined source of data. You will use the ChilliCream GraphQL platform to implement the service, which includes Hot Chocolate. New in this edition is how to implement paging, filtering, sorting, and subscriptions.

Chapter 13, Building Efficient Microservices Using gRPC, introduces building microservices using the efficient gRPC standard. You will learn about the `.proto` file format for defining service contracts and the Protobuf binary format for message serialization. You will also learn how to enable web browsers to call gRPC services using gRPC JSON transcoding. New to this edition is how to improve the startup and memory footprint of a gRPC service with native AOT publish, handling custom data types including non-supported types like decimal, and implementing interceptors and handling faults.

Apps

Chapter 14, Building Web User Interfaces Using ASP.NET Core, is about building web user interfaces with ASP.NET Core MVC. You will learn Razor syntax, tag helpers, and Bootstrap for quick user interface prototyping.

Chapter 15, Building Web Components Using Blazor, is about how to build user interface components using the new unified full-stack hosting of Blazor introduced in .NET 8. Blazor components can now be individually configured to execute on the client- and server-side in the same project. For times when you need to interact with browser features like local storage, you will learn how to perform JavaScript interop. An optional online-only section, *Leveraging Open-Source Blazor Component Libraries*, introduces some popular open-source libraries of Blazor components.

Chapter 16, Building Mobile and Desktop Apps Using .NET MAUI, introduces you to building cross-platform mobile and desktop apps for Android, iOS, macOS, and Windows. You will learn the basics of XAML, which can be used to define the user interface for a graphical app. An online-only section, *Implementing Model-View-ViewModel for .NET MAUI*, covers best practice for architecting and implementing graphical apps by using Model-View-ViewModel. You will also see the benefits of using MVVM Toolkit and .NET MAUI Community Toolkit. Another online-only section, *Integrating .NET MAUI Apps with Blazor and Native Platforms*, covers building hybrid native and web apps that make the most of the operating system they run on. You will integrate native platform features like the system clipboard, filesystem, retrieve device and display information, and pop-up notifications. For desktop apps, you will add menus and manage windows.

Conclusion

Epilogue, describes your options for learning more about building apps and services with C# and .NET, and tools and skills you should learn to become a well-rounded professional .NET developer. An online-only section, *Introducing the Survey Project Challenge*, documents the product requirements for a survey/polling software solution that the reader can optionally attempt to implement and publish to a public GitHub repository to get feedback from the author and other readers.

Appendix, Answers to the Test Your Knowledge Questions, has the answers to the test questions at the end of each chapter.

You can read the appendix at the following link: `https://github.com/markjprice/apps-services-net8/blob/main/docs/B19587_Appendix.pdf`.

What you need for this book

You can develop and deploy C# and .NET apps and services using Visual Studio 2022, or Visual Studio Code and the command-line tools on most operating systems, including Windows, macOS, and many varieties of Linux. An operating system that supports Visual Studio Code and an internet connection is all you need to complete this book. If you prefer to use a third-party tool like JetBrains Rider, then you can.

Downloading the color images of this book

We also provide you with a PDF file that has color images of the screenshots and diagrams used in this book. The color images will help you better understand the changes in the output.

You can download this file from `https://packt.link/gbp/9781837637133`.

Conventions

In this book, you will find several text styles that distinguish between different kinds of information. Here are some examples of these styles and an explanation of their meaning.

CodeInText: Indicates code words in text, database table names, folder names, filenames, file extensions, pathnames, dummy URLs, user input, and Twitter handles. For example: "The Controllers, Models, and Views folders contain ASP.NET Core classes and the .cshtml files for execution on the server."

A block of code is set as follows:

```
// storing items at index positions
names[0] = "Kate";
names[1] = "Jack";
names[2] = "Rebecca";
names[3] = "Tom";
```

When we wish to draw your attention to a particular part of a code block, the relevant lines or items are highlighted:

```
// storing items at index positions
names[0] = "Kate";
names[1] = "Jack";
names[2] = "Rebecca";
names[3] = "Tom";
```

Any command-line input or output is written as follows:

```
dotnet new console
```

Bold: Indicates a new **term**, an important **word**, or words that you see on the screen, for example, in menus or dialog boxes, also appear in the text like this. For example: "Clicking on the **Next** button moves you to the next screen."

    Important notes and links to external sources of further reading appear in a box like this.

    Good Practice: Recommendations for how to program like an expert appear like this.

Get in touch

Feedback from our readers is always welcome.

General feedback: If you have questions about any aspect of this book, mention the book title in the subject of your message and email us at customercare@packtpub.com.

Errata: Although we have taken every care to ensure the accuracy of our content, mistakes do happen. If you have found a mistake in this book, we would be grateful if you would report this to us. Please visit, www.packtpub.com/support/errata, selecting your book, clicking on the **Errata Submission Form** link, and entering the details.

Piracy: If you come across any illegal copies of our works in any form on the Internet, we would be grateful if you would provide us with the location address or website name.

Please contact us at copyright@packt.com with a link to the material.

If you are interested in becoming an author: If there is a topic that you have expertise in and you are interested in either writing or contributing to a book, please visit authors.packtpub.com.

For more information about Packt, please visit packt.com

Share your thoughts

Once you've read *Apps and Services with .NET 8 - Second Edition*, we'd love to hear your thoughts! Scan the QR code below to go straight to the Amazon review page for this book and share your feedback.

https://packt.link/r/1-837-63713-X

Your review is important to us and the tech community and will help us make sure we're delivering excellent quality content.

Download a free PDF copy of this book

Thanks for purchasing this book!

Do you like to read on the go but are unable to carry your print books everywhere? Is your eBook purchase not compatible with the device of your choice?

Don't worry, now with every Packt book you get a DRM-free PDF version of that book at no cost.

Read anywhere, any place, on any device. Search, copy, and paste code from your favorite technical books directly into your application.

The perks don't stop there, you can get exclusive access to discounts, newsletters, and great free content in your inbox daily

Follow these simple steps to get the benefits:

1. Scan the QR code or visit the link below

https://packt.link/free-ebook/9781837637133

2. Submit your proof of purchase
3. That's it! We'll send your free PDF and other benefits to your email directly

1

Introducing Apps and Services with .NET

In this first chapter, the goals are setting up your development environment to use Visual Studio 2022 and Visual Studio Code and understanding your choices for building apps and services; we will review good places to look for help.

The GitHub repository for this book has solutions using full application projects for all code tasks:

```
https://github.com/markjprice/apps-services-net8/
```

After going to the GitHub repository, simply press the . (dot) key on your keyboard or change .com to .dev to change the repository into a live code editor based on Visual Studio Code using GitHub Codespaces.

Visual Studio Code in a web browser is great to run alongside your chosen code editor as you work through the book's coding tasks. You can compare your code to the solution code and easily copy and paste parts if needed.

Throughout this book, I use the term **modern .NET** to refer to .NET 8 and its predecessors like .NET 6, which come from .NET Core. I use the term **legacy .NET** to refer to .NET Framework, Mono, Xamarin, and .NET Standard. Modern .NET is a unification of those legacy platforms and standards.

This chapter covers the following topics:

- Introducing this book and its contents
- App and service technologies
- Setting up your development environment
- Exploring top-level programs, functions, and namespaces
- Making good use of the GitHub repository for this book
- Where to go for help

Introducing this book and its contents

This book caters to two audiences:

- Readers who have completed my book for beginners, *C# 12 and .NET 8 – Modern Cross-Platform Development Fundamentals*, and now want to take their learning further.
- Readers who already have basic skills and knowledge about C# and .NET and want to learn practical skills and knowledge to build real-world applications and services.

Companion books to continue your learning journey

This book is the second of three books in a trilogy that continues your learning journey through .NET 8:

1. The first book covers the fundamentals of the C# language, the .NET libraries, and ASP.NET Core for web development. It is designed to be read linearly because skills and knowledge from earlier chapters build up and are needed to understand later chapters.

2. This second book covers more specialized topics like internationalization and popular third-party packages including Serilog and NodaTime. You will learn how to build native AOT-compiled services with ASP.NET Core Minimal APIs and how to improve performance, scalability, and reliability using caching, queues, and background services. You will implement more services using GraphQL, gRPC, SignalR, and Azure Functions. Finally, you will learn how to build graphical user interfaces for websites, desktop, and mobile apps with Blazor and .NET MAUI.

3. The third book covers important tools and skills that a professional .NET developer should have. These include design patterns and solution architecture, debugging, memory analysis, all the important types of testing whether unit, performance, or web and mobile, and then hosting and deployment topics like Docker and Azure Pipelines. Finally, we look at how to prepare for an interview to get the .NET developer career that you want.

A summary of the .NET 8 trilogy and their most important topics is shown in *Figure 1.1*:

- **C# language**, including new C# 12 features, object-oriented programming, debugging, and unit testing.
- **.NET libraries**, including numbers, text, regular expressions, collections, file I/O, and data with EF Core and SQLite.
- **Websites and web services** with ASP.NET Core and Blazor.

- **More libraries**: Internationalization, multitasking, and third-party packages.
- **More data**: SQL Server and Cosmos DB.
- **More services**: Caching, Queuing, Minimal API, GraphQL, gRPC, SignalR, and Azure Functions.
- **More user interfaces**: ASP.NET Core MVC, Blazor, and .NET MAUI.

- **Tools**: IDEs, debugging, memory analysis, and AI assistants.
- **Testing**: Unit, integration, performance, system, and web, including DI and IoC.
- **Design**: Patterns and architecture.
- **Deploy**: CI/CD, Azure hosting and deployment pipelines and automation.
- **Career**: Interview preparation.

Figure 1.1: Companion books for learning C# 12 and .NET 8

Tools and Skills for .NET 8 Pros is planned to be published in the first half of 2024. Look out for it in your favorite bookstore and complete your .NET 8 trilogy.

We provide you with a PDF file that has color images of the screenshots and diagrams used in this book. You can download this file from `https://packt.link/gbp/9781837637133`.

What you will learn in this book

After this first chapter, this book can be divided into four parts:

1. **Managing data:** How to store and manage data locally and in the cloud with SQL Server and Azure Cosmos DB. Later chapters use the SQL Server database and entity models that you will create at the end of *Chapter 3, Building Entity Models for SQL Server Using EF Core*. The chapter about Cosmos DB uses the SQL API, and there is an online-only chapter about Gremlin, which is a graph API.

2. **Specialized libraries:** Dates, times, and internationalization; improving performance with threads and tasks; and third-party libraries for image handling, data validation rules, and so on. These chapters can be treated like a cookbook of recipes. If you are not interested in any topic, you can skip it, and you can read them in any order.

3. **Service technologies:** How to build and secure services with ASP.NET Core Web API Minimal APIs, GraphQL, gRPC, SignalR, and Azure Functions. To improve service scalability and reliability we cover queues, caching, and event scheduling. There is also an online-only chapter about OData services.

4. **User interface technologies:** How to build user interfaces with ASP.NET Core, Blazor, and .NET MAUI.

My learning philosophy

Most people learn complex topics best by imitation and repetition rather than reading a detailed explanation of the theory; therefore, I will not overload you with detailed explanations of every step throughout this book. The idea is to get you to write some code and see it run.

You don't need to know all the nitty-gritty details immediately. That will be something that comes with time as you build your own apps and go beyond what any book can teach you.

Fixing my mistakes

In the words of Samuel Johnson, author of the English dictionary in 1755, I have committed *"a few wild blunders, and risible absurdities, from which no work of such multiplicity is free."* I take sole responsibility for these and hope you appreciate the challenge of my attempt to lash the wind by writing this book about rapidly evolving technologies like C# and .NET, and the apps and services that you can build with them.

 If you have an issue with something in this book, then please contact me before resorting to a negative review on Amazon. Authors cannot respond to Amazon reviews so I cannot contact you to resolve the problem. I want to help you to get the best from my book, and I want to listen to your feedback and do better in the next edition. Please email me (my email address can be found in the GitHub repository for the book), chat with me in the Discord channel for the book (`https://packt.link/apps_and_services_dotnet8`), or raise an issue at the following link: `https://github.com/markjprice/apps-services-net8/issues`.

Finding the solution code on GitHub

The solution code in the GitHub repository for this book for all code editors is available at the following link: `https://github.com/markjprice/apps-services-net8/tree/main/code`.

Project naming and port numbering conventions

If you complete all the coding tasks in this book, then you will end up with dozens of projects. Many of those will be websites and services that require port numbers for hosting on the `localhost` domain.

With large, complex solutions, it can be difficult to navigate the entire code. So, a good reason to structure your projects well is to make it easier to find components. It is good to have an overall name for your solution that reflects the application or solution.

In the 1990s, Microsoft registered **Northwind** as a fictional company name for use in database and code samples. It was first used as the sample database for their Access product and then also used in SQL Server. We will build multiple projects for this fictional company, so we will use the name `Northwind` as a prefix for all the project names.

 Good Practice: There are many ways to structure and name projects and solutions, for example, using a folder hierarchy as well as a naming convention. If you work in a team, make sure you know how your team does it.

It is good to have a naming convention for your projects in a solution so that any developer can tell what each one does instantly. A common choice is to use the type of project, for example, class library, console app, website, and so on, as shown in *Table 1.1*:

Name	Description
`Northwind.Common`	A class library project for common types like interfaces, enums, classes, records, and structs, used across multiple projects.
`Northwind.Common.EntityModels`	A class library project for common EF Core entity models. Entity models are often used on both the server and client side, so it is best to separate dependencies on specific database providers.
`Northwind.Common.DataContext`	A class library project for the EF Core database context with dependencies on specific database providers.
`Northwind.Mvc`	An ASP.NET Core project for a complex website that uses the MVC pattern and can be more easily unit tested.
`Northwind.WebApi.Service`	An ASP.NET Core project for an HTTP API service. A good choice for integrating with websites because it can use any JavaScript library or Blazor to interact with the service.
`Northwind.WebApi.Client.Console`	A client to a web service. The last part of the name indicates that it is a console app.
`Northwind.gRPC.Service`	An ASP.NET Core project for a gRPC service.

`Northwind.gRPC.Client.Mvc`	A client to a gRPC service. The last part of the name indicates that it is an ASP.NET Core MVC website project.
`Northwind.BlazorWasm.Client`	An ASP.NET Core Blazor WebAssembly client-side project.
`Northwind.BlazorWasm.Server`	An ASP.NET Core Blazor WebAssembly server-side project.
`Northwind.BlazorWasm.Shared`	A class library shared between client- and server-side Blazor projects.

Table 1.1: Example naming conventions for common project types

To enable you to run any of these projects simultaneously, we must make sure that we do not configure duplicated port numbers. I have used the following convention:

```
https://localhost:5[chapternumber]1/
```

```
http://localhost:5[chapternumber]2/
```

For example, for the encrypted connection to the website built in *Chapter 14*, *Building Web User Interfaces Using ASP.NET Core*, I used port 5141, as shown in the following link:

```
https://localhost:5141/
```

Treating warnings as errors

By default, compiler warnings may appear if there are potential problems with your code when you first build a project, but they do not prevent compilation and they are hidden if you rebuild. Warnings are given for a reason, so ignoring warnings encourages poor development practices.

Some developers would prefer to be forced to fix warnings, so .NET provides a project setting to do this, as shown highlighted in the following markup:

```
<Project Sdk="Microsoft.NET.Sdk">

  <PropertyGroup>
    <OutputType>Exe</OutputType>
    <TargetFramework>net8.0</TargetFramework>
    <ImplicitUsings>enable</ImplicitUsings>
    <Nullable>enable</Nullable>
    <TreatWarningsAsErrors>true</TreatWarningsAsErrors>
  </PropertyGroup>
```

I have enabled the option to treat warnings as errors in (almost) all the solutions in the GitHub repository.

The exceptions are the gRPC projects. This is due to a combination of factors. In .NET 7 or later, the compiler will warn if you compile source files that contain only lowercase letters in the name of a type. For example, if you define a person class, as shown in the following code:

```
public class person
{
}
```

This compiler warning has been introduced so that a future version of C# can safely add a new keyword knowing it will not conflict with the name of a type that you have used because only C# keywords should contain only lowercase letters.

Unfortunately, the Google tools for generating C# source files from .proto files generate aliases for class names that only contain lowercase letters, as shown in the following code:

```
#region Designer generated code


using pb = global::Google.Protobuf;
```

If you treat warnings as errors, then the compiler complains and refuses to compile the source code, as shown in the following output:

```
Error CS8981 The type name 'pb' only contains lower-cased ascii characters.
Such names may become reserved for the language. Northwind.Grpc.Service C:\
apps-services-net8\Chapter14\Northwind.Grpc.Service\obj\Debug\net8.0\Protos\
Greet.cs
```

> **Good Practice:** Always treat warnings as errors in your .NET projects (except for gRPC projects until Google updates their code generation tools).

If you find that you get too many errors after enabling this, you can disable specific warnings by using the <WarningsNotAsErrors> element with a comma-separated list of warning codes, as shown in the following markup:

```
<WarningsNotAsErrors>0219,CS8981</WarningsNotAsErrors>
```

> **More Information:** You can learn more about controlling warnings as errors at the following link: https://learn.microsoft.com/en-us/dotnet/csharp/language-reference/compiler-options/errors-warnings#warningsaserrors-and-warningsnotaserrors.

App and service technologies

Microsoft calls platforms for building applications and services **app models** or **workloads**.

Understanding .NET

.NET, .NET Core, .NET Framework, and Xamarin are related and overlapping platforms for developers used to build applications and services. If you are not familiar with the history of .NET, then I will point you to each of these .NET concepts at the following link, which is from the *C# 12 and .NET 8 – Modern Cross-Platform Development Fundamentals* book:

https://github.com/markjprice/cs12dotnet8/blob/main/docs/ch01-dotnet-history.md

Building websites and apps using ASP.NET Core

Websites are made up of multiple web pages loaded statically from the filesystem or generated dynamically by a server-side technology such as ASP.NET Core. A web browser makes GET requests using **Unique Resource Locators** (**URLs**), which identify each page and can manipulate data stored on the server using POST, PUT, and DELETE requests.

With many websites, the web browser is treated as a presentation layer, with almost all the processing performed on the server side. Some JavaScript might be used on the client side to implement some presentation features, such as carousels, or to perform data validation.

ASP.NET Core provides multiple technologies for building websites:

- **ASP.NET Core Razor Pages** can dynamically generate HTML for simple websites.
- **ASP.NET Core MVC** is an implementation of the **Model-View-Controller** (**MVC**) design pattern, which is popular for developing complex websites. You will learn about using it to build user interfaces in *Chapter 14, Building Web User Interfaces Using ASP.NET Core*.
- **Razor class libraries** provide a way to package reusable functionality for ASP.NET Core projects including user interface components.
- **Blazor** lets you build user interface components using C# and .NET and then run them in a web browser or embedded web component instead of a JavaScript-based UI framework like Angular, React, and Vue. You will learn about Blazor in detail in *Chapter 15, Building Web Components Using Blazor*, and an online-only section titled *Leveraging Open-Source Blazor Component Libraries*.

 Blazor is not just for building websites; it can also be used to create hybrid mobile and desktop apps when combined with .NET MAUI.

This book assumes that you are already familiar with the fundamentals of ASP.NET Core development, so although the book reviews the basics, it quickly moves on to intermediate topics.

Building web and other services

There are no formal definitions, but services are sometimes described based on their complexity:

- **Service**: All functionality needed by a client app in one monolithic service.
- **Microservice**: Multiple services that each focus on a smaller set of functionalities. The guiding principle for what the boundary of functionality should be for a microservice is that each microservice should own its own data. Only that microservice should read/write to that data. If you have a data store that multiple services access, then they are not microservices.
- **Nanoservice**: A single function provided as a service. Unlike services and microservices that are hosted 24/7/365, nanoservices are often inactive until called upon to reduce resources and costs. For this reason, they are also known as serverless services.

Although the theory of microservices and serverless services has made them a fashionable choice over the past decade or so, monolithic services have recently had a resurgence in popularity as developers have found the reality of microservices does not always match the theory.

You will learn how to build ASP.NET Core Web API and Minimal API web services that use HTTP as the underlying communication technology and follow the design principles of Roy Field's REST architecture. You will also learn how to build services using web and other technologies that extend basic web APIs, including:

- **gRPC**: For building highly efficient and performant microservices with support for almost any platform.
- **SignalR**: For implementing real-time communications between components.
- **GraphQL**: For letting the client control what data is retrieved across multiple data sources. Although GraphQL can use HTTP, it does not have to, and it does not follow the web design principles defined by Roy Field in his dissertation about REST APIs.
- **Azure Functions**: For hosting serverless nanoservices in the cloud.
- **OData**: For easily wrapping EF Core and other data models as a web service. This is an online-only section.

Windows Communication Foundation

In 2006, Microsoft released .NET Framework 3.0 with some major new frameworks, one of which was **Windows Communication Foundation (WCF)**. It abstracted the business logic implementation of a service from the communication technology infrastructure so that you could easily switch to an alternative in the future or even have multiple mechanisms to communicate with the service.

WCF heavily uses XML configuration to declaratively define endpoints, including their address, binding, and contract. This is known as the ABCs of WCF endpoints. Once you understand how to do this, WCF is a powerful yet flexible technology.

Microsoft decided not to officially port WCF to modern .NET, but there is a community-owned OSS project named **CoreWCF** managed by the .NET Foundation. If you need to migrate an existing service from .NET Framework to modern .NET or build a client to a WCF service, then you can use CoreWCF. Be aware that it can never be a full port since parts of WCF are Windows-specific.

Technologies like WCF allow for the building of distributed applications. A client application can make **remote procedure calls (RPCs)** to a server application. Instead of using a port of WCF to do this, we should use an alternative RPC technology like gRPC, which is covered in this book.

 More Information: You can learn more about CoreWCF in its GitHub repository found at the following link: https://github.com/CoreWCF/CoreWCF. You can read the announcement about client support for calling WCF or CoreWCF with System.ServiceModel 6.0 at the following link: https://devblogs.microsoft.com/dotnet/wcf-client-60-has-been-released/.

Common service principles

One of the most important service architecture principles is to make method calls chunky instead of chatty. In other words, try to bundle all the data needed for an operation in a single call, rather than requiring multiple calls to transmit all that information. This is because the overhead of a remote call is one of the biggest negative effects of services. This is also why having smaller and smaller services can hugely negatively impact a solution architecture.

Summary of choices for services

Each service technology has its pros and cons based on its feature support, as shown in *Table 1.2*:

Feature	Web API	OData	GraphQL	gRPC	SignalR
Clients can request just the data they need	No	Yes	Yes	No	No
Minimum HTTP version	1.1	1.1	1.1	2.0	1.1
Browser support	Yes	Yes	Yes	No	Yes
Data format	XML, JSON	XML, JSON	GraphQL (JSONish)	Binary	Varies
Service documentation	Swagger	Swagger	No	No	No
Code generation	Third-party	Third-party	Third-party	Google	Microsoft
Caching	Easy	Easy	Hard	Hard	Hard

Table 1.2: Pros and cons of common service technologies

Use these recommendations for various scenarios as guidance, as shown in *Table 1.3*:

Scenario	Recommendation
Public service	HTTP/1.1-based services are best for services that need to be publicly accessible, especially if they need to be called from a browser or mobile device.
Public data service	OData and GraphQL are both good choices for exposing complex hierarchical datasets that could come from different data stores. OData is designed and supported by Microsoft via official .NET packages. GraphQL is designed by Facebook and supported by third-party packages.
Service-to-service	gRPC is designed for low-latency and high-throughput communication. gRPC is great for lightweight internal microservices where efficiency is critical.
Point-to-point real-time communication	gRPC has excellent support for bidirectional streaming. gRPC services can push messages in real time without polling. SignalR is designed for real-time communication of many kinds, so it tends to be easier to implement than gRPC although it is less efficient.

Broadcast real-time communication	SignalR has great support for broadcasting real-time communication to many clients.
Polyglot environment	gRPC tooling supports all popular development languages, making gRPC a good choice for multi-language and platform environments.
Network-bandwidth-constrained environment	gRPC messages are serialized with Protobuf, a lightweight message format. A gRPC message is always smaller than an equivalent JSON message.
Serverless nanoservice	Azure Functions do not need to be hosted 24/7 so they are a good choice for nanoservices that usually do not need to be running constantly. **Amazon Web Services (AWS)** Lambdas are an alternative.

Table 1.3: Service scenarios and the recommended implementation technology

Building Windows-only apps

Technologies for building Windows-only apps, primarily for desktop, include:

- **Windows Forms**, 2002
- **Windows Presentation Foundation (WPF)**, 2006
- **Windows Store**, 2012
- **Universal Windows Platform (UWP)**, 2015
- **Windows App SDK** (formerly **WinUI 3** and **Project Reunion**), 2021

Understanding legacy Windows application platforms

With the Microsoft Windows 1.0 release in 1985, the only way to create Windows applications was to use the C language and call functions in three core DLLs named KERNEL, USER, and GDI. Once Windows became 32-bit with Windows 95, the DLLs were suffixed with 32 and became known as **Win32 API**.

In 1991, Microsoft introduced Visual Basic, which provided developers with a visual, drag-and-drop-from-a-toolbox-of-controls way to build the user interface for Windows applications. It was immensely popular, and the Visual Basic runtime is still distributed as part of Windows 11 today.

With the first version of C# and .NET Framework released in 2002, Microsoft provided technology for building Windows desktop applications named **Windows Forms**. The equivalent at the time for web development was named **Web Forms**, hence the complementary names. The code could be written in either Visual Basic or C# languages. Windows Forms had a similar drag-and-drop visual designer, although it generated C# or Visual Basic code to define the user interface, which can be difficult for humans to understand and edit directly.

In 2006, Microsoft released a more powerful technology for building Windows desktop applications, named **Windows Presentation Foundation (WPF)**, as a key component of .NET Framework 3.0 alongside **WCF** and Windows **Workflow (WF)**.

Although a WPF app can be created by writing only C# statements, it can also use **eXtensible Application Markup Language (XAML)** to specify its user interface, which is easy for both humans and code to understand. Visual Studio 2022 is partially built with WPF.

In 2012, Microsoft released Windows 8 with its Windows Store apps that run in a protected sandbox.

In 2015, Microsoft released Windows 10 with an updated Windows Store app concept named **Universal Windows Platform** (**UWP**). UWP apps can be built using C++ and DirectX UI, JavaScript and HTML, or C# using a custom fork of modern .NET that is not cross-platform but provides full access to the underlying WinRT APIs.

UWP apps can only execute on the Windows 10 or Windows 11 platforms, not earlier versions of Windows, but UWP apps can run on Xbox and Windows Mixed Reality headsets with motion controllers.

Many Windows developers rejected Windows Store and UWP apps because they have limited access to the underlying system. Microsoft recently created **Project Reunion** and **WinUI 3**, which work together to allow Windows developers to bring some of the benefits of modern Windows development to their existing WPF apps and allow them to have the same benefits and system integrations that UWP apps have. This initiative is now known as **Windows App SDK**.

 More Information: This book does not cover Windows App SDK because it is not cross-platform. If you would like to learn more, you can start at the following link: `https://learn.microsoft.com/en-us/windows/apps/windows-app-sdk/`.

Understanding modern .NET support for legacy Windows platforms

The on-disk size of the .NET SDKs for Linux and macOS is about 330 MB. The on-disk size of the .NET SDK for Windows is about 440 MB. This is because it includes **.NET Desktop Runtime**, which allows the legacy Windows application platforms Windows Forms and WPF to be run on modern .NET.

There are many enterprise applications built using Windows Forms and WPF that need to be maintained or enhanced with new features, but until recently they were stuck on .NET Framework, which is now a legacy platform. With modern .NET and its .NET Desktop Runtime, these apps can now use the full modern capabilities of .NET. Windows desktop app developers can also optionally install the Windows Compatibility Pack. You can learn more about this at the following link: `https://learn.microsoft.com/en-us/dotnet/core/porting/windows-compat-pack`.

Building cross-platform mobile and desktop apps

There are two major mobile platforms, Apple's iOS and Google's Android, each with its own programming languages and platform APIs. There are also two major desktop platforms, Apple's macOS and Microsoft's Windows, each with its own programming languages and platform APIs, as shown in the following list:

- **iOS:** Objective-C or Swift and UIkit
- **Android:** Java or Kotlin and Android API
- **macOS:** Objective-C or Swift and AppKit or Catalyst
- **Windows:** C, C++, or many other languages and Win32 API or Windows App SDK

Cross-platform mobile and desktop apps can be built once for the **.NET Multi-platform App UI** (**MAUI**) platform and then can run on many mobile and desktop platforms.

.NET MAUI makes it easy to develop those apps by sharing user interface components as well as business logic; they can target the same .NET APIs as used by console apps, websites, and web services.

The apps can exist standalone, but they usually call services to provide an experience that spans all your computing devices, from servers and laptops to phones and gaming systems.

.NET MAUI supports existing MVVM and XAML patterns. The team also plans to add support in the future for **Model-View-Update (MVU)** with C#, which is like Apple's Swift UI. MVU using Comet is still only a proof of concept. It is not as mature or well supported as Swift UI. I will not cover it in this book. You can read more about it at the following link: `https://github.com/dotnet/Comet`.

.NET MAUI alternatives

Before Microsoft created .NET MAUI, third parties created open-source initiatives to enable .NET developers to build cross-platform apps using XAML, named **Uno** and **Avalonia**.

Understanding the Uno platform

Uno is *"the first C# & XAML, free and open-source platform for creating true single-source, multi-platform applications,"* as stated on its own website at the following link: `https://platform.uno/`.

Developers can reuse 99% of the business logic and UI layer across native mobile, web, and desktop.

The Uno platform uses the Xamarin native platform but not Xamarin.Forms. For WebAssembly, Uno uses the mono-wasm runtime just like Blazor WebAssembly. For Linux, Uno uses Skia to draw the user interface on the canvas.

 A book to read to learn about the Uno platform can be found at the following link: `https://www.packtpub.com/product/creating-cross-platform-c-applications-with-uno-platform/9781801078498`.

Understanding Avalonia

Avalonia *"is a cross-platform UI framework for .NET. It creates pixel-perfect, native apps"* and *"is supported on all major platforms."* Avalonia *"is the trusted UI framework for complex apps,"* as stated on its official website home page at the following link: `https://avaloniaui.net/`.

You can think of Avalonia as a spiritual successor to WPF. WPF, Silverlight, and UWP developers can continue to benefit from their years of pre-existing knowledge and skills.

It was used by JetBrains to modernize their legacy WPF-based tools and take them cross-platform. This means their C# code editor runs on Windows, macOS, and Linux.

The Avalonia extension for Visual Studio 2022 and deep integration with JetBrains Rider makes development easier and more productive.

Now that we've reviewed the theory about the apps and services technologies that can be used with .NET 8, let's get practical and see how you can set up your development environment.

Setting up your development environment

Before you start programming, you'll need a code editor for C#. Microsoft has a family of code editors and **Integrated Development Environments (IDEs)**, which include:

- Visual Studio 2022 for Windows
- Visual Studio Code for Windows, Mac, or Linux
- Visual Studio Code for the Web or GitHub Codespaces

Third parties have created their own C# code editors, for example, JetBrains Rider, which is available for Windows, Mac, or Linux but does have a license cost. JetBrains Rider is popular with more experienced .NET developers.

> **Warning!** Although JetBrains is a fantastic company with great products, both Rider and the ReSharper extension for Visual Studio are software, and all software has bugs and quirky behavior. For example, they might show errors like "Cannot resolve symbol" in your Razor Pages, Razor views, and Blazor components. Yet you can build and run those files because there is no actual problem. If you have installed the Unity Support plugin, then it will complain about boxing operations, which are a genuine problem for Unity game developers. But in this book we will not create any Unity projects so the boxing warnings do not apply.

In *Chapters 1* to *15*, you can use Visual Studio 2022 or cross-platform Visual Studio Code and JetBrains Rider to build all the apps and services. In *Chapter 16, Building Mobile and Desktop Apps Using .NET MAUI*; and its *online sections, Implementing Model-View-ViewModel for .NET MAUI* and *Integrating .NET MAUI Apps with Blazor and Native Platforms*, although you could use Visual Studio Code to build the mobile and desktop app, it is not easy. Visual Studio 2022 has better support for .NET MAUI than Visual Studio Code does (for now).

Choosing the appropriate tool and application type for learning

What is the best tool and application type for building apps and services with C# and .NET?

I want you to be free to choose any C# code editor or IDE to complete the coding tasks in this book, including Visual Studio Code, Visual Studio 2022, or even JetBrains Rider.

In this book, I give general instructions that work with all tools so you can use whichever tool you prefer.

Using Visual Studio 2022 for general development

Visual Studio 2022 can create most types of applications, including console apps, websites, web services, desktop, and mobile apps.

Although you can use Visual Studio 2022 with a .NET MAUI project to write a cross-platform mobile app, you still need macOS and Xcode to compile it.

Visual Studio 2022 only runs on Windows 10 version 1909 or later, or Windows Server 2016 or later, and only on 64-bit versions. Version 17.4 is the first version to support native Arm64.

Warning! Visual Studio 2022 for Mac does not officially support .NET 8 and it will reach end-of-life in August 2024. If you have been using Visual Studio 2022 for Mac then you should switch to Visual Studio Code for Mac, JetBrains Rider for Mac, or use Visual Studio 2022 for Windows in a virtual machine on your local computer or in the cloud using a technology like Microsoft Dev Box. The retirement announcement can be read here: `https://devblogs.microsoft.com/visualstudio/visual-studio-for-mac-retirement-announcement/`.

Using Visual Studio Code for cross-platform development

The most modern and lightweight code editor to choose from, and the only one from Microsoft that is cross-platform, is Visual Studio Code. It can run on all common operating systems, including Windows, macOS, and many varieties of Linux, including **Red Hat Enterprise Linux** (RHEL) and Ubuntu.

Visual Studio Code is a good choice for modern cross-platform development because it has an extensive and growing set of extensions to support many languages beyond C#.

Being cross-platform and lightweight, it can be installed on all platforms that your apps will be deployed to for quick bug fixes and so on. Choosing Visual Studio Code means a developer can use a cross-platform code editor to develop cross-platform apps.

Visual Studio Code has strong support for web development, although it currently has weak support for mobile and desktop development.

Visual Studio Code is supported on ARM processors, so you can develop on Apple Silicon computers and Raspberry Pi.

Visual Studio Code is by far the most popular integrated development environment, with over 73% of professional developers selecting it in the Stack Overflow 2023 survey that you can read at the following link: `https://survey.stackoverflow.co/2023/`.

Using GitHub Codespaces for development in the cloud

GitHub Codespaces is a fully configured development environment based on Visual Studio Code that can be spun up in an environment hosted in the cloud and accessed through any web browser. It supports Git repos, extensions, and a built-in command-line interface so you can edit, run, and test from any device.

More Information: You can learn more about GitHub Codespaces at the following link: `https://github.com/features/codespaces`.

What I used

To write and test the code for this book, I used the following hardware and software:

- Visual Studio 2022 for Windows on:

  - Windows 11 on the HP Spectre (Intel) laptop

- Visual Studio Code on:

  - macOS on the Apple Silicon Mac mini (M1) desktop
  - Windows 11 on the HP Spectre (Intel) laptop

- JetBrains Rider on:

  - Windows 11 on the HP Spectre (Intel) laptop
  - macOS on the Apple Silicon Mac mini (M1) desktop

I hope that you have access to a variety of hardware and software too because seeing the differences on various platforms deepens your understanding of development challenges, although any one of the above combinations is enough to learn how to build practical apps and websites.

 Getting Started: *Chapter 1* of the *C# 12 and .NET 8 – Modern Cross-Platform Development Fundamentals* book has online sections showing how to get started with multiple projects using various code editors like Visual Studio 2022, Visual Studio Code, or JetBrains Rider. You can read the sections at the following link: `https://github.com/markjprice/cs12dotnet8/blob/main/docs/code-editors/README.md`.

JetBrains Rider and its warnings about boxing

If you use JetBrains Rider and you have installed the Unity Support plugin, then it will complain a lot about boxing. A common scenario when boxing happens is when value types like `int` and `DateTime` are passed as positional arguments to `string` formats. This is a problem for Unity projects because they use a different memory garbage collector to the normal .NET runtime. For non-Unity projects, like all the projects in this book, you can ignore these boxing warnings because they are not relevant. You can read more about this Unity-specific issue at the following link: `https://docs.unity3d.com/Manual/performance-garbage-collection-best-practices.html#boxing`.

Deploying cross-platform

Your choice of code editor and operating system for development does not limit where your code gets deployed.

.NET 8 supports the following platforms for deployment:

- **Windows:** Windows 10 version 1607 or later. Windows 11 version 22000 or later. Windows Server 2012 R2 SP1 or later. Nano Server version 1809 or later.
- **Mac:** macOS Catalina version 10.15 or later and in the Rosetta 2 x64 emulator. Mac Catalyst 11.0 or later.

- **Linux:** Alpine Linux 3.17 or later. Debian 11 or later. Fedora 37 or later. openSUSE 15 or later. Oracle Linux 8 or later. **Red Hat Enterprise Linux (RHEL)** 8 or later. SUSE Enterprise Linux 12 SP2 or later. Ubuntu 20.04 or later.
- **Android:** API 21 or later.
- **iOS** and **tvOS:** 11.0 or later.

 Warning! .NET support for Windows 7 and 8.1 ended in January 2023: `https://github.com/dotnet/core/issues/7556`.

Windows ARM64 support in .NET 5 and later means you can develop on, and deploy to, Windows Arm devices like Microsoft's Windows Dev Kit 2023 (formerly known as Project Volterra) and Surface Pro X.

 You can review the latest supported operating systems and versions at the following link: `https://github.com/dotnet/core/blob/main/release-notes/8.0/supported-os.md`.

Downloading and installing Visual Studio 2022

Many professional Microsoft developers use Visual Studio 2022 in their day-to-day development work. Even if you choose to use Visual Studio Code to complete the coding tasks in this book, you might want to familiarize yourself with Visual Studio 2022 too.

If you do not have a Windows computer, then you can skip this section and continue to the next section where you will download and install Visual Studio Code on macOS or Linux.

Since October 2014, Microsoft has made a professional quality edition of Visual Studio 2022 available to students, open-source contributors, and individuals for free. It is called Community Edition. Any of the editions are suitable for this book. If you have not already installed it, let's do so now:

1. Download Visual Studio 2022 version 17.8 or later from the following link: `https://visualstudio.microsoft.com/downloads/`.
2. Start the installer.
3. On the **Workloads** tab, select the following:

   - **ASP.NET and web development**
   - **Azure development**
   - **.NET Multi-platform App UI development**
   - **.NET desktop development** (because this includes console apps)
   - **Desktop development with C++** with all default components (because this enables publishing console apps and web services that start faster and have smaller memory footprints)

4. On the **Individual components** tab, in the **Code tools** section, select the following:

   • **Git for Windows**

5. Click **Install** and wait for the installer to acquire the selected software and install it.

6. When the installation is complete, click **Launch**.

7. The first time that you run Visual Studio, you will be prompted to sign in. If you have a Microsoft account, you can use that account. If you don't, then register for a new one at the following link: `https://signup.live.com/`.

8. The first time that you run Visual Studio, you will be prompted to configure your environment. For **Development Settings**, choose **Visual C#**. For the color theme, I chose **Blue**, but you can choose whatever tickles your fancy.

9. If you want to customize your keyboard shortcuts, navigate to **Tools | Options...**, and then select the **Environment | Keyboard** option.

Visual Studio 2022 keyboard shortcuts

In this book, I will avoid showing keyboard shortcuts since they are often customized. Where they are consistent across code editors and commonly used, I will try to show them.

If you want to identify and customize your keyboard shortcuts, then you can, as shown at the following link: `https://learn.microsoft.com/en-us/visualstudio/ide/identifying-and-customizing-keyboard-shortcuts-in-visual-studio`.

Downloading and installing Visual Studio Code

Visual Studio Code has rapidly improved over the past couple of years and has pleasantly surprised Microsoft with its popularity. If you are brave and like to live on the bleeding edge, then there is the **Insiders** edition, which is a daily build of the next version.

Even if you plan to only use Visual Studio 2022 for development, I recommend that you download and install Visual Studio Code and try the coding tasks in this chapter using it, and then decide if you want to stick with just using Visual Studio 2022 for the rest of the book.

Let's now download and install Visual Studio Code, the .NET SDK, and the C# Dev Kit extension:

1. Download and install either the Stable build or the Insiders edition of Visual Studio Code from the following link: `https://code.visualstudio.com/`.

    More Information: If you need more help installing Visual Studio Code on any operating system, you can read the official setup guide at the following link: `https://code.visualstudio.com/docs/setup/setup-overview`.

2. Download and install the .NET SDK for version 8.0 from the following link: `https://www.microsoft.com/net/download`.

3. To install the **C# Dev Kit** extension using the user interface, you must first launch the Visual Studio Code application.

4. In Visual Studio Code, click the **Extensions** icon or navigate to **View | Extensions**.

5. **C# Dev Kit** is one of the most popular extensions available, so you should see it at the top of the list, or you can enter C# Dev Kit in the search box.

> **C# Dev Kit** has a dependency on the **C#** extension version 2.0 or later, so you do not have to install the **C#** extension separately. Note that **C#** extension version 2.0 or later no longer uses OmniSharp since it has a new **Language Service Protocol (LSP)** host. **C# Dev Kit** also has dependencies on the **.NET Install Tool for Extension Authors** and **IntelliCode for C# Dev Kit** extensions so they will be installed too.

6. Click **Install** and wait for the supporting packages to download and install.

> **Good Practice:** Be sure to read the license agreement for **C# Dev Kit**. It has a more restrictive license than the **C#** extension: https://aka.ms/vs/csdevkit/license.

Installing other extensions

In later chapters of this book, you will use more Visual Studio Code extensions. If you want to install them now, all the extensions that we will use are shown in *Table 1.4*:

Extension name and identifier	Description
C# Dev Kit ms-dotnettools.csdevkit	Official C# extension from Microsoft. Manage your code with a solution explorer and test your code with integrated unit test discovery and execution. Includes the **C#** and **IntelliCode for C# Dev Kit** extensions.
C# ms-dotnettools.csharp	C# editing support, including syntax highlighting, IntelliSense, Go To Definition, Find All References, debugging support for .NET, and support for csproj projects on Windows, macOS, and Linux.
IntelliCode for C# Dev Kit ms-dotnettools.vscodeintellicode-csharp	Provides AI-assisted development features for Python, TypeScript/JavaScript, C#, and Java developers.
MSBuild project tools tintoy.msbuild-project-tools	Provides IntelliSense for MSBuild project files, including autocomplete for <PackageReference> elements.

SQL Server (mssql) for Visual Studio Code `ms-mssql.mssql`	For developing SQL Server, Azure SQL Database, and SQL data warehouses everywhere with a rich set of functionalities.
REST Client `humao.rest-client`	Send an HTTP request and view the response directly in Visual Studio Code.
ilspy-vscode `icsharpcode.ilspy-vscode`	Decompile MSIL assemblies – support for modern .NET, .NET Framework, .NET Core, and .NET Standard.
vscode-proto3 `zxh404.vscode-proto3`	Syntax highlighting, syntax validation, code snippets, code completion, code formatting, brace matching, and line and block commenting.
Azure Functions for Visual Studio Code `ms-azuretools.vscode-azurefunctions`	Create, debug, manage, and deploy serverless apps directly from VS Code. It has dependencies on the Azure Account (`ms-vscode.azure-account`) and Azure Resources (`ms-azuretools.vscode-azureresourcegroups`) extensions.

Table 1.4: Visual Studio Code extensions used in this book

Managing Visual Studio Code extensions at the command prompt

You can install a Visual Studio Code extension at the command prompt or terminal, as shown in *Table 1.5*:

Command	Description
`code --list-extensions`	List installed extensions.
`code --install-extension <extension-id>`	Install the specified extension.
`code --uninstall-extension <extension-id>`	Uninstall the specified extension.

Table 1.5: Working with extensions at the command prompt

For example, to install the **C# Dev Kit** extension, enter the following at the command prompt:

```
code --install-extension ms-dotnettools.csdevkit
```

 I have created PowerShell scripts to install and uninstall the Visual Studio Code extensions in the preceding table. You can find them at the following link: `https://github.com/markjprice/apps-services-net8/tree/main/scripts/extension-scripts`.

Understanding Microsoft Visual Studio Code versions

Microsoft releases a new feature version of Visual Studio Code (almost) every month and bug-fix versions more frequently. For example:

- Version 1.78.0, April 2023 feature release
- Version 1.78.1, April 2023 bug fix release

The version used in this book is 1.83.0, September 2023 feature release, but the version of Microsoft Visual Studio Code is less important than the version of the C# extension that you installed.

While the C# extension is not required, it provides IntelliSense as you type, code navigation, and debugging features, so it's something that's very handy to install and keep updated to support the latest C# language features.

Visual Studio Code keyboard shortcuts

In this book, I will avoid showing keyboard shortcuts used for tasks like creating a new file since they are often different on different operating systems. The situations where I will show keyboard shortcuts are when you need to repeatedly press the key, for example, while debugging. These are also more likely to be consistent across operating systems.

If you want to customize your keyboard shortcuts for Visual Studio Code, then you can, as shown at the following link: https://code.visualstudio.com/docs/getstarted/keybindings.

I recommend that you download a PDF of keyboard shortcuts for your operating system from the following list:

- Windows: https://code.visualstudio.com/shortcuts/keyboard-shortcuts-windows.pdf
- macOS: https://code.visualstudio.com/shortcuts/keyboard-shortcuts-macos.pdf
- Linux: https://code.visualstudio.com/shortcuts/keyboard-shortcuts-linux.pdf

Consuming Azure resources

Some of the chapters in this book will require you to sign up for an Azure account and create Azure resources. Frequently, there are free tiers or local development versions of these services, but sometimes you will have to create a resource that generates costs for the time it exists.

Packt books use technical reviewers who complete all the coding exercises just like a reader would. Here is what one of the TRs of the **second edition** (**2E**) of this book said about their Azure costs. "I got my Azure bill. To run through 2E on a "paid" account cost me $3.01."

Microsoft currently says, *"Eligible new users get $200 Azure credit in your billing currency for the first 30 days and a limited quantity of free services for 12 months with your Azure free account."* You can learn more at the following link:

https://learn.microsoft.com/en-us/azure/cost-management-billing/manage/avoid-charges-free-account

 Good Practice: Delete Azure resources as soon as you do not need them to keep your costs low.

A summary of which chapters need Azure resources and if a local development alternative is available is shown in *Table 1.6*:

Chapter	Azure resource	Free tier	Local development alternative
2 to 16	SQL Database	As part of the free first year.	SQL Server Developer Edition on Windows, or SQL Edge in a Docker container on Windows, Linux, and macOS.
4	Cosmos DB database	1,000 RU/s and 25 GB of storage.	Azure Cosmos DB emulator on Windows or the preview version on Linux.
11	Azure Functions	1 million requests and 400,000 GBs of resource consumption per month.	Azurite open-source emulator for testing Azure Blob, Queue Storage, and Table storage applications like Azure Functions.
12	Azure SignalR Service	20 concurrent connections and 20,000 messages per day with 99.9% SLA.	Add SignalR to any ASP.NET Core project for local development.

Table 1.6: Chapters that use Azure resources and local development alternatives

 You can find out how to check your usage of free Azure resources at the following link: https://learn.microsoft.com/en-us/azure/cost-management-billing/manage/ check-free-service-usage.

Using other project templates

When you install the .NET SDK, there are many project templates included. Let's review them:

1. At a command prompt or terminal, enter the following command:

    ```
    dotnet new list
    ```

     .NET 7 and later SDKs support either dotnet new --list or dotnet new list. The .NET 6 and earlier SDKs only support dotnet new --list.

2. You will see a list of currently installed templates, including templates for Windows desktop development if you are running on Windows, the most common of which are shown in *Table 1.7*:

Template Name	Short Name	Language
.NET MAUI App	maui	C#
.NET MAUI Blazor App	maui-blazor	C#
ASP.NET Core Empty	web	C#, F#
ASP.NET Core gRPC Service	grpc	C#
ASP.NET Core Web API	webapi	C#, F#

ASP.NET Core Web API (native AOT)	`webapiaot`	C#
ASP.NET Core Web App (Model-View-Controller)	`mvc`	C#, F#
Blazor Web App	`blazor`	C#
Class Library	`classlib`	C#, F#, VB
Console App	`console`	C#, F#, VB
`EditorConfig` File	`editorconfig`	
`global.json` File	`globaljson`	
Solution File	`sln`	
xUnit Test Project	`xunit`	

Table 1.7: Project template full and short names

 .NET MAUI projects are not supported for Linux. The team has said they have left that work to the open-source community. If you need to create a truly cross-platform graphical app, then take a look at Avalonia at the following link: `https://avaloniaui.net/`.

Installing additional template packs

Developers can install lots of additional template packs:

1. Start a browser and navigate to `https://www.nuget.org/packages`.
2. Enter vue in the **Search for packages...** textbox and note that about 210 packages are returned.
3. Click **Filter**, select a **Package Type** of **Template**, click **Apply**, and note the list of about 25 available templates, including one published by Microsoft.
4. Click on **Vue.Simple.Template** and then click **Project website**, and note the instructions for installing and using this template, as shown in the following commands:

```
dotnet new --install "Vue.Simple.Template"
dotnet new simplevue
```

5. Close the browser.

Exploring top-level programs, functions, and namespaces

Since .NET 6, the default project template for console apps uses the top-level program feature introduced with .NET 5. It is important to understand how it works with the automatically generated `Program` class and its `<Main>$` method.

Let's explore how the top-level program feature works when you define functions:

1. Use your preferred coding tool to create a new project, as defined in the following list:

    *   Project template: **Console App** / `console`
    *   Project file and folder: `TopLevelFunctions`
    *   Solution file and folder: `Chapter01`
    *   **Do not use top-level statements:** Cleared
    *   **Enable native AOT publishing:** Cleared

2. In `Program.cs`, delete the existing statements, define a local function at the bottom of the file, and call it, as shown in the following code:

    ```
    using static System.Console;

    WriteLine("Top-level functions example");

    WhatsMyNamespace(); // Call the function.

    void WhatsMyNamespace() // Define a local function.
    {
      WriteLine("Namespace of Program class: {0}",
        arg0: typeof(Program).Namespace ?? "null");
    }
    ```

3. Run the console app and note that the namespace for the `Program` class is `null`, as shown in the following output:

    ```
    Top-level functions example
    Namespace of Program class: null
    ```

What is automatically generated for a local function?

The compiler automatically generates a `Program` class with a `<Main>$` function, then moves your statements and function inside the `<Main>$` method, and renames the local function, as shown highlighted in the following code:

```
using static System.Console;

partial class Program
{
  static void <Main>$(String[] args)
  {
    WriteLine("Top-level functions example");

    <<Main>$>g__WhatsMyNamespace|0_0(); // Call the function.
```

```
    void <<Main>$>g__WhatsMyNamespace|0_0() // Define a local function.
  {
    WriteLine("Namespace of Program class: {0}",
      arg0: typeof(Program).Namespace ?? "null");
  }
 }
}
```

For the compiler to know where what statements need to go, you must follow some rules:

- Import statements (using) must go at the top of the Program.cs file.
- Statements that will go in the <Main>$ function must go in the middle of the Program.cs file. Any functions will become **local functions** in the <Main>$ method.

The last point is important because local functions have limitations, for example, they cannot have XML comments to document them.

Writing static functions in a separate Program class file

A better approach is to write any functions in a separate class file and define them as static members of the Program class:

1. Add a new class file named Program.Functions.cs. The name has no effect, but it is a good practice to name it so that it is clear that this file is related to the Program.cs class file.
2. In Program.Functions.cs, define a partial Program class, then cut and paste the WhatsMyNamespace function to move it from Program.cs into Program.Functions.cs, and finally add the static keyword, as shown highlighted in the following code:

```
using static System.Console;

// Do not define a namespace so this class goes in the default empty
namespace
// just like the auto-generated partial Program class.

partial class Program
{
  static void WhatsMyNamespace() // Define a static function.
  {
    WriteLine("Namespace of Program class: {0}",
      arg0: typeof(Program).Namespace ?? "null");
  }
}
```

3. In `Program.cs`, confirm that its entire content is now just three statements, as shown in the following code:

    ```
    using static System.Console;

    WriteLine("Top-level functions example");

    WhatsMyNamespace(); // Call the function.
    ```

4. Run the console app and note that it has the same behavior as before.

What is automatically generated for a static function?

When you use a separate file to define a partial `Program` class with `static` functions, the compiler defines a `Program` class with a `<Main>$` function and moves your top-level statements inside the `<Main>$` method, and then merges your function as a member of the `Program` class, as shown in the following code:

```
using static System.Console;

partial class Program
{
  static void <Main>$(String[] args)
  {
    WriteLine("Top-level functions example");

    WhatsMyNamespace(); // Call the function.
  }

  static void WhatsMyNamespace() // Define a static function.
  {
    WriteLine("Namespace of Program class: {0}",
      arg0: typeof(Program).Namespace ?? "null");
  }
}
```

This is much cleaner, and you can document your functions with XML comments, which also provide tooltips in your code editor when calling the function.

Good Practice: Create any functions that you will call in `Program.cs` in a separate file and manually define them inside a partial `Program` class. This will merge them into the automatically generated `Program` class *at the same level* as the `<Main>$` method, instead of as local functions *inside* the `<Main>$` method.

It is important to note the lack of namespace declarations. Both the automatically generated `Program` class and the explicitly defined `Program` class are in the default `null` namespace. If you define your `partial Program` class in a namespace, then it will be in a different namespace and therefore not merge with the auto-generated `partial Program` class.

 Good Practice: Do not define a namespace for any `partial Program` classes that you create so that they will be defined in the default `null` namespace.

Optionally, all the `static` methods in the `Program` class could be explicitly declared as `private` but this is the default anyway. Since all the functions will be called within the `Program` class itself the access modifier is not important.

Making good use of the GitHub repository for this book

Git is a commonly used source code management system. **GitHub** is a company, website, and desktop application that makes it easier to manage Git. Microsoft purchased GitHub in 2018, so it will continue to be closely integrated with Microsoft tools.

I created a GitHub repository for this book, and I use it for the following:

- To store the solution code for the book, which will be maintained after the print publication date.
- To provide extra materials that extend the book, like errata fixes, small improvements, lists of useful links, and longer articles that cannot fit in the printed book.
- To provide a place for readers to get in touch with me if they have issues with the book.

Raising issues with the book

If you get stuck following any of the instructions in this book, or if you spot a mistake in the text or the code in the solutions, please raise an issue in the GitHub repository:

1. Use your favorite browser to navigate to the following link: `https://github.com/markjprice/apps-services-net8/issues`.
2. Click **New Issue**.
3. Enter as much detail as possible that will help me to diagnose the issue. For example:
   - The specific section title, page number, and step number.
   - Your code editor, for example, Visual Studio 2022, Visual Studio Code, or something else, including the version number.
   - As much of your code and configuration that you feel is relevant and necessary.
   - A description of the expected behavior and the behavior experienced.
   - Screenshots (you can drag and drop image files into the issue box).

The following is less relevant but might be useful:

- Your operating system, for example, Windows 11 64-bit, or macOS Big Sur version 11.2.3.
- Your hardware, for example, Intel, Apple silicon, or ARM CPU.

I want all my readers to be successful with my book, so if I can help you (and others) without too much trouble, then I will gladly do so.

Giving me feedback

If you'd like to give me more general feedback about the book, then you can email me at markjprice@ gmail.com. My publisher, Packt, has set up Discord channels for readers to interact with authors and other readers. You are welcome to join us at the following link: https://packt.link/apps_and_ services_dotnet8.

I love to hear from my readers about what they like about my books, as well as suggestions for improvements and how they are working with C# and .NET, so don't be shy. Please get in touch!

Thank you in advance for your thoughtful and constructive feedback.

Downloading solution code from the GitHub repository

I use GitHub to store solutions to all the hands-on, step-by-step coding examples throughout chapters and the practical exercises that are featured at the end of each chapter. You will find the repository at the following link: https://github.com/markjprice/apps-services-net8.

If you just want to download all the solution files without using Git, click the green **Code** button and then select **Download ZIP**.

I recommend that you add the preceding link to your favorites or bookmarks.

 Good Practice: It is best to clone or download the code solutions to a short folder path, like C:\cs12dotnet8\ or C:\book\, to avoid build-generated files exceeding the maximum path length. You should also avoid special characters like #. For example, do not use a folder name like C:\C# projects\. That folder name might work for a simple console app project but once you start adding features that automatically generate code you are likely to have strange issues. Keep your folder names short and simple.

Where to go for help

This section is all about how to find quality information about programming on the web.

Reading documentation on Microsoft Learn

The definitive resource for getting help with Microsoft developer tools and platforms is in the technical documentation on Microsoft Learn, and you can find it at the following link: https://learn. microsoft.com/en-us/docs.

Getting help for the dotnet tool

At the command prompt, you can ask the dotnet tool for help with its commands. The syntax is:

```
dotnet help <command>
```

This will cause your web browser to open a page in the documentation about the specified command. Common dotnet commands include new, build, and run.

> **Warning!** The dotnet help new command worked with .NET Core 3.1 to .NET 6, but it returns an error with .NET 7 or later: Specified command 'new' is not a valid SDK command. Specify a valid SDK command. For more information, run dotnet help. Hopefully, the .NET team will fix that bug soon!

Another type of help is command-line documentation. It follows this syntax:

```
dotnet <command> -?|-h|--help
```

For example, dotnet new -? or dotnet new -h or dotnet new --help outputs documentation about the new command at the command prompt.

> As you should now expect, dotnet help help opens a web browser for the help command, and dotnet help -h outputs documentation for the help command at the command prompt!

Let's try some examples:

1. To open the official documentation in a web browser window for the dotnet build command, enter the following at the command prompt or in the Visual Studio Code terminal, and note the page opened in your web browser, as shown in *Figure 1.2*:

```
dotnet help build
```

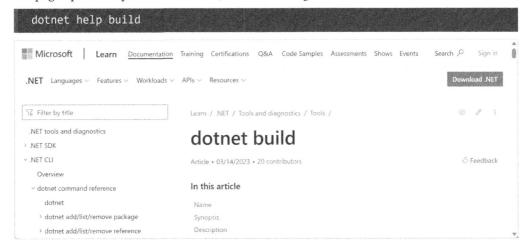

Figure 1.2: Web page documentation for the dotnet build command

2. To get help output at the command prompt, use the `-?`, `-h`, or `--help` flag, as shown in the following command:

```
dotnet build -?
```

3. You will see the following partial output:

```
Description:
  .NET Builder

Usage:
  dotnet build [<PROJECT | SOLUTION>...] [options]

Arguments:
  <PROJECT | SOLUTION>  The project or solution file to operate on. If a
  file is not specified, the command will search the current directory for
  one.

Options:
  --ucr, --use-current-runtime            Use current runtime as the target
  runtime.
  -f, --framework <FRAMEWORK>             The target framework to build for.
  The target framework must also be specified in the project file.
  ...
  -?, -h, --help                          Show command-line help.
```

4. Repeat both types of help request for the following commands: `add`, `help`, `list`, `new`, and `run`.

AI tools like ChatGPT and GitHub Copilot

One of the biggest changes in coding and development in the past year is the emergence of generative **artificial intelligence** (**AI**) tools that can help with coding tasks like completing a code statement, implementing an entire function, writing unit tests, and suggesting debugging fixes for existing code.

ChatGPT

ChatGPT currently has two models: 3.5 (free) and 4.0 ($20 per month).

Let's say you need to understand more about how to design a microservice. You might enter the following prompt:

```
You are an expert .NET solution architect with experience advising global
enterprises. What are the top three most common mistakes when designing a
microservice architecture that are serious enough to cause a project to be
abandoned?
```

It responds with a summary of those top three mistakes, as shown in detail in *Figure 1.3* and the following list:

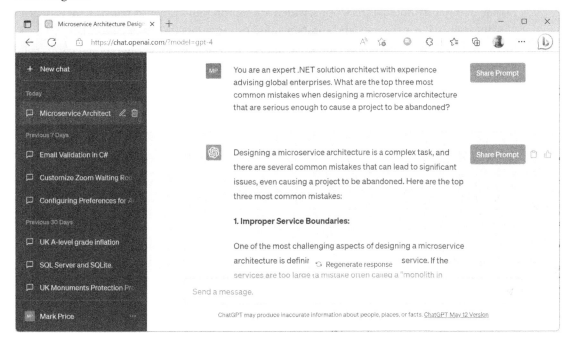

Figure 1.3: ChatGPT advising about microservice architecture design

"Designing a microservice architecture is a complex task, and there are several common mistakes that can lead to significant issues, even causing a project to be abandoned. Here are the top three most common mistakes:

- **Improper Service Boundaries:** One of the most challenging aspects of designing a microservice architecture is defining the boundaries of each service. If the services are too large (a mistake often called a "monolith in disguise"), you lose many of the benefits of microservices due to tight coupling of different concerns. On the other hand, if the services are too small (sometimes referred to as "nanoservices"), you might have to deal with excessive inter-service communication, resulting in high latency and complexity.

- A lack of proper boundaries can also lead to data consistency issues. If multiple services are interacting with the same database tables, it can be difficult to maintain data consistency.

- To avoid this mistake, it's important to understand the business domain thoroughly and design services around business capabilities. Techniques such as **Domain-Driven Design (DDD)** can help identify service boundaries more effectively.

- **Inadequate Consideration for Data Management:** Each microservice should own its own data to ensure loose coupling. Sharing databases across services leads to tight coupling and makes it difficult to change the schema without affecting other services.

- However, managing data across services introduces challenges with data consistency and transaction management. Developers often underestimate these challenges. They might try to implement distributed transactions, which are complex and can hurt performance, instead of using eventual consistency and compensation transactions (the Saga pattern).

- **Neglecting Operational Complexity:** Microservice architectures add operational complexity. You're moving from managing a single monolithic application to managing multiple services, each potentially written in different languages, using different data storage technologies, and running in different environments.

- This requires a mature DevOps capability, including automated deployment, monitoring, and good logging practices. You need to plan for how services will be monitored, how logs will be aggregated and analyzed, and how deployments and rollbacks will be handled.

- Ignoring the operational challenges of microservices can lead to significant issues down the line. For instance, it can become very difficult to debug issues that span multiple services without good tracing and logging. Deploying changes can become a nightmare without automated deployment and good testing practices.

In conclusion, designing a microservice architecture isn't a trivial task. It requires a deep understanding of the business domain, careful planning, and a mature DevOps capability. However, when done right, microservices can provide significant benefits, including better scalability, flexibility, and maintainability."

GitHub Copilot

Microsoft has a service specifically for programmers named GitHub Copilot that can help autocomplete code directly in your code editor. It is being enhanced with more intelligence using GPT-4. It has plugins for code editors including Visual Studio 2022, Visual Studio Code, and JetBrains IntelliJ-based IDEs.

GitHub Copilot is free for students, teachers, and some open-source project maintainers. For everyone else, it has a 30-day free trial and then it costs $10 per month or $100 per year for individuals. Once you have an account, you can then sign up for the more advanced experimental GitHub Copilot X features.

You should check online for which Copilot features are available for various code editors. As you can imagine, this is a fast-changing world and a lot of what I might write in the book today will be out of date by the time you read it: https://github.com/features/copilot.

 JetBrains has its own equivalent named AI Assistant, which you can read about at the following link: https://blog.jetbrains.com/idea/2023/06/ai-assistant-in-jetbrains-ides/.

You can sign up for GitHub Copilot at the following link:

https://github.com/github-copilot/signup/

Subscribing to the official .NET blog and announcements

To keep up to date with .NET, an excellent blog to subscribe to is the official .NET blog, written by the .NET engineering teams, and you can find it at the following link: `https://devblogs.microsoft.com/dotnet/`.

I also recommend that you subscribe to the official .NET announcements repository at the following link: `https://github.com/dotnet/announcements`.

Practicing and exploring

Test your knowledge and understanding by answering some questions, getting some hands-on practice, and exploring with deeper research the topics in this chapter.

Exercise 1.1 – Test your knowledge

Use the web to answer the following questions:

1. Why is it good practice to add the following setting to your project files? And when should you not set it?

   ```
   <TreatWarningsAsErrors>true</TreatWarningsAsErrors>
   ```

2. Which service technology requires a minimum HTTP version of 2?

3. In 2010, your organization created a service using .NET Framework and WCF. What is the best technology to migrate it to and why?

4. Which code editor or IDE should you install for .NET development?

5. What should you beware of when creating Azure resources?

Exercise 1.2 – Review the online-only sections

To preserve space in the print book, there are some optional online-only sections available in the GitHub repository. They are not needed for the rest of the book, but you will find them useful for general knowledge:

- **What's New in Modern C# and .NET**: In this section, the goal is to review what is new since C# 6 and .NET Core 1.0, which were released in 2016. Instead of just listing the new features introduced with each version of .NET, this section takes a themed approach to make it easier to understand how small individual improvements introduced over multiple versions are designed to work together. This section will also be updated throughout the lifetime of .NET 8, from November 2023 to November 2026. This will include new language and library features introduced in .NET 9 and .NET 10 (`https://github.com/markjprice/apps-services-net8/blob/main/docs/ch01-whats-new.md`).

- **Benchmarking Performance and Testing**: In this section, you will learn how to use types in the `System.Diagnostics` namespace and the Benchmark.NET library to monitor your code to measure performance and efficiency (`https://github.com/markjprice/apps-services-net8/blob/main/docs/ch01-benchmarking.md`).

- **Observing and Modifying Code Execution Dynamically**: This is about some common types that are included with .NET for performing code reflection and applying and reading attributes, working with expression trees, and creating source generators (`https://github.com/markjprice/apps-services-net8/blob/main/docs/ch01-dynamic-code.md`).

Exercise 1.3 — Explore topics

Use the links on the following page to learn more about the topics covered in this chapter:

`https://github.com/markjprice/apps-services-net8/blob/main/docs/book-links.md#chapter-1---introducing-apps-and-services-with-net`

Summary

In this chapter, you:

- Were introduced to the app and service technologies that you will learn about in this book.
- Set up your development environment.
- Learned where to look for help.

In the next chapter, you will learn how to use SQL Server to store and manage relational data.

Learn more on Discord

To join the Discord community for this book – where you can share feedback, ask questions to the author, and learn about new releases – follow the QR code below:

`https://packt.link/apps_and_services_dotnet8`

2

Managing Relational Data Using SQL Server

This chapter is about managing relational data stored in SQL Server, Azure SQL Database, or Azure SQL Edge. First, you will learn how to manage the data using native Transact-SQL statements. Next, you will learn how to manage data at a low level using ADO.NET libraries (`Microsoft.Data.SqlClient`). Finally, you will use Dapper to make it easier to work with entity models.

This chapter will cover the following topics:

- Understanding modern databases
- Managing data with Transact-SQL
- Managing SQL Server data with low-level APIs
- Managing SQL Server data with Dapper
- Cleaning up data resources

Understanding modern databases

Two of the most common places to store data are in a **Relational Database Management System** (**RDBMS**) such as **SQL Server, PostgreSQL, MySQL**, and **SQLite**, or in a **NoSQL** database such as **Azure Cosmos DB, MongoDB, Redis**, and **Apache Cassandra**.

In this chapter, we will focus on the most popular RDBMS for Windows, which is SQL Server. This product is also available in a version for Linux. For cross-platform development, you can use either Azure SQL Database, which stores the data in the cloud, or Azure SQL Edge, which can run in a Docker container on Windows, macOS, or Linux, on both Intel and ARM architecture CPUs.

Using a sample relational database

To learn how to manage an RDBMS using .NET, it would be useful to have a sample one so that you can practice on a database that has a medium complexity and a decent number of sample records.

Microsoft offers several sample databases, most of which are too complex for our needs, so instead, we will use a database that was first created in the early 1990s known as **Northwind**.

Let's take a minute to look at a diagram of the Northwind database and its eight most important tables. You can use the diagram in *Figure 2.1* to refer to as we write code and queries throughout this book:

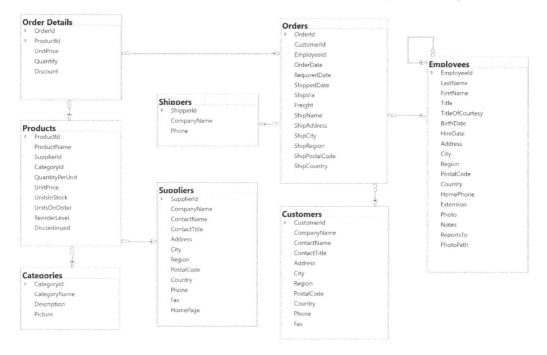

Figure 2.1: The Northwind database tables and relationships

Note that:

- Each category has a unique identifier, name, description, and picture. The picture is stored as a byte array in JPEG format.
- Each product has a unique identifier, name, unit price, number of units in stock, and other columns.
- Each product is associated with a category by storing the category's unique identifier.
- The relationship between `Categories` and `Products` is one-to-many, meaning each category can have zero, one, or more products.
- Each product is supplied by a supplier company indicated by storing the supplier's unique identifier.
- The quantity and unit price of a product is stored for each detail of an order.
- Each order is made by a customer, taken by an employee, and shipped by a shipping company.
- Each employee has a name, address, contact details, birth, and hire dates, a reference to their manager (except for the boss, whose `ReportsTo` field is `null`), and a photo stored as a byte array in JPEG format. The table has a one-to-many relationship to itself because one employee can manage many other employees.

Connecting to a SQL Server database

To connect to a SQL Server database, we need to know multiple pieces of information, as shown in the following list:

- The name of the server (and the name of the instance if it has more than the default one). This can include the protocol, IP address, and port number if connecting over a network.
- The name of the database.
- Security information, such as the username and password, or if we should pass the currently logged-on user's credentials automatically using Windows Authentication.

We specify this information in a **connection string**.

For backward compatibility, there are multiple possible keywords we can use in a SQL Server connection string for the various parameters, as shown in the following list:

- `Data Source`, `server`, or `addr`: These keywords are the name of the server (and an optional instance). You can use a dot (`.`) to mean the local server.
- `Initial Catalog` or `database`: These keywords are the name of the database that will be active initially. A SQL statement could change that using the command: `USE <databasename>`.
- `Integrated Security` or `trusted_connection`: These keywords are set to `true` or `SSPI` to pass the thread's current user credentials using Windows Authentication.
- `User Id` and `Password`: These keywords are used to authenticate with any edition of SQL Server. This is important for Azure SQL Database or Azure SQL Edge because they do not support Windows Authentication. The full edition of SQL Server on Windows supports both username with password and Windows Authentication.
- `Authentication`: This keyword is used to authenticate by using Azure AD identities that can enable password-less authentication. Values can be `Active Directory Integrated`, `Active Directory Password`, and `Sql Password`.
- `Persist Security Info`: If set to `false`, this keyword tells the connection to remove the `Password` from the connection string after authenticating.
- `Encrypt`: If set to `true`, this keyword tells the connections to use SSL to encrypt transmissions between client and server.
- `TrustServerCertificate`: Set to true if hosting locally and you get the error "A connection was successfully established with the server, but then an error occurred during the login process. (provider: SSL Provider, error: 0 - The certificate chain was issued by an authority that is not trusted.)".
- `Connection Timeout`: This keyword defaults to 30 seconds.
- `MultipleActiveResultSets`: This keyword is set to `true` to enable a single connection to be used to work with multiple tables simultaneously to improve efficiency. It is used for lazy loading rows from related tables.

As described in the list above, when you write code to connect to a SQL Server database, you need to know its server name. The server name depends on the edition and version of SQL Server that you will connect to, as shown in *Table 2.1*:

SQL Server edition	Server name \ Instance name
LocalDB 2012	`(localdb)\v11.0`
LocalDB 2016 or later	`(localdb)\mssqllocaldb`
Express	`.\sqlexpress`
Full/Developer (default instance)	`.`
Full/Developer (named instance)	`.\apps-services-book`
Azure SQL Edge (local Docker)	`tcp:127.0.0.1,1433`
Azure SQL Database	`tcp:[custom server name].database.windows.net,1433`

Table 2.1: Server name examples for various editions of SQL Server

Good Practice: Use a dot (.) as shorthand for the local computer name (localhost). Remember that server names for SQL Server can be made up of two parts: the name of the computer and the name of a SQL Server instance. You provide instance names during custom installation.

Installing and setting up SQL Server locally

Microsoft offers various editions of its popular and capable SQL Server product for Windows, Linux, and Docker containers. If you have Windows, then you can use a free version that runs standalone, known as SQL Server Developer Edition. You can also use the Express edition or the free SQL Server LocalDB edition that can be installed with Visual Studio 2022 for Windows.

If you do not have a Windows computer or if you want to use a cross-platform database system, then you can skip ahead to the topic *Setting up Azure SQL Database*, or the online-only section *Installing Azure SQL Edge in Docker* found at the following link:

`https://github.com/markjprice/apps-services-net8/blob/main/docs/ch02-sql-edge.md`

If you prefer to install SQL Server locally on Linux, then you will find instructions at the following link: `https://learn.microsoft.com/en-us/sql/linux/sql-server-linux-setup`.

Installing SQL Server Developer Edition for Windows

On Windows, if you want to use the full edition of SQL Server instead of the simplified LocalDB or Express editions, then you can find all SQL Server editions at the following link: `https://www.microsoft.com/en-us/sql-server/sql-server-downloads`.

Take the following steps:

1. Download the **Developer** edition.
2. Run the installer.
3. Select the **Custom** installation type.
4. Select a folder for the installation files and then click **Install**.
5. Wait for the 1.5 GB of installer files to download.
6. In **SQL Server Installation Center**, click **Installation**, and then click **New SQL Server stand-alone installation or add features to an existing installation**, as shown in *Figure 2.2*:

Figure 2.2: Installing a new instance of SQL Server

7. Select **Developer** as the free edition and then click **Next**.
8. Accept the license terms and then click **Next.**
9. Review the **Microsoft Update** options and then click **Next**.
10. Review the install rules, fix any issues although you might want to ignore any firewall warnings since you might not want to expose those ports anyway, and then click **Next**.
11. In **Feature Selection**, select **Database Engine Services**, and then click **Next**.
12. In **Azure Extension for SQL Server**, you can turn this off.
13. In **Instance Configuration**, select **Default instance**, and then click **Next**. If you already have a default instance configured, then you could create a named instance, perhaps called `apps-services-book`.
14. In **Server Configuration**, note the **SQL Server Database Engine** is configured to start automatically. If not already set by default, then set the **SQL Server Browser** to start automatically, and then click **Next**.
15. In **Database Engine Configuration**, on the **Server Configuration** tab, set **Authentication Mode** to **Mixed**, set the **sa** account password to a strong password, click **Add Current User**, and then click **Next**.
16. In **Ready to Install**, review the actions that will be taken, and then click **Install**.
17. In **Complete**, note the successful actions taken, and then click **Close**.
18. In **SQL Server Installation Center**, in **Installation**, click **Install SQL Server Management Tools**.

19. In the browser window, click to download the latest version of SSMS, as shown in *Figure 2.3*:

Figure 2.3: Downloading SQL Server Management Studio (SSMS)

 The direct link to download SSMS is as follows: `https://learn.microsoft.com/en-us/sql/ssms/download-sql-server-management-studio-ssms`.

20. Run the SSMS installer and click **Install**.
21. When the installer has finished, click **Restart** if needed or **Close**.

 Azure Data Studio (ADS) is automatically installed alongside SSMS. ADS is cross-platform and open-source, so you can use it to work with SQL Server databases on any desktop operating system.

Visual Studio Code extension for working with SQL Server

There are many tools that make it easy to work with SQL Server. If you are using Visual Studio Code, then you can install the **SQL Server (mssql)** `ms-mssql.mssql` extension. If you install the extension, it adds a new view to the Primary Side Bar titled **SQL Server**, as shown in *Figure 2.4*:

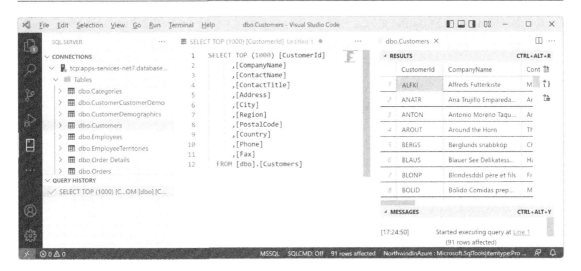

Figure 2.4: SQL Server (mssql) extension for Visual Studio Code

Creating the Northwind sample database locally

Now we can run a database script to create the Northwind sample database locally on Windows using **SQL Server Management Studio (SSMS)**:

1. If you have not previously downloaded or cloned the GitHub repository for this book, then do so now using the following link: `https://github.com/markjprice/apps-services-net8/`.

2. In your `apps-services-net8` folder, create a folder named `Chapter02`.

3. Copy the script to create the Northwind database for SQL Server from the following path in your local Git repository: `/scripts/sql-scripts/Northwind4SQLServer.sql` into the `Chapter02` folder.

4. Start **SQL Server Management Studio**.

5. In the **Connect to Server** dialog, for **Server name**, enter . (a dot), meaning the local computer name, and then click **Connect**.

> **Warning!** If you had to create a named instance, like `apps-services-book`, then enter `.\apps-services-book`. If you see an error about the server certificate, then click the **Options >>** button and select the **Trust server certificate** check box.

6. Navigate to **File | Open | File....**

7. Browse to select the `Northwind4SQLServer.sql` file and then click **Open**.

8. In the toolbar, click **Execute**, and note the **Command(s) completed successfully** message.

9. In **Object Explorer**, expand the **Northwind** database, and then expand **Tables**.

10. Right-click **Products**, click **Select Top 1000 Rows**, and note the returned results, as shown in *Figure 2.5*:

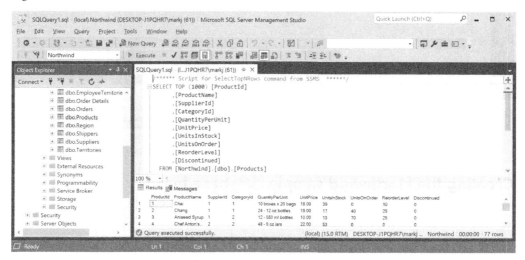

Figure 2.5: The Products table in SQL Server Management Studio

11. In the **Object Explorer** toolbar, click the **Disconnect** button.

12. Exit **SQL Server Management Studio**.

We did not have to use **SQL Server Management Studio** to execute the database script. We can also use tools in Visual Studio 2022, including the **SQL Server Object Explorer** and **Server Explorer**, or cross-platform tools like the Visual Studio Code extension for SQL Server, or **Azure Data Studio**, which you can download and install separately from the following link: `https://aka.ms/getazuredatastudio`.

Setting up Azure SQL Database

If you do not have a Windows computer, then you can create a cloud-hosted instance of SQL Server. You will need an Azure account. You can sign up at the following link: `https://signup.azure.com`. Next, you need to take the following steps:

1. Log in to your Azure account: `https://portal.azure.com/`

2. Navigate to `https://portal.azure.com/#create/hub`.

3. Search for **Resource group** and then click the **Create** button.

4. Enter a resource group name of `apps-services-book` and select a suitable region close to you, and then click the **Review + create** button, as shown in *Figure 2.6*:

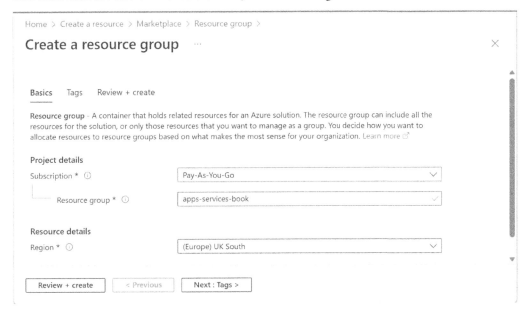

Figure 2.6: Creating a resource group in the Azure portal

5. Review your choices and then click the **Create** button.

6. Create another resource, search for **SQL Database**, and click **Create**.

7. In the **Create SQL Database** page, in the **Basics** tab, for the **Database name**, enter Northwind, and select the resource group that you created before.

8. In the **Server** section, click **Create New**.

9. Enter the following details for the SQL Database server, as shown in *Figure 2.7*:

   • **Server name:** `apps-services-book-[your initials]` or something else entirely. The server name must be globally unique because it becomes part of a public URL.

   • **Location:** A region close to you. I chose **(Europe) UK South**. Not all regions support all types of resources. You will see an error if the region you select does not support SQL Database server resources.

   • **Authentication method:** Use SQL authentication.

   • **Server admin login:** [Your email or another username], for example, I entered `markjprice`.

   • **Password/Confirm password:** [Enter a strong password].

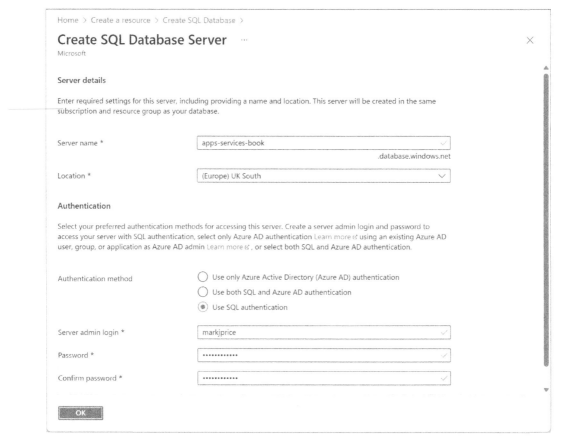

Figure 2.7: Entering the server details for a SQL Database instance

10. Click **OK**.

11. Leave **Want to use SQL elastic pool** set to **No**.

12. For **Workload environment**, select **Development** (instead of **Production**).

13. In the **Create SQL Database** page, in the **Compute + storage** section, click **Configure database**.

14. For **Service tier**, select **Basic (For less demanding workloads)**. Note the maximum database size is 2 GB and the estimated cost is about $5 per month (or less than 1 cent per hour). You can delete the resources as soon as you have completed this chapter to reduce the cost further.

15. Click **Apply**.

16. In the **Create SQL Database** page, set **Backup storage redundancy** to **Locally-redundant backup storage**.

17. Click the **Next : Networking** button.

18. In the **Network connectivity** section, select **Public endpoint**.

19. In the **Firewall rules** section, set **Add current client IP address** to **Yes**.

20. Click the **Next : Security** button.

21. Review the options but leave them as the defaults.

22. Click the **Next : Additional settings** button.

23. Review the options but leave them as the defaults.

24. Click the **Review + create** button.

25. Click the **Create** button.

26. Wait for the deployment to complete, as shown in *Figure 2.8*:

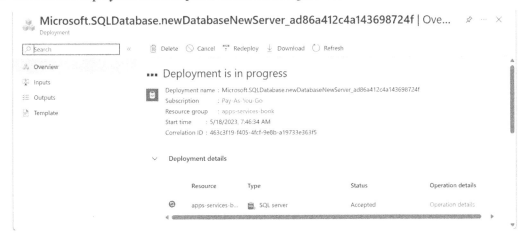

Figure 2.8: Deployment progress for SQL Database

27. When deployment has completed, click **Go to resource**.

28. Click **Overview** and note the database details, as shown in *Figure 2.9*:

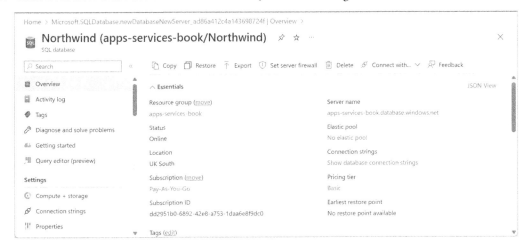

Figure 2.9: SQL Database details

29. Click **See connection strings** (or click **Connection strings** in the left navigation).

30. Copy the **ADO.NET (SQL authentication)** connection string to your clipboard.

31. Start **Notepad** or your preferred plain text editor, paste the connection string, and add carriage returns after each semicolon to separate each part to make them easier to work with, as shown in the following text:

```
Server=tcp:apps-services-book.database.windows.net,1433;
Initial Catalog=Northwind;
Persist Security Info=False;
User ID=markjprice;
Password={your_password};
MultipleActiveResultSets=False;
Encrypt=True;
TrustServerCertificate=False;
Connection Timeout=30;
```

 Your `Server` value will be different because the custom server name part, for example, `apps-services-book`, is public and must be globally unique.

32. Optionally, save the Notepad file for future reference.

JetBrains Rider tool window for working with SQL Server

If you use JetBrains Rider on any operating system, then you can use the following steps to connect with a SQL Server database:

1. In JetBrains Rider, select **View | Tool Windows | Database**.
2. In the **Database** tool window, click **Connect to database...**.
3. Select the **Use connection string** option button.
4. Set the **Database type** to **Microsoft SQL Server**.
5. In the **String** box, enter the database connection string.
6. Change {your_password} to the password you chose.
7. Optionally, click **Test Connection** and correct any errors if necessary. If you get an **Inconsistent language** error, then you can ignore it as we are using SQL Server as the dialect.
8. Click **Connect to Database**.

Creating the Northwind sample database in the cloud

Now we can run a database script to create the Northwind sample database in the Azure SQL Database:

1. Use your preferred database tool to connect to the SQL server in Azure:
   - In Visual Studio 2022, view **Server Explorer**.
   - On Windows, start **SQL Server Management Studio**.
   - In Visual Studio Code, view the **SQL Server** tool.

- In JetBrains Rider, navigate to **View | Tool Windows | Database**, and then click **Connect to database...**.

2. Add a data connection, and fill in the dialog box with all the required connection string information, as shown in *Figure 2.10*:

Figure 2.10: Connecting to your Azure SQL database from Visual Studio

 You might also be prompted to **Choose Data Source**. Choose **Microsoft SQL Server**. You can select a checkbox to always use this selection.

3. Right-click the data connection and choose **New Query**.

 If you are using JetBrains Rider, then right-click the SQL Server, in the popup menu, select **SQL Scripts | Run SQL Script...**, and then select the `Northwind4AzureSQLdatabase.sql` file.

4. Copy and paste the contents of the `Northwind4AzureSQLdatabase.sql` file into the query window and execute it.

 The main difference between the `Northwind4SQLServer.sql` and `Northwind4AzureSQLdatabase.sql` scripts is that the local SQL Server script will delete and recreate the Northwind database. The Azure SQL database script will not because the database needs to be created as an Azure resource. You can download SQL script files from the following link: `https://github.com/markjprice/apps-services-net8/tree/main/scripts/sql-scripts`.

5. Wait to see the **Command completed successfully** message. This can take a few minutes.

6. In **Server Explorer**, right-click **Tables** and select **Refresh**, and note that 13 tables have been created, for example, **Categories**, **Customers**, and **Products**. Also note that dozens of views and stored procedures have also been created.

You now have a running Azure SQL database in the cloud that you can connect to from a .NET project.

Managing data with Transact-SQL

Transact-SQL (T-SQL) is SQL Server's dialect of **Structured Query Language (SQL)**. Some pronounce it *tee-sequel*, others *tee-es-queue-el*.

Unlike C#, T-SQL is not case-sensitive; for example, you can use `int` or `INT` to specify the 32-bit integer data type, and you can use `SELECT` or `select` to start a query expression. Text data stored in SQL Server tables can be treated as case-sensitive or not, depending on the configuration.

 The complete reference for T-SQL is found at the following link: `https://learn.microsoft.com/en-us/sql/t-sql/language-reference`. From that documentation starting page, use the left side navigation to view topics like **Data types**, **Queries**, and **Statements**.

T-SQL data types

T-SQL has data types that are used for columns, variables, parameters, and so on, as shown in *Table 2.2*:

Category	Examples
Numbers	`bigint`, `bit`, `decimal`, `float`, `int`, `money`, `numeric`, `real`, `smallint`, `smallmoney`, `tinyint`
Date and time	`date`, `datetime2`, `datetime`, `datetimeoffset`, `smalldatetime`, `time`
Text	`char`, `nchar`, `ntext`, `nvarchar`, `text`, `varchar`
Binary	`binary`, `image`, `varbinary`
Other	`cursor`, `hierarchyid`, `sql_variant`, `table`, `rowversion`, `uniqueidentifier`, `xml`

Table 2.2: Categories of SQL Server data types

 There is an `xml` data type but no JSON data type. Use `nvarchar` to store JSON values. T-SQL also has support for spatial `geometry` and `geography` types.

Documenting with comments

To comment out the rest of a line, use `--`, which is the equivalent of `//`.

To comment out a block, use /* at the start and */ at the end, just like in C#.

Declaring variables

Local variable names are prefixed with @ and they are defined using SET, SELECT, or DECLARE, as shown in the following code:

```
DECLARE @WholeNumber INT; -- Declare a variable and specify its type.
SET @WholeNumber = 3; -- Set the variable to a literal value.
SET @WholeNumber = @WholeNumber + 1; -- Increment the variable.
SELECT @WholeNumber = COUNT(*) FROM Employees; -- Set to the number of
employees.
SELECT @WholeNumber = EmployeeId FROM Employees WHERE FirstName = 'Janet';
```

Global variables are prefixed with @@. For example, @@ROWCOUNT is a context-dependent value that returns the number of rows affected by a statement executed within the current scope, for example, the number of rows updated or deleted.

Specifying data types

Most types have a fixed size. For example, an int uses four bytes, a smallint uses two bytes, and a tinyint uses one byte.

For text and binary types, you can either specify a type prefixed with var or nvar (meaning variable size), which will automatically change its size based on its current value up to a maximum, as shown in the following example: varchar(40); or you can specify a fixed number of characters that will always be allocated, as shown in the following example: char(40).

For text types, the n prefix indicates Unicode, meaning it will use two bytes per character. Text types not prefixed with n use one byte per character.

Controlling flow

T-SQL has similar flow control keywords as C#, for example, BREAK, CONTINUE, GOTO, IF...ELSE, CASE, THROW, TRY...CATCH, WHILE, and RETURN. The main difference is the use of BEGIN and END to indicate the start and end of a block, the equivalent of curly braces in C#.

Operators

T-SQL has similar operators as C#, for example, = (assignment), +, -, *, /, %, <, >, <=, ==, !=, &, |, ^, and so on. It has logical operators like AND, OR, NOT, and LINQ-like operators like ANY, ALL, SOME, EXISTS, BETWEEN, and IN.

LIKE is used for text pattern matching. The pattern can use % for any number of characters. The pattern can use _ for a single character. The pattern can use [ ] to specify a range and set of allowed characters, for example, [0-9A-Z.-,], which looks like a simplified regular expression syntax but keep in mind that it is *not* regular expression syntax.

If a table or column name contains spaces, then you must surround the name in square brackets, like [Order Details]. The SQL scripts to create the Northwind database include the command set quoted_identifier on, so you can also use double quotes, like "Order Details". Single quotes are used for literal text, like 'USA'.

Data Manipulation Language (DML)

DML is used to query and change data.

The most common statement in DML is SELECT, which is used to retrieve data from one or more tables. SELECT is extremely complicated because it is so powerful. This book is not about learning T-SQL, so the quickest way to get a feel for SELECT is to see some examples, as shown in *Table 2.3*:

Example	Description
SELECT * FROM Employees	Get all columns of all the employees.
SELECT FirstName, LastName FROM Employees	Get the first and last name columns of all employees.
SELECT emp.FirstName, emp.LastName FROM Employees AS emp	Give an alias for the table name. Table name prefixes are not needed when there is only one table, but become useful to disambiguate when there are multiple tables that have columns with the same name, for example, Customers.CustomerId and Orders.CustomerId.
SELECT emp.FirstName, emp.LastName FROM Employees emp	Give an alias for the table name without needing the AS keyword.
SELECT FirstName, LastName AS Surname FROM Employees	Give an alias for the column name.
SELECT FirstName, LastName FROM Employees WHERE Country = 'USA'	Filter the results to only include employees in the USA.
SELECT DISTINCT Country FROM Employees	Get a list of countries used as values in the Country column of the Employees table without duplicates.
SELECT UnitPrice * Quantity AS Subtotal FROM [Order Details]	Calculate a subtotal for each order detail row.

SELECT OrderId, SUM(UnitPrice * Quantity) AS Total FROM [Order Details] GROUP BY OrderId ORDER BY Total DESC	Calculate a total for each order and sort with the largest order value at the top.
SELECT CompanyName FROM Customers UNION SELECT CompanyName FROM Suppliers	Return all the company names of all customers and suppliers.
SELECT CategoryName, ProductName FROM Categories, Products	Match *every* category with *every* product using a Cartesian join and output their names (not what you normally want!). 616 rows (8 categories x 77 products).
SELECT CategoryName, ProductName FROM Categories c, Products p WHERE c.CategoryId = p.CategoryId	Match each product with its category using a WHERE clause for the CategoryId column in each table and output the category name and product name. 77 rows.
SELECT CategoryName, ProductName FROM Categories c INNER JOIN Products p ON c.CategoryId = p.CategoryId	Match each product with its category using an INNER JOIN...ON clause for the CategoryId column in each table and output the category name and product name. This is a modern alternative syntax to using WHERE, and it allows outer joins, which would also include non-matches. 77 rows.

Table 2.3: Example SELECT statements with descriptions

 More Information: You can read the full documentation for SELECT at the following link: https://learn.microsoft.com/en-us/sql/t-sql/queries/select-transact-sql.

Use your favorite database querying tool, like Visual Studio's **Server Explorer** or Visual Studio Code's mssql extension, to connect to your Northwind database and try out some of the queries above, as shown in *Figure 2.11* and *Figure 2:12*:

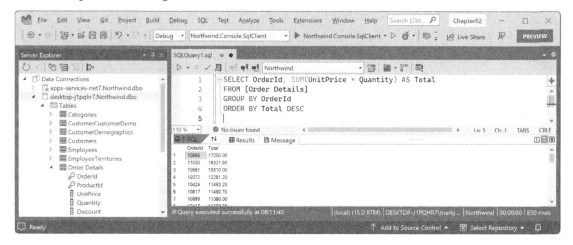

Figure 2.11: Executing T-SQL queries using Visual Studio's Server Explorer

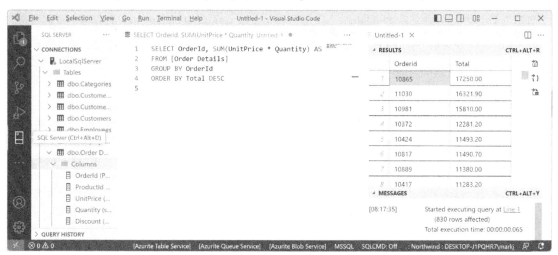

Figure 2.12: Executing T-SQL queries using Visual Studio Code's mssql extension

DML for adding, updating, and deleting data

DML statements for adding, updating, and deleting data include those shown in *Table 2.4*:

Example	Description
`INSERT Employees(FirstName, LastName)` `VALUES('Mark', 'Price')`	Add a new row to the `Employees` table. The `EmployeeId` primary key value is automatically assigned. Use `@@IDENTITY` to get this value.

UPDATE Employees SET Country = 'UK' WHERE FirstName = 'Mark' AND LastName = 'Price'	Update my employee row to set my Country to UK.
DELETE Employees WHERE FirstName = 'Mark' AND LastName = 'Price'	Delete my employee row.
DELETE Employees	Delete all rows in the Employees table and record those deletions in the transaction log.
TRUNCATE TABLE Employees	Delete all rows in the Employees table more efficiently because it does not log the individual row deletions.

Table 2.4: Example DML statements with descriptions

 The above examples use the Employees table in the Northwind database. That table has referential integrity constraints that would mean that, for example, deleting all rows in the table cannot happen because every employee has related data in other tables like Orders.

Data Definition Language (DDL)

DDL statements change the structure of the database, including creating new objects like tables, functions, and stored procedures. The following table shows some examples of DDL statements to give you an idea, but the examples are simple and cannot be executed within the Northwind database, as shown in *Table 2.5*:

Example	Description

CREATE TABLE dbo.Shippers (
 	
  ShipperId INT PRIMARY KEY CLUSTERED,
 	
  CompanyName NVARCHAR(40)
 	
);
	Create a table to store shippers.

ALTER TABLE Shippers ADD Country NVARCHAR(40)	Add a column to a table.
CREATE NONCLUSTERED INDEX IX_Country ON Shippers(Country)	Add a non-clustered index for a column in a table.

`CREATE INDEX IX_FullName`
 	
`ON Employees(LastName, FirstName DESC)`
 	
`WITH (DROP_EXISTING = ON)`
	Change an aggregate index with multiple columns and control the sort order.

`DROP TABLE Employees`	Delete the `Employees` table. If it does not exist, then this throws an error.
`DROP TABLE IF EXISTS Employees`	Delete the `Employees` table if it already exists. This avoids the potential error from using the statement in the previous row.
`IF OBJECT_ID(N'Employees', N'U')` `    IS NOT NULL`	Check if a table exists. The `N` prefix before a text literal means Unicode. `'U'` means a user table as opposed to a system table.

Table 2.5: Example DDL statements with descriptions

Managing data with low-level APIs

The `Microsoft.Data.SqlClient` package provides database connectivity to SQL Server for .NET applications. It is also known as the **ADO.NET driver for SQL Server** and Azure SQL Database.

 More Information: You can find the GitHub repository for ADO.NET at the following link: https://github.com/dotnet/SqlClient.

The `Microsoft.Data.SqlClient` package supports the following .NET platforms:

- .NET Framework 4.6.2 and later.
- .NET Core 3.1 and later.
- .NET Standard 2.0 and later.

Understanding the types in ADO.NET

ADO.NET defines abstract types that represent minimal objects for working with data, like `DbConnection`, `DbCommand`, and `DbDataReader`. Database software manufacturers can inherit from and provide specific implementations that are optimized for and expose additional features for their database. Microsoft has done this for SQL Server. The most important types with their most used members are shown in *Table 2.6*:

Type	Properties	Methods	Description

`SqlConnection`	`ConnectionString,`
	
	`State,`
	
	`ServerVersion`
		`Open, Close,`
		
		`CreateCommand,`
		
		`RetrieveStatistics`
			Manage the connection to the database.

SqlConnectionStringBuilder	InitialCatalog, DataSource, Encrypt, UserID, Password, ConnectTimeout, and so on	Clear, ContainsKey, Remove	Build a valid connection string for a SQL Server database. After setting all the relevant individual properties, get the ConnectionString property.
SqlCommand	Connection, CommandType, CommandText, Parameters, Transaction	ExecuteReader, ExecuteNonQuery, ExecuteXmlReader, CreateParameter	Configure the command to execute.
SqlParameter	ParameterName, Value, DbType, SqlValue, SqlDbType, Direction, IsNullable		Configure a parameter for a command.
SqlDataReader	FieldCount, HasRows, IsClosed, RecordsAffected	Read, Close, GetOrdinal, GetInt32, GetString, GetDecimal, GetFieldValue<T>	Process the result set from executing a query.

Table 2.6: Important types in ADO.NET SqlClient

SqlConnection has two useful events: StateChange and InfoMessage.

All the ExecuteXxx methods of SqlCommand will execute any command. The one you use depends on what you expect to get back:

- If the command includes at least one SELECT statement that returns a result set, then call ExecuteReader to execute the command. This method returns a DbDataReader-derived object for reading row-by-row through the result set.
- If the command does not include at least one SELECT statement, then it is more efficient to call ExecuteNonQuery. This method returns an integer for the number of rows affected.

- If the command includes at least one SELECT statement that returns XML because it uses the AS XML command, then call ExecuteXmlReader to execute the command.

Creating a console app for working with ADO.NET

First, we will create a console app project for working with ADO.NET:

1. Use your preferred code editor to create a console app project, as defined in the following list:

    - Project template: **Console App** / console.
    - Solution file and folder: Chapter02.
    - Project file and folder: Northwind.Console.SqlClient.
    - **Do not use top-level statements:** Cleared.
    - **Enable native AOT publish:** Cleared.

     Good Practice: For all the projects that you create for this book, keep your root path short and avoid using # in your folder and file names, or you might see compiler errors like RSG002: TargetPath not specified for additional file. For example, do *not* use C:\My C# projects\ as your root path!

2. In the project file, treat warnings as errors, add a package reference for the latest version of Microsoft.Data.SqlClient, and statically and globally import System.Console, as shown highlighted in the following markup:

```
<Project Sdk="Microsoft.NET.Sdk">

  <PropertyGroup>
    <OutputType>Exe</OutputType>
    <TargetFramework>net8.0</TargetFramework>
    <ImplicitUsings>enable</ImplicitUsings>
    <Nullable>enable</Nullable>
    <TreatWarningsAsErrors>true</TreatWarningsAsErrors>
  </PropertyGroup>

  <ItemGroup>
    <PackageReference Include="Microsoft.Data.SqlClient" Version="5.1.2"
/>
  </ItemGroup>

  <ItemGroup>
    <Using Include="System.Console" Static="true" />
  </ItemGroup>

</Project>
```

You can check the most recent version of the package at the following link:
`https://www.nuget.org/packages/Microsoft.Data.SqlClient#versions-`
`body-tab.`

3. Build the project to restore the referenced package.
4. Add a new class file named `Program.Helpers.cs`, and modify its contents to define a method to configure the console to enable special characters like the Euro currency symbol and set the current culture, and a method that will output some text to the console in a specified color, with a default color of black, as shown in the following code:

```
using System.Globalization; // To use CultureInfo.

partial class Program
{
  private static void ConfigureConsole(string culture = "en-US",
    bool useComputerCulture = false)
  {
    // To enable Unicode characters like Euro symbol in the console.
    OutputEncoding = System.Text.Encoding.UTF8;

    if (!useComputerCulture)
    {
      CultureInfo.CurrentCulture = CultureInfo.GetCultureInfo(culture);
    }
    WriteLine($"CurrentCulture: {CultureInfo.CurrentCulture.
DisplayName}");
  }

  private static void WriteLineInColor(string value,
    ConsoleColor color = ConsoleColor.White)
  {
    ConsoleColor previousColor = ForegroundColor;
    ForegroundColor = color;
    WriteLine(value);
    ForegroundColor = previousColor;
  }
}
```

The default foreground color in the preceding code is white because I have assumed that most readers will have a default background color of black. On my computer, I set the default background color of the console to white so that I can take screenshots for this book. Set whatever default color is best for your computer.

5. Add a new class file named `Program.EventHandlers.cs`, and modify its contents to define methods that will act as event handlers for a database connection state change by showing the original and current states, and for when the database sends an `InfoMessage`, as shown in the following code:

```csharp
using Microsoft.Data.SqlClient; // To use SqlInfoMessageEventArgs.
using System.Data; // To use StateChangeEventArgs.

partial class Program
{
  private static void Connection_StateChange(
    object sender, StateChangeEventArgs e)
  {
    WriteLineInColor(
      $"State change from {e.OriginalState} to {e.CurrentState}.",
      ConsoleColor.DarkYellow);
  }

  private static void Connection_InfoMessage(
    object sender, SqlInfoMessageEventArgs e)
  {
    WriteLineInColor($"Info: {e.Message}.", ConsoleColor.DarkBlue);
  }
}
```

6. In `Program.cs`, delete the existing statements. Add statements to connect to SQL Server locally, to Azure SQL Database, or to SQL Edge, using either SQL authentication with a user ID and password or Windows Authentication without a user ID and password, as shown in the following code:

```csharp
using Microsoft.Data.SqlClient; // To use SqlConnection and so on.

ConfigureConsole();

#region Set up the connection string builder

SqlConnectionStringBuilder builder = new()
{
```

```
    InitialCatalog = "Northwind",
    MultipleActiveResultSets = true,
    Encrypt = true,
    TrustServerCertificate = true,
    ConnectTimeout = 10 // Default is 30 seconds.
};

WriteLine("Connect to:");
WriteLine("  1 - SQL Server on local machine");
WriteLine("  2 - Azure SQL Database");
WriteLine("  3 - Azure SQL Edge");
WriteLine();
Write("Press a key: ");

ConsoleKey key = ReadKey().Key;
WriteLine(); WriteLine();

switch (key)
{
  case ConsoleKey.D1 or ConsoleKey.NumPad1:
    builder.DataSource = ".";
    break;
  case ConsoleKey.D2 or ConsoleKey.NumPad2:
    builder.DataSource =
      // Use your Azure SQL Database server name.
      "tcp:apps-services-book.database.windows.net,1433";
    break;
  case ConsoleKey.D3 or ConsoleKey.NumPad3:
    builder.DataSource = "tcp:127.0.0.1,1433";
    break;
  default:
    WriteLine("No data source selected.");
    return;
}

WriteLine("Authenticate using:");
WriteLine("  1 - Windows Integrated Security");
WriteLine("  2 - SQL Login, for example, sa");
WriteLine();
Write("Press a key: ");
```

```
key = ReadKey().Key;
WriteLine(); WriteLine();

if (key is ConsoleKey.D1 or ConsoleKey.NumPad1)
{
  builder.IntegratedSecurity = true;
}
else if (key is ConsoleKey.D2 or ConsoleKey.NumPad2)
{
  Write("Enter your SQL Server user ID: ");
  string? userId = ReadLine();
  if (string.IsNullOrWhiteSpace(userId))
  {
    WriteLine("User ID cannot be empty or null.");
    return;
  }

  builder.UserID = userId;

  Write("Enter your SQL Server password: ");
  string? password = ReadLine();
  if (string.IsNullOrWhiteSpace(password))
  {
    WriteLine("Password cannot be empty or null.");
    return;
  }

  builder.Password = password;
  builder.PersistSecurityInfo = false;
}
else
{
  WriteLine("No authentication selected.");
  return;
}

#endregion

#region Create and open the connection

SqlConnection connection = new(builder.ConnectionString);
```

```
WriteLine(connection.ConnectionString);
WriteLine();

connection.StateChange += Connection_StateChange;
connection.InfoMessage += Connection_InfoMessage;

try
{
  WriteLine("Opening connection. Please wait up to {0} seconds...",
    builder.ConnectTimeout);
  WriteLine();
  connection.Open();

  WriteLine($"SQL Server version: {connection.ServerVersion}");
}
catch (SqlException ex)
{
  WriteLineInColor($"SQL exception: {ex.Message}",
    ConsoleColor.Red);
  return;
}

#endregion

connection.Close();
```

Good Practice: In this coding task, we prompt the user to enter the password to connect to the database. In a real-world app you are more likely to store the password in an environment variable or secure storage like Azure Key Vault. You must definitely never store passwords in your source code!

7. Run the console app, select options that work with your SQL Server setup, and note the results, including the state change event output written in dark yellow to make them easier to see, as shown in the following output:

```
Connect to:
  1 - SQL Server on local machine
  2 - Azure SQL Database
  3 - Azure SQL Edge

Press a key: 1
```

```
Authenticate using:
  1 - Windows Integrated Security
  2 - SQL Login, for example, sa

Press a key: 1

Data Source=.;Initial Catalog=Northwind;Integrated Security=True;Multiple
Active Result Sets=True;Connect Timeout=10;Encrypt=True;Trust Server
Certificate=True

Opening connection. Please wait up to 10 seconds...

State change from Closed to Open.
SQL Server version: 15.00.2101
State change from Open to Closed.
```

The following steps show the experience when connecting to Azure SQL Database or Azure SQL Edge, which require a username and password. If you are connecting to a local SQL Server using Windows Integrated Security, then you will not need to enter a password.

8. Run the console app, select choices that require a user ID and password, for example, with Azure SQL Database, and note the result, as shown in the following output:

```
Enter your SQL Server user ID: markjprice
Enter your SQL Server password: [censored]
Data Source=tcp:apps-services-book.database.windows.
net,1433;Initial Catalog=Northwind;Persist Security Info=False;User
ID=markjprice;Password=[censored];Multiple Active Result
Sets=True;Connect Timeout=10;Encrypt=True;Trust Server Certificate=True

Opening connection. Please wait up to 10 seconds...

State change from Closed to Open.
SQL Server version: 12.00.5168
State change from Open to Closed.
```

9. Run the console app, select choices that require a user ID and password, enter a wrong password, and note the result, as shown in the following output:

```
Enter your SQL Server user ID: markjprice
Enter your SQL Server password: 123456
```

```
Data Source=tcp:apps-services-book.database.windows.
net,1433;Initial Catalog=Northwind;Persist Security Info=False;User
ID=markjprice;Password=123456;Multiple Active Result Sets=True;Connect
Timeout=10;Encrypt=True;Trust Server Certificate=True

Opening connection. Please wait up to 10 seconds...

SQL exception: Login failed for user 'markjprice'.
```

10. In `Program.cs`, change the server name (the `DataSource` property) to something wrong.

11. Run the console app and note the result (depending on where your database is hosted, the exception message might be slightly different), as shown in the following output:

```
SQL exception: A network-related or instance-specific error occurred
while establishing a connection to SQL Server. The server was not found
or was not accessible. Verify that the instance name is correct and that
SQL Server is configured to allow remote connections. (provider: TCP
Provider, error: 0 - No such host is known.)
```

 When opening a SQL Server connection, the default timeout is 30 seconds for server connection problems, so be patient! We changed the timeout to 10 seconds to avoid having to wait so long.

Executing queries and working with data readers using ADO.NET

Now that we have a successful connection to the SQL Server database, we can run commands that retrieve rows from a table and process the results using a data reader:

1. In `Program.cs`, import the namespace for working with ADO.NET command types, as shown in the following code:

```
using System.Data; // To use CommandType.
```

 Good Practice: To save space in this book, I will use the names `cmd` and `r` to represent an SQL command and an SQL data reader. In your code, give variables proper word names like `command` and `reader`.

2. Before the statement that closes the connection, add statements to define a command that selects the ID, name, and price from the Products table, executes it, and outputs the product IDs, names, and prices using a data reader, as shown in the following code:

```
SqlCommand cmd = connection.CreateCommand();

cmd.CommandType = CommandType.Text;
cmd.CommandText = "SELECT ProductId, ProductName, UnitPrice FROM
Products";

SqlDataReader r = cmd.ExecuteReader();

string horizontalLine = new string('-', 60);
WriteLine(horizontalLine);
WriteLine("| {0,5} | {1,-35} | {2,10} |",
  arg0: "Id", arg1: "Name", arg2: "Price");
WriteLine(horizontalLine);

while (r.Read())
{
  WriteLine("| {0,5} | {1,-35} | {2,10:C} |",
    r.GetInt32("ProductId"),
    r.GetString("ProductName"),
    r.GetDecimal("UnitPrice"));
}

WriteLine(horizontalLine);

r.Close();
```

 We format the unit price using the C format, which uses the current culture to format currency values. The call to ConfigureConsole sets the current culture to US English so the output for all readers uses $. To test alternative cultures like French that use the Euro currency symbol, modify the call at the top of the Program.cs file, as shown in the following code: ConfigureConsole("fr-FR");.

3. Run the console app and note the results, as shown in the following partial output:

```
------------------------------------------------------------
|    Id | Name                                |      Price |
------------------------------------------------------------
|     1 | Chai                                |     $18.00 |
|     2 | Chang                               |     $19.00 |
```

```
...
|   76 | Lakkalikööri                          | $18.00 |
|   77 | Original Frankfurter grüne Soße       | $13.00 |
----------------------------------------------------------
```

4. In Program.cs, modify the SQL statement to define a parameter for the unit price and use it to filter the results to products that cost more than that unit price, as shown highlighted in the following code:

```
Write("Enter a unit price: ");
string? priceText = ReadLine();

if(!decimal.TryParse(priceText, out decimal price))
{
  WriteLine("You must enter a valid unit price.");
  return;
}

SqlCommand cmd = connection.CreateCommand();

cmd.CommandType = CommandType.Text;

cmd.CommandText = "SELECT ProductId, ProductName, UnitPrice FROM
Products"
  + " WHERE UnitPrice >= @minimumPrice";

cmd.Parameters.AddWithValue("minimumPrice", price);
```

5. Run the console app, enter a unit price like 50, and note the results, as shown in the following partial output:

```
Enter a unit price: 50

----------------------------------------------------------
|   Id | Name                             |    Price |
----------------------------------------------------------
|    9 | Mishi Kobe Niku                  |   $97.00 |
|   18 | Carnarvon Tigers                 |   $62.50 |
|   20 | Sir Rodney's Marmalade           |   $81.00 |
|   29 | Thüringer Rostbratwurst          |  $123.79 |
|   38 | Côte de Blaye                    |  $263.50 |
|   51 | Manjimup Dried Apples            |   $53.00 |
|   59 | Raclette Courdavault             |   $55.00 |
----------------------------------------------------------
```

Outputting statistics

An ADO.NET connection can track useful statistics during its lifetime, including those listed in *Table 2.7*:

Key	Description
`BuffersReceived, BuffersSent, BytesReceived, BytesSent`	Data is transmitted as bytes stored in buffers.
`CursorOpens`	Cursors are an expensive operation because they require state on the server, and should be avoided when possible.
`Prepares, PreparedExecs, UnpreparedExecs`	Number of prepares (compilations), executions of prepared commands, and executions of unprepared commands.
`SelectCount, SelectRows`	Number of `SELECT` statements and rows returned by `SELECT` statements.
`ServerRoundtrips, SumResultSets, Transactions`	Number of server round trips, result sets, and transactions.
`ConnectionTime, ExecutionTime, NetworkServerTime`	Time in milliseconds spent connected, executing commands, or due to the network.

Table 2.7: Connection statistics that can be tracked

Let's enable this and output some of those statistics:

1. In `Program.Helpers.cs`, import the namespaces for working with ADO.NET and common collections, as shown in the following code:

   ```
   using Microsoft.Data.SqlClient; // To use SqlConnection.
   using System.Collections; // To use IDictionary.
   ```

2. In `Program.Helpers.cs`, in the partial `Program` class, add a method to output statistics about the current connection, with an array of string values to control which of the dozen or more statistics we want to output, as shown in the following code:

   ```
   private static void OutputStatistics(SqlConnection connection)
   {
     // Remove all the string values to see all the statistics.
     string[] includeKeys = {
       "BytesSent", "BytesReceived", "ConnectionTime", "SelectRows"
     };

     IDictionary statistics = connection.RetrieveStatistics();

     foreach (object? key in statistics.Keys)
     {
       if (!includeKeys.Any() || includeKeys.Contains(key))
   ```

```
      {
        if (int.TryParse(statistics[key]?.ToString(), out int value))
        {
          WriteLineInColor($"{key}: {value:N0}", ConsoleColor.Cyan);
        }
      }
    }
  }
}
```

3. In `Program.cs`, after writing the SQL Server version to the console, add a statement to enable statistics for the connection, as shown highlighted in the following code:

    ```
    WriteLine($"SQL Server version: {connection.ServerVersion}");

    connection.StatisticsEnabled = true;
    ```

4. In `Program.cs`, before closing the connection, add a statement to output statistics for the connection, as shown highlighted in the following code:

    ```
    OutputStatistics(connection);

    connection.Close();
    ```

5. Run the console app and note the statistics, as shown in the following partial output:

    ```
    BytesReceived: 3,888
    BytesSent: 336
    SelectRows: 77
    ExecutionTime: 25
    ```

Working with ADO.NET asynchronously

You can improve the responsiveness of data access code by making it asynchronous. You will see more details of how asynchronous operations work in *Chapter 5, Multitasking and Concurrency*. For now, just enter the code as instructed.

Let's see how to change the statements to work asynchronously:

1. In `Program.cs`, change the statement to open the connection to make it asynchronous, as shown highlighted in the following code:

    ```
    await connection.OpenAsync();
    ```

2. In `Program.cs`, change the statement to execute the command to make it asynchronous, as shown highlighted in the following code:

    ```
    SqlDataReader r = await cmd.ExecuteReaderAsync();
    ```

3. In `Program.cs`, change the statements to read the next row and get the field values to make them asynchronous, as shown highlighted in the following code:

```
while (await r.ReadAsync())
{
  WriteLine("| {0,5} | {1,-35} | {2,8:C} |",
    await r.GetFieldValueAsync<int>("ProductId"),
    await r.GetFieldValueAsync<string>("ProductName"),
    await r.GetFieldValueAsync<decimal>("UnitPrice"));
}
```

4. In `Program.cs`, change the statements to close the data reader and connection to make them asynchronous, as shown highlighted in the following code:

```
await r.CloseAsync();
await connection.CloseAsync();
```

5. Run the console app and confirm that it has the same results as before, but it would run better in a multithreaded system, for example, not blocking the user interface in a GUI app, and not blocking I/O threads in a website.

Executing stored procedures using ADO.NET

If you need to execute the same query or another SQL statement multiple times, it is best to create a **stored procedure**, often with parameters, so that it can be precompiled and optimized. Stored procedure parameters have a direction to indicate if they are inputs, outputs, or return values.

Let's see an example that uses all three types of parameter direction. First, we will create the stored procedure in the database:

1. In your preferred database tool, connect to the `Northwind` database.

2. In your preferred database tool, add a new stored procedure:

    - If you are using **SQL Server Management Studio**, then in **Object Explorer**, navigate to **Databases | Northwind | Programmability**, right-click **Stored Procedures**, and select **New | Stored Procedure**.

    - If you are using Visual Studio 2022, then in **Server Explorer**, right-click **Stored Procedures** and select **Add New Stored Procedure**.

    - If you are using Visual Studio Code, then in **SQL Server**, right-click your connection profile and select **New Query**.

- If you are using JetBrains Rider, then in the **Database** toolbar, click the **Jump to Query Console...** button, and then remove any existing statements. As well as the following SQL statements, start with a command to set the active database to Northwind: USE Northwind GO. This should prevent JetBrains Rider from creating the stored procedure in the master database!

3. Modify the SQL statements to define a stored procedure named GetExpensiveProducts with two parameters, an input parameter for the minimum unit price and an output parameter for the row count of matching products, as shown in the following code:

```sql
CREATE PROCEDURE [dbo].[GetExpensiveProducts]
  @price money,
  @count int OUT
AS
  PRINT 'Getting expensive products: ' +
    TRIM(CAST(@price AS NVARCHAR(10)))

  SELECT @count = COUNT(*)
  FROM Products
      WHERE UnitPrice >= @price

  SELECT *
  FROM Products
  WHERE UnitPrice >= @price

RETURN 0
```

 The stored procedure uses two **SELECT** statements. The first sets the @count output parameter to a count of the matching product rows. The second returns the matching product rows. It also calls the **PRINT** command, which will raise the InfoMessage event.

4. Right-click in the SQL statements and select **Execute** or **Execute Query**.
5. Right-click **Stored Procedures** and select **Refresh**. In JetBrains Rider, it is named **routines**.

6. Expand **GetExpensiveProducts** and note the `@price` money input, `@count` int input/output, and return value parameters, as shown in **SQL Server Management Studio** in *Figure 2.13*:

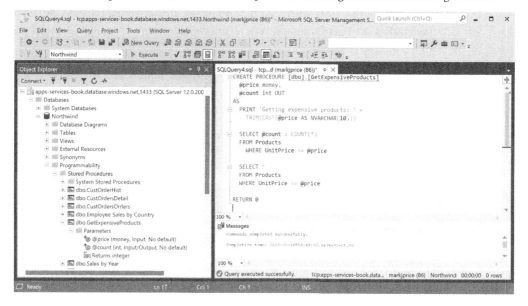

Figure 2.13: Parameters of the GetExpensiveProducts stored procedure

7. Close the SQL query without saving changes.

8. In `Program.cs`, add statements to allow the user to choose between running the text command and the stored procedure. Add statements defining the stored procedure and its parameters, and then execute the command, as shown highlighted in the following code:

```
SqlCommand cmd = connection.CreateCommand();

WriteLine("Execute command using:");
WriteLine("  1 - Text");
WriteLine("  2 - Stored Procedure");
WriteLine();
Write("Press a key: ");

key = ReadKey().Key;
WriteLine(); WriteLine();

SqlParameter p1, p2 = new(), p3 = new();

if (key is ConsoleKey.D1 or ConsoleKey.NumPad1)
{
    cmd.CommandType = CommandType.Text;
```

```
    cmd.CommandText = "SELECT ProductId, ProductName, UnitPrice FROM
Products"
      + " WHERE UnitPrice >= @minimumPrice";

  cmd.Parameters.AddWithValue("minimumPrice", price);
}
else if (key is ConsoleKey.D2 or ConsoleKey.NumPad2)
{
  cmd.CommandType = CommandType.StoredProcedure;
  cmd.CommandText = "GetExpensiveProducts";

  p1 = new()
  {
    ParameterName = "price",
    SqlDbType = SqlDbType.Money,
    SqlValue = price
  };

  p2 = new()
  {
    Direction = ParameterDirection.Output,
    ParameterName = "count",
    SqlDbType = SqlDbType.Int
  };

  p3 = new()
  {
    Direction= ParameterDirection.ReturnValue,
    ParameterName = "rv",
    SqlDbType = SqlDbType.Int
  };

  cmd.Parameters.AddRange(new[] { p1, p2, p3 });
}

SqlDataReader r = await cmd.ExecuteReaderAsync();
```

9. After the statement that closes the data reader, add statements to output the output parameter and the return value, as shown highlighted in the following code:

```
await r.CloseAsync();

if (key is ConsoleKey.D2 or ConsoleKey.NumPad2)
{
  WriteLine($"Output count: {p2.Value}");
  WriteLine($"Return value: {p3.Value}");
}

await connection.CloseAsync();
```

 If a stored procedure returns result sets as well as parameters, then the data reader for the result sets must be closed before the parameters can be read.

10. Run the console app and note the results if the price entered is 60, and note the InfoMessage event handler writes a message in dark blue, as shown in the following output:

```
Enter a unit price: 60
Execute command using:
  1 - Text
  2 - Stored Procedure

Press a key: 2

Info: Getting expensive products: 60.00.
-------------------------------------------------------------
|   Id | Name                             |      Price |
-------------------------------------------------------------
|    9 | Mishi Kobe Niku                  |    $97.00 |
|   18 | Carnarvon Tigers                 |    $62.50 |
|   20 | Sir Rodney's Marmalade           |    $81.00 |
|   29 | Thüringer Rostbratwurst          |   $123.79 |
|   38 | Côte de Blaye                    |   $263.50 |
-------------------------------------------------------------
Output count: 5
Return value: 0
State change from Open to Closed.
```

Outputting streams with a data reader

In a real app or service, we would likely not output to the console. More likely, as we read each row with a data reader, we might output to a stream that writes HTML tags inside a web page, or text formats like XML and JSON for returning data from a service.

Let's add the ability to generate a JSON file:

1. In `Program.cs`, import the namespace for working efficiently with JSON and to statically import the `Environment` and `Path` classes, as shown in the following code:

    ```
    using System.Text.Json; // To use Utf8JsonWriter, JsonSerializer.

    using static System.Environment;
    using static System.IO.Path;
    ```

2. In `Program.cs`, before the `while` statement that processes the data reader, add statements to define a file path for a JSON file, create a file stream, and start a JSON array, then in the `while` block, write a JSON object that represents each product row, and finally, end the array and close the stream, as shown highlighted in the following code:

    ```
    // Define a file path to write to.
    string jsonPath = Combine(CurrentDirectory, "products.json");

    await using (FileStream jsonStream = File.Create(jsonPath))
    {
      Utf8JsonWriter jsonWriter = new(jsonStream);
      jsonWriter.WriteStartArray();

      while (await r.ReadAsync())
      {
        WriteLine("| {0,5} | {1,-35} | {2,10:C} |",
          await r.GetFieldValueAsync<int>("ProductId"),
          await r.GetFieldValueAsync<string>("ProductName"),
          await r.GetFieldValueAsync<decimal>("UnitPrice"));

        jsonWriter.WriteStartObject();

        jsonWriter.WriteNumber("productId",
          await r.GetFieldValueAsync<int>("ProductId"));
        jsonWriter.WriteString("productName",
          await r.GetFieldValueAsync<string>("ProductName"));
        jsonWriter.WriteNumber("unitPrice",
          await r.GetFieldValueAsync<decimal>("UnitPrice"));
    ```

```
    jsonWriter.WriteEndObject();
  }


  jsonWriter.WriteEndArray();
  jsonWriter.Flush();
  jsonStream.Close();
}


WriteLineInColor($"Written to: {jsonPath}", ConsoleColor.DarkGreen);
```

3. Run the console app, enter a price of 60, and note the path to the JSON file, as shown in the following output:

```
Written to: C:\apps-services-net8\Chapter02\Northwind.Console.SqlClient\
bin\Debug\net8.0\products.json
```

4. Open the products.json file and note that the JSON is written with no whitespace, so it all appears on one line, as shown in the following file:

```
[{"productId":9,"productName":"Mishi Kobe
Niku","unitPrice":97.0000},{"productId":18,"productName":"Carnarvon
Tigers","unitPrice":62.5000},{"productId":20,"productName":"Sir Rodney\
u0027s Marmalade","unitPrice":81.0000},{"productId":29,"productName":"Th\
u00FCringer
Rostbratwurst","unitPrice":123.7900},{"productId":38,"productName":"C\
u00F4te de Blaye","unitPrice":263.5000}]
```

5. If you are using Visual Studio 2022, then you can right-click and select **Format Document**, and note that it is now easier to read, as shown in *Figure 2.14*:

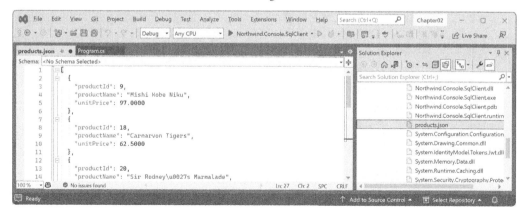

Figure 2.14: The products.json file generated from a data reader

Generating objects with a data reader

For maximum flexibility, we likely want to convert the rows in a data reader into object instances stored in an array or collection. After that, we could serialize the object graph however we want. ADO.NET does not have a built-in ability to map a data reader row to an object, so we will have to do it manually.

Let's see an example:

1. Add a new class file named `Product.cs`, and modify its contents to define a class to represent just the three columns we want from each row in the `Products` table, as shown in the following code:

    ```
    namespace Northwind.Models;

    public class Product
    {
      public int ProductId { get; set; }
      public string? ProductName { get; set; }
      public decimal? UnitPrice { get; set; }
    }
    ```

     Good Practice: In this task, we will use this type only for read-only instances, so we could have used an immutable `record`. But later we will need to change property values after the object is created, so we have to define a `class` instead.

2. At the top of `Program.cs`, import the `Northwind.Models` namespace so we can use `Product`.

3. In `Program.cs`, before creating the file stream, instantiate a list of products with an initial storage for 77 items (but this is not a limit) because when first created the Northwind database has 77 products, as shown highlighted in the following code:

    ```
    List<Product> products = new(capacity: 77);

    await using (FileStream jsonStream = File.Create(jsonPath))
    ```

4. In the `while` block, add statements to instantiate the `Product` type per row in the data reader and add it to the list, as shown highlighted in the following code:

    ```
    while (await r.ReadAsync())
    {
      Product product = new()
      {
        ProductId = await r.GetFieldValueAsync<int>("ProductId"),
        ProductName = await r.GetFieldValueAsync<string>("ProductName"),
        UnitPrice = await r.GetFieldValueAsync<decimal>("UnitPrice")
      };
    ```

```
    products.Add(product);

    ...

}
```

5. Before closing the data reader, add a statement to use the static `Serialize` method of the `JsonSerializer` class to write the list of products to the console, as shown highlighted in the following code:

```
WriteLineInColor(JsonSerializer.Serialize(products),
  ConsoleColor.Magenta);

await r.CloseAsync();
```

6. Run the console app, enter a price of `60`, and note the JSON generated from the list of products, as shown in the following output:

```
Written to: C:\apps-services-net8\Chapter02\Northwind.Console.SqlClient\
bin\Debug\net8.0\products.json
[{"ProductId":9,"ProductName":"Mishi Kobe
Niku","UnitPrice":97.0000},{"ProductId":18,"ProductName":"Carnarvon
Tigers","UnitPrice":62.5000},{"ProductId":20,"ProductName":"Sir Rodney\
u0027s Marmalade","UnitPrice":81.0000},{"ProductId":29,"ProductName":"Th\
u00FCringer
Rostbratwurst","UnitPrice":123.7900},{"ProductId":38,"ProductName":"C\
u00F4te de Blaye","UnitPrice":263.5000}]
```

Instead of manually instantiating objects, to simplify even more, we can use a simple **object-relational mapper (ORM)** like Dapper.

Managing data with Dapper

Dapper uses ADO.NET underneath when working with SQL Server. Because it is a higher-level technology, it is not as efficient as using ADO.NET directly, but it can be easier. Dapper is an alternative ORM to EF Core. It is more efficient because it extends the low-level ADO.NET `IDbConnection` interface with very basic functionality without trying to be all things to all people.

Dapper connection extension methods

Dapper adds three extension methods to any class that implements `IDbConnection` (like `SqlConnection`). They are `Query<T>`, `Query`, and `Execute`. Dapper will automatically open and close the associated connection as needed.

The `Query<T>` extension method is the most used because it runs any specified SQL command and then returns the results as an `IEnumerable<T>` (a sequence of objects). It is designed to run commands that retrieve data like `SELECT`. It has several parameters, as shown in *Table 2.8*:

Parameter	Description
`string sql`	This is the only mandatory parameter. It is either the text of a SQL command or the name of a stored procedure.
`object param = null`	A complex object for passing parameters used in the query. This can be an anonymous type.
`IDbTransaction transaction = null`	To manage distributed transactions.
`bool buffered = true`	By default, it will buffer the entire reader on return. With large datasets, you can minimize memory and only load objects as needed by setting `buffered` to `false`.
`int? commandTimeout = null`	To change the default command timeout.
`CommandType? commandType = null)`	To switch to a stored procedure instead of the default of text.

Table 2.8: Dapper's Query<T> extension method parameters

The `Query` extension method is a loosely-typed equivalent so it is less frequently used.

The `Execute` extension method runs any specified SQL command and then returns the number of rows affected as an `int`. It is designed to run commands like `INSERT`, `UPDATE`, and `DELETE`. It has the same parameters as the `Query<T>` extension method.

Querying using Dapper

Let's see a simple example that queries the `Suppliers` table instead of the `Products` table:

1. In the `Northwind.Console.SqlClient` project, add a package reference for `Dapper`, as shown highlighted in the following markup:

    ```
    <ItemGroup>
      <PackageReference Include="Microsoft.Data.SqlClient" Version="5.1.2" />
      <PackageReference Include="Dapper" Version="2.1.21" />
    </ItemGroup>
    ```

     At the time of writing, the latest version of Dapper is 2.1.21, released on November 11, 2023. You can check if it has been updated since then at the following link: `https://www.nuget.org/packages/Dapper`.

2. Build the project to restore packages.

3. Add a new class file named `Supplier.cs`, and modify its contents to define a class to represent four columns from each row in the `Suppliers` table, as shown in the following code:

    ```
    namespace Northwind.Models;

    public class Supplier
    ```

```
{
  public int SupplierId { get; set; }
  public string? CompanyName { get; set; }
  public string? City { get; set; }
  public string? Country { get; set; }
}
```

4. At the bottom of `Program.cs`, add statements to retrieve `Supplier` entities in `Germany`, enumerate the collection outputting basic information about each one, and then serialize the collection as JSON to the console, as shown in the following code:

```
WriteLineInColor("Using Dapper", ConsoleColor.DarkGreen);

connection.ResetStatistics(); // So we can compare using Dapper.

IEnumerable<Supplier> suppliers = connection.Query<Supplier>(
  sql: "SELECT * FROM Suppliers WHERE Country=@Country",
  param: new { Country = "Germany" });

foreach (Supplier s in suppliers)
{
  WriteLine("{0}: {1}, {2}, {3}",
    s.SupplierId, s.CompanyName, s.City, s.Country);
}

WriteLineInColor(JsonSerializer.Serialize(suppliers),
  ConsoleColor.Green);

OutputStatistics(connection);
```

5. Run the console app, and in the section where we used Dapper, note the same connection was used, so its events were raised while the Dapper query was executed, the enumerated collection output, and then JSON generated from the list of suppliers, as shown in the following output:

```
Using Dapper
11: Heli Süßwaren GmbH & Co. KG, Berlin, Germany
12: Plutzer Lebensmittelgroßmärkte AG, Frankfurt, Germany
13: Nord-Ost-Fisch Handelsgesellschaft mbH, Cuxhaven, Germany
[{"SupplierId":11,
  "CompanyName":"Heli S\u00FC\u00DFwaren GmbH \u0026 Co. KG",
  "City":"Berlin","Country":"Germany"},
 {"SupplierId":12,
  "CompanyName":"Plutzer Lebensmittelgro\u00DFm\u00E4rkte AG",
```

```
   "City":"Frankfurt","Country":"Germany"},
  {"SupplierId":13,
   "CompanyName":"Nord-Ost-Fisch Handelsgesellschaft mbH",
   "City":"Cuxhaven","Country":"Germany"}]
BytesReceived: 1,430
BytesSent: 240
SelectRows: 3
ExecutionTime: 5
```

6. At the bottom of `Program.cs`, add statements to run the `GetExpensiveProducts` stored procedure, passing a `price` parameter value of `100`, enumerate the collection outputting basic information about each one, and then serialize the collection as JSON to the console, as shown in the following code:

```csharp
IEnumerable<Product> productsFromDapper =
  connection.Query<Product>(sql: "GetExpensiveProducts",
  param: new { price = 100M, count = 0 },
  commandType: CommandType.StoredProcedure);

foreach (Product p in productsFromDapper)
{
  WriteLine("{0}: {1}, {2}",
    p.ProductId, p.ProductName, p.UnitPrice);
}

WriteLineInColor(JsonSerializer.Serialize(productsFromDapper),
  ConsoleColor.Green);
```

 Warning! With Dapper, you must pass a **param** object with all parameters, even if they are only used as output parameters. For example, we must define count, or an exception will be thrown. You must also remember to explicitly set the command type to stored procedure!

Run the console app, and in the section where we used Dapper to run the stored procedure to get the products that cost more than 100, note the same connection was used so its events were raised while the Dapper query was executed, the enumerated collection output, and then JSON generated from the list of products, as shown in the following output:

```
Info: Getting expensive products: 100.00.
29: Thüringer Rostbratwurst, 123.7900
38: Côte de Blaye, 263.5000
```

```
[{"ProductId":29,"ProductName":"Th\u00FCringer
Rostbratwurst","UnitPrice":123.7900},{"ProductId":38,"ProductName":"C\u00F4te
de Blaye","UnitPrice":263.5000}]
```

More Information: You can learn more about Dapper at the following link: `https://github.com/DapperLib/Dapper/blob/main/Readme.md`.

Cleaning up data resources

When you are done with a SQL Server database, you can clean up the resources used.

The Northwind database is used in most chapters of this book so if you plan to immediately continue with more chapters after this one, do not delete Northwind yet! If you created the database on your local computer, then you can leave it forever.

Removing Azure resources

To remove the resources used by SQL Database to save costs:

Warning! If you do not remove the resources used by an Azure SQL database, then you will incur costs.

1. In the Azure portal, find the resource group named `apps-services-book`.
2. Click **Delete**.
3. Enter the name of the resource group.
4. Click **Delete**.

Practicing and exploring

Test your knowledge and understanding by answering some questions, getting some hands-on practice, and exploring this chapter's topics with deeper research.

Exercise 2.1 – Test your knowledge

Answer the following questions:

1. Which NuGet package should you reference in a .NET project to get the best performance when working with data in SQL Server?
2. What is the safest way to define a database connection string?
3. What must T-SQL parameters and variables be prefixed with?
4. What must you do before reading an output parameter?

5. What type does Dapper add its extension methods to?

6. What are the two most commonly used extension methods provided by Dapper?

Exercise 2.2 — Explore topics

Use the links on the following page to learn more details about the topics covered in this chapter:

```
https://github.com/markjprice/apps-services-net8/blob/main/docs/book-links.md#chapter-
2---managing-relational-data-using-sql-server
```

Exercise 2.3 — Alternatives for storing secrets

Secrets like passwords and other values used in database connection strings, or values like keys to access a service, are often stored in environment variables. Other places for storing these values include App Secrets. You can learn more about them in the article *Safe storage of app secrets in development in ASP.NET Core*, found at the following link:

```
https://learn.microsoft.com/en-us/aspnet/core/security/app-secrets
```

For related guidance about handling connection strings, you can read the following link:

```
https://learn.microsoft.com/en-us/ef/core/miscellaneous/connection-strings
```

Summary

In this chapter, you learned:

- How to connect to an existing SQL Server database.
- How to execute a simple query and process the results using fast and low-level ADO.NET.
- How to execute a simple query and process the results using Dapper.

In the next chapter, you will learn how to use the more powerful and complex ORM from Microsoft named EF Core.

3

Building Entity Models for SQL Server Using EF Core

This chapter is about managing relational data stored in SQL Server, Azure SQL Database, or Azure SQL Edge by using the higher-level object-to-data store mapping technology named **Entity Framework Core** (**EF Core**). Then, you will learn how to store entity models that use inheritance hierarchies using three different mapping strategies. Finally, you will build class libraries for a SQL Server database that will be used in code examples throughout the rest of this book.

This chapter will cover the following topics:

- Managing SQL Server data with EF Core
- Mapping inheritance hierarchies with EF Core
- Building a reusable entity data model

Managing data with EF Core

EF Core is an **object-relational mapper** (**ORM**) that uses ADO.NET underneath when working with SQL Server. Because it is a higher-level technology, it is not as efficient as using ADO.NET directly, but it can be easier for developers to work with because they can treat the data as objects instead of rows in multiple tables. This should feel more natural for an object-oriented developer.

EF Core 8 only targets .NET 8. EF Core 7 targeted .NET 6, so it could be used with both the **Long Term Support** (**LTS**) release of .NET 6 and the **Standard Term Support** (**STS**) release of .NET 7, as shown in *Figure 3.1*:

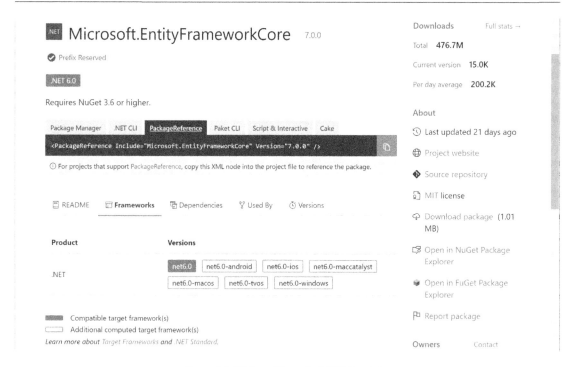

Figure 3.1: EF Core 7 targeted .NET 6 or later

When EF Core 9 is released in November 2024, we can expect it to target .NET 8 or later, so you can upgrade EF Core while still getting long-term support for the .NET 8 platform. The EF Core team is responsible for making sure that you will be able to swap 8 for 9 in the version number of their packages and your code should still work. They are usually very good at that, and they will document any needed changes to your code in the official release notes for EF Core 9.

Understanding Entity Framework Core

As well as traditional RDBMSs like SQL Server, EF Core supports modern cloud-based, nonrelational, schema-less data stores, such as Azure Cosmos DB and MongoDB, sometimes with third-party providers.

There are two approaches to working with EF Core:

- **Database First**: A database already exists, so you build a model that matches its structure and features.
- **Code First**: No database exists, so you build a model and then use EF Core to create a database that matches its structure and features.

We will use EF Core with an existing database because that is the most common scenario. You will also see an example of Code First later in this chapter that will create its database at runtime.

Scaffolding models using an existing database

Scaffolding is the process of using a tool to create classes that represent the model of an existing database using reverse engineering. A good scaffolding tool allows you to extend the automatically generated classes and then regenerate those classes without losing your extended classes.

If you know that you will never regenerate the classes using the tool, then feel free to change the code for the automatically generated classes as much as you want. The code generated by the tool is just the best approximation.

> **Good Practice:** Do not be afraid to overrule a tool when you know better. For example, when using SQLite for the Northwind database, date/time columns are mapped to `string` properties, and money columns are mapped to `double` properties. In the Northwind database, these would be better mapped to `DateTime` and `decimal` respectively, but in another database, they might need more flexibility. As another example, in the Northwind database, a `CustomerId` should always be five uppercase alphabetic characters. The tool cannot infer this automatically, so you could add a regular expression to validate it. Keep in mind that tool behavior is one of the more volatile components of .NET, so these examples may not be valid by the time you read this book.

Setting up the dotnet-ef tool

.NET has a command-line tool named dotnet. It can be extended with capabilities useful for working with EF Core. It can perform design-time tasks like creating and applying migrations from an older model to a newer model and generating code for a model from an existing database.

The dotnet ef command-line tool is not automatically installed. You must install this package as either a **global** or **local tool**. If you have already installed an older version of the tool, then you should uninstall any existing version.

Let's make sure you have the latest version of the tool installed:

1. At a command prompt or terminal, check if you have already installed dotnet-ef as a global tool, as shown in the following command:

    ```
    dotnet tool list --global
    ```

2. Check in the list if an older version of the tool has been installed, like the one for .NET 7, as shown in the following output:

    ```
    Package Id                            Version      Commands
    -------------------------------------------------------------
    dotnet-ef                             7.0.0        dotnet-ef
    microsoft.web.librarymanager.cli      2.1.175      libman
    redth.net.maui.check                  0.5.6        maui-check
    ```

3. If an older version is already installed, then uninstall the tool, as shown in the following command:

    ```
    dotnet tool uninstall --global dotnet-ef
    ```

4. Install the latest version, as shown in the following command:

    ```
    dotnet tool install --global dotnet-ef
    ```

5. If necessary, follow any OS-specific instructions to add the `dotnet tools` directory to your `PATH` environment variable, as described in the output of installing the `dotnet-ef` tool.

 If you want to install a preview version, you can specify a version wildcard, for example, for EF Core 9 previews, as shown in the following command:

```
dotnet tool install --global dotnet-ef --version 9-*
```

6. Instead of uninstalling and then installing, you can update using the following command:

```
dotnet tool update --global dotnet-ef
```

Defining EF Core models

EF Core uses a combination of **conventions, annotation attributes**, and **Fluent API** statements to build an **entity model** at runtime so that any actions performed on the classes can later be automatically translated into actions performed on the actual database. An **entity class** represents the structure of a table, and an instance of the class represents a row in that table.

First, we will review the three ways to define a model, with code examples, and then we will create some classes that implement those techniques.

Using EF Core conventions to define the model

The code we will write will use the following conventions:

- The name of a table is assumed to match the name of a `DbSet<T>` property in the `DbContext` class, for example, `Products`.
- The names of the columns are assumed to match the names of properties in the entity model class, for example, `ProductId`.
- The `string` .NET type is assumed to be an `nvarchar` type in the database.
- The `int` .NET type is assumed to be an `int` type in the database.
- The primary key is assumed to be a property that is named `Id` or `ID`. Or, when the entity model class is named `Product`, then the property can be named `ProductId` or `ProductID`. If this property is of an integer type or the `Guid` type, then it is also assumed to be an `IDENTITY` column (a column type that automatically assigns a value when inserting).

 Good Practice: There are many other conventions that you should know, and you can even define your own, but that is beyond the scope of this book. You can read about them at the following link: https://learn.microsoft.com/en-us/ef/core/modeling/.

Using EF Core annotation attributes to define the model

Conventions often aren't enough to completely map the classes to the database objects. For example, some databases like SQLite use dynamic column types so the tool has to guess about what property types its columns should map to, based on the current data values in that column.

A simple way of adding more smarts to your model is to apply annotation attributes, as shown in *Table 3.1*:

Attribute	Description
`[Required]`	Ensures the value is not null.
`[StringLength(50)]`	Ensures the value is up to 50 characters in length.
`[RegularExpression(expression)]`	Ensures the value matches the specified regular expression.
`[Column(TypeName = "money", Name = "UnitPrice")]`	Specifies the column type and column name used in the table.

Table 3.1: Common EF Core annotation attributes

For example, in the database, the maximum length of a product name is 40, and the value cannot be null, as shown highlighted in the following partial DDL code, which defines how to create a table named Products:

```
CREATE TABLE Products (
    ProductId       INTEGER       PRIMARY KEY,
    ProductName     NVARCHAR (40) NOT NULL,
    SupplierId      "INT",
    ...
);
```

In a Product class, we could apply attributes to specify this, as shown in the following code:

```
[Required]
[StringLength(40)]
public string ProductName { get; set; }
```

> **Good Practice:** If you have nullability checks enabled, then you do not need to decorate a non-nullable reference type with the `[Required]` attribute as shown above. This is because the C# nullability will flow to the EF Core model. A `string` property will be required; a `string?` property will be optional, in other words, nullable. You can read more about this at the following link: https://learn.microsoft.com/en-us/ef/core/modeling/entity-properties?tabs=data-annotations%2Cwith-nrt#required-and-optional-properties.

When there isn't an obvious map between .NET types and database types, an attribute can be used.

For example, in the database, the column type of UnitPrice for the Products table is money. .NET does not have a money type, so it should use decimal instead, as shown in the following code:

```
[Column(TypeName = "money")]
public decimal? UnitPrice { get; set; }
```

Another example is for the `Categories` table, as shown highlighted in the following DDL code:

```
CREATE TABLE Categories (
    CategoryId   INTEGER        PRIMARY KEY,
    CategoryName NVARCHAR (15) NOT NULL,
    Description  "NTEXT",
    Picture      "IMAGE"
);
```

The `Description` column can be longer than the maximum 8,000 characters that can be stored in an `nvarchar` variable, so it needs to map to `ntext` instead, as shown in the following code:

```
[Column(TypeName = "ntext")]
public string? Description { get; set; }
```

Using the EF Core Fluent API to define the model

The last way that the model can be defined is by using the Fluent API. This API can be used instead of attributes, as well as being used in addition to them. One reason you might need to do this is if the entity models need to be defined in a .NET Standard 2.0 class library so they can be used on legacy platforms. In this case, the class library should not include references to data annotation libraries. Another reason is that your team might have a policy to separate raw data models from validation rules.

For example, to define the `ProductName` property, instead of decorating the property with two attributes, an equivalent Fluent API statement could be written in the `OnModelCreating` method of the database context class, as shown in the following code:

```
modelBuilder.Entity<Product>()
    .Property(product => product.ProductName)
    .IsRequired() // only needed if you have disabled nullability checks
    .HasMaxLength(40);
```

This keeps the entity model class simpler. You will see an example of this in the coding task below.

Understanding data seeding with the Fluent API

Another benefit of the Fluent API is to provide initial data to populate a database. EF Core automatically works out what insert, update, or delete operations must be executed.

For example, if we wanted to make sure that a new database has at least one row in the `Product` table, then we would call the `HasData` method, as shown in the following code:

```
modelBuilder.Entity<Product>()
    .HasData(new Product
    {
      ProductId = 1,
      ProductName = "Chai",
      UnitPrice = 8.99M
    });
```

Calls to HasData take effect either during a data migration executed by the dotnet ef database update command or when you call the Database.EnsureCreated method.

Our model will map to an existing database that is already populated with data, so we will not need to use this technique in our code.

Defining the Northwind database model

A Northwind class will be used to represent the database. To use EF Core, the class must inherit from DbContext. This class understands how to communicate with databases and dynamically generate SQL statements to query and manipulate data.

Your DbContext-derived class should have an overridden method named OnConfiguring, which will set the database connection string.

Inside your DbContext-derived class, you must define at least one property of the DbSet<T> type. These properties represent the tables. To tell EF Core what columns each table has, the DbSet<T> properties use generics to specify a class that represents a row in the table. That entity model class has properties that represent its columns.

The DbContext-derived class can optionally have an overridden method named OnModelCreating. This is where you can write Fluent API statements as an alternative to decorating your entity classes with attributes. This can enhance the clarity and maintainability of the model configuration because all of it could be in one place instead of scattered throughout your code base. You can also mix and match both techniques, but then you'd lose this primary benefit.

 If you did not create the Northwind database, or if you deleted it, then you will need to create it now. Instructions are in *Chapter 2, Managing Relational Data Using SQL Server*.

Let's build the model for the Northwind database in a console app:

1. Use your preferred code editor to create a console app project, as defined in the following list:

    *   Project template: **Console App** / console.
    *   Solution file and folder: Chapter03.
    *   Project file and folder: Northwind.Console.EFCore.
    *   **Do not use top-level statements:** Cleared.
    *   **Enable native AOT publish:** Cleared.

2. In the Northwind.Console.EFCore project, add package references to the EF Core data provider for SQL Server, and globally and statically import the System.Console class, as shown highlighted in the following markup:

    ```
    <ItemGroup>
      <PackageReference
    ```

```
    Include="Microsoft.EntityFrameworkCore.Design"
    Version="8.0.0" />
  <PackageReference
    Include="Microsoft.EntityFrameworkCore.SqlServer"
    Version="8.0.0" />
</ItemGroup>

<ItemGroup>
  <Using Include="System.Console" Static="true" />
</ItemGroup>
```

3. Build the project to restore packages.

 The next step assumes a database connection string for a local SQL Server authenticated with Windows integrated security. Modify it for Azure SQL Database or Azure SQL Edge with a user ID and password if necessary.

4. At a command prompt or terminal in the Northwind.Console.EFCore folder, generate a model for all the tables in a new folder named Models, as shown in the following command:

```
dotnet ef dbcontext scaffold "Data Source=.;Initial
Catalog=Northwind;Integrated Security=true;TrustServerCertificate=true;"
Microsoft.EntityFrameworkCore.SqlServer --output-dir Models --namespace
Northwind.Models --data-annotations --context NorthwindDb
```

 Command-line tools need to have their commands entered all in one line. The dotnet-ef tool often needs long commands to be entered. I recommend that you type from the print book or copy and paste long commands like this from the eBook into a plain text editor like Notepad. Then make sure that the whole command is properly formatted as a single line with correct spacing before you then copy and paste it to the command line. Copying and pasting directly from the eBook is likely to include newline characters, missing spaces, and so on that break the command. All command lines that must be entered from this book are available to copy from as a single line at the following link: https://github.com/markjprice/apps-services-net8/blob/main/docs/command-lines.md.

Note the following:

*   The command action: dbcontext scaffold.
*   The connection string: This will be different depending on whether you are connecting to a local SQL Server (with or without an instance name) or Azure SQL Database.
*   The database provider: Microsoft.EntityFrameworkCore.SqlServer.
*   The output folder: --output-dir Models.

- The namespace: `--namespace Northwind.Models`.
- The use of data annotations as well as the Fluent API: `--data-annotations`.
- Renaming the context from `[database_name]Context`: `--context NorthwindDb`.

5. Note the build messages and warnings, as shown in the following output:

```
Build started…
Build succeeded.
To protect potentially sensitive information in your connection string,
you should move it out of source code. You can avoid scaffolding the
connection string by using the Name= syntax to read it from configuration
- see https://go.microsoft.com/fwlink/?linkid=2131148. For more
guidance on storing connection strings, see http://go.microsoft.com/
fwlink/?LinkId=723263.
```

 Good Practice: Do not commit your project to Git until you have fixed this warning. If you used a username and password to connect to your SQL Server database, then that information is now in your source code! We will fix this by replacing the fixed connection string with a dynamically generated one that reads the sensitive values from environment variables.

6. Open the `Models` folder and note the 28 class files that were automatically generated.

7. Open `Category.cs` and note that it represents a row in the `Categories` table, as shown in the following code:

```csharp
using System;
using System.Collections.Generic;
using System.ComponentModel.DataAnnotations;
using System.ComponentModel.DataAnnotations.Schema;
using Microsoft.EntityFrameworkCore;

namespace Northwind.Models;

[Index("CategoryName", Name = "CategoryName")]
public partial class Category
{
    [Key]
    public int CategoryId { get; set; }

    [StringLength(15)]
    public string CategoryName { get; set; } = null!;

    [Column(TypeName = "ntext")]
```

```
    public string? Description { get; set; }

    [Column(TypeName = "image")]
    public byte[]? Picture { get; set; }

    [InverseProperty("Category")]
    public virtual ICollection<Product> Products { get; set; }
        = new List<Product>();
}
```

Note the following:

- It decorates the entity class with the [Index] attribute that was introduced in EF Core 5. This indicates properties that should have an index for its column in the table. In earlier versions, only the Fluent API was supported for defining indexes. Since we are working with an existing database, this attribute is not needed. But if we want to recreate a new empty Northwind database from our code, then this information will be used to create indexes in the Categories table.

- The table name in the database is Categories but the dotnet-ef tool used the **Humanizer** third-party library to automatically singularize the class name to Category, which is a more natural name when creating a single entity.

- The entity class is declared using the partial keyword so that you can create a matching partial class for adding additional code. This allows you to rerun the tool and regenerate the entity class without losing that extra code you wrote in your partial class.

- The CategoryId property is decorated with the [Key] attribute to explicitly indicate that it is the primary key for this entity although its name follows the primary key convention too.

- The Products property uses the [InverseProperty] attribute to define the foreign key relationship to the Category property on the Product entity class.

8. Open ProductsAboveAveragePrice.cs and note that it represents a row returned by a database view rather than a table, so it is decorated with the [Keyless] attribute.

9. Open NorthwindDb.cs and review the class, as shown in the following edited-for-space code:

```
using System;
using System.Collections.Generic;
using Microsoft.EntityFrameworkCore;

namespace Northwind.Models;

public partial class NorthwindDb : DbContext
{
    public NorthwindDb()
    {
```

```csharp
  }

  public NorthwindDb(DbContextOptions<NorthwindDb> options)
    : base(options)
  {
  }

  public virtual DbSet<AlphabeticalListOfProduct>
    AlphabeticalListOfProducts { get; set; }

  public virtual DbSet<Category> Categories { get; set; }

...

  public virtual DbSet<Territory> Territories { get; set; }

  protected override void OnConfiguring(
    DbContextOptionsBuilder optionsBuilder)
#warning To protect potentially sensitive information in your connection
string, you should move it out of source code. You can avoid scaffolding
the connection string by using the Name= syntax to read it from
configuration - see https://go.microsoft.com/fwlink/?linkid=2131148. For
more guidance on storing connection strings, see http://go.microsoft.com/
fwlink/?LinkId=723263.
        => optionsBuilder.UseSqlServer("Data
Source=.;Initial Catalog=Northwind;Integrated
Security=true;TrustServerCertificate=true;");

  protected override void OnModelCreating(ModelBuilder modelBuilder)
  {
    modelBuilder.Entity<AlphabeticalListOfProduct>(entity =>
    {
      entity.ToView("Alphabetical list of products");
    });

...

    OnModelCreatingPartial(modelBuilder);
  }

  partial void OnModelCreatingPartial(ModelBuilder modelBuilder);
}
```

Note the following:

- The `NorthwindDb` data context class is `partial` to allow you to extend it and regenerate it in the future. We used the name `NorthwindDb` because `Northwind` is used for a namespace.

- `NorthwindDb` has two constructors: a default parameter-less one and one that allows options to be passed in. This is useful in apps where you want to specify the connection string at runtime.

- The `DbSet<T>` properties that represent tables like `Categories`.

- In the `OnConfiguring` method, if options have not been specified in the constructor, then it defaults to using the connection string used during scaffolding. It has a compiler warning to remind you that you should not hardcode security information in this connection string.

- In the `OnModelCreating` method, the Fluent API is used to configure the entity classes, and then a partial method named `OnModelCreatingPartial` is invoked. This allows you to implement that partial method in your own partial `Northwind` class to add your own Fluent API configuration, which will not be lost if you regenerate the model classes.

10. At the top of the `NorthwindDb.cs` file, import the namespace for working with ADO.NET types, as shown in the following code:

```
using Microsoft.Data.SqlClient; // To use SqlConnectionStringBuilder.
```

11. Modify the `OnConfiguring` method to dynamically set the connection string and set any sensitive parameters using environment variables, as shown in the following code:

```
protected override void OnConfiguring(
  DbContextOptionsBuilder optionsBuilder)
{
  if (!optionsBuilder.IsConfigured)
  {
    SqlConnectionStringBuilder builder = new();

    builder.DataSource = "."; // "ServerName\InstanceName" e.g. @".\
sqlexpress"
    builder.InitialCatalog = "Northwind";
    builder.TrustServerCertificate = true;
    builder.MultipleActiveResultSets = true;

    // Because we want to fail faster. Default is 15 seconds.
    builder.ConnectTimeout = 3;

    // If using Windows Integrated authentication.
    builder.IntegratedSecurity = true;
```

```
    // If using SQL Server authentication.
    // builder.UserID = Environment.GetEnvironmentVariable("MY_SQL_USR");
    // builder.Password = Environment.GetEnvironmentVariable("MY_SQL_
PWD");

    optionsBuilder.UseSqlServer(builder.ConnectionString);
  }
}
```

12. Close the automatically generated class files.

 More Information: If you have not worked with environment variables before, then you can learn about them from an online section available at the following link: https://github. com/markjprice/cs12dotnet8/blob/main/docs/ch09-environment-variables.md.

Querying the Northwind model

Now we can query the model:

1. In `Program.cs`, delete the existing statements. Add statements to create an instance of the `NorthwindDb` data context class and use it to query the products table for those that cost more than a given price, as shown in the following code:

```
using Microsoft.Data.SqlClient; // To use SqlConnectionStringBuilder.
using Microsoft.EntityFrameworkCore; // ToQueryString,
GetConnectionString
using Northwind.Models; // To use NorthwindDb.

SqlConnectionStringBuilder builder = new();

builder.InitialCatalog = "Northwind";
builder.MultipleActiveResultSets = true;
builder.Encrypt = true;
builder.TrustServerCertificate = true;
builder.ConnectTimeout = 10;

WriteLine("Connect to:");
WriteLine("  1 - SQL Server on local machine");
WriteLine("  2 - Azure SQL Database");
WriteLine("  3 - Azure SQL Edge");
WriteLine();
Write("Press a key: ");
```

```
ConsoleKey key = ReadKey().Key;
WriteLine(); WriteLine();

if (key is ConsoleKey.D1 or ConsoleKey.NumPad1)
{
  builder.DataSource = "."; // Local SQL Server
  // @".\apps-services-book"; // Local SQL Server with an instance name
}
else if (key is ConsoleKey.D2 or ConsoleKey.NumPad2)
{
  builder.DataSource = // Azure SQL Database
    "tcp:apps-services-book.database.windows.net,1433";
}
else if (key is ConsoleKey.D3 or ConsoleKey.NumPad3)
{
  builder.DataSource = "tcp:127.0.0.1,1433"; // Azure SQL Edge
}
else
{
  WriteLine("No data source selected.");
  return;
}

WriteLine("Authenticate using:");
WriteLine("  1 - Windows Integrated Security");
WriteLine("  2 - SQL Login, for example, sa");
WriteLine();
Write("Press a key: ");

key = ReadKey().Key;
WriteLine(); WriteLine();

if (key is ConsoleKey.D1 or ConsoleKey.NumPad1)
{
  builder.IntegratedSecurity = true;
}
else if (key is ConsoleKey.D2 or ConsoleKey.NumPad2)
{
  Write("Enter your SQL Server user ID: ");
  string? userId = ReadLine();
```

```
    if (string.IsNullOrWhiteSpace(userId))
    {
      WriteLine("User ID cannot be empty or null.");
      return;
    }

    builder.UserID = userId;

    Write("Enter your SQL Server password: ");
    string? password = ReadLine();
    if (string.IsNullOrWhiteSpace(password))
    {
      WriteLine("Password cannot be empty or null.");
      return;
    }

    builder.Password = password;
    builder.PersistSecurityInfo = false;
  }
  else
  {
    WriteLine("No authentication selected.");
    return;
  }

  DbContextOptionsBuilder<NorthwindDb> options = new();
  options.UseSqlServer(builder.ConnectionString);

  using (NorthwindDb db = new(options.Options))
  {
    Write("Enter a unit price: ");
    string? priceText = ReadLine();

    if (!decimal.TryParse(priceText, out decimal price))
    {
      WriteLine("You must enter a valid unit price.");
      return;
    }

    // We have to use var because we are projecting into an anonymous type.
    var products = db.Products
```

```
      .Where(p => p.UnitPrice > price)
      .Select(p => new { p.ProductId, p.ProductName, p.UnitPrice });


  WriteLine("-------------------------------------------------------------");
  WriteLine("| {0,5} | {1,-35} | {2,8} |", "Id", "Name", "Price");
  WriteLine("-------------------------------------------------------------");


  foreach (var p in products)
  {
    WriteLine("| {0,5} | {1,-35} | {2,8:C} |",
        p.ProductId, p.ProductName, p.UnitPrice);
  }


  WriteLine("-------------------------------------------------------------");

  WriteLine(products.ToQueryString());
  WriteLine();
  WriteLine($"Provider:   {db.Database.ProviderName}");
  WriteLine($"Connection: {db.Database.GetConnectionString()}");
}
```

2. Run the console app and note the results, as shown in the following partial output:

```
Enter a unit price: --
|    Id | Name                                |      Price--
|     9 | Mishi Kobe Niku                     |   £97.00 |
|    18 | Carnarvon Tigers                    |   £62.50 |
|    20 | Sir Rodney's Marmalade              |   £81.00 |
|    29 | Thüringer Rostbratwurst             |  £123.79 |
|    38 | Côte de Blaye                       |  £263.50--
DECLARE @__price_0 decimal(2) = 60.0;


SELECT [p].[ProductId], [p].[ProductName], [p].[UnitPrice]
FROM [Products] AS [p]
WHERE [p].[UnitPrice] > @__price_0


Provider:   Microsoft.EntityFrameworkCore.SqlServer
Connection: Data Source=tcp:apps-services-book.database.windows.
net,1433;Initial Catalog=Northwind;Persist Security Info=False;User
ID=<censored>;Password=<censored>;Multiple Active Result
Sets=False;Encrypt=True;Trust Server Certificate=False;Connection
Timeout=10;
```

The output of your connection string will be different.

Controlling the tracking of entities

We need to start with the definition of entity **identity resolution**. EF Core resolves each entity instance by reading its unique primary key value. This ensures no ambiguities about the identities of entities or relationships between them.

 EF Core can only track entities with keys because it uses a key to uniquely identify the entity in the database. Keyless entities, like those returned by views, are never tracked.

By default, EF Core assumes that you want to track entities in local memory so that if you make changes, like adding a new entity, modifying an existing entity, or removing an existing entity, then you can call SaveChanges and all those changes will be made in the underlying data store.

If you execute a query within a data context, like getting all customers in Germany, and then execute another query within the same data context, like getting all customers whose name starts with A, if one of those customer entities already exists in the context, it will be identified and not replaced or loaded twice. However, if the telephone number of that customer is updated in the database between the executions of the two queries, then the entity being tracked in the data context is not refreshed with the new telephone number.

If you do not need to track these changes, or you want to load new instances of an entity for every query execution with the latest data values, even if the entity is already loaded, then you can disable tracking.

To disable tracking for an individual query, call the AsNoTracking method as part of the query, as shown in the following code:

```
var products = db.Products
  .AsNoTracking()
  .Where(p => p.UnitPrice > price)
  .Select(p => new { p.ProductId, p.ProductName, p.UnitPrice });
```

To disable tracking by default for the data context, set the change tracker's query tracking behavior to NoTracking, as shown in the following code:

```
db.ChangeTracker.QueryTrackingBehavior = QueryTrackingBehavior.NoTracking;
```

To disable tracking for an individual query, but retain identity resolution, call the `AsNoTrackingWith IdentityResolution` method as part of the query, as shown in the following code:

```
var products = db.Products
  .AsNoTrackingWithIdentityResolution()
  .Where(p => p.UnitPrice > price)
  .Select(p => new { p.ProductId, p.ProductName, p.UnitPrice });
```

To disable tracking but perform identity resolution by default for the data context, set the change tracker's query-tracking behavior to `NoTrackingWithIdentityResolution`, as shown in the following code:

```
db.ChangeTracker.QueryTrackingBehavior =
  QueryTrackingBehavior.NoTrackingWithIdentityResolution;
```

To set defaults for all new instances of a data context, in the `OnConfiguring` method, call the `UseQueryTrackingBehavior` method, as shown in the following code:

```
protected override void OnConfiguring(DbContextOptionsBuilder optionsBuilder)
{
  optionsBuilder.UseSqlServer(connectionString)
    .UseQueryTrackingBehavior(QueryTrackingBehavior.NoTracking);
}
```

A scenario using default tracking

The default is **change tracking** with identity resolution. Once an entity is loaded into the data context, underlying changes are not reflected and only one copy exists. Entities have local changes tracked and a call to `SaveChanges` updates the database, as shown in *Table 3.2*:

Action	Entity in data context	Row in database
Query for customers in Germany	Alfred's Futterkiste, 123-4567	Alfred's Futterkiste, 123-4567
Change telephone in database	Alfred's Futterkiste, 123-4567	Alfred's Futterkiste, 123-9876
Query for customers starting with A	Alfred's Futterkiste, 123-4567	Alfred's Futterkiste, 123-9876
Query for customers in Germany	Alfred's Futterkiste, 123-4567	Alfred's Futterkiste, 123-9876
Change telephone in entity	Alfred's Futterkiste, 123-1928	Alfred's Futterkiste, 123-9876
Save changes	Alfred's Futterkiste, 123-1928	Alfred's Futterkiste, 123-1928

Table 3.2: Default tracking scenario

The same scenario using no tracking

No tracking and no identity resolution. Every query loads another instance of a database row into the data context, including underlying changes, allowing duplicates and mixed out-of-date and updated data. No local entity changes are tracked, so `SaveChanges` does nothing, as shown in *Table 3.3*:

Action	Entities in data context	Row in database
Query for customers in Germany	Alfred's Futterkiste, 123-4567	Alfred's Futterkiste, 123-4567
Change telephone in database	Alfred's Futterkiste, 123-4567	Alfred's Futterkiste, 123-9876
Query for customers starting with A	Alfred's Futterkiste, 123-4567 Alfred's Futterkiste, 123-9876	Alfred's Futterkiste, 123-9876
Query for customers in Germany	Alfred's Futterkiste, 123-4567 Alfred's Futterkiste, 123-9876 Alfred's Futterkiste, 123-9876	Alfred's Futterkiste, 123-9876
Change telephone in entity	Alfred's Futterkiste, 123-4567 Alfred's Futterkiste, 123-9876 Alfred's Futterkiste, 123-1928	Alfred's Futterkiste, 123-9876
Save changes	Alfred's Futterkiste, 123-4567 Alfred's Futterkiste, 123-9876 Alfred's Futterkiste, 123-1928	Alfred's Futterkiste, 123-9876

Table 3.3: No tracking scenario

The same scenario using no tracking with identity resolution

No tracking with identity resolution. Once an entity is loaded into the data context, underlying changes are not reflected and only one copy exists. No local entity changes are tracked, so SaveChanges does nothing, as shown in *Table 3.4*:

Action	Entities in data context	Row in database
Query for customers in Germany	Alfred's Futterkiste, 123-4567	Alfred's Futterkiste, 123-4567
Change telephone in database	Alfred's Futterkiste, 123-4567	Alfred's Futterkiste, 123-9876
Query for customers starting with A	Alfred's Futterkiste, 123-4567	Alfred's Futterkiste, 123-9876
Query for customers in Germany	Alfred's Futterkiste, 123-4567	Alfred's Futterkiste, 123-9876
Change telephone in entity	Alfred's Futterkiste, 123-1928	Alfred's Futterkiste, 123-9876
Save changes	Alfred's Futterkiste, 123-1928	Alfred's Futterkiste, 123-9876

Table 3.4: Identity resolution scenario

Summary of tracking

Which should you choose? Of course, it depends on your specific scenario.

You will sometimes read blogs that excitedly tell you that you can dramatically improve your EF Core queries by calling AsNoTracking. But if you run a query that returns thousands of entities and then run the same query again within the same data context, you now have thousands of duplicates! This wastes memory and impacts performance.

Understand how the three tracking choices work and select the best for your data context or individual queries. In the next topic, you will learn how to map inheritance hierarchies.

Mapping inheritance hierarchies with EF Core

Imagine that you have an inheritance hierarchy for some C# classes to store information about students and employees, both of which are types of people. All people have a name and an ID to uniquely identify them, students have a subject they are studying, and employees have a hire date, as shown in the following code:

```
public abstract class Person
{
  public int Id { get; set; }
  public string? Name { get; set; }
}

public class Student : Person
{
  public string? Subject { get; set; }
}

public class Employee : Person
{
  public DateTime HireDate { get; set; }
}
```

By default, EF Core will map these to a single table using the **table-per-hierarchy** (**TPH**) mapping strategy. EF Core 5 introduced support for the **table-per-type** (**TPT**) mapping strategy. EF Core 7 introduced support for the **table-per-concrete-type** (**TPC**) mapping strategy. Let's explore the differences between these mapping strategies.

Table-per-hierarchy (TPH) mapping strategy

For the Person-Student-Employee hierarchy, TPH will use a single table structure with a discriminator column to indicate which type of person, a student or employee, the row is, with nullable columns for extra values that only apply to some of the types, as shown highlighted in the following code:

```
CREATE TABLE [People] (
  [Id] int NOT NULL IDENTITY,
  [Name] nvarchar(max) NOT NULL,
  [Discriminator] nvarchar(max) NOT NULL,
  [Subject] nvarchar(max) NULL,
  [HireDate] nvarchar(max) NULL,
  CONSTRAINT [PK_People] PRIMARY KEY ([Id])
);
```

Some data in the table might look like *Table 3.5*:

Id	Name	Discriminator	Subject	HireDate
1	Roman Roy	Student	History	NULL
2	Kendall Roy	Employee	NULL	02/04/2014
3	Siobhan Roy	Employee	NULL	12/09/2020

Table 3.5: Sample data in the People table

TPH requires the `Discriminator` column to store the class name of the type for each row. TPH requires the columns for properties of derived types to be nullable, like `Subject` and `HireDate`. This will cause an issue if those properties are required (non-null) at the class level. EF Core does not handle this by default.

The main benefits of the TPH mapping strategy are simplicity and performance, which is why it is used by default.

Good Practice: If the discriminator column has many different values, then you can improve performance even more by defining an index on the discriminator. But if there are only a few different values, an index may make overall performance worse because it affects updating time. In this case, there are only two potential values, `Student` and `Employee`, so in a table with 100,000 rows, an index would make little difference.

Table-per-type (TPT) mapping strategy

For the `Person-Student-Employee` hierarchy, TPT will use a table for every type, as shown in the following code:

```
CREATE TABLE [People] (
  [Id] int NOT NULL IDENTITY,
  [Name] nvarchar(max) NOT NULL,
  CONSTRAINT [PK_People] PRIMARY KEY ([Id])
);

CREATE TABLE [Students] (
  [Id] int NOT NULL,
  [Subject] nvarchar(max) NULL,
  CONSTRAINT [PK_Students] PRIMARY KEY ([Id])
  CONSTRAINT [FK_Students_People] FOREIGN KEY ([Id]) REFERENCES [People] ([Id])
);

CREATE TABLE [Employees] (
  [Id] int NOT NULL,
  [HireDate] nvarchar(max) NULL,
```

```
  CONSTRAINT [PK_Employees] PRIMARY KEY ([Id])
  CONSTRAINT [FK_Employees_People] FOREIGN KEY ([Id]) REFERENCES [People]
([Id])
);
```

Some data in the tables might look like the following:

Id	Name
1	Roman Roy
2	Kendall Roy
3	Siobhan Roy

Table 3.6: People table

Id	Subject
1	History

Table 3.7: Students table

Id	HireDate
2	02/04/2014
3	12/09/2020

Table 3.8: Employees table

The main benefit of the TPT mapping strategy is reduced storage due to the full normalization of the data. The main disadvantage is that a single entity is spread over multiple tables and reconstructing it takes more effort and therefore reduces overall performance. TPT is usually a poor choice, so only use it if the table structure is already normalized and cannot be restructured.

Table-per-concrete-type (TPC) mapping strategy

For the Person-Student-Employee hierarchy, TPC will use a table for each non-abstract type, as shown in the following code:

```
CREATE TABLE [Students] (
  [Id] int NOT NULL DEFAULT (NEXT VALUE FOR [PersonIds]),
  [Name] nvarchar(max) NOT NULL,
  [Subject] nvarchar(max) NULL,
  CONSTRAINT [PK_Students] PRIMARY KEY ([Id])
  CONSTRAINT [FK_Students_People] FOREIGN KEY ([Id]) REFERENCES [People] ([Id])
);

CREATE TABLE [Employees] (
  [Id] int NOT NULL DEFAULT (NEXT VALUE FOR [PersonIds]),
```

```
    [Name] nvarchar(max) NOT NULL,
    [HireDate] nvarchar(max) NULL,
  CONSTRAINT [PK_Employees] PRIMARY KEY ([Id])
  CONSTRAINT [FK_Employees_People] FOREIGN KEY ([Id]) REFERENCES [People]
([Id])
);
```

 Since there is not a single table with an IDENTITY column to assign Id values, we can use the (NEXT VALUE FOR [PersonIds]) command to define a sequence shared between the two tables so they do not assign the same Id values.

Some data in the tables might look like the following:

Id	Name	Subject
1	Roman Roy	History

Table 3.9: Students table

Id	Name	HireDate
2	Kendall Roy	02/04/2014
3	Siobhan Roy	12/09/2020

Table 3.10: Employees table

The main benefit of the TPC mapping strategy is performance because when querying a single concrete type, only one table is needed so we avoid expensive joins. It works best for large inheritance hierarchies of many concrete types, each with many type-specific properties.

Configuring inheritance hierarchy mapping strategies

First, all types must be included in the model, as shown in the following code:

```
public DbSet<Person> People { get; set; }
public DbSet<Student> Students { get; set; }
public DbSet<Employee> Employees { get; set; }
```

For TPH, you are now finished, because it is the default! If you want to make this explicit, then in the data context class OnModelCreating method, call the appropriate "use mapping strategy" method on the base class of the hierarchy. Person is the base class, so you would call UseTphMappingStrategy on that entity type, as shown in the following code:

```
modelBuilder.Entity<Person>().UseTphMappingStrategy();
```

To use either of the other two mapping strategies, call the appropriate method, as shown in the following code:

```
modelBuilder.Entity<Person>().UseTptMappingStrategy();
modelBuilder.Entity<Person>().UseTpcMappingStrategy();
```

Next, you can optionally specify the table name to use for each entity class, as shown in the following code:

```
modelBuilder.Entity<Student>().ToTable("Students");
modelBuilder.Entity<Employee>().ToTable("Employees");
```

The TPC strategy should have a shared sequence, so we should configure that too, as shown in the following code:

```
modelBuilder.HasSequence<int>("PersonIds");

modelBuilder.Entity<Person>().UseTpcMappingStrategy()
  .Property(e => e.Id).HasDefaultValueSql("NEXT VALUE FOR [PersonIds]");
```

Example of hierarchy mapping strategies

Now let's see this in action using a new database and project named HierarchyMapping:

1. Use your preferred code editor to add a console app project, as defined in the following list:

    *   Project template: **Console App** / console.
    *   Solution file and folder: Chapter03.
    *   Project file and folder: Northwind.Console.HierarchyMapping.
    *   **Do not use top-level statements:** Cleared.
    *   **Enable native AOT publish:** Cleared.

2. Configure the startup project to run Northwind.Console.HierarchyMapping.

3. In the Northwind.Console.HierarchyMapping project, add package references to the EF Core data provider for SQL Server, and globally and statically import the System.Console class, as shown in the following markup:

    ```
    <ItemGroup>
      <PackageReference
        Include="Microsoft.EntityFrameworkCore.Design"
        Version="8.0.0" />
      <PackageReference
        Include="Microsoft.EntityFrameworkCore.SqlServer"
        Version="8.0.0" />
    </ItemGroup>
    ```

```
<ItemGroup>
  <Using Include="System.Console" Static="true" />
</ItemGroup>
```

4. Build the project to restore packages.

5. In the Northwind.Console.HierarchyMapping project, add a new folder named Models.

6. In Models, add a new class file named Person.cs, and modify its contents, as shown in the following code:

```
using System.ComponentModel.DataAnnotations; // To use [Required].

namespace Northwind.Models;

public abstract class Person
{
  public int Id { get; set; }

  [Required]
  [StringLength(40)]
  public string? Name { get; set; }
}
```

7. In Models, add a new class file named Student.cs, and modify its contents, as shown in the following code:

```
namespace Northwind.Models;

public class Student : Person
{
  public string? Subject { get; set; }
}
```

8. In Models, add a new class file named Employee.cs, and modify its contents, as shown in the following code:

```
namespace Northwind.Models;

public class Employee : Person
{
  public DateTime HireDate { get; set; }
}
```

9. In `Models`, add a new class file named `HierarchyDb.cs`, and modify its contents, as shown in the following code:

```
using Microsoft.EntityFrameworkCore; // To use DbSet<T>.

namespace Northwind.Models;

public class HierarchyDb : DbContext
{
  public DbSet<Person>? People { get; set; }
  public DbSet<Student>? Students { get; set; }
  public DbSet<Employee>? Employees { get; set; }

  public HierarchyDb(DbContextOptions<HierarchyDb> options)
      : base(options)
  {
  }

  protected override void OnModelCreating(ModelBuilder modelBuilder)
  {
    modelBuilder.Entity<Person>()
      .UseTphMappingStrategy();

    // Populate database with sample data.

    Student p1 = new() { Id = 1, Name = "Roman Roy",
      Subject = "History" };

    Employee p2 = new() { Id = 2, Name = "Kendall Roy",
      HireDate = new(year: 2014, month: 4, day: 2) };

    Employee p3 = new() { Id = 3, Name = "Siobhan Roy",
      HireDate = new(year: 2020, month: 9, day: 12) };

    modelBuilder.Entity<Student>().HasData(p1);
    modelBuilder.Entity<Employee>().HasData(p2, p3);
  }
}
```

10. In `Program.cs`, delete the existing statements. Add statements to configure the connection string for the `HierarchyDb` data context and then use it to delete and then create a database named `HierarchyMapping` (not `Northwind`!), show the automatically generated SQL script, and then output the students, employees, and people, as shown in the following code:

```csharp
using Microsoft.Data.SqlClient; // To use SqlConnectionStringBuilder.
using Microsoft.Extensions.Options;
using Microsoft.EntityFrameworkCore; // GenerateCreateScript()
using Northwind.Models; // HierarchyDb, Person, Student, Employee

DbContextOptionsBuilder<HierarchyDb> options = new();

SqlConnectionStringBuilder builder = new();

builder.DataSource = "."; // "ServerName\InstanceName" e.g. @".\
sqlexpress"
builder.InitialCatalog = "HierarchyMapping";
builder.TrustServerCertificate = true;
builder.MultipleActiveResultSets = true;

// Because we want to fail faster. Default is 15 seconds.
builder.ConnectTimeout = 3;

// If using Windows Integrated authentication.
builder.IntegratedSecurity = true;

// If using SQL Server authentication.
// builder.UserID = Environment.GetEnvironmentVariable("MY_SQL_USR");
// builder.Password = Environment.GetEnvironmentVariable("MY_SQL_PWD");

options.UseSqlServer(builder.ConnectionString);

using (HierarchyDb db = new(options.Options))
{
  bool deleted = await db.Database.EnsureDeletedAsync();
  WriteLine($"Database deleted: {deleted}");

  bool created = await db.Database.EnsureCreatedAsync();
  WriteLine($"Database created: {created}");

  WriteLine("SQL script used to create the database:");
  WriteLine(db.Database.GenerateCreateScript());

  if (db.Students is null || !db.Students.Any())
  {
    WriteLine("There are no students.");
```

```
    }
    else
    {
      foreach (Student student in db.Students)
      {
        WriteLine("{0} studies {1}",
          student.Name, student.Subject);
      }
    }

    if (db.Employees is null || !db.Employees.Any())
    {
      WriteLine("There are no employees.");
    }
    else
    {
      foreach (Employee employee in db.Employees)
      {
        WriteLine("{0} was hired on {1}",
          employee.Name, employee.HireDate);
      }
    }

    if (db.People is null || !db.People.Any())
    {
      WriteLine("There are no people.");
    }
    else
    {
      foreach (Person person in db.People)
      {
        WriteLine("{0} has ID of {1}",
          person.Name, person.Id);
      }
    }
  }
```

11. Start the console app, and note the results including the single table named People that is created, as shown in the following output:

```
Database deleted: False
Database created: True
```

```
SQL script used to create the database:
CREATE TABLE [People] (
    [Id] int NOT NULL IDENTITY,
    [Name] nvarchar(40) NOT NULL,
    [Discriminator] nvarchar(8) NOT NULL,
    [HireDate] datetime2 NULL,
    [Subject] nvarchar(max) NULL,
    CONSTRAINT [PK_People] PRIMARY KEY ([Id])
);
GO


IF EXISTS (SELECT * FROM [sys].[identity_columns] WHERE [name] IN
(N'Id', N'Discriminator', N'Name', N'Subject') AND [object_id] = OBJECT_
ID(N'[People]'))
    SET IDENTITY_INSERT [People] ON;
INSERT INTO [People] ([Id], [Discriminator], [Name], [Subject])
VALUES (1, N'Student', N'Roman Roy', N'History');
IF EXISTS (SELECT * FROM [sys].[identity_columns] WHERE [name] IN
(N'Id', N'Discriminator', N'Name', N'Subject') AND [object_id] = OBJECT_
ID(N'[People]'))
    SET IDENTITY_INSERT [People] OFF;
GO


IF EXISTS (SELECT * FROM [sys].[identity_columns] WHERE [name] IN
(N'Id', N'Discriminator', N'HireDate', N'Name') AND [object_id] = OBJECT_
ID(N'[People]'))
    SET IDENTITY_INSERT [People] ON;
INSERT INTO [People] ([Id], [Discriminator], [HireDate], [Name])
VALUES (2, N'Employee', '2014-04-02T00:00:00.0000000', N'Kendall Roy'),
(3, N'Employee', '2020-09-12T00:00:00.0000000', N'Siobhan Roy');
IF EXISTS (SELECT * FROM [sys].[identity_columns] WHERE [name] IN
(N'Id', N'Discriminator', N'HireDate', N'Name') AND [object_id] = OBJECT_
ID(N'[People]'))
    SET IDENTITY_INSERT [People] OFF;
GO


Roman Roy studies History
Kendall Roy was hired on 02/04/2014 00:00:00
Siobhan Roy was hired on 12/09/2020 00:00:00
Roman Roy has ID of 1
Kendall Roy has ID of 2
Siobhan Roy has ID of 3
```

12. In your preferred database tool, view the contents of the People table, as shown in *Figure 3.2*:

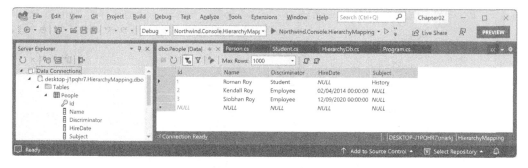

Figure 3.2: The People table when using the TPH mapping strategy

13. Close the connection to the HierarchyMapping database.

14. In HierarchyDb.cs, comment out the method call that configures TPH and add a call to the method that configures TPT, as shown highlighted in the following code:

```
protected override void OnModelCreating(ModelBuilder modelBuilder)
{
  modelBuilder.Entity<Person>()
    // .UseTphMappingStrategy();
    .UseTptMappingStrategy();
```

15. Start the console app, and note the results including the three tables named People, Students, and Employees that are created, as shown in the following partial output:

```
Database deleted: True
Database created: True
SQL script used to create the database:
CREATE TABLE [People] (
    [Id] int NOT NULL IDENTITY,
    [Name] nvarchar(40) NOT NULL,
    CONSTRAINT [PK_People] PRIMARY KEY ([Id])
);
GO


CREATE TABLE [Employees] (
    [Id] int NOT NULL,
    [HireDate] datetime2 NOT NULL,
    CONSTRAINT [PK_Employees] PRIMARY KEY ([Id]),
    CONSTRAINT [FK_Employees_People_Id] FOREIGN KEY ([Id]) REFERENCES
[People] ([Id])
);
GO
```

```
CREATE TABLE [Students] (
    [Id] int NOT NULL,
    [Subject] nvarchar(max) NULL,
    CONSTRAINT [PK_Students] PRIMARY KEY ([Id]),
    CONSTRAINT [FK_Students_People_Id] FOREIGN KEY ([Id]) REFERENCES
[People] ([Id])
);
GO
```

16. In your preferred database tool, view the contents of the tables, as shown in *Figure 3.3*:

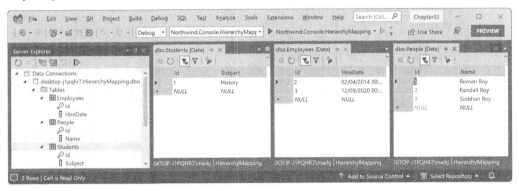

Figure 3.3: The tables when using the TPT mapping strategy

17. Close the connection to the HierarchyMapping database.

18. In HierarchyDb.cs, comment out the method call that configures TPT. Add a call to the method that configures TPC and configure a sequence to track assigned ID values starting at four because we always add three sample rows, as shown highlighted in the following code:

```
protected override void OnModelCreating(ModelBuilder modelBuilder)
{
  modelBuilder.Entity<Person>()
    // .UseTphMappingStrategy();
    // .UseTptMappingStrategy();
    .UseTpcMappingStrategy()
    .Property(person => person.Id)
    .HasDefaultValueSql("NEXT VALUE FOR [PersonIds]");

  modelBuilder.HasSequence<int>("PersonIds", builder =>
  {
    builder.StartsAt(4);
  });
```

19. Start the console app, and note the results including the two tables named Students and Employees that are created as well as the shared sequence that starts at 4, as shown in the following partial output:

```
CREATE SEQUENCE [PersonIds] AS int START WITH 4 INCREMENT BY 1 NO
MINVALUE NO MAXVALUE NO CYCLE;
GO


CREATE TABLE [Employees] (
    [Id] int NOT NULL DEFAULT (NEXT VALUE FOR [PersonIds]),
    [Name] nvarchar(40) NOT NULL,
    [HireDate] datetime2 NOT NULL,
    CONSTRAINT [PK_Employees] PRIMARY KEY ([Id])
);
GO


CREATE TABLE [Students] (
    [Id] int NOT NULL DEFAULT (NEXT VALUE FOR [PersonIds]),
    [Name] nvarchar(40) NOT NULL,
    [Subject] nvarchar(max) NULL,
    CONSTRAINT [PK_Students] PRIMARY KEY ([Id])
);
GO
```

20. In your preferred database tool, view the contents of the tables, as shown in *Figure 3.4*:

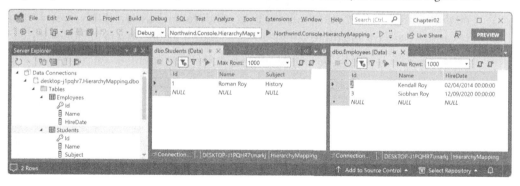

Figure 3.4: The tables when using the TPC mapping strategy

21. Close the connection to the HierarchyMapping database.

22. In Program.cs, after the statement to write the database create script to the console, add some statements to add two new people using the current database context, as shown highlighted in the following code:

```
WriteLine(db.Database.GenerateCreateScript());

if ((db.Employees is not null) && (db.Students is not null))
{
  db.Students.Add(new Student { Name = "Connor Roy",
    Subject = "Politics" });

  db.Employees.Add(new Employee { Name = "Kerry Castellabate",
    HireDate = DateTime.UtcNow });

  int result = db.SaveChanges();
  WriteLine($"{result} people added.");
}
```

23. Start the console app, and note the results, including the two new people added using the database context with IDs that start at 4, as shown in the following partial output:

```
2 people added.
Roman Roy studies History
Connor Roy studies Politics
Kendall Roy was hired on 02/04/2014 00:00:00
Siobhan Roy was hired on 12/09/2020 00:00:00
Kerry Castellabate was hired on 19/05/2023 10:13:53
Kendall Roy has ID of 2
Siobhan Roy has ID of 3
Kerry Castellabate has ID of 4
Roman Roy has ID of 1
Connor Roy has ID of 5
```

You've now seen how an object-relational mapper like EF Core can define an object inheritance hierarchy and map it in three different ways to an underlying database structure with one or more related tables. You've also seen how Code First works especially well with this since it is so easy to delete and recreate the database each time the project starts.

Building a reusable entity data model

Practical applications usually need to work with data in a relational database or another data store. Earlier in this chapter, we defined EF Core models in the same console app project that we used them in.

Now, we will define an entity data model for the Northwind database as a pair of reusable class libraries. One part of the pair will define the entities, like Product and Customer. The second part of the pair will define the tables in the database and the default configuration for how to connect to the database, and use the Fluent API to configure additional options for the model. This pair of class libraries will be used in many of the apps and services that you create in subsequent chapters.

Good Practice: You should create a separate class library project for your entity data models. This allows easier sharing between backend web servers and frontend desktop, mobile, and Blazor clients.

Creating a class library for entity models using SQL Server

You will now create the entity models using the `dotnet-ef` tool:

1. Add a new project, as defined in the following list:

    - Project template: **Class Library** / `classlib`.
    - Project file and folder: `Northwind.Common.EntityModels.SqlServer`.
    - Solution file and folder: `Chapter03`.

2. In the `Northwind.Common.EntityModels.SqlServer` project, treat warnings as errors, and add package references for the SQL Server database provider and EF Core design-time support, as shown highlighted in the following markup:

```xml
<Project Sdk="Microsoft.NET.Sdk">

  <PropertyGroup>
    <TargetFramework>net8.0</TargetFramework>
    <ImplicitUsings>enable</ImplicitUsings>
    <Nullable>enable</Nullable>
    <TreatWarningsAsErrors>true</TreatWarningsAsErrors>
  </PropertyGroup>

  <ItemGroup>
    <PackageReference
      Include="Microsoft.EntityFrameworkCore.SqlServer" Version="8.0.0"
/>
    <PackageReference
      Include="Microsoft.EntityFrameworkCore.Design" Version="8.0.0">
      <PrivateAssets>all</PrivateAssets>
      <IncludeAssets>runtime; build; native; contentfiles; analyzers;
buildtransitive</IncludeAssets>
    </PackageReference>
  </ItemGroup>

</Project>
```

More Information: If you are unfamiliar with how packages like `Microsoft.EntityFrameworkCore.Design` can manage their assets, then you can learn more at the following link: `https://learn.microsoft.com/en-us/nuget/consume-packages/package-references-in-project-files#controlling-dependency-assets`.

3. Delete the `Class1.cs` file.

4. Build the `Northwind.Common.EntityModels.SqlServer` project.

5. Open a command prompt or terminal for the `Northwind.Common.EntityModels.SqlServer` folder.

The next step assumes a database connection string for a local SQL Server authenticated with Windows integrated security. Modify it for Azure SQL Database or Azure SQL Edge with a user ID and password if necessary.

6. At the command line, generate entity class models for all tables, as shown in the following commands:

```
dotnet ef dbcontext scaffold "Data Source=.;Initial
Catalog=Northwind;Integrated Security=true;TrustServerCertificate=True;"
Microsoft.EntityFrameworkCore.SqlServer --namespace Northwind.
EntityModels --data-annotations
```

Note the following:

- The command to perform: `dbcontext scaffold`.
- The connection string: `"Data Source=.;Initial Catalog=Northwind;Integrated Security=true;TrustServerCertificate=True;"`.
- The database provider: `Microsoft.EntityFrameworkCore.SqlServer`.
- The namespace for the generated classes: `--namespace Northwind.EntityModels`.
- To use data annotations as well as the Fluent API: `--data-annotations`.

7. Note that 28 classes were generated, from `AlphabeticalListOfProduct.cs` to `Territory.cs`.

8. In `NorthwindContext.cs`, delete the `OnConfiguring` method including the warning and connection string.

9. In `Customer.cs`, the `dotnet-ef` tool correctly identified that the `CustomerId` column is the primary key and it is limited to a maximum of five characters, but we also want the values to always be uppercase. So, add a regular expression to validate its primary key value to only allow uppercase Western characters, as shown highlighted in the following code:

```
[Key]
[StringLength(5)]
[RegularExpression("[A-Z]{5}")]
public string CustomerId { get; set; } = null!;
```

Creating a class library for the data context using SQL Server

Next, you will move the context model that represents the database to a separate class library:

1. Add a new project, as defined in the following list:

    -   Project template: **Class Library** / `classlib`.
    -   Project file and folder: `Northwind.Common.DataContext.SqlServer`.
    -   Solution file and folder: `Chapter03`.
    -   In the `DataContext` project, add a project reference to the `EntityModels` project, and add a package reference to the EF Core data provider for SQL Server, as shown in the following markup:

    ```xml
    <ItemGroup>
      <PackageReference
        Include="Microsoft.EntityFrameworkCore.SqlServer" Version="8.0.0" />
    </ItemGroup>

    <ItemGroup>
      <ProjectReference Include="..\Northwind.Common.EntityModels
    .SqlServer\Northwind.Common.EntityModels.SqlServer.csproj" />
    </ItemGroup>
    ```

     Warning! The path to the project reference should not have a line break in your project file.

2. In the `Northwind.Common.DataContext.SqlServer` project, delete the `Class1.cs` file.
3. Build the `Northwind.Common.DataContext.SqlServer` project.
4. Move the `NorthwindContext.cs` file from the `Northwind.Common.EntityModels.SqlServer` project/folder to the `Northwind.Common.DataContext.SqlServer` project/folder.
5. In the `Northwind.Common.DataContext.SqlServer` project, add a class named `NorthwindContextExtensions.cs`, and modify its contents to define an extension method that adds the Northwind database context to a collection of dependency services, as shown in the following code:

    ```csharp
    using Microsoft.Data.SqlClient; // SqlConnectionStringBuilder
    using Microsoft.EntityFrameworkCore; // UseSqlServer
    using Microsoft.Extensions.DependencyInjection; // IServiceCollection

    namespace Northwind.EntityModels;

    public static class NorthwindContextExtensions
    ```

```
{
  /// <summary>
  /// Adds NorthwindContext to the specified IServiceCollection. Uses the
SqlServer database provider.
  /// </summary>
  /// <param name="services">The service collection.</param>
  /// <param name="connectionString">Set to override the default.</param>
  /// <returns>An IServiceCollection that can be used to add more
services.</returns>
  public static IServiceCollection AddNorthwindContext(
    this IServiceCollection services,
    string? connectionString = null)
  {
    if (connectionString == null)
    {
      SqlConnectionStringBuilder builder = new();

      builder.DataSource = ".";
      builder.InitialCatalog = "Northwind";
      builder.TrustServerCertificate = true;
      builder.MultipleActiveResultSets = true;

      // If using Azure SQL Edge.
      // builder.DataSource = "tcp:127.0.0.1,1433";

      // Because we want to fail fast. Default is 15 seconds.
      builder.ConnectTimeout = 3;

      // If using Windows Integrated authentication.
      builder.IntegratedSecurity = true;

      // If using SQL Server authentication.
      // builder.UserID = Environment.GetEnvironmentVariable("MY_SQL_
USR");
      // builder.Password = Environment.GetEnvironmentVariable("MY_SQL_
PWD");

      connectionString = builder.ConnectionString;
    }

    services.AddDbContext<NorthwindContext>(options =>
```

```
    {
      options.UseSqlServer(connectionString);

      // Log to console when executing EF Core commands.
      options.LogTo(Console.WriteLine,
        new[] { Microsoft.EntityFrameworkCore
          .Diagnostics.RelationalEventId.CommandExecuting });
    },
    // Register with a transient lifetime to avoid concurrency
    // issues with Blazor Server projects.
    contextLifetime: ServiceLifetime.Transient,
    optionsLifetime: ServiceLifetime.Transient);

    return services;
  }
}
```

6.   Build the two class libraries and fix any compiler errors.

 Good Practice: We have provided an optional argument for the `AddNorthwindContext` method so that we can override the SQL Server database connection string. This will allow us more flexibility, for example, to load these values from a configuration file.

Calculated properties on entity creation

EF Core 7 added an `IMaterializationInterceptor` interface that allows interception before and after an entity is created, and when properties are initialized. This is useful for calculated values.

For example, when a service or client app requests entities to show to the user, it might want to cache a copy of the entity for a period of time. To do this, it needs to know when the entity was last refreshed. It would be useful if this information was automatically generated and stored with each entity at the time of loading.

To achieve this goal, we must complete four steps:

1.   First, define an interface with the extra property.
2.   Next, at least one entity model class must implement the interface.
3.   Then, define a class that implements the interceptor interface with a method named `InitializedInstance` that will execute on any entity, and if that entity implements the custom interface with the extra property, then it will set its value.
4.   Finally, we must create an instance of the interceptor and register it in the data context class.

Now let's implement this for Northwind `Employee` entities:

1. In the `Northwind.Common.EntityModels.SqlServer` project, add a new file named `IHasLastRefreshed.cs`, and modify its contents to define the interface, as shown in the following code:

    ```
    namespace Northwind.EntityModels;

    public interface IHasLastRefreshed
    {
      DateTimeOffset LastRefreshed { get; set; }
    }
    ```

2. In the `Northwind.Common.EntityModels.SqlServer` project, add a new file named `EmployeePartial.cs`, and modify its contents to implement the interface, as shown highlighted in the following code:

    ```
    using System.ComponentModel.DataAnnotations.Schema; // [NotMapped]

    namespace Northwind.EntityModels;

    public partial class Employee : IHasLastRefreshed
    {
      [NotMapped]
      public DateTimeOffset LastRefreshed { get; set; }
    }
    ```

     Good Practice: Add extension code like this to a separate partial entity class file so that you can later regenerate the `Employee.cs` file using the `dotnet-ef` tool without overwriting your additional code.

3. In the `Northwind.Common.DataContext.SqlServer` project, add a new file named `SetLastRefreshedInterceptor.cs`, and modify its contents to define the interceptor, as shown in the following code:

    ```
    // IMaterializationInterceptor, MaterializationInterceptionData
    using Microsoft.EntityFrameworkCore.Diagnostics;

    namespace Northwind.EntityModels;

    public class SetLastRefreshedInterceptor : IMaterializationInterceptor
    {
      public object InitializedInstance(
    ```

```
      MaterializationInterceptionData materializationData,
      object entity)
  {
    if (entity is IHasLastRefreshed entityWithLastRefreshed)
    {
      entityWithLastRefreshed.LastRefreshed = DateTimeOffset.UtcNow;
    }
    return entity;
  }
}
```

4. In the `Northwind.Common.DataContext.SqlServer` project, in `NorthwindContext.cs`, delete the existing `OnConfiguring` method.

5. In the `Northwind.Common.DataContext.SqlServer` project, add a new file named `NorthwindContextPartial.cs`, then declare and register the interceptor in the `OnConfiguring` method, as shown in the following code:

```
using Microsoft.Data.SqlClient; // SqlConnectionStringBuilder
using Microsoft.EntityFrameworkCore; // DbContext

namespace Northwind.EntityModels;

public partial class NorthwindContext : DbContext
{
  private static readonly SetLastRefreshedInterceptor
    setLastRefreshedInterceptor = new();

  protected override void OnConfiguring(DbContextOptionsBuilder
optionsBuilder)
  {
    if (!optionsBuilder.IsConfigured)
    {
      SqlConnectionStringBuilder builder = new();

      builder.DataSource = ".";
      builder.InitialCatalog = "Northwind";
      builder.TrustServerCertificate = true;
      builder.MultipleActiveResultSets = true;

      // Because we want to fail fast. Default is 15 seconds.
      builder.ConnectTimeout = 3;
```

```
        // If using Windows Integrated authentication.
        builder.IntegratedSecurity = true;

        // If using SQL Server authentication.
        // builder.UserID = Environment.GetEnvironmentVariable("MY_SQL_
    USR");
        // builder.Password = Environment.GetEnvironmentVariable("MY_SQL_
    PWD");

        optionsBuilder.UseSqlServer(builder.ConnectionString);
      }
      optionsBuilder.AddInterceptors(setLastRefreshedInterceptor);
    }
}
```

6. Save the changes.

Creating a test project to check the integration of the class libraries

Since we will not be creating a client project in this chapter that uses the EF Core model, we should create a test project to make sure the database context and entity models integrate correctly:

1. Use your preferred coding tool to add a new **xUnit Test Project [C#]** / xunit project named Northwind.Common.EntityModels.Tests to the Chapter03 solution.

2. In Northwind.Common.EntityModels.Tests.csproj, modify the configuration to treat warnings as errors and to add an item group with a project reference to the Northwind.Common.DataContext.SqlServer project, as shown in the following markup:

    ```
    <ItemGroup>
      <ProjectReference Include="..\Northwind.Common.DataContext
    .SqlServer\Northwind.Common.DataContext.SqlServer.csproj" />
    </ItemGroup>
    ```

     Warning! The path to the project reference should not have a line break in your project file.

3. Build the Northwind.Common.EntityModels.Tests project to build and restore project dependencies.

Writing unit tests for entity models

A well-written unit test will have three parts:

- **Arrange:** This part will declare and instantiate variables for input and output.
- **Act:** This part will execute the unit that you are testing. In our case, that means calling the method that we want to test.
- **Assert:** This part will make one or more assertions about the output. An assertion is a belief that, if not true, indicates a failed test. For example, when adding 2 and 2, we would expect the result to be 4.

Now, we will write some unit tests for the `NorthwindContext` and entity model classes:

1. Rename the file `UnitTest1.cs` to `NorthwindEntityModelsTests.cs` and then open it.
2. In Visual Studio Code, rename the class to `NorthwindEntityModelsTests`. (Visual Studio prompts you to rename the class when you rename the file.)
3. Modify the `NorthwindEntityModelsTests` class to import the `Northwind.EntityModels` namespace and have some test methods for ensuring the context class can connect, ensuring the provider is SQL Server, and ensuring the first product is named `Chai`, as shown in the following code:

```
using Northwind.EntityModels;

namespace Northwind.Common.EntityModels.Tests
{
  public class NorthwindEntityModelsTests
  {
    [Fact]
    public void CanConnectIsTrue()
    {
      using (NorthwindContext db = new()) // arrange
      {
        bool canConnect = db.Database.CanConnect(); // act

        Assert.True(canConnect); // assert
      }
    }

    [Fact]
    public void ProviderIsSqlServer()
    {
      using (NorthwindContext db = new())
      {
        string? provider = db.Database.ProviderName;
```

```
          Assert.Equal("Microsoft.EntityFrameworkCore.SqlServer",
      provider);
        }
    }


    [Fact]
    public void ProductId1IsChai()
    {
      using (NorthwindContext db = new())
      {
        Product product1 = db.Products.Single(p => p.ProductId == 1);

        Assert.Equal("Chai", product1.ProductName);
      }
    }


    [Fact]
    public void EmployeeHasLastRefreshedIn10sWindow()
    {
      using (NorthwindContext db = new())
      {
        Employee employee1 = db.Employees.Single(p => p.EmployeeId == 1);

        DateTimeOffset now = DateTimeOffset.UtcNow;

        Assert.InRange(actual: employee1.LastRefreshed,
          low: now.Subtract(TimeSpan.FromSeconds(5)),
          high: now.AddSeconds(5));
      }
    }
  }
}
```

Running unit tests using Visual Studio 2022

Now we are ready to run the unit tests and see the results:

1. In Visual Studio 2022, navigate to **Test** | **Run All Tests**.

2. In **Test Explorer**, note that the results indicate that four tests ran, and all passed, as shown in *Figure 3.5*:

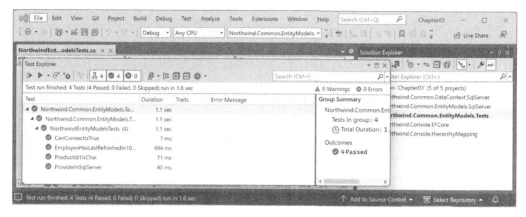

Figure 3.5: All unit tests passed

Running unit tests using Visual Studio Code

Now we are ready to run the unit tests and see the results:

1. In Visual Studio Code, in the `Northwind.Common.EntityModels.Tests` project's **TERMINAL** window, run the tests, as shown in the following command:

```
dotnet test
```

 If you are using **C# Dev Kit**, then you can also build the test project and then run the tests from the **Testing** section in the **Primary Side Bar.**

2. In the output, note that the results indicate that four tests ran, and all passed.

As an optional task, can you think of other tests you could write to make sure the database context and entity models are correct?

Practicing and exploring

Test your knowledge and understanding by answering some questions, getting some hands-on practice, and exploring this chapter's topics with deeper research.

Exercise 3.1 — Test your knowledge

Answer the following questions:

1. What can the dotnet-ef tool be used for?
2. What type would you use for the property that represents a table, for example, the Products property of a data context?
3. What type would you use for the property that represents a one-to-many relationship, for example, the Products property of a Category entity?
4. What is the EF Core convention for primary keys?
5. Why might you choose the Fluent API in preference to annotation attributes?
6. Why might you implement the IMaterializationInterceptor interface in an entity type?

Exercise 3.2 — Practice benchmarking ADO.NET against EF Core

In the Chapter03 solution, create a console app named Ch03Ex02_ADONETvsEFCore that uses Benchmark. NET to compare retrieving all the products from the Northwind database using ADO.NET (SqlClient) and using EF Core.

 You can learn how to use Benchmark.NET by reading the online-only section *Benchmarking Performance and Testing* at the following link: https://github.com/markjprice/apps-services-net8/blob/main/docs/ch01-benchmarking.md.

Exercise 3.3 — Review performance choices

The data tier can have an outsized influence on the overall performance of an app or service.

Docs: https://learn.microsoft.com/en-us/ef/core/performance/

Exercise 3.4 — Explore topics

Use the links on the following page to learn more details about the topics covered in this chapter:

https://github.com/markjprice/apps-services-net8/blob/main/docs/book-links.md#chapter-3---building-entity-models-for-sql-server-using-ef-core

Summary

In this chapter, you learned:

- How to execute a simple query and process the results using the slower but more object-oriented EF Core.
- How to configure and decide between three mapping strategies for type hierarchies.
- How to implement calculated properties on entity creation.

In the next chapter, you will learn how to use cloud-native data storage with Azure Cosmos DB.

Learn more on Discord

To join the Discord community for this book – where you can share feedback, ask questions to the author, and learn about new releases – follow the QR code below:

https://packt.link/apps_and_services_dotnet8

4

Managing NoSQL Data Using Azure Cosmos DB

This chapter is about managing NoSQL data by using Azure Cosmos DB. You will learn about some of the key concepts of Cosmos DB like its APIs, ways to model your data, and throughput provisioning, which influences costs. You will create some Cosmos DB resources using the local emulator and in the Azure cloud. Then you will learn how to work with more traditional data using the Core (SQL) API.

In an optional online-only section, you can learn how to work with graph data using the Gremlin API.

This chapter will cover the following topics:

- Understanding NoSQL databases
- Creating Cosmos DB resources
- Manipulating data with the Core (SQL) API
- Exploring server-side programming
- Cleaning up Azure resources

Understanding NoSQL databases

Two of the most common places to store data are in a **Relational Database Management System** (**RDBMS**) such as SQL Server, PostgreSQL, MySQL, and SQLite, or in a **NoSQL** database such as Azure Cosmos DB, Redis, MongoDB, and Apache Cassandra.

Relational databases were invented in the 1970s. They are queried with **Structured Query Language** (**SQL**). At the time, data storage costs were high, so they reduced data duplication as much as possible via a process known as *normalization*. Data is stored in tabular structures with rows and columns that are tricky to refactor once in production. They can be difficult and expensive to scale.

NoSQL databases do not just mean "no SQL;" they can also mean "not only SQL." They were invented in the 2000s, after the internet and the web had become popular and adopted much of the learning from that era of software.

They are designed for massive scalability and high performance, and to make programming easier by providing maximum flexibility and allowing schema changes at any time because they do not enforce a structure.

Cosmos DB and its APIs

Azure Cosmos DB is a NoSQL data store that supports multiple APIs. Its native API is SQL-based. It also supports alternative APIs like MongoDB, Cassandra, and Gremlin.

Azure Cosmos DB stores data in **atom-record-sequence** (**ARS**) format. You interact with this data via an API that you choose when you create the database:

- The **API for MongoDB** supports recent MongoDB wire protocol versions, which allow existing clients to work with the data as if they are interacting with an actual MongoDB database. Tools like mongodump and mongorestore can be used to move any existing data into Azure Cosmos DB. You can check the latest MongoDB support at the following link: https://learn.microsoft. com/en-us/azure/cosmos-db/mongodb/mongodb-introduction#how-the-api-works.

- The **API for Cassandra** supports the **Cassandra Query Language** (**CQL**) wire protocol version 4, which allows existing clients to work with the data as if they are interacting with an actual Cassandra database.

- For a new project, sometimes known as a "green field" project, Microsoft recommends the **Core (SQL) API**.

- For existing projects that use alternative APIs, you could choose to use the appropriate API so that your clients and tools do not need to be updated while gaining the benefits of data stored in Azure Cosmos DB. This reduces migration costs.

- If the relationships between data items have metadata that needs analyzing, then using the **Gremlin API for Cosmos DB** to treat Cosmos DB as a graph data store is a good choice.

 Good Practice: If you are unsure which API to choose, select Core (SQL) as the default.

In this book, we will first use the native Core (SQL) API for Cosmos DB. This allows the developer to query JSON documents using a language like SQL. The Core (SQL) API uses JSON's type system and JavaScript's function system.

Document modeling

A typical JSON document representing a product from the Northwind database, the example database that we used in *Chapter 2, Managing Relational Data Using SQL Server*, when stored in Azure Cosmos DB might look like the following:

```
{
  "id": "1",
  "productId": "1",
```

```
    "productName": "Chai",
    "supplier": {
      "supplierId": 1,
      "companyName": "Exotic Liquids",
      "contactName": "Charlotte Cooper",
      "Address": "49 Gilbert St.",
      "City": "London",
      "Country": "UK",
      "Phone": "(171) 555-2222"
    },
    "category": {
      "categoryId": 1,
      "categoryName": "Beverages",
      "description": "Soft drinks, coffees, teas, beers, and ales",
      "image": "https://myaccount.blob.core.windows.net/categories/beverages.png"
    },
    "quantityPerUnit": "10 boxes x 20 bags",
    "unitPrice": 18.0000,
    "unitsInStock": 39,
    "unitsOnOrder": 0,
    "reorderLevel": 10,
    "discontinued": false
  }
```

Unlike with a relational database model, it is common to **embed** related data, which involves duplicating data such as the category and supplier information across multiple products. This is good practice if the related data is bounded.

For example, for a product, there will only ever be one supplier and one category, so those relationships are bounded to one, which means limited to one each. If we were modeling a category and decided to embed its related products, then that could be poor practice because having all the product details as an array would be unbounded. Instead, we might choose to only store a unique identifier for each product and reference the product details stored elsewhere.

You should also consider how frequently the related data is updated. The more frequently it needs to be updated, the more you should avoid embedding it. If related data is unbounded but infrequently updated, then embedding might still be a good choice.

Deliberately but carefully **denormalizing** parts of your data model implies that you will need to execute fewer queries and updates for common operations, reducing costs both in money and performance.

Use embedding (denormalized data) when:

- The relationships are contained, like property owned by a person, or the children of a parent.
- The relationships are one-to-one or one-to-few, i.e., the related data is bounded.

- The related data needs infrequent updates.
- The related data often or always needs to be included in query results.

 Good Practice: Denormalized data models provide better read performance but worse write performance.

Imagine that you want to model an article and its comments on a popular news website. The comments are unbounded and, for an engaging article, would frequently be added to, especially during the hours or days after it is published while it is topical news. Or imagine an investor with stock they trade. The current price of that stock would be frequently updated.

In these scenarios, you would want to **normalize** the related data either wholly or partially. For example, you could choose to embed the most liked comments that will be shown at the top of the list directly under the article. Other comments could be stored separately and referenced using their primary keys. You could choose to embed stock information for long-term investments that are held for many years, like the price the investment was purchased at and the price on the first day of each month since then (but not the live current price), but reference stock information for short-term investments for day trading.

Use referencing (normalized data) when:

- The relationships are one-to-many or many-to-many and unbounded.
- The related data needs frequent updates.

 Good Practice: Normalized data models require more queries, which worsens read performance but provides better write performance.

 You can read more about modeling documents in Azure Cosmos DB at the following link: `https://learn.microsoft.com/en-us/azure/cosmos-db/sql/modeling-data`.

Consistency levels

Azure Cosmos DB is distributed globally and scales elastically. It relies on replication to provide low latency and high availability all over the world. To achieve this, you must accept and choose tradeoffs.

To ease the life of a programmer, you want total consistency of data. If data is modified anywhere in the world, then any subsequent read operation should see that change. The best consistency is known as **linearizability**. Linearizability increases the latency of write operations and reduces the availability of read operations because it must wait for replication to occur globally.

A more relaxed consistency level improves latency and availability at the cost of potentially increased complexity for the programmer because data might be inconsistent.

Most NoSQL databases only offer two levels of consistency: strong and eventual. Azure Cosmos DB offers five to provide exactly the level of consistency that suits your project.

You choose the level of data consistency, and this will be guaranteed by the **Service-Level Agreement (SLA)**, as shown in the following, ordered from the strongest to the weakest:

- **Strong** consistency guarantees linearizability across all regions globally. All other consistency levels are collectively known as "relaxed." You might ask, "Why not set Strong consistency in all scenarios?" If you are familiar with relational databases, then you should be familiar with transaction isolation levels. These are similar conceptually to NoSQL consistency levels. The strongest level of transaction isolation level is SERIALIZABLE. Weaker levels include READUNCOMMITTED and REPEATABLE READ. You would not want to use SERIALIZABLE in all scenarios for the same reason you wouldn't want to use Strong consistency in all scenarios. They both slow down operations, and sometimes, to an unacceptable point. Your users will complain about a lack of performance, or even an inability to perform a task at all. So, you need to look carefully at each task you are attempting and determine the minimal required level for that task. Some developers prefer to default to the strongest level and weaken it for scenarios that are "too slow." Other developers prefer to default to the weakest level and strengthen it for scenarios that introduce too much inconsistency. As you become more familiar with NoSQL development, you will be able to judge quicker what level is best for different scenarios.

- **Bounded staleness** consistency guarantees the ability to read your own write within the write region, monotonic read within the region (meaning the values do not increase or decrease, like a monotone voice, and remain in a consistent order), and consistent prefix, and the staleness of read data is restricted to a specific number of versions for which the reads lag behind the writes within a specified time interval. For example, the time interval might be ten minutes and the number of versions might be three. That would mean that a maximum of three writes can be made in any ten-minute period before a read operation must reflect those changes.

- **Session** consistency guarantees the ability to read your own write within the write region, monotonic read, and consistent prefix.

- **Consistent prefix** consistency only guarantees the order that writes can then be read.

- **Eventual** consistency does not guarantee that the order of writes will match the order of reads. When writes pause, reads will eventually catch up as the replicas synchronize. It is possible for a client to read values older than the ones it read before. **Probabilistic Bounded Staleness (PBS)** is a measurement that shows how eventual your consistency is currently. You can monitor it in the Azure portal.

 You can read more details about consistency levels at the following link: https://learn. microsoft.com/en-us/azure/cosmos-db/consistency-levels.

Hierarchy of components

The hierarchy of components for Azure Cosmos DB is:

- **Account:** You can create up to 50 accounts via the Azure portal.
- **Database:** You can have an unlimited number of databases per account. We will create a database named `Northwind`.
- **Container:** You can have an unlimited number of containers per database. We will create a container named `Products`.
- **Partition:** These are created and managed automatically within a container, and you can have an unlimited number. Partitions are either logical or physical. A **logical partition** contains items with the same partition key and defines the scope for transactions. Multiple logical partitions are mapped to a **physical partition**. Small containers may only need one physical partition. You should not concern yourself with physical partitions since you have no control over them. Focus on deciding what your partition key should be because that defines the items stored in a logical partition.
- **Item:** This is a stored entity in a container. We will add items that represent each product, like Chai tea.

"Item" is a deliberately generic term and is used by the Core (SQL) API to refer to a JSON document but can also be used for the other APIs. The other APIs also have their own more specific terms:

- Cassandra uses **row**.
- MongoDB uses **document**.
- Graph databases like Gremlin use **vertex** and **edge**.

Throughput provisioning

Throughput is measured as **request units per second (RU/s)**. A single **request unit** (RU) is about the cost of performing a `GET` request for a 1KB document using its unique identifier. Creating, updating, and deleting cost more RUs; for example, a query might cost 46.54 RUs, or a delete operation might cost 14.23 RUs.

Throughput must be provisioned in advance, although you can scale up and down at any time in increments or decrements of 100 RU/s. You will be billed per hour.

 You can discover how much a request costs in RUs by getting the `RequestCharge` property. You can learn more at the following link: `https://learn.microsoft.com/en-us/azure/cosmos-db/sql/find-request-unit-charge`. We will output this property in all the example code that we run in this chapter.

You must provision throughput to run CRUD operations (creates, reads, updates, and deletes). You must estimate throughput by calculating the number of operations you'll need to support throughout the year. For example, a commerce website might need to expect much greater throughput at Thanksgiving in the US or Singles Day in China.

Most throughput settings are applied at the container level, or you can do so at the database level and have the settings shared across all containers. Throughput is distributed equally among partitions.

Once provisioned throughput is exhausted, Cosmos DB will start rate-limiting access requests, and your code will have to wait and retry later. Luckily, we will use the .NET SDK for Cosmos DB, which automatically reads the `retry-after` response header and retries after that time limit.

Using the Azure portal, you can provision between 400 RU/s and 250,000 RU/s. At the time of writing, the 400 RU/s minimum would cost about US$35 per month. You would then also need to add the cost of storage depending on how many GBs you want to store, for example, US$5 for a few GBs.

 The free tier of Cosmos DB allows up to 1,000 RU/s and 25 GB of storage. You can use a calculator at the following link: `https://cosmos.azure.com/capacitycalculator/`.

Factors that affect RUs:

- **Item size:** A 2KB document costs twice as much as a 1KB document.
- **Indexed properties:** Indexing all item properties costs more than indexing a subset of properties.
- **Consistency:** Strict consistency costs twice as many RUs as looser consistency.
- **Query complexity:** The number of predicates (filters), the number of results, the number of custom functions, projections, the size of the dataset, and so on, all increase the cost in RUs.

Partition strategies

A good partition strategy allows a Cosmos DB database to grow and efficiently run queries and transactions. A good partition strategy is about choosing a suitable **partition key**. It is set for a container and cannot be changed.

The partition key should be chosen to evenly distribute operations across the database to avoid hot partitions, meaning a partition that handles more requests, so it is busier than other partitions.

A property that will be unique for an item and will often be used to look up an item might be a good choice. For example, for US citizens, a person's social security number. However, partition keys do not have to be unique. The partition key value will be combined with an item ID to uniquely identify an item.

Partitions are automatically created by Cosmos DB when needed. There is no negative impact on your applications and services from the automatic creation and deletion of partitions. Each partition can grow up to a maximum of 20 GB. Cosmos DB will automatically split partitions when needed.

A container should have a partition key that possesses these attributes:

- High cardinality so that items are distributed evenly across partitions.
- Evenly distributed requests across partitions.
- Evenly distributed storage across partitions.

Data storage design

With relational databases, the schemas are rigid and inflexible. The Northwind database's products are all food-related, so the schema might not change much. But if you are building a commerce system for a company that sells everything from clothes to electronic equipment to books, then a semi-structured data store like the following would be better:

- Clothing: Sizes like S, M L, XL; brand; color.
- Shoes: Sizes like 7, 8, 9; brand; color.
- Televisions: Sizes like 40", 52"; screen technology like OLED, LCD; brand.
- Books: Number of pages; author; publisher.

Being schema-less, Azure Cosmos DB can add new types of products with different structures and properties simply by adding a new product with that structure to a container. You will see examples of this in the code that you write later in this chapter.

Migrating data to Cosmos DB

The open-source **Azure Cosmos DB Data Migration Tool** can import data into Azure Cosmos DB from many different sources, including Azure Table Storage, SQL databases, MongoDB, text files in JSON and CSV formats, HBase, and more.

 We will not use this migration tool in this book, so if you think it will be useful to you, then you can learn how to use it at the following link: `https://github.com/Azure/azure-documentdb-datamigrationtool`.

That's quite enough theory. Now, let's look at something more practical, how to create Cosmos DB resources so we can work with them in code.

Creating Cosmos DB resources

To see Azure Cosmos DB in action, first, we must create Cosmos DB resources. We can manually create them in the cloud using the Azure portal or programmatically create them using the Azure Cosmos DB .NET SDK. Azure Cosmos DB resources created in the cloud have a cost unless you use a trial or free account.

You can also create Azure Cosmos DB resources locally using an emulator, which will cost you nothing. At the time of writing, the Azure Cosmos DB Emulator only supports Windows. If you want to use Linux or macOS, then you can try to use the Linux Emulator, which is currently in preview, or you could host the emulator in a Windows virtual machine.

Using an emulator on Windows to create Azure Cosmos DB resources

If you do not have a Windows computer, then just read through this section without completing the steps yourself, and then in the next section, you will use the Azure portal to create Azure Cosmos DB resources.

Let's use the Azure Cosmos DB Emulator on Windows to create Azure Cosmos DB resources like a database and container:

1. Download and install the latest version of the Azure Cosmos DB Emulator on your local Windows computer from the following link (direct to the MSI installer file): `https://aka.ms/cosmosdb-emulator`.

 The most recent version of the emulator at the time of writing is 2.14.12, released on March 20, 2023. Earlier versions of the emulator are not supported by the developer team. If you have an older version installed, then remove it and install the latest.

2. Make sure the Azure Cosmos DB Emulator is running.

3. The **Azure Cosmos DB Emulator** user interface should start automatically, but if not, start your favorite browser and navigate to `https://localhost:8081/_explorer/index.html`.

4. Note that the Azure Cosmos DB emulator is running, hosted at `localhost` on port `8081`, with a **Primary Key** that you will need to securely connect to the service, as shown in *Figure 4.1*:

Figure 4.1: The Azure Cosmos DB Emulator user interface on Windows

 The default primary key for the emulator is the same value for everyone. You can specify your own key value by starting the emulator at the command line with the `/key` switch. You can learn about starting the emulator at the command line at the following link: `https://learn.microsoft.com/en-us/azure/cosmos-db/emulator-command-line-parameters`.

5. In the navigation bar on the left, click **Explorer**, and then click **New Container**.

6. Complete the following information:

    - For **Database id**, select **Create new** and enter Northwind.
    - Select the **Share throughput across containers** check box.
    - For **Database throughput**, select **Autoscale**.
    - Set **Database max RU/s** as 4000. This will use a minimum of 400 RU/s and autoscale up to 4,000 RU/s when needed.
    - For **Container id**, enter Products.
    - For **Partition key**, enter /productId.

7. Click **OK**.

8. In the tree on the left, expand the **Northwind** database, expand the **Products** container, and select **Items**, as shown in *Figure 4.2*:

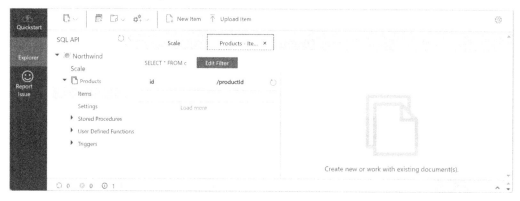

Figure 4.2: The empty items in the Products container in the Northwind database

9. In the toolbar, click **New Item**.

10. Replace the contents of the editor window with a JSON document that represents a product named Chai, as shown in the following JSON:

```json
{
    "productId": 1,
    "productName": "Chai",
    "supplier": {
        "supplierId": 1,
        "companyName": "Exotic Liquids",
        "contactName": "Charlotte Cooper",
        "Address": "49 Gilbert St.",
        "City": "London",
        "Country": "UK",
        "Phone": "(171) 555-2222"
    },
    "category": {
```

```
        "categoryId": 1,
        "categoryName": "Beverages",
        "description": "Soft drinks, coffees, teas, beers, and ales"
    },
    "quantityPerUnit": "10 boxes x 20 bags",
    "unitPrice": 18,
    "unitsInStock": 39,
    "unitsOnOrder": 0,
    "reorderLevel": 10,
    "discontinued": false
}
```

11. In the toolbar, click **Save**, and note the extra properties that are automatically added to any item, including id, _etag, and _ts, as shown highlighted in the following JSON:

```
{
    "productId": 1,
    "productName": "Chai",
    "supplier": {
        "supplierId": 1,
        ...
    "reorderLevel": 10,
    "discontinued": false,
    "id": "2ad4c71d-d0e4-4ebd-a146-bcf052f8d7d6",
    "_rid": "bmAuAJ9o6I8BAAAAAAAAAA==",
    "_self": "dbs/bmAuAA==/colls/bmAuAJ9o6I8=/docs/
bmAuAJ9o6I8BAAAAAAAAAA==/",
    "_etag": "\"00000000-0000-0000-8fc2-ec4d49ea01d8\"",
    "_attachments": "attachments/",
    "_ts": 1656952035
}
```

12. Click **New Item**.

13. Replace the contents of the editor window with a JSON document that represents a product named Chang, as shown in the following JSON:

```
{
    "productId": 2,
    "productName": "Chang",
    "supplier": {
        "supplierId": 1,
        "companyName": "Exotic Liquids",
        "contactName": "Charlotte Cooper",
```

```
      "Address": "49 Gilbert St.",
      "City": "London",
      "Country": "UK",
      "Phone": "(171) 555-2222"
    },
    "category": {
      "categoryId": 1,
      "categoryName": "Beverages",
      "description": "Soft drinks, coffees, teas, beers, and ales"
    },
    "quantityPerUnit": "24 - 12 oz bottles",
    "unitPrice": 19,
    "unitsInStock": 17,
    "unitsOnOrder": 40,
    "reorderLevel": 25,
    "discontinued": false
  }
```

14. Click **Save**.

15. Click **New Item**.

16. Replace the contents of the editor window with a JSON document that represents a product named Aniseed Syrup, as shown in the following JSON:

```
  {
    "productId": 3,
    "productName": "Aniseed Syrup",
    "supplier": {
      "supplierId": 1,
      "companyName": "Exotic Liquids",
      "contactName": "Charlotte Cooper",
      "Address": "49 Gilbert St.",
      "City": "London",
      "Country": "UK",
      "Phone": "(171) 555-2222"
    },
    "category": {
      "categoryId": 2,
      "categoryName": "Condiments",
      "description": "Sweet and savory sauces, relishes, spreads, and
  seasonings"
    },
    "quantityPerUnit": "12 - 550 ml bottles",
```

```
      "unitPrice": 10,
      "unitsInStock": 13,
      "unitsOnOrder": 70,
      "reorderLevel": 25,
      "discontinued": false
   }
```

17. Click **Save**.

18. Click the first item in the list and note that all the items have been automatically assigned GUID values for their id properties, as shown in *Figure 4.3*:

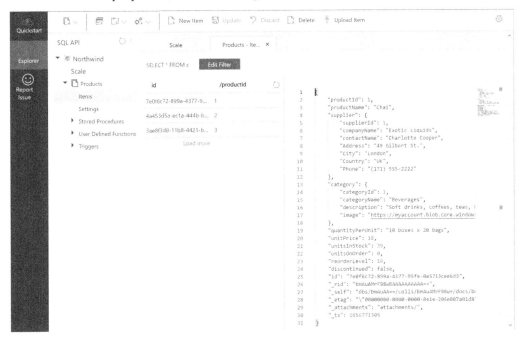

Figure 4.3: A saved JSON document item in the Azure Cosmos DB emulator

19. In the toolbar, click **New SQL Query**, and note the default query text is `SELECT * FROM c`.

20. Modify the query text to return all products supplied by `Exotic Liquids`; in the toolbar, click **Execute Query**, and note that all three products are included in the array of results, as shown in *Figure 4.4* and in the following query:

```
SELECT * FROM c WHERE c.supplier.companyName = "Exotic Liquids"
```

Figure 4.4: A query to return all products supplied by Exotic Liquids

 Keywords are case-insensitive, so `WHERE` is treated the same as `Where` or `where`. Property names are case-sensitive so `CompanyName` is different from `companyName`, and will return zero results.

21. Modify the query text to return all products in category 2, as shown in the following query:

```
SELECT * FROM c WHERE c.category.categoryId = 2
```

22. Execute the query and note that one product is included in the array of results.

Using the Azure portal to create Azure Cosmos DB resources

 If you would prefer to only use the Azure Cosmos DB Emulator to avoid any costs, then feel free to skip this section, or just read through it without completing the steps yourself.

Now, let's use the Azure portal to create Azure Cosmos DB resources like an account, database, and container in the cloud:

1. If you do not have an Azure account, then you can sign up for one for free at the following link: https://azure.microsoft.com/free/.
2. Navigate to the Azure portal and sign in: https://portal.azure.com/.
3. In the Azure portal menu, click **+ Create a resource**.
4. On the **Create a resource** page, search for, or click, **Azure Cosmos DB**, and then on the **Azure Cosmos DB** page, click **Create**.

5. On the **Which API best suits your workload?** page, in the **Azure Cosmos DB for NoSQL** box, note the description, **Azure Cosmos DB's core, or native API for working with documents. Supports fast, flexible development with familiar SQL query language and client libraries for .NET, JavaScript, Python, and Java.**, and then click the **Create** button.

6. On the **Basics** tab:

   - Select your **Subscription**. Mine is named Pay-As-You-Go.

   - Select a **Resource Group** or create a new one. I used the name apps-services-book.

   - Enter an Azure Cosmos DB **Account Name**. I used apps-services-book.

   - Select a **Location**. I chose **(Europe) UK South** as it is the closest to me.

   - Set **Capacity mode** to **Provisioned throughput**.

   - Set **Apply Free Tier Discount** to **Do not apply**.

 Good Practice: Only apply the free tier discount now if you want this account to be the *only* account within your subscription to be on the free tier. You might be better off saving this discount for another account that you might use for a real project, rather than a temporary learning account while reading this book. With Azure Cosmos DB free tier, you will get the first 1,000 RU/s and 25 GB of storage for free in an account. You can only enable a free tier on one account per subscription. Microsoft estimates this has a value of $64/month.

   - Select the **Limit total account throughput** check box.

7. Click the **Next: Global Distribution** button and review the options but leave them at their defaults.

8. Click the **Next: Networking** button and review the options but leave them at their defaults.

9. Click the **Next: Backup Policy** button and review the options but leave them at their defaults.

10. Click the **Next: Encryption** button and review the options but leave them at their defaults.

11. Click the **Review + create** button.

12. Note the **Validation Success** message, review the summary, and then click the **Create** button.

13. Wait for the deployment to complete. This will take a few minutes.

14. Click the **Go to resource** button. Note that you are probably directed to the **Quick Start** page with steps to follow to create a container and so on, depending on if this is the first time that you have created an Azure Cosmos DB account.

15. In the left navigation, click **Overview**, and note the information about your Azure Cosmos DB account, as shown in *Figure 4.5*:

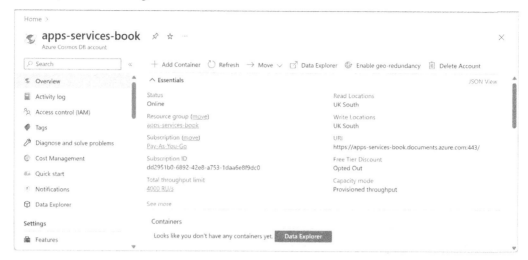

Figure 4.5: Azure Cosmos DB account Overview page

16. In the navigation on the left, in the **Settings** section, click **Keys**, and note the **URI** and **PRIMARY KEY** needed to programmatically work with this Azure Cosmos DB account, as shown in *Figure 4.6*:

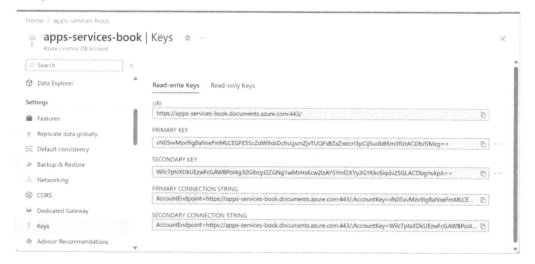

Figure 4.6: Keys to programmatically work with the Azure Cosmos DB account

 Good Practice: Unlike the primary key that is shared by all developers of the Cosmos DB emulator, your Cosmos DB primary keys in Azure are unique and must be kept secret. I deleted the Cosmos DB account that I used to write this chapter so the keys in the screenshot above are useless.

17. In the navigation on the left, click **Data Explorer**, and if a video pops up, then close it.

18. In the toolbar, click **New Container**.

19. Complete the steps listed in the emulator section, *Using an emulator on Windows to create Azure Cosmos DB resources,* starting at *step 6* where you fill in the information about the new container, and going up to the end of that section.

Using a .NET app to create Azure Cosmos DB resources

Next, we will create a console app project for creating the same Azure Cosmos DB resources in either the local emulator or in the cloud, depending on which URI and primary key you choose to use:

1. Use your preferred code editor to create a new project, as defined in the following list:

    - Project template: **Console App** / `console`
    - Solution file and folder: `Chapter04`
    - Project file and folder: `Northwind.CosmosDb.SqlApi`

2. In the project file, treat warnings as errors, add a package reference for Azure Cosmos, add a project reference to the Northwind data context project that you created in *Chapter 3, Building Entity Models for SQL Server Using EF Core,* and import the Console class statically and globally, as shown highlighted in the following markup:

```xml
<Project Sdk="Microsoft.NET.Sdk">

  <PropertyGroup>
    <OutputType>Exe</OutputType>
    <TargetFramework>net8.0</TargetFramework>
    <ImplicitUsings>enable</ImplicitUsings>
    <Nullable>enable</Nullable>
    <TreatWarningsAsErrors>true</TreatWarningsAsErrors>
  </PropertyGroup>

  <ItemGroup>
    <PackageReference Include="Microsoft.Azure.Cosmos" Version="3.37.0"
/>
  </ItemGroup>

  <ItemGroup>
    <ProjectReference Include="..\..\Chapter03\Northwind.Common.
DataContext
.SqlServer\Northwind.Common.DataContext.SqlServer.csproj" />
  </ItemGroup>

  <ItemGroup>
```

```
    <Using Include="System.Console" Static="true" />
  </ItemGroup>

</Project>
```

3. Build the `Northwind.CosmosDb.SqlApi` project at the command prompt or terminal using the following command: `dotnet build`.

> **Warning!** If you are using Visual Studio 2022 and you reference a project outside of the current solution, then using the **Build** menu gives the following error:
>
> ```
> NU1105 Unable to find project information for 'C:\apps-services-
> net8\Chapter03\Northwind.Common.DataContext.SqlServer\Northwind.
> Common.DataContext.SqlServer.csproj'. If you are using Visual
> Studio, this may be because the project is unloaded or not part of
> the current solution.
> ```
>
> You must enter a `dotnet build` command at the command prompt or terminal. In **Solution Explorer**, you can right-click the project and select **Open in Terminal**.

4. Add a class file named `Program.Helpers.cs`, delete any existing statements, and then add statements to define a partial `Program` class with a method to output a section title to the console, as shown in the following code:

```
// This is defined in the default empty namespace, so it merges with
// the SDK-generated partial Program class.

partial class Program
{
  static void SectionTitle(string title)
  {
    ConsoleColor previousColor = ForegroundColor;
    ForegroundColor = ConsoleColor.DarkYellow;
    WriteLine("*");
    WriteLine($"* {title}");
    WriteLine("*");
    ForegroundColor = previousColor;
  }
}
```

5. Add a class file named `Program.Methods.cs`.

6. In `Program.Methods.cs`, add statements to import the namespace for working with Azure Cosmos. Then, define a method for the `Program` class that creates a Cosmos client and uses it to create a database named `Northwind` and a container named `Products`, in either the local emulator or in the cloud, as shown in the following code:

```csharp
using Microsoft.Azure.Cosmos; // To use CosmosClient and so on.
using System.Net; // To use HttpStatusCode.

// This is defined in the default empty namespace, so it merges with
// the SDK-generated partial Program class.

partial class Program
{
  // To use Azure Cosmos DB in the local emulator.
  private static string endpointUri = "https://localhost:8081/";
  private static string primaryKey = "C2y6yDjf5/R+ob0N8A7Cgv30VRDJIWEHL
M+4QDU5DE2nQ9nDuVTqobD4b8mGGyPMbIZnqyMsEcaGQy67XIw/Jw==";

  /*
  // To use Azure Cosmos DB in the cloud.
  private static string account = "apps-services-book"; // use your
account
  private static string endpointUri =
    $"https://{account}.documents.azure.com:443/";
  private static string primaryKey = "LGrx7H...gZw=="; // use your key
  */

  static async Task CreateCosmosResources()
  {
    SectionTitle("Creating Cosmos resources");

    try
    {
      using (CosmosClient client = new(
        accountEndpoint: endpointUri,
        authKeyOrResourceToken: primaryKey))
      {
        DatabaseResponse dbResponse = await client
          .CreateDatabaseIfNotExistsAsync(
            "Northwind", throughput: 400 /* RU/s */);

        string status = dbResponse.StatusCode switch
        {
          HttpStatusCode.OK => "exists",
          HttpStatusCode.Created => "created",
          _ => "unknown"
```

```
    };

WriteLine("Database Id: {0}, Status: {1}.",
  arg0: dbResponse.Database.Id, arg1: status);

IndexingPolicy indexingPolicy = new()
{
  IndexingMode = IndexingMode.Consistent,
  Automatic = true, // Items are indexed unless explicitly
excluded.
  IncludedPaths = { new IncludedPath { Path = "/*" } }
};

ContainerProperties containerProperties = new("Products",
  partitionKeyPath: "/productId")
{
  IndexingPolicy = indexingPolicy
};

ContainerResponse containerResponse = await dbResponse.Database
  .CreateContainerIfNotExistsAsync(
    containerProperties, throughput: 1000 /* RU/s */);

status = dbResponse.StatusCode switch
{
  HttpStatusCode.OK => "exists",
  HttpStatusCode.Created => "created",
  _ => "unknown",
};

WriteLine("Container Id: {0}, Status: {1}.",
  arg0: containerResponse.Container.Id, arg1: status);

Container container = containerResponse.Container;

ContainerProperties properties = await container.
ReadContainerAsync();
WriteLine($"  PartitionKeyPath: {properties.PartitionKeyPath}");
WriteLine($"  LastModified: {properties.LastModified}");
WriteLine("  IndexingPolicy.IndexingMode: {0}",
  arg0: properties.IndexingPolicy.IndexingMode);
```

```
        WriteLine("  IndexingPolicy.IncludedPaths: {0}",
          arg0: string.Join(",", properties.IndexingPolicy
            .IncludedPaths.Select(path => path.Path)));
        WriteLine($"  IndexingPolicy: {properties.IndexingPolicy}");
      }
    }
    catch (HttpRequestException ex)
    {
      WriteLine($"Error: {ex.Message}");
      WriteLine("Hint: If you are using the Azure Cosmos Emulator then
please make sure that it is running.");
    }
    catch (Exception ex)
    {
      WriteLine("Error: {0} says {1}",
        arg0: ex.GetType(),
        arg1: ex.Message);
    }
  }
}
```

Note the following in the preceding code:

- When using the emulator, the `endpointUri` and `primaryKey` are the same for everyone.
- The constructor for a `CosmosClient` requires the `endpointUri` and `primaryKey`. Never store your primary key in your source code and then check it in to a public Git repository! You should get it from an environment variable or other secure place like Azure Key Vault.
- When creating a database, you must specify a name and throughput in RUs per second.
- When creating a container, you must specify a name and partition key path, and you can optionally set an indexing policy and override the throughput, which defaults to the database throughput.
- The response to a request to create an Azure Cosmos DB resource includes an HTTP status code like `200 OK` if the resource already exists, or `201 Created` if the resource did not exist but has now been successfully created. The response also includes information about the resource like its `Id`.

7. In `Program.cs`, delete the existing statements and then add a statement to call the method to create Azure Cosmos resources, as shown in the following code:

```
await CreateCosmosResources();
```

8. Run the console app and note the results, as shown in the following output:

```
*
* Creating Cosmos resources
*
Database Id: Northwind, Status: exists.
Container Id: Products, Status: exists.
  PartitionKeyPath: /productId
  LastModified: 04/07/2022 11:11:31
  IndexingPolicy.IndexingMode: Consistent
  IndexingPolicy.IncludedPaths: /*
```

9. In the Azure Cosmos DB Emulator or Azure portal, use **Data Explorer** to delete the Northwind database. (You must hover your mouse cursor over the database and then click the **...** ellipsis button.) You will be prompted to enter its name to confirm deletion because this operation cannot be undone.

It is important to delete the Northwind database at this point. Later in this chapter, you will programmatically add the 77 products from the SQL Server Northwind database to the Cosmos DB Northwind database. If you still have the three sample products in its Products container, then you will have issues.

10. Run the console app and note that because we have just deleted the database, the code we have executed has (re)created the database, as shown in the following output:

```
*
* Creating Cosmos resources
*
Database Id: Northwind, Status: created.
Container Id: Products, Status: created.
  PartitionKeyPath: /productId
  LastModified: 04/07/2022 11:11:31
  IndexingPolicy.IndexingMode: Consistent
  IndexingPolicy.IncludedPaths: /*
```

You do not need to delete the database again because it will be empty of any products.

We now have a Cosmos DB database resource to work with, either in the local emulator or in the Azure cloud. Now, let's learn how to perform CRUD operations on it using the SQL API.

Manipulating data with the Core (SQL) API

The most common API for working with data in Azure Cosmos DB is Core (SQL).

 The full documentation for the Core (SQL) API can be found at the following link: `https://learn.microsoft.com/en-us/azure/cosmos-db/sql/`.

Performing CRUD operations with the Cosmos SQL API

You can perform CRUD operations on JSON documents in Cosmos with the SQL API by calling the following most common overloads of methods on an instance of the `Microsoft.Azure.Cosmos.Container` class:

- `ReadItemAsync<T>(id, partitionKey)`: Where `T` is the item type to get, `id` is its unique identifier, and `partitionKey` is its partition key value.
- `ReadManyItemsAsync<T>(idsAndPartitionKeys)`: Where `T` is the item type to get, and `idsAndPartitionKeys` are the unique identifiers and partition key values of a read-only list of items to retrieve.
- `CreateItemAsync(object)`: Where `object` is an instance of the item type to insert.
- `DeleteItemAsync<T>(id, partitionKey)`: Where `T` is the item type to delete, `id` is its unique identifier, and `partitionKey` is its partition key value.
- `PatchItemAsync<T>(id, partitionKey, patchOperations)`: Where `T` is the item type to update, `id` is its unique identifier, `partitionKey` is its partition key value, and `patchOperations` is a read-only list of property changes.
- `ReplaceItemAsync<T>(object, id)`: Where `T` is the item type to replace, `id` is its unique identifier, and `object` is an instance of the item type to replace it with.
- `UpsertItemAsync<T>(object, id)`: Where `T` is the item type to either insert or replace, `id` is its unique identifier, and `object` is an instance of the item type to insert or replace the existing item with.

 Good Practice: Cosmos DB uses HTTP as its underlying communication protocol and so the "patch" and "replace" operations are implemented using `PATCH` and `PUT`. Just like those HTTP methods, `PATCH` is more efficient because only the properties that need to change are sent in the request.

Each method returns a response that has the following common properties:

- `Resource`: The item that was created/retrieved/updated/deleted.
- `RequestCharge`: A double value indicating the request charge measured in RUs.
- `StatusCode`: An HTTP status code value; for example, `404` when a `ReadItemAsync<T>` request fails to find the item.

- `Headers`: A dictionary of HTTP response headers.
- `Diagnostics`: Useful information for diagnostics.
- `ActivityId`: A GUID value that is useful for tracking this activity through multi-tiered services.

Let's copy all the products from the Northwind database in SQL Server to Cosmos.

Since the entity classes in the EF Core for SQL Server class libraries are designed for the normalized data structure in the Northwind SQL database, we will create new classes to represent items in Cosmos that have embedded related data. They will use JSON casing conventions since they represent JSON documents:

1. In the `Northwind.CosmosDb.SqlApi` project, add a new folder named `Models`.

2. In the `Models` folder, add a class file named `CategoryCosmos.cs`.

3. Modify its content to define a `CategoryCosmos` class, as shown in the following code:

```
namespace Northwind.CosmosDb.Items;

public class CategoryCosmos
{
  public int categoryId { get; set; }
  public string categoryName { get; set; } = null!;
  public string? description { get; set; }
}
```

 We must deliberately not follow usual .NET casing conventions because we cannot dynamically manipulate the serialization and the resulting JSON must use camel case.

4. In the `Models` folder, add a class file named `SupplierCosmos.cs`, and modify its content to define a `SupplierCosmos` class, as shown in the following code:

```
namespace Northwind.CosmosDb.Items;

public class SupplierCosmos
{
  public int supplierId { get; set; }
  public string companyName { get; set; } = null!;
  public string? contactName { get; set; }
  public string? contactTitle { get; set; }
  public string? address { get; set; }
  public string? city { get; set; }
  public string? region { get; set; }
  public string? postalCode { get; set; }
  public string? country { get; set; }
```

```
    public string? phone { get; set; }
    public string? fax { get; set; }
    public string? homePage { get; set; }
  }
```

5. In the `Models` folder, add a class file named `ProductCosmos.cs`, and modify its content to define a `ProductCosmos` class, as shown in the following code:

```
namespace Northwind.CosmosDb.Items;

public class ProductCosmos
{
  public string id { get; set; } = null!;
  public string productId { get; set; } = null!;
  public string productName { get; set; } = null!;
  public string? quantityPerUnit { get; set; }
  public decimal? unitPrice { get; set; }
  public short? unitsInStock { get; set; }
  public short? unitsOnOrder { get; set; }
  public short? reorderLevel { get; set; }
  public bool discontinued { get; set; }
  public CategoryCosmos? category { get; set; }
  public SupplierCosmos? supplier { get; set; }
}
```

 Good Practice: All JSON document items in Cosmos must have an `id` property. To control the value, it is good practice to explicitly define that property in the model. Otherwise, the system will assign a GUID value, as you saw earlier in this chapter when using the **Data Explorer** to manually add a new item.

6. In `Program.Methods.cs`, add statements to import namespaces for the Northwind data context and entities types, the Northwind Cosmos types, and EF Core extensions, as shown in the following code:

```
using Northwind.EntityModels; // To use NorthwindContext and so on.
using Northwind.CosmosDb.Items; // To use ProductCosmos and so on.
using Microsoft.EntityFrameworkCore; // To use Include extension method.
```

7. In `Program.Methods.cs`, add statements to define a method to get all the products in the Northwind SQL database, including their related category and supplier, and then insert them as new items in the `Products` container in Cosmos, as shown in the following code:

```
static async Task CreateProductItems()
{
  SectionTitle("Creating product items");
```

```csharp
double totalCharge = 0.0;

try
{
  using (CosmosClient client = new(
    accountEndpoint: endpointUri,
    authKeyOrResourceToken: primaryKey))
  {
    Container container = client.GetContainer(
      databaseId: "Northwind", containerId: "Products");

    using (NorthwindContext db = new())
    {
      if (!db.Database.CanConnect())
      {
        WriteLine("Cannot connect to the SQL Server database to " +
          " read products using database connection string: " +
          db.Database.GetConnectionString());
        return;
      }

      ProductCosmos[] products = db.Products

        // Get the related data for embedding.
        .Include(p => p.Category)
        .Include(p => p.Supplier)

        // Filter any products with null category or supplier
        // to avoid null warnings.
        .Where(p => (p.Category != null) && (p.Supplier != null))

        // Project the EF Core entities into Cosmos JSON types.
        .Select(p => new ProductCosmos
        {
          id = p.ProductId.ToString(),
          productId = p.ProductId.ToString(),
          productName = p.ProductName,
          quantityPerUnit = p.QuantityPerUnit,

          // If the related category is null, store null,
```

```
          // // else store the category mapped to Cosmos model.
          category = p.Category == null ? null :
            new CategoryCosmos
          {
            categoryId = p.Category.CategoryId,
            categoryName = p.Category.CategoryName,
            description = p.Category.Description
          },

          supplier = p.Supplier == null ? null :
            new SupplierCosmos
          {
            supplierId = p.Supplier.SupplierId,
            companyName = p.Supplier.CompanyName,
            contactName = p.Supplier.ContactName,
            contactTitle = p.Supplier.ContactTitle,
            address = p.Supplier.Address,
            city = p.Supplier.City,
            country = p.Supplier.Country,
            postalCode = p.Supplier.PostalCode,
            region = p.Supplier.Region,
            phone = p.Supplier.Phone,
            fax = p.Supplier.Fax,
            homePage = p.Supplier.HomePage
          },

          unitPrice = p.UnitPrice,
          unitsInStock = p.UnitsInStock,
          reorderLevel = p.ReorderLevel,
          unitsOnOrder = p.UnitsOnOrder,
          discontinued = p.Discontinued,
        })
        .ToArray();

    foreach (ProductCosmos product in products)
    {
      try
      {
        // Try to read the item to see if it exists.
        ItemResponse<ProductCosmos> productResponse =
          await container.ReadItemAsync<ProductCosmos>(
```

```
                    id: product.id, new PartitionKey(product.productId));

            WriteLine("Item with id: {0} exists. Query consumed {1}
RUs.",
                productResponse.Resource.id, productResponse.
RequestCharge);

            totalCharge += productResponse.RequestCharge;
          }
          catch (CosmosException ex)
            when (ex.StatusCode == HttpStatusCode.NotFound)
          {
            // Create the item if it does not exist.
            ItemResponse<ProductCosmos> productResponse =
              await container.CreateItemAsync(product);

            WriteLine("Created item with id: {0}. Insert consumed {1}
RUs.",
                productResponse.Resource.id, productResponse.
RequestCharge);

            totalCharge += productResponse.RequestCharge;
          }
          catch (Exception ex)
          {
            WriteLine("Error: {0} says {1}",
              arg0: ex.GetType(),
              arg1: ex.Message);
          }
        }
      }
    }
  }
  catch (HttpRequestException ex)
  {
    WriteLine($"Error: {ex.Message}");
    WriteLine("Hint: If you are using the Azure Cosmos Emulator then
please make sure it is running.");
  }
  catch (Exception ex)
  {
    WriteLine("Error: {0} says {1}",
```

```
        arg0: ex.GetType(),
        arg1: ex.Message);
    }

    WriteLine("Total requests charge: {0:N2} RUs", totalCharge);
}
```

8. In `Program.cs`, comment out the call to create the Azure Cosmos resources, and then add a statement to call the method to insert all the products, as shown in the following code:

```
await CreateProductItems();
```

9. Run the console app and note the results, which should be 77 product items inserted, as shown in the following partial output:

```
*
* Creating product items
*
Created item with id: 1. Insert consumed 14.29 RUs.
Created item with id: 2. Insert consumed 14.29 RUs.
Created item with id: 3. Insert consumed 14.29 RUs.
...
Created item with id: 76. Insert consumed 14.29 RUs.
Created item with id: 77. Insert consumed 14.48 RUs.
Total requests charge: 1,114.58 RUs
```

10. Run the console app again and note the results, which should show that the product items already exist, as shown in the following partial output:

```
*
* Creating product items
*
Item with id: 1 exists. Query consumed 1 RUs.
Item with id: 2 exists. Query consumed 1 RUs.
Item with id: 3 exists. Query consumed 1 RUs.
...
Item with id: 76 exists. Query consumed 1 RUs.
Item with id: 77 exists. Query consumed 1 RUs.
Total requests charge: 77.00 RUs
```

11. In the Azure Cosmos DB Emulator or Azure portal **Data Explorer**, confirm that there are 77 product items in the `Products` container.

12. In `Program.Methods.cs`, add statements to define a method to list all the items in the `Products` container, as shown in the following code:

```
static async Task ListProductItems(string sqlText = "SELECT * FROM c")
{
  SectionTitle("Listing product items");

  try
  {
    using (CosmosClient client = new(
      accountEndpoint: endpointUri,
      authKeyOrResourceToken: primaryKey))
    {
      Container container = client.GetContainer(
        databaseId: "Northwind", containerId: "Products");

      WriteLine("Running query: {0}", sqlText);

      QueryDefinition query = new(sqlText);

      using FeedIterator<ProductCosmos> resultsIterator =
        container.GetItemQueryIterator<ProductCosmos>(query);

      if (!resultsIterator.HasMoreResults)
      {
        WriteLine("No results found.");
      }

      while (resultsIterator.HasMoreResults)
      {
        FeedResponse<ProductCosmos> products =
          await resultsIterator.ReadNextAsync();

        WriteLine("Status code: {0}, Request charge: {1} RUs.",
          products.StatusCode, products.RequestCharge);

        WriteLine($"{products.Count} products found.");

        foreach (ProductCosmos product in products)
        {
          WriteLine("id: {0}, productName: {1}, unitPrice: {2}",
            arg0: product.id, arg1: product.productName,
```

```
                    arg2: product.unitPrice.ToString());
            }
          }
        }
      }
    catch (HttpRequestException ex)
    {
      WriteLine($"Error: {ex.Message}");
      WriteLine("Hint: If you are using the Azure Cosmos Emulator then
    please make sure it is running.");
    }
    catch (Exception ex)
    {
      WriteLine("Error: {0} says {1}",
        arg0: ex.GetType(),
        arg1: ex.Message);
    }
  }
```

13. In `Program.cs`, add statements to import the namespaces to work with cultures and encodings, simulate French culture, comment out the call to create the product items, and then add a statement to call the method to list the product items, as shown in the following code:

```
using System.Globalization; // To use CultureInfo.
using System.Text; // To use Encoding.

OutputEncoding = Encoding.UTF8; // To enable Euro symbol output.

// Simulate French culture to test Euro currency symbol output.
Thread.CurrentThread.CurrentCulture = CultureInfo.GetCultureInfo("fr-
FR");

//await CreateCosmosResources();

//await CreateProductItems();

await ListProductItems();
```

14. Run the console app and note the results, which should be 77 product items, as shown in the following partial output:

```
*
* Listing product items
*
```

```
Running query: SELECT * FROM c
Status code: OK, Request charge: 3.93 RUs.
77 products found.
id: 1, productName: Chai, unitPrice: 18,00 €
id: 2, productName: Chang, unitPrice: 19,00 €
id: 3, productName: Aniseed Syrup, unitPrice: 10,00 €
...
id: 76, productName: Lakkalikööri, unitPrice: 18,00 €
id: 77, productName: Original Frankfurter grüne Soße, unitPrice: 13,00 €
```

15. In `Program.Methods.cs`, add statements to define a method to delete all the items in the Products container, as shown in the following code:

```
static async Task DeleteProductItems()
{
  SectionTitle("Deleting product items");

  double totalCharge = 0.0;

  try
  {
    using (CosmosClient client = new(
      accountEndpoint: endpointUri,
      authKeyOrResourceToken: primaryKey))
    {
      Container container = client.GetContainer(
        databaseId: "Northwind", containerId: "Products");

      string sqlText = "SELECT * FROM c";

      WriteLine("Running query: {0}", sqlText);

      QueryDefinition query = new(sqlText);

      using FeedIterator<ProductCosmos> resultsIterator =
        container.GetItemQueryIterator<ProductCosmos>(query);

      while (resultsIterator.HasMoreResults)
      {
        FeedResponse<ProductCosmos> products =
          await resultsIterator.ReadNextAsync();

        foreach (ProductCosmos product in products)
```

```
            {
               WriteLine("Delete id: {0}, productName: {1}",
                  arg0: product.id, arg1: product.productName);

               ItemResponse<ProductCosmos> response =
                  await container.DeleteItemAsync<ProductCosmos>(
                  id: product.id, partitionKey: new(product.id));

               WriteLine("Status code: {0}, Request charge: {1} RUs.",
                  response.StatusCode, response.RequestCharge);

               totalCharge += response.RequestCharge;
            }
         }
      }
   }
   catch (HttpRequestException ex)
   {
      WriteLine($"Error: {ex.Message}");
      WriteLine("Hint: If you are using the Azure Cosmos Emulator then
please make sure it is running.");
   }
   catch (Exception ex)
   {
      WriteLine("Error: {0} says {1}",
         arg0: ex.GetType(),
         arg1: ex.Message);
   }

   WriteLine("Total requests charge: {0:N2} RUs", totalCharge);
}
```

16. In `Program.cs`, comment out the call to list the product items, and then add a statement to call the method to delete the product items, as shown in the following code:

```
await DeleteProductItems();
```

17. Run the console app and note the results, which should be 77 product items deleted, as shown in the following partial output:

```
*
* Deleting product items
*
Running query: SELECT * FROM c
```

```
Delete id: 1, productName: Chai
Status code: NoContent, Request charge: 14.29 RUs.
...
Delete id: 77, productName: Original Frankfurter grüne Soße
Status code: NoContent, Request charge: 14.48 RUs.
Total requests charge: 1,128.87 RUs
```

18. In the Azure Cosmos DB Emulator or Azure portal **Data Explorer**, confirm that the `Products` container is empty.

Understanding SQL queries

The following keywords and more are available when writing SQL queries for Azure Cosmos DB:

- `SELECT` to select from item properties. Supports * for all and `TOP` for limiting the results to the first specific number of items.
- `AS` to define aliases.
- `FROM` to define the items to select from. Some of the previous queries used `FROM c`, where `c` is an implied alias for the items in the container. Since a SQL query is executed within the context of a container like `Products`, you can use any alias you like, so `FROM Items c` or `FROM p` would work equally well.
- `WHERE` to define a filter.
- `LIKE` to use pattern matching. % means zero, one, or more characters. _ means a single character. [a-f] or [aeiou] means a single character within the defined range or set. [^aeiou] means not in the range or set.
- `IN, BETWEEN` are range and set filters.
- `AND, OR, NOT` for Boolean logic.
- `ORDER BY` to sort the results.
- `DISTINCT` to remove duplicates.
- `COUNT, AVG, SUM`, and other aggregate functions.

To query the `Products` container using the Core (SQL) API, you might write the following code:

```
SELECT p.id, p.productName, p.unitPrice FROM Items p
```

Let's try executing a SQL query against our product items:

1. In `Program.cs`, uncomment the call to (re)create the product items and modify the call to `ListProductItems` to pass a SQL query that filters the products to only show the products in the Beverages category and only their ID, name, and unit price, as shown in the following code:

```
//await CreateCosmosResources();
await CreateProductItems();
await ListProductItems("SELECT p.id, p.productName, p.unitPrice FROM
Items p WHERE p.category.categoryName = 'Beverages'");
//await DeleteProductItems();
```

2. Run the console app and note the results, which should be the 12 product items in the Beverages category, as shown in the following output:

```
*
* Listing product items
*
Running query: SELECT p.id, p.productName, p.unitPrice FROM Items p WHERE
p.category.categoryName = 'Beverages'
Status code: OK, Request charge: 3.19 RUs.
12 products found.
id: 1, productName: Chai, unitPrice: 18
id: 2, productName: Chang, unitPrice: 19
id: 24, productName: Guaraná Fantástica, unitPrice: 4.5
id: 34, productName: Sasquatch Ale, unitPrice: 14
id: 35, productName: Steeleye Stout, unitPrice: 18
id: 38, productName: Côte de Blaye, unitPrice: 263.5
id: 39, productName: Chartreuse verte, unitPrice: 18
id: 43, productName: Ipoh Coffee, unitPrice: 46
id: 67, productName: Laughing Lumberjack Lager, unitPrice: 14
id: 70, productName: Outback Lager, unitPrice: 15
id: 75, productName: Rhönbräu Klosterbier, unitPrice: 7.75
id: 76, productName: Lakkalikööri, unitPrice: 18
```

3. In the Azure Cosmos DB Emulator or Azure portal **Data Explorer**, create a new SQL query, use the same SQL text, and execute it, as shown in *Figure 4.7*:

Figure 4.7: Executing a SQL query in Data Explorer

4. Click **Query Stats**, and note the request charge (3.19 RUs), the number of records (12), and the output document size (752 bytes), as shown in *Figure 4.8*:

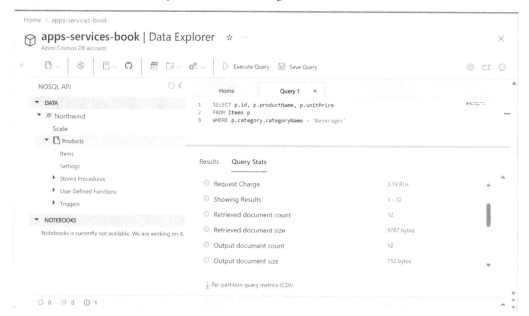

Figure 4.8: Query statistics in Data Explorer

Other useful query statistics include:

*   Index hit document count.
*   Index lookup time.
*   Document load time.
*   Query engine execution time.
*   Document write time.

Exploring other SQL queries with Cosmos DB

Try executing the following queries:

```
SELECT p.id, p.productName, p.unitPrice FROM Items p
WHERE p.unitPrice > 50


SELECT DISTINCT p.category FROM Items p


SELECT DISTINCT p.category.categoryName FROM Items p
WHERE p.discontinued = true


SELECT p.productName, p.supplier.city FROM Items p
WHERE p.supplier.country = 'Germany'
```

```
SELECT COUNT(p.id) AS HowManyProductsComeFromGermany FROM Items p
WHERE p.supplier.country = 'Germany'


SELECT AVG(p.unitPrice) AS AverageUnitPrice FROM Items p
```

Although queries defined using strings are the most common way of working with Cosmos DB, you can also create permanently stored objects using server-side programming.

Exploring server-side programming

Azure Cosmos DB server-side programming consists of **stored procedures**, **triggers**, and **user-defined functions (UDFs)** written in JavaScript.

Implementing user-defined functions

UDFs can only be called from within a query, and they implement custom business logic like calculating tax.

Let's define a UDF to calculate the sales tax of products:

1. In the Azure Cosmos DB Emulator or Azure portal **Data Explorer**, create a new UDF, as shown in *Figure 4.9*:

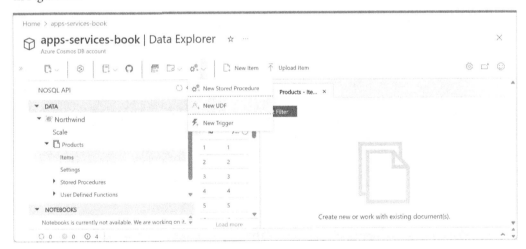

Figure 4.9: Creating a new UDF

2. For the **User Defined Function Id**, enter salesTax.
3. For the **User Defined Function Body**, enter JavaScript to define the salesTax function, as shown in the following code:

```
function salesTax(unitPrice){
    return unitPrice * 0.2;
}
```

4.   In the toolbar, click **Save**.

5.   Create a new SQL query and enter SQL text to return the unit price and sales tax for products that cost more than 100, as shown in the following query:

```
SELECT p.unitPrice cost, udf.salesTax(p.unitPrice) AS tax
FROM Items p WHERE p.unitPrice > 100
```

 Note that **AS** to alias an expression is optional. I prefer to specify **AS** for improved legibility.

6.   Click the **Save Query** button.

 If you are using cloud resources instead of the emulator, then for compliance reasons, Microsoft saves queries in a container in your Azure Cosmos account in a separate database called **___Cosmos**. The estimated additional cost is $0.77 daily.

7.   Execute the query and note the results, as shown in the following output:

```
[
    {
        "cost": 123.79,
        "tax": 24.758000000000003
    },
    {
        "cost": 263.5,
        "tax": 52.7
    }
]
```

Implementing stored procedures

Stored procedures are the only way to ensure **ACID** (**Atomic, Consistent, Isolated, Durable**) transactions that combine multiple discrete activities into a single action that can be committed or rolled back. You cannot use client-side code to implement transactions. Server-side programming also provides improved performance since the code executes where the data is stored.

We have just seen that you can define a UDF using the Data Explorer. We could define a stored procedure in a similar way, but let's see how we would do it using code:

1.   In `Program.Methods.cs`, import the namespace for working with server-side programming objects, as shown in the following code:

```
                     // To use StoredProcedureResponse and so on.
                     using Microsoft.Azure.Cosmos.Scripts;
```

2. In `Program.Methods.cs`, add statements to define a method to create a stored procedure that can insert multiple products by chaining callback functions until all items in an array are inserted, as shown in the following code:

```csharp
static async Task CreateInsertProductStoredProcedure()
{
  SectionTitle("Creating the insertProduct stored procedure");

  try
  {
    using (CosmosClient client = new(
      accountEndpoint: endpointUri,
      authKeyOrResourceToken: primaryKey))
    {
      Container container = client.GetContainer(
        databaseId: "Northwind", containerId: "Products");

      StoredProcedureResponse response = await container
        .Scripts.CreateStoredProcedureAsync(new StoredProcedureProperties
        {
          Id = "insertProduct",
          // __ means getContext().getCollection().
          Body = """
function insertProduct(product) {
  if (!product) throw new Error(
    "product is undefined or null.");

  tryInsert(product, callbackInsert);

  function tryInsert(product, callbackFunction) {
    var options = { disableAutomaticIdGeneration: false };

    // __ is an alias for getContext().getCollection()
    var isAccepted = __.createDocument(
      __.getSelfLink(), product, options, callbackFunction);

    if (!isAccepted)
      getContext().getResponse().setBody(0);
  }
```

```
    function callbackInsert(err, item, options) {
      if (err) throw err;
      getContext().getResponse().setBody(1);
    }
}
"""

        });

      WriteLine("Status code: {0}, Request charge: {1} RUs.",
        response.StatusCode, response.RequestCharge);
    }
  }
  catch (HttpRequestException ex)
  {
    WriteLine($"Error: {ex.Message}");
    WriteLine("Hint: If you are using the Azure Cosmos Emulator then
please make sure it is running.");
  }
  catch (Exception ex)
  {
    WriteLine("Error: {0} says {1}",
      arg0: ex.GetType(),
      arg1: ex.Message);
  }
}
```

3. In `Program.cs`, comment out all the existing statements, and add a statement to run the new method, as shown in the following code:

```
await CreateInsertProductStoredProcedure();
```

4. Run the console app and note the results, which should be the successful creation of the stored procedure, as shown in the following output:

```
*
* Creating the insertProduct stored procedure
*
Status code: Created, Request charge: 6.29 RUs.
```

5. In `Program.Methods.cs`, add statements to define a method to execute the stored procedure, as shown in the following code:

```
static async Task ExecuteInsertProductStoredProcedure()
{
```

```
    SectionTitle("Executing the insertProduct stored procedure");

  try
  {
    using (CosmosClient client = new(
      accountEndpoint: endpointUri,
      authKeyOrResourceToken: primaryKey))
    {
      Container container = client.GetContainer(
        databaseId: "Northwind", containerId: "Products");

      string pid = "78";

      ProductCosmos product = new()
      {
        id = pid, productId = pid,
        productName = "Barista's Chilli Jam",
        unitPrice = 12M, unitsInStock = 10
      };

      StoredProcedureExecuteResponse<string> response = await container.
Scripts
          .ExecuteStoredProcedureAsync<string>("insertProduct",
          new PartitionKey(pid), new[] { product });

      WriteLine("Status code: {0}, Request charge: {1} RUs.",
        response.StatusCode, response.RequestCharge);
    }
  }
  catch (HttpRequestException ex)
  {
    WriteLine($"Error: {ex.Message}");
    WriteLine("Hint: If you are using the Azure Cosmos Emulator then
please make sure it is running.");
  }
  catch (Exception ex)
  {
    WriteLine("Error: {0} says {1}",
      arg0: ex.GetType(),
      arg1: ex.Message);
  }
}
```

6. In `Program.cs`, comment out the statement to create the stored procedure, add a statement to execute the stored procedure, and then list products with a `productId` of 78, as shown in the following code:

```
//await CreateInsertProductStoredProcedure();
await ExecuteInsertProductStoredProcedure();
await ListProductItems("SELECT p.id, p.productName, p.unitPrice FROM
Items p WHERE p.productId = '78'");
```

7. Run the console app and note the results, which should be the successful execution of the stored procedure, as shown in the following output:

```
*
* Executing the insertProduct stored procedure
*
Status code: OK, Request charge: 10.23 RUs.
*
* Listing product items
*
Running query: SELECT p.id, p.productName, p.unitPrice FROM Items p WHERE
p.productId = '78'
Status code: OK, Request charge: 2.83 RUs.
1 products found.
id: 78, productName: Barista's Chilli Jam, unitPrice: €12.00
```

Cleaning up Azure resources

When you are done with an Azure Cosmos DB account, you must clean up the resources used, or you will incur costs for as long as those resources exist. You can delete resources individually or delete the resource group to delete the entire set of resources. If you delete an Azure Cosmos DB account, then all the databases and containers within it are also deleted:

1. In the Azure portal, navigate to **All Resources**.
2. In your `apps-services-book` resource group, click your Azure Cosmos DB account.
3. Click **Overview**, and then in the toolbar, click **Delete Account**.
4. In the **Confirm the Account Name** box, enter your account name.
5. Click the **Delete** button.

Practicing and exploring

Test your knowledge and understanding by answering some questions, getting some hands-on practice, and exploring this chapter's topics with deeper research.

Exercise 4.1 – Test your knowledge

Answer the following questions:

1. What are the five APIs supported by Azure Cosmos DB?
2. At what level do you select the API: account, database, container, or partition?
3. What does *embed* mean regarding data modeling with Cosmos DB?
4. What is the unit of measurement for throughput for Cosmos DB and what does 1 unit represent?
5. What package should you reference to programmatically work with Cosmos DB resources?
6. What language do you use to write Cosmos DB Core (SQL) API user-defined functions and stored procedures?

Exercise 4.2 – Practice data modeling and partitioning

Microsoft documentation has an extensive example of modeling and partitioning Azure Cosmos DB:

```
https://learn.microsoft.com/en-us/azure/cosmos-db/sql/how-to-model-partition-example
```

Exercise 4.3 – Explore topics

Use the links on the following page to learn more details about the topics covered in this chapter:

```
https://github.com/markjprice/apps-services-net8/blob/main/docs/book-links.md#chapter-
4---managing-nosql-data-using-azure-cosmos-db
```

Exercise 4.4 – Download cheat sheets

Download query cheat sheets for the Azure Cosmos DB APIs and review them:

```
https://learn.microsoft.com/en-us/azure/cosmos-db/sql/query-cheat-sheet
```

Exercise 4.5 – Explore the Gremlin API for Cosmos DB

If you are interested, then I have written an optional online-only section where you explore the Azure Cosmos DB graph API that uses the Gremlin API, found at the following link:

```
https://github.com/markjprice/apps-services-net8/blob/main/docs/ch04-gremlin.md
```

To gain more experience with the Gremlin graph API, you could read the following online book:

```
https://kelvinlawrence.net/book/Gremlin-Graph-Guide.html
```

Exercise 4.6 – Explore NoSQL databases

This chapter focused on Azure Cosmos DB. If you wish to learn more about NoSQL databases, such as MongoDB, and how to use them with EF Core, then I recommend the following links:

- **Use NoSQL databases as a persistence infrastructure:** `https://learn.microsoft.com/en-us/dotnet/standard/microservices-architecture/microservice-ddd-cqrs-patterns/nosql-database-persistence-infrastructure`
- **Document Database Providers for Entity Framework Core:** `https://github.com/BlueshiftSoftware/EntityFrameworkCore`

Summary

In this chapter, you learned:

- How to store flexibly structured data in Azure Cosmos DB.
- How to create Cosmos DB resources in the emulator and in the Azure cloud.
- How to manipulate data using the Cosmos SQL API.
- How to implement server-side programming in Cosmos DB using JavaScript.

In the next chapter, you will use the Task type to improve the performance of your applications.

5

Multitasking and Concurrency

This chapter is about allowing multiple actions to occur at the same time to improve performance, scalability, and user productivity for the applications that you build.

In this chapter, we will cover the following topics:

- Understanding processes, threads, and tasks
- Running tasks asynchronously
- Synchronizing access to shared resources
- Understanding async and await

Understanding processes, threads, and tasks

A **process**, with one example being each of the console applications we have created, has resources like memory and threads allocated to it.

A **thread** executes your code statement by statement. By default, each process only has one thread, and this can cause problems when we need to do more than one task at the same time. Threads are also responsible for keeping track of things like the currently authenticated user and any internationalization rules that should be followed for the current language and region.

Windows and most other modern operating systems use **preemptive multitasking**, which simulates the parallel execution of tasks. It divides the processor time among the threads, allocating a **time slice** to each thread one after another. The current thread is suspended when its time slice finishes. The processor then allows another thread to run for a time slice.

When Windows switches from one thread to another, it saves the context of the thread and reloads the previously saved context of the next thread in the thread queue. This takes both time and resources to complete.

As a developer, if you have a small number of complex pieces of work and you want complete control over them, then you could create and manage individual Thread instances. If you have one main thread and multiple small pieces of work that can be executed in the background, then you can use the ThreadPool class to add delegate instances that point to those pieces of work implemented as methods to a queue, and they will be automatically allocated to threads in the thread pool.

In this chapter, we will use the Task type to manage threads at a higher abstraction level.

Threads may have to compete for and wait for access to shared resources, such as variables, files, and database objects. There are types for managing this that you will see in action later in this chapter.

Depending on the task, doubling the number of threads (workers) to perform a task does not halve the number of seconds that it will take to complete that task. In fact, it can increase the duration of the task due to resource contention, as shown in *Figure 5.1*:

Carl T. Bergstrom @CT_Bergstrom · Dec 17

My son clearly has a better grasp on the real world than his teacher does.

8. If 6 workers can make a car in 90 hours, how long would it take 12 workers to make the same car?

    (A) 12 hours
    (B) 25 hours
    (C) 30 hours
    (D) 45 hours
    (E) 180 hours

    ↩ 253   ⇄ 10K   ♥ 16K   •••

Figure 5.1: A tweet about tasks in the real world

Good Practice: Never assume that more threads will improve performance! Run performance tests on a baseline code implementation without multiple threads, and then again on a code implementation with multiple threads. You should also perform performance tests in a staging environment that is as close as possible to the production environment.

Running tasks asynchronously

To understand how multiple tasks can be run **simultaneously** (at the same time), we will create a console app that needs to execute three methods.

There will be three methods that need to be executed: the first takes 3 seconds, the second takes 2 seconds, and the third takes 1 second. To simulate that work, we can use the Thread class to tell the current thread to go to sleep for a specified number of milliseconds.

Running multiple actions synchronously

Before we make the tasks run simultaneously, we will run them **synchronously**, that is, one after the other:

1. Use your preferred code editor to add a console app project, as defined in the following list:

    - Project template: **Console App** / `console`
    - Solution file and folder: `Chapter05`
    - Project file and folder: `WorkingWithTasks`
    - **Do not use top-level statements:** Cleared.
    - **Enable native AOT publish:** Cleared.

2. In the `WorkingWithTasks` project, globally and statically import the `System.Console` class and treat warnings as errors.

3. In the `WorkingWithTasks` project, add a new class file named `Program.Helpers.cs`.

4. In `Program.Helpers.cs`, delete any existing statements, and then define a partial `Program` class with methods to output a section title and a task title, and to output information about the current thread, each in different colors to make them easier to identify in output, as shown in the following code:

```
partial class Program
{
  private static void SectionTitle(string title)
  {
    ConsoleColor previousColor = ForegroundColor;
    ForegroundColor = ConsoleColor.DarkYellow;
    WriteLine($"*** {title}");
    ForegroundColor = previousColor;
  }

  private static void TaskTitle(string title)
  {
    ConsoleColor previousColor = ForegroundColor;
    ForegroundColor = ConsoleColor.Green;
    WriteLine($"{title}");
    ForegroundColor = previousColor;
  }

  private static void OutputThreadInfo()
  {
    Thread t = Thread.CurrentThread;
```

```
    ConsoleColor previousColor = ForegroundColor;
    ForegroundColor = ConsoleColor.DarkCyan;

    WriteLine(
      "Thread Id: {0}, Priority: {1}, Background: {2}, Name: {3}",
      t.ManagedThreadId, t.Priority, t.IsBackground, t.Name ?? "null");

    ForegroundColor = previousColor;
  }
}
```

5. In the `WorkingWithTasks` project, add a new class file named `Program.Methods.cs`.

6. In `Program.Methods.cs`, delete any existing statements, and then add three methods that simulate work, as shown in the following code:

```
partial class Program
{
  private static void MethodA()
  {
    TaskTitle("Starting Method A...");
    OutputThreadInfo();
    Thread.Sleep(3000); // Simulate three seconds of work.
    TaskTitle("Finished Method A.");
  }

  private static void MethodB()
  {
    TaskTitle("Starting Method B...");
    OutputThreadInfo();
    Thread.Sleep(2000); // Simulate two seconds of work.
    TaskTitle("Finished Method B.");
  }

  private static void MethodC()
  {
    TaskTitle("Starting Method C...");
    OutputThreadInfo();
    Thread.Sleep(1000); // Simulate one second of work.
    TaskTitle("Finished Method C.");
  }
}
```

7. In `Program.cs`, delete the existing statements and then add statements to call the helper method to output information about the thread, define and start a stopwatch, call the three simulated work methods, and then output the milliseconds elapsed, as shown in the following code:

```csharp
using System.Diagnostics; // To use Stopwatch.

OutputThreadInfo();
Stopwatch timer = Stopwatch.StartNew();

SectionTitle("Running methods synchronously on one thread.");
MethodA();
MethodB();
MethodC();

WriteLine($"{timer.ElapsedMilliseconds:#,##0}ms elapsed.");
```

8. Run the code, wait for all three methods to finish executing, and then review the result, noting that when there is only one unnamed foreground thread doing the work, the total time required is just over 6 seconds, as shown in the following output:

```
Thread Id: 1, Priority: Normal, Background: False, Name: null
*** Running methods synchronously on one thread.
Starting Method A...
Thread Id: 1, Priority: Normal, Background: False, Name: null
Finished Method A.
Starting Method B...
Thread Id: 1, Priority: Normal, Background: False, Name: null
Finished Method B.
Starting Method C...
Thread Id: 1, Priority: Normal, Background: False, Name: null
Finished Method C.
6,028ms elapsed.
```

Running multiple actions asynchronously using tasks

The `Thread` class has been available since the first version of .NET in 2002 and can be used to create new threads and manage them, but it can be tricky to work with directly.

.NET Framework 4.0 introduced the `Task` class in 2010, which represents an asynchronous operation. A task is a high-level abstraction around the operating system thread that performs the operation, and the `Task` class enables easier creation and management of any underlying threads. Managing multiple threads wrapped in tasks will allow our code to execute at the same time, aka **asynchronously**.

Each `Task` has a `Status` property and a `CreationOptions` property. A `Task` has a `ContinueWith` method that can be customized with the `TaskContinuationOptions` enum, and it can be managed with the `TaskFactory` class.

Starting tasks

We will look at three ways to start the methods using Task instances. There are links in the GitHub repository to articles that discuss the pros and cons. Each has a slightly different syntax, but they all define a Task and start it:

1. In Program.cs, comment out the previous statements that call methods A to C, and then add statements to create and start three tasks, one for each method, as shown highlighted in the following code:

```
Stopwatch timer = Stopwatch.StartNew();

/*
SectionTitle("Running methods synchronously on one thread.");
MethodA();
MethodB();
MethodC();
*/

SectionTitle("Running methods asynchronously on multiple threads.");

Task taskA = new(MethodA);
taskA.Start();
Task taskB = Task.Factory.StartNew(MethodB);
Task taskC = Task.Run(MethodC);

WriteLine($"{timer.ElapsedMilliseconds:#,##0}ms elapsed.");
```

 Instead of commenting out the previous statements, you could let them run, but then make sure to call the timer.Restart() method after outputting a new section title to reset the timings for each section.

2. Run the code, view the result, and note that the elapsed milliseconds appear almost immediately. This is because each of the three methods is now being executed by three new background worker threads allocated from the **thread pool (TP)**, as shown in the following output:

```
*** Running methods asynchronously on multiple threads.
Starting Method A...
Thread Id: 4, Priority: Normal, Background: True, Name: .NET TP Worker
Starting Method C...
Thread Id: 7, Priority: Normal, Background: True, Name: .NET TP Worker
Starting Method B...
Thread Id: 6, Priority: Normal, Background: True, Name: .NET TP Worker
6ms elapsed.
```

It is even likely that the console app will end before one or even all the tasks have a chance to start and write to the console!

Waiting for tasks

Sometimes, you need to wait for a task to complete before continuing. To do this, you can use the `Wait` method on a `Task` instance, or the `WaitAll` or `WaitAny` static methods on an array of tasks, as described in *Table 5.1*:

Method	Description
`t.Wait()`	This waits for the task instance named `t` to complete execution.
`Task.WaitAny(Task[])`	This waits for any of the tasks in the array to complete execution.
`Task.WaitAll(Task[])`	This waits for all the tasks in the array to complete execution.

Table 5.1: Task class Wait methods

Using wait methods with tasks

Let's see how we can use these wait methods to fix the problem with our console app:

1. In `Program.cs`, after creating the three tasks and before outputting the elapsed time, add statements to combine references to the three tasks into an array and pass them to the `WaitAll` method, as shown in the following code:

    ```
    Task[] tasks = { taskA, taskB, taskC };
    Task.WaitAll(tasks);
    ```

2. Run the code and view the result, and note the original thread will pause on the call to `WaitAll`, waiting for all three tasks to finish before outputting the elapsed time, which is a little over 3 seconds, as shown in the following output:

    ```
    Starting Method A...
    Starting Method B...
    Thread Id: 4, Priority: Normal, Background: True, Name: .NET TP Worker
    Thread Id: 6, Priority: Normal, Background: True, Name: .NET TP Worker
    Starting Method C...
    Thread Id: 7, Priority: Normal, Background: True, Name: .NET TP Worker
    Finished Method C.
    Finished Method B.
    Finished Method A.
    3,013ms elapsed.
    ```

The three new threads execute their code simultaneously, and they can potentially start in any order. `MethodC` should finish first because it takes only 1 second, then `MethodB`, which takes 2 seconds, and finally, `MethodA`, because it takes 3 seconds.

However, the actual CPU used has a big effect on the results. It is the CPU that allocates time slices to each process to allow them to execute their threads. You have no control over when the methods run.

Continuing with another task

If all three tasks can be performed at the same time, then waiting for all tasks to finish will be all we need to do. However, often, a task is dependent on the output from another task. To handle this scenario, we need to define **continuation tasks**.

We will create some methods to simulate a call to a web service that returns a monetary amount, which then needs to be used to retrieve how many products cost more than that amount in a database. The result returned from the first method needs to be fed into the input of the second method. This time, instead of waiting for fixed amounts of time, we will use the Random class to wait for a random interval between 2 and 4 seconds for each method call to simulate the work:

1. In `Program.Methods.cs`, add two methods that simulate calling a web service and a database-stored procedure, as shown in the following code:

    ```csharp
    private static decimal CallWebService()
    {
      TaskTitle("Starting call to web service...");
      OutputThreadInfo();
      Thread.Sleep(Random.Shared.Next(2000, 4000));
      TaskTitle("Finished call to web service.");
      return 89.99M;
    }

    private static string CallStoredProcedure(decimal amount)
    {
      TaskTitle("Starting call to stored procedure...");
      OutputThreadInfo();
      Thread.Sleep((Random.Shared.Next(2000, 4000));
      TaskTitle("Finished call to stored procedure.");
      return $"12 products cost more than {amount:C}.";
    }
    ```

2. In `Program.cs`, comment out the statements for the previous three tasks, and then add statements to start a task to call the web service and then pass its return value to a task that starts the database-stored procedure, as shown highlighted in the following code:

    ```csharp
    SectionTitle("Passing the result of one task as an input into another.");

    Task<string> taskServiceThenSProc = Task.Factory
      .StartNew(CallWebService) // returns Task<decimal>
      .ContinueWith(previousTask => // returns Task<string>
    ```

```
    CallStoredProcedure(previousTask.Result));

WriteLine($"Result: {taskServiceThenSProc.Result}");

WriteLine($"{timer.ElapsedMilliseconds:#,##0}ms elapsed.");
```

3. Run the code and view the result, as shown in the following output:

```
Starting call to web service...
Thread Id: 4, Priority: Normal, Background: True, Name: .NET TP Worker
Finished call to web service.
Starting call to stored procedure...
Thread Id: 6, Priority: Normal, Background: True, Name: .NET TP Worker
Finished call to stored procedure.
Result: 12 products cost more than £89.99.
5,463ms elapsed.
```

 The currency symbol is culture-specific so on my computer it uses a £. On your computer it will use your culture. You will learn how to control cultures in *Chapter 7, Handling Dates, Times, and Internationalization.*

You might see two different threads running the web service and stored procedure calls as in the output above (for example, threads 4 and 6), or the same thread might be reused since it is no longer busy.

Nested and child tasks

As well as defining dependencies between tasks, you can define nested and child tasks. A **nested task** is a task that is created inside another task. A **child task** is a nested task that must finish before its parent task is allowed to finish.

Let's explore how these types of tasks work:

1. In `Program.Methods.cs`, add two methods, one of which starts a task to run the other, as shown in the following code:

```
private static void OuterMethod()
{
  TaskTitle("Outer method starting...");
  Task innerTask = Task.Factory.StartNew(InnerMethod);
  TaskTitle("Outer method finished.");
}

private static void InnerMethod()
{
```

```
    TaskTitle("Inner method starting...");
    Thread.Sleep(2000);
    TaskTitle("Inner method finished.");
}
```

2. In `Program.cs`, add statements to start a task to run the outer method and wait for it to finish before stopping, as shown in the following code:

```
SectionTitle("Nested and child tasks");

Task outerTask = Task.Factory.StartNew(OuterMethod);
outerTask.Wait();
WriteLine("Console app is stopping.");
```

3. Run the code and view the result, as shown in the following output:

```
Outer method starting...
Inner method starting...
Outer method finished.
Console app is stopping.
```

> Although we wait for the outer task to finish, its inner task does not have to finish as well. In fact, the outer task might finish, and the console app could end before the inner task even starts, as shown in the following output:
>
> ```
> Outer method starting...
> Outer method finished.
> Console app is stopping.
> ```

4. To link these nested tasks as parent and child, we must use a special option. In `Program.Methods.cs`, modify the existing code to add a `TaskCreationOption` value of `AttachedToParent`, as shown highlighted in the following code:

```
private static void OuterMethod()
{
    TaskTitle("Outer method starting...");

    Task innerTask = Task.Factory.StartNew(InnerMethod,
      TaskCreationOptions.AttachedToParent);

    TaskTitle("Outer method finished.");
}
```

5. Run the code, view the result, and note that the inner task must finish before the outer task can, as shown in the following output:

```
Outer method starting...
Inner method starting...
Outer method finished.
Inner method finished.
Console app is stopping.
```

6. Alternatively, the outer method could finish before the inner method starts, as shown in the following output:

```
Outer method starting...
Outer method finished.
Inner method starting...
Inner method finished.
Console app is stopping.
```

 The OuterMethod can finish its work before the InnerMethod, as shown by what it writes to the console, but its task must wait, as shown by the console not stopping until both the outer and inner tasks finish.

Wrapping tasks around other objects

Sometimes you might have a method that you want to be asynchronous, but the result to be returned is not itself a task. You can wrap the return value in a successfully completed task, return an exception, or indicate that the task was canceled by using one of the Task static methods, as shown in *Table 5.2*:

Method	Description
FromResult<TResult>(TResult)	Creates a Task<TResult> object whose Result property is the non-task result and whose Status property is RanToCompletion.
FromException<TResult>(Exception)	Creates a Task<TResult> that's completed with a specified exception.
FromCanceled<TResult>(CancellationToken)	Creates a Task<TResult> that's completed due to cancellation with a specified cancellation token.

Table 5.2: Methods to create a Task in various scenarios

These methods are useful when you need to:

- Implement an interface that has asynchronous methods, but your implementation is synchronous. This is common for websites and services.
- Mock asynchronous implementations during unit testing.

Imagine that you need to create a method to validate XML input and the method must conform to an interface that requires a `Task<T>` to be returned, as shown in the following code:

```
public interface IValidation
{
  Task<bool> IsValidXmlTagAsync(this string input);
}
```

 The code in this section is for illustration only. You do not need to enter it in your project.

We could use these helpful `FromX` methods to return the results wrapped in a task, as shown in the following code:

```
using System.Text.RegularExpressions;

namespace Packt.Shared;

public static class StringExtensions : IValidation
{
  public static Task<bool> IsValidXmlTagAsync(this string input)
  {
    if (input == null)
    {
      return Task.FromException<bool>(
        new ArgumentNullException($"Missing {nameof(input)} parameter"));
    }

    if (input.Length == 0)
    {
      return Task.FromException<bool>(
        new ArgumentException($"{nameof(input)} parameter is empty."));
    }

    return Task.FromResult(Regex.IsMatch(input,
      @"^<([a-z]+)([^<]+)*(?:>(.*)<\/\1>|\s+\/>)$"));
  }
}
```

If the method you need to implement returns a `Task` (equivalent to `void` in a synchronous method), then you can return a predefined completed `Task` object, as shown in the following code:

```
public Task DeleteCustomerAsync()
{
  // ...
  return Task.CompletedTask;
}
```

When running tasks in parallel, the code will often need to access resources, and those resources are sometimes shared between tasks and threads. We, therefore, need to learn how to safely access those shared resources.

Synchronizing access to shared resources

When you have multiple threads executing at the same time, there is a possibility that two or more of the threads may access the same variable or another resource at the same time, and as a result, may cause a problem. For this reason, you should carefully consider how to make your code **thread-safe**.

The simplest mechanism for implementing thread safety is to use an object variable as a flag or traffic light to indicate when a shared resource has an exclusive lock applied.

In William Golding's *Lord of the Flies*, Piggy and Ralph find a conch shell and use it to call a meeting. The boys impose a "rule of the conch" on themselves, deciding that no one can speak unless they're holding the conch.

I like to name the object variable I use for implementing thread-safe code the "conch." When a thread has the conch, no other thread should access the shared resource(s) represented by that conch. Note that I say *should*. Only code that respects the conch enables synchronized access. A conch is *not* a lock.

We will explore a couple of types that can be used to synchronize access to shared resources:

- `Monitor`: An object that can be used by multiple threads to check if they should access a shared resource within the same process.
- `Interlocked`: An object for manipulating simple numeric types at the CPU level.

Accessing a resource from multiple threads

Let's create a console app to explore sharing resources between multiple threads:

1. Use your preferred code editor to add a new **Console App** / console project to the Chapter05 solution named SynchronizingResourceAccess.
2. Globally and statically import the System.Console class and treat warnings as errors.
3. Add a new class file named SharedObjects.cs.
4. In SharedObjects.cs, delete any existing statements and then define a static class with a field to store a message that is a shared resource, as shown in the following code:

```
public static class SharedObjects
{
  public static string? Message; // a shared resource
}
```

5. Add a new class file named `Program.Methods.cs`.

6. In `Program.Methods.cs`, delete any existing statements and then define two methods that both loop five times, waiting for a random interval of up to two seconds and appending either A or B to the shared message resource, as shown in the following code:

```
partial class Program
{
  private static void MethodA()
  {
    for (int i = 0; i < 5; i++)
    {
      // Simulate two seconds of work on the current thread.
      Thread.Sleep(Random.Shared.Next(2000));

      // Concatenate the letter "A" to the shared message.
      SharedObjects.Message += "A";

      // Show some activity in the console output.
      Write(".");
    }
  }

  private static void MethodB()
  {
    for (int i = 0; i < 5; i++)
    {
      Thread.Sleep(Random.Shared.Next(2000));
      SharedObjects.Message += "B";
      Write(".");
    }
  }
}
```

7. In `Program.cs`, delete the existing statements. Add statements to import the namespace for diagnostic types like `Stopwatch`, and statements to execute both methods on separate threads using a pair of tasks, and wait for them to complete before outputting the elapsed milliseconds, as shown in the following code:

```
using System.Diagnostics; // To use Stopwatch.

WriteLine("Please wait for the tasks to complete.");
```

```
Stopwatch watch = Stopwatch.StartNew();
Task a = Task.Factory.StartNew(MethodA);
Task b = Task.Factory.StartNew(MethodB);

Task.WaitAll(new Task[] { a, b });
WriteLine();
WriteLine($"Results: {SharedObjects.Message}.");
WriteLine($"{watch.ElapsedMilliseconds:N0} elapsed milliseconds.");
```

8. Run the code and view the result, as shown in the following output:

```
Please wait for the tasks to complete.
..........
Results: BABABAABBA.
5,753 elapsed milliseconds.
```

This shows that both threads were modifying the message concurrently. In an actual application, this could be a problem. But we can prevent concurrent access by applying a mutually exclusive lock to a conch object, as well as adding code to the two methods to voluntarily check the conch before modifying the shared resource, which we will do in the following section.

Applying a mutually exclusive lock to a conch

Now, let's use a conch to ensure that only one thread accesses the shared resource at a time:

1. In `SharedObjects.cs`, declare and instantiate an `object` variable to act as a conch, as shown in the following code:

    ```
    public static object Conch = new(); // A shared object to lock.
    ```

2. In `Program.Methods.cs`, in both `MethodA` and `MethodB`, add a `lock` statement for the conch around the `for` statements, as shown highlighted in the following code for `MethodB`:

    ```
    lock (SharedObjects.Conch)
    {
      for (int i = 0; i < 5; i++)
      {
        Thread.Sleep(Random.Shared.Next(2000));
        SharedObjects.Message += "B";
        Write(".");
      }
    }
    ```

Good Practice: Note that since checking the conch is voluntary, if you only use the lock statement in one of the two methods, the shared resource will continue to be accessed by both methods. Make sure that all methods that access a shared resource respect the conch by calling lock on it before trying to use any shared resources.

3. Run the code and view the result, as shown in the following output:

```
Please wait for the tasks to complete.
..........
Results: BBBBBAAAAA.
10,345 elapsed milliseconds.
```

Although the time elapsed was longer, only one method at a time could access the shared resource. Either MethodA or MethodB can start first. Once a method has finished its work on the shared resource, then the conch gets released, and the other method has the chance to do its work.

Understanding the lock statement

You might wonder what the lock statement does when it "locks" an object variable (hint: it does not lock the object!), as shown in the following code:

```
lock (SharedObjects.Conch)
{
  // Work with a shared resource.
}
```

The C# compiler changes the lock statement into a try-finally statement that uses the Monitor class to *enter* and *exit* the conch object (I like to think of it as *take* and *release* the conch object), as shown in the following code:

```
try
{
  Monitor.Enter(SharedObjects.Conch);
  // Work with a shared resource.
}
finally
{
  Monitor.Exit(SharedObjects.Conch);
}
```

When a thread calls Monitor.Enter on a reference type, it checks to see if some other thread has already taken the conch. If it has, the thread waits. If it has not, the thread takes the conch and gets on with its work on the shared resource. Once the thread has finished its work, it calls Monitor.Exit, releasing the conch.

If another thread was waiting, it could now take the conch and do its work. This requires all threads to respect the conch by calling `Monitor.Enter` and `Monitor.Exit` appropriately.

 Good Practice: You cannot use value types (`struct` types) as a conch. `Monitor.Enter` requires a reference type because it locks the memory address. Any internal data structures for that object are *not* locked.

Avoiding deadlocks

Knowing how the `lock` statement is translated by the compiler to method calls on the `Monitor` class is also important because using the `lock` statement can cause a deadlock.

Deadlocks can occur when there are two or more shared resources (each with a conch to monitor which thread is currently doing work on each shared resource), and the following sequence of events happens:

- Thread X "locks" conch A and starts working on shared resource A.
- Thread Y "locks" conch B and starts working on shared resource B.
- While still working on resource A, thread X needs to also work with resource B, and so it attempts to "lock" conch B but is blocked because thread Y already has conch B.
- While still working on resource B, thread Y needs to also work with resource A, and so it attempts to "lock" conch A but is blocked because thread X already has conch A.

One way to prevent deadlocks is to specify a timeout when attempting to get a lock. To do this, you must manually use the `Monitor` class instead of using the `lock` statement. Let's see how:

1. In `Program.Methods.cs`, modify your code to replace the `lock` statements with code that tries to enter the conch with a timeout, outputs an error, and then exits the monitor, allowing other threads to enter the monitor, as shown highlighted in the following code for `MethodB`:

```
try
{
  if (Monitor.TryEnter(SharedObjects.Conch, TimeSpan.FromSeconds(15)))
  {
    for (int i = 0; i < 5; i++)
    {
      Thread.Sleep(Random.Shared.Next(2000));
      SharedObjects.Message += "B";
      Write(".");
    }
  }
  else
  {
    WriteLine("Method B timed out when entering a monitor on conch.");
  }
```

```
    }
    finally
    {
      Monitor.Exit(SharedObjects.Conch);
    }
```

2. Run the code and view the result, which should return the same results as before (although either A or B could grab the conch first) but is better code because it will prevent potential deadlocks.

 Good Practice: Only use the `lock` keyword if you can write your code such that it avoids potential deadlocks. If you cannot avoid potential deadlocks, then always use the `Monitor.TryEnter` method instead of `lock`, in combination with a `try-finally` statement, so that you can supply a timeout and one of the threads will back out of a deadlock if it occurs. You can read more about good threading practices at the following link: `https://learn.microsoft.com/en-us/dotnet/standard/threading/managed-threading-best-practices`.

Synchronizing events

.NET events are not thread-safe, so you should avoid using them in multi-threaded scenarios.

After learning that .NET events are not thread-safe, some developers attempt to use exclusive locks when adding and removing event handlers or when raising an event, as shown in the following code:

```
// event delegate field
public event EventHandler? Shout;

// conch
private object eventConch = new();

// method
public void Poke()
{
  lock (eventConch) // bad idea
  {
    // If something is listening...
    if (Shout != null)
    {
      // ...then call the delegate to raise the event.
      Shout(this, EventArgs.Empty);
    }
  }
}
```

Good Practice: Is it good or bad that some developers use locks in event handling? Well, it is complicated. It depends on complex factors so I cannot give a value judgement. You can read more about events and thread safety at the following link: `https://learn.microsoft.com/en-us/archive/blogs/cburrows/field-like-events-considered-harmful`. But it is complicated, as explained by Stephen Cleary in the following blog post: `https://blog.stephencleary.com/2009/06/threadsafe-events.html`.

Making CPU operations atomic

Atomic is from the Greek word **atomos,** which means *undividable*. It is important to understand which operations are atomic in multithreading because if they are not atomic, then they could be interrupted by another thread partway through their operation. Is the C# increment operator atomic, as shown in the following code?

```
int x = 3;
x++; // is this an atomic CPU operation?
```

It is not atomic! Incrementing an integer requires the following three CPU operations:

1. Load a value from an instance variable into a register.
2. Increment the value.
3. Store the value in the instance variable.

A thread could be interrupted after executing the first two steps. A second thread could then execute all three steps. When the first thread resumes execution, it will overwrite the value in the variable, and the effect of the increment or decrement performed by the second thread will be lost!

There is a type named `Interlocked` that can perform atomic actions like `Add`, `Increment`, `Decrement`, `Exchange`, `CompareExchange`, `And`, `Or`, and `Read` on the integer types in the following list:

- `System.Int32` (int), `System.UInt32` (uint)
- `System.Int64` (long), `System.UInt64` (ulong)

`Interlocked` does not work on numeric types like `byte`, `sbyte`, `short`, `ushort`, and `decimal`.

`Interlocked` can perform atomic operations like `Exchange` and `CompareExchange` that swap values in memory on the following types:

- `System.Single` (float), `System.Double` (double)
- `nint`, `nuint`
- `System.Object` (object)

Let's see it in action:

1. Declare another field in the `SharedObjects` class that will count how many operations have occurred, as shown in the following code:

    ```
    public static int Counter; // Another shared resource.
    ```

2. In `Program.Methods.cs`, in both methods A and B, inside the `for` statement and after modifying the `string` value, add a statement to safely increment the counter, as shown in the following code:

    ```
    Interlocked.Increment(ref SharedObjects.Counter);
    ```

3. In `Program.cs`, before outputting the elapsed time, write the current value of the counter to the console, as shown in the following code:

    ```
    WriteLine($"{SharedObjects.Counter} string modifications.");
    ```

4. Run the code and view the result, as shown highlighted in the following output:

    ```
    Please wait for the tasks to complete.
    ..........
    Results: BBBBBAAAAA.
    10 string modifications.
    13,531 elapsed milliseconds.
    ```

Observant readers will realize that the existing conch object protects all shared resources accessed within a block of code locked by the conch, and therefore, it is unnecessary to use `Interlocked` in this specific example. But if we had not already been protecting another shared resource like `Message`, then using `Interlocked` would be necessary.

Applying other types of synchronization

`Monitor` and `Interlocked` are mutually exclusive locks that are simple and effective, but sometimes, you need more advanced options to synchronize access to shared resources, as shown in *Table 5.3*:

Type	Description
`ReaderWriterLock`, `ReaderWriterLockSlim`	These allow multiple threads to be in **read mode**, one thread to be in **write mode** with exclusive ownership of the write lock, and one thread that has read access to be in **upgradeable read mode**, from which the thread can upgrade to write mode without having to relinquish its read access to the resource.
`Mutex`	Like `Monitor`, this provides exclusive access to a shared resource, except it is used for inter-process synchronization.
`Semaphore`, `SemaphoreSlim`	These limit the number of threads that can access a resource or pool of resources concurrently by defining slots. This is known as **resource throttling** rather than **resource locking**.
`AutoResetEvent`, `ManualResetEvent`	Event wait handles allow threads to synchronize activities by signaling each other and by waiting for each other's signals.

Table 5.3: Synchronization types

Now that we've explored the importance of synchronizing access to shared resources in multi-threaded applications, it's time to delve into how some new keywords introduced in C# 5 make writing asynchronous code easier.

Understanding async and await

C# 5 introduced two C# keywords when working with the Task type. They are especially useful for the following:

- Implementing multitasking for a **graphical user interface (GUI)**
- Improving the scalability of web applications and web services

In *Chapter 16, Building Mobile and Desktop Apps Using .NET MAUI*, we will see how the async and await keywords can implement multitasking for a GUI.

But for now, let's learn the theory of why these two C# keywords were introduced, and then later, you will see them used in practice.

Improving responsiveness for console apps

One of the limitations with console apps is that you can only use the await keyword inside methods that are marked as async, but C# 7 and earlier do not allow the Main method to be marked as async! Luckily, a new feature introduced in C# 7.1 was support for async in Main:

1. Use your preferred code editor to add a new **Console App** / console project to the Chapter05 solution named AsyncConsole.

2. In Program.cs, delete the existing statements, statically import Console, and then add statements to create an HttpClient instance, make a request for Apple's home page, and output how many bytes it has, as shown in the following code:

```
using static System.Console;

HttpClient client = new();

HttpResponseMessage response =
  await client.GetAsync("http://www.apple.com/");

WriteLine("Apple's home page has {0:N0} bytes.",
  response.Content.Headers.ContentLength);
```

3. Build the project and note that it builds successfully. In .NET 5 and earlier, the project template created an explicit Program class with a non-async Main method, so you would have seen an error message, as shown in the following output:

```
Program.cs(14,9): error CS4033: The 'await' operator can only be used
within an async method. Consider marking this method with the 'async'
modifier and changing its return type to 'Task'. [/Users/markjprice/apps-
services-net7/Chapter04/AsyncConsole/AsyncConsole.csproj]
```

4. You would have had to add the `async` keyword to the `Main` method and change its return type to `Task`. With .NET 6 and later, the console app project template uses the top-level program feature to automatically define the `Program` class with an asynchronous `<Main>$` method for you.

5. Run the code and view the result, which is likely to have a different number of bytes since Apple changes its home page frequently, as shown in the following output:

```
Apple's home page has 40,252 bytes.
```

Working with async streams

With .NET Core 3, Microsoft introduced the asynchronous processing of streams.

> You can complete a tutorial about async streams at the following link: `https://learn.microsoft.com/en-us/dotnet/csharp/tutorials/generate-consume-asynchronous-stream`.

Before C# 8 and .NET Core 3, the `await` keyword only worked with tasks that return scalar values. Async stream support in .NET Standard 2.1 allows an `async` method to return one value after another asynchronously.

Let's see a simulated example that returns three random integers as an async stream:

1. Use your preferred code editor to add a new **Console App** / `console` project to the `Chapter05` solution named `AsyncEnumerable`.

2. Globally and statically import the `System.Console` class and treat warnings as errors.

3. Add a new file named `Program.Methods.cs`.

4. In `Program.Methods.cs`, delete any existing statements and then define a method that uses the `yield` keyword to return a random sequence of three numbers asynchronously, as shown in the following code:

```
partial class Program
{
  private static async IAsyncEnumerable<int> GetNumbersAsync()
  {
    Random r = Random.Shared;

    // Simulate some work that takes 1.5 to 3 seconds.
    await Task.Delay(r.Next(1500, 3000));

    // Return a random number between 1 and 1000.
    yield return r.Next(1, 1001);

    await Task.Delay(r.Next(1500, 3000));
```

```
      yield return r.Next(1, 1001);

      await Task.Delay(r.Next(1500, 3000));
      yield return r.Next(1, 1001);
    }
}
```

5. In `Program.cs`, delete the existing statements and then add statements to enumerate the sequence of numbers, as shown in the following code:

```
// Use async streams to iterate over a collection asynchronously.
await foreach (int number in GetNumbersAsync())
{
  WriteLine($"Number: {number}");
}
```

6. Run the code and view the result, as shown in the following output:

```
Number: 509
Number: 813
Number: 307
```

Improving responsiveness for GUI apps

So far in this book, we have only built console apps. Life for a programmer gets more complicated when building web applications, web services, and apps with GUIs such as Windows desktop and mobile apps.

One reason for this is that for a GUI app, there is a special thread: the **user interface** (UI) thread.

There are two rules for working in GUIs:

- Do not perform long-running tasks on the UI thread.
- Do not access UI elements on any thread except the UI thread.

To handle these rules, programmers used to have to write complex code to ensure that long-running tasks were executed by a non-UI thread, but once complete, the results of the task were safely passed to the UI thread to present to the user. It could quickly get messy!

Luckily, with C# 5 and later, you have the use of `async` and `await`. They allow you to continue to write your code as if it is synchronous, which keeps your code clean and easy to understand, but underneath, the C# compiler creates a complex state machine and keeps track of running threads. It's kind of magical! The combination of these two keywords makes the asynchronous method run on a worker thread and, when it's complete, return the results on the UI thread.

Let's see an example. We will build a Windows desktop app using **Windows Presentation Foundation** (**WPF**) that gets employees from the Northwind database in a SQL Server database using low-level types like `SqlConnection`, `SqlCommand`, and `SqlDataReader`.

The Northwind database has medium complexity and a decent number of sample records. You used it extensively in *Chapter 2, Managing Relational Data Using SQL Server*, where it was introduced and set up.

Warning! You will only be able to complete this task if you have Microsoft Windows and the Northwind database stored in Microsoft SQL Server. This is the only section in this book that is not cross-platform and modern (WPF is 17 years old!). You can use either Visual Studio 2022 or Visual Studio Code.

At this point, we are focusing on making a GUI app responsive. You will learn about XAML and building cross-platform GUI apps in *Chapter 16, Building Mobile and Desktop Apps Using .NET MAUI*. Since this book does not cover WPF elsewhere, I thought this task would be a good opportunity to at least see an example app built using WPF even if we do not look at it in detail. Let's go!

1. If you are using Visual Studio 2022, add a new **WPF Application [C#]** project named WpfResponsive to the Chapter05 solution. If you are using Visual Studio Code, use the following command: dotnet new wpf. If you are using JetBrains Rider, select **Desktop Application** and then select a **Type** of **WPF Application**.
2. Add a package reference for Microsoft.Data.SqlClient to the project.
3. In the project file, note the output type is a Windows EXE, the target framework is .NET for Windows (it will not run on other platforms, like macOS and Linux), and the project uses WPF, as shown in the following markup:

```
<Project Sdk="Microsoft.NET.Sdk">

  <PropertyGroup>
    <OutputType>WinExe</OutputType>
    <TargetFramework>net8.0-windows</TargetFramework>
    <Nullable>enable</Nullable>
    <UseWPF>true</UseWPF>
  </PropertyGroup>

  <ItemGroup>
    <PackageReference Include="Microsoft.Data.SqlClient" Version="5.2.0"
/>
  </ItemGroup>

</Project>
```

4. Build the WpfResponsive project to restore packages.

5. In `MainWindow.xaml`, in the `<Grid>` element, add elements to define two buttons, a text box and a list box, laid out vertically in a stack panel, as shown in the following markup:

```
<StackPanel>
  <Button Name="GetEmployeesSyncButton"
          Click="GetEmployeesSyncButton_Click">
    Get Employees Synchronously</Button>
  <Button Name="GetEmployeesAsyncButton"
          Click="GetEmployeesAsyncButton_Click">
    Get Employees Asynchronously</Button>
  <TextBox HorizontalAlignment="Stretch" Text="Type in here" />
  <ListBox Name="EmployeesListBox" Height="400" />
</StackPanel>
```

 Visual Studio 2022 has good support for building WPF apps and will provide IntelliSense as you edit code and XAML markup. Visual Studio Code does not.

6. In `MainWindow.xaml.cs`, import namespaces to work with ADO.NET and the stopwatch, as shown in the following code:

```
using Microsoft.Data.SqlClient; // To use SqlConnection and so on.
using System.Diagnostics; // To use Stopwatch.
```

7. In the `MainWindow` class, in the constructor, define two `string` fields for the database connection string and SQL statement, as shown in the following code:

```
private string connectionString;

private string sql = "WAITFOR DELAY '00:00:05';" +
  "SELECT EmployeeId, FirstName, LastName FROM Employees";
```

 The SQL has two statements. The first waits for five seconds to simulate a long-running query.

8. In the `MainWindow` class, in the constructor, after the call to `InitializeComponent`, use an `SqlConnectionStringBuilder` to set the database connection string, as shown in the following code:

```
public MainWindow()
{
  InitializeComponent();
```

```
    // Change as needed to work with your Northwind database.
    SqlConnectionStringBuilder builder = new();

    builder.DataSource = ".";
    builder.InitialCatalog = "Northwind";
    builder.Encrypt = false;
    builder.MultipleActiveResultSets = true;
    builder.ConnectTimeout = 5;

    // To use Windows Integrated authentication.
    builder.IntegratedSecurity = true;

    // To use SQL Server authentication.
    // builder.UserID = Environment.GetEnvironmentVariable("MY_SQL_USR");
    // builder.Password = Environment.GetEnvironmentVariable("MY_SQL_PWD");

    connectionString = builder.ConnectionString;
  }
```

9. Create event handlers for clicking on the two buttons. They must use the string constants to open a connection to the Northwind database and then populate the list box with the IDs and names of all employees, as shown in the following code:

```
private void GetEmployeesSyncButton_Click(object sender, RoutedEventArgs
e)
{
  Stopwatch timer = Stopwatch.StartNew();

  using (SqlConnection connection = new(connectionString))
  {
    try
    {
      connection.Open();

      SqlCommand command = new(sql, connection);
      SqlDataReader reader = command.ExecuteReader();

      while (reader.Read())
      {
        string employee = string.Format("{0}: {1} {2}",
          reader.GetInt32(0), reader.GetString(1),
```

```
              reader.GetString(2));

          EmployeesListBox.Items.Add(employee);
        }

        reader.Close();
        connection.Close();
      }
      catch (Exception ex)
      {
        MessageBox.Show(ex.Message);
      }
    }
    EmployeesListBox.Items.Add(
      $"Sync: {timer.ElapsedMilliseconds:N0}ms");
}

private async void GetEmployeesAsyncButton_Click(
  object sender, RoutedEventArgs e)
{
  Stopwatch timer = Stopwatch.StartNew();

  using (SqlConnection connection = new(connectionString))
  {
    try
    {
      await connection.OpenAsync();

      SqlCommand command = new(sql, connection);
      SqlDataReader reader = await command.ExecuteReaderAsync();

      while (await reader.ReadAsync())
      {
        string employee = string.Format("{0}: {1} {2}",
          await reader.GetFieldValueAsync<int>(0),
          await reader.GetFieldValueAsync<string>(1),
          await reader.GetFieldValueAsync<string>(2));

        EmployeesListBox.Items.Add(employee);
      }
      await reader.CloseAsync();
```

```
        await connection.CloseAsync();
      }
      catch (Exception ex)
      {
        MessageBox.Show(ex.Message);
      }
    }
    EmployeesListBox.Items.Add(
      $"Async: {timer.ElapsedMilliseconds:N0}ms");
  }
```

Note the following:

- Defining an async void method is generally bad practice because it is "fire and forget." You will not be notified when it is completed and there is no way to cancel it because it does not return a Task or Task<T> that can be used to control it.

- The SQL statement uses the SQL Server WAITFOR DELAY command to simulate processing that takes five seconds. It then selects three columns from the Employees table.

- The GetEmployeesSyncButton_Click event handler uses synchronous methods to open a connection and fetch the employee rows.

- The GetEmployeesAsyncButton_Click event handler is marked as async and uses asynchronous methods with the await keyword to open a connection and fetch the employee rows.

- Both event handlers use a stopwatch to record the number of milliseconds the operation takes and add it to the list box.

10. Start the WPF app without debugging.

11. Click in the text box, enter some text, and note that the GUI is responsive.

12. Click the **Get Employees Synchronously** button.

13. Try to click in the text box, and note the GUI is not responsive.

14. Wait for at least five seconds until the list box is filled with employees.

15. Click in the text box, enter some text, and note the GUI is responsive again.

16. Click the **Get Employees Asynchronously** button.

17. Click in the text box, enter some text, and note that the GUI is still responsive while it performs the operation. Continue typing until the list box is filled with the employees, as shown in *Figure 5.2*:

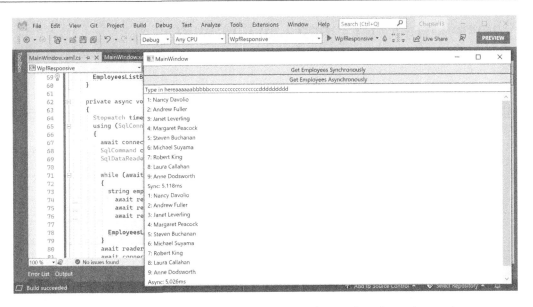

Figure 5.2: Loading employees into a WPF app synchronously and asynchronously

18. Note the difference in timings for the two operations. The UI is blocked when fetching data synchronously, while the UI remains responsive when fetching data asynchronously.

19. Close the WPF app.

Improving scalability for web applications and web services

The `async` and `await` keywords can also be applied on the server side when building websites, applications, and services. From the client application's point of view, nothing changes (or they might even notice a small increase in the time taken for a request to return). So, from a single client's point of view, the use of `async` and `await` to implement multitasking on the server side makes their experience worse!

On the server side, additional, cheaper worker threads are created to wait for long-running tasks to finish so that expensive I/O threads can handle other client requests instead of being blocked. This improves the overall scalability of a web application or service. More clients can be supported simultaneously.

Common types that support multitasking

There are many common types that have asynchronous methods that you can await, as shown in *Table 5.4*:

Type	Methods
DbContext<T>	AddAsync, AddRangeAsync, FindAsync, and SaveChangesAsync
DbSet<T>	AddAsync, AddRangeAsync, ForEachAsync, SumAsync, ToListAsync ToDictionaryAsync, AverageAsync, and CountAsync
HttpClient	GetAsync, PostAsync, PutAsync, DeleteAsync, and SendAsync
StreamReader	ReadAsync, ReadLineAsync, and ReadToEndAsync
StreamWriter	WriteAsync, WriteLineAsync, and FlushAsync

Table 5.4: Common types with asynchronous methods

 Good Practice: Any time you see a method that ends in the Async suffix, check to see whether it returns Task or Task<T>. If it does return Task or Task<T>, then you could use it instead of the synchronous non-Async suffixed method. Remember to call it using await and decorate your method with async.

Using await in catch blocks

When async and await were first introduced in C# 5, it was only possible to use the await keyword in a try block, but not in a catch block. In C# 6 and later, it is now possible to use await in both try and catch blocks.

Practicing and exploring

Test your knowledge and understanding by answering some questions, getting some hands-on practice, and exploring this chapter's topics with deeper research.

Exercise 5.1 – Test your knowledge

Answer the following questions:

1. What information can you find out about a process?
2. How accurate is the Stopwatch class?
3. By convention, what suffix should be applied to a method that returns Task or Task<T>?
4. To use the await keyword inside a method, what keyword must be applied to the method declaration?
5. How do you create a child task?
6. Why should you avoid the lock keyword?
7. When should you use the Interlocked class?
8. When should you use the Mutex class instead of the Monitor class?

9. What is the benefit of using `async` and `await` in a website or web service?

10. Can you cancel a task? If so, how?

Exercise 5.2 — Explore topics

Use the links on the following web page to learn more about the topics covered in this chapter:

```
https://github.com/markjprice/apps-services-net8/blob/main/docs/book-links.md#chapter-
5---multitasking-and-concurrency
```

Exercise 5.3 — Read more about parallel programming

Packt has a book that goes deeper into the topics in this chapter, *Parallel Programming and Concurrency with C# 10 and .NET 6: A modern approach to building faster, more responsive, and asynchronous .NET applications using C#*, by Alvin Ashcroft:

```
https://www.packtpub.com/product/parallel-programming-and-concurrency-with-c-10-and-
net-6/9781803243672
```

Summary

In this chapter, you learned:

- How to define and start a task.
- How to wait for one or more tasks to finish.
- How to control task completion order.
- How to synchronize access to shared resources.
- The magic behind `async` and `await`.

In the next chapter, you will learn how to use some popular third-party libraries.

6

Using Popular Third-Party Libraries

This chapter is about some popular third-party libraries for .NET that enable you to perform actions that either are not possible with the core .NET libraries or are better than the built-in functionality. These actions include manipulating images with **ImageSharp**, logging with **Serilog**, mapping objects to other objects with **AutoMapper**, making unit test assertions with **FluentAssertions**, validating data with **FluentValidation**, and generating PDFs with **QuestPDF**.

This chapter covers the following topics:

- Which third-party libraries are most popular?
- Working with images
- Logging with Serilog
- Mapping between objects
- Making fluent assertions in unit testing
- Validating data
- Generating PDFs

Which third-party libraries are most popular?

To help me decide which third-party libraries to include in this book, I researched which are downloaded most frequently at `https://www.nuget.org/stats/packages`, and, as shown in *Table 6.1*, they are:

Rank	Package	Downloads
1	`newtonsoft.json`	167,927,712
2	`serilog`	42,436,567
3	`awssdk.core`	36,423,449
4	`castle.core`	28,383,411
5	`newtonsoft.json.bson`	26,547,661
6	`swashbuckle.aspnetcore.swagger`	25,828,940

7	`swashbuckle.aspnetcore.swaggergen`	25,823,941
8	`polly`	22,487,368
9	`automapper`	21,679,921
10	`swashbuckle.aspnetcore.swaggerui`	21,373,873
12	`moq`	19,408,440
15	`fluentvalidation`	17,739,259
16	`humanizer.core`	17,602,598
23	`stackexchange.redis`	15,771,377
36	`fluentassertions`	12,244,097
40	`dapper`	10,819,569
52	`rabbitmq.client`	8,591,362
83	`hangfire.core`	5,479,381
94	`nodatime`	4,944,830

Table 6.1: The most downloaded NuGet packages

What is covered in my books

My book *C# 12 and .NET 8 – Modern Cross-Platform Development Fundamentals* introduces processing JSON using `newtonsoft.json` and documenting web services using `swashbuckle`.

For now, using Castle Core to generate dynamic proxies and typed dictionaries, or deploying to and integrating with **Amazon Web Services (AWS)**, is out of scope for this book.

As well as raw download numbers, questions from readers and the usefulness of the library also contributed to my decision to include a library in this chapter, as summarized in the following list:

- Most popular library for manipulating images: **ImageSharp**
- Most popular library for manipulating text: **Humanizer**
- Most popular library for logging: **Serilog**
- Most popular library for object mapping: **AutoMapper**
- Most popular library for unit test assertions: **FluentAssertions**
- Most popular library for data validation: **FluentValidation**
- Open-source library for generating PDFs: **QuestPDF**

In *Chapter 7, Handling Dates, Times, and Internationalization*, I cover the most popular library for handling dates and times: **Noda Time**.

In *Chapter 9, Caching, Queuing, and Resilient Background Services*, I cover a few more popular libraries, as summarized in the following list:

- Most popular library for resilience and transient fault handling: **Polly**

- Most popular library for scheduling jobs and implementing background services: **Hangfire**
- Most popular library for distributed caching: **Redis**
- Most popular library for queuing: **RabbitMQ**

Working with images

ImageSharp is a third-party cross-platform 2D graphics library. When .NET Core 1.0 was in development, there was negative feedback from the community about the missing System.Drawing namespace for working with 2D images. The ImageSharp project was started to fill that gap for modern .NET applications.

In their official documentation for System.Drawing, Microsoft says, "The System.Drawing namespace is not recommended for new development due to not being supported within a Windows or ASP.NET service, and it is not cross-platform. ImageSharp and SkiaSharp are recommended as alternatives."

 Six Labors released ImageSharp 3.0 in March 2023. It now requires .NET 6 or later and major future versions will target LTS releases of .NET, like .NET 8. You can read the announcement at the following link: https://sixlabors.com/posts/announcing-imagesharp-300/.

Generating grayscale thumbnails

Let's see what can be achieved with ImageSharp:

1. Use your preferred code editor to create a console app project, as defined in the following list:

    - Project template: **Console App** / console
    - Solution file and folder: Chapter06
    - Project file and folder: WorkingWithImages
    - **Do not use top-level statements:** Cleared
    - **Enable native AOT publish:** Cleared

2. In the WorkingWithImages project, create an images folder and download the nine images from the following link to it: https://github.com/markjprice/apps-services-net8/tree/master/images/Categories.

3. If you are using Visual Studio 2022, then the images folder and its files must be copied to the WorkingWithImages\bin\Debug\net8 folder where the compiled console app will run. We can configure Visual Studio to do this for us, as shown in the following steps:

    1. In **Solution Explorer**, select all nine images.

2.   In **Properties**, set **Copy to Output Directory** to **Copy always**, as shown in *Figure 6.1*:

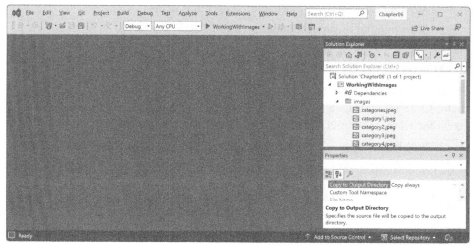

Figure 6.1: Setting images to always copy to the output directory

3.   Open the project file and note the `<ItemGroup>` entries that will copy the nine images to the correct folder, as partially shown in the following markup:

```
<ItemGroup>
  <None Update="images\categories.jpeg">
    <CopyToOutputDirectory>Always</CopyToOutputDirectory>
  </None>
  <None Update="images\category1.jpeg">
    <CopyToOutputDirectory>Always</CopyToOutputDirectory>
  </None>
...
```

4.   In the `WorkingWithImages` project, treat warnings as errors, globally and statically import the `System.Console` class, and add a package reference for `SixLabors.ImageSharp`, as shown highlighted in the following markup:

```
<Project Sdk="Microsoft.NET.Sdk">

  <PropertyGroup>
    <OutputType>Exe</OutputType>
    <TargetFramework>net8.0</TargetFramework>
    <ImplicitUsings>enable</ImplicitUsings>
    <Nullable>enable</Nullable>
    <TreatWarningsAsErrors>true</TreatWarningsAsErrors>
  </PropertyGroup>

  <ItemGroup>
```

```
    <Using Include="System.Console" Static="true" />
  </ItemGroup>

  <ItemGroup>
    <PackageReference Include="SixLabors.ImageSharp" Version="3.0.2" />
  </ItemGroup>
  ...
```

 To save space, in other steps like this in this chapter, I will not show the markup to treat warnings as errors or to globally and statically import the System.Console class. I will only show the ItemGroup and PackageReference for task-specific libraries.

5. Build the WorkingWithImages project.

6. If you are using Visual Studio 2022, then in **Solution Explorer**, toggle **Show All Files**.

7. In the obj\Debug\net8.0 folder, open WorkingWithImages.GlobalUsings.g.cs, and note that referencing the SixLabors.ImageSharp package adds three global namespace imports alongside the usual ones added by the .NET SDK, as shown in the following code:

```
// <auto-generated/>
global using global::SixLabors.ImageSharp;
global using global::SixLabors.ImageSharp.PixelFormats;
global using global::SixLabors.ImageSharp.Processing;
...
```

 If you reference older versions of SixLabors.ImageSharp like 2.0.0, then it does not do this so you must manually import those three namespaces in each code file. This feature is one reason why version 3.0 and later have a minimum requirement of .NET 6.

8. In Program.cs, delete the existing statements and then add statements to convert all the files in the images folder into grayscale thumbnails at one-tenth size, as shown in the following code:

```
string imagesFolder = Path.Combine(
  Environment.CurrentDirectory, "images");

WriteLine($"I will look for images in the following folder:\
n{imagesFolder}");
WriteLine();

if (!Directory.Exists(imagesFolder))
{
  WriteLine();
  WriteLine("Folder does not exist!");
```

```
    return;
}

IEnumerable<string> images =
  Directory.EnumerateFiles(imagesFolder);

foreach (string imagePath in images)
{
  if (Path.GetFileNameWithoutExtension(imagePath).EndsWith("-thumbnail"))
  {
    WriteLine($"Skipping:\n  {imagePath}");
    WriteLine();
    continue; // This file has already been converted.
  }

  string thumbnailPath = Path.Combine(
    Environment.CurrentDirectory, "images",
    Path.GetFileNameWithoutExtension(imagePath)
    + "-thumbnail" + Path.GetExtension(imagePath));

  using (Image image = Image.Load(imagePath))
  {
    WriteLine($"Converting:\n  {imagePath}");
    WriteLine($"To:\n  {thumbnailPath}");
    image.Mutate(x => x.Resize(image.Width / 10, image.Height / 10));
    image.Mutate(x => x.Grayscale());
    image.Save(thumbnailPath);
    WriteLine();
  }
}

WriteLine("Image processing complete.");

if (OperatingSystem.IsWindows())
{
  Process.Start("explorer.exe", imagesFolder);
}
else
{
  WriteLine("View the images folder.");
}
```

9. Run the console app and note the images should be converted into grayscale thumbnails, as shown in the following partial output:

```
I will look for images in the following folder:
C:\apps-services-net8\Chapter06\WorkingWithImages\bin\Debug\net8.0\images

Converting:
  C:\apps-services-net8\Chapter06\WorkingWithImages\bin\Debug\net8.0\
images\categories.jpeg
To:
  C:\apps-services-net8\Chapter06\WorkingWithImages\bin\Debug\net8.0\
images\categories-thumbnail.jpeg

Converting:
  C:\apps-services-net8\Chapter06\WorkingWithImages\bin\Debug\net8.0\
images\category1.jpeg
To:
  C:\apps-services-net8\Chapter06\WorkingWithImages\bin\Debug\net8.0\
images\category1-thumbnail.jpeg

...

Converting:
  C:\apps-services-net8\Chapter06\WorkingWithImages\bin\Debug\net8.0\
images\category8.jpeg
To:
  C:\apps-services-net8\Chapter06\WorkingWithImages\bin\Debug\net8.0\
images\category8-thumbnail.jpeg

Image processing complete.
```

10. In the filesystem, open the appropriate `images` folder and note the much-smaller-in-bytes grayscale thumbnails, as shown in *Figure 6.2*:

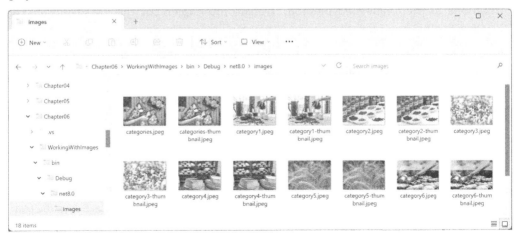

Figure 6.2: Images after processing

ImageSharp packages for drawing and the web

ImageSharp also has NuGet packages for programmatically drawing images and working with images on the web, as shown in the following list:

- `SixLabors.ImageSharp.Drawing`
- `SixLabors.ImageSharp.Web`

 More Information: Learn more details at the following link: `https://docs.sixlabors.com/`.

Working with text and numbers using Humanizer

Humanizer manipulates text in `string` values, names of `enum` values, dates, times, numbers, and quantities.

Working with text

The built-in `string` type has methods to manipulate text like `Substring` and `Trim`. But there are plenty of other common manipulations that we might want to perform on text. For example:

- You might have an ugly string generated by some code and you want to make it look friendlier to display to a user. This is common with `enum` types that cannot use spaces in multi-word values.
- You might build a web content management system, and when a user enters an article title, you need to convert what they enter into a format suitable for a URL path.
- You might have a long `string` value that needs to be truncated to show in the limited space of a mobile user interface.

Humanizer case transformations

Complex transformations can be performed in sequence by passing multiple Humanizer transformations to the `Transform` method. Transforms implement the `IStringTransformer` or `ICulturedStringTransformer` interfaces so you can implement your own custom transforms.

The built-in transforms are all casing transformations, and they are listed in *Table 6.2* along with convenient alternative methods that extend the `string` type:

Transform	Description	Example
`To.LowerCase`	Transforms all characters in the `string` to lowercase.	the cat sat on the mat
`To.UpperCase`	Transforms all characters in the `string` to uppercase.	THE CAT SAT ON THE MAT
`To.TitleCase`	Transforms the first character of each word in the `string` to uppercase.	The Cat Sat on the Mat

To.SentenceCase	Transforms the first character in the string to uppercase. It ignores periods (full stops) so it does not recognize sentences!	The cat sat on the mat

Table 6.2: Humanizer casing transforms

 Good Practice: It is important to consider the casing of the original text. If it is already uppercase, the title and sentence casing options will *not* convert to lowercase! You might need to transform to lowercase first, then transform to title or sentence case.

As well as calling the Transform method with a transform object like To.TitleCase, there are convenience methods for manipulating the case of text, as shown in *Table 6.3*:

String extension method	Description
Titleize	Equivalent to transforming with To.TitleCase
Pascalize	Converts strings to upper camel case, also removing underscores
Camelize	Same as Pascalize except that the first character is lowercase

Table 6.3: Humanizer text extension methods

Humanizer spacing conversions

There are convenient methods for manipulating the spacing of text, by adding underscores and dashes, as shown in *Table 6.4*:

String extension method	Description
Underscore	Separates the input words with an underscore
Dasherize, Hyphenate	Replaces underscores with dashes (hyphens) in the string
Kebaberize	Separates the input words with dashes (hyphens)

Table 6.4: Humanizer spacing conversion methods

Humanizer's Singularize and Pluralize methods

Humanizer has two extension methods for the string class that automate converting between the singular and plural versions of a word, as shown in *Table 6.5*:

String extension method	Description
Singularize	If the string contains a plural word, it is converted to the singular equivalent.
Pluralize	If the string contains a singular word, it is converted to the plural equivalent.

Table 6.5: Humanizer's Singularize and Pluralize methods

These methods are used by Microsoft Entity Framework Core to singularize and pluralize the names of entity classes and their members.

Exploring text manipulations with a console app

Let's explore some examples of text manipulation using Humanizer:

1. Use your preferred code editor to add a new **Console App** / console project named HumanizingData to the Chapter06 solution. In Visual Studio 2022, set the startup project to the current selection.

2. In the HumanizingData project, treat warnings as errors, globally and statically import the System.Console class, and add a package reference for Humanizer, as shown in the following markup:

```
<ItemGroup>
  <PackageReference Include="Humanizer" Version="2.14.1" />
</ItemGroup>
```

 We are referencing a Humanizer package that includes all languages. If you only need the English language, then you can reference Humanizer.Core instead. If you also need a subset of languages, reference specific language packages using the pattern Humanizer.Core.<lang>, for example, Humanizer.Core.fr for French.

3. Build the HumanizingData project to restore packages.

4. Add a new class file to the project named Program.Functions.cs.

5. In Program.Functions.cs, add statements to import the namespace for working with globalization, and to define a method to configure the console to enable easy switching of the current culture and enable the use of special characters, as shown in the following code:

```
using System.Globalization; // To use CultureInfo.

partial class Program
{
  private static void ConfigureConsole(string culture = "en-US")
  {
    // To enable special characters like … (ellipsis) as a single
character.
    OutputEncoding = System.Text.Encoding.UTF8;

    Thread t = Thread.CurrentThread;
    t.CurrentCulture = CultureInfo.GetCultureInfo(culture);
```

```
        t.CurrentUICulture = t.CurrentCulture;

        WriteLine("Current culture: {0}", t.CurrentCulture.DisplayName);
        WriteLine();
    }
}
```

6. In `Program.cs`, delete the existing statements, and then call the `ConfigureConsole` method, as shown in the following code:

```
ConfigureConsole(); // Defaults to en-US culture.
```

7. In `Program.Functions.cs`, add a statement to import the namespace for working with extension methods provided by Humanizer, as shown in the following code:

```
using Humanizer; // To use common Humanizer extension methods.
```

8. In `Program.Functions.cs`, add statements to define a method to output an original `string` and then the results of transforming it using the built-in casing transforms, as shown in the following code:

```
private static void OutputCasings(string original)
{
  WriteLine("Original casing: {0}", original);
  WriteLine("Lower casing: {0}", original.Transform(To.LowerCase));
  WriteLine("Upper casing: {0}", original.Transform(To.UpperCase));
  WriteLine("Title casing: {0}", original.Transform(To.TitleCase));
  WriteLine("Sentence casing: {0}", original.Transform(To.SentenceCase));
  WriteLine("Lower, then Sentence casing: {0}",
    original.Transform(To.LowerCase, To.SentenceCase));
  WriteLine();
}
```

9. In `Program.cs`, call the `OutputCasings` method with three different `string` values, as shown in the following code:

```
OutputCasings("The cat sat on the mat.");
OutputCasings("THE CAT SAT ON THE MAT.");
OutputCasings("the cat sat on the mat. the frog jumped.");
```

10. Run the code and view the result, as shown in the following output:

```
Current culture: English (United States)

Original casing: The cat sat on the mat.
Lower casing: the cat sat on the mat.
Upper casing: THE CAT SAT ON THE MAT.
```

```
Title casing: The Cat Sat on the Mat.
Sentence casing: The cat sat on the mat.
Lower, then Sentence casing: The cat sat on the mat.

Original casing: THE CAT SAT ON THE MAT.
Lower casing: the cat sat on the mat.
Upper casing: THE CAT SAT ON THE MAT.
Title casing: THE CAT SAT ON THE MAT.
Sentence casing: THE CAT SAT ON THE MAT.
Lower, then Sentence casing: The cat sat on the mat.

Original casing: the cat sat on the mat. the frog jumped.
Lower casing: the cat sat on the mat. the frog jumped.
Upper casing: THE CAT SAT ON THE MAT. THE FROG JUMPED.
Title casing: The Cat Sat on the Mat. the Frog Jumped.
Sentence casing: The cat sat on the mat. the frog jumped.
Lower, then Sentence casing: The cat sat on the mat. the frog jumped.
```

11. In `Program.Functions.cs`, add statements to define a method that outputs an ugly `string` value using various Humanizer extension methods, as shown in the following code:

```csharp
private static void OutputSpacingAndDashes()
{
  string ugly = "ERROR_MESSAGE_FROM_SERVICE";

  WriteLine("Original string: {0}", ugly);

  WriteLine("Humanized: {0}", ugly.Humanize());

  // LetterCasing is legacy and will be removed in future.
  WriteLine("Humanized, lower case: {0}",
    ugly.Humanize(LetterCasing.LowerCase));

  // Use Transform for casing instead.
  WriteLine("Transformed (lower case, then sentence case): {0}",
    ugly.Transform(To.LowerCase, To.SentenceCase));

  WriteLine("Humanized, Transformed (lower case, then sentence case):
{0}",
    ugly.Humanize().Transform(To.LowerCase, To.SentenceCase));
}
```

12. In `Program.cs`, comment out the previous method calls and then add a statement to call the new method, as shown highlighted in the following code:

```
/*
OutputCasings("The cat sat on the mat.");
OutputCasings("THE CAT SAT ON THE MAT.");
OutputCasings("the cat sat on the mat. the frog jumped.");
*/

OutputSpacingAndDashes();
```

13. Run the code and view the result, as shown in the following output:

```
Original string: ERROR_MESSAGE_FROM_SERVICE
Humanized: ERROR MESSAGE FROM SERVICE
Humanized, lower case: error message from service
Transformed (lower case, then sentence case): Error_message_from_service
Humanized, Transformed (lower case, then sentence case): Error message
from service
```

14. Add a new class file to the project named `WondersOfTheAncientWorld.cs`.

15. Modify the `WondersOfTheAncientWorld.cs` file, as shown in the following code:

```
namespace Packt.Shared;

public enum WondersOfTheAncientWorld : byte
{
  None                      = 0b_0000_0000, // i.e. 0
  GreatPyramidOfGiza        = 0b_0000_0001, // i.e. 1
  HangingGardensOfBabylon   = 0b_0000_0010, // i.e. 2
  StatueOfZeusAtOlympia     = 0b_0000_0100, // i.e. 4
  TempleOfArtemisAtEphesus  = 0b_0000_1000, // i.e. 8
  MausoleumAtHalicarnassus  = 0b_0001_0000, // i.e. 16
  ColossusOfRhodes          = 0b_0010_0000, // i.e. 32
  LighthouseOfAlexandria    = 0b_0100_0000  // i.e. 64
}
```

16. In `Program.Functions.cs`, import the namespace for using the enum that we just defined, as shown in the following code:

```
using Packt.Shared; // To use WondersOfTheAncientWorld.
```

17. In `Program.Functions.cs`, define a method to create the `WondersOfTheWorld` variable and output its name using various Humanizer extension methods, as shown in the following code:

```
private static void OutputEnumNames()
{
  var favoriteAncientWonder = WondersOfTheAncientWorld.
StatueOfZeusAtOlympia;

  WriteLine("Raw enum value name: {0}", favoriteAncientWonder);

  WriteLine("Humanized: {0}", favoriteAncientWonder.Humanize());

  WriteLine("Humanized, then Titleized: {0}",
    favoriteAncientWonder.Humanize().Titleize());

  WriteLine("Truncated to 8 characters: {0}",
    favoriteAncientWonder.ToString().Truncate(length: 8));

  WriteLine("Kebaberized: {0}",
    favoriteAncientWonder.ToString().Kebaberize());
}
```

18. In `Program.cs`, comment out the previous method call, and then add a call to `OutputEnumNames`, as shown highlighted in the following code:

```
//OutputSpacingAndDashes();

OutputEnumNames();
```

19. Run the code and view the result, as shown in the following output:

```
Raw enum value name: StatueOfZeusAtOlympia
Humanized: Statue of zeus at olympia
Humanized, then Titlerized: Statue of Zeus at Olympia
Truncated to 8 characters: StatueO...
Kebaberized: statue-of-zeus-at-olympia
```

Note the `Truncate` method uses the single-character ... (ellipsis) by default. If you ask to truncate to a length of 8, it can return the first seven characters followed by the ellipsis character. You can specify a different character using an overload of the `Truncate` method.

Working with numbers

Now let's see how Humanizer can help us with numbers:

1. In `Program.Functions.cs`, define a method to create some numbers and then output them using various Humanizer extension methods, as shown in the following code:

```csharp
private static void NumberFormatting()
{
  int number = 123;

  WriteLine($"Original number: {number}");
  WriteLine($"Roman: {number.ToRoman()}");
  WriteLine($"Words: {number.ToWords()}");
  WriteLine($"Ordinal words: {number.ToOrdinalWords()}");
  WriteLine();

  string[] things = { "fox", "person", "sheep",
    "apple", "goose", "oasis", "potato", "die", "dwarf",
    "attorney general", "biceps"};

  for (int i = 1; i <= 3; i++)
  {
    for (int j = 0; j < things.Length; j++)
    {
      Write(things[j].ToQuantity(i, ShowQuantityAs.Words));

      if (j < things.Length - 1) Write(", ");
    }
    WriteLine();
  }
  WriteLine();

  int thousands = 12345;
  int millions = 123456789;

  WriteLine("Original: {0}, Metric: About {1}", thousands,
    thousands.ToMetric(decimals: 0));

  WriteLine("Original: {0}, Metric: {1}", thousands,
    thousands.ToMetric(MetricNumeralFormats.WithSpace
      | MetricNumeralFormats.UseShortScaleWord,
      decimals: 0));
```

```
      WriteLine("Original: {0}, Metric: {1}", millions,
        millions.ToMetric(decimals: 1));
   }
```

2. In `Program.cs`, comment out the previous method call and add a call to `NumberFormatting`, as shown highlighted in the following code:

    ```
    //OutputEnumNames();
    ```

    ```
    NumberFormatting();
    ```

3. Run the code and view the result, as shown in the following output:

    ```
    Original number: 123
    Roman: CXXIII
    Words: one hundred and twenty-three
    Ordinal words: hundred and twenty-third

    one fox, one person, one sheep, one apple, one goose, one oasis, one
    potato, one die, one dwarf, one attorney general, one bicep
    two foxes, two people, two sheep, two apples, two geese, two oases, two
    potatoes, two dice, two dwarves, two attorney generals, two biceps
    three foxes, three people, three sheep, three apples, three geese,
    three oases, three potatoes, three dice, three dwarves, three attorney
    generals, three biceps

    Original: 12345, Metric: About 12k
    Original: 12345, Metric: About 12 thousand
    Original: 123456789, Metric: 123.5M
    ```

 Humanizer's default vocabulary is quite decent, but it does not correctly pluralize attorney general (the plural is *attorneys general*) or biceps (the singular is *biceps* and the plural is *bicepses*).

4. In `Program.Functions.cs`, import the namespace for working with Humanizer vocabularies, as shown in the following code:

    ```
    using Humanizer.Inflections; // To use Vocabularies.
    ```

5. In `Program.Functions.cs`, at the top of the `NumberFormatting` method, add statements to register two irregular words, as shown in the following code:

```
Vocabularies.Default.AddIrregular("biceps", "bicepses");
Vocabularies.Default.AddIrregular("attorney general", "attorneys
general");
```

6. Run the code, view the result, and note that the two irregular words now output correctly.

Working with dates and times

Now let's see how Humanizer can help us with dates and times:

1. In `Program.Functions.cs`, define a method to get the current date and time and some number of days, and then output them using various Humanizer extension methods, as shown in the following code:

```
private static void DateTimeFormatting()
{
  DateTimeOffset now = DateTimeOffset.Now;

  // By default, all Humanizer comparisons are to Now (UTC).
  WriteLine($"Now (UTC): {now}");

  WriteLine("Add 3 hours, Humanized: {0}",
    now.AddHours(3).Humanize());

  WriteLine("Add 3 hours and 1 minute, Humanized: {0}",
    now.AddHours(3).AddMinutes(1).Humanize());

  WriteLine("Subtract 3 hours, Humanized: {0}",
    now.AddHours(-3).Humanize());

  WriteLine("Add 24 hours, Humanized: {0}",
    now.AddHours(24).Humanize());

  WriteLine("Add 25 hours, Humanized: {0}",
    now.AddHours(25).Humanize());

  WriteLine("Add 7 days, Humanized: {0}",
    now.AddDays(7).Humanize());

  WriteLine("Add 7 days and 1 minute, Humanized: {0}",
    now.AddDays(7).AddMinutes(1).Humanize());

  WriteLine("Add 1 month, Humanized: {0}",
    now.AddMonths(1).Humanize());
```

```
    WriteLine();

    // Examples of TimeSpan humanization.
    int[] daysArray = { 12, 13, 14, 15, 16 };

    foreach (int days in daysArray)
    {
      WriteLine("{0} days, Humanized: {1}",
        days, TimeSpan.FromDays(days).Humanize());

      WriteLine("{0} days, Humanized with precision 2: {1}",
        days, TimeSpan.FromDays(days).Humanize(precision: 2));

      WriteLine("{0} days, Humanized with max unit days: {1}",
        days, TimeSpan.FromDays(days).Humanize(
          maxUnit: Humanizer.Localisation.TimeUnit.Day));

      WriteLine();
    }

    // Examples of clock notation.
    TimeOnly[] times = { new TimeOnly(9, 0),
      new TimeOnly(9, 15), new TimeOnly(15, 30) };

    foreach (TimeOnly time in times)
    {
      WriteLine("{0}: {1}", time, time.ToClockNotation());
    }
}
```

2. In `Program.cs`, comment out the previous method call and add a call to `DateTimeFormatting`, as shown highlighted in the following code:

    ```
    //NumberFormatting();

    DateTimeFormatting();
    ```

3. Run the code and view the result, as shown in the following output:

    ```
    Current culture: English (United States)

    Now (UTC): 5/30/2023 8:12:51 AM +01:00
    ```

```
Add 3 hours, Humanized: 2 hours from now
Add 3 hours and 1 minute, Humanized: 3 hours from now
Subtract 3 hours, Humanized: 3 hours ago
Add 24 hours, Humanized: 23 hours from now
Add 25 hours, Humanized: tomorrow
Add 7 days, Humanized: 6 days from now
Add 7 days and 1 minute, Humanized: 7 days from now
Add 1 month, Humanized: one month from now

12 days, Humanized: 1 week
12 days, Humanized with precision 2: 1 week, 5 days
12 days, Humanized with max unit days: 12 days

13 days, Humanized: 1 week
13 days, Humanized with precision 2: 1 week, 6 days
13 days, Humanized with max unit days: 13 days

14 days, Humanized: 2 weeks
14 days, Humanized with precision 2: 2 weeks
14 days, Humanized with max unit days: 14 days

15 days, Humanized: 2 weeks
15 days, Humanized with precision 2: 2 weeks, 1 day
15 days, Humanized with max unit days: 15 days

16 days, Humanized: 2 weeks
16 days, Humanized with precision 2: 2 weeks, 2 days
16 days, Humanized with max unit days: 16 days

9:00 AM: nine o'clock
9:15 AM: a quarter past nine
3:30 PM: half past three
```

4. In `Program.cs`, specify the French language and region when configuring the console, as shown highlighted in the following code:

```
ConfigureConsole("fr-FR"); // Defaults to en-US culture.
```

5. Run the code, view the result, and note that the text is localized to French.

Logging with Serilog

Although .NET includes logging frameworks, third-party logging providers give more power and flexibility by using **structured event data**. Serilog is the most popular.

Structured event data

Most systems write plain text messages to their logs.

Serilog can be told to write serialized structured data to the log. The @ symbol prefixing a parameter tells Serilog to serialize the object passed in, instead of just the result of calling the ToString method.

Later, that complex object can be queried for improved search and sort capabilities in the logs.

For example:

```
var lineitem = new { ProductId = 11, UnitPrice = 25.49, Quantity = 3 };

log.Information("Added {@LineItem} to shopping cart.", lineitem);
```

 You can learn more about how Serilog handles structured data at the following link: https://github.com/serilog/serilog/wiki/Structured-Data.

Serilog sinks

All logging systems need to record the log entries somewhere. That could be to the console output, a file, or a more complex data store like a relational database or cloud data store. Serilog calls these **sinks**.

Serilog has hundreds of official and third-party sink packages for all the possible places you might want to record your logs. To use them, just include the appropriate package. The most popular are shown in the following list:

- serilog.sinks.file
- serilog.sinks.console
- serilog.sinks.periodicbatching
- serilog.sinks.debug
- serilog.sinks.rollingfile (deprecated; use serilog.sinks.file instead)
- serilog.sinks.applicationinsights
- serilog.sinks.mssqlserver

 There are more than 470 packages currently listed on Microsoft's public NuGet feed: https://www.nuget.org/packages?q=serilog.sinks.

Logging to the console and a rolling file with Serilog

Let's start:

1. Use your preferred code editor to add a new **Console App** / console project named Serilogging to a Chapter06 solution.

2. In the `Serilogging` project, treat warnings as errors, globally and statically import the `System.Console` class, and add a package reference for `Serilog`, including sinks for `console` and `file` (which also supports rolling files), as shown in the following markup:

```
<ItemGroup>
  <PackageReference Include="Serilog" Version="3.1.1" />
  <PackageReference Include="Serilog.Sinks.Console" Version="5.0.0" />
  <PackageReference Include="Serilog.Sinks.File" Version="5.0.0" />
</ItemGroup>
```

3. Build the `Serilogging` project.

4. In the `Serilogging` project, add a new folder named `Models`.

5. In the `Serilogging` project, in the `Models` folder, add a new class file named `ProductPageView.cs`, and modify its contents, as shown in the following code:

```
namespace Serilogging.Models;

public class ProductPageView
{
  public int ProductId { get; set; }
  public string? PageTitle { get; set; }
  public string? SiteSection { get; set; }
}
```

6. In `Program.cs`, delete the existing statements and then import some namespaces for working with Serilog, as shown in the following code:

```
using Serilog; // To use Log, LoggerConfiguration, RollingInterval.
using Serilog.Core; // To use Logger.
using Serilogging.Models; // To use ProductPageView.
```

7. In `Program.cs`, create a logger configuration that will write to the console as well as configure a rolling interval that means a new file is created each day, and write various levels of log entries, as shown in the following code:

```
// Create a new logger that will write to the console and to
// a text file, one-file-per-day, named with the date.
using Logger log = new LoggerConfiguration()
    .WriteTo.Console()
    .WriteTo.File("log.txt", rollingInterval: RollingInterval.Day)
    .CreateLogger();

// Assign the new logger to the static entry point for logging.
Log.Logger = log;
Log.Information("The global logger has been configured.");
```

```
// Log some example entries of differing severity.
Log.Warning("Danger, Serilog, danger!");
Log.Error("This is an error!");
Log.Fatal("Fatal problem!");

ProductPageView pageView = new() {
  PageTitle = "Chai",
  SiteSection = "Beverages",
  ProductId = 1 };

Log.Information("{@PageView} occurred at {Viewed}",
  pageView, DateTimeOffset.UtcNow);

// For a log with a buffer, like a text file logger, you
// must flush before ending the app.
Log.CloseAndFlush();
```

8. Run the console app and note the messages, as shown in the following output:

```
[07:09:43 INF] The global logger has been configured.
[07:09:43 WRN] Danger, Serilog, danger!
[07:09:43 ERR] This is an error!
[07:09:43 FTL] Fatal problem!
[07:09:43 INF] {"ProductId": 1, "PageTitle": "Chai", "SiteSection":
"Beverages", "$type": "ProductPageView"} occurred at 09/07/2023 15:08:44
+00:00
```

9. Open the logYYYYMMDD.txt file, where YYYY is the year, MM is the month, and DD is the day, and note it contains the same messages:

    *   For Visual Studio 2022, the log file will be written to the Serilogging\bin\Debug\ net8.0 folder.

    *   For Visual Studio Code and dotnet run, the log file will be written to the Serilogging folder.

 More Information: Learn more details at the following link: https://serilog.net/.

Good Practice: Disable logging when it is not needed. Logging can get costly fast. For example, one organization was spending $10,000 per month on cloud resources, much more than predicted, and they didn't know why. It turned out they were logging every SQL statement executed in production. By "flipping a switch" to stop that logging they saved $8,500 per month! You can read Milan Jovanović's story at the following link: `https://www.linkedin.com/posts/milan-jovanovic_i-helped-a-team-save-100k-in-azure-cloud-activity-7109887614664474625-YDiU/`.

Mapping between objects

One of the most boring parts of being a programmer is mapping between objects. It is common to need to integrate systems or components that have conceptually similar objects but with different structures.

Models for data are different for different parts of an application. Models that represent data in storage are often called **entity models**. Models that represent data that must be passed between layers are often called **data transfer objects** (DTOs). Models that represent only the data that must be presented to a user are often called **view models**. All these models are likely to have commonalities but different structures.

AutoMapper is a popular package for mapping objects because it has conventions that make the work as easy as possible. For example, if you have a source member called `CompanyName`, it will be mapped to a destination member with the name `CompanyName`.

AutoMapper's creator, Jimmy Bogard, has written an article about its design philosophy that is worth reading, available at the following link: `https://jimmybogard.com/automappers-design-philosophy/`.

Let's see an example of AutoMapper in action. You will create four projects:

- A class library for the entity and view models.
- A class library to create mapper configurations for reuse in unit tests and actual projects.
- A unit test project to test the mappings.
- A console app to perform a live mapping.

We will construct an example object model that represents an e-commerce website customer and their shopping cart with a couple of items, and then map it to a summary view model to present to the user.

Defining models for an AutoMapper configuration

To test the mapping, we will define some `record` types. As a reminder, a `record` (or `record class`) is a reference type that has value-based equality. A `class` is a reference type that has memory address-based equality (except for `string`, which overrides this behavior).

It is good practice to always validate your configuration for mappings before using them, so we will start by defining some models and a mapping between them, and then create a unit test for the mappings:

1. Use your preferred code editor to add a new **Class Library** / classlib project named MappingObjects.Models to the Chapter06 solution.

2. In the MappingObjects.Models project, delete the file named Class1.cs.

3. In the MappingObjects.Models project, add a new class file named Customer.cs and modify its contents to define an immutable record type named Customer by using constructor syntax, as shown in the following code:

    ```
    namespace Northwind.EntityModels;


    // This record will only have a constructor with the parameters below.
    // Objects will be immutable after instantiation using this constructor.
    // It will not have a default parameterless constructor.
    public record class Customer(
      string FirstName,
      string LastName
    );
    ```

4. In the MappingObjects.Models project, add a new class file named LineItem.cs and modify its contents, as shown in the following code:

    ```
    namespace Northwind.EntityModels;

    public record class LineItem(
      string ProductName,
      decimal UnitPrice,
      int Quantity
    );
    ```

5. In the MappingObjects.Models project, add a new class file named Cart.cs and modify its contents, as shown in the following code:

    ```
    namespace Northwind.EntityModels;

    public record class Cart(
      Customer Customer,
      List<LineItem> Items
    );
    ```

6. In the MappingObjects.Models project, add a new class file named Summary.cs in the Northwind.ViewModels namespace (not Northwind.EntityModels), delete any existing statements, and then define a record type that can have its properties set *after* instantiating with a default parameterless constructor, as shown in the following code:

```
namespace Northwind.ViewModels;

public record class Summary
{
  // These properties can be initialized once but then never changed.
  public string? FullName { get; init; }
  public decimal Total { get; init; }

  // This record class will have a default parameterless constructor.
  // The following commented statement is automatically generated:
  // public Summary() { }
}
```

 For the entity models, we used record class types defined using the constructor syntax to make them immutable. But an instance of Summary will need to be created using a default parameterless constructor and then its members set by AutoMapper. Therefore, it must be a record class with public properties that can be set during initialization but not after that. To do this, we use the init keyword.

Defining mappers for an AutoMapper configuration

Now we can define the mappings between models:

1. Use your preferred code editor to add a new **Class Library** / classlib project named MappingObjects.Mappers to the Chapter06 solution.

2. In the MappingObjects.Mappers project, treat warnings as errors, add a reference to the latest AutoMapper package, and add a reference to the Models project, as shown in the following markup:

```
<ItemGroup>
  <PackageReference Include="AutoMapper" Version="12.0.1" />
</ItemGroup>

<ItemGroup>
  <ProjectReference Include=
    "..\MappingObjects.Models\MappingObjects.Models.csproj" />
</ItemGroup>
```

3. Build the MappingObjects.Mappers project to restore packages and compile referenced projects.

4. In the MappingObjects.Mappers project, delete the file named Class1.cs.

5. In the `MappingObjects.Mappers` project, add a new class file named `CartToSummaryMapper.cs` and modify its contents to create a mapper configuration that maps the `FullName` of the `Summary` to a combination of the `FirstName` and `LastName` from `Customer`, as shown in the following code:

```csharp
using AutoMapper; // To use MapperConfiguration.
using AutoMapper.Internal; // To use the Internal() extension method.
using Northwind.EntityModels; // To use Cart.
using Northwind.ViewModels; // To use Summary.

namespace MappingObjects.Mappers;

public static class CartToSummaryMapper
{
  public static MapperConfiguration GetMapperConfiguration()
  {
    MapperConfiguration config = new(cfg =>
    {
      // To fix an issue with the MaxInteger method:
      // https://github.com/AutoMapper/AutoMapper/issues/3988
      cfg.Internal().MethodMappingEnabled = false;
      // Configure the mapper using projections.
      cfg.CreateMap<Cart, Summary>()
        // Map the first and last names formatted to the full name.
        .ForMember(dest => dest.FullName, opt => opt.MapFrom(src =>
          string.Format("{0} {1}",
            src.Customer.FirstName,
            src.Customer.LastName)
        ));
    });
    return config;
  }
}
```

Performing tests for an AutoMapper configuration

Now we can define unit tests for the mapper:

1. Use your preferred code editor to add a new **xUnit Test Project** / xunit named `MappingObjects.Tests` to the `Chapter06` solution.

2. In the `MappingObjects.Tests` project file, add a package reference to `AutoMapper`, as shown highlighted in the following markup:

```
<ItemGroup>
  <PackageReference Include="AutoMapper" Version="12.0.1" />
  <PackageReference Include="Microsoft.NET.Test.Sdk" Version="17.8.0" />
```

3. In the `MappingObjects.Tests` project file, add project references to `MappingObjects.Models` and `MappingObjects.Mappers`, as shown in the following markup:

```
<ItemGroup>
  <ProjectReference Include=
    "..\MappingObjects.Mappers\MappingObjects.Mappers.csproj" />
  <ProjectReference Include=
    "..\MappingObjects.Models\MappingObjects.Models.csproj" />
</ItemGroup>
```

4. Build the `MappingObjects.Tests` project to restore packages and build referenced projects.

5. In the `MappingObjects.Tests` project, rename `UnitTest1.cs` to `TestAutoMapperConfig.cs`.

6. Modify the contents of `TestAutoMapperConfig.cs` to get the mapper and then assert that the mapping is complete, as shown in the following code:

```
using AutoMapper; // To use MapperConfiguration.
using MappingObjects.Mappers; // To use CartToSummaryMapper.

namespace MappingObjects.Tests;

public class TestAutoMapperConfig
{
  [Fact]
  public void TestSummaryMapping()
  {
    MapperConfiguration config = CartToSummaryMapper.
GetMapperConfiguration();

    config.AssertConfigurationIsValid();
  }
}
```

7. Run the test:

   • In Visual Studio 2022, navigate to **Test | Run All Tests**.

   • In Visual Studio Code, in **Terminal**, enter `dotnet test`.

8. Note the test fails because the `Total` member of the `Summary` view model is unmapped, as shown in *Figure 6.3*:

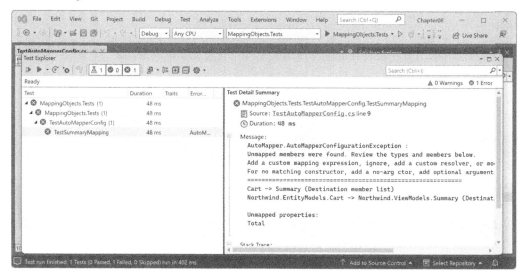

Figure 6.3: The test fails because the Total member is unmapped

9. In the `MappingObjects.Mappers` project, in the mapper configuration, after the mapping for the `FullName` member, add a mapping for the `Total` member, as shown highlighted in the following code:

```
cfg.CreateMap<Cart, Summary>()
    // Map the first and last names formatted to the full name.
    .ForMember(dest => dest.FullName, opt => opt.MapFrom(src =>
        string.Format("{0} {1}",
            src.Customer.FirstName, src.Customer.LastName)
    )) // We have removed a semi-colon from here.
    // Map the sum of items to the Total member.
    .ForMember(dest => dest.Total, opt => opt.MapFrom(
        src => src.Items.Sum(item => item.UnitPrice * item.Quantity)));
});
```

10. Run the test and note that, this time, it passes.

Performing live mappings between models

Now that we have validated the configuration of our mapping, we can use it in a live console app:

1. Use your preferred code editor to add a new **Console App** / console project named `MappingObjects.Console` to the `Chapter06` solution.

2. In the `MappingObjects.Console` project, treat warnings as errors, globally and statically import the `System.Console` class, add a project reference for the two class libraries, and add a package reference for `AutoMapper`, as shown in the following markup:

```
<ItemGroup>
  <ProjectReference Include=
    "..\MappingObjects.Mappers\MappingObjects.Mappers.csproj" />
  <ProjectReference Include=
    "..\MappingObjects.Models\MappingObjects.Models.csproj" />
</ItemGroup>

<ItemGroup>
  <PackageReference Include="AutoMapper" Version="12.0.1" />
</ItemGroup>
```

3. Build the `MappingObjects.Console` project.

4. In `Program.cs`, delete the existing statements, add some statements to construct an example object model that represents a customer and their shopping cart with a couple of items, and then map it to a summary view model to present to the user, as shown in the following code:

```
using AutoMapper; // To use MapperConfiguration, IMapper.
using MappingObjects.Mappers; // To use CartToSummaryMapper.
using Northwind.EntityModels; // To use Customer, Cart, LineItem.
using Northwind.ViewModels; // To use Summary.
using System.Text; // To use Encoding.

// Set the console's output encoding to UTF-8 to support
// Unicode characters like the Euro currency symbol.
OutputEncoding = Encoding.UTF8;

// Create an object model from "entity" model types that
// might have come from a data store like SQL Server.

Cart cart = new(
  Customer: new(
    FirstName: "John",
    LastName: "Smith"
  ),
  Items: new()
  {
    new(ProductName: "Apples", UnitPrice: 0.49M, Quantity: 10),
    new(ProductName: "Bananas", UnitPrice: 0.99M, Quantity: 4)
  }
);

WriteLine("*** Original data before mapping.");
```

```
WriteLine($"{cart.Customer}");
foreach (LineItem item in cart.Items)
{
  WriteLine($"  {item}");
}

// Get the mapper configuration for converting a Cart to a Summary.
MapperConfiguration config = CartToSummaryMapper.
GetMapperConfiguration();

// Create a mapper using the configuration.
IMapper mapper = config.CreateMapper();

// Perform the mapping.
Summary summary = mapper.Map<Cart, Summary>(cart);

// Output the result.
WriteLine();
WriteLine("*** After mapping.");
WriteLine($"Summary: {summary.FullName} spent {summary.Total:C}.");
```

5. Run the console app and note the successful result, as shown in the following code:

```
*** Original data before mapping.
Customer { FirstName = John, LastName = Smith }
  LineItem { ProductName = Apples, UnitPrice = 0.49, Quantity = 10 }
  LineItem { ProductName = Bananas, UnitPrice = 0.99, Quantity = 4 }

*** After mapping.
Summary: John Smith spent £8.86.
```

6. Optionally, write a unit test to perform a similar check as the preceding code to assert that the Summary has the correct full name and total.

Good Practice: There is a debate about when AutoMapper should be used that you can read about in an article (which has more links at the bottom) at the following link: https://www.anthonysteele.co.uk/AgainstAutoMapper.html.

More Information: Learn more details at the following link: https://automapper.org/.

Making fluent assertions in unit testing

FluentAssertions are a set of extension methods that make writing and reading the code in unit tests and the error messages of failing tests more similar to a natural human language like English.

It works with most unit testing frameworks, including xUnit. When you add a package reference for a test framework, FluentAssertions will automatically find the package and use it for throwing exceptions.

After importing the `FluentAssertions` namespace, call the `Should()` extension method on a variable and then one of the hundreds of other extension methods to make assertions in a human-readable way. You can chain multiple assertions using the `And()` extension method or have separate statements, each calling `Should()`.

Making assertions about strings

Let's start by making assertions about a single `string` value:

1. Use your preferred code editor to add a new **xUnit Test Project** / xunit named `FluentTests` to a `Chapter06` solution.

2. In the `FluentTests` project, add a package reference to `FluentAssertions`, as highlighted in the following markup:

    ```
    <ItemGroup>
      <PackageReference Include="FluentAssertions" Version="6.12.0" />
      <PackageReference Include="Microsoft.NET.Test.Sdk" Version="17.8.0" />
    ```

     FluentAssertions 7.0 should be available by the time this book is published. You can check at the following link: https://www.nuget.org/packages/FluentAssertions/.

3. Build the `FluentTests` project.

4. Rename `UnitTest1.cs` to `FluentExamples.cs`.

5. In `FluentExamples.cs`, import the namespace to make the `FluentAssertions` extension methods available and write a test method for a `string` value, as shown in the following code:

    ```
    using FluentAssertions; // To use common fluent assertions extension
    methods.

    namespace FluentTests;

    public class FluentExamples
    {
      [Fact]
      public void TestString()
      {
    ```

```
    string city = "London";
    string expectedCity = "London";

    city.Should().StartWith("Lo")
      .And.EndWith("on")
      .And.Contain("do")
      .And.HaveLength(6);

    city.Should().NotBeNull()
      .And.Be("London")
      .And.BeSameAs(expectedCity)
      .And.BeOfType<string>();

    city.Length.Should().Be(6);
  }
}
```

6. Run the test:

    *   In Visual Studio 2022, navigate to **Test | Run All Tests**.
    *   In Visual Studio Code, in **Terminal**, enter dotnet test.

7. Note the test passes.

8. In the TestString method, for the city variable, delete the last n in London.

9. Run the test and note it fails, as shown in the following output:

    ```
    Expected city "Londo" to end with "on".
    ```

10. Add the n back in London.

11. Run the test again to confirm the fix.

Making assertions about collections and arrays

Now let's continue by making assertions about collections and arrays:

1. In FluentExamples.cs, add a test method to explore collection assertions, as shown in the following code:

    ```
    [Fact]
    public void TestCollections()
    {
      string[] names = { "Alice", "Bob", "Charlie" };

      names.Should().HaveCountLessThan(4,
        "because the maximum items should be 3 or fewer");
    ```

```
      names.Should().OnlyContain(name => name.Length <= 6);
  }
```

2. Run the tests and note the collections test fails, as shown in the following output:

```
Expected names to contain only items matching (name.Length <= 6), but
{"Charlie"} do(es) not match.
```

3. Change `Charlie` to `Charly`.

4. Run the tests and note they succeed.

Making assertions about dates and times

Let's start by making assertions about date and time values:

1. In `FluentExamples.cs`, import the namespace for adding more extension methods for named months and other useful date/time-related functionality, as shown in the following code:

```
using FluentAssertions.Extensions; // To use February, March extension
methods.
```

2. Add a test method to explore date/time assertions, as shown in the following code:

```
[Fact]
public void TestDateTimes()
{
  DateTime when = new(
    hour: 9, minute: 30, second: 0,
    day: 25, month: 3, year: 2024);

  when.Should().Be(25.March(2024).At(9, 30));

  when.Should().BeOnOrAfter(23.March(2024));

  when.Should().NotBeSameDateAs(12.February(2024));

  when.Should().HaveYear(2024);

  DateTime due = new(
    hour: 11, minute: 0, second: 0,
    day: 25, month: 3, year: 2024);

  when.Should().BeAtLeast(2.Hours()).Before(due);
}
```

3. Run the tests and note the date/time test fails, as shown in the following output:

```
Expected when <2024-03-25 09:30:00> to be at least 2h before <2024-03-25
11:00:00>, but it is behind by 1h and 30m.
```

4. For the due variable, change the hour from 11 to 13.

5. Run the tests and note that the date/time test succeeds.

 More Information: You can learn more details about FluentAssertions at the following link: https://fluentassertions.com/.

Validating data

FluentValidation allows you to define strongly typed validation rules in a human-readable way.

You create a validator for a type by inheriting from `AbstractValidator<T>`, where `T` is the type that you want to validate. In the constructor, you call the `RuleFor` method to define one or more rules. If a rule should run only in specified scenarios, then you call the `When` method.

Understanding the built-in validators

FluentValidation ships with lots of useful built-in validator extension methods for defining rules, as shown in the following partial list, some of which you will explore in the coding task in this section:

- `Null`, `NotNull`, `Empty`, `NotEmpty`
- `Equal`, `NotEqual`
- `Length`, `MaxLength`, `MinLength`
- `LessThan`, `LessThanOrEqualTo`, `GreaterThan`, `GreaterThanOrEqualTo`
- `InclusiveBetween`, `ExclusiveBetween`
- `ScalePrecision`
- `Must` (aka predicate)
- `Matches` (aka regular expression), `EmailAddress`, `CreditCard`
- `IsInEnum`, `IsEnumName`

Performing custom validation

The easiest way to create custom rules is to use `Predicate` to write a custom validation function. You can also call the `Custom` method to get maximum control.

Customizing validation messages

There are a few extension methods that are used to customize the validation messages' output when data fails to pass the rules:

- `WithName`: Change the name used for a property in the message.

- WithSeverity: Change the default severity from Error to Warning or some other level.
- WithErrorCode: Assign an error code that can be output in the message.
- WithState: Add some state that can be used in the message.
- WithMessage: Customize the format of the default message.

Defining a model and validator

Let's see an example of FluentValidation in action. You will create three projects:

- A class library for a model to validate that represents an order made by a customer.
- A class library for the validator for the model.
- A console app to perform a live validation.

Let's start:

1. Use your preferred code editor to add a new **Class Library** / classlib project named FluentValidation.Models to the Chapter06 solution.

2. In the FluentValidation.Models project, delete the file named Class1.cs.

3. In the FluentValidation.Models project, add a new class file named CustomerLevel.cs and modify its contents to define an enum with three customer levels, Bronze, Silver, and Gold, as shown in the following code:

```
namespace FluentValidation.Models;

public enum CustomerLevel
{
  Bronze,
  Silver,
  Gold
}
```

4. In the FluentValidation.Models project, add a new class file named Order.cs and modify its contents, as shown in the following code:

```
namespace FluentValidation.Models;

public class Order
{
  public long OrderId { get; set; }
  public string? CustomerName { get; set; }
  public string? CustomerEmail { get; set; }
  public CustomerLevel CustomerLevel { get; set; }
  public decimal Total { get; set; }
  public DateTime OrderDate { get; set; }
  public DateTime ShipDate { get; set; }
}
```

5. Use your preferred code editor to add a new **Class Library** / `classlib` project named `FluentValidation.Validators` to the `Chapter06` solution.

6. In the `FluentValidation.Validators` project, add a project reference to the `Models` project and a package reference to the `FluentValidation` package, as shown in the following markup:

```
<ItemGroup>
  <PackageReference Include="FluentValidation" Version="11.8.1" />
</ItemGroup>

<ItemGroup>
  <ProjectReference Include=
    "..\FluentValidation.Models\FluentValidation.Models.csproj" />
</ItemGroup>
```

7. Build the `FluentValidation.Validators` project.

8. In the `FluentValidation.Validators` project, delete the file named `Class1.cs`.

9. In the `FluentValidation.Validators` project, add a new class file named `OrderValidator.cs` and modify its contents, as shown in the following code:

```
using FluentValidation.Models;

namespace FluentValidation.Validators;

public class OrderValidator : AbstractValidator<Order>
{
  public OrderValidator()
  {
    RuleFor(order => order.OrderId)
      .NotEmpty(); // Not default(long) which is 0.

    RuleFor(order => order.CustomerName)
      .NotNull()
      .WithName("Name"); // Use Name instead of CustomerName in messages.

    RuleFor(order => order.CustomerName)
      .MinimumLength(5)
      .WithSeverity(Severity.Warning);

    RuleFor(order => order.CustomerEmail)
      .NotEmpty()
      .EmailAddress();
```

```
    RuleFor(order => order.CustomerLevel)
      .IsInEnum();

    RuleFor(order => order.Total)
      .GreaterThan(0);

    RuleFor(order => order.ShipDate)
      .GreaterThan(order => order.OrderDate);

    When(order => order.CustomerLevel == CustomerLevel.Gold, () =>
    {
      RuleFor(order => order.Total).LessThan(50M);
      RuleFor(order => order.Total).GreaterThanOrEqualTo(20M);
    }).Otherwise(() =>
    {
      RuleFor(order => order.Total).LessThan(20M);
    });
  }
}
```

Testing the validator

Now we are ready to create a console app to test the validator on the model:

1. Use your preferred code editor to add a new **Console App** / console project named FluentValidation.Console to a Chapter06 solution.

2. In the FluentValidation.Console project, treat warnings as errors, globally and statically import the System.Console class, and add project references for FluentValidation.Validators and FluentValidation.Models, as shown in the following markup:

```
<ItemGroup>
  <ProjectReference Include=
    "..\FluentValidation.Models\FluentValidation.Models.csproj" />
  <ProjectReference Include=
    "..\FluentValidation.Validators\FluentValidation.Validators.csproj"
/>
</ItemGroup>
```

3. Build the FluentValidation.Console project to build referenced projects.

4. In Program.cs, delete the existing statements, and then add statements to create an order and validate it, as shown in the following code:

```
using FluentValidation.Models; // To use Order.
using FluentValidation.Results; // To use ValidationResult.
```

```
using FluentValidation.Validators; // To use OrderValidator.
using System.Globalization; // To use CultureInfo.
using System.Text; // To use Encoding.

OutputEncoding = Encoding.UTF8; // Enable Euro symbol.

// Control the culture used for formatting of dates and currency,
// and for localizing error messages to local language.
Thread t = Thread.CurrentThread;
t.CurrentCulture = CultureInfo.GetCultureInfo("en-US");
t.CurrentUICulture = t.CurrentCulture;
WriteLine($"Current culture: {t.CurrentCulture.DisplayName}");
WriteLine();

Order order = new()
{
  // Start with a deliberately invalid order.
};

OrderValidator validator = new();

ValidationResult result = validator.Validate(order);

// Output the order data.
WriteLine($"CustomerName:  {order.CustomerName}");
WriteLine($"CustomerEmail: {order.CustomerEmail}");
WriteLine($"CustomerLevel: {order.CustomerLevel}");
WriteLine($"OrderId:       {order.OrderId}");
WriteLine($"OrderDate:     {order.OrderDate}");
WriteLine($"ShipDate:      {order.ShipDate}");
WriteLine($"Total:         {order.Total:C}");
WriteLine();

// Output if the order is valid and any rules that were broken.
WriteLine($"IsValid:  {result.IsValid}");
foreach (var item in result.Errors)
{
  WriteLine($"  {item.Severity}: {item.ErrorMessage}");
}
```

5. Run the console app and note the failed rules, as shown in the following output:

```
Current culture: English (United States)

CustomerName:
CustomerEmail:
CustomerLevel: Bronze
OrderId:       0
OrderDate:     01/01/0001 12:00:00 AM
ShipDate:      01/01/0001 12:00:00 AM
Total:         $0.00


IsValid:  False
   Error: 'Order Id' must not be empty.
   Error: 'Name' must not be empty.
   Error: 'Customer Email' must not be empty.
   Error: 'Total' must be greater than '0'.
   Error: 'Ship Date' must be greater than '01/01/0001 12:00:00 AM'.
```

6. Comment out the two statements that set the culture to see the output in your local language and region. For example, if you are in France (fr-FR), it would look like the following:

```
Current culture: français (France)

CustomerName:
CustomerEmail:
CustomerLevel: Bronze
OrderId:       0
OrderDate:     01/01/0001 00:00:00
ShipDate:      01/01/0001 00:00:00
Total:         0,00 €

IsValid:  False
   Error: 'Order Id' ne doit pas être vide.
   Error: 'Name' ne doit pas avoir la valeur null.
   Error: 'Customer Email' ne doit pas être vide.
   Error: 'Total' doit être plus grand que '0'.
   Error: 'Ship Date' doit être plus grand que '01/01/0001 00:00:00'.
```

7. Set some property values for the order, as shown highlighted in the following code:

```
Order order = new()
{
  OrderId = 10001,
```

```
    CustomerName = "Abc",
    CustomerEmail = "abc&example.com",
    CustomerLevel = (CustomerLevel)4,
    OrderDate = new(2022, month: 12, day: 1),
    ShipDate = new(2022, month: 11, day: 5),
    Total = 49.99M
};
```

8. Set the current culture to US English to make sure you see the same output as in this book. You can experiment with your own culture later.

9. Run the console app and note the failed rules, as shown in the following output:

```
Current culture: English (United States)

CustomerName:  Abc
CustomerEmail: abc&example.com
CustomerLevel: 4
OrderId:       10001
OrderDate:     12/1/2022 12:00:00 AM
ShipDate:      11/5/2022 12:00:00 AM
Total:         $49.99

IsValid:  False
  Warning: The length of 'Customer Name' must be at least 5 characters.
You entered 3 characters.
  Error: 'Customer Email' is not a valid email address.
  Error: 'Customer Level' has a range of values which does not include
'4'.
  Error: 'Ship Date' must be greater than '12/1/2022 12:00:00 AM'.
  Error: 'Total' must be less than '20'.
```

10. Modify some property values for the order, as shown highlighted in the following code:

```
Order order = new()
{
  OrderId = 10001,
  CustomerName = "Abcdef",
  CustomerEmail = "abc@example.com",
  CustomerLevel = CustomerLevel.Gold,
  OrderDate = new(2022, month: 12, day: 1),
  ShipDate = new(2022, month: 12, day: 5),
  // CustomerLevel is Gold so Total can be >20.
  Total = 49.99M
};
```

11. Run the console app and note the order is now valid, as shown in the following output:

```
IsValid:   True
```

Validating data with ASP.NET Core

For automatic data validation with ASP.NET Core, FluentValidation supports .NET Core 3.1 and later.

 More Information: Learn more details at the following link: `https://cecilphillip.com/fluent-validation-rules-with-asp-net-core/`.

Generating PDFs

One of the most common questions I get when teaching C# and .NET is, "What open-source library is available to generate PDF files?"

There are many licensed libraries for generating PDF files, but over the years, it has been difficult to find cross-platform open-source ones.

QuestPDF says, *"If you are consuming the QuestPDF library as a Direct Package Dependency for usage in a Closed Source software in the capacity of a for-profit company/individual with more than 1M USD annual gross revenue, you must purchase the QuestPDF Professional or Enterprise License, depending on the number of software developers. Please refer to the QuestPDF License and Pricing webpage for more details.* (`https://www.questpdf.com/pricing.html`)"

The older 2022.12.X release will always be available under the MIT license, free for commercial usage. If you want to support library development, please consider purchasing the Professional License for version 2023.1.X or later.

Using QuestPDF on Apple silicon Macs

QuestPDF uses SkiaSharp, which has implementations for Windows, Mac, and Linux operating systems. The console app that you create in this section to generate PDFs is therefore cross-platform. But on an Apple silicon Mac, like my Mac mini M1, I had to install the x64 version of .NET SDK and start the project using `dotnet new -a x64`. This tells the .NET SDK to use the x64 architecture, otherwise the SkiaSharp libraries give an error because they have not yet been built to target ARM64.

Creating class libraries to generate PDF documents

Let's see an example of QuestPDF in action. You will create three projects:

- A class library for a model that represents a catalog of product categories with names and images.
- A class library for the document template.
- A console app to perform a live generation of a PDF file.

Let's start:

1. Use your preferred code editor to add a new **Class Library** / classlib project named GeneratingPdf.Models to the Chapter06 solution.

2. In the GeneratingPdf.Models project, delete the file named Class1.cs.

3. In the GeneratingPdf.Models project, add a new class file named Category.cs and modify its contents to define a class with two properties for the name and identifier of a category, as shown in the following code:

    ```
    namespace GeneratingPdf.Models;

    public class Category
    {
      public int CategoryId { get; set; }
      public string CategoryName { get; set; } = null!;
    }
    ```

     Later, you will create an **images** folder with filenames that use the pattern categoryN.jpeg, where N is a number from 1 to 8 that matches the CategoryId values.

4. In the GeneratingPdf.Models project, add a new class file named Catalog.cs and modify its contents to define a class with a property to store the eight categories, as shown in the following code:

    ```
    namespace GeneratingPdf.Models;

    public class Catalog
    {
      public List<Category> Categories { get; set; } = null!;
    }
    ```

5. Use your preferred code editor to add a new **Class Library** / classlib project named GeneratingPdf.Document to the Chapter06 solution.

6. In the GeneratingPdf.Document project, add a package reference for QuestPDF and a project reference for the Models class library, as shown in the following markup:

    ```
    <ItemGroup>
      <!-- The newest version with an MIT license. -->
      <PackageReference Include="QuestPDF" Version="2022.12.6" />
    </ItemGroup>

    <ItemGroup>
    ```

```
        <ProjectReference Include=
          "..\GeneratingPdf.Models\GeneratingPdf.Models.csproj" />
      </ItemGroup>
```

7. Build the `GeneratingPdf.Document` project.

8. In the `GeneratingPdf.Document` project, delete the file named `Class1.cs`.

9. In the `GeneratingPdf.Document` project, add a new class file named `CatalogDocument.cs`.

10. In `CatalogDocument.cs`, define a class that implements the `IDocument` interface to define a template with a header and a footer, and then output the eight categories, including name and image, as shown in the following code:

```csharp
using GeneratingPdf.Models; // Catalog
using QuestPDF.Drawing; // DocumentMetadata
using QuestPDF.Fluent; // Page
using QuestPDF.Helpers; // Colors
using QuestPDF.Infrastructure; // IDocument, IDocumentContainer

namespace GeneratingPdf.Document;

public class CatalogDocument : IDocument
{
  public Catalog Model { get; }

  public CatalogDocument(Catalog model)
  {
    Model = model;
  }

  public void Compose(IDocumentContainer container)
  {
    container
      .Page(page =>
      {
        page.Margin(50 /* points */);

        page.Header()
          .Height(100).Background(Colors.Grey.Lighten1)
          .AlignCenter().Text("Catalogue")
          .Style(TextStyle.Default.FontSize(20));

        page.Content()
          .Background(Colors.Grey.Lighten3)
```

```
      .Table(table =>
      {
        table.ColumnsDefinition(columns =>
        {
          columns.ConstantColumn(100);
          columns.RelativeColumn();
        });

        foreach (var item in Model.Categories)
        {
          table.Cell().Text(item.CategoryName);

          string imagePath = Path.Combine(
            Environment.CurrentDirectory, "images",
            $"category{item.CategoryId}.jpeg");

          table.Cell().Image(imagePath);
        }
      });

    page.Footer()
      .Height(50).Background(Colors.Grey.Lighten1)
      .AlignCenter().Text(x =>
      {
        x.CurrentPageNumber();
        x.Span(" of ");
        x.TotalPages();
      });
    });
  }

  public DocumentMetadata GetMetadata() => DocumentMetadata.Default;
}
```

Creating a console app to generate PDF documents

Now we can create a console app project that will use the class libraries to generate a PDF document:

1. Use your preferred code editor to add a new **Console App** / console project named GeneratingPdf. Console to a Chapter06 solution.

2. In the GeneratingPdf.Console project, create an images folder and download the eight category images 1 to 8 from the following link to it: https://github.com/markjprice/apps-services-net8/tree/master/images/Categories.

3. If you are using Visual Studio 2022 or JetBrains Rider, then the images folder and its files must be copied to the `GeneratingPdf.Console\bin\Debug\net8` folder:

    1. In **Solution Explorer**, select all the images.

    2. In **Properties**, set **Copy To Output Directory** to **Copy Always**.

    3. Open the project file and note the `<ItemGroup>` entries that will copy the eight images to the correct folder, as partially shown in the following markup:

    ```xml
    <ItemGroup>
      <None Update="images\category1.jpeg">
        <CopyToOutputDirectory>Always</CopyToOutputDirectory>
      </None>
    ...
    ```

4. In the `GeneratingPdf.Console` project, treat warnings as errors, globally and statically import the `System.Console` class, and add a project reference for the `Document` template class library, as shown in the following markup:

    ```xml
    <ItemGroup>
      <ProjectReference Include=
        "..\GeneratingPdf.Document\GeneratingPdf.Document.csproj" />
    </ItemGroup>
    ```

5. Build the `GeneratingPdf.Console` project.

6. In `Program.cs`, delete the existing statements and then add statements to create a catalog model, pass it to a catalog document, generate a PDF file, and then attempt to open the file using the appropriate operating system command, as shown in the following code:

    ```csharp
    using GeneratingPdf.Document; // To use CatalogDocument.
    using GeneratingPdf.Models; // To use Catalog, Category.
    using QuestPDF.Fluent; // To use the GeneratePdf extension method.
    using QuestPDF.Infrastructure; // To use LicenseType.

    // For evaluation purposes, feel free to use the QuestPDF Community
    // License in a non-production environment.
    QuestPDF.Settings.License = LicenseType.Community;

    string filename = "catalog.pdf";

    Catalog model = new()
    {
      Categories = new()
      {
        new() { CategoryId = 1, CategoryName = "Beverages"},
    ```

```
      new() { CategoryId = 2, CategoryName = "Condiments"},
      new() { CategoryId = 3, CategoryName = "Confections"},
      new() { CategoryId = 4, CategoryName = "Dairy Products"},
      new() { CategoryId = 5, CategoryName = "Grains/Cereals"},
      new() { CategoryId = 6, CategoryName = "Meat/Poultry"},
      new() { CategoryId = 7, CategoryName = "Produce"},
      new() { CategoryId = 8, CategoryName = "Seafood"}
    }
};

CatalogDocument document = new(model);
document.GeneratePdf(filename);

WriteLine("PDF catalog has been created: {0}",
  Path.Combine(Environment.CurrentDirectory, filename));

try
{
  if (OperatingSystem.IsWindows())
  {
    System.Diagnostics.Process.Start("explorer.exe", filename);
  }
  else
  {
    WriteLine("Open the file manually.");
  }
}
catch (Exception ex)
{
  WriteLine($"{ex.GetType()} says {ex.Message}");
}
```

The Process class and its Start method should also be able to start processes on Mac and Linux, but getting the paths right can be tricky, so I've left that as an optional exercise for the reader. You can learn more about the Process class and its Start method at the following link: https://learn.microsoft.com/en-us/dotnet/api/system.diagnostics.process.start.

7.   Run the console app and note the PDF file generated, as shown in *Figure 6.4*:

Figure 6.4: A PDF file generated from C# code

 More Information: Learn more details at the following link: https://www.questpdf.com/.

Practicing and exploring

Test your knowledge and understanding by answering some questions, getting some hands-on practice, and doing deeper research into the topics in this chapter.

Exercise 6.1 – Test your knowledge

Use the web to answer the following questions:

1. What is the most downloaded third-party NuGet package of all time?
2. What method do you call on the ImageSharp Image class to make a change like resizing the image or replacing colors with grayscale?
3. What is a key benefit of using Serilog for logging?
4. What is a Serilog sink?
5. Should you always use a package like AutoMapper to map between objects?
6. Which FluentAssertions method should you call to start a fluent assertion on a value?
7. Which FluentAssertions method should you call to assert that all items in a sequence conform to a condition, like a string item must have less than six characters?
8. Which FluentValidation class should you inherit from to define a custom validator?
9. With FluentValidation, how can you set a rule to only apply in certain conditions?
10. With QuestPDF, which interface must you implement to define a document for a PDF and what methods of that interface must you implement?

Exercise 6.2 – Explore topics

Use the links on the following page to learn more details about the topics covered in this chapter:

```
https://github.com/markjprice/apps-services-net8/blob/main/docs/book-links.md#chapter-
6---implementing-popular-third-party-libraries
```

Summary

In this chapter, you explored some third-party libraries that are popular with .NET developers to perform functions, including:

- Manipulating images using a Microsoft-recommended third-party library named ImageSharp.
- Making text, numbers, dates, and times friendlier with Humanizer.
- Logging structured data with Serilog.
- Mapping between objects, for example, entity models to view models.
- Making fluent assertions in unit testing.
- Validating data in a local culture language-readable way.
- Generating a PDF file.

In the next chapter, we will learn how to handle internationalization with dates and times and localization, including a new type in .NET 8 for making it easier to unit test components with a dependency on the current time.

Learn more on Discord

To join the Discord community for this book – where you can share feedback, ask questions to the author, and learn about new releases – follow the QR code below:

```
https://packt.link/apps_and_services_dotnet8
```

7

Handling Dates, Times, and Internationalization

This chapter is about some of the common types that are included with .NET. These include types to manipulate dates and times and implement internationalization, which includes globalization and localization.

When writing code to handle times, it is especially important to consider time zones. Bugs are often introduced because two times are compared in different time zones without taking that into account. It is important to understand the concept of **Coordinated Universal Time (UTC)** and to convert time values into UTC before performing time manipulation.

You should also be aware of any **Daylight Saving Time (DST)** adjustments that might be needed.

This chapter covers the following topics:

- Working with dates and times
- Working with time zones
- Working with cultures
- Working with Noda Time

Working with dates and times

After numbers and text, the next most popular types of data to work with are dates and times. The two main types are as follows:

- `DateTime`: Represents a combined date and time value for a fixed point in time.
- `TimeSpan`: Represents a duration of time.

These two types are often used together. For example, if you subtract one `DateTime` value from another, the result is a `TimeSpan`. If you add a `TimeSpan` to a `DateTime`, then the result is a `DateTime` value.

Specifying date and time values

A common way to create a date and time value is to specify individual values for the date and time components, like day and hour, as described in *Table 7.1*:

Date/time parameter	Value range
year	1 to 9,999
month	1 to 12
day	1 to the number of days in that month
hour	0 to 23
minute	0 to 59
second	0 to 59
millisecond	0 to 999
microsecond	0 to 999

Table 7.1: Parameters for formatting date and time values

For example, to instantiate a `DateTime` that represents when .NET 9 might be released for **General Availability**, as shown in the following code:

```
DateTime dotnet9GA = new(year: 2024, month: 11, day: 12,
  hour: 11, minute: 0, second: 0);
```

 Good Practice: The preceding code example might make you think, "What time zone does the value represent?" This is the big problem with `DateTime` and why it is good practice to avoid it in favor of `DateTimeOffset`, which stores the time zone too. We will look at this issue in more detail later in this chapter.

An alternative is to provide the value as a `string` to be parsed, but this can be misinterpreted depending on the default culture of the thread. For example, in the UK, dates are specified as day/month/year, whereas in the US, dates are specified as month/day/year.

Let's see what you might want to do with dates and times:

1. Use your preferred code editor to create a new project, as defined in the following list:

   - Project template: **Console App** / `console`
   - Project file and folder: `WorkingWithTime`
   - Solution file and folder: `Chapter07`
   - **Do not use top-level statements:** Cleared.
   - **Enable native AOT publish:** Cleared.

2. In the project file, treat warnings as errors, and add an element to statically and globally import the `System.Console` class.

3. Add a new class file named `Program.Helpers.cs` and replace its contents, as shown in the following code:

```
using System.Globalization; // To use CultureInfo.

partial class Program
{
  private static void ConfigureConsole(string culture = "en-US",
    bool overrideComputerCulture = true)
  {
    // To enable special characters like Euro currency symbol.
    OutputEncoding = System.Text.Encoding.UTF8;

    Thread t = Thread.CurrentThread;

    if (overrideComputerCulture)
    {
      t.CurrentCulture = CultureInfo.GetCultureInfo(culture);
      t.CurrentUICulture = t.CurrentCulture;
    }

    CultureInfo ci = t.CurrentCulture;
    WriteLine($"Current culture: {ci.DisplayName}");
    WriteLine($"Short date pattern: {
      ci.DateTimeFormat.ShortDatePattern}");
    WriteLine($"Long date pattern: {
      ci.DateTimeFormat.LongDatePattern}");
    WriteLine();
  }

  private static void SectionTitle(string title)
  {
    ConsoleColor previousColor = ForegroundColor;
    ForegroundColor = ConsoleColor.DarkYellow;
    WriteLine($"*** {title}");
    ForegroundColor = previousColor;
  }
}
```

4. In `Program.cs`, delete the existing statements, and then add statements to initialize some special date/time values, as shown in the following code:

```
ConfigureConsole(); // Defaults to en-US culture.


SectionTitle("Specifying date and time values");


WriteLine($"DateTime.MinValue:  {DateTime.MinValue}");
WriteLine($"DateTime.MaxValue:  {DateTime.MaxValue}");
WriteLine($"DateTime.UnixEpoch: {DateTime.UnixEpoch}");
WriteLine($"DateTime.Now:       {DateTime.Now}");
WriteLine($"DateTime.Today:     {DateTime.Today}");
WriteLine($"DateTime.Today:     {DateTime.Today:d}");
WriteLine($"DateTime.Today:     {DateTime.Today:D}");
```

5. Run the code, and note the results, as shown in the following output:

```
Current culture: English (United States)
Short date pattern: M/d/yyyy
Long date pattern: dddd, MMMM d, yyyy

*** Specifying date and time values
DateTime.MinValue:  1/1/0001 12:00:00 AM
DateTime.MaxValue:  12/31/9999 11:59:59 PM
DateTime.UnixEpoch: 1/1/1970 12:00:00 AM
DateTime.Now:       5/30/2023 9:18:05 AM
DateTime.Today:     5/30/2023 12:00:00 AM
DateTime.Today:     5/30/2023
DateTime.Today:     Tuesday, May 30, 2023
```

 The date and time formats output are determined by the culture settings of your console app. We called the `ConfigureConsole` method to make sure we all see the same default output in US English.

6. In `Program.cs`, at the top of the statement that calls `ConfigureConsole`, set the parameter to not override your local computer's culture, as shown in the following code:

```
ConfigureConsole(overrideComputerCulture: false);
```

7. Run the code, and note the output is localized to your computer's culture.

8. In `Program.cs`, set the parameter to specify alternative languages, like French in Canada (`fr-CA`) or English in Great Britain (`en-GB`), as shown in the following code:

```
ConfigureConsole("fr-CA");
```

More Information: There is a table of common culture codes at the following link: https://en.wikipedia.org/wiki/Language_localisation#Language_tags_and_codes

9. Run the code, and note that the output is localized to the specified culture.
10. Reset the console configuration back to the default so that it uses US English culture, as shown in the following code:

```
ConfigureConsole(); // Defaults to en-US culture.
```

Formatting date and time values

You have just seen that dates and times have default formats based on the current culture.

You can take complete control of date and time formatting using custom format code, as shown in *Table 7.2*:

Format code	Description
/	Date part separator. Varies by culture; for example, en-US uses /, but fr-FR uses - (dash).
\	Escape character. Useful if you want to use a special format code as a literal character; for example, h \h m \m would format a time of 9:30 am as 9 h 30 m.
:	Time part separator. Varies by culture; for example, en-US uses :, but fr-FR uses . (dot).
d, dd	The day of the month, from 1 to 31, or with a leading zero from 01 through 31.
ddd, dddd	The abbreviated or full name of the day of the week, for example, Mon or Monday, localized for the current culture.
f, ff, fff	The tenths of a second, hundredths of a second, or milliseconds.
g	The period or era, for example, A.D.
h, hh	The hour, using a 12-hour clock from 1 to 12, or from 01 to 12.
H, HH	The hour, using a 24-hour clock from 0 to 23, or from 01 to 23.
K	Time zone information. null for an unspecified time zone, Z for UTC, and a value like -8:00 for local time adjusted from UTC.
m, mm	The minute, from 0 through 59, or with a leading zero from 00 through 59.
M, MM	The month, from 1 through 12, or with a leading zero from 01 through 12.
MMM, MMMM	The abbreviated or full name of the month, for example, Jan or January, localized for the current culture.
s, ss	The second, from 0 through 59, or with a leading zero from 00 through 59.
t, tt	The first or both characters of the AM/PM designator.

y, yy	The year of the current century, from 0 through 99, or with a leading zero from 00 through 99.
yyy	The year with a minimum of three digits, and as many as needed. For example, 1 A.D. is 001. The first sacking of Rome was in 410. The year this book was published is 2023.
yyyy, yyyyy	The year as a four- or five-digit number.
z, zz	Hours offset from UTC, with no leading zeros, or with leading zeros.
zzz	Hours and minutes offset from UTC, with a leading zero, for example, +04:30.

Table 7.2: Custom format code for date and time values

 More Information: A full list of custom format code can be found at the following link: https://learn.microsoft.com/en-us/dotnet/standard/base-types/custom-date-and-time-format-strings

You can apply standard date and time formatting using simpler format code, like the d and D we used in the code example, as shown in *Table 7.3*:

Format code	Description
d	Short date pattern. Varies by culture; for example, en-US uses M/d/yyyy and fr-FR uses dd/MM/yyyy.
D	Long date pattern. Varies by culture; for example, en-US uses mmmm, MMMM d, yyyy and fr-FR uses mmmm, dd MMMM yyyy.
f	Full date/time pattern (short time – hours and minutes). Varies by culture.
F	Full date/time pattern (long time – hours, minutes, seconds, and AM/PM). Varies by culture.
o, O	A standardized pattern, suitable to serialize date/time values for roundtrips, for example, 2023-05-30T13:45:30.0000000-08:00.
r, R	RFC1123 pattern.
t	Short time pattern. Varies by culture; for example, en-US uses h:mm tt and fr-FR uses HH:mm.
T	Long time pattern. Varies by culture; for example, en-US uses h:mm:ss tt and fr-FR uses HH:mm:ss.
u	Universal sortable date/time pattern, for example, 2009-06-15 13:45:30Z.
U	Universal full date/time pattern. Varies by culture; for example, en-US might be Monday, June 15, 2009 8:45:30 PM.

Table 7.3: Standard format code for date and time values

More Information: A full list of format code can be found at the following link: `https://learn.microsoft.com/en-us/dotnet/standard/base-types/standard-date-and-time-format-strings`.

Let's run some examples:

1. In `Program.cs`, add statements to define Christmas Day in 2024 and display it in various ways, as shown in the following code:

```
DateTime xmas = new(year: 2024, month: 12, day: 25);
WriteLine($"Christmas (default format): {xmas}");
WriteLine($"Christmas (custom short format): {xmas:ddd d/M/yy}");
WriteLine($"Christmas (custom long format): {
  xmas:dddd, dd MMMM yyyy}");
WriteLine($"Christmas (standard long format): {xmas:D}");
WriteLine($"Christmas (sortable): {xmas:u}");
WriteLine($"Christmas is in month {xmas.Month} of the year.");
WriteLine($"Christmas is day {xmas.DayOfYear} of {xmas.Year}.");
WriteLine($"Christmas {xmas.Year} is on a {xmas.DayOfWeek}.");
```

2. Run the code, and note the results, as shown in the following output:

```
Christmas (default format): 12/25/2024 12:00:00 AM
Christmas (custom short format): Wed, 25/12/24
Christmas (custom long format): Wednesday, 25 December 2024
Christmas (standard long format): Wednesday, December 25, 2024
Christmas (sortable): 2024-12-25 00:00:00Z
Christmas is in month 12 of the year.
Christmas is day 360 of 2024.
Christmas 2024 is on a Wednesday.
```

3. Disable overriding your computer culture or pass a specific culture code, like French in France, as shown in the following code:

```
ConfigureConsole("fr-FR"); // Defaults to en-US culture.
```

4. Run the code, and note that the results should be localized to that culture.

5. Reset the console configuration back to the default of US English.

Date and time calculations

Now, let's try performing simple calculations on date and time values:

1. In `Program.cs`, add statements to perform addition and subtraction with Christmas 2024, as shown in the following code:

```
SectionTitle("Date and time calculations");

DateTime beforeXmas = xmas.Subtract(TimeSpan.FromDays(12));
DateTime afterXmas = xmas.AddDays(12);

WriteLine($"12 days before Christmas: {beforeXmas:d}");
WriteLine($"12 days after Christmas: {afterXmas:d}");

TimeSpan untilXmas = xmas - DateTime.Now;

WriteLine($"Now: {DateTime.Now}");
WriteLine($"There are {untilXmas.Days} days and {untilXmas.Hours
  } hours until Christmas {xmas.Year.");

WriteLine("There are {untilXmas.TotalHours:N0} hours " +
  $"until Christmas {xmas.Year}.");
```

2. Run the code, and note the results, as shown in the following output:

```
*** Date and time calculations
12 days before Christmas: 12/13/2024
12 days after Christmas: 1/6/2025
Now: 5/30/2023 1:57:01 PM
There are 574 days and 10 hours until Christmas 2024.
There are 13,786 hours until Christmas 2024.
```

3. Add statements to define the time on Christmas Day that your children (or dog or cat or iguana?) might wake up to open presents, and display it in various ways, as shown in the following code:

```
DateTime kidsWakeUp = new(
  year: 2024, month: 12, day: 25,
  hour: 6, minute: 30, second: 0);

WriteLine($"Kids wake up: {kidsWakeUp}");

WriteLine($"The kids woke me up at {
  kidsWakeUp.ToShortTimeString()}");
```

4. Run the code, and note the results, as shown in the following output:

```
Kids wake up: 25/12/2024 06:30:00 AM
The kids woke me up at 06:30 AM
```

Microseconds and nanoseconds

In earlier versions of .NET, the smallest unit of time measurement was a tick. A tick is 100 nanoseconds, so developers used to have to do the calculation for nanoseconds themselves. .NET 7 introduced millisecond and microsecond parameters to constructors, and microsecond and nanosecond properties to the `DateTime`, `DateTimeOffset`, `TimeSpan`, and `TimeOnly` types.

Let's see some examples:

1. In `Program.cs`, add statements to construct a date and time value with more precision than was possible and to display its value, as shown in the following code:

```
SectionTitle("Milli-, micro-, and nanoseconds");

DateTime preciseTime = new(
  year: 2022, month: 11, day: 8,
  hour: 12, minute: 0, second: 0,
  millisecond: 6, microsecond: 999);

WriteLine($"Millisecond: {preciseTime.Millisecond}, Microsecond: {
  preciseTime.Microsecond}, Nanosecond: {preciseTime.Nanosecond}");

preciseTime = DateTime.UtcNow;

// Nanosecond value will be 0 to 900 in 100 nanosecond increments.
WriteLine($"Millisecond: {preciseTime.Millisecond}, Microsecond: {
  preciseTime.Microsecond}, Nanosecond: {preciseTime.Nanosecond}");
```

2. Run the code, and note the results, as shown in the following output:

```
*** Milli-, micro-, and nanoseconds
Millisecond: 6, Microsecond: 999, Nanosecond: 0
Millisecond: 243, Microsecond: 958, Nanosecond: 400
```

Globalization with dates and times

The current culture controls how dates and times are formatted and parsed:

1. At the top of `Program.cs`, import the namespace to work with globalization, as shown in the following code:

```
using System.Globalization; // To use CultureInfo.
```

2. Add statements to show the current culture that is used to display date and time values, and then parse the United States' Independence Day and display it in various ways, as shown in the following code:

```
SectionTitle("Globalization with dates and times");

// Same as Thread.CurrentThread.CurrentCulture.
WriteLine($"Current culture: {CultureInfo.CurrentCulture.Name}");

string textDate = "4 July 2024";
DateTime independenceDay = DateTime.Parse(textDate);

WriteLine($"Text: {textDate}, DateTime: {independenceDay:d MMMM}");

textDate = "7/4/2024";
independenceDay = DateTime.Parse(textDate);

WriteLine($"Text: {textDate}, DateTime: {independenceDay:d MMMM}");

// Explicitly override the current culture by setting a provider.
independenceDay = DateTime.Parse(textDate,
  provider: CultureInfo.GetCultureInfo("en-US"));

WriteLine($"Text: {textDate}, DateTime: {independenceDay:d MMMM}");
```

 Good Practice: Although you can create a `CultureInfo` instance using its constructor, unless you need to make changes to it, you should get a read-only shared instance by calling the `GetCultureInfo` method.

3. At the top of `Program.cs`, set the culture to British English, as shown in the following code:

```
ConfigureConsole("en-GB");
```

4. Run the code, and note the results, as shown in the following output:

```
*** Globalization with dates and times
Current culture is: en-GB
Text: 4 July 2024, DateTime: 4 July
Text: 7/4/2024, DateTime: 7 April
Text: 7/4/2024, DateTime: 4 July
```

When the current culture is *English (Great Britain)*, if a date is given as 4 July 2024, then it is correctly parsed regardless of whether the current culture is British or American. But if the date is given as **7/4/2024**, then it is parsed as 7 April. You can override the current culture by specifying the correct culture as a provider when parsing, as shown in the third example above.

5. Add statements to loop from the year 2023 to 2028, displaying if the year is a leap year and how many days there are in February, and then showing if Christmas and Independence Day are during DST, as shown in the following code:

```
for (int year = 2023; year <= 2028; year++)
{
  Write($"{year} is a leap year: {DateTime.IsLeapYear(year)}. ");
  WriteLine($"There are {DateTime.DaysInMonth(year: year, month: 2)
    } days in February {year}.");
}

WriteLine($"Is Christmas daylight saving time? {
  xmas.IsDaylightSavingTime()}");

WriteLine($"Is July 4th daylight saving time? {
  independenceDay.IsDaylightSavingTime()}");
```

6. Run the code, and note the results, as shown in the following output:

```
2023 is a leap year: False. There are 28 days in February 2023.
2024 is a leap year: True. There are 29 days in February 2024.
2025 is a leap year: False. There are 28 days in February 2025.
2026 is a leap year: False. There are 28 days in February 2026.
2027 is a leap year: False. There are 28 days in February 2027.
2028 is a leap year: True. There are 29 days in February 2028.
Is Christmas daylight saving time? False
Is July 4th daylight saving time? True
```

Complexities of Daylight Saving Time (DST)

DST is not used in all countries; it is also determined by hemisphere, and politics plays a role. For example, the United States is currently debating whether it should make DST permanent. They might decide to leave the decision up to individual states. It could all get extra confusing for Americans over the next few years.

Each country has its own rules for what day and what hour DST happens. These rules are encoded by .NET so that it can adjust automatically when needed.

In the US in springtime, the clocks "spring" forward one hour at 2 AM. In the fall, they "fall" back one hour at 2 AM. Wikipedia explains this at the following link: `https://en.wikipedia.org/wiki/Daylight_saving_time_in_the_United_States`

In the UK in springtime, the clocks spring forward one hour at 1 AM. In the autumn, they fall back one hour at 2 AM. The UK government explains this at the following link: `https://www.gov.uk/when-do-the-clocks-change`

Imagine that you need to set an alarm to wake you up at 1:30 AM to catch a flight from Heathrow airport in the UK. Your flight happens to depart on the day that DST takes effect.

In the UK spring, the clocks are at 12:59 AM, and then the next minute they spring forward to 2:00AM. 1:30 AM never happens, your alarm does not go off, and you miss your flight! 1:30 AM is an invalid time in .NET, and if you try to store that value in a variable, it will throw an exception.

In the UK autumn, the clocks are at 1:59, and then the next minute, they fall back to 1:00 and repeat that hour. In this case, 1:30 AM happens twice.

Localizing the DayOfWeek enum

`DayOfWeek` is an enum, so it cannot be localized as you might expect or hope. Its `string` values are hardcoded in English, as shown in the following code:

```
namespace System
{
  public enum DayOfWeek
  {
    Sunday = 0,
    Monday = 1,
    Tuesday = 2,
    Wednesday = 3,
    Thursday = 4,
    Friday = 5,
    Saturday = 6
  }
}
```

There are two solutions to this problem. First, you could apply the `dddd` date format code to a whole date value. For example,

```
WriteLine($"The day of the week is {DateTime.Now:dddd}.");
```

Second, you can use a helper method of the `DateTimeFormatInfo` class to convert a `DayOfWeek` value into a localized `string` for output as text.

Let's see an example of the problem and solution:

1. In `Program.cs`, add statements to explicitly set the current culture to Danish, and then output the current day of the week in that culture, as shown in the following code:

```
SectionTitle("Localizing the DayOfWeek enum");

CultureInfo previousCulture = Thread.CurrentThread.CurrentCulture;

// Explicitly set culture to Danish (Denmark).
Thread.CurrentThread.CurrentCulture =
  CultureInfo.GetCultureInfo("da-DK");

// DayOfWeek is not localized to Danish.
WriteLine("Culture: {Thread.CurrentThread.CurrentCulture
  .NativeName}, DayOfWeek: {DateTime.Now.DayOfWeek}";

// Use dddd format code to get day of the week localized.
WriteLine($"Culture: {Thread.CurrentThread.CurrentCulture
  .NativeName}, DayOfWeek: {DateTime.Now:dddd}");

// Use GetDayName method to get day of the week localized.
WriteLine("Culture: {Thread.CurrentThread.CurrentCulture
  .NativeName}, DayOfWeek: {DateTimeFormatInfo.CurrentInfo
  .GetDayName(DateTime.Now.DayOfWeek)}");

Thread.CurrentThread.CurrentCulture = previousCulture;
```

2. Run the code, and note the results, as shown in the following output:

```
*** Localizing the DayOfWeek enum
Culture: dansk (Danmark), DayOfWeek: Thursday
Culture: dansk (Danmark), DayOfWeek: torsdag
Culture: dansk (Danmark), DayOfWeek: torsdag
```

Working with only a date or a time

.NET 6 introduced some new types to work with only a date value or only a time value, named `DateOnly` and `TimeOnly`.

These are better than using a `DateTime` value with a zero time to store a date-only value because it is type-safe and avoids misuse. `DateOnly` also maps better to database column types, for example, a date column in SQL Server. `TimeOnly` is good for setting alarms and scheduling regular meetings or the opening hours for an organization, and it maps to a `time` column in SQL Server.

Let's use them to plan a release party for .NET 9, probably on Tuesday, November 12, 2024, one week after the US presidential election:

1. In `Program.cs`, add statements to define the .NET 9 release party and a time for it to start, and then combine the two values to make a calendar entry so that we don't miss it, as shown in the following code:

```
SectionTitle("Working with only a date or a time");

DateOnly party = new(year: 2024, month: 11, day: 12);
WriteLine($"The .NET 9 release party is on {party.ToLongDateString()}.");

TimeOnly starts = new(hour: 11, minute: 30);
WriteLine($"The party starts at {starts}.");

DateTime calendarEntry = party.ToDateTime(starts);
WriteLine($"Add to your calendar: {calendarEntry}.");
```

2. Run the code and note the results, as shown in the following output:

```
*** Working with only a date or a time
The .NET 9 release party is on Tuesday, November 12, 2024.
The party starts at 11:30 AM.
Add to your calendar: 11/12/2024 11:30:00 AM.
```

Getting date/time formatting information

Each culture has its own date/time formatting rules. These are defined in the `DateTimeFormat` property of a `CultureInfo` instance.

Let's output some commonly used information:

1. In `Program.cs`, add statements to get the date/time formatting information for the current culture and output some of its most useful properties, as shown in the following code:

```
SectionTitle("Working with date/time formats");

DateTimeFormatInfo dtfi = DateTimeFormatInfo.CurrentInfo;
// Or use Thread.CurrentThread.CurrentCulture.DateTimeFormat.

WriteLine($"Date separator: {dtfi.DateSeparator}");
WriteLine($"Time separator: {dtfi.TimeSeparator}");

WriteLine($"Long date pattern: {dtfi.LongDatePattern}");
WriteLine($"Short date pattern: {dtfi.ShortDatePattern}");
```

```
WriteLine($"Long time pattern: {dtfi.LongTimePattern}");
WriteLine($"Short time pattern: {dtfi.ShortTimePattern}");

Write("Day names:");
for (int i = 0; i < dtfi.DayNames.Length - 1; i++)
{
  Write($"  {dtfi.GetDayName((DayOfWeek)i)}");
}
WriteLine();

Write("Month names:");
for (int i = 1; i < dtfi.MonthNames.Length; i++)
{
  Write($"  {dtfi.GetMonthName(i)}");
}
WriteLine();
```

2. Run the code, and note the results, as shown in the following output:

```
*** Working with date/time formats
Date separator: /
Time separator: :
Long date pattern: dddd, MMMM d, yyyy
Short date pattern: M/d/yyyy
Long time pattern: h:mm:ss tt
Short time pattern: h:mm tt
Day names:  Sunday  Monday  Tuesday  Wednesday  Thursday  Friday
Month names:  January  February  March  April  May  June  July  August
September  October  November  December
```

3. Change the culture to something else, run the code, and note the results.

Unit testing with a time provider

Writing unit tests for components that need the current time is tricky because the time is constantly changing!

Imagine you want visitors to your e-commerce website to get a 20% discount if they make an order at the weekend. During workdays, they pay full price. How can we test this functionality?

To control the time used in unit tests, .NET 8 introduces the `TimeProvider` class.

Let's start defining a function to perform this calculation:

1. In the `Chapter07` solution, add a new **Class Library**/`classlib` project named `TimeFunctionsLib`.

2. In the `TimeFunctionsLib` project, rename `Class1.cs` to `DiscountService.cs`.

3. In `DiscountService.cs`, define a function to perform the calculation, as shown in the following code:

```
namespace Northwind.Services;

public class DiscountService
{
  public decimal GetDiscount()
  {
    // This has a dependency on the current time provided by the system.
    var now = DateTime.UtcNow;

    return now.DayOfWeek switch
    {
      DayOfWeek.Saturday or DayOfWeek.Sunday => 0.2M,
      _ => 0M
    };
  }
}
```

4. In the `Chapter07` solution, add a new **xUnit Test Project**/xunit project named `TestingWithTimeProvider`.

5. In the `TestingWithTimeProvider` project, add a reference to the `TimeFunctionsLib` project, as shown in the following markup:

```
<ItemGroup>
  <ProjectReference Include=
    "..\TimeFunctionsLib\TimeFunctionsLib.csproj" />
</ItemGroup>
```

6. Build the `TestingWithTimeProvider` project.

7. In the `TestingWithTimeProvider` project, rename `Test1.cs` to `TimeTests.cs`.

8. In `TimeTests.cs`, modify the statements to import the namespace for the discount service, and then define two tests, one for workdays and one for weekends, as shown in the following code:

```
using Northwind.Services; // To use DiscountService.

namespace TestingWithTimeProvider;

public class TimeTests
{
  [Fact]
```

```
        public void TestDiscountDuringWorkdays()
        {
          // Arrange
          DiscountService service = new();

          // Act
          decimal discount = service.GetDiscount();

          // Assert
          Assert.Equal(0M, discount);
        }

        [Fact]
        public void TestDiscountDuringWeekends()
        {
          DiscountService service = new();

          decimal discount = service.GetDiscount();

          Assert.Equal(0.2M, discount);
        }
    }
```

9. Run the two tests, and note that only one can ever succeed at any one time. If you run the tests during workdays, the weekend test will fail. If you run the tests during the weekend, the workday test will fail!

Now that you've seen the problem, how can we solve it?

The way Microsoft solves it is by each team that creates .NET libraries defining its own internal ISystemClock interface with, at a minimum, a property named UtcNow, and sometimes other members, along with implementations that typically use the built-in system clock but are all slightly different. A typical example is shown in the following code:

```
using System;

namespace Microsoft.Extensions.Internal
{
  public interface ISystemClock
  {
    DateTimeOffset UtcNow { get; }
  }

  public class SystemClock
```

```
  {
    public DateTimeOffset UtcNow
    {
      return DateTimeOffset.UtcNow;
    }
  }
}
```

Finally, with .NET 8, the core .NET team has introduced a proper equivalent of the preceding code with an implementation that uses the system clock. Unfortunately, they do not define an interface. Instead, they define an abstract class named `TimeProvider`.

Let's use it:

1. In the `TimeFunctionsLib` project, in `DiscountService.cs`, comment out the use of the `UtcNow` property, and add a statement to add a constructor-injected service, as highlighted in the following code:

    ```
    namespace Northwind.Services;

    public class DiscountService
    {
      private TimeProvider _timeProvider;

      public DiscountService(TimeProvider timeProvider)
      {
        _timeProvider = timeProvider;
      }

      public decimal GetDiscount()
      {
        // This has a dependency on the current time provided by the system.
        // var now = DateTime.UtcNow;

        var now = _timeProvider.GetUtcNow();

        // This has a dependency on the current time provided by the system.
        return now.DayOfWeek switch
        {
          DayOfWeek.Saturday or DayOfWeek.Sunday => 0.2M,
          _ => 0M
        };
      }
    }
    ```

2. In the `TestingWithTimeProvider` project, in `TimeTests.cs`, add statements to both tests to show how we could use the new `TimeProvider` and its `System` property (which would still have a dependency on the system clock!), as shown in the following code:

```
// This would use the .NET 8 or later dependency service,
// but its implementation is still the system clock.
DiscountService service = new(TimeProvider.System);
```

3. In the `TestingWithTimeProvider` project, add a reference to `Moq`, a package to mock dependencies, as shown in the following markup:

```
<!-- The newest version before the controversy. -->
<PackageReference Include="Moq" Version="4.18.4" />
```

 Moq 4.18.4 was the last version released before a controversy erupted when the developer added obfuscated code that executed during builds. You can read more about this at the following link: `https://github.com/devlooped/moq/issues/1370`. I plan to keep an eye on the situation over the next few months and then decide whether I should switch to an alternative.

4. In `TimeTests.cs`, import the namespace to use the `Mock.Of<T>` extension method, as shown in the following code:

```
using Moq; // To use Mock.Of<T> method.
```

5. In the `TestDiscountDuringWorkdays` method, comment out the statement that used the `System` provider, and replace it with statements to mock a time provider that always returns a fixed date and time during workdays, as highlighted in the following code:

```
TimeProvider timeProvider = Mock.Of<TimeProvider>();

// Mock the time provider so it always returns the date of
// 2023-11-07 09:30:00 UTC which is a Tuesday.
Mock.Get(timeProvider).Setup(s => s.GetUtcNow()).Returns(
  new DateTimeOffset(year: 2023, month: 11, day: 7,
  hour: 9, minute: 30, second: 0, offset: TimeSpan.Zero));

DiscountService service = new(timeProvider);
```

6. In the `TestDiscountDuringWeekends` method, comment out the statement that used the `System` provider and replace it with statements to mock a time provider that always returns a fixed date and time at the weekend, as highlighted in the following code:

```
TimeProvider timeProvider = Mock.Of<TimeProvider>();

// Mock the time provider so it always returns the date of
```

```
// 2023-11-04 09:30:00 UTC which is a Saturday.
Mock.Get(timeProvider).Setup(s => s.GetUtcNow()).Returns(
  new DateTimeOffset(year: 2023, month: 11, day: 4,
  hour: 9, minute: 30, second: 0, offset: TimeSpan.Zero));

DiscountService service = new(timeProvider);
```

7. Run the unit tests, and note that they both succeed.

Working with time zones

In the code example about the .NET release party, using a `TimeOnly` was not actually a good idea because the `TimeOnly` value did not include information about the time zone. It is only useful if you are in the correct time zone. `TimeOnly` is, therefore, a poor choice for an event. For events, we need to understand and handle time zones.

Understanding DateTime and TimeZoneInfo

The `DateTime` class has many useful members related to time zones, as shown in *Table 7.4*:

Member	Description
`Now` property	A `DateTime` value that represents the current date and time in the local time zone.
`UtcNow` property	A `DateTime` value that represents the current date and time in the UTC time zone.
`Kind` property	A `DateTimeKind` value that indicates whether the `DateTime` value is `Unspecified`, `Utc`, or `Local`.
`IsDaylightSavingTime` method	A `bool` that indicates if the `DateTime` value is during DST.
`ToLocalTime` method	Converts a UTC `DateTime` value to the equivalent local time.
`ToUniversalTime` method	Converts a local `DateTime` value to the equivalent UTC time.

Table 7.4: DateTime members related to time zones

The `TimeZoneInfo` class has many useful members, as shown in *Table 7.5*:

Member	Description
`Id` property	A `string` that uniquely identifies the time zone.
`Local` property	A `TimeZoneInfo` value that represents the current local time zone. Varies depending on where the code executes.
`Utc` property	A `TimeZoneInfo` value that represents the UTC time zone.
`StandardName` property	A `string` for the name of the time zone when Daylight Saving is not active.

DaylightName property	A string for the name of the time zone when Daylight Saving is active.
DisplayName property	A string for the general name of the time zone.
BaseUtcOffset property	A TimeSpan that represents the difference between this time zone and the UTC time zone, ignoring any potential Daylight Saving adjustments.
SupportsDaylightSavingTime property	A bool that indicates whether this time zone has Daylight Saving adjustments.
ConvertTime method	Converts a DateTime value to another DateTime value in a different time zone. You can specify the source and destination time zones.
ConvertTimeFromUtc method	Converts a DateTime value in the UTC time zone to a DateTime value in a specified time zone.
ConvertTimeToUtc method	Converts a DateTime value in a specified time zone to a DateTime value in the UTC time zone.
IsDaylightSavingTime method	Returns a bool, indicating whether the DateTime value is in Daylight Saving.
GetSystemTimeZones method	Returns a collection of time zones registered with the operating system.

Table 7.5: TimeZoneInfo useful members

 Some database providers for EF Core only allow you to store DateTime values that use the Kind property to determine whether it is UTC, so you might need to convert to and from DateTimeOffset if you need to work with these values.

Exploring DateTime and TimeZoneInfo

Use the TimeZoneInfo class to work with time zones:

1. Use your preferred code editor to add a new **Console App** / console project named WorkingWithTimeZones to the Chapter07 solution:

    1. In Visual Studio 2022, set **Startup Project** to **Current selection**.
    2. Treat warnings as errors, and statically and globally import the System.Console class.

2. Add a new class file named Program.Helpers.cs.
3. Modify its contents to define some helper methods to output a section title in a visually different way, output a list of all time zones in the current system, and output details about a DateTime or TimeZoneInfo object, as shown in the following code:

    ```
    using System.Collections.ObjectModel; // To use ReadOnlyCollection<T>

    partial class Program
    ```

```
{
  private static void SectionTitle(string title)
  {
    ConsoleColor previousColor = ForegroundColor;
    ForegroundColor = ConsoleColor.DarkYellow;
    WriteLine($"*** {title}");
    ForegroundColor = previousColor;
  }

  private static void OutputTimeZones()
  {
    // get the time zones registered with the OS
    ReadOnlyCollection<TimeZoneInfo> zones =
      TimeZoneInfo.GetSystemTimeZones();

    WriteLine($"*** {zones.Count} time zones:");

    // order the time zones by Id instead of DisplayName
    foreach (TimeZoneInfo zone in zones.OrderBy(z => z.Id))
    {
      WriteLine($"{zone.Id}");
    }
  }

  private static void OutputDateTime(DateTime dateTime, string title)
  {
    SectionTitle(title);
    WriteLine($"Value: {dateTime}");
    WriteLine($"Kind: {dateTime.Kind}");
    WriteLine($"IsDaylightSavingTime: {dateTime.
IsDaylightSavingTime()}");
    WriteLine($"ToLocalTime(): {dateTime.ToLocalTime()}");
    WriteLine($"ToUniversalTime(): {dateTime.ToUniversalTime()}");
  }

  private static void OutputTimeZone(TimeZoneInfo zone, string title)
  {
    SectionTitle(title);
    WriteLine($"Id: {zone.Id}");
    WriteLine($"IsDaylightSavingTime(DateTime.Now): {
      zone.IsDaylightSavingTime(DateTime.Now)}");
```

```
    WriteLine($"StandardName: {zone.StandardName}");
    WriteLine($"DaylightName: {zone.DaylightName}");
    WriteLine($"BaseUtcOffset: {zone.BaseUtcOffset}");
  }

  private static string GetCurrentZoneName(TimeZoneInfo zone, DateTime
when)
  {
    // time zone names change if Daylight Saving time is active
    // e.g. GMT Standard Time becomes GMT Summer Time
    return zone.IsDaylightSavingTime(when) ?
      zone.DaylightName : zone.StandardName;
  }
}
```

4. In `Program.cs`, delete the existing statements. Add statements to output the current date and time in the local and UTC time zones, and then output details about the local and UTC time zones, as shown in the following code:

```
OutputTimeZones();

OutputDateTime(DateTime.Now, "DateTime.Now");
OutputDateTime(DateTime.UtcNow, "DateTime.UtcNow");

OutputTimeZone(TimeZoneInfo.Local, "TimeZoneInfo.Local");
OutputTimeZone(TimeZoneInfo.Utc, "TimeZoneInfo.Utc");
```

5. Run the console app and note the results, including the time zones registered on your operating system (there are 141 on my Windows 11 laptop), and that it is currently 4:17 PM on 31 May 2022 in England, meaning I am in the GMT Standard Time zone. However, because DST is active, it is currently known as GMT Summer Time, which is one hour ahead of UTC, as shown in the following output:

```
*** 141 time zones:
Afghanistan Standard Time
Alaskan Standard Time
...
West Pacific Standard Time
Yakutsk Standard Time
Yukon Standard Time
*** DateTime.Now
Value: 31/05/2022 16:17:03
Kind: Local
IsDaylightSavingTime: True
```

```
ToLocalTime(): 31/05/2022 16:17:03
ToUniversalTime(): 31/05/2022 15:17:03
*** DateTime.UtcNow
Value: 31/05/2022 15:17:03
Kind: Utc
IsDaylightSavingTime: False
ToLocalTime(): 31/05/2022 16:17:03
ToUniversalTime(): 31/05/2022 15:17:03
*** TimeZoneInfo.Local
Id: GMT Standard Time
IsDaylightSavingTime(DateTime.Now): True
StandardName: GMT Standard Time
DaylightName: GMT Summer Time
BaseUtcOffset: 00:00:00
*** TimeZoneInfo.Utc
Id: UTC
IsDaylightSavingTime(DateTime.Now): False
StandardName: Coordinated Universal Time
DaylightName: Coordinated Universal Time
BaseUtcOffset: 00:00:00
```

 The `BaseUtcOffset` of the **GMT Standard Time** zone is zero because normally Daylight Saving is not active. That is why it is prefixed with `Base`.

6. In `Program.cs`, add statements to prompt the user to enter a time zone (using Eastern Standard Time as a default), get that time zone, output details about it, and then compare a time entered by the user with the equivalent time in the other time zone, and catch potential exceptions, as shown in the following code:

```
Write("Enter a time zone or press Enter for US East Coast: ");
string zoneId = ReadLine()!;

if (string.IsNullOrEmpty(zoneId))
{
  zoneId = "Eastern Standard Time";
}

try
{
  TimeZoneInfo otherZone = TimeZoneInfo.FindSystemTimeZoneById(zoneId);
```

```
      OutputTimeZone(otherZone,
        $"TimeZoneInfo.FindSystemTimeZoneById(\"{zoneId}\")");


      SectionTitle($"What's the time in {zoneId}?");


      Write("Enter a local time or press Enter for now: ");
      string? timeText = ReadLine();
      DateTime localTime;
      if (string.IsNullOrEmpty(timeText) ||
        !DateTime.TryParse(timeText, out localTime))
      {
        localTime = DateTime.Now;
      }


      DateTime otherZoneTime = TimeZoneInfo.ConvertTime(
        dateTime: localTime, sourceTimeZone: TimeZoneInfo.Local,
        destinationTimeZone: otherZone);


      WriteLine($"{localTime} {GetCurrentZoneName(TimeZoneInfo.Local,
        localTime)} is {otherZoneTime} {GetCurrentZoneName(otherZone,
        otherZoneTime)}.");
    }
    catch (TimeZoneNotFoundException)
    {
      WriteLine($"The {zoneId} zone cannot be found on the local system.");
    }
    catch (InvalidTimeZoneException)
    {
      WriteLine($"The {zoneId} zone contains invalid or missing data.");
    }
    catch (System.Security.SecurityException)
    {
      WriteLine("The application does not have permission to read time zone
    information.");
    }
    catch (OutOfMemoryException)
    {
      WriteLine($"Not enough memory is available to load information on the
    {zoneId} zone.");
    }
```

7. Run the console app, press *Enter* for US East Coast, then enter `12:30pm` for the local time, and note the results, as shown in the following output:

```
Enter a time zone or press Enter for US East Coast:
*** TimeZoneInfo.FindSystemTimeZoneById("Eastern Standard Time")
Id: Eastern Standard Time
IsDaylightSavingTime(DateTime.Now): True
StandardName: Eastern Standard Time
DaylightName: Eastern Summer Time
BaseUtcOffset: -05:00:00
*** What's the time in Eastern Standard Time?
Enter a local time or press Enter for now: 12:30pm
31/05/2023 12:30:00 GMT Summer Time is 31/05/2023 07:30:00 Eastern Summer
Time.
```

 My local time zone is GMT Standard Time, so there is currently a five-hour time difference between me and the US East Coast. Your local time zone will be different.

8. Run the console app, copy one of the time zones to the clipboard, paste it at the prompt, and then press *Enter* for the local time. Note the results, as shown in the following output:

```
Enter a time zone or press Enter for US East Coast: AUS Eastern Standard
Time
*** TimeZoneInfo.FindSystemTimeZoneById("AUS Eastern Standard Time")
Id: AUS Eastern Standard Time
IsDaylightSavingTime(DateTime.Now): False
StandardName: AUS Eastern Standard Time
DaylightName: AUS Eastern Summer Time
BaseUtcOffset: 10:00:00
*** What's the time in AUS Eastern Standard Time?
Enter a local time or press Enter for now:
31/05/2023 17:00:04 GMT Summer Time is 01/06/2023 02:00:04 AUS Eastern
Standard Time.
```

 Sydney, Australia, is currently nine hours ahead, so at about 5 PM for me, it is about 2 AM on the following day for them.

That's a lot to learn about dates, times, and time zones. But we aren't done yet. Now, we need to look at the wider topic of cultures, which are a combination of language and region and do not just affect date and time formatting.

Working with cultures

Internationalization is the process of enabling your code to correctly run all over the world. It has two parts, **globalization** and **localization**, and both of them are about working with cultures.

Globalization is about writing your code to accommodate multiple languages and region combinations. The combination of a language and a region is known as a culture. It is important for your code to know both the language and region because, for example, the date and currency formats are different in Quebec and Paris, despite them both using the French language.

There are **International Organization for Standardization (ISO)** codes for all culture combinations. For example, in the code da-DK, da indicates the Danish language and DK indicates the Denmark region, and in the code fr-CA, fr indicates the French language and CA indicates the Canada region.

> ISO is not just an acronym. ISO is a reference to the Greek word *isos* (which means *equal*). You can see a list of ISO culture codes at the following link: https://lonewolfonline.net/list-net-culture-country-codes/.

Localization is about customizing the user interface to support a language, for example, changing the label of a button to **Close** (en) or **Fermer** (fr). Since localization is more about the language, it doesn't always need to know about the region, although, ironically enough, the words *standardization* (en-US) and *standardisation* (en-GB) suggest otherwise.

> **Good Practice:** I am not a professional translator of software user interfaces, so take all examples in this chapter as general guidance. My research into French user interface labeling common practice led me to the following links, but it would be best to hire a professional if you are not a native language speaker: https://french.stackexchange.com/questions/12969/translation-of-it-terms-like-close-next-search-etc and https://www.linguee.com/english-french/translation/close+button.html.

Detecting and changing the current culture

Internationalization is a huge topic on which thousand-page books have been written. In this section, you will get a brief introduction to the basics, using the CultureInfo and RegionInfo types in the System.Globalization namespace.

Let's write some code:

1. Use your preferred code editor to add a new **Console App** / console project named WorkingWithCultures to the Chapter07 solution.

    • In the project file, treat warnings as errors, and then statically and globally import the System.Console class, and globally import the System.Globalization namespace so that we can use the CultureInfo class, as shown in the following markup:

```
<ItemGroup>
  <Using Include="System.Console" Static="true" />
  <Using Include="System.Globalization" />
</ItemGroup>
```

2. Add a new class file named `Program.Helpers.cs`, and modify its contents to add a method to the partial `Program` class that will output information about the cultures used for globalization and localization, as shown in the following code:

```
partial class Program
{
  private static void OutputCultures(string title)
  {
    ConsoleColor previousColor = ForegroundColor;
    ForegroundColor = ConsoleColor.DarkYellow;

    WriteLine($"*** {title}");

    // Get the cultures from the current thread.
    CultureInfo globalization = CultureInfo.CurrentCulture;
    CultureInfo localization = CultureInfo.CurrentUICulture;

    WriteLine($"The current globalization culture is {
      globalization.Name}: {globalization.DisplayName}");

    WriteLine($"The current localization culture is {
      localization.Name}: {localization.DisplayName}");

    WriteLine($"Days of the week: {string.Join(", ",
      globalization.DateTimeFormat.DayNames)}");

    WriteLine($"Months of the year: {string.Join(", ",
      globalization.DateTimeFormat.MonthNames
      // Some have 13 months; most 12, and the last is empty.
      .TakeWhile(month => !string.IsNullOrEmpty(month)))}");

    WriteLine($"1st day of this year: {new DateTime(
      year: DateTime.Today.Year, month: 1, day: 1)
      .ToString("D", globalization)}");

    WriteLine($"Number group separator: {globalization
      .NumberFormat.NumberGroupSeparator}");
```

```
    WriteLine($"Number decimal separator: {globalization
      .NumberFormat.NumberDecimalSeparator}");

    RegionInfo region = new(globalization.LCID);

    WriteLine($"Currency symbol: {region.CurrencySymbol}");

    WriteLine($"Currency name: {region.CurrencyNativeName} ({
      region.CurrencyEnglishName})");

    WriteLine($"IsMetric: {region.IsMetric}");

    WriteLine();

    ForegroundColor = previousColor;
  }
}
```

3. In `Program.cs`, delete the existing statements, and add statements to set the output encoding
    of the console to support Unicode. Then, output information about the globalization and local-
    ization cultures. Finally, prompt the user to enter a new culture code and show how that affects
    the formatting of common values, such as dates and currency, as shown in the following code:

```
// To enable special characters like €.
OutputEncoding = System.Text.Encoding.UTF8;

OutputCultures("Current culture");

WriteLine("Example ISO culture codes:");

string[] cultureCodes = {
  "da-DK", "en-GB", "en-US", "fa-IR",
  "fr-CA", "fr-FR", "he-IL", "pl-PL", "sl-SI" };

foreach (string code in cultureCodes)
{
  CultureInfo culture = CultureInfo.GetCultureInfo(code);
  WriteLine($"  {culture.Name}: {culture.EnglishName} / {
    culture.NativeName}");
}
```

```
WriteLine();

Write("Enter an ISO culture code: ");
string? cultureCode = ReadLine();

if (string.IsNullOrWhiteSpace(cultureCode))
{
  cultureCode = "en-US";
}

CultureInfo ci;

try
{
  ci = CultureInfo.GetCultureInfo(cultureCode);
}
catch (CultureNotFoundException)
{
  WriteLine($"Culture code not found: {cultureCode}");
  WriteLine("Exiting the app.");
  return;
}

// change the current cultures on the thread
CultureInfo.CurrentCulture = ci;
CultureInfo.CurrentUICulture = ci;

OutputCultures("After changing the current culture");

Write("Enter your name: ");
string? name = ReadLine();
if (string.IsNullOrWhiteSpace(name))
{
  name = "Bob";
}

Write("Enter your date of birth: ");
string? dobText = ReadLine();

if (string.IsNullOrWhiteSpace(dobText))
{
```

```
    // If they do not enter a DOB then use
    // sensible defaults for their culture.
    dobText = ci.Name switch
      {
        "en-US" or "fr-CA" => "1/27/1990",
        "da-DK" or "fr-FR" or "pl-PL" => "27/1/1990",
        "fa-IR" => "1990/1/27",
        _ => "1/27/1990"
      };
}

Write("Enter your salary: ");
string? salaryText = ReadLine();

if (string.IsNullOrWhiteSpace(salaryText))
{
  salaryText = "34500";
}

DateTime dob = DateTime.Parse(dobText);
int minutes = (int)DateTime.Today.Subtract(dob).TotalMinutes;
decimal salary = decimal.Parse(salaryText);

WriteLine($"{name} was born on a {dob:dddd}. {name} is {
  minutes:N0} minutes old. {name} earns {salary:C}.");
```

When you run an application, it automatically sets its thread to use the culture of the operating system. I am running my code in London, UK, so the thread is set to English (Great Britain).

The code prompts the user to enter an alternative ISO code. This allows your applications to replace the default culture at runtime.

The application then uses standard format codes to output the day of the week using format code dddd, the number of minutes with thousand separators using format code N0, and the salary with the currency symbol. These adapt automatically, based on the thread's culture.

4. Run the code and enter en-US for the ISO code (or press *Enter*), and then enter some sample data, including a date in a format valid for US English, as shown in the following output:

```
*** Current culture
The current globalization culture is en-GB: English (United Kingdom)
The current localization culture is en-GB: English (United Kingdom)
Days of the week: Sunday, Monday, Tuesday, Wednesday, Thursday, Friday,
Saturday
```

```
Months of the year: January, February, March, April, May, June, July,
August, September, October, November, December
1st day of this year: 01 January 2023
Number group separator: ,
Number decimal separator: .
Currency symbol: £
Currency name: British Pound (British Pound)
IsMetric: True

Example ISO culture codes:
  da-DK: Danish (Denmark) / dansk (Danmark)
  en-GB: English (United Kingdom) / English (United Kingdom)
  en-US: English (United States) / English (United States)
  fa-IR: Persian (Iran) / فارسی (ایران)
  fr-CA: French (Canada) / français (Canada)
  fr-FR: French (France) / français (France)
  he-IL: Hebrew (Israel) / עברית (ישראל)
  pl-PL: Polish (Poland) / polski (Polska)
  sl-SI: Slovenian (Slovenia) / slovenščina (Slovenija)

Enter an ISO culture code: en-US
*** After changing the current culture
The current globalization culture is en-US: English (United States)
The current localization culture is en-US: English (United States)
Days of the week: Sunday, Monday, Tuesday, Wednesday, Thursday, Friday,
Saturday
Months of the year: January, February, March, April, May, June, July,
August, September, October, November, December
1st day of this year: Sunday, January 1, 2023
Number group separator: ,
Number decimal separator: .
Currency symbol: $
Currency name: US Dollar (US Dollar)
IsMetric: False

Enter your name: Alice
Enter your date of birth: 3/30/1967
Enter your salary: 34500
Alice was born on a Thursday. Alice is 29,541,600 minutes old. Alice
earns $34,500.00
```

5. Run the code again, and try Danish in Denmark (da-DK), as shown in the following output:

```
Enter an ISO culture code: da-DK
*** After changing the current culture
The current globalization culture is da-DK: dansk (Danmark)
The current localization culture is da-DK: dansk (Danmark)
Days of the week: søndag, mandag, tirsdag, onsdag, torsdag, fredag,
lørdag
Months of the year: januar, februar, marts, april, maj, juni, juli,
august, september, oktober, november, december
1st day of this year: søndag den 1. januar 2023
Number group separator: .
Number decimal separator: ,
Currency symbol: kr.
Currency name: dansk krone (Danish Krone)
IsMetric: True

Enter your name: Mikkel
Enter your date of birth: 16/3/1980
Enter your salary: 65000
Mikkel was born on a søndag. Mikkel is 22.723.200 minutes old. Mikkel
earns 65.000,00 kr..
```

In this example, only the date and salary are globalized into Danish. The rest of the text is hardcoded as English. Later, we will translate that English text into other languages. For now, let's see some other differences between cultures.

6. Run the code again, and try Polish in Poland (pl-PL). Note that the grammar rules in Polish make the day number possessive for the month name, so the month styczeń becomes stycznia, as shown in the following output:

```
The current globalization culture is pl-PL: polski (Polska)
...
Months of the year: styczeń, luty, marzec, kwiecień, maj, czerwiec,
lipiec, sierpień, wrzesień, październik, listopad, grudzień
1st day of this year: niedziela, 1 stycznia 2023
...
Enter your name: Bob
Enter your date of birth: 1972/4/16
Enter your salary: 50000
Bob was born on a niedziela. Bob is 26 886 240 minutes old. Bob earns 50
000,00 zł.
```

7. Run the code again, and try Persian in Iran (`fa-IR`). Note that dates in Iran must be specified as year/month/day, and that this year (2023) is the year 1401 in the Persian calendar, as shown in the following output:

```
The current globalization culture is fa-IR: فارسی (ایران)
The current localization culture is fa-IR: فارسی (ایران)
Days of the week: یکشنبه, دوشنبه, سه‌شنبه, چهارشنبه, پنجشنبه, جمعه, شنبه
Months of the year: فروردین, اردیبهشت, خرداد, تیر, مرداد, شهریور, مهر, آبان, آذر, دی, بهمن, اسفند
1st day of this year: شنبه, 11 دی 1401
Number group separator: ,
Number decimal separator: ,
Currency symbol: ریال
Currency name: ریال ایران (Iranian Rial)
IsMetric: True


Enter your name: Cyrus
Enter your date of birth: 1372/4/16
Enter your salary: 50000
Cyrus was born on a چهارشنبه. Cyrus is 15,723,360 minutes old. Cyrus
earns ریال50,000.
```

 Although I tried to confirm with a Persian reader whether this example is correct, due to factors like right-to-left languages being tricky to work with in console apps and copying and pasting from a console window into a word processor, I apologize in advance to my Persian readers if this example is all messed up!

Temporarily using the invariant culture

Sometimes, you might need to temporarily use a different culture without switching the current thread to that culture. For example, when automatically generating documents, queries, and commands that include data values, you might need to ignore your current culture and use a more standardized culture. For this purpose, you can use the invariant culture, which is based on US English.

For example, you might need to generate a JSON document with a decimal number value and format the number with two decimal places, as shown in the following code:

```
decimal price = 54321.99M;
string document = $$"""
  {
    "price": "{{price:N2}}"
  }
  """;
```

If you were to execute this on a Slovenian computer, you would get the following output:

```
{
  "price": " 54.321,99"
}
```

If you then tried to insert this JSON document into a cloud database, it would fail because it would not understand the number format that uses commas for decimals and dots for groups.

So you can override the current culture and specify the invariant culture only when outputting the number as a `string` value, as shown in the following code:

```
decimal price = 54321.99M;
string document = $$"""
  {
    "price": "{{price.ToString("N2", CultureInfo.InvariantCulture)}}"
  }
  """;
```

If you were to execute this on a Slovenian (or any other culture) computer, you would now get the following output, which would be successfully recognized by a cloud database and not throw exceptions:

```
{
  "price": " 54,321.99"
}
```

Now, let's see how to translate text from one language to another so that the label prompts are in the correct language for the current culture.

Localizing your user interface

A localized application is divided into two parts:

- An assembly containing code that is the same for all locales and contains resources for when no other resource file is found.
- One or more assemblies that contain the user interface resources, which are different for different locales. These are known as **satellite assemblies**.

This model allows the initial application to be deployed with default invariant resources, and over time, additional satellite assemblies can be deployed as the resources are translated. In the coding task, you will create a console app with embedded invariant culture, and satellite assemblies for Danish, French, French-Canadian, Polish, and Iranian (Persian). To add more cultures in the future, just follow the same steps.

User interface resources include any text for messages, logs, dialog boxes, buttons, labels, or even filenames of images, videos, and so on. Resource files are XML files with the `.resx` extension. The filename includes a culture code, for example, `PacktResources.en-GB.resx` or `PacktResources.da-DK.resx`.

If a resource file or individual entry is missing, the automatic culture fallback search path for resources goes from specific culture (language and region) to neutral culture (language only) to invariant culture (supposedly independent but, basically, US English). If the current thread culture is en-AU (Australian English), then it will search for the resource file in the following order:

1. Australian English: `PacktResources.en-AU.resx`
2. Neutral English: `PacktResources.en.resx`
3. Invariant: `PacktResources.resx`

Defining and loading resources

To load resources from these satellite assemblies, we use some standard .NET types named `IStringLocalizer<T>` and `IStringLocalizerFactory`. Implementations of these are loaded from the .NET generic host as dependency services:

1. In the `WorkingWithCultures` project, add package references to Microsoft extensions to work with generic hosting and localization, as shown in the following markup:

    ```xml
    <ItemGroup>
      <PackageReference Include="Microsoft.Extensions.Hosting"
                        Version="8.0.0" />
      <PackageReference Include="Microsoft.Extensions.Localization"
                        Version="8.0.0" />
    </ItemGroup>
    ```

2. Build the `WorkingWithCultures` project to restore packages.
3. In the project folder, create a new folder named `Resources`.
4. In the `Resources` folder, add a new XML file named `PacktResources.resx`, and modify the contents to contain default invariant language resources (usually equivalent to US English), as shown in the following markup:

    ```xml
    <?xml version="1.0" encoding="utf-8"?>
    <root>
      <data name="EnterYourDob" xml:space="preserve">
        <value>Enter your date of birth: </value>
      </data>
      <data name="EnterYourName" xml:space="preserve">
        <value>Enter your name: </value>
      </data>
      <data name="EnterYourSalary" xml:space="preserve">
        <value>Enter your salary: </value>
      </data>
      <data name="PersonDetails" xml:space="preserve">
        <value>{0} was born on a {1:dddd}. {0} is {2:N0} minutes old. {0}
    earns {3:C}.</value>
    ```

```
      </data>
   </root>
```

5. In the `WorkingWithCultures` project folder, add a new class file named `PacktResources.cs` that will load text resources for the user interface, as shown in the following code:

```csharp
using Microsoft.Extensions.Localization; // To use IStringLocalizer and
so on.

public class PacktResources
{
  private readonly IStringLocalizer<PacktResources> localizer = null!;

  public PacktResources(IStringLocalizer<PacktResources> localizer)
  {
    this.localizer = localizer;
  }

  public string? GetEnterYourNamePrompt()
  {
    string resourceStringName = "EnterYourName";

    // 1. Get the LocalizedString object.
    LocalizedString localizedString = localizer[resourceStringName];

    // 2. Check if the resource string was found.
    if (localizedString.ResourceNotFound)
    {
      ConsoleColor previousColor = ForegroundColor;
      ForegroundColor = ConsoleColor.Red;
      WriteLine($"Error: resource string \"{resourceStringName}\" not
found."
        + Environment.NewLine
        + $"Search path: {localizedString.SearchedLocation}");
      ForegroundColor = previousColor;

      return $"{localizedString}: ";
    }
    // 3. Return the found resource string.
    return localizedString;
  }

  public string? GetEnterYourDobPrompt()
```

```
  {
    // LocalizedString has an implicit cast to string
    // that falls back to the key if the resource
    // string is not found.
    return localizer["EnterYourDob"];
  }

  public string? GetEnterYourSalaryPrompt()
  {
    return localizer["EnterYourSalary"];
  }

  public string? GetPersonDetails(
    string name, DateTime dob, int minutes, decimal salary)
  {
    return localizer["PersonDetails", name, dob, minutes, salary];
  }
}
```

For the GetEnterYourNamePrompt method, I broke the implementation down into steps to get useful information, like checking if the resource string is found and showing the search path if not. The other method implementations use a simplified fallback to the key name for the resource string if the resource is not found.

6. In Program.cs, at the top, import the namespaces to work with hosting and dependency injection, and then configure a host that enables localization and the PacktResources service, as shown in the following code:

```
using Microsoft.Extensions.Hosting; // To use IHost, Host.

// To use AddLocalization, AddTransient<T>.
using Microsoft.Extensions.DependencyInjection;

using IHost host = Host.CreateDefaultBuilder(args)
  .ConfigureServices(services =>
  {
    services.AddLocalization(options =>
    {
      options.ResourcesPath = "Resources";
    });

    services.AddTransient<PacktResources>();
```

```
    })
    .Build();
```

 Good Practice: By default, `ResourcesPath` is an empty string, meaning it looks for `.resx` files in the current directory. We are going to make the project tidier by putting resources into a subfolder.

7. After changing the current culture, add a statement to get the `PacktResources` service, and use it to output localized prompts for the user to enter their name, date of birth, and salary. Then, output their details, as highlighted in the following code:

```
OutputCultures("After changing the current culture");

PacktResources resources =
    host.Services.GetRequiredService<PacktResources>();

Write(resources.GetEnterYourNamePrompt());
string? name = ReadLine();
if (string.IsNullOrWhiteSpace(name))
{
  name = "Bob";
}

Write(resources.GetEnterYourDobPrompt());
string? dobText = ReadLine();

if (string.IsNullOrWhiteSpace(dobText))
{
  // If they do not enter a DOB then use
  // sensible defaults for their culture.
  dobText = ci.Name switch
    {
      "en-US" or "fr-CA" => "1/27/1990",
      "da-DK" or "fr-FR" or "pl-PL" => "27/1/1990",
      "fa-IR" => "1990/1/27",
      _ => "1/27/1990"
    };
}

Write(resources.GetEnterYourSalaryPrompt());
string? salaryText = ReadLine();
```

```
if (string.IsNullOrWhiteSpace(salaryText))
{
  salaryText = "34500";
}

DateTime dob = DateTime.Parse(dobText);
int minutes = (int)DateTime.Today.Subtract(dob).TotalMinutes;
decimal salary = decimal.Parse(salaryText);

WriteLine(resources.GetPersonDetails(name, dob, minutes, salary));
```

Testing globalization and localization

Now, we can run the console app and see the resources being loaded:

1. Run the console app and enter da-DK for the ISO code. Note that the prompts are in US English because we currently only have invariant culture resources.

     To save time and to make sure you have the correct structure, you can copy, paste, and rename the .resx files instead of creating empty new ones. Or you could copy these files from the GitHub repository for the book.

2. In the Resources folder, add a new XML file named PacktResources.da.resx, and modify the contents to contain non-region-specific Danish language resources, as shown in the following markup:

    ```xml
    <?xml version="1.0" encoding="utf-8"?>
    <root>
      <data name="EnterYourDob" xml:space="preserve">
        <value>Indtast din fødselsdato: </value>
      </data>
      <data name="EnterYourName" xml:space="preserve">
        <value>Indtast dit navn: </value>
      </data>
      <data name="EnterYourSalary" xml:space="preserve">
        <value>Indtast din løn: </value>
      </data>
      <data name="PersonDetails" xml:space="preserve">
        <value>{0} blev født på en {1:dddd}. {0} er {2:N0} minutter gammel.
    {0} tjener {3:C}.</value>
      </data>
    </root>
    ```

3. In the `Resources` folder, add a new XML file named `PacktResources.fr.resx`, and modify the contents to contain non-region-specific French language resources, as shown in the following markup:

```xml
<?xml version="1.0" encoding="utf-8"?>
<root>
  <data name="EnterYourDob" xml:space="preserve">
    <value>Entrez votre date de naissance: </value>
  </data>
  <data name="EnterYourName" xml:space="preserve">
    <value>Entrez votre nom: </value>
  </data>
  <data name="EnterYourSalary" xml:space="preserve">
    <value>Entrez votre salaire: </value>
  </data>
  <data name="PersonDetails" xml:space="preserve">
    <value>{0} est né un {1:dddd}. {0} a {2:N0} minutes. {0} gagne
{3:C}.</value>
  </data>
</root>
```

4. In the `Resources` folder, add a new XML file named `PacktResources.fr-CA.resx`, and modify the contents to contain the French language in Canada region resources, as shown in the following markup:

```xml
<?xml version="1.0" encoding="utf-8"?>
<root>
  <data name="EnterYourDob" xml:space="preserve">
    <value>Entrez votre date de naissance / Enter your date of birth: </
value>
  </data>
  <data name="EnterYourName" xml:space="preserve">
    <value>Entrez votre nom / Enter your name: </value>
  </data>
  <data name="EnterYourSalary" xml:space="preserve">
    <value>Entrez votre salaire / Enter your salary: </value>
  </data>
  <data name="PersonDetails" xml:space="preserve">
    <value>{0} est né un {1:dddd}. {0} a {2:N0} minutes. {0} gagne
{3:C}.</value>
  </data>
</root>
```

5. In the `Resources` folder, add a new XML file named `PacktResources.pl-PL.resx`, and modify the contents to contain the Polish language in Poland region resources, as shown in the following markup:

```xml
<?xml version="1.0" encoding="utf-8"?>
<root>
  <data name="EnterYourDob" xml:space="preserve">
    <value>Wpisz swoją datę urodzenia: </value>
  </data>
  <data name="EnterYourName" xml:space="preserve">
    <value>Wpisz swoje imię i nazwisko: </value>
  </data>
  <data name="EnterYourSalary" xml:space="preserve">
    <value>Wpisz swoje wynagrodzenie: </value>
  </data>
  <data name="PersonDetails" xml:space="preserve">
    <value>{0} urodził się na {1:dddd}. {0} ma {2:N0} minut. {0} zarabia
{3:C}.</value>
  </data>
</root>
```

6. In the `Resources` folder, add a new XML file named `PacktResources.fa-IR.resx`, and modify the contents to contain the Farsi language in Iranian region resources, as shown in the following markup:

```xml
<?xml version="1.0" encoding="utf-8"?>
<root>
  <data name="EnterYourDob" xml:space="preserve">
    <value>تاریخ تولد خود را وارد کنید / Enter your date of birth: </value>
  </data>
  <data name="EnterYourName" xml:space="preserve">
    <value>اسمت را وارد کن / Enter your name: </value>
  </data>
  <data name="EnterYourSalary" xml:space="preserve">
    <value>حقوق خود را وارد کنید / Enter your salary: </value>
  </data>
  <data name="PersonDetails" xml:space="preserve">
    <value>{0} دقیقه است. {0} {2:N0} به دنیا آمد. {1:dddd}به در {0}
{3:C}.</value>
  </data>
</root>
```

7. Run the code, and enter `da-DK` for the ISO code. Note that the prompts are in Danish, as shown in the following output:

```
The current localization culture is da-DK: dansk (Danmark)
...
Indtast dit navn: Bob
Indtast din fødselsdato: 3/4/1987
Indtast din løn: 45449
Bob blev født på en fredag. Bob er 19.016.640 minutter gammel. Bob tjener
45.449,00 kr.
```

8. Run the code, and enter `fr-FR` for the ISO code. Note that the prompts are in French only, as shown in the following output:

```
The current localization culture is fr-FR: français (France)
...
Entrez votre nom: Monique
Entrez votre date de naissance: 2/12/1990
Entrez votre salaire: 45000
Monique est né un dimanche. Monique a 17 088 480 minutes. Monique gagne
45 000,00 €.
```

9. Run the code, and enter `fr-CA` for the ISO code. Note that the prompts are in French and English because Canada might have a requirement to support both as official languages, as shown in the following output:

```
The current localization culture is fr-CA: français (Canada)
...
Entrez votre nom / Enter your name: Sophie
Entrez votre date de naissance / Enter your date of birth: 4/5/2001
Entrez votre salaire / Enter your salary: 65000
Sophie est né un jeudi. Sophie a 11 649 600 minutes. Sophie gagne 65
000,00 $ CA.
```

10. Run the code, and enter `fa-IR` for the ISO code. Note that the prompts are in Persian/Farsi and English, and there is the additional complication of a right-to-left language, as shown in the following output:

```
The current localization culture is fa-IR: فارسی (ایران)
...
اسم تان را وارد کن / Enter your name: Hoshyar
تاریخ تولد خود را وارد کنید / Enter your date of birth: 1370/3/6
حقوق خود را وارد کنید / Enter your salary: 90000
Hoshyar در چه روشنبه ای آمد. Hoshyar 11,190,240 دقیقه است. Hoshyar
ری ال90,000.
```

If you need to work with Persian dates, then there are NuGet packages with open-source GitHub repositories that you can try, although I cannot vouch for their correctness, like https://github.com/VahidN/DNTPersianUtils.Core and https://github.com/imanabidi/PersianDate.NET.

11. In the Resources folder, in PacktResources.da.resx, modify the contents to deliberately change the key for the prompt to enter your name, by appending Wrong, as highlighted in the following markup:

```xml
<?xml version="1.0" encoding="utf-8"?>
<root>
  <data name="EnterYourDob" xml:space="preserve">
    <value>Indtast din fødselsdato: </value>
  </data>
  <data name="EnterYourNameWrong" xml:space="preserve">
    <value>Indtast dit navn: </value>
  </data>
  <data name="EnterYourSalary" xml:space="preserve">
    <value>Indtast din løn: </value>
  </data>
  <data name="PersonDetails" xml:space="preserve">
    <value>{0} blev født på en {1:dddd}. {0} er {2:N0} minutter gammel.
{0} tjener {3:C}.</value>
  </data>
</root>
```

12. Run the code, and enter da-DK for the ISO code. Note that the prompts are in Danish, except for the Enter your name prompt in English, due to it falling back to the default resource file, as shown in the following output:

```
The current localization culture is da-DK: dansk (Danmark)
...
Enter your name: Bob
Indtast din fødselsdato: 3/4/1987
Indtast din løn: 45449
Bob blev født på en fredag. Bob er 18.413.280 minutter gammel. Bob tjener
45.449,00 kr.
```

13. In the Resources folder, in PacktResources.resx, modify the contents to deliberately change the key for the prompt to enter your name, by appending Wrong.

14. Run the code, and enter da-DK for the ISO code. Note that the prompts are in Danish, except for the Enter your name prompt, which shows an error and uses the key name as a last-resort fallback, as shown in the following output:

```
The current localization culture is da-DK: dansk (Danmark)
...
Error: resource string "EnterYourName" not found.
Search path: WorkingWithCultures.Resources.PacktResources
EnterYourName: Bob
Indtast din fødselsdato: 3/4/1987
Indtast din løn: 45449
Bob blev født på en fredag. Bob er 18.413.280 minutter gammel. Bob tjener
45.449,00 kr.
```

15. Remove the Wrong suffix in both resource files.

16. In **Solution Explorer**, toggle **Show All Files**, and expand the bin/Debug/net8.0/da folder, as shown in *Figure 7.1*:

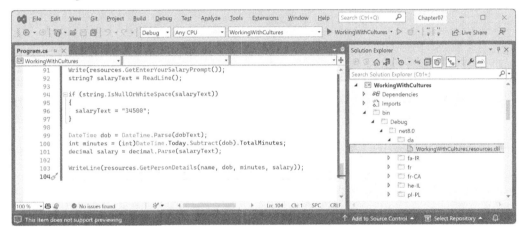

Figure 7.1: The satellite assembly folders for culture resources

17. Note the satellite assembly named WorkingWithCultures.resources.dll for the neutral Danish resources.

Any other culture resource assemblies are named the same but stored in folders that match the appropriate culture code. You can use tools like **ResX Resource Manager** (found at the following link: https://dotnetfoundation.org/projects/resx-resource-manager) to create many more .resx files, compile them into satellite assemblies, and then deploy them to users without needing to recompile the original console app.

 Good Practice: Consider whether your application needs to be internationalized, and plan for that before you start coding! Think about all the data that will need to be globalized (date formats, number formats, and sorting text behavior). Write down all the pieces of text in the user interface that will need to be localized.

Microsoft has an online tool (found at the following link: `https://www.microsoft.com/en-us/Language/`) that can help you translate text in your user interfaces, as shown in *Figure 7.2*:

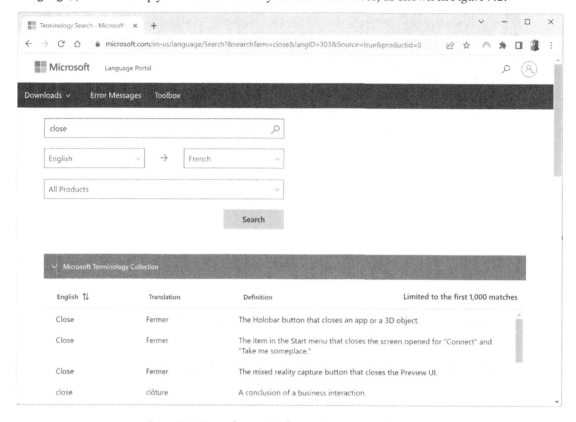

Figure 7.2: Microsoft user interface online text translation tool

We have now seen lots of date and time features provided by the .NET BCL. Does it provide everything we need to handle internationalization? Unfortunately, no. That's why you will likely want to use Noda Time.

Working with Noda Time

Noda Time is for developers who feel that the built-in libraries for handling dates and times are not good enough. Noda Time is like Joda Time, a replacement date/time handling library for Java.

> Noda Time 3.0 or later supports .NET Standard 2.0 and .NET 6 or later. This means that you can use it with legacy platforms like .NET Framework and Xamarin, as well as modern .NET.

To understand one of the core deficiencies with the built-in .NET date/time types, imagine that instead of defining separate types for numbers, like `int` (`System.Int32`), `double` (`System.Double`), and `decimal` (`System.Decimal`), the .NET team defined only a `System.Number` type with a property named `Kind` to indicate what kind of number it is, how it is stored in memory, how to handle it, and so on.

That is what the team did with System.DateTime. That type has a Kind property that indicates if it is a local time, UTC time, or unspecified. It varies in behavior depending on how you treat it. This makes date/time values as implemented in .NET fundamentally tricky to work with and understand.

 More Information: Jon Skeet, the creator of Noda Time, has a lot more to say about the limitations of date/time support in .NET and DateTime, specifically in a 2011 blog post found at the following link: https://blog.nodatime.org/2011/08/what-wrong-with-datetime-anyway.html

Important concepts and defaults in Noda Time

The built-in DateTime type stores both global and local values, or values that are unspecified. Unless treated with great care, this opens the door to subtle bugs and misunderstandings.

The first big difference with Noda Time is that it forces you to make a choice at the type level. Noda Time, therefore, has more types and, at first, can seem more confusing. Types in Noda Time are global or local. Every person anywhere in the world would share the same global values at the same instant, whereas each person would have a different local value, depending on factors like their time zone.

The built-in date/time types in .NET are only accurate to the tick, which is about 100 nanoseconds. Noda Time is accurate to 1 nanosecond, 100 times more accurate.

The "zero" baseline in Noda Time is midnight at the start of 1 January 1970 in the UTC time zone. The Noda Time Instant is the number of nanoseconds before (if a negative value) or since (if a positive value) that time and represents a point in time on the global timeline.

The default calendaring system in Noda Time is the ISO-8601 calendar because it is the standard, and you can read more about it at the following link: https://en.wikipedia.org/wiki/ISO_8601. Automatic conversions to other calendaring systems like Julian, Coptic, and Buddhist are supported.

Noda Time has some common types that are like some .NET date/time types, as summarized in *Table 7.6*:

Noda Time type	Description
Instant struct	Represents an instant on the global timeline, with nanosecond resolution.
Interval struct	Two Instant values, an inclusive start and an exclusive end.
LocalDateTime struct	A date/time value in a particular calendaring system, but it does not represent a fixed point on the global timeline. For example, midnight on New Year's Eve 2023 happens for different people in different time zones. If you do not know the user's time zone, you will likely have to use this type.
LocalDate and LocalTime structs	Like LocalDateTime struct but only the date or time part. When prompting the user to enter date and time values, you often start with them separately and then combine them into a single LocalDateTime struct.

DateTimeZone class	Represents a time zone. It is easy to convert from the .NET TimeZoneInfo using BclDateTimeZone. Use DateTimeZoneProviders.Tzdb to get a time zone, based on the standard names listed at the following link: https://en.wikipedia.org/wiki/List_of_tz_database_time_zones
ZonedDateTime struct	A date/time value in a particular calendaring system and in a specific time zone, so it does represent a fixed point on the global timeline.
Offset struct	Represents an offset. It is positive if the local time is ahead of UTC, and negative if the local time is behind UTC.
OffsetDateTime struct	You might know the offset from UTC, but that does not always cleanly map to a single time zone. This type should be used in this scenario instead of ZonedDateTime.
Duration struct	A fixed number of nanoseconds. Has properties to convert to common time units like Days, Hours, Minutes, and Seconds, rounded down or up to zero because they return an int, and non-rounded properties like TotalDays, TotalMinutes, and so on, because they return a double. Used for calculations on Instant and ZonedDateTime values. Use this instead of the .NET TimeSpan type.
Period class	A variable duration because the "two months" represented by January and February 2024 are different lengths to the "two months" of June and July 2024, or even the "two months" represented by January and February in a non-leap year (2024 is a leap year, so February 2024 has 29 days).

Table 7.6: Common Noda Time types

 Good Practice: Use Instant to record the point in time when something happened. It is good for timestamps. It can then be represented to the user in their local time zone. Common types used to record a user-entered date/time value are the following: ZonedDateTime, OffsetDateTime, LocalDateTime, LocalDate, and LocalTime.

Converting between Noda Time date/time types

To summarize common ways to convert between Noda Time types, review the following non-exhaustive diagram:

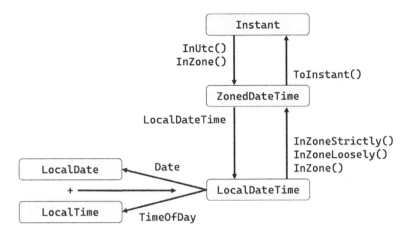

Figure 7.3: Common ways to convert between Noda Time date/time types

Exploring Node Time in a console app

Let's write some code:

1. Use your preferred code editor to add a new **Console App** / console project named WorkingWithNodaTime to the Chapter07 solution.

    -   In the project file, treat warnings as errors, then statically and globally import the System.Console class, and add a package reference for NodaTime, as shown in the following markup:

    ```xml
    <ItemGroup>
      <PackageReference Include="NodaTime" Version="3.1.9" />
    </ItemGroup>
    ```

2. Add a new class file named Program.Helpers.cs, and replace its contents, as shown in the following code:

    ```csharp
    partial class Program
    {
      private static void SectionTitle(string title)
      {
        ConsoleColor previousColor = ForegroundColor;
        ForegroundColor = ConsoleColor.DarkYellow;
        WriteLine($"*** {title}");
        ForegroundColor = previousColor;
      }
    }
    ```

3. In `Program.cs`, delete the existing statements, add statements to get the current instant in time, and convert it to various Noda Time types, including UTC, a couple of time zones, and local time, as shown in the following code:

```
using NodaTime; // To use SystemClock, Instant and so on.

SectionTitle("Converting Noda Time types");

// Get the current instant in time.
Instant now = SystemClock.Instance.GetCurrentInstant();

WriteLine($"Now (Instant): {now}");
WriteLine();

ZonedDateTime nowInUtc = now.InUtc();

WriteLine($"Now (DateTimeZone): {nowInUtc.Zone}");
WriteLine($"Now (ZonedDateTime): {nowInUtc}");
WriteLine($"Now (DST): {nowInUtc.IsDaylightSavingTime()}");
WriteLine();

// Use the Tzdb provider to get the time zone for US Pacific.
// To use .NET compatible time zones, use the Bcl provider.

DateTimeZone zonePT = DateTimeZoneProviders.Tzdb["US/Pacific"];
ZonedDateTime nowInPT = now.InZone(zonePT);

WriteLine($"Now (DateTimeZone): {nowInPT.Zone}");
WriteLine($"Now (ZonedDateTime): {nowInPT}");
WriteLine($"Now (DST): {nowInPT.IsDaylightSavingTime()}");
WriteLine();

DateTimeZone zoneUK = DateTimeZoneProviders.Tzdb["Europe/London"];
ZonedDateTime nowInUK = now.InZone(zoneUK);

WriteLine($"Now (DateTimeZone): {nowInUK.Zone}");
WriteLine($"Now (ZonedDateTime): {nowInUK}");
WriteLine($"Now (DST): {nowInUK.IsDaylightSavingTime()}");
WriteLine();

LocalDateTime nowInLocal = nowInUtc.LocalDateTime;
```

```
WriteLine($"Now (LocalDateTime): {nowInLocal}");
WriteLine($"Now (LocalDate): {nowInLocal.Date}");
WriteLine($"Now (LocalTime): {nowInLocal.TimeOfDay}");
WriteLine();
```

4. Run the console app, and note the results, including that "local" time does not take into account any DST offset; for example, in my case, living in the UK, I must use the London time zone to get British Summer Time (10:21am), not "local" time (9:21am), as shown in the following output:

```
*** Converting Noda Time types
Now (Instant): 2023-06-01T09:21:05Z

Now (DateTimeZone): UTC
Now (ZonedDateTime): 2023-06-01T09:21:05 UTC (+00)
Now (DST): False

Now (DateTimeZone): US/Pacific
Now (ZonedDateTime): 2023-06-01T02:21:05 US/Pacific (-07)
Now (DST): True

Now (DateTimeZone): Europe/London
Now (ZonedDateTime): 2023-06-01T10:21:05 Europe/London (+01)
Now (DST): True

Now (LocalDateTime): 01/06/2023 09:21:05
Now (LocalDate): 01 June 2023
Now (LocalTime): 09:21:05
```

5. In `Program.cs`, add statements to explore what can be done with periods of time, as shown in the following code:

```
SectionTitle("Working with periods");

// The modern .NET era began with the release of .NET Core 1.0
// on June 27, 2016 at 10am Pacific Time, or 5pm UTC.
LocalDateTime start = new(year: 2016, month: 6, day: 27,
  hour: 17, minute: 0, second: 0);
LocalDateTime end = LocalDateTime.FromDateTime(DateTime.UtcNow);

WriteLine("Modern .NET era");
WriteLine($"Start: {start}");
WriteLine($"End: {end}");
WriteLine();
```

```
Period period = Period.Between(start, end);

WriteLine($"Period: {period}");
WriteLine($"Years: {period.Years}");
WriteLine($"Months: {period.Months}");
WriteLine($"Weeks: {period.Weeks}");
WriteLine($"Days: {period.Days}");
WriteLine($"Hours: {period.Hours}");
WriteLine();

Period p1 = Period.FromWeeks(2);
Period p2 = Period.FromDays(14);

WriteLine($"p1 (period of two weeks): {p1}");
WriteLine($"p2 (period of 14 days): {p2}");
WriteLine($"p1 == p2: {p1 == p2}");
WriteLine($"p1.Normalize() == p2: {p1.Normalize() == p2}");
```

6. Run the console app and note the results, including that at the time of running the console app on 1 June 2023, the modern .NET era has lasted 6 years, 11 months, and 4 days, the serialization format for the Period type, and how two periods can be compared and should be normalized before the comparison, as shown in the following output:

```
*** Working with periods
Modern .NET era
Start: 27/06/2016 17:00:00
End: 01/06/2023 09:21:05

Period: P6Y11M4DT16H21M5S889s9240t
Years: 6
Months: 11
Weeks: 0
Days: 4
Hours: 16

p1 (period of two weeks): P2W
p2 (period of 14 days): P14D
p1 == p2: False
p1.Normalize() == p2: True
```

More Information: Normalizing a `Period` with the `Normalize` method means multiplying any weeks by 7 and adding them to the number of days, then setting `Weeks` to zero, and other calculations. Learn more at the following link: `https://nodatime.org/3.1.x/api/NodaTime.Period.html#NodaTime_Period_Normalize`

Unit testing and JSON serialization with Noda Time

Noda Time has two optional packages to write unit tests (`NodaTime.Testing`) and work with JSON.NET (`NodaTime.Serialization.JsonNet`).

The documentation for Noda Time is found at the following link: `https://nodatime.org/`

Practicing and exploring

Test your knowledge and understanding by answering some questions, getting some hands-on practice, and exploring the topics in this chapter with deeper research.

Exercise 7.1 – Test your knowledge

Use the web to answer the following questions:

1. What is the difference between localization, globalization, and internationalization?
2. What is the smallest measurement of time available in .NET?
3. How long is a "tick" in .NET?
4. In what scenario might you use a `DateOnly` value instead of a `DateTime` value?
5. For a time zone, what does its `BaseUtcOffset` property tell you?
6. How can you get information about the local time zone in which your code executes?
7. For a `DateTime` value, what does its `Kind` property tell you?
8. How can you control the current culture for your executing code?
9. What is the ISO culture code for Welsh?
10. How do localization resource file fallbacks work?

Exercise 7.2 – Explore topics

Use the links on the following page to learn more details about the topics covered in this chapter:

`https://github.com/markjprice/apps-services-net8/blob/main/docs/book-links.md#chapter-7---handling-dates-times-and-internationalization`

Exercise 7.3 – Learn from expert Jon Skeet

Jon Skeet is a world-renowned expert on internationalization. Watch him present *Working with Time is Easy* at the following link: `https://www.youtube.com/watch?v=saeKBuPewcU`

Summary

In this chapter, you:

- Explored dates and times, including the .NET 8 `TimeProvider` to improve unit tests.
- Learned how to handle time zones.
- Learned how to internationalize your code using globalization and localization.
- Explored some of the features of Noda Time.

In the next chapter, you will learn how to build web services using the ASP.NET Core Minimal API, and how to secure and protect them.

8

Building and Securing Web Services Using Minimal APIs

This chapter is about building and securing web services using ASP.NET Core Minimal APIs. This includes implementing techniques to protect a web service from attacks as well as authentication and authorization.

This chapter will cover the following topics:

- Building web services using ASP.NET Core Minimal APIs
- Relaxing the same origin security policy using CORS
- Preventing denial of service attacks using rate limiting
- Improving startup time and resources using native AOT
- Understanding identity services

Building web services using ASP.NET Core Minimal APIs

In older versions of ASP.NET Core, you would build a web service using controllers with an action method for each endpoint, a bit like building a website with ASP.NET Core MVC using controllers and models but without the views. Since .NET 6, you have another, often better, choice: **ASP.NET Core Minimal APIs**.

Benefits of Minimal API-based web services

In earlier versions of ASP.NET Core, implementing even a simple web service required a lot of boiler-plate code compared to alternative web development platforms. For example, a minimal Hello World web service implementation that has a single endpoint that returns plain text could be implemented using **Express.js** in just nine lines of code, as shown in the following code:

```
const express = require('express')
const app = express()
```

```
const port = 3000

app.get('/', (req, res) => {
  res.send('Hello World!')
})

app.listen(port, () => {
  console.log(`Example app listening on port ${port}`)
})
```

With ASP.NET Core 5 or earlier, that would require more than fifty lines of code!

The equivalent using ASP.NET Core 6 or later using ASP.NET Core Minimal APIs is now only five lines of code and six lines of configuration, as shown in the following two code blocks:

```
int port = 3000;
var app = WebApplication.Create();
app.MapGet("/", () => "Hello World!");
Console.WriteLine($"Example app listening on port {port}");
await app.RunAsync($"https://localhost:{port}/");
```

The platform is specified in the project file, and the implicit using statements SDK feature does some heavy lifting. It is enabled by default, as shown highlighted in the following markup:

```
<Project Sdk="Microsoft.NET.Sdk.Web">
  <PropertyGroup>
    <TargetFramework>net8.0</TargetFramework>
    <ImplicitUsings>enable</ImplicitUsings>
  </PropertyGroup>
</Project>
```

Good Practice: Another benefit of minimal APIs is that they do not use dynamically generated code, unlike controller-based Web APIs. This allows them to use native AOT to produce smaller, faster services that are better for implementing and hosting microservices in containers. We will cover native AOT with minimal APIs later in this chapter. Whenever possible, implement your web services using minimal APIs instead of controllers.

Understanding Minimal API route mappings

The WebApplication instance has methods that you can call to map a route to a lambda expression or statement:

- MapGet: Map a route to a GET request to retrieve an entity.
- MapPost: Map a route to a POST request to insert an entity.
- MapPut: Map a route to a PUT request to update an entity.

- MapPatch: Map a route to a PATCH request to update an entity.
- MapDelete: Map a route to a DELETE request to delete an entity.
- MapMethods: Map a route to any other HTTP method or methods, for example, CONNECT or HEAD.

For example, you might want to map an HTTP GET request for the relative path api/customers to a delegate defined by a lambda expression or a function that returns a JSON document containing a list of customers, and equivalent mappings to insert and delete, as shown in the following code:

```
app.MapGet("api/customers", GetCustomers);
app.MapPost("api/customers", InsertCustomer);
app.MapDelete("api/customers/{id}", DeleteCustomer);
```

You might want to map an HTTP CONNECT request for the relative path api/customers to a lambda statement block, as shown in the following code:

```
app.MapMethods("api/customers", new[] { "CONNECT" }, () =>
  {
    // Do something.
  });
```

If you have multiple endpoints that share a common relative path, then you can define a **route group**. The MapGroup method was introduced in .NET 7:

```
RouteGroupBuilder group = app.MapGroup("api/customers")


group.MapGet("/", GetCustomers)
  .MapGet("/{id}", GetCustomerById)
  .MapPost("/", InsertCustomer)
  .MapDelete("/{id}", DeleteCustomer);
```

 More Information: You can learn more about mapping routes at the following link: https://learn.microsoft.com/en-us/aspnet/core/fundamentals/minimal-apis/route-handlers.

Understanding parameter mapping

The delegate can have parameters defined that can be set automatically. Although most mappings can be configured without explicitly being specified, you can optionally use attributes to define where ASP.NET Core Minimal APIs should set the parameter values from:

- [FromServices]: The parameter will be set from the registered dependency services.
- [FromRoute]: The parameter will be set from a matching named route segment.
- [FromQuery]: The parameter will be set from a matching named query string parameter.
- [FromBody]: The parameter will be set from the body of the HTTP request.

For example, to update an entity in a database, you would need a database context to be retrieved from the registered dependency services, an identifier passed as a query string or route segment, and the new entity in the body of the request, as shown in the following code:

```
app.MapPut("api/customers/{id}", async (
  [FromServices] NorthwindContext db,
  [FromRoute] string id, // or [FromQuery] string id,
  [FromBody] Customer customer) =>
{
  Customer? existingCustomer = await db.Customers.FindAsync(id);
  ...
});
```

Understanding return values

A minimal API service can return data in some common formats, as shown in *Table 8.1*:

Type	Lambda
Plain text	`() => "Hello World!"`
	`() => Results.Text("Hello World!")`
JSON document	`() => new { FirstName = "Bob", LastName = "Jones" }`
	`() => Results.Json(new { FirstName = "Bob", LastName = "Jones" })`
IResult with status codes	`() => Results.Ok(new { FirstName = "Bob", LastName = "Jones" })`
	`() => Results.NoContent()`
	`() => Results.Redirect("new/path")`
	`() => Results.NotFound()`
	`() => Results.BadRequest()`
	`() => Results.Problem()`
	`() => Results.StatusCode(405)`
File	`() => Results.File("/path/filename.ext")`

Table 8.1: Examples of minimal API return values

Documenting a Minimal APIs service

You can call additional methods as many times as you need to specify what return types and status codes can be expected from an endpoint, for example:

- `Produces<T>(StatusCodes.Status200OK)`: When successful, this route returns a response containing a type T and status code 200.
- `Produces(StatusCodes.Status404NotFound)`: When no match for the route is found, this route returns an empty response and status code 404.

Setting up an ASP.NET Core Web API project

First, we will create a simple ASP.NET Core Web API project that we will later protect using various techniques like rate limiting, CORS, and authentication and authorization.

The API for this web service is defined as shown in *Table 8.2*:

Method	Path	Request body	Response body	Success code
GET	/	None	Hello World!	200
GET	/api/products	None	Array of in-stock Product objects	200
GET	/api/products/outofstock	None	Array of out-of-stock Product objects	200
GET	/api/products/discontinued	None	Array of discontinued Product objects	200
GET	/api/products/{id}	None	Product object	200
GET	/api/products/{name}	None	Array of Product objects that contain the name	200
POST	/api/products	Product object (no Id value)	Product object	201
PUT	/api/products/{id}	Product object	None	204
DELETE	/api/products/{id}	None	None	204

Table 8.2: API methods implemented by the example project

Let's go:

1. Use your preferred code editor to create a new solution named Chapter08.

2. Add a Web API project, as defined in the following list:

    *   Project template: **ASP.NET Core Web API** / webapi
    *   Solution file and folder: Chapter08
    *   Project file and folder: Northwind.WebApi.Service
    *   **Authentication type: None.**
    *   **Configure for HTTPS:** Selected.
    *   **Enable Docker:** Cleared.
    *   **Enable OpenAPI support:** Selected.
    *   **Do not use top-level statements:** Cleared.
    *   **Use controllers:** Cleared.

To create a Web API project using minimal APIs with `dotnet new` for pre-.NET 8 SDKs, you must use either the `-minimal` switch or the `--use-minimal-apis` switch. For .NET 8 SDKs, minimal APIs are the default and to use controllers, you must specify the `--use-controllers` or `-controllers` switch.

Warning! If you are using JetBrains Rider, its user interface might not yet have an option to create a web API project using minimal APIs. I recommend creating the project using `dotnet new` and then adding the project to your solution.

3. Add a project reference to the Northwind database context project for SQL Server that you created in *Chapter 3, Building Entity Models for SQL Server Using EF Core*, as shown in the following markup:

    ```
    <ItemGroup>
      <ProjectReference Include="..\..\Chapter03\Northwind.Common.DataContext
    .SqlServer\Northwind.Common.DataContext.SqlServer.csproj" />
    </ItemGroup>
    ```

The path cannot have a line break. If you did not complete the task of creating the class libraries in *Chapter 3*, then download the solution projects from the GitHub repository.

4. In the project file, change `invariantGlobalization` to `false`, and treat warnings as errors, as shown in the following markup:

    ```
    <Project Sdk="Microsoft.NET.Sdk.Web">

      <PropertyGroup>
        <TargetFramework>net8.0</TargetFramework>
        <Nullable>enable</Nullable>
        <ImplicitUsings>enable</ImplicitUsings>
        <InvariantGlobalization>false</InvariantGlobalization>
        <TreatWarningsAsErrors>true</TreatWarningsAsErrors>
      </PropertyGroup>
    ```

```
app.MapGet("api/products", (
  [FromServices] NorthwindContext db,
  [FromQuery] int? page) =>
  db.Products
    .Where(p => p.UnitsInStock > 0 && !p.Discontinued)
    .OrderBy(product => product.ProductId)
    .Skip(((page ?? 1) - 1) * pageSize)
    .Take(pageSize)
  )
  .WithName("GetProducts")
  .WithOpenApi(operation =>
  {
    operation.Description =
      "Get products with UnitsInStock > 0 and Discontinued = false.";
    operation.Summary = "Get in-stock products that are not
discontinued.";
    return operation;
  })
  .Produces<Product[]>(StatusCodes.Status200OK);

app.MapGet("api/products/outofstock",
  ([FromServices] NorthwindContext db) => db.Products
    .Where(p => p.UnitsInStock == 0 && !p.Discontinued)
  )
  .WithName("GetProductsOutOfStock")
  .WithOpenApi()
  .Produces<Product[]>(StatusCodes.Status200OK);

app.MapGet("api/products/discontinued",
  ([FromServices] NorthwindContext db) =>
    db.Products.Where(product => product.Discontinued)
  )
  .WithName("GetProductsDiscontinued")
  .WithOpenApi()
  .Produces<Product[]>(StatusCodes.Status200OK);

app.MapGet("api/products/{id:int}",
  async Task<Results<Ok<Product>, NotFound>> (
  [FromServices] NorthwindContext db,
  [FromRoute] int id) =>
```

```
        await db.Products.FindAsync(id) is Product product ?
            TypedResults.Ok(product) : TypedResults.NotFound())
    .WithName("GetProductById")
    .WithOpenApi()
    .Produces<Product>(StatusCodes.Status200OK)
    .Produces(StatusCodes.Status404NotFound);

    app.MapGet("api/products/{name}", (
        [FromServices] NorthwindContext db,
        [FromRoute] string name) =>
          db.Products.Where(p => p.ProductName.Contains(name)))
    .WithName("GetProductsByName")
    .WithOpenApi()
    .Produces<Product[]>(StatusCodes.Status200OK);

    return app;
  }
}
```

10. In `WebApplication.Extensions.cs`, define an extension method for the `WebApplication` class to configure a response to the HTTP POST request documented in the API table, as shown in the following code:

```
public static WebApplication MapPosts(this WebApplication app)
{
  app.MapPost("api/products", async ([FromBody] Product product,
    [FromServices] NorthwindContext db) =>
  {
    db.Products.Add(product);
    await db.SaveChangesAsync();
    return Results.Created($"api/products/{product.ProductId}", product);
  }).WithOpenApi()
    .Produces<Product>(StatusCodes.Status201Created);

  return app;
}
```

11. In `WebApplication.Extensions.cs`, define an extension method for the `WebApplication` class to configure a response to the HTTP PUT request documented in the API table, as shown in the following code:

```
public static WebApplication MapPuts(this WebApplication app)
{
```

```
      app.MapPut("api/products/{id:int}", async (
        [FromRoute] int id,
        [FromBody] Product product,
        [FromServices] NorthwindContext db) =>
      {

        Product? foundProduct = await db.Products.FindAsync(id);

        if (foundProduct is null) return Results.NotFound();

        foundProduct.ProductName = product.ProductName;
        foundProduct.CategoryId = product.CategoryId;
        foundProduct.SupplierId = product.SupplierId;
        foundProduct.QuantityPerUnit = product.QuantityPerUnit;
        foundProduct.UnitsInStock = product.UnitsInStock;
        foundProduct.UnitsOnOrder = product.UnitsOnOrder;
        foundProduct.ReorderLevel = product.ReorderLevel;
        foundProduct.UnitPrice = product.UnitPrice;
        foundProduct.Discontinued = product.Discontinued;

        await db.SaveChangesAsync();

        return Results.NoContent();
      }).WithOpenApi()
        .Produces(StatusCodes.Status404NotFound)
        .Produces(StatusCodes.Status204NoContent);

      return app;
    }
```

12. In `WebApplication.Extensions.cs`, define an extension method for the `WebApplication` class to configure a response to the HTTP `DELETE` request documented in the API table, as shown in the following code:

```
    public static WebApplication MapDeletes(this WebApplication app)
    {
      app.MapDelete("api/products/{id:int}", async (
        [FromRoute] int id,
        [FromServices] NorthwindContext db) =>
      {
        if (await db.Products.FindAsync(id) is Product product)
        {
          db.Products.Remove(product);
```

```
        await db.SaveChangesAsync();
        return Results.NoContent();
      }
      return Results.NotFound();
    }).WithOpenApi()
      .Produces(StatusCodes.Status404NotFound)
      .Produces(StatusCodes.Status204NoContent);

    return app;
  }
```

13. In `Program.cs`, import the namespace to use the extension methods you just defined, as shown in the following code:

```
using Packt.Extensions; // To use MapGets and so on.
```

14. In `Program.cs`, before the call to `app.Run()`, call your custom extension methods to map `GET`, `POST`, `PUT`, and `DELETE` requests, noting that you can override the default page size of 10 entities when requesting all products, as shown in the following code:

```
app.MapGets() // Default pageSize: 10.
   .MapPosts()
   .MapPuts()
   .MapDeletes();
```

15. In `Program.cs`, make sure the last statement in the file runs the web app, as shown in the following code:

```
app.Run();
```

Testing web services using Swagger

Now we can start the web service, see its documentation using Swagger, and perform basic manual testing:

1. If your database server is not running (for example, because you are hosting it in Docker, a virtual machine, or in the cloud), then make sure to start it.

2. Start the web service project using the `https` profile:

   - If you are using Visual Studio 2022, then select the **https** profile in the drop-down list and then navigate to **Debug | Start Without Debugging** or press *Ctrl + F5*. A web browser should navigate to the Swagger documentation web page automatically.

   - If you are using Visual Studio Code, then enter the command `dotnet run --launch-profile https`, manually start a web browser, and navigate to the Swagger documentation web page: `https://localhost:5081/swagger`.

On Windows, if prompted to do so, you will have to set Windows Defender Firewall to allow access to your local web service.

3. In the console or terminal, note the information about your web service, as shown in the following output:

```
info: Microsoft.Hosting.Lifetime[14]
      Now listening on: https://localhost:5081
info: Microsoft.Hosting.Lifetime[0]
      Application started. Press Ctrl+C to shut down.
info: Microsoft.Hosting.Lifetime[0]
      Hosting environment: Development
info: Microsoft.Hosting.Lifetime[0]
      Content root path: C:\apps-services-net8\Chapter08\Northwind.
WebApi.Service
```

4. In your web browser, note the Swagger documentation, as shown in *Figure 8.1*:

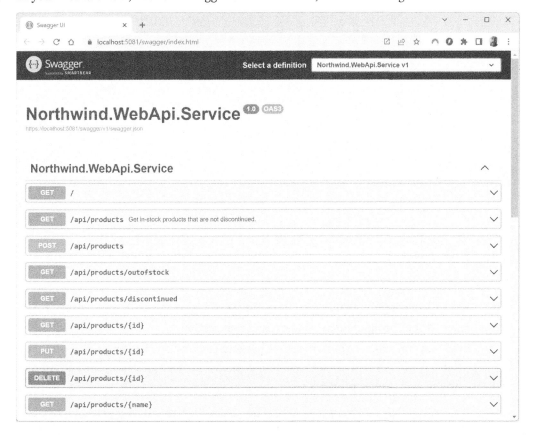

Figure 8.1: Swagger documentation for the Northwind Web API service

5. Click **GET /api/products** to expand that section.

6. Click the **Try it out** button, note the optional query string parameter named **page**, and then click the **Execute** button.

7. Note the response includes the first ten products that are in stock and not discontinued: 1, 2, 3, 4, 6, 7, 8, 10, 11, and 12.

8. For the **page** parameter, enter 3, and then click the **Execute** button.

9. Note the response includes the third page of ten products that are in stock and are not discontinued: 25, 26, 27, 30, 32, 33, 34, 35, 36, and 37.

10. Click **GET /api/products** to collapse that section.

11. Try executing the **GET /api/products/outofstock** path and note it returns one product, **31 Gorgonzola Telino**, which has zero units in stock and is not discontinued.

12. Try executing the **GET /api/products/discontinued** path and note it returns eight products, 5, 9, 17, 24, 28, 29, 42, and 53, which all have their Discontinued properties set to true.

13. Click **GET /api/products/{id}** to expand that section.

14. Click **Try it out**, enter the required **id** parameter as 77, click **Execute**, and note the response contains the product named **Original Frankfurter grüne Soße**, as shown in the following JSON document:

    ```
    {
        "productId": 77,
        "productName": "Original Frankfurter grüne Soße",
        "supplierId": 12,
        "categoryId": 2,
        "quantityPerUnit": "12 boxes",
        "unitPrice": 13,
        "unitsInStock": 32,
        "unitsOnOrder": 0,
        "reorderLevel": 15,
        "discontinued": false,
        "category": null,
        "supplier": null,
        "orderDetails": []
    }
    ```

15. Click **GET /api/products/{id}** to collapse that section.

16. Click **GET /api/products/{name}** to expand that section.

17. Click **Try it out**, enter the required **name** parameter as man, click **Execute**, and note the response contains the products named **Queso Manchego La Pastora** and **Manjimup Dried Apples**.

18. Leave the web service running.

Testing web services with code editor tools

Using the Swagger user interface to test web services can quickly get clumsy. A better tool is either the Visual Studio Code extension named **REST Client** or the **Endpoints Explorer** and `.http` file support available with Visual Studio 2022 version 17.6 or later.

> **More Information:** You can learn about Visual Studio 2022 and its HTTP editor at the following link: `https://learn.microsoft.com/en-us/aspnet/core/test/http-files`.

JetBrains Rider has a similar tool window named **Endpoints**.

> If you are using JetBrains Rider, you can read about its tools for HTTP files at the following link: `https://www.jetbrains.com/help/rider/Http_client_in__product__code_editor.html`. It is slightly different from the other two code editors. In particular, how Rider handles setting variables is more awkward, as shown at the following link: `https://www.jetbrains.com/help/rider/Exploring_HTTP_Syntax.html#example-working-with-environment-files`. You might prefer to use Visual Studio Code with the REST Client extension for this section.

Let's see how these help us test a web service:

1. Make sure you have the web service testing tools installed:

    - If you are using Visual Studio 2022, then make sure you have version 17.6 or later (released in May 2023).
    - If you are using Visual Studio Code, then make sure you have installed the REST Client extension by Huachao Mao (`humao.rest-client`).
    - If you are using Visual Studio 2022, navigate to **View** | **Other Windows** | **Endpoints Explorer**, and note the current project is scanned for potential Web API endpoints, as shown in *Figure 8.2*.

2. In your preferred code editor, start the `Northwind.WebApi.Service` project using the `https` profile (if it is not already running) and leave it running.

3. In the `apps-services-net8` folder, if it does not already exist, create an `HttpRequests` folder.

4. In the `HttpRequests` folder, create a file named `webapi-get-products.http` and modify its contents to declare a variable to hold the base address of the Web API service products endpoint and a request to get the first page of ten products, as shown in the following code:

```
### Configure a variable for the web service base address.
@base_address = https://localhost:5081/api/products/

### Get first page of 10 products that are in stock and not discontinued.
GET {{base_address}}
```

Good Practice: REST Client does not require GET at the beginning of a request because it will assume GET as the default. But at the time of writing, Visual Studio's HTTP editor requires GET to be explicitly specified. For now, I recommend that you specify the HTTP method for all tools, and I will do so for all `.http` files for my books.

5. Click **Send Request**, and note the response is the same as what was returned by Swagger, a JSON document response containing the first ten products that are in stock and not discontinued, as shown in Visual Studio 2022 in *Figure 8.2* and Visual Studio Code in *Figure 8.3*:

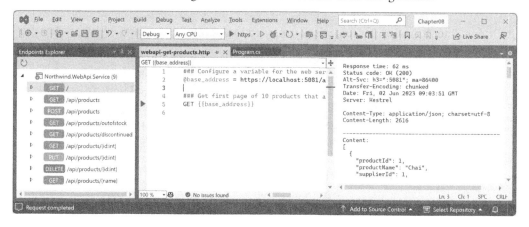

Figure 8.2: Visual Studio 2022 getting products from the web API service

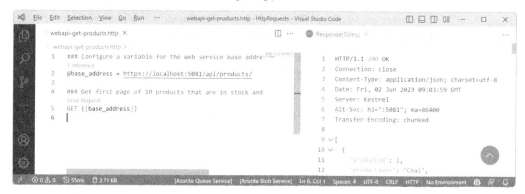

Figure 8.3: Visual Studio Code REST Client getting products from the web API service

6. In `webapi-get-products.http`, add more requests separated by ###, as shown in the following file:

```
### Get third page of 10 products that are in stock and not discontinued
GET {{base_address}}?page=3
```

```
### Get products that are out-of-stock but not discontinued
GET {{base_address}}outofstock

### Get products that are discontinued
GET {{base_address}}discontinued

### Get product 77
GET {{base_address}}77

### Get products that contain "man"
GET {{base_address}}man
```

 You can execute an HTTP request in Visual Studio 2022 by clicking the green triangle "play" button, by right-clicking and selecting **Send Request**, or by pressing *Ctrl + Alt + S*. In Visual Studio Code, click **Send Request** above each query, or navigate to **View** | **Command Palette** and select **Rest Client: Send Request**, or use its keyboard shortcut (*Ctrl + Alt + R* on Windows).

7. In the HttpRequests folder, create a file named webapi-insert-product.http and modify its contents to contain a **POST** request to insert a new product, as shown in the following code:

```
POST https://localhost:5081/api/products/
Content-Type: application/json

{
  "productName": "Harry's Hamburgers",
  "supplierId": 7,
  "categoryId": 6,
  "quantityPerUnit": "6 per box",
  "unitPrice": 24.99,
  "unitsInStock": 0,
  "unitsOnOrder": 20,
  "reorderLevel": 10,
  "discontinued": false
}
```

8. Click **Send Request**, and note the response indicates that the new product was added successful-
    ly because the status code is 201, and its location includes its product ID, as shown in *Figure 8.4*:

Figure 8.4: REST Client inserting a new product by calling the web API service

> Originally, there were 77 products in the Northwind database. The next product
> ID would be 78. The actual product ID assigned automatically will depend on
> whether you have previously added any other products, so your assigned number
> might be higher.

9. In the HttpRequests folder, create a file named webapi-update-product.http and modify its
    contents to contain a PUT request to update the product with ID 78 (or whatever number was
    assigned to your Harry's Hamburgers) with a different quantity per unit, unit price, and units
    in stock, as shown in the following code:

```
PUT https://localhost:5081/api/products/78
Content-Type: application/json

{
  "productName": "Harry's Hamburgers",
  "supplierId": 7,
  "categoryId": 6,
  "quantityPerUnit": "12 per box",
  "unitPrice": 44.99,
  "unitsInStock": 50,
  "unitsOnOrder": 20,
  "reorderLevel": 10,
  "discontinued": false
}
```

10. Send the request and note you should get a 204 status code in the response, meaning a suc-
    cessful update.

11. Confirm the product was updated by executing a GET request for the product ID.

12. In the HttpRequests folder, create a file named webapi-delete-product.http and modify its contents to contain a DELETE request for the new product, as shown in the following code:

```
DELETE https://localhost:5081/api/products/78
```

13. Note the successful response, as shown in *Figure 8.5*:

Figure 8.5: Deleting a product using the Web API service

14. Send the request again and note the response contains a 404 status code because the product has now been deleted.

15. Shut down the web server.

Excluding paths from OpenAPI documentation

Sometimes you want to have a path that works but is not shown in the Swagger documentation. Let's see how to remove the service base address that returns a plain text Hello World! response from the Swagger documentation web page:

1. In WebApplication.Extensions.cs, for the root path that returns Hello World, exclude it from the OpenAPI documentation, as shown highlighted in the following code:

```
app.MapGet("/", () => "Hello World!")
    .ExcludeFromDescription();
```

2. Start the Northwind.WebApi.Service project using the https profile without debugging and note the path is now not documented.

We have a working web service implemented using ASP.NET Core Minimal APIs. Now let's attack it! (So that we can learn how to prevent those attacks.)

Visual Studio 2022 scaffolding for Minimal APIs

It is important to learn how to implement a service using minimal APIs from scratch so that you properly understand it. But once you know how to do it manually, the process can be automated and the boilerplate code can be written for you, especially if you are building a web API that wraps an EF Core entity model.

For example, Visual Studio 2022 has a project item template named **API with read/write endpoints, using Entity Framework** that allows you to select:

- An entity model class like `Customer`.
- An endpoints class that will contain all the mapping methods.
- A `DbContext`-derived class like `NorthwindContext`.
- A database provider like SQLite or SQL Server.

More Information: You can learn more about this project item template at the following link: `https://devblogs.microsoft.com/visualstudio/web-api-development-in-visual-studio-2022/#scaffolding-in-visual-studio/`.

Relaxing the same origin security policy using CORS

Modern web browsers support multiple tabs so users can visit multiple websites at the same time efficiently. If code executing in one tab could access resources in another tab, then that could be a vector of attack.

All web browsers implement a security feature called the **same origin policy**. This means that only requests that come from the same origin are allowed. For example, if a block of JavaScript is served from the same origin that hosts a web service or served an `<iframe>`, then that JavaScript can call the service and access the data in the `<iframe>`. If a request is made from a different origin, then the request fails. But what counts as the "same origin?"

An origin is defined by:

- **Scheme** aka protocol, for example, `http` or `https`.
- **Port**, for example, `801` or `5081`. The default port for `http` is `80` and for `https` is `443`.
- **Host/domain/subdomain**, for example, `www.example.com`, `www.example.net`, `example.com`.

If the origin is `https://www.example.com/about-us/`, then the following are *not* the same origin:

- Different scheme: `http://www.example.com/about-us/`
- Different host/domain: `https://www.example.co.uk/about-us/`
- Different subdomain: `https://careers.example.com/about-us/`
- Different port: `https://www.example.com:444/about-us/`

It is the web browser that sets the `Origin` header automatically when making a request. This cannot be overridden.

Warning! The same origin policy does *not* apply to any requests that come from a non-web browser because, in those cases, the programmer could change the `Origin` header anyway. If you create a console app or even an ASP.NET Core project that uses .NET classes like `HttpClient` to make a request, the same origin policy does not apply unless you explicitly set the `Origin` header.

Let's see some examples of calling the web service from a web page with a different origin and from a .NET app.

Configuring HTTP logging for the web service

First, let's enable HTTP logging for the web service and configure it to show the origin of requests:

1. In the `Northwind.WebApi.Service` project, add a new class file named `IServiceCollection.Extensions.cs`.

2. In `IServiceCollection.Extensions.cs`, import the namespace for controlling which HTTP fields are logged, and then define an extension method for the `IServiceCollection` interface to add HTTP logging, including the `Origin` header and all fields including the response body, as shown in the following code:

    ```
    using Microsoft.AspNetCore.HttpLogging; // To use HttpLoggingFields.

    namespace Packt.Extensions;

    public static class IServiceCollectionExtensions
    {
      public static IServiceCollection AddCustomHttpLogging(
        this IServiceCollection services)
      {
        services.AddHttpLogging(options =>
        {
          // Add the Origin header so it will not be redacted.
          options.RequestHeaders.Add("Origin");

          // By default, the response body is not included.
          options.LoggingFields = HttpLoggingFields.All;
        });

        return services;
      }
    }
    ```

3. In `Program.cs`, before the call to `builder.Build()`, add a statement to add custom HTTP logging, as shown in the following code:

    ```
    builder.Services.AddCustomHttpLogging();
    ```

4. In `Program.cs`, after the call to `UseHttpsRedirection()`, add a statement to use HTTP logging, as shown in the following code:

    ```
    app.UseHttpLogging();
    ```

5. In `appsettings.Development.json`, add an entry to set the level for HTTP logging to `Information`, as shown highlighted in the following configuration:

```json
{
  "Logging": {
    "LogLevel": {
      "Default": "Information",
      "Microsoft.AspNetCore": "Warning",

      // To enable logging HTTP requests, this must be
      // set to Information (3) or higher.
      "Microsoft.AspNetCore.HttpLogging": "Information"
    }
  }
}
```

Good Practice: The JSON specification does not allow comments but the JSON with Comments format does. You can use JavaScript-style comments using // or /* */. You can read more at the following link: `https://code.visualstudio.com/docs/languages/json#_json-with-comments`. If you are using a fussy code editor, just delete the comment I added above.

Creating a web page JavaScript client

Next, let's create a web page client that will attempt to use JavaScript on a different port to call the web service:

1. Use your preferred code editor to add a new project, as defined in the following list:

- Project template: **ASP.NET Core Web App (Model-View-Controller)** / `mvc`
- Solution file and folder: `Chapter08`
- Project file and folder: `Northwind.WebApi.Client.Mvc`
- Other Visual Studio 2022 options:
    - **Authentication Type: None.**
    - **Configure for HTTPS:** Selected.
    - **Enable Docker:** Cleared.
    - **Do not use top-level statements:** Cleared.
    - In Visual Studio 2022, configure the startup project to be the current selection.

2. In the `Northwind.WebApi.Client.Mvc` project, in the `Properties` folder, in `launchSettings.json`, change the `applicationUrl` for the `https` profile to use port `5082`, as shown in the following markup:

```
"applicationUrl": "https://localhost:5082",
```

3. In the `Northwind.WebApi.Client.Mvc` project file, treat warnings as errors.

4. In the `Views/Home` folder, in `Index.cshtml`, replace the existing markup with the markup below, which has a link to a route that has not been defined yet to define a text box and button, and a JavaScript block that makes a call to the web service to get products that contain a partial name, as shown in the following code:

```
@{
  ViewData["Title"] = "Products using JavaScript";
}


<div class="text-center">
  <h1 class="display-4">@ViewData["Title"]</h1>
  <div>
      Go to <a href="/home/products">Products using .NET</a>
  </div>
  <div>
    <input id="productName" placeholder="Enter part of a product name" />
    <input id="getProductsButton" type="button" value="Get Products" />
  </div>
  <div>
    <table id="productsTable" class="table">
        <thead>
            <tr>
                <th scope="col">Product Name</th>
            </tr>
        </thead>
        <tbody id="tableBody">

        </tbody>
    </table>
  </div>
  <script>
    var baseaddress = "https://localhost:5081/";

    function xhr_load() {
        console.log(this.responseText);

        var products = JSON.parse(this.responseText);

        var out = "";
        var i;
```

```
            for (i = 0; i < products.length; i++) {
                out += '<tr><td><a href="' + baseaddress + 'api/products/' +
                    products[i].productId + '">' +
                    products[i].productName + '</a></td></tr>';
            }
            document.getElementById("tableBody").innerHTML = out;
        }


        function getProductsButton_click() {
            xhr.open("GET", baseaddress + "api/products/" +
              document.getElementById("productName").value);

            xhr.send();
        }


        document.getElementById("getProductsButton")
          .addEventListener("click", getProductsButton_click);

        var xhr = new XMLHttpRequest();
        xhr.addEventListener("load", xhr_load);
    </script>
</div>
```

5. Start the `Northwind.WebApi.Service` project using the `https` profile without debugging.
6. Start the `Northwind.WebApi.Client.Mvc` project using the `https` profile without debugging.

 If you are using Visual Studio Code, then the web browser will not start automatically. Start Chrome, and then navigate to `https://localhost:5082`.

7. In Chrome, show **Developer Tools** and **Console**.
8. In the **Products using JavaScript** web page, in the text box, enter man, click the **Get Products** button, and note the error, as shown in the following output and in *Figure 8.6*:

```
Access to XMLHttpRequest at 'https://localhost:5081/api/products/man'
from origin 'https://localhost:5082' has been blocked by CORS policy:
No 'Access-Control-Allow-Origin' header is present on the requested
resource.
GET https://localhost:5081/api/products/man net::ERR_FAILED 200
```

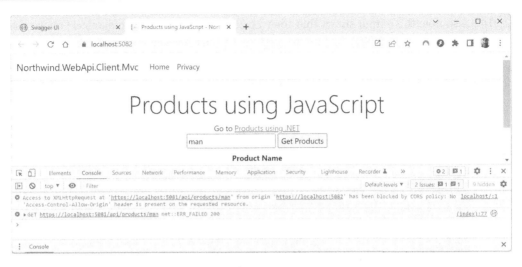

Figure 8.6: CORS error in the Chrome Developer Tools console

9. At the command prompt or terminal for the Northwind.WebApi.Service project, note the HTTP log for the request and that the Host is on a different port number to the Origin so they are not the same origin, as shown highlighted in the following output:

```
info: Microsoft.AspNetCore.HttpLogging.HttpLoggingMiddleware[1]
      Request:
      Protocol: HTTP/2
      Method: GET
      Scheme: https
      PathBase:
      Path: /api/products/man
      Accept: */*
      Host: localhost:5081
      User-Agent: Mozilla/5.0 (Windows NT 10.0; Win64; x64)
AppleWebKit/537.36 (KHTML, like Gecko) Chrome/113.0.0.0 Safari/537.36
      Accept-Encoding: gzip, deflate, br
      Accept-Language: en-US,en;q=0.9,sv;q=0.8
      Origin: https://localhost:5082
      Referer: [Redacted]
      sec-ch-ua: [Redacted]
      sec-ch-ua-mobile: [Redacted]
      sec-ch-ua-platform: [Redacted]
      sec-fetch-site: [Redacted]
      sec-fetch-mode: [Redacted]
      sec-fetch-dest: [Redacted]
```

10. Also note the output shows that the web service did execute the database query and return the products in a JSON document response to the browser, as shown in the following output:

```
info: Microsoft.AspNetCore.HttpLogging.HttpLoggingMiddleware[2]
      Response:
      StatusCode: 200
      Content-Type: application/json; charset=utf-8
info: Microsoft.AspNetCore.HttpLogging.HttpLoggingMiddleware[4]
      ResponseBody: [{"productId":12,"productName":
      "Queso Manchego La Pastora","supplierId":5,"categoryId":4,
      "quantityPerUnit":"10 - 500 g pkgs.","unitPrice":38.0000,
      "unitsInStock":86,"unitsOnOrder":0,"reorderLevel":0,
      "discontinued":false,"category":null,"supplier":null,
      "orderDetails":[]},
      {"productId":51,"productName":"Manjimup Dried Apples",
      "supplierId":24,"categoryId":7,
      "quantityPerUnit":"50 - 300 g pkgs.","unitPrice":53.0000,
      "unitsInStock":20,"unitsOnOrder":0,"reorderLevel":10,
      "discontinued":false,"category":null,"supplier":null,
      "orderDetails":[]}]
```

 Although the browser receives a response containing the data requested, it is the browser that enforces the same origin policy by refusing to reveal the HTTP response to the JavaScript. The web service is not "secured" by CORS.

11. Close the browser(s) and shut down the web servers.

Creating a .NET client

Next, let's create a .NET client to the web service to see that the same origin policy does not apply to non-web browsers:

1. In the `Northwind.WebApi.Client.Mvc` project, add a reference to the entity models project so that we can use the `Product` class, as shown in the following markup:

```
<ItemGroup>
  <ProjectReference Include="..\..\Chapter03\Northwind.Common.
EntityModels
.SqlServer\Northwind.Common.EntityModels.SqlServer.csproj" />
</ItemGroup>
```

2. Build the `Northwind.WebApi.Client.Mvc` project at the command prompt or terminal by entering the following command: `dotnet build`.

3. In the `Northwind.WebApi.Client.Mvc` project, in `Program.cs`, import the namespace for work-
    ing with HTTP headers, as shown in the following code:

    ```
    using System.Net.Http.Headers; // To use MediaTypeWithQualityHeaderValue.
    ```

4. In `Program.cs`, before the call to `builder.Build()`, add statements to configure an HTTP client
    factory to call the web service, as shown in the following code:

    ```
    builder.Services.AddHttpClient(name: "Northwind.WebApi.Service",
      configureClient: options =>
      {
        options.BaseAddress = new("https://localhost:5081/");
        options.DefaultRequestHeaders.Accept.Add(
          new MediaTypeWithQualityHeaderValue(
            "application/json", 1.0));
      });
    ```

5. In the `Controllers` folder, in `HomeController.cs`, import the namespace for the entity models,
    as shown in the following code:

    ```
    using Northwind.EntityModels; // To use Product.
    ```

6. In `HomeController.cs`, add statements to store the registered HTTP client factory in a private
    readonly field, as shown highlighted in the following code:

    ```
    private readonly ILogger<HomeController> _logger;
    private readonly IHttpClientFactory _httpClientFactory;

    public HomeController(ILogger<HomeController> logger,
      IHttpClientFactory httpClientFactory)
    {
      _logger = logger;
      _httpClientFactory = httpClientFactory;
    }
    ```

7. In `HomeController.cs`, add an asynchronous action method named `Products` that will use the
    HTTP factory to request products whose name contains a value entered as an optional name
    parameter in a custom MVC route, as shown in the following code:

    ```
    [Route("home/products/{name?}")]
    public async Task<IActionResult> Products(string? name)
    {
      HttpClient client = _httpClientFactory.CreateClient(
        name: "Northwind.WebApi.Service");

      HttpRequestMessage request = new(
    ```

```
    method: HttpMethod.Get, requestUri: $"api/products/{name}");

  HttpResponseMessage response = await client.SendAsync(request);

  IEnumerable<Product>? model = await response.Content
    .ReadFromJsonAsync<IEnumerable<Product>>();

  ViewData["baseaddress"] = client.BaseAddress;

  return View(model);
}
```

8. In the `Views/Home` folder, add a new file named `Products.cshtml`. (The Visual Studio 2022 project item template is named **Razor View - Empty**. The JetBrains Rider project item template is named **Razor MVC View**.)

9. In `Products.cshtml`, modify its contents to output a table of products that match part of a product name entered in a text box, as shown in the following markup:

```
@using Northwind.EntityModels
@model IEnumerable<Product>?
@{
  ViewData["Title"] = "Products using .NET";
}
<div class="text-center">
  <h1 class="display-4">@ViewData["Title"]</h1>
  <div>
    Go to <a href="/">Products using JavaScript</a>
  </div>
  <form action="/home/products">
    <input name="name" placeholder="Enter part of a product name" />
    <input type="submit" value="Get Products" />
  </form>
  <div>
    <table class="table">
      <thead>
        <tr>
          <th scope="col">Product Name</th>
        </tr>
      </thead>
      <tbody>
        @if (Model is not null)
        {
```

```
        @foreach (Product p in Model)
        {
          <tr><td><a href="@(ViewData["baseaddress"])api/products/
@p.ProductId">@p.ProductName</a></td></tr>
        }
      }
    </tbody>
  </table>
  </div>
</div>
```

10. Start the `Northwind.WebApi.Service` project using the `https` profile without debugging.

11. Start the `Northwind.WebApi.Client.Mvc` project using the `https` profile without debugging.

12. On the home page, click the link to go to **Products using .NET**, and note the first ten in-stock, not discontinued products are shown in the table, from **Chai** to **Queso Manchego La Pastora**.

13. In the text box, enter `man`, click **Get Products**, and note that two products are shown in the table, as shown in *Figure 8.7*:

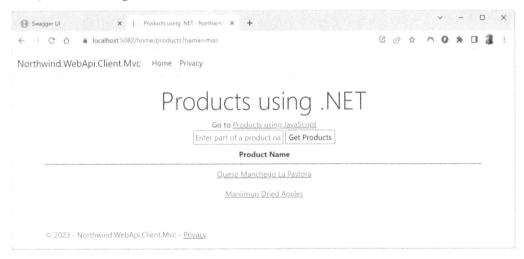

Figure 8.7: Getting two products from a web service using .NET

 It is the .NET HTTP client that is calling the web service, so the same origin policy does not apply. If you were to check the logs at the command line or terminal as you did before, you would see the ports are different, but it does not matter.

14. Click one of the product names to make a direct request to the web service for an individual product and note the response, as shown in the following document:

```
{"productId":12,"productName":"Queso Manchego La Pastora",
"supplierId":5,"categoryId":4,
```

```
"quantityPerUnit":"10 - 500 g pkgs.","unitPrice":38.0000,
"unitsInStock":86,"unitsOnOrder":0,"reorderLevel":0,
"discontinued":false,"category":null,"supplier":null,"orderDetails":[]}
```

15. Close the browser and shut down the web servers.

Understanding CORS

Cross-Origin Resource Sharing (CORS) is an HTTP-header-based feature that asks the browser to disable its same-origin security policy in specific scenarios. The HTTP headers indicate which origins should be allowed in addition to the same origin.

Let's enable CORS in the web service so that it can send extra headers to indicate to the browser that it is allowed to access resources from a different origin:

1. In the Northwind.WebApi.Service project, in WebApplication.Extensions.cs, add an extension method to add CORS support to the web service, as shown in the following code:

```
public static IServiceCollection AddCustomCors(
  this IServiceCollection services)
{
  services.AddCors(options =>
  {
    options.AddPolicy(name: "Northwind.Mvc.Policy",
      policy =>
      {
        policy.WithOrigins("https://localhost:5082");
      });
  });
  return services;
}
```

2. In Program.cs, after creating the builder, call the custom extension method to add CORS support, as shown in the following code:

```
builder.Services.AddCustomCors();
```

3. In Program.cs, after the call to UseHttpLogging, and before mapping the GET requests, add a statement to use the CORS policy, as shown in the following code:

```
app.UseCors(policyName: "Northwind.Mvc.Policy");
```

4. Start the Northwind.WebApi.Service project using the https profile without debugging.

5. Start the Northwind.WebApi.Client.Mvc project using the https profile without debugging.

6. Show **Developer Tools** and the **Console**.

7. On the home page, in the text box, enter man, click **Get Products**, and note that the console shows the JSON document returned from the web service, and the table is filled with the two products, as shown in *Figure 8.8*:

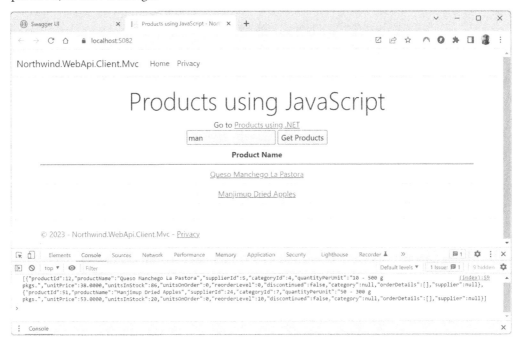

Figure 8.8: A successful cross-origin request to the web service using JavaScript

8. Close the browser and shut down the web servers.

Enabling CORS for specific endpoints

In the previous example, we enabled the same CORS policy for the whole web service. You might need finer control at the endpoint level:

1. In the `Northwind.WebApi.Service` project, in `Program.cs`, change the call to `UseCors` to not specify the policy name, as shown highlighted in the following code:

    ```
    // app.UseCors(policyName: "Northwind.Mvc.Policy");

    // Without a named policy the middleware is added but not active.
    app.UseCors();
    ```

2. In `WebApplication.Extensions.cs`, at the end of the call to `MapGet` that gets products that contain part of a product name, add a call to `RequiresCors`, as shown highlighted in the following code:

    ```
    app.MapGet("api/products/{name}", (
      [FromServices] NorthwindContext db,
      [FromRoute] string name) =>
    ```

```
        db.Products.Where(p => p.ProductName.Contains(name)))
    .WithName("GetProductsByName")
    .WithOpenApi()
    .Produces<Product[]>(StatusCodes.Status200OK)
    .RequireCors(policyName: "Northwind.Mvc.Policy");
```

3. Start the `Northwind.WebApi.Service` project using the `https` profile without debugging.

4. Start the `Northwind.WebApi.Client.Mvc` project using the `https` profile without debugging.

5. Show **Developer Tools** and **Console**.

6. On the home page, in the text box, enter cha, click **Get Products**, and note that the console shows the JSON document returned from the web service and the table is filled with three products.

7. Close the browser and shut down the web servers.

Understanding other CORS policy options

You can control the:

- Allowed origins, for example, `https://*.example.com/`.
- Allowed HTTP methods, for example, `GET`, `POST`, `DELETE`, and so on.
- Allowed HTTP request headers, for example, `Content-Type`, `Content-Language`, `x-custom-header`, and so on.
- Exposed HTTP response headers, meaning which headers to include unredacted in a response (because, by default, response headers are redacted), for example, `x-custom-header`.

 You can learn more about options for CORS policies at the following link: `https://learn.microsoft.com/en-us/aspnet/core/security/cors#cors-policy-options`

Now that you know that CORS does not secure a web service, let's look at a useful technique that can prevent a common form of attack.

Preventing denial of service attacks using rate limiting

A **denial of service** (DoS) attack is a malicious attempt to disrupt a web service by overwhelming it with requests. If the requests all came from the same place, for example, the same IP address, then it would be relatively easy to cut them off as soon as the attack is detected. But these attacks are often implemented as **distributed DoS** (DDoS) attacks from many locations so you cannot separate attackers from genuine clients.

A different approach is to apply rate limiting to everyone but let through more requests for genuine identified clients.

Genuine clients should only make the minimum requests they need. How many is reasonable will depend on your service. One way to prevent DDoS attacks would be to limit how many requests are allowed from any client per minute.

This technique is not just useful to prevent attacks. Even genuine clients might accidentally make too many requests, or for a commercial web service, you might want to charge different amounts for different rates, like when controlling a subscription. Commercial web services from Twitter/X to Reddit now charge a *lot* of money for access to their web APIs.

When a client makes requests over a set rate limit, the client should receive either 429 Too Many Requests or 503 Service Unavailable HTTP responses.

> **Good Practice:** If you need to build a massively scalable web service and protect its APIs, you should use a cloud service like Azure API Management instead of trying to implement your own rate limiting. You can learn more about this at the following link: https://learn.microsoft.com/en-us/azure/api-management/.

Rate limiting using the AspNetCoreRateLimit package

AspNetCoreRateLimit, a third-party package that targets .NET 6 or later, provides flexible rate-limiting middleware based on the IP address or client ID:

1. In the Northwind.WebApi.Service project, add a reference to the AspNetCoreRateLimit package, as shown in the following markup:

    ```
    <PackageReference Include="AspNetCoreRateLimit" Version="5.0.0" />
    ```

2. Build the Northwind.WebApi.Service project to restore packages.

3. In appsettings.Development.json, add configuration for default rate limit options and client-specific policies, as shown highlighted in the following configuration:

    ```
    {
      "Logging": {
        "LogLevel": {
          "Default": "Information",
          "Microsoft.AspNetCore": "Warning",
          "Microsoft.AspNetCore.HttpLogging": "Information"
        }
      },
      "ClientRateLimiting": {
        "EnableEndpointRateLimiting": false,
        "StackBlockedRequests": false,
        "ClientIdHeader": "X-Client-Id",
        "HttpStatusCode": 429,
        "EndpointWhitelist": [ "get:/api/license", "*:/api/status" ],
        "ClientWhitelist": [ "dev-id-1", "dev-id-2" ],
        "GeneralRules": [
          {
            "Endpoint": "*",
    ```

```json
            "Period": "10s",
            "Limit": 2
        },
        {
            "Endpoint": "*",
            "Period": "12h",
            "Limit": 100
        }
    ]
},
"ClientRateLimitPolicies": {
  "ClientRules": [
    {
        "ClientId": "console-client-abc123",
        "Rules": [
            {
                "Endpoint": "*",
                "Period": "10s",
                "Limit": 5
            },
            {
                "Endpoint": "*",
                "Period": "12h",
                "Limit": 250
            }
        ]
    }
  ]
}
}
```

Note:

- `EnableEndpointRateLimiting` is `false`, meaning all endpoints will share the same rules.
- If a client needs to identify itself, it can set a header named `X-Client-Id` to a unique `string` value.
- If a rate limit is reached for a client, the service will start returning `429` status code responses to that client.
- Two endpoints will be excluded from the global rate limits because they are on the endpoint whitelist. One endpoint is for getting a license, and the other endpoint is for checking the status of the service. We will not actually implement these features and you would want to apply different rate limits to these endpoints; otherwise, someone could call them to bring down your server instead.

- Two client IDs, named dev-id-1 and dev-id-2, will be excluded from the rate limits because they are on the client whitelist. These could be special client accounts for internal developers that are not shared outside the organization.

- Two general (default) rules are configured: the first sets a rate limit of 2 requests every 10 seconds, and the second sets a rate limit of 100 requests every 12 hours.

- Two client-specific rules are configured that are looser than the default rules: for the client ID named console-client-abc123, it is allowed to make up to 5 requests every 10 seconds, and up to 250 requests every 12 hours.

4. In IServiceCollection.Extensions.cs, import the namespace for working with rate-limiting options, as shown in the following code:

```
using AspNetCoreRateLimit; // To use ClientRateLimitOptions and so on.
```

5. In IServiceCollection.Extensions.cs, define an extension method to load rate-limiting configuration from app settings and set rate-limiting options, as shown in the following code:

```
public static IServiceCollection AddCustomRateLimiting(
  this IServiceCollection services, ConfigurationManager configuration)
{
  // Add services to store rate limit counters and rules in memory.
  services.AddMemoryCache();
  services.AddInMemoryRateLimiting();

  // Load default rate limit options from appsettings.json.
  services.Configure<ClientRateLimitOptions>(
    configuration.GetSection("ClientRateLimiting"));

  // Load client-specific policies from appsettings.json.
  services.Configure<ClientRateLimitPolicies>(
    configuration.GetSection("ClientRateLimitPolicies"));

  // Register the configuration.
  services.AddSingleton
    <IRateLimitConfiguration, RateLimitConfiguration>();

  return services;
}
```

6. In Program.cs, after creating the builder, add statements to load rate-limiting configuration from app settings and set rate-limiting options, as shown in the following code:

```
builder.Services.AddCustomRateLimiting(builder.Configuration);
```

7. In `IServiceCollection.Extensions.cs`, in the call to configure HTTP logging, add a statement to allow two rate-limiting headers to not be redacted, as shown highlighted in the following code:

```
services.AddHttpLogging(options =>
{
  // Add the Origin header so it will not be redacted.
  options.RequestHeaders.Add("Origin");

  // Add the rate limiting headers so they will not be redacted.
  options.RequestHeaders.Add("X-Client-Id");
  options.ResponseHeaders.Add("Retry-After");

  // By default, the response body is not included.
  options.LoggingFields = HttpLoggingFields.All;
});
```

8. In `WebApplication.Extensions.cs`, import the namespace for working with rate-limiting policy stores, as shown in the following code:

```
using AspNetCoreRateLimit; // To use IClientPolicyStore and so on.
```

9. In `WebApplication.Extensions.cs`, add statements to define an extension method to seed the client policy store, which just means loading the policies from the configuration, and then use client rate limits, as shown in the following code:

```
public static async Task UseCustomClientRateLimiting(this WebApplication
app)
{
  using (IServiceScope scope = app.Services.CreateScope())
  {
    IClientPolicyStore clientPolicyStore = scope.ServiceProvider
      .GetRequiredService<IClientPolicyStore>();

    await clientPolicyStore.SeedAsync();
  }

  app.UseClientRateLimiting();
}
```

10. In `Program.cs`, after calling `UseHttpLogging`, add a call to use client rate limiting, as shown in the following code:

```
await app.UseCustomClientRateLimiting();
```

Creating a rate-limited console client

Now we can create a console app that will be a client to the web service:

1. Use your preferred code editor to add a new console app to the Chapter08 solution named Northwind.WebApi.Client.Console.

2. In the Northwind.WebApi.Client.Console project, treat warnings as errors, globally and statically import the System.Console class, and add a reference to the entity models project, as shown in the following markup:

```
<ItemGroup>
  <ProjectReference Include="..\..\Chapter03\Northwind.Common.
EntityModels
.SqlServer\Northwind.Common.EntityModels.SqlServer.csproj" />
</ItemGroup>
```

3. Build the Northwind.WebApi.Client.Console project at the command prompt or terminal to compile the referenced project and copy its assembly to the appropriate bin folder.

4. In the Northwind.WebApi.Client.Console project, add a new class file named Program.Helpers.cs.

5. In Program.Helpers.cs, add statements to define a method for the partial Program class to write some text in a foreground color, as shown in the following markup:

```
partial class Program
{
  private static void WriteInColor(string text, ConsoleColor
foregroundColor)
  {
    ConsoleColor previousColor = ForegroundColor;
    ForegroundColor = foregroundColor;
    Write(text);
    ForegroundColor = previousColor;
  }
}
```

6. In Program.cs, delete the existing statements. Add statements to prompt the user for a client name to identify it, and then create an HTTP client to make a request to get the first page of products from the web service once per second until the user presses *Ctrl* + *C* to stop the console app, as shown in the following code:

```
using Northwind.EntityModels; // To use Product.
using System.Net.Http.Json; // To use ReadFromJsonAsync<T> method.

Write("Enter a client name or press Enter: ");
string? clientName = ReadLine();
```

```csharp
if (string.IsNullOrEmpty(clientName))
{
  clientName = $"console-client-{Guid.NewGuid()}";
}

WriteLine($"X-Client-Id will be: {clientName}");

HttpClient client = new();

client.BaseAddress = new("https://localhost:5081");

client.DefaultRequestHeaders.Accept.Add(new("application/json"));

// Specify the rate limiting client id for this console app.
client.DefaultRequestHeaders.Add("X-Client-Id", clientName);

while (true)
{
  WriteInColor(string.Format("{0:hh:mm:ss}: ",
    DateTime.UtcNow), ConsoleColor.DarkGreen);

  int waitFor = 1; // Second.

  try
  {
    HttpResponseMessage response = await client.GetAsync("api/products");

    if (response.IsSuccessStatusCode)
    {
      Product[]? products =
        await response.Content.ReadFromJsonAsync<Product[]>();

      if (products != null)
      {
        foreach (Product product in products)
        {
          Write(product.ProductName);
          Write(", ");
        }
        WriteLine();
```

```
      }
    }
    else
    {
      WriteInColor(string.Format("{0}: {1}", (int)response.StatusCode,
        await response.Content.ReadAsStringAsync()),
        ConsoleColor.DarkRed);

      WriteLine();
    }
  }
  catch (Exception ex)
  {
    WriteLine(ex.Message);
  }

  await Task.Delay(TimeSpan.FromSeconds(waitFor));
}
```

7. If your database server is not running (for example, because you are hosting it in Docker, a virtual machine, or in the cloud), then make sure to start it.

8. Start the `Northwind.WebApi.Service` project using the `https` profile without debugging.

9. Start the `Northwind.WebApi.Client.Console` project without debugging.

10. In the console app, press *Enter* to generate a GUID-based client ID.

11. Start the `Northwind.WebApi.Client.Console` project using the `https` profile without debugging again so we have two clients.

12. In the console app, press *Enter* to generate a GUID-based client ID.

13. Note that each client can make two requests before it starts to receive 429 status codes, as shown in the following output and in *Figure 8.9*:

```
Enter a client name or press Enter:
X-Client-Id will be: console-client-d54c61ba-66bb-4e39-9c1a-7af6e2bf647e
07:32:18: Chai, Chang, Aniseed Syrup, Chef Anton's Cajun Seasoning,
Grandma's Boysenberry Spread, Uncle Bob's Organic Dried Pears, Northwoods
Cranberry Sauce, Ikura, Queso Cabrales, Queso Manchego La Pastora,
07:32:20: Chai, Chang, Aniseed Syrup, Chef Anton's Cajun Seasoning,
Grandma's Boysenberry Spread, Uncle Bob's Organic Dried Pears, Northwoods
Cranberry Sauce, Ikura, Queso Cabrales, Queso Manchego La Pastora,
07:32:21: 429: API calls quota exceeded! maximum admitted 2 per 10s.
07:32:22: 429: API calls quota exceeded! maximum admitted 2 per 10s.
07:32:23: 429: API calls quota exceeded! maximum admitted 2 per 10s.
07:32:24: 429: API calls quota exceeded! maximum admitted 2 per 10s.
```

```
07:32:25: 429: API calls quota exceeded! maximum admitted 2 per 10s.
07:32:26: 429: API calls quota exceeded! maximum admitted 2 per 10s.
07:32:27: 429: API calls quota exceeded! maximum admitted 2 per 10s.
07:32:28: Chai, Chang, Aniseed Syrup, Chef Anton's Cajun Seasoning,
Grandma's Boysenberry Spread, Uncle Bob's Organic Dried Pears, Northwoods
Cranberry Sauce, Ikura, Queso Cabrales, Queso Manchego La Pastora,
07:32:29: Chai, Chang, Aniseed Syrup, Chef Anton's Cajun Seasoning,
Grandma's Boysenberry Spread, Uncle Bob's Organic Dried Pears, Northwoods
Cranberry Sauce, Ikura, Queso Cabrales, Queso Manchego La Pastora,
07:32:30: 429: API calls quota exceeded! maximum admitted 2 per 10s.
07:32:31: 429: API calls quota exceeded! maximum admitted 2 per 10s.
07:32:32: 429: API calls quota exceeded! maximum admitted 2 per 10s.
```

```
C:\apps-services-net8\Chapter08\Northwind.WebApi.Client.Console\bin\Debug\net8.0\Northwind.WebApi.Client.Console.exe

Enter a client name or press Enter:
X-Client-Id will be: console-client-8aeb2e7e-3679-4fba-ba4b-93dc2fa7429f
12:48:40: Chai, Chang, Aniseed Syrup, Chef Anton's Cajun Seasoning, Grandma's Boysenberry Spread, Uncle Bob's
Organic Dried Pears, Northwoods Cranberry Sauce, Ikura, Queso Cabrales, Queso Manchego La Pastora,
12:48:42: Chai, Chang, Aniseed Syrup, Chef Anton's Cajun Seasoning, Grandma's Boysenberry Spread, Uncle Bob's
Organic Dried Pears, Northwoods Cranberry Sauce, Ikura, Queso Cabrales, Queso Manchego La Pastora,
12:48:43: 429: API calls quota exceeded! maximum admitted 2 per 10s.
12:48:44: 429: API calls quota exceeded! maximum admitted 2 per 10s.
12:48:45: 429: API calls quota exceeded! maximum admitted 2 per 10s.
12:48:46: 429: API calls quota exceeded! maximum admitted 2 per 10s.
12:48:47: 429: API calls quota exceeded! maximum admitted 2 per 10s.
12:48:48: 429: API calls quota exceeded! maximum admitted 2 per 10s.
12:48:49: 429: API calls quota exceeded! maximum admitted 2 per 10s.
12:48:50: 429: API calls quota exceeded! maximum admitted 2 per 10s.
12:48:51: Chai, Chang, Aniseed Syrup, Chef Anton's Cajun Seasoning, Grandma's Boysenberry Spread, Uncle Bob's
Organic Dried Pears, Northwoods Cranberry Sauce, Ikura, Queso Cabrales, Queso Manchego La Pastora,
12:48:52: Chai, Chang, Aniseed Syrup, Chef Anton's Cajun Seasoning, Grandma's Boysenberry Spread, Uncle Bob's
Organic Dried Pears, Northwoods Cranberry Sauce, Ikura, Queso Cabrales, Queso Manchego La Pastora,
12:48:53: 429: API calls quota exceeded! maximum admitted 2 per 10s.
```

Figure 8.9: A console app exceeding its web service rate limit

14. Stop the two console apps. Leave the web service running.

15. In the command line for the web service, note the HTTP logs that show each request from the console client with its client ID sent as a header named X-Client-Id, the request being blocked because that client has exceeded its quota, and a response that contains a header named Retry-After containing the number of seconds the client should wait before retrying, as shown highlighted in the following output:

```
info: Microsoft.AspNetCore.HttpLogging.HttpLoggingMiddleware[1]
      Request:
      Protocol: HTTP/1.1
      Method: GET
      Scheme: https
      PathBase:
      Path: /api/products
      Accept: application/json
      Host: localhost:5081
```

```
      X-Client-Id: console-client-d54c61ba-66bb-4e39-9c1a-7af6e2bf647e
info: AspNetCoreRateLimit.ClientRateLimitMiddleware[0]
      Request get:/api/products from ClientId console-client-d54c61ba-
66bb-4e39-9c1a-7af6e2bf647e has been blocked, quota 2/10s exceeded by 3.
Blocked by rule *, TraceIdentifier 0HMIKGNJQEK5P:0000000E. MonitorMode:
False
info: Microsoft.AspNetCore.HttpLogging.HttpLoggingMiddleware[2]
      Response:
      StatusCode: 429
      Content-Type: text/plain
      Retry-After: 6
info: Microsoft.AspNetCore.HttpLogging.HttpLoggingMiddleware[4]
      ResponseBody: API calls quota exceeded! maximum admitted 2 per 10s.
```

16. In the `Northwind.WebApi.Client.Console` project, in `Program.cs`, before writing the error message to the console in dark red, add statements to read the `Retry-After` header to get the number of seconds to wait for, as shown highlighted in the following code:

```
string retryAfter = response.Headers
  .GetValues("Retry-After").ToArray()[0];

if (int.TryParse(retryAfter, out waitFor))
{
  retryAfter = string.Format(
    "I will retry after {0} seconds.", waitFor);
}

WriteInColor(string.Format("{0}: {1} {2}", (int)response.StatusCode,
  await response.Content.ReadAsStringAsync(), retryAfter),
  ConsoleColor.DarkRed);
```

 Note the `waitFor` variable is set from the `Retry-After` header value. This is later used to pause the console app using an asynchronous delay, as shown in the following code:

```
await Task.Delay(TimeSpan.FromSeconds(waitFor));
```

17. Start the `Northwind.WebApi.Client.Console` project without debugging.

18. In the console app, press *Enter* to generate a GUID-based client ID.

19. Note the console app will now sensibly wait for the suggested number of seconds before making its next call to the service, as shown in the following output:

```
Enter a client name:
X-Client-Id will be: console-client-add7613f-51a9-4c4a-8ec7-0244203d2e19
07:45:01: Chai, Chang, Aniseed Syrup, Chef Anton's Cajun Seasoning,
Grandma's Boysenberry Spread, Uncle Bob's Organic Dried Pears, Northwoods
Cranberry Sauce, Ikura, Queso Cabrales, Queso Manchego La Pastora,
07:45:02: Chai, Chang, Aniseed Syrup, Chef Anton's Cajun Seasoning,
Grandma's Boysenberry Spread, Uncle Bob's Organic Dried Pears, Northwoods
Cranberry Sauce, Ikura, Queso Cabrales, Queso Manchego La Pastora,
07:45:03: 429: API calls quota exceeded! maximum admitted 2 per 10s. I
will retry after 8 seconds.
07:45:11: Chai, Chang, Aniseed Syrup, Chef Anton's Cajun Seasoning,
Grandma's Boysenberry Spread, Uncle Bob's Organic Dried Pears, Northwoods
Cranberry Sauce, Ikura, Queso Cabrales, Queso Manchego La Pastora,
07:45:12: Chai, Chang, Aniseed Syrup, Chef Anton's Cajun Seasoning,
Grandma's Boysenberry Spread, Uncle Bob's Organic Dried Pears, Northwoods
Cranberry Sauce, Ikura, Queso Cabrales, Queso Manchego La Pastora,
07:45:13: 429: API calls quota exceeded! maximum admitted 2 per 10s. I
will retry after 8 seconds.
```

20. Stop and restart the `Northwind.WebApi.Client.Console` project without debugging.

21. In the console app, enter the name `dev-id-1`, and note that the rate limit does not apply to this console app client. This could be a special account for internal developers.

22. Stop and restart the `Northwind.WebApi.Client.Console` project without debugging.

23. In the console app, enter the name `console-client-abc123`, and note that the rate limit is different for this console app client ID, as shown in the following output:

```
info: AspNetCoreRateLimit.ClientRateLimitMiddleware[0]
      Request get:/api/products from ClientId console-client-abc123
has been blocked, quota 5/10s exceeded by 1. Blocked by rule *,
TraceIdentifier 0HMIKGS1TPSHJ:00000006. MonitorMode: False
```

Rate limiting using ASP.NET Core middleware

ASP.NET Core 7 introduced its own basic rate-limiting middleware, initially distributed as a separate NuGet package but now included with ASP.NET Core. It has a dependency on another Microsoft package, `System.Threading.RateLimiting`. It is not as feature-rich as the third-party package and we will not cover it in this book, although I have written an online-only section at the following link:

`https://github.com/markjprice/apps-services-net8/blob/main/docs/ch08-rate-limiting.md`

You can learn about the ASP.NET Core rate limiter at the following link: `https://learn.microsoft.com/en-us/aspnet/core/performance/rate-limit`.

Protecting your web services from attacks is important. What about improving the performance of your web service? Is there anything we can do about that?

Improving startup time and resources using native AOT

Native AOT produces apps and services that are:

- **Self-contained**, meaning they can run on systems that do not have the .NET runtime installed.
- **Ahead-of-time (AOT) compiled to native code**, meaning a faster startup time and a potentially smaller memory footprint. This can have a positive impact when you have lots of instances (for example, when deploying massively scalable microservices) that are frequently stopped and restarted.

Native AOT compiles **intermediate code (IL)** to native code at the time of publishing, rather than at runtime using the **Just-In-Time (JIT)** compiler. But native AOT apps and services must target a specific runtime environment like Windows x64 or Linux ARM.

Since native AOT happens at publish time, while debugging and working live on a project in your code editor, it uses the runtime JIT compiler, not native AOT, even if you have AOT enabled in the project! But some features that are incompatible with native AOT will be disabled or throw exceptions, and a source analyzer is enabled to show warnings about potential code incompatibilities.

Limitations of native AOT

Native AOT has limitations, some of which are shown in the following list:

- No dynamic loading of assemblies.
- No runtime code generation, for example, using `System.Reflection.Emit`.
- It requires trimming, which has its own limitations.
- The assembly must be self-contained, so they must embed any libraries they call, which increases their size.

Although your own apps and services might not use the features listed above, major parts of .NET itself do. For example, ASP.NET Core MVC (including Web API services that use controllers) and EF Core do runtime code generation to implement their functionality.

The .NET teams are hard at work making as much of .NET compatible with native AOT as possible, as soon as possible. But .NET 8 only includes basic support for ASP.NET Core if you use minimal APIs, and no support for EF Core.

My guess is that .NET 9 will include support for ASP.NET Core MVC and some parts of EF Core, but it could take until .NET 10 before we can all confidently use most of .NET and know we can build our apps and services with native AOT to gain the benefits.

The native AOT publishing process includes code analyzers to warn you if you use any features that are not supported, but not all packages have been annotated to work well with this yet.

The most common annotation used to indicate that a type or member does not support AOT is the [RequiresDynamicCode] attribute.

 More Information: You can learn more about AOT warnings at the following link: `https://learn.microsoft.com/en-us/dotnet/core/deploying/native-aot/fixing-warnings`.

Reflection and native AOT

Reflection is frequently used for runtime inspection of type metadata, dynamic invocation of members, and code generation.

Native AOT does allow some reflection features, but the trimming performed during the native AOT compilation process cannot statically determine when a type has members that might be only accessed via reflection. These members would be removed by AOT, which would then cause a runtime exception.

 Good Practice: Developers must annotate their types with [DynamicallyAccessedMembers] to indicate a member that is only dynamically accessed via reflection and should therefore be left untrimmed.

Native AOT for ASP.NET Core

.NET 7 only supported native AOT with console apps and class libraries on Windows or Linux. It did not support macOS or ASP.NET Core. .NET 8 is the first version to support macOS and parts of ASP.NET Core.

The following ASP.NET Core features are fully supported: gRPC, CORS, HealthChecks, HttpLogging, Localization, OutputCaching, RateLimiting, RequestDecompression, ResponseCaching, ResponseCompression, Rewrite, StaticFiles, and WebSockets.

The following ASP.NET Core features are partially supported: minimal APIs.

The following ASP.NET Core features are not supported (yet): MVC, Blazor Server, SignalR, Authentication (except JWT), Session, and SPA.

As you have previously seen, you implement an ASP.NET Core Minimal APIs web service by mapping an HTTP request to a lambda expression, for example, as shown in the following code:

```
app.MapGet("/", () => "Hello World!");
```

At runtime, ASP.NET Core uses the RequestDelegateFactory (RDF) class to convert your MapX calls into RequestDelegate instances. But this is dynamic code so is not compatible with native AOT.

In ASP.NET Core 8, when native AOT is enabled, the runtime use of RDF is replaced with a source generator named **Request Delegate Generator** (RDG) that performs similar work but at compile time. This makes sure the code generated is statically analyzable by the native AOT publish process.

 More Information: You can learn how to create your own source generator at the following link: https://github.com/markjprice/apps-services-net8/blob/main/docs/ch01-dynamic-code.md#creating-source-generators.

Requirements for native AOT

There are additional requirements for different operating systems:

- On Windows, you must install the Visual Studio 2022 **Desktop development with C++** workload with all default components.
- On Linux, you must install the compiler toolchain and developer packages for libraries that the .NET runtime depends on. For example, for Ubuntu 18.04 or later: sudo apt-get install clang zlib1g-dev.

 Warning! Cross-platform native AOT publishing is not supported. This means that you must run the publish on the operating system that you will deploy to. For example, you cannot publish a native AOT project on Linux to later run on Windows.

Enabling native AOT for a project

To enable native AOT publishing in a project, add the <PublishAot> element to the project file, as shown highlighted in the following markup:

```
<PropertyGroup>
  <TargetFramework>net8.0</TargetFramework>
  <PublishAot>true</PublishAot>
```

Enabling JSON serialization with native AOT

JSON serialization with native AOT requires the use of the System.Text.Json source generator. All model types passed as parameters or return values must be registered with a JsonSerializerContext, as shown in the following code:

```
[JsonSerializable(typeof(Product)] // A single Product.
[JsonSerializable(typeof(Product[]))] // An array of Products.
public partial class MyJsonSerializerContext : JsonSerializerContext { }
```

Your custom JSON serializer context must be added to the service dependencies, as shown in the following code:

```
builder.Services.ConfigureHttpJsonOptions(options =>
{
  options.SerializerOptions.AddContext<MyJsonSerializerContext>();
});
```

Building a native AOT project

Now let's see a practical example using the new project template:

1. In the solution named Chapter08, add a native AOT-compatible web service project, as defined in the following list:

    *   Project template: **ASP.NET Core Web API (native AOT)** / webapiaot

         This is a new project template introduced with .NET 8. It is different from the **Web API** / webapi project template. It does not have an option to use controllers since native AOT support is currently minimal APIs-only. It also does not have an option for HTTPS because HTTPS is often handled by a reverse-proxy in cloud-native deployments. In JetBrains Rider, select **ASP.NET Core Web Application** and then select the **Type** of **Web API (native AOT)**.

    *   Solution file and folder: Chapter08
    *   Project file and folder: Northwind.MinimalAot.Service
    *   **Enable Docker:** Cleared.
    *   **Do not use top-level statements:** Cleared.
    *   In the Properties folder, in launchSettings.json, note only http is configured; delete the launchUrl and modify the port to use 5083, as shown highlighted in the following configuration:

        ```
        {
          "$schema": "http://json.schemastore.org/launchsettings.json",
          "profiles": {
            "http": {
              "commandName": "Project",
              "dotnetRunMessages": true,
              "launchBrowser": true,
              "launchUrl": "",
              "applicationUrl": "http://localhost:5083",
              "environmentVariables": {
        ```

```
                    "ASPNETCORE_ENVIRONMENT": "Development"
                }
            }
        }
    }
```

2. In the project file, change invariant globalization to `false`, treat warnings as errors, note that native AOT publishing is enabled, and add a package reference for SQL Server for ADO.NET, as shown highlighted in the following markup:

```
<Project Sdk="Microsoft.NET.Sdk.Web">

  <PropertyGroup>
    <TargetFramework>net8.0</TargetFramework>
    <Nullable>enable</Nullable>
    <ImplicitUsings>enable</ImplicitUsings>
    <InvariantGlobalization>false</InvariantGlobalization>
    <TreatWarningsAsErrors>true</TreatWarningsAsErrors>
    <PublishAot>true</PublishAot>
  </PropertyGroup>

  <ItemGroup>
    <PackageReference Include="Microsoft.Data.SqlClient" Version="5.1.2"
/>
  </ItemGroup>

</Project>
```

3. Add a new class file named `Product.cs`, and modify its contents to define a class to represent just the three columns we want from each row in the `Products` table, as shown in the following code:

```
namespace Northwind.Models;

public class Product
{
    public int ProductId { get; set; }
    public string? ProductName { get; set; }
    public decimal? UnitPrice { get; set; }
}
```

4. Add a new class file named `NorthwindJsonSerializerContext.cs`.

5.   In NorthwindJsonSerializerContext.cs, define a class that enables a Product and a list of
     Product objects to be serialized as JSON, as shown in the following code:

```
using System.Text.Json.Serialization; // To use JsonSerializerContext.
using Northwind.Models; // To use Product.

namespace Northwind.Serialization;

[JsonSerializable(typeof(Product))]
[JsonSerializable(typeof(List<Product>))]
internal partial class NorthwindJsonSerializerContext
  : JsonSerializerContext { }
```

6.   Delete the Northwind.MinimalAot.Service.http file.

7.   Add a new class file named WebApplication.Extensions.cs.

8.   In WebApplication.Extensions.cs, define an extension method for the WebApplication
     class that maps some HTTP GET requests to return a plain text response, and a list of either
     all products or products with a minimum price from the Northwind database using ADO.NET,
     as shown in the following code:

```
using Microsoft.Data.SqlClient; // To use SqlConnection and so on.
using Northwind.Models; // To use Product.
using System.Data; // To use CommandType.

namespace Packt.Extensions;

public static class WebApplicationExtensions
{
  public static WebApplication MapGets(this WebApplication app)
  {
    // app.MapGet(pattern, handler);

    app.MapGet("/", () => "Hello from a native AOT minimal API web
service.");

    app.MapGet("/products", GetProducts);

    app.MapGet("/products/{minimumUnitPrice:decimal?}", GetProducts);

    return app;
  }
```

```
   private static List<Product> GetProducts(decimal? minimumUnitPrice =
null)
  {
    SqlConnectionStringBuilder builder = new();

    builder.InitialCatalog = "Northwind";
    builder.MultipleActiveResultSets = true;
    builder.Encrypt = true;
    builder.TrustServerCertificate = true;
    builder.ConnectTimeout = 10; // Default is 30 seconds.
    builder.DataSource = "."; // Local SQL Server
    builder.IntegratedSecurity = true;

    /*
    // To use SQL Server Authentication:
    builder.UserID = Environment.GetEnvironmentVariable("MY_SQL_USR");
    builder.Password = Environment.GetEnvironmentVariable("MY_SQL_PWD");
    builder.PersistSecurityInfo = false;
    */

    SqlConnection connection = new(builder.ConnectionString);

    connection.Open();

    SqlCommand cmd = connection.CreateCommand();

    cmd.CommandType = CommandType.Text;
    cmd.CommandText =
      "SELECT ProductId, ProductName, UnitPrice FROM Products";

    if (minimumUnitPrice.HasValue)
    {
      cmd.CommandText += " WHERE UnitPrice >= @minimumUnitPrice";

      cmd.Parameters.AddWithValue("minimumUnitPrice", minimumUnitPrice);
    }

    SqlDataReader r = cmd.ExecuteReader();

    List<Product> products = new();
```

```
      while (r.Read())
      {
        Product p = new()
        {
          ProductId = r.GetInt32("ProductId"),
          ProductName = r.GetString("ProductName"),
          UnitPrice = r.GetDecimal("UnitPrice")
        };
        products.Add(p);
      }

      r.Close();

      return products;
    }
  }
```

With native AOT, we cannot use EF Core, so we are using the lower-level ADO.NET SqlClient API. This is faster and more efficient anyway. In the future, perhaps with .NET 9 or .NET 10, we will be able to use our EF Core model for Northwind instead.

9. In `Program.cs`, note the call to the `CreateSlimBuilder` method, which ensures that only the essential features of ASP.NET Core are enabled by default, so it minimizes the deployed web service size, as shown in the following code:

```
var builder = WebApplication.CreateSlimBuilder(args);
```

The `CreateSlimBuilder` method does not include support for HTTPS or HTTP/3, although you can add those back in yourself if you need them. It does support JSON file configuration for `appsettings.json` and logging.

10. In `Program.cs`, after the call to `builder.Build()`, delete the statements that generated some sample todos and map some endpoints, as shown in the following code:

```
var sampleTodos = new Todo[]
{
  new(1, "Walk the dog"),
  new(2, "Do the dishes", DateOnly.FromDateTime(DateTime.Now)),
  new(3, "Do the laundry", DateOnly.FromDateTime(DateTime.Now.
AddDays(1))),
  new(4, "Clean the bathroom"),
```

```
    new(5, "Clean the car", DateOnly.FromDateTime(DateTime.Now.AddDays(2)))
};

var todosApi = app.MapGroup("/todos");
todosApi.MapGet("/", () => sampleTodos);
todosApi.MapGet("/{id}", (int id) =>
    sampleTodos.FirstOrDefault(a => a.Id == id) is { } todo
        ? Results.Ok(todo)
        : Results.NotFound());
```

11. In `Program.cs`, at the bottom of the file, delete the statements that define the `Todo` record and `AppJsonSerializerContext` class, as shown in the following code:

```
public record Todo(int Id, string? Title, DateOnly? DueBy = null, bool
IsComplete = false);


[JsonSerializable(typeof(Todo[]))]
internal partial class AppJsonSerializerContext : JsonSerializerContext
{


}
```

12. In `Program.cs`, delete the namespace imports, import the namespaces for our JSON serializer context and extension methods, modify the statement that inserts the JSON serialization context to use the Northwind one, and then before running the web app, call the `MapGets` method, as shown highlighted in the following code:

```
using Northwind.Serialization;
using Packt.Extensions; // To use MapGets().

var builder = WebApplication.CreateSlimBuilder(args);

builder.Services.ConfigureHttpJsonOptions(options =>
{
  options.SerializerOptions.TypeInfoResolverChain
    .Insert(0, NorthwindJsonSerializerContext.Default);
});

var app = builder.Build();

app.MapGets();

app.Run();
```

13. If your database server is not running (for example, because you are hosting it in Docker, a virtual machine, or in the cloud), then make sure to start it.

14. Start the web service project using the `http` profile:

    - If you are using Visual Studio 2022, then select the **http** profile in the drop-down list and then navigate to **Debug | Start Without Debugging** or press *Ctrl + F5*.

    - If you are using Visual Studio Code, then enter the command `dotnet run --launch-profile http`, manually start a web browser, and navigate to the web service: `https://localhost:5083/`.

15. In the web browser, note the plain text response: `Hello from a native AOT minimal API web service`.

16. In the address bar, append `/products`, and note the array of products in the response, as shown in the following partial output:

```
[{"productId":1,"productName":"Chai","unitPrice":18.0000},
 {"productId":2,"productName":"Chang","unitPrice":19.0000},
 {"productId":3,"productName":"Aniseed Syrup","unitPrice":10.0000},
 {"productId":4,"productName":"Chef Anton's Cajun Seasoning",
  "unitPrice":22.0000},
 {"productId":5,"productName":"Chef Anton's Gumbo Mix",
  "unitPrice":21.3500},
 {"productId":6,"productName":"Grandma's Boysenberry Spread",
  "unitPrice":25.0000},
 {"productId":7,"productName":"Uncle Bob's Organic Dried Pears",
  "unitPrice":30.0000},
 {"productId":8,"productName":"Northwoods Cranberry Sauce",
  "unitPrice":40.0000},
 {"productId":9,"productName":"Mishi Kobe Niku","unitPrice":97.0000},
 {"productId":10,"productName":"Ikura","unitPrice":31.0000},
 {"productId":11,"productName":"Queso Cabrales","unitPrice":21.0000},
 {"productId":12,"productName":"Queso Manchego La Pastora",
  "unitPrice":38.0000},
```

17. In the address bar, append `/products/100`, and note the array of two products in the response, as shown in the following partial output:

```
[{"productId":29,"productName":"Thüringer
Rostbratwurst","unitPrice":123.7900},{"productId":38,"productName":"Côte
de Blaye","unitPrice":263.5000}]
```

18. Close the browser and shut down the web server.

Publishing a native AOT project

A service that functions correctly during development when the service is untrimmed and JIT-compiled could still fail once you publish it using native AOT. You should therefore perform a publish before assuming your project will work.

If your project does not produce any AOT warnings at publish time, you can then be confident that your service will work after publishing for AOT.

Let's review the source-generated code and publish our web service:

1. In the `Northwind.MinimalAot.Service` project file, add an element to emit compiler-generated files, as shown highlighted in the following markup:

    ```
    <PropertyGroup>
      <TargetFramework>net8.0</TargetFramework>
      ...
      <EmitCompilerGeneratedFiles>true</EmitCompilerGeneratedFiles>
    </PropertyGroup>
    ```

2. Build the `Northwind.MinimalAot.Service` project.

3. If you are using Visual Studio 2022, toggle **Show All Files** in **Solution Explorer**.

4. Expand the `obj\Debug\net8.0\generated` folder, and note the folders and files that have been created by the source generators for AOT and JSON serialization, and note that you will be opening some of these files in the next few steps, as shown in *Figure 8.10*:

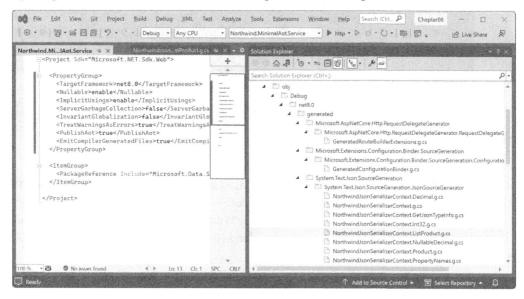

Figure 8.10: Folders and files created by source generators in an AOT web service project

5. Open the `GeneratedRouteBuilderExtensions.g.cs` file, and note it contains code to define the mapped routes for the minimal API web service.

6. Open the `NorthwindJsonSerializerContext.Decimal.g.cs` file, and note it contains code to serialize a `decimal` value passed as the minimum unit price parameter to one of the routes.

7. Open the `NorthwindJsonSerializerContext.ListProduct.g.cs` file, and note it contains code to serialize a list of `Product` objects returned as a response for two of the routes.

8. In the `Northwind.MinimalAot.Service` folder, at the command prompt or terminal, publish the web service using native AOT, as shown in the following command:

```
dotnet publish
```

9. Note the message about generating native code and trim warnings for packages like `Microsoft.Data.SqlClient`, as shown in the following partial output:

```
Generating native code
C:\Users\markj\.nuget\packages\microsoft.data.sqlclient\5.1.1\runtimes\
win\lib\net6.0\Microsoft.Data.SqlClient.dll : warning IL2104: Assembly
'Microsoft.Data.SqlClient' produced trim warnings. For more information
see https://aka.ms/dotnet-illink/libraries [C:\apps-services-net8\
Chapter08\Northwind.MinimalAot.Service\Northwind.MinimalAot.Service.
csproj]
/_/src/libraries/System.Data.Common/src/System/Data/DataTable.
cs(6704): Trim analysis warning IL2026: System.Data.DataTable.System.
Xml.Serialization.IXmlSerializable.ReadXml(XmlReader): Using member
'System.Data.DataTable.ReadXmlSerializableInternal(XmlReader)' which has
'RequiresUnreferencedCodeAttribute' can break functionality when trimming
application code. DataTable.ReadXml uses XmlSerialization underneath
which is not trimming safe. Members from serialized types may be trimmed
if not referenced directly. [C:\apps-services-net8\Chapter08\Northwind.
MinimalAot.Service\Northwind.MinimalAot.Service.csproj]
```

 We did not use the `DataTable.ReadXml` method, which is calling a potentially trimmed member, so we can ignore the preceding warning.

10. Start **File Explorer** and open the `bin\Release\net8.0\win-x64\publish` folder and note the EXE file is about 30 MB. This and the `Microsoft.Data.SqlClient.SNI.dll` file are the only files that need to be deployed onto another Windows computer for the web service to work. The `appsettings.json` files are only needed to override configuration if needed. The PDB file is only needed if debugging.

11. Run the `Northwind.MinimalAot.Service.exe`, and note the web service starts up very fast and it will use port `5000` by default, as shown in *Figure 8.11*:

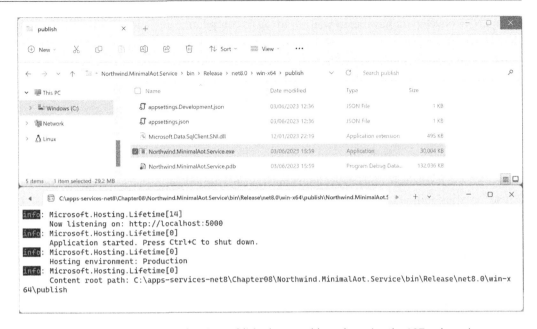

Figure 8.11: File Explorer showing published executable and running the AOT web service

12. Start a web browser, navigate to `http://localhost:5000/`, and note the web service works correctly by returning the plain text response.

13. Navigate to `http://localhost:5000/products/100`, and note the web service responds with the two products that have a minimum unit price of 100.

14. Close the web browser and shut down the web service.

15. In the `Northwind.WebApi.Service` project file, at the command prompt or terminal, publish the web service, as shown in the following command:

```
dotnet publish
```

16. Start **File Explorer**, open the `bin\Release\net8.0\win-x64\publish` folder, and note the `Northwind.WebApi.Service.exe` file is less than 154 KB. That is because it is framework-dependent, meaning it needs .NET installed on the computer to work. Also, there are many files that must be deployed along with the EXE file that add up to about 14 MB.

17. Run the `Northwind.MinimalAot.Service.exe` and note the web service starts up slower than the AOT version and it will use port `5000` by default.

18. Start a web browser, navigate to `http://localhost:5000/`, and note the web service works correctly by returning the plain text response.

19. Navigate to `http://localhost:5000/products/100`, and note the web service responds with the two products that have a minimum unit price of 100 but the response is slower than the AOT version.

20. Close the web browser and shut down the web service.

Many .NET developers have been waiting for AOT compilation for a long time. Microsoft is finally delivering on the promise, and it will expand to cover more project types over the next few major versions, so it's a technology to keep an eye on.

Understanding identity services

Identity services are used to authenticate and authorize users. It is important for these services to implement open standards so that you can integrate disparate systems. Common standards include **OpenID Connect** and **OAuth 2.0**.

Microsoft has no plans to officially support third-party authentication servers like **IdentityServer4** because "creating and sustaining an authentication server is a full-time endeavor, and Microsoft already has a team and a product in that area, Azure Active Directory, which allows 500,000 objects for free."

JWT bearer authorization

JSON Web Token (JWT) is a standard that defines a compact and secure method to transmit information as a JSON object. The JSON object is digitally signed so it can be trusted. The most common scenario for using JWT is authorization.

A user logs in to a trusted party using credentials like a username and password or biometric scan or two-factor authentication, and the trusted party issues a JWT. This is then sent with every request to the secure web service.

In their compact form, JWTs consist of three parts separated by dots. These parts are the *header*, *payload*, and *signature*, as shown in the following format: `aaa.bbb.ccc`. The header and payload are Base64 encoded.

Authenticating service clients using JWT bearer authentication

During local development, the `dotnet user-jwts` command-line tool is used to create and manage local JWTs. The values are stored in a JSON file in the local machine's user profile folder.

Let's secure the web service using JWT bearer authentication and test it with a local token:

1. In the `Northwind.WebApi.Service` project, add a reference to the package for JWT bearer authentication, as shown in the following markup:

    ```
    <PackageReference Include="Microsoft.AspNetCore.Authentication.JwtBearer"
                      Version="8.0.0" />
    ```

2. Build the `Northwind.WebApi.Service` project to restore packages.

3. In `Program.cs`, after creating the `builder`, add statements to add authorization and authentication using JWT, as shown highlighted in the following code:

    ```
    var builder = WebApplication.CreateBuilder(args);

    builder.Services.AddAuthorization();
    ```

```
builder.Services.AddAuthentication(defaultScheme: "Bearer")
  .AddJwtBearer();
```

4. In `Program.cs`, after building the app, add a statement to use authorization, as shown highlighted in the following code:

```
var app = builder.Build();

app.UseAuthorization();
```

5. In `WebApplication.Extensions.cs`, import the namespace for security claims, as shown in the following code:

```
using System.Security.Claims; // To use ClaimsPrincipal.
```

6. In `WebApplication.Extensions.cs`, after mapping an HTTP GET request for the root path to return a plain text `Hello World` response, add a statement to map an HTTP GET request for the secret path to return the authenticated user's name if they are authorized, as shown in the following code:

```
app.MapGet("/", () => "Hello World!")
  .ExcludeFromDescription();

app.MapGet("/secret", (ClaimsPrincipal user) =>
  string.Format("Welcome, {0}. The secret ingredient is love.",
    user.Identity?.Name ?? "secure user"))
  .RequireAuthorization();
```

7. In the `Northwind.WebApi.Service` project folder, at the command prompt or terminal, create a local JWT, as shown in the following command:

```
dotnet user-jwts create
```

8. Note the automatically assigned `ID`, `Name`, and `Token`, as shown in the following partial output:

```
New JWT saved with ID 'd7e22000'.
Name: markjprice

Token: eyJhbGciOiJIUzI1NiIsInR5cCI6IkpXVCJ9.
eyJ1bmlxdWVfbmFtZSI6Im1hcmtqcHJpY2UiLCJzdWIiOiJtYXJan...lci1qd3RzIn0.
pGEbYKRjU98dEjxLSx7GAEm41LXMS0J80iIjuZbqrj4
```

9. At the command prompt or terminal, print all the information for the ID that was assigned, as shown in the following command:

```
dotnet user-jwts print d7e22000 --show-all
```

10. Note the scheme is `Bearer` so the token must be sent with every request, the audience(s) lists the authorized client domains and port numbers, the token expires after three months, the JSON objects represent the header and payload, and finally, there's the compact token with its Base64-encoded three parts separated by dots, as shown in the following partial output:

```
Found JWT with ID 'd7e22000'.
ID: d7e22000
Name: markjprice
Scheme: Bearer
Audience(s): http://localhost:30225, https://localhost:44344, http://
localhost:5080, https://localhost:5081
Not Before: 2023-09-26T10:58:18.0000000+00:00
Expires On: 2023-12-26T10:58:18.0000000+00:00
Issued On: 2023-09-26T10:58:19.0000000+00:00
Scopes: none
Roles: [none]
Custom Claims: [none]
Token Header: {"alg":"HS256","typ":"JWT"}
Token Payload: {"unique_
name":"markjprice","sub":"markjprice","jti":"d7e22000","aud":["http://
localhost:30225","https://localhost:44344","http://
localhost:5080","https://localhost:5081"],"nbf":1664189898,"exp":16720522
98,"iat":1664189899,"iss":"dotnet-user-jwts"}
Compact Token: eyJhbGciOiJIUzI1NiIsInR5cCI6IkpXVCJ9.
eyJ1bmlxdWVfbmFtZSI6Im1hcmtqcHJpY2UiLCJzdWIiOiJtYXJranByaWNl...
uZXQtdXNlci1qd3RzIn0.pGEbYKRjU98dEjxLSx7GAEm41LXMS0J80iIjuZbqrj4
```

11. In the `Northwind.WebApi.Service` project, in `appsettings.Development.json`, note the new section named `Authentication`, as shown highlighted in the following configuration:

```json
{
  "Logging": {
    "LogLevel": {
      "Default": "Information",
      "Microsoft.AspNetCore": "Warning",
      "Microsoft.AspNetCore.HttpLogging": "Information"
    }
  },
  "Authentication": {
    "Schemes": {
      "Bearer": {
        "ValidAudiences": [
          "http://localhost:30225",
```

```
                    "https://localhost:44344",
                    "http://localhost:5080"
                    "https://localhost:5081"
                ],
                "ValidIssuer": "dotnet-user-jwts"
            }
        }
    }
}
```

12. Start the `Northwind.WebApi.Service` project using the `https` profile without debugging.

13. In the browser, change the relative path to `/secret` and note the response is rejected with a 401 status code.

14. Start Visual Studio Code and open the `HttpRequests` folder.

15. In the `HttpRequests` folder, create a file named `webapi-secure-request.http` and modify its contents to contain a request to get the secret ingredient, as shown in the following code (but use your `Bearer` token, of course):

```
### Get the secret ingredient.
GET https://localhost:5081/secret/
Authorization: Bearer eyJhbGciOiJIUzI1NiIsInR5cCI6IkpXVCJ9.
eyJ1bmlxdWVfbmFtZSI6Im1hcmtqcHJpY2UiLCJzdWIiOiJtYXJranByaWN1...
uZXQtdXNlci1qd3RzIn0.pGEbYKRjU98dEjxLSx7GAEm41LXMS0J80iIjuZbqrj4
```

16. Click **Send Request**, and note the response, as shown in the following output:

```
Welcome, secure user. The secret ingredient is love.
```

17. Close the browser and shut down the web service.

Practicing and exploring

Test your knowledge and understanding by answering some questions, getting some hands-on practice, and exploring this chapter's topics with deeper research.

Exercise 8.1 – Test your knowledge

Answer the following questions:

1. List six method names that can be specified in an HTTP request.

2. List six status codes and their descriptions that can be returned in an HTTP response.

3. How is the ASP.NET Core Minimal APIs service technology different from the ASP.NET Core Web APIs service technology?

4. With the ASP.NET Core Minimal APIs service technology, how do you map an HTTP PUT request to `api/customers` to a lambda statement block?

5. With the ASP.NET Core Minimal APIs service technology, how do you map a method or lambda parameter to a value in a route, query string, or the body of the request?

6. Does enabling CORS increase security for a web service?

7. You have added statements to `Program.cs` to enable HTTP logging but HTTP requests and responses are not being logged. What is the most likely reason and how can you fix it?

8. How do you limit the rate of requests for a specific client using the `AspNetCoreRateLimit` package?

9. How do you limit the rate of requests for a specific endpoint using the `Microsoft.AspNetCore.RateLimiting` package?

10. What does JWT mean?

Exercise 8.2 – Review Microsoft HTTP API design policy

Microsoft has internal HTTP/REST API design guidelines. Microsoft teams reference this document when designing their HTTP APIs. They are a great starting point for your own standards for HTTP APIs. You can review them at the following link:

```
https://github.com/microsoft/api-guidelines
```

The guidelines have a section specific to CORS and you can review them at the following link:

```
https://github.com/microsoft/api-guidelines/blob/vNext/Guidelines.md#8-cors
```

Exercise 8.3 – Explore topics

Use the links on the following page to learn more details about the topics covered in this chapter:

```
https://github.com/markjprice/apps-services-net8/blob/main/docs/book-links.md#chapter-
8---building-and-securing-web-services-using-minimal-apis
```

Exercise 8.4 – Exposing data via the web using OData services

Learn how to quickly implement a Web API service that can wrap an EF Core entity model using OData in this online-only chapter:

```
https://github.com/markjprice/apps-services-net8/blob/main/docs/ch08-odata.md
```

Exercise 8.5 – Auth0 project templates

If you need to implement Auth0 for authentication and authorization, then you can use project templates to scaffold your code. An article describing these project templates and how to use them is found at the following link:

```
https://auth0.com/blog/introducing-auth0-templates-for-dotnet/
```

Summary

In this chapter, you learned how to:

- Build a web service that implements the REST architectural style using minimal APIs.
- Relax the same-origin security policy for specified domains and ports using CORS.
- Implement two different rate-limiting packages to prevent denial of service attacks.
- Secure services using JWT bearer authorization.

In the next chapter, you will learn how to build reliable and scalable services by adding features like caching, queues, and automatic handling of transient faults using libraries like Polly.

Caching, Queuing, and Resilient Background Services

In this chapter, you will be introduced to multiple technologies and techniques that will improve the scalability and reliability of your services, no matter what service technology you choose to implement them with.

This chapter will cover the following topics:

- Understanding service architecture
- Caching with ASP.NET Core
- Fault tolerance with Polly
- Queuing with RabbitMQ
- Implementing long-running background services

Understanding service architecture

In *Chapter 8*, *Building and Securing Web Services Using Minimal APIs*, you learned how to build a web service using ASP.NET Core Minimal APIs. Before looking at alternative technologies to build services, it is worth taking a step back and reviewing service architecture and what causes bottlenecks in service performance and scalability.

What parts of a system are slowest?

Traditionally, the slowest parts of a system are:

- The network (slowest)
- The disk
- Memory
- CPU cache memory (fastest)

Each step can be 5 to 10 times slower than the next.

However, networks are much faster than they used to be, and systems often run within remote data centers. Imagine your service needs some data. Is it faster to read from the local server disk or to make a call to another server?

- Server-to-server call within the same data center: 500,000 nanoseconds (ns)
- Disk seek: 10,000,000 ns

Numbers every (developer) should know

Jeff Dean, a Google Fellow, quotes in his presentations the actual times in nanoseconds (ns) for various technologies to access or read data. They are shown in *Table 9.1*, and I have added a column to scale the numbers to be more comprehensible to a human:

Technology	Actual	Humanized
CPU cycle	0.1 ns	1 second
L1 cache reference	½ ns	5 seconds
L2 cache reference	5 ns	1 minute
Mutex lock/unlock	25 ns	4 minutes
Main memory reference	100 ns	¼ hour
Send 1K byte over 1 Gbps network	10,000 ns	28 hours
Read 1 MB sequentially from memory	250,000 ns	29 days
Round trip within same datacenter	500,000 ns	2 months
Read 1 MB sequentially from SSD	1,000,000 ns	4 months
Disk seek	10,000,000 ns	3¼ years
Read 1 MB sequentially from disk	20,000,000 ns	6¼ years
Send packet CA->Netherlands->CA	150,000,000 ns	47½ years

Table 9.1: Nanosecond times for various technologies to access or read data

 More Information: *Designs, Lessons, and Advice from Building Large Distributed Systems*, by Jeff Dean, http://www.cs.cornell.edu/projects/ladis2009/talks/dean-keynote-ladis2009.pdf.

The point is not to debate if reading from drives or SSDs is faster or not than network calls. It is more about being aware of the differences between getting data that's close and data that's far away. The orders of magnitude are comparatively massive.

For example, if a CPU needs to process some data and it is already in the L1 cache, then it takes the equivalent of 1 second. If it needs to read the data from memory, it takes the equivalent of a quarter of an hour. If it needs to fetch that data from a server in the same data center, it takes the equivalent of 2 months. And if it is in California and the data is in the Netherlands, it takes the equivalent of 47½ years!

This is why caching is so important. Caching is about temporarily storing data as close to where it will be needed as possible.

Caching with ASP.NET Core

Caching can enable our systems to copy some data from a remote data center to a local data center, or from a server or disk to memory. Caches store data as key-value pairs.

However, one of the hardest parts of caching is getting the balance right between storing enough data and keeping it fresh. The more data we copy, the more resources we use. And we need to consider how we will keep the copies synchronized with the original data.

General caching guidelines

Caching works best with data that costs a lot to generate and does not change often.

Follow these guidelines when caching:

- Your code should never depend on cached data. It should always be able to get the data from the original source when the data is not found in the cache.
- Wherever you cache data (in-memory or in a database) it is a limited resource, so deliberately limit the amount of data cached and for how long by implementing expirations and size limits. You should monitor cache hits (when data is successfully found in the cache) to obtain the right balance for your specific scenarios.

In the coding tasks in this section, you will implement all of these guidelines.

Let's start by reviewing the caching technologies built-in to ASP.NET Core.

Building a controller-based Web API service

To explore various caching technologies, let's build a basic web service:

1. Use your preferred code editor to create a new Web API controller-based project, as defined in the following list:

    - Project template: **ASP.NET Core Web API** / `webapi --use-controllers`
    - Solution file and folder: `Chapter09`
    - Project file and folder: `Northwind.WebApi.Service`
    - **Authentication type: None**
    - **Configure for HTTPS:** Selected
    - **Enable Docker:** Cleared
    - **Use controllers:** Selected
    - **Enable OpenAPI support:** Selected
    - **Do not use top-level statements:** Cleared

Make sure to select the **Use controllers** checkbox or specify the `--use-controllers` or `-controllers` switch. We will not use minimal APIs, which is the default way a Web API is implemented using the .NET 8 project templates. If you use JetBrains Rider, you might want to use the `dotnet new` command until Rider supports a **Use controllers** option.

2. Add a project reference to the Northwind database context project for the SQL Server that you created in *Chapter 3, Building Entity Models for SQL Server Using EF Core*, as shown in the following markup:

```xml
<ItemGroup>
  <ProjectReference Include="..\..\Chapter03\Northwind.Common.DataContext
.SqlServer\Northwind.Common.DataContext.SqlServer.csproj" />
</ItemGroup>
```

The path cannot have a line break. If you did not complete the task of creating the class libraries in *Chapter 3*, then download the solution projects from the GitHub repository.

3. In the project file, change invariant globalization to `false`, and treat warnings as errors, as shown in the following markup:

```xml
<Project Sdk="Microsoft.NET.Sdk.Web">

  <PropertyGroup>
    <TargetFramework>net8.0</TargetFramework>
    <Nullable>enable</Nullable>
    <ImplicitUsings>enable</ImplicitUsings>
    <InvariantGlobalization>false</InvariantGlobalization>
    <TreatWarningsAsErrors>true</TreatWarningsAsErrors>
  </PropertyGroup>
```

Explicitly setting invariant globalization to `true` is new in the ASP.NET Core Web API project template with .NET 8. It is designed to make a web service non-culture-specific so that it can be deployed anywhere in the world and have the same behavior. By setting this property to `false`, the web service will default to the culture of the current computer it is hosted on. You can read more about invariant globalization mode at the following link: `https://github.com/dotnet/runtime/blob/main/docs/design/features/globalization-invariant-mode.md`.

4. At the command prompt or terminal, build the Northwind.WebApi.Service project to make sure the entity model class library projects outside the current solution are properly compiled, as shown in the following command:

```
dotnet build
```

5. In the Properties folder, in launchSettings.json, modify the applicationUrl of the profile named https to use port 5091 for https and port 5092 for http, as highlighted in the following configuration:

```
"profiles": {
  ...
  "https": {
    "commandName": "Project",
    "dotnetRunMessages": true,
    "launchBrowser": true,
    "launchUrl": "swagger",
    "applicationUrl": "https://localhost:5091;http://localhost:5092",
    "environmentVariables": {
      "ASPNETCORE_ENVIRONMENT": "Development"
    }
```

 Visual Studio 2022 and JetBrains Rider will read this settings file and automatically run a web browser if launchBrowser is true, and then navigate to the applicationUrl and launchUrl. Visual Studio Code and dotnet run will not, so you will need to run a web browser and navigate manually to https://localhost:5091/swagger.

6. Delete the file named WeatherForecast.cs.

7. In the Controllers folder, delete the file named WeatherForecastController.cs.

8. In Program.cs, import the namespace to add the NorthwindContext to configured services, as highlighted in the following code:

```
using Northwind.EntityModels; // To use the AddNorthwindContext method.

var builder = WebApplication.CreateBuilder(args);

// Add services to the container.
builder.Services.AddNorthwindContext();
builder.Services.AddControllers();
```

9. In the Controllers folder, add a new class file named ProductsController.cs.

10. In `ProductsController.cs`, modify its contents to define a controller-based Web API to work with products in the Northwind database, as we did for minimal APIs, as shown in the following code:

```csharp
using Microsoft.AspNetCore.Mvc; // To use [HttpGet] and so on.
using Northwind.EntityModels; // To use NorthwindContext, Product.

namespace Northwind.WebApi.Service.Controllers;

[Route("api/products")]
[ApiController]
public class ProductsController : ControllerBase
{
  private int pageSize = 10;

  private readonly ILogger<ProductsController> _logger;
  private readonly NorthwindContext _db;

  public ProductsController(ILogger<ProductsController> logger,
    NorthwindContext context)
  {
    _logger = logger;
    _db = context;
  }

  // GET: api/products
  [HttpGet]
  [Produces(typeof(Product[]))]
  public IEnumerable<Product> Get(int? page)
  {
    return _db.Products
      .Where(p => p.UnitsInStock > 0 && !p.Discontinued)
      .OrderBy(product => product.ProductId)
      .Skip(((page ?? 1) - 1) * pageSize)
      .Take(pageSize);
  }

  // GET: api/products/outofstock
  [HttpGet]
  [Route("outofstock")]
  [Produces(typeof(Product[]))]
```

```csharp
public IEnumerable<Product> GetOutOfStockProducts()
{
  return _db.Products
    .Where(p => p.UnitsInStock == 0 && !p.Discontinued);
}

// GET: api/products/discontinued
[HttpGet]
[Route("discontinued")]
[Produces(typeof(Product[]))]
public IEnumerable<Product> GetDiscontinuedProducts()
{
  return _db.Products
    .Where(product => product.Discontinued);
}

// GET api/products/5
[HttpGet("{id:int}")]
public async ValueTask<Product?> Get(int id)
{
  return await _db.Products.FindAsync(id);
}

// GET api/products/cha
[HttpGet("{name}")]
public IEnumerable<Product> Get(string name)
{
  return _db.Products.Where(p => p.ProductName.Contains(name));
}

// POST api/products
[HttpPost]
public async Task<IActionResult> Post([FromBody] Product product)
{
  _db.Products.Add(product);
  await _db.SaveChangesAsync();
  return Created($"api/products/{product.ProductId}", product);
}

// PUT api/products/5
[HttpPut("{id}")]
```

```csharp
  public async Task<IActionResult> Put(int id, [FromBody] Product
product)
  {
    Product? foundProduct = await _db.Products.FindAsync(id);

    if (foundProduct is null) return NotFound();

    foundProduct.ProductName = product.ProductName;
    foundProduct.CategoryId = product.CategoryId;
    foundProduct.SupplierId = product.SupplierId;
    foundProduct.QuantityPerUnit = product.QuantityPerUnit;
    foundProduct.UnitsInStock = product.UnitsInStock;
    foundProduct.UnitsOnOrder = product.UnitsOnOrder;
    foundProduct.ReorderLevel = product.ReorderLevel;
    foundProduct.UnitPrice = product.UnitPrice;
    foundProduct.Discontinued = product.Discontinued;

    await _db.SaveChangesAsync();

    return NoContent();
  }

  // DELETE api/products/5
  [HttpDelete("{id}")]
  public async Task<IActionResult> Delete(int id)
  {
    if (await _db.Products.FindAsync(id) is Product product)
    {
      _db.Products.Remove(product);
      await _db.SaveChangesAsync();
      return NoContent();
    }
    return NotFound();
  }
}
```

11. If your database server is not running, for example, because you are hosting it in Docker, a virtual machine, or the cloud, then make sure to start it.

12. Start the web service project using the https profile without debugging.

    - If you are using Visual Studio 2022, then select the **https** profile in the drop-down list, and then navigate to **Debug** | **Start Without Debugging** or press *Ctrl* + *F5*. A web browser should navigate to the Swagger documentation web page automatically.

- If you are using Visual Studio Code, then enter the command `dotnet run --launch-profile https`, manually start a web browser, and navigate to the Swagger documentation web page: `https://localhost:5091/swagger`.

On Windows, if prompted to do so, you will have to set the Windows Defender Firewall to allow access to your local web service.

13. Use Swagger to test the various endpoints, and note the SQL statements logged to the output as you do so, for example:

   - Get the first page of 10 products.
   - Get the 6th page of 10 products.
   - Get the product with an ID of 77.
   - Get the single out-of-stock product.
   - Get the seven discontinued products.
   - Get products whose names start with `cha`.
   - Create (`POST`), update (`PUT`), and delete a product. For hints about how to perform these tests, read the following link: `https://github.com/markjprice/apps-services-net8/blob/main/docs/ch09-swagger-tests.md`.

If you completed *Chapter 8, Building and Securing Web Services Using Minimal APIs,* then instead of manually using Swagger, you can use the `.http` files we created to test the minimal API web service. Just change the port from `5081` to `5091`.

Now that we have a basic web service, we can start activating caching in it.

Caching objects using in-memory caching

The `IMemoryCache` interface represents a cache that uses local server memory. If you have multiple servers hosting your service or website, then you must enable "sticky sessions." This means that an incoming request from a client or visitor will be directed to the same server as previous requests from that client or visitor, allowing the request to find the correct cached data in that server's memory.

The `Microsoft.Extensions.Caching.Memory` package has a modern implementation of `IMemoryCache`. Avoid the older `System.Runtime.Caching`.

Sizes are defined using custom units. If you store simple `string` values, then you could use the length of the string. If you don't know the size, you could just use 1 unit for each entry to simply limit the number of entries.

When you add an object to a cache, you should set an expiration. There are two types, absolute and sliding, and you can set one or the other, both, or neither:

- **Absolute expiration:** This is a fixed date/time, for example, 1am on December 24, 2023. When the date/time is reached, the object is evicted. To use this, set the `AbsoluteExpiration` property of a cache entry to a `DateTime` value. Choose this if you need to guarantee that at some point the data in the cache will be refreshed.

- **Sliding expiration:** This is a time span, for example, 20 seconds. When the time span expires, the object is evicted. However, whenever an object is read from the cache, its expiration is reset for another 20 seconds. This is why it is described as *sliding*. A common duration for a **Content Management System (CMS)**, where content like a web page is loaded from a database, is 12 hours. Content frequently viewed by visitors, like the home page, is then likely to remain in memory. To use this, set the `SlidingExpiration` property of a cache entry to a `TimeSpan` value. Choose this if it is acceptable for data to potentially never be refreshed. A good CMS will have an additional mechanism to reliably force a refresh when new content is published, but this functionality is not built into .NET caching.

- **Both expirations:** If you only set a sliding expiration, an object may stay in the cache forever, so you might also want to set the `AbsoluteExpirationRelativeToNow` property to a `TimeSpan` further in the future, after which the object should definitely be evicted. Choose this if you want the best of both worlds.

- **Never:** You can set a cache entry to have a priority of `CacheItemPriority.NeverRemove`.

You can also configure a method to call back to when an object is evicted from the cache. This allows you to execute some business logic to decide if you want to add the object back into the cache, perhaps after refreshing it from the original data source. You do this by calling the `RegisterPostEvictionCallback` method.

Let's explore the in-memory cache:

1. In the `Northwind.WebApi.Service` project, in `Program.cs`, import the namespace to work with the in-memory cache, as shown in the following code:

    ```
    using Microsoft.Extensions.Caching.Memory; // To use IMemoryCache and so
    on.
    ```

2. In `Program.cs`, after the call to `CreateBuilder`, in the section for configuring services, register an implementation for the in-memory cache, configured to store a maximum of 50 products, as shown in the following code:

    ```
    builder.Services.AddSingleton<IMemoryCache>(new MemoryCache(
      new MemoryCacheOptions
      {
        TrackStatistics = true,
        SizeLimit = 50 // Products.
      }));
    ```

3. In `ProductsController.cs`, import the namespace to work with the in-memory cache, as shown in the following code:

```
using Microsoft.Extensions.Caching.Memory; // To use IMemoryCache.
```

4. In `ProductsController.cs`, declare some fields to store the in-memory cache and a key for the out-of-stock products, as shown in the following code:

```
private readonly IMemoryCache _memoryCache;
private const string OutOfStockProductsKey = "OOSP";

public ProductsController(ILogger<ProductsController> logger,
  NorthwindContext context,
  IMemoryCache memoryCache)
{
  _logger = logger;
  _db = context;
  _memoryCache = memoryCache;
}
```

5. In `ProductsController.cs`, in the `GetOutOfStockProducts` action method, add statements to try to get the cached out-of-stock products, and if they are not cached, get them from the database and set them in the cache, using a sliding expiration of five seconds, as highlighted in the following code:

```
// GET: api/products/outofstock
[HttpGet]
[Route("outofstock")]
[Produces(typeof(Product[]))]
public IEnumerable<Product> GetOutOfStockProducts()
{
  // Try to get the cached value.
  if (!_memoryCache.TryGetValue(OutOfStockProductsKey,
    out Product[]? cachedValue))
  {
    // If the cached value is not found, get the value from the database.
    cachedValue = _db.Products
      .Where(p => p.UnitsInStock == 0 && !p.Discontinued)
      .ToArray();

    MemoryCacheEntryOptions cacheEntryOptions = new()
    {
      SlidingExpiration = TimeSpan.FromSeconds(5),
      Size = cachedValue?.Length
```

```
    };

    _memoryCache.Set(OutOfStockProductsKey, cachedValue,
cacheEntryOptions);
    }

    MemoryCacheStatistics? stats = _memoryCache.GetCurrentStatistics();

    _logger.LogInformation("Memory cache. Total hits: {stats?
        .TotalHits}. Estimated size: {stats?.CurrentEstimatedSize}.");

    return cachedValue ?? Enumerable.Empty<Product>();
}
```

6.   Start the web service project using the https profile without debugging.

7.   Arrange the windows so that you can see the command prompt or terminal at the same time as the web page.

8.   On the Swagger web page, click **GET /api/product/outofstock** to expand that section.

9.   Click the **Try it out** button.

10.   Click the **Execute** button, and note in the output that EF Core executes a SQL statement to get the products, the total hit counter is zero, and one product has now been cached, as shown in the following output:

```
info: Northwind.WebApi.Service.Controllers.ProductsController[0]
      Memory cache. Total hits: 0. Estimated size: 1.
```

11.   Click **Execute** within five seconds, and continue to click it a few more times:

   •   Note that EF Core does not need to re-execute the SQL statement because the products are cached, and if something reads them within a five-second sliding expiration, they will stay in memory forever.

   •   Note the total hit counter for the cache increments each time the out-of-stock products are found in the cache, as shown in the following output:

```
info: Northwind.WebApi.Service.Controllers.ProductsController[0]
      Memory cache. Total hits: 1. Estimated size: 1.
info: Northwind.WebApi.Service.Controllers.ProductsController[0]
      Memory cache. Total hits: 2. Estimated size: 1.
info: Northwind.WebApi.Service.Controllers.ProductsController[0]
      Memory cache. Total hits: 3. Estimated size: 1.
```

12.   Wait at least five seconds.

13.   Click **Execute**, and note in the output that EF Core executes a SQL statement to get the products because they have not been read within the five-second sliding expiration window.

14. Close the browser and shut down the web server.

Caching objects using distributed caching

Distributed caches have benefits over in-memory caches. Cached objects:

- Are consistent across requests to multiple servers.
- Survive server restarts and service deployments.
- Do not waste local server memory.
- Are stored in a shared area, so in a server farm scenario with multiple servers, you do not need to enable sticky sessions.

 Warning! A disadvantage of distributed caches is that in-memory caches can store any object, but a distributed cache can only store byte arrays. Your object needs to be serialized and sent across a network to the remote cache.

Microsoft provides the IDistributedCache interface with pre-defined methods to manipulate items in any distributed cache implementation. The methods are:

- Set or SetAsync: To store an object in the cache.
- Get or GetAsync: To retrieve an object from the cache.
- Remove or RemoveAsync: To remove an object from the cache.
- Refresh or RefreshAsync: To reset the sliding expiration for an object in the cache.

There are many implementations of distributed caching to choose from, including the following:

- SQL Server: https://learn.microsoft.com/en-us/aspnet/core/performance/caching/distributed#distributed-sql-server-cache
- Redis: https://learn.microsoft.com/en-us/aspnet/core/performance/caching/distributed#distributed-redis-cache
- NCache: http://www.alachisoft.com/ncache/aspnet-core-idistributedcache-ncache.html

We will use the **Distributed Memory Cache**, which is a Microsoft built-in implementation of IDistributedCache that stores items in memory on the server where the service runs.

It is not an actual distributed cache, but it is useful for scenarios like unit testing, where you want to remove the dependency on yet another external service, or while learning, as we are doing in this book.

Later, you only need to change the configured distributed cache, not the service implementation code that uses it, because all interactions go through the registered IDistributedCache implementation.

Let's go!

1. In the `Northwind.WebApi.Service` project, in `Program.cs`, after the call to `CreateBuilder`, in the section for configuring services, register the implementation for the distributed memory cache, as shown in the following code:

   ```
   builder.Services.AddDistributedMemoryCache();
   ```

2. In `ProductsController.cs`, import the namespace for working with a distributed cache implementation and serialized JSON, as shown in the following code:

   ```
   using Microsoft.Extensions.Caching.Distributed; // To use
   IDistributedCache.
   using System.Text.Json; // To use JsonSerializer.
   ```

3. In `ProductsController.cs`, declare some fields to store the distributed cache implementation and an item key for discontinued products, as highlighted in the following code:

   ```
   private readonly IMemoryCache _memoryCache;
   private const string OutOfStockProductsKey = "OOSP";

   private readonly IDistributedCache _distributedCache;
   private const string DiscontinuedProductsKey = "DISCP";

   public ProductsController(ILogger<ProductsController> logger,
     NorthwindContext context,
     IMemoryCache memoryCache,
     IDistributedCache distributedCache)
   {
     _logger = logger;
     _db = context;
     _memoryCache = memoryCache;
     _distributedCache = distributedCache;
   }
   ```

4. In `ProductsController.cs`, define a `private` method to get the discontinued products from the database, and set them in the distributed cache, using a sliding expiration of 5 seconds and an absolute expiration of 20 seconds, as shown in the following code:

   ```
   private Product[]? GetDiscontinuedProductsFromDatabase()
   {
     Product[]? cachedValue = _db.Products
       .Where(product => product.Discontinued)
       .ToArray();

     DistributedCacheEntryOptions cacheEntryOptions = new()
   ```

```
{
  // Allow readers to reset the cache entry's lifetime.
  SlidingExpiration = TimeSpan.FromSeconds(5),

  // Set an absolute expiration time for the cache entry.
  AbsoluteExpirationRelativeToNow = TimeSpan.FromSeconds(20),
};

byte[]? cachedValueBytes =
  JsonSerializer.SerializeToUtf8Bytes(cachedValue);

_distributedCache.Set(DiscontinuedProductsKey,
  cachedValueBytes, cacheEntryOptions);

return cachedValue;
}
```

5. In `ProductsController.cs`, in the `GetDiscontinuedProducts` action method, add statements to try to get the cached discontinued products, and if not cached, get them from the database. If a byte array is found in the cache, try to deserialize it into products, but if that fails too, get the products from the database, as highlighted in the following code:

```
// GET: api/products/discontinued
[HttpGet]
[Route("discontinued")]
[Produces(typeof(Product[]))]
public IEnumerable<Product> GetDiscontinuedProducts()
{
  // Try to get the cached value.

  byte[]? cachedValueBytes = _distributedCache.
Get(DiscontinuedProductsKey);

  Product[]? cachedValue = null;

  if (cachedValueBytes is null)
  {
    cachedValue = GetDiscontinuedProductsFromDatabase();
  }
  else
  {
    cachedValue = JsonSerializer
```

```
        .Deserialize<Product[]?>(cachedValueBytes);

    if (cachedValue is null)
    {
        cachedValue = GetDiscontinuedProductsFromDatabase();
    }
}


    return cachedValue ?? Enumerable.Empty<Product>();
}
```

 Unlike the in-memory cache that can store any live object, objects stored in distributed cache implementations must be serialized into `byte` arrays because they need to be transmittable across networks.

6. Start the web service project, using the `https` profile without debugging.

7. Arrange the windows so that you can see the command prompt or terminal at the same time as the web page.

8. On the Swagger web page, click **GET /api/product/discontinued** to expand that section.

9. Click the **Try it out** button.

10. Click the **Execute** button, and note in the output that EF Core executes a SQL statement to get the products.

11. Click **Execute** within five seconds, continue to click it a few more times, and note that EF Core does not need to re-execute the SQL statement because the products are cached. If something reads them within a five-second sliding expiration, they will stay in memory forever.

12. Wait at least five seconds.

13. Click **Execute**, and note in the output that EF Core executes a SQL statement to get the products because they have not been read within the five-second sliding expiration window.

14. Continue to click **Execute** repeatedly, and note that after 20 seconds, EF Core must execute a SQL statement to refresh the products.

15. Close the browser and shut down the web server.

A new abstraction for distributed caching

The ASP.NET Core team is working on adding a new abstraction for distributed caching to make it easier to use. It is not expected to be ready for .NET 8. It might be included in a point release, like 8.1, but more likely will be built-in with .NET 9.

Some `GetAsync` extension methods and supporting methods have been written by Marc Gravell. He maintains the most popular package to integrate .NET with Redis, so he has a lot of experience with distributed caching.

While we wait for an official implementation, you can read or download the source code to his extensions at the following link: `https://github.com/mgravell/DistributedCacheDemo/blob/main/DistributedCacheExtensions.cs`. The file is only 137 lines long, so it is easy to add to your own projects straight away.

The main difference in the new extension methods is that you do not need to call the `Set` or `SetAsync` methods anymore because they are abstracted away inside the new `GetAsync` methods, as shown in the following code:

```
// IDistributedCache methods.
objectFromDatabase = GetFromDatabase(...);
cache.Set(key: "ITEM_KEY", value: objectFromDatabase, options: ...);
dataFromCache = cache.Get(key: "ITEM_KEY");

// New extension methods.
dataFromCache = await cache.GetAsync(key: "ITEM_KEY",
  getMethod: GetFromDatabase(...), options: ..., cancellation: ...);
```

Also, note that the new extension methods are all asynchronous and generic, with a type `T` that will be serialized as JSON by default, but this can be overridden to use alternatives like the binary format protobuf.

More Information: You can learn more about the plans for these new extension methods at the following link: `https://devblogs.microsoft.com/dotnet/caching-abstraction-improvements-in-aspnetcore/`.

Caching web responses using HTTP caching

In-memory and distributed caching work with any type of app or service, using any transport technology, because all the magic happens on the server.

Response aka HTTP caching is tied to HTTP GET requests and responses because it is based on HTTP headers. Therefore, it only works with apps and services that use HTTP as their transport technology, like web services built using Web APIs, minimal APIs, and OData.

More Information: You can read the official standard for HTTP caching at the following link: `https://www.rfc-editor.org/rfc/rfc9111`.

Requirements for HTTP aka response caching include the following:

- The request must be a `GET` or `HEAD` one. `POST`, `PUT`, and `DELETE` requests, and so on, are never cached by HTTP caching.
- The response must have a `200 OK` status code.

- If the request has an `Authorization` header, then the response is not cached.
- If the request has a `Vary` header, then the response is not cached when the values are not valid or *.

The web server sets response caching headers, and then intermediate proxies and clients should respect the headers to tell them how they should cache the responses.

 Good Practice: Response aka HTTP caching is not typically useful for web user interfaces because web browsers often set request headers that prevent HTTP caching. For web user interfaces, output caching is better suited, and we will cover that in *Chapter 14, Building Web User Interfaces Using ASP.NET Core*.

The `Cache-Control` HTTP header for requests and responses has some common directives, as shown in *Table 9.2*:

Directive	Description
`public`	Clients and intermediaries can cache this response.
`private`	Only a client should cache this response.
`max-age`	The client does not accept responses older than the specified number of seconds.
`no-cache`	A client request is asking for a non-cached response. A server is telling the client and intermediaries not the cache the response.
`no-store`	A cache must not store the request or response.

Table 9.2: Common Cache-Control HTTP header directives

As well as `Cache-Control`, there are other headers that might affect caching, as shown in *Table 9.3*:

Header	Description
`Age`	Estimated number of seconds old the response is.
`Expires`	An absolute date/time after which the response should be considered expired.
`Vary`	All fields must match for a cached response to be sent. Otherwise, a fresh response is sent. For example, a query string of `color`.

Table 9.3: Common HTTP headers for caching

For example, a client could ask for a fresh list of discontinued products, and the service should not use any cached version, as shown in the following HTTP response:

```
GET api/products/discontinued
Cache-Control: no-cache
```

A service could return some products as a JSON array, with a header to say that intermediaries should not cache the response but clients can, as shown in the following HTTP response:

```
content-type: application/json; charset=utf-8
```

```
date: Fri,09 Jun 2023 06:05:13 GMT
server: Kestrel
cache-control: private


[
  {
    "productId": 5,
    "productName": "Chef Anton's Gumbo Mix",
    ...
```

Decorate a controller or method with the `[ResponseCache]` attribute to control caching responses from the server (code to control caching requests has to go in the client code). This attribute has common parameters, as shown in *Table 9.4*:

Property	Description
`Duration`	How long to cache in seconds.
`Location`	Where the response can be cached. `Any` (`cache-control: public`), `Client` (`cache-control: private`), `None` (`cache-control: no-cache`).
`NoStore`	Sets `cache-control: no-store`.
`VaryByHeader`	Sets the `Vary` header.
`VaryByQueryKeys`	Query keys to vary by.

Table 9.4: Common parameters of the [ResponseCache] attribute

Let's apply response caching to the web service:

1. In the `Northwind.WebApi.Service` project, in `Program.cs`, after the call to add the distributed memory cache, add a statement to add response caching middleware as a dependency service, as shown in the following code:

    ```
    builder.Services.AddResponseCaching();
    ```

2. In `Program.cs`, after the call to use HTTPS redirection, add a statement to use response caching middleware, as shown in the following code:

    ```
    app.UseResponseCaching();
    ```

     Good Practice: If using CORS middleware, then `UseCors` must be called before `UseResponseCaching`.

3. In `ProductsController.cs`, decorate the `Get` method with an `int` `id` parameter with the `[ResponseCache]` attribute, as highlighted in the following code:

```
// GET api/products/5
[HttpGet("{id:int}")]
[ResponseCache(Duration = 5, // Cache-Control: max-age=5
  Location = ResponseCacheLocation.Any, // Cache-Control: public
  VaryByHeader = "User-Agent" // Vary: User-Agent
  )]
public async ValueTask<Product?> Get(int id)
{
  return await _db.Products.FindAsync(id);
}
```

 The `[ResponseCache]` attribute can be applied to Razor Pages, MVC controller classes, and MVC action methods for both web services and websites.

4. Start the web service project, using the `https` profile without debugging.

5. In the `HttpRequests` folder, open the `webapi-get-products.http` file.

6. Modify the base address to use port 5091, and then send the request for a specific product, like 77, as shown in the following code:

```
GET {{base_address}}77
```

7. Note that the response includes headers to control caching, as highlighted in the following output:

```
Response time: 89 ms
Status code: OK (200)
Alt-Svc: h3=":5091"; ma=86400
Transfer-Encoding: chunked
Vary: User-Agent
Cache-Control: public, max-age=5
Date: Fri, 09 Jun 2023 06:26:45 GMT
Server: Kestrel

Content-Type: application/json; charset=utf-8
Content-Length: 270


-------------------------------------------------
Content:
```

```
{
    "productId": 77,
    "productName": "Original Frankfurter grüne Soße",
    "supplierId": 12,
    "categoryId": 2,
    "quantityPerUnit": "12 boxes",
    "unitPrice": 85.0,
    "unitsInStock": 32,
    "unitsOnOrder": 0,
    "reorderLevel": 15,
    "discontinued": false,
    "category": null,
    "orderDetails": [],
    "supplier": null
}
```

8. Close the browser and shut down the web server.

 Good Practice: Response caching should only be enabled for anonymous requests. Authenticated requests and responses should not be cached.

Caching is one of the best ways to improve the performance and scalability of your services. Next, we will learn how to improve a service's resilience when inevitable failures occur.

Fault tolerance with Polly

Polly is *"a .NET resilience and transient-fault-handling library that allows developers to express policies such as Retry, Circuit Breaker, Timeout, Bulkhead Isolation, and Fallback in a fluent and thread-safe manner,"* as stated on the official Polly GitHub repository, which can be found at the following link: https:// github.com/App-vNext/Polly.

Transient faults are errors caused by temporary conditions, such as temporary service unavailability or network connectivity issues. It is essential to handle transient faults in distributed systems, or they can become almost unusable.

Understanding retry and circuit breaker patterns

The **Retry** pattern enables clients to automatically retry a failed action with the expectation that the fault will succeed if retried after a short delay. Be careful, because if you implement the Retry pattern naively, then it can make the problem worse!

For example, if you set a fixed time between retries, then all the clients who received a fault will attempt to retry at the same time, overloading the service. To avoid this issue, retries are often set with an exponentially increasing time between retries, or they might use jitter (aka randomizer) algorithms.

The **Circuit Breaker** pattern prevents calls when a threshold of faults is reached. In effect, it is a way for a service to detect if a fault is *not* transient, or not transient enough to keep retrying.

 More Information: There is a nice summary table of resilience policies for Polly on its GitHub repository: `https://github.com/App-vNext/Polly#resilience-policies`.

Defining and executing policies

In any type of .NET project that calls any unreliable code, you can reference the Polly package and then define a policy using the `Policy` class. Polly is not used in the unreliable code or service itself. It is used by any clients that call the code or service.

For example, you might need to call two methods that might throw arithmetic or custom exceptions, and you want to automatically retry up to three times, so you define a policy to handle this, as shown in the following code:

```
RetryPolicy policy = Policy
    .Handle<CustomException>().Or<ArithmeticException>()
    .Retry(3);
```

Then, you can use that policy to execute the methods, as shown in the following code:

```
policy.Execute(() => GetProducts());
policy.Execute(() => GetCustomers());
```

Each call to `Execute` gets its own counter for retries, so if the call to `GetProducts` needs two retries, the call to `GetCustomers` still has a full three retries of its own.

For unlimited retries, you can call the `RetryForever` method, but this is not recommended.

For asynchronous methods, there are matching asynchronous methods; for example, instead of `Retry`, use `RetryAsync`.

To execute some statements when a retry occurs, for example, to log information, the `Retry` method can have a callback, as shown in the following code:

```
RetryPolicy policy = Policy
    .Handle<CustomException>().Or<ArithmeticException>()
    .Retry(3, onRetry: (exception, retryCount) =>
    {
        // Log the current retry count and exception information.
    });
```

Defining wait intervals between retries

Instead of immediately retrying after a fault, it is good practice to wait a moment before retrying.

For example, to wait and retry, as shown in the following code:

```
RetryPolicy policy = Policy
  .Handle<CustomException>().Or<ArithmeticException>()
  .WaitAndRetry(new[]
  {
    TimeSpan.FromSeconds(1), // 1 second between 1st and 2nd try.
    TimeSpan.FromSeconds(2), // 2 seconds between 2nd and 3rd try.
    TimeSpan.FromSeconds(5) // 5 seconds between 3rd and 4th try.
  });
```

Instead of hardcoded delay values, you can also define a function to generate them, as shown in the following code:

```
RetryPolicy policy = Policy
  .Handle<CustomException>().Or<ArithmeticException>()
  .WaitAndRetry(3, retryAttempt =>
    TimeSpan.FromSeconds(Math.Pow(2, retryAttempt)));


//  2 ^ 1 = 2 seconds then
//  2 ^ 2 = 4 seconds then
//  2 ^ 3 = 8 seconds then
```

However, if we pass an array of fixed delays, even if they are calculated, imagine what happens when a fault occurs in a busy web service. All the clients receive an exception, they all wait for the first second, and they all attempt to recall the web service one second later. This causes floods that could make the situation worse!

Jittering is the idea of adding small amounts of randomization to time delays. There are many implementations that you can find online, and the best is built-in with an extra Polly package. We will use it to generate time delays in our example project.

Applying policies to HTTP clients

When calling a web service, it's a good practice to define an HTTP client factory and register it in a dependency services collection.

In this scenario, you will not call the methods that might throw an exception yourself. Instead, you must define a policy and then attach it to a registered HTTP client, so that it automatically follows that policy.

To do so, we will use an extension class named HttpPolicyExtensions to create policies specifically for common HTTP requests and failures, as shown in the following code:

```
AsyncRetryPolicy<HttpResponseMessage> retryPolicy = HttpPolicyExtensions
  // Handle network failures, 408 and 5xx status codes.
  .HandleTransientHttpError()
  // Define the policy using all the same options as before.
  .RetryAsync(3);
```

To attach the policy to an HTTP client, call the `AddPolicyHandler` extension method after defining the factory. You will see how to do this in practice later in this section.

Adding random faults to the web service

First, let's add random faults to the web service:

1. In the `Northwind.WebApi.Service` project, in `ProductsController.cs`, in the `Get` action method that has a `name` parameter, add statements to randomly throw an exception two-thirds of the time, as highlighted in the following code:

    ```
    // GET api/products/cha
    [HttpGet("{name}")]
    public IEnumerable<Product> Get(string name)
    {
      // Works correctly 1 out of 3 times.
      if (Random.Shared.Next(1, 4) == 1)
      {
        return _db.Products.Where(p => p.ProductName.Contains(name));
      }

      // Throws an exception at all other times.
      throw new Exception("Randomized fault.");
    }
    ```

2. Build the project.

Building an MVC project to call the faulty web service

Next, let's create an ASP.NET Core MVC client that calls the randomly faulty web service endpoint. Initially, it will just receive the exception if the web service throws an exception. Later, we will add transient fault handling using Polly:

1. Use your preferred code editor to add a new project, as defined in the following list:

    *   Project template: **ASP.NET Core Web App (Model-View-Controller)** / `mvc`
    *   Solution file and folder: `Chapter09`
    *   Project file and folder: `Northwind.WebApi.Client.Mvc`
    *   Other Visual Studio 2022 options:

        *   **Authentication Type: None.**
        *   **Configure for HTTPS:** Selected.
        *   **Enable Docker:** Cleared.
        *   **Do not use top-level statements:** Cleared.

2. In the `Northwind.WebApi.Client.Mvc` project, in the `Properties` folder, in `launchSettings.json`, change the `applicationUrl` for the `https` profile to use port `5093` for `https` and `5094` for `http`, as shown in the following markup:

```
"applicationUrl": "https://localhost:5093;http://localhost:5094",
```

3. In the `Northwind.WebApi.Client.Mvc` project file, treat warnings as errors, and add a reference to the entity models project so that we can use the `Product` class, as shown in the following markup:

```
<ItemGroup>
  <ProjectReference Include="..\..\Chapter03\Northwind.Common.
EntityModels
.SqlServer\Northwind.Common.EntityModels.SqlServer.csproj" />
</ItemGroup>
```

4. Build the `Northwind.WebApi.Client.Mvc` project at the command prompt or terminal by entering the following command: `dotnet build`.

5. In the `Northwind.WebApi.Client.Mvc` project, in `Program.cs`, import the namespace to work with HTTP headers, as shown in the following code:

```
using System.Net.Http.Headers; // To use MediaTypeWithQualityHeaderValue.
```

6. In `Program.cs`, before calling the `builder.Build()`, add statements to configure an HTTP client factory to call the web service, as shown in the following code:

```
builder.Services.AddHttpClient(name: "Northwind.WebApi.Service",
  configureClient: options =>
  {
    options.BaseAddress = new("https://localhost:5091/");
    options.DefaultRequestHeaders.Accept.Add(
      new MediaTypeWithQualityHeaderValue(
        "application/json", 1.0));
  });
```

7. In the `Models` folder, add a new class file named `HomeProductsViewModel.cs`.

8. In `HomeProductsViewModel.cs`, define a class to store information needed in the view, like the partial product name the visitor wants to search for, a sequence of products, and an error message, as shown in the following code:

```
using Northwind.EntityModels; // To use Product.

namespace Northwind.WebApi.Client.Mvc.Models;

public class HomeProductsViewModel
{
```

```
    public string? NameContains { get; set; }
    public Uri? BaseAddress { get; set; }
    public IEnumerable<Product>? Products { get; set; }
    public string? ErrorMessage { get; set; }
  }
```

9. In the `Controllers` folder, in `HomeController.cs`, import the namespace for the entity models, as shown in the following code:

```
using Northwind.EntityModels; // To use Product.
```

10. In `HomeController.cs`, add statements to store the registered HTTP client factory in a private `readonly` field, as shown highlighted in the following code:

```
private readonly ILogger<HomeController> _logger;
private readonly IHttpClientFactory _httpClientFactory;

public HomeController(ILogger<HomeController> logger,
  IHttpClientFactory httpClientFactory)
{
  _logger = logger;
  _httpClientFactory = httpClientFactory;
}
```

11. In `HomeController.cs`, add an asynchronous action method named `Products`, which will use the HTTP factory to request products whose name contains a value entered as an optional name parameter, in a custom MVC route, as shown in the following code:

```
[Route("home/products/{name?}")]
public async Task<IActionResult> Products(string? name = "cha")
{
  HomeProductsViewModel model = new();

  HttpClient client = _httpClientFactory.CreateClient(
    name: "Northwind.WebApi.Service");

  model.NameContains = name;
  model.BaseAddress = client.BaseAddress;

  HttpRequestMessage request = new(
    method: HttpMethod.Get,
    requestUri: $"api/products/{name}");

  HttpResponseMessage response = await client.SendAsync(request);
```

```
  if (response.IsSuccessStatusCode)
  {
    model.Products = await response.Content
      .ReadFromJsonAsync<IEnumerable<Product>>();
  }
  else
  {
    model.Products = Enumerable.Empty<Product>();

    string content = await response.Content.ReadAsStringAsync();

    // Use the range operator .. to start from zero and
    // go to the first carriage return.
    string exceptionMessage = content[..content.IndexOf("\r")];

    model.ErrorMessage = string.Format("{0}: {1}:",
      response.ReasonPhrase, exceptionMessage);
  }

  return View(model);
}
```

12. In the `Views/Home` folder, add a new file named `Products.cshtml`. (The Visual Studio 2022 project item template is named **Razor View - Empty**. The JetBrains Rider project item template is named **Razor MVC View**.)

13. In `Products.cshtml`, modify its contents to output a table of products that match part of a product name entered in a textbox, as shown in the following markup:

```
@using Northwind.EntityModels
@model HomeProductsViewModel
@{
  ViewData["Title"] = "Products using Polly";
}
<div class="text-center">
  <h1 class="display-4">@ViewData["Title"]</h1>
  <div class="alert alert-info">
    <p>
      This page calls a web service endpoint that will randomly fail two
out of three times. It will use Polly to retry the call automatically.
    </p>
  </div>
```

```
@if (Model is not null)
{
  if (!string.IsNullOrWhiteSpace(Model.ErrorMessage))
  {
    <div class="alert alert-danger">
      @Model.ErrorMessage
    </div>
  }
  <form action="/home/products">
    <input name="name" placeholder="Enter part of a product name"
      value="@Model.NameContains" />
    <input type="submit" value="Get Products" />
    @if (!string.IsNullOrWhiteSpace(Model.NameContains))
    {
    <p>
      Searched for product names that start with:
      <span class="badge bg-primary rounded-pill">
        @Model.NameContains</span>
    </p>
    }
  </form>
  <div>
    @if (Model.Products is not null)
    {
      <table class="table">
        <thead>
          <tr>
            <th scope="col">Product Name</th>
          </tr>
        </thead>
        <tbody>
          @if (Model.Products.Any())
          {
            @foreach (Product p in Model.Products)
            {
              <tr>
                <td>
                  <a href=
"@(Model.BaseAddress)api/products/@p.ProductId">
@p.ProductName</a>
                </td>
```

```
            </tr>
          }
        }
        else
        {
          <tr><td>0 products found.</td></tr>
        }
      </tbody>
    </table>
  }
  </div>
 }
</div>
```

14. In `Views/Home`, in `Index.cshtml`, add code to define a link to the products page, as shown in the following markup:

    ```
    <p><a href="home/products">Search for products by name</a></p>
    ```

15. Start the `Northwind.WebApi.Service` project, using the `https` profile without debugging.

16. Start the `Northwind.WebApi.Client.Mvc` project, using the `https` profile without debugging.

 If you are using Visual Studio Code, then the web browser will not start automatically. Start Chrome, and then navigate to `https://localhost:5093`.

17. On the home page, click **Search for products by name**.

18. If the search works, you will see the successful results shown in *Figure 9.1*:

Products using Polly

This page calls a web service endpoint that will randomly fail two out of three times. It will use Polly to retry the call automatically.

| cha | Get Products | Searched for: **cha** |

Product Name

Chai

Chang

Chartreuse verte

Figure 9.1: A successful call to the faulty random web service

19. fails, you will see an error message, as shown in *Figure 9.2*:

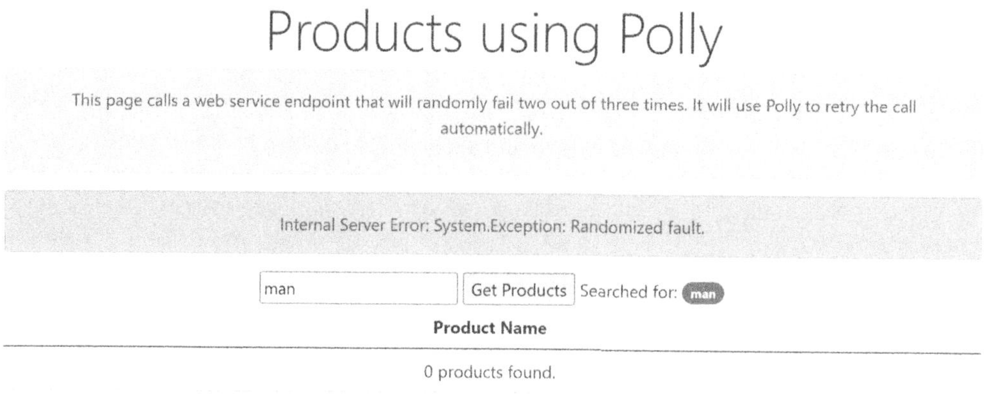

Products using Polly

This page calls a web service endpoint that will randomly fail two out of three times. It will use Polly to retry the call automatically.

Internal Server Error: System.Exception: Randomized fault.

| man | Get Products | Searched for: **man**

Product Name

0 products found.

Figure 9.2: A successful call to the faulty random web service

20. In the command prompt or terminal, when a fault occurs you will see the exception, as shown in the following partial output:

```
fail: Microsoft.AspNetCore.Diagnostics.
DeveloperExceptionPageMiddleware[1]
      An unhandled exception has occurred while executing the request.
      System.Exception: Randomized fault.
```

21. Enter different partial names and click **Get Products** until you have seen both a successful search and a failed search.

22. Close the browsers and shut down the web servers.

Implementing the Retry pattern for transient fault handling

Now that we have a web service and MVC client with random faults, let's add transient fault handling by using the Retry pattern:

1. In the `Northwind.WebApi.Client.Mvc` project file, globally and statically import the `System.Console` class, and add a package reference for the Microsoft package to integrate Polly with ASP.NET Core (which has a dependency on the `Polly` package), and for a library to add jittering to retry time spans, as shown in the following markup:

```
<ItemGroup>
  <PackageReference Include="Microsoft.Extensions.Http.Polly"
                    Version="8.0.0" />
  <PackageReference Include="Polly.Contrib.WaitAndRetry"
                    Version="1.1.1" />
</ItemGroup>
```

2. Build the `Northwind.WebApi.Client.Mvc` project to restore packages.

3. In `Program.cs`, import common Polly namespaces to work with ASP.NET Core, as shown in the following code:

```
using Polly; // To use AddTransientHttpErrorPolicy method.
using Polly.Contrib.WaitAndRetry; // To use Backoff.
using Polly.Extensions.Http; // To use HttpPolicyExtensions.
using Polly.Retry; // To use AsyncRetryPolicy<T>
```

4. In `Program.cs`, before the statement to add an HTTP client to services, add statements to generate five jittered and exponentially increasing time-span values, output them to the console, use them to define an asynchronous wait and retry policy, and then add the retry policy to the HTTP client factory, as highlighted in the following code:

```
// Create five jittered delays, starting with about 1 second.
IEnumerable<TimeSpan> delays = Backoff.DecorrelatedJitterBackoffV2(
  medianFirstRetryDelay: TimeSpan.FromSeconds(1), retryCount: 5);

WriteLine("Jittered delays for Polly retries:");
foreach (TimeSpan item in delays)
{
  WriteLine($"  {item.TotalSeconds:N2} seconds.");
}

AsyncRetryPolicy<HttpResponseMessage> retryPolicy = HttpPolicyExtensions
  // Handle network failures, 408 and 5xx status codes.
  .HandleTransientHttpError().WaitAndRetryAsync(delays);

builder.Services.AddHttpClient(name: "Northwind.WebApi.Service",
  configureClient: options =>
  {
    options.BaseAddress = new("https://localhost:5091/");
    options.DefaultRequestHeaders.Accept.Add(
      new MediaTypeWithQualityHeaderValue(
        "application/json", 1.0));
  })
  .AddPolicyHandler(retryPolicy);
```

5. If your database server is not running (for example, because you are hosting it in Docker, a virtual machine, or in the cloud), then make sure to start it.

6. Start the `Northwind.WebApi.Service` project, using the `https` profile without debugging.

7. Start the `Northwind.WebApi.Client.Mvc` project, using the `https` profile without debugging.

8. In the command prompt or terminal for the MVC project, note the jittered time spans, as shown in the following output:

```
Jittered delays for Polly retries:
  1.38 seconds.
  0.15 seconds.
  2.65 seconds.
  3.06 seconds.
  6.46 seconds.
```

 Your five delays will be different, but they should start at about 1 second and increase from that.

9. Arrange the web service command prompt or terminal and the MVC website browser so that you can see both side by side.

10. On the home page, click **Search for products by name**.

11. Note that the MVC website might have to make multiple requests before showing the page, which will take up to about 15 seconds. For example, when I ran my projects, the MVC web site made four requests that failed before succeeding on the fifth attempt. You will see the exceptions logged in the web service output.

12. Enter a partial product name, click **Get Products**, and note that the web page will likely appear successfully again, even if one or more requests must be made beforehand.

13. It is possible that you could exceed the maximum of five requests, in which case you will see the error message as before.

 Microsoft has created their own packages that wrap Polly to make it even easier to use. They are the `Microsoft.Extensions.Http.Resilience` and `Microsoft.Extensions.Resilience` packages. You can learn about this at the following link: `https://devblogs.microsoft.com/dotnet/building-resilient-cloud-services-with-dotnet-8/`

Now that you've seen two techniques that improve services, caching, and handling transient faults, let's look a third powerful technique, queuing.

Queuing with RabbitMQ

Queuing can improve the scalability of your service, just as it can in the physical world. When too many clients all need to call a service at once, we can use a queue to smooth out the load.

There are many queuing systems available for all the major development platforms. One of the most popular is RabbitMQ. It implements the **Advanced Message Queuing Protocol (AMQP)**.

With AMQP, messages are published to exchanges, which then distribute message copies to queues using rules named bindings. Then a broker can deliver the messages to consumers subscribed to a queue (sometimes called a topic) or a consumer can read from a queue when they want.

Since networks and systems often fail, AMQP uses message acknowledgments to tell the broker when a consumer has successfully processed a message, and only then does the broker remove the message from the queue.

RabbitMQ supports four types of exchange:

- **Direct**: A direct exchange delivers messages based on a message routing key. Multiple queues can be bound to the exchange, but messages are only delivered to a queue if they have a matching routing key. They are mostly used for unicast messages. The default (empty name) exchange is a direct exchange. It is pre-bound with a routing key that is the same name as the queue. This is the type we will use in this book.

- **Fanout**: A fanout exchange delivers messages to all queues that are bound to it, and the routing key is ignored. These are good for broadcasting messages.

- **Topic**: A topic exchange delivers messages based on a routing key and criteria defined in the binding between the exchange and a queue. They are used for the publish/subscribe pattern, where there are many consumers but they want to receive different messages, based on factors like geographic location, registered interests, and so on.

- **Headers**: A headers exchange delivers messages based on multiple attributes in a message header instead of a routing key.

The RabbitMQ API uses the following types:

- `IConnection`: This represents an AMQP connection.
- `ConnectionFactory`: This creates `IConnection` instances. It has default values for common properties designed to work with the Docker image. For example, `UserName` is `guest`, `Password` is `guest`, `VirtualHost` is `/`, `HostName` is `localhost`, and `Port` is `5672`.
- `IModel`: This represents the AMQP channel and has methods to perform common tasks, like declaring a queue with `QueueDeclare` or sending a message using `BasicPublish`.
- `IBasicConsumer`: This represents a message consumer.
- `EventBasicConsumer`: This is an implementation of a message consumer that integrates with the .NET event system, making it easy for a client app to process a message as soon as it is sent and received.

 Good Practice: Queuing systems can get complicated fast. In this book, we will cover the basics, but if you decide to implement any queuing system in production, then you will want to learn much more about how to implement them deeply.

You can install RabbitMQ locally on your computer, but for maximum ease of use, I recommend using a Docker image.

To install RabbitMQ on your computer, read the instructions at the following link for your operating system: `https://www.rabbitmq.com/download.html`.

Setting up RabbitMQ using Docker

The Docker image we will use has RabbitMQ version 3.12.0 and is designed to be used as a throwaway container, where you simply start the container and your project can start using it with the default configuration.

 More Information: You can read more about the Docker image at the following link: `https://registry.hub.docker.com/_/rabbitmq/`.

Let's get started with RabbitMQ in a Docker container:

1. Install **Docker** from the following link: `https://docs.docker.com/engine/install/`.
2. Start **Docker**.
3. At the command prompt or terminal, pull down the latest container image for RabbitMQ on Docker and run it, opening ports 5672 and 15672 to the container, which are used by default by AMQP, as shown in the following command:

```
docker run -it --rm --name rabbitmq -p 5672:5672 -p 15672:15672
rabbitmq:3.12-management
```

4. Note that the first time you run this command, the RabbitMQ image will not be found on your local computer, as shown in the following output:

```
Unable to find image 'rabbitmq:3.12-management' locally
```

5. Note that the image will then be downloaded automatically, as shown in the following output:

```
3.12-management: Pulling from library/rabbitmq
99803d4b97f3: Pull complete
8fb904ec525a: Pull complete
ba4d114a87c0: Pull complete
c869b027f1e1: Pull complete
729c8b3166a8: Pull complete
7de098b90abf: Pull complete
4f206ad5199f: Pull complete
```

```
1f40437d763f: Pull complete
f4cbf27a2d68: Pull complete
5a4db5ea38b2: Pull complete
99886074092c: Pull complete
Digest:
sha256:da98d468cf2236171da94e34953619ddd01b5db155ee326b653675d1e5017f0f
Status: Downloaded newer image for rabbitmq:3.12-management
```

6. Note that RabbitMQ runs on Erlang, and its copyright and license information is displayed when the container starts up, as shown in the following output:

```
2023-06-11 14:03:22.785019+00:00 [info] <0.230.0>  Starting RabbitMQ
3.12.0 on Erlang 25.3.2.2 [jit]
2023-06-11 14:03:22.785019+00:00 [info] <0.230.0>  Copyright (c) 2007-
2023 VMware, Inc. or its affiliates.
2023-06-11 14:03:22.785019+00:00 [info] <0.230.0>  Licensed under the MPL
2.0. Website: https://rabbitmq.com

  ##  ##       RabbitMQ 3.12.0
  ##  ##
  ##########   Copyright (c) 2007-2023 VMware, Inc. or its affiliates.
  ######  ##
  ##########   Licensed under the MPL 2.0. Website: https://rabbitmq.com
```

7. Note the RabbitMQ service listens on port 5672 and has started four plugins, as shown in the following output:

```
2023-06-11 14:03:27.574844+00:00 [info] <0.744.0> started TCP listener on
[::]:5672
 completed with 4 plugins.
2023-06-11 14:03:27.659139+00:00 [info] <0.599.0> Server startup
complete; 4 plugins started.
2023-06-11 14:03:27.659139+00:00 [info] <0.599.0>  * rabbitmq_prometheus
2023-06-11 14:03:27.659139+00:00 [info] <0.599.0>  * rabbitmq_management
2023-06-11 14:03:27.659139+00:00 [info] <0.599.0>  * rabbitmq_web_
dispatch
2023-06-11 14:03:27.659139+00:00 [info] <0.599.0>  * rabbitmq_management_
agent
```

8. Leave the command prompt or terminal running.

9. Optionally, in **Docker Desktop**, note that a container for RabbitMQ runs and listens on ports 5672 (the actual queue service) and 15672 (its management service), as shown in *Figure 9.3*:

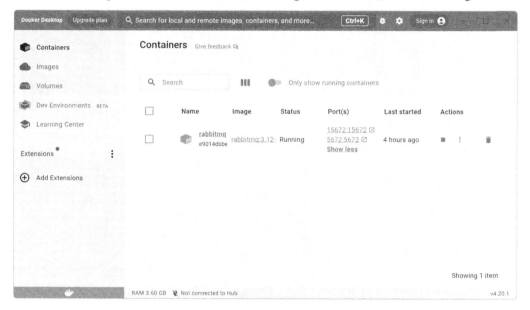

Figure 9.3: RabbitMQ running in a Docker container

Sending messages to a queue using an MVC website

Now that we have the RabbitMQ system running, we can add the RabbitMQ client package to the MVC website project so that it can send messages to a queue.

But first, let's create a class library to define models we will use with the queue:

1. Use your preferred code editor to create a new class library project, as defined in the following list:

    *   Project template: **Class Library** / classlib
    *   Solution file and folder: Chapter09
    *   Project file and folder: Northwind.Queue.Models

2. Add a project reference to the Northwind entity models project for SQL Server that you created in *Chapter 3, Building Entity Models for SQL Server Using EF Core*, as shown in the following markup:

```
<ItemGroup>
  <ProjectReference Include="..\..\Chapter03\Northwind.Common.
EntityModels
.SqlServer\Northwind.Common.EntityModels.SqlServer.csproj" />
</ItemGroup>
```

3. At the command prompt or terminal, build the project to make sure the entity model class library projects outside the current solution are properly compiled, as shown in the following command:

```
dotnet build
```

4. Delete the file named `Class1.cs`.
5. Add a new file named `ProductQueueMessage.cs`.
6. In `ProductQueueMessage.cs`, define a class that will represent a message in a queue with a simple plain text property and a complex `Product` entity model type as a second property, as shown in the following code:

```
using Northwind.EntityModels; // To use Product.

namespace Northwind.Queue.Models;

public class ProductQueueMessage
{
  public string? Text { get; set; }
  public Product Product { get; set; } = null!;
}
```

7. In the `Northwind.WebApi.Client.Mvc` project file, add a reference to the queue models project so that we can use the `ProductQueueMessage` class, as shown in the following markup:

```
<ItemGroup>
  <ProjectReference Include=
  "..\Northwind.Queue.Models\Northwind.Queue.Models.csproj" />
</ItemGroup>
```

8. In the `Northwind.WebApi.Client.Mvc` project file, add a package reference for RabbitMQ clients, as shown in the following markup:

```
<PackageReference Include="RabbitMQ.Client" Version="6.7.0" />
```

 You can check the latest package version at the following link: https://www.nuget.org/packages/RabbitMQ.Client/

9. Build the `Northwind.WebApi.Client.Mvc` project.
10. In the `Models` folder, add a new class file named `HomeSendMessageViewModel.cs`.

11. Define a class to represent the information that needs to be displayed in a view for sending a message including a couple of properties for showing message to the visitor when a message is successfully sent and when an error occurs, as shown in the following code:

```
using Northwind.Queue.Models; // To use ProductQueueMessage.

namespace Northwind.WebApi.Client.Mvc.Models;

public class HomeSendMessageViewModel
{
  public string? Info { get; set; }
  public string? Error { get; set; }
  public ProductQueueMessage? Message { get; set; }
}
```

12. In `Views\Home`, in `Index.cshtml`, add a link to a page that will let the visitor send a message to a queue, as shown in the following markup:

```
<p><a href="home/sendmessage">Send a message</a></p>
```

13. In `HomeControllers.cs`, import namespaces to work with RabbitMQ and serialize JSON, as shown in the following code:

```
using RabbitMQ.Client; // To use ConnectionFactory and so on.
using System.Text.Json; // To use JsonSerializer.
```

14. In `HomeControllers.cs`, add statements to define an action method that responds to a GET request by showing a web form to send a message, as shown in the following code:

```
public IActionResult SendMessage()
{
  return View();
}
```

15. In `HomeControllers.cs`, add statements to define an action method that responds to a POST request by sending a message from information in the form, as shown in the following code:

```
// POST: home/sendmessage
// Body: message=Hello&productId=1
[HttpPost]
public async Task<IActionResult> SendMessage(
  string? message, int? productId)
{
  HomeSendMessageViewModel model = new();
  model.Message = new();
```

```csharp
      if (message is null || productId is null)
      {
        model.Error = "Please enter a message and a product ID.";
        return View(model);
      }

      model.Message.Text = message;

      model.Message.Product = new() { ProductId = productId.Value };

      HttpClient client = _httpClientFactory.CreateClient(
        name: "Northwind.WebApi.Service");

      HttpRequestMessage request = new(
        method: HttpMethod.Get,
        requestUri: $"api/products/{productId}");

      HttpResponseMessage response = await client.SendAsync(request);

      if (response.IsSuccessStatusCode)
      {
        Product? product = await response.Content.
ReadFromJsonAsync<Product>();

        if (product is not null)
        {
          model.Message.Product = product;
        }
      }

      // Create a RabbitMQ factory.
      ConnectionFactory factory = new() { HostName = "localhost" };

      using IConnection connection = factory.CreateConnection();

      using IModel channel = connection.CreateModel();

      string queueNameAndRoutingKey = "product";

      // If the queue does not exist, it will be created.
      // If the Docker container is restarted, the queue will be lost.
```

```
  // The queue can be shared with multiple consumers.
  // The queue will not be deleted when the last message is consumer.

  channel.QueueDeclare(queue: queueNameAndRoutingKey, durable: false,
    exclusive: false, autoDelete: false, arguments: null);

  byte[] body = JsonSerializer.SerializeToUtf8Bytes(model.Message);

  // The exchange is empty because we are using the default exchange.
  channel.BasicPublish(exchange: string.Empty,
    routingKey: queueNameAndRoutingKey,
    basicProperties: null, body: body);

  model.Info = "Message sent to queue successfully.";

  return View(model);
}
```

16. In `Views\Home`, add a new empty Razor View named `SendMessage.cshtml`.

17. Define a web page with a form to send a message, as shown in the following markup:

```
@model HomeSendMessageViewModel
@{
  ViewData["Title"] = "Send a Message";
}
<div class="text-center">
  <h1 class="display-4">@ViewData["Title"]</h1>

  @if (Model is not null)
  {
    if (Model.Error is not null)
    {
      <div class="alert alert-danger">
        <h2>Error</h2>
        <p>@Model.Error</p>
      </div>
    }
    if (Model.Info is not null)
    {
      <div class="alert alert-info">
        <h2>Information</h2>
        <p>@Model.Info</p>
```

```
          </div>
        }
      }
      <form asp-controller="Home" asp-action="SendMessage" method="post">
        <div>
          <label for="message">Message</label>
          <input id="message" name="message" />
        </div>
        <div>
          <label for="productId">Product ID</label>
          <input id="productId" name="productId" />
        </div>
        <input type="submit" value="Send" />"
      </form>
    </div>
```

Consuming message from a queue using a console app

Finally, we can create a console app that will process messages from the queue:

1. Use your preferred code editor to create a new console app project, as defined in the following list:

   - Project template: **Console App** / console
   - Solution file and folder: Chapter09
   - Project file and folder: Northwind.Queue.Consumer

2. Treat warnings as errors, add a package reference for RabbitMQ, add project references to the Northwind entity models project and the queue message models project, and statically and globally import the System.Console class, as shown in the following markup:

```xml
<Project Sdk="Microsoft.NET.Sdk">

  <PropertyGroup>
    <OutputType>Exe</OutputType>
    <TargetFramework>net8.0</TargetFramework>
    <ImplicitUsings>enable</ImplicitUsings>
    <Nullable>enable</Nullable>
    <TreatWarningsAsErrors>true</TreatWarningsAsErrors>
  </PropertyGroup>

  <ItemGroup>
    <PackageReference Include="RabbitMQ.Client" Version="6.7.0" />
  </ItemGroup>
```

```xml
  <ItemGroup>
    <ProjectReference Include=
        "..\..\Chapter03\Northwind.Common.EntityModels.SqlServer\
        Northwind.Common.EntityModels.SqlServer.csproj" />
    <ProjectReference Include=
        "..\Northwind.Queue.Models\Northwind.Queue.Models.csproj" />
  </ItemGroup>

  <ItemGroup>
    <Using Include="System.Console" Static="true" />
  </ItemGroup>

</Project>
```

3. At the command prompt or terminal, build the project, as shown in the following command:

```
dotnet build
```

4. In `Program.cs`, delete any existing statements, and then add statements to read messages from the product queue, as shown in the following code:

```csharp
using Northwind.Queue.Models; // To use ProductQueueMessage.
using RabbitMQ.Client; // To use ConnectionFactory.
using RabbitMQ.Client.Events; // To use EventingBasicConsumer.
using System.Text.Json; // To use JsonSerializer.

string queueName = "product";

ConnectionFactory factory = new () { HostName = "localhost" };

using IConnection connection = factory.CreateConnection();

using IModel channel = connection.CreateModel();

WriteLine("Declaring queue...");

QueueDeclareOk response = channel.QueueDeclare(
  queue: queueName,
  durable: false,
  exclusive: false,
  autoDelete: false,
  arguments: null);
```

```
WriteLine("Queue name: {response.QueueName}, Message count: {
  response.MessageCount}, Consumer count: {response.ConsumerCount}.");

WriteLine("Waiting for messages...");

EventingBasicConsumer consumer = new(channel);

consumer.Received += (model, args) =>
{
  byte[] body = args.Body.ToArray();

  ProductQueueMessage? message = JsonSerializer
    .Deserialize<ProductQueueMessage>(body);

  if (message is not null)
  {
    WriteLine("Received product. Id: {message.Product.ProductId
      }, Name: { message.Product.ProductName}, Message: {
      message.Text}");
  }
  else
  {
    WriteLine($"Received unknown: {args.Body.ToArray()}.");
  }
};

// Start consuming as messages arrive in the queue.
channel.BasicConsume(queue: queueName,
  autoAck: true,
  consumer: consumer);

WriteLine(">>> Press Enter to stop consuming and quit. <<<");
ReadLine();
```

5. If your database server is not running (for example, because you are hosting it in Docker, a virtual machine, or in the cloud), then make sure to start it.

6. Start the Northwind.WebApi.Service project, using the https profile without debugging.

7. Start the Northwind.WebApi.Client.Mvc project, using the https profile without debugging.

8. Start the `Northwind.Queue.Consumer` console app project with or without debugging:

    •   Optionally, you can configure your solution to start up all three projects at once, as shown for Visual Studio 2022 in *Figure 9.4*:

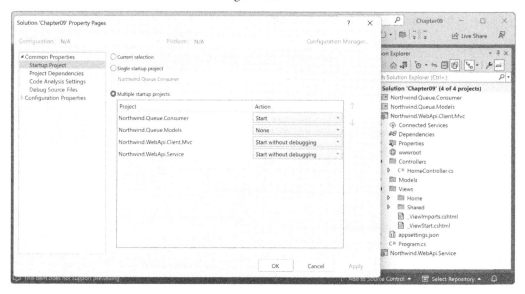

Figure 9.4: Configuring three startup projects to test message queues

9. Arrange the console app and the MVC web page so that you can see both, then click **Send a message**, and enter a simple text message and a valid product ID (1 to 77), as shown in *Figure 9.5*:

Figure 9.5: An ASP.NET Core MVC website sending a message to a queue

10. Click **Send,** and note the message that appears in the console app, as shown in *Figure 9.6*:

Figure 9.6: A console app consuming a message from the queue

11. In the command prompt or terminal for Docker, press *Ctrl + C* to shut down the container, and note the result, as shown in the following output:

```
2023-06-11 17:42:31.006172+00:00 [info] <0.744.0> stopped TCP listener on
[::]:5672
2023-06-11 17:42:31.008574+00:00 [info] <0.1552.0> Closing all
connections in vhost '/' on node 'rabbit@e9014dbbe5f5' because the vhost
is stopping
2023-06-11 17:42:31.017407+00:00 [info] <0.557.0> Stopping message store
for directory '/var/lib/rabbitmq/mnesia/rabbit@e9014dbbe5f5/msg_stores/
vhosts/628WB79CIFDYO9LJI6DKMI09L/msg_store_persistent'
2023-06-11 17:42:31.024661+00:00 [info] <0.557.0> Message store for
directory '/var/lib/rabbitmq/mnesia/rabbit@e9014dbbe5f5/msg_stores/
vhosts/628WB79CIFDYO9LJI6DKMI09L/msg_store_persistent' is stopped
2023-06-11 17:42:31.024937+00:00 [info] <0.553.0> Stopping message store
for directory '/var/lib/rabbitmq/mnesia/rabbit@e9014dbbe5f5/msg_stores/
vhosts/628WB79CIFDYO9LJI6DKMI09L/msg_store_transient'
2023-06-11 17:42:31.031218+00:00 [info] <0.553.0> Message store for
directory '/var/lib/rabbitmq/mnesia/rabbit@e9014dbbe5f5/msg_stores/
vhosts/628WB79CIFDYO9LJI6DKMI09L/msg_store_transient' is stopped
2023-06-11 17:42:31.037584+00:00 [info] <0.489.0> Management plugin: to
stop collect_statistics.
```

12. In **Docker Desktop**, note the container is gone from the list, but the image remains for quicker use next time.

 More Information: You can read more about using RabbitMQ with .NET at the following link: `https://www.rabbitmq.com/dotnet-api-guide.html`.

The combination of caching, queuing, and handling transient faults goes a long way to making your services more resilient, scalable, and performant. In the last section of this chapter, we will look at long-running background services.

Implementing long-running background services

It is common to need long-running background services to perform operations like:

- Performing a task on a regular timed schedule.
- Processing queued messages.
- Performing intense work like building AI and ML models or processing video and images.

In the distant past, on the Windows operating system, to have some code running in the background meant building a **Windows Service**. For example, the database engine of SQL Server is implemented as a Windows Service. With the move to cross-platform, .NET needs a cross-platform solution to run code in the background.

Background services often do not have a user interface, although they might provide one for the configuration and management of the service.

Building a worker service

Now, let's build a worker service project so that we can see how we would host a long-running background service:

1. Use your preferred code editor to add a new project, as defined in the following list:

   - Project template: **Worker Service** / worker
   - Solution file and folder: Chapter09
   - Project file and folder: Northwind.Background.Workers
   - **Enable Docker:** Cleared
   - **Do not use top-level statements:** Cleared
   - **Enable native AOT publish:** Cleared

2. In the Northwind.Background.Workers project file, note that the .NET SDK is Microsoft.NET. Sdk.Worker, and then make the following changes, as highlighted in the following markup:

   - Treat warnings as errors.
   - Add a package reference for RabbitMQ.

- Add references to the entity models and queue models projects:

```xml
<Project Sdk="Microsoft.NET.Sdk.Worker">

  <PropertyGroup>
    <TargetFramework>net8.0</TargetFramework>
    <Nullable>enable</Nullable>
    <ImplicitUsings>enable</ImplicitUsings>
    <UserSecretsId>dotnet-Northwind.Background.Workers-66434cdf-
0fdd-4993-a399-ec9581b4b914</UserSecretsId>
    <TreatWarningsAsErrors>true</TreatWarningsAsErrors>
  </PropertyGroup>

  <ItemGroup>
    <PackageReference Include="Microsoft.Extensions.Hosting"
                      Version="8.0.0" />
    <PackageReference Include="RabbitMQ.Client" Version="6.7.0" />
  </ItemGroup>

  <ItemGroup>
    <ProjectReference Include=
"..\..\Chapter03\Northwind.Common.EntityModels
.SqlServer\Northwind.Common.EntityModels.SqlServer.csproj" />
    <ProjectReference Include=
"..\Northwind.Queue.Models\Northwind.Queue.Models.csproj" />
  </ItemGroup>

</Project>
```

3. Build the `Northwind.Background.Workers` project at the command prompt or terminal by entering the following command: `dotnet build`.

4. In `Program.cs`, note that the initialization statements are like an ASP.NET Core project, and that it registers a hosted service named `Worker` and then runs the host, as shown in the following code:

```csharp
using Northwind.Background.Workers;

var builder = Host.CreateApplicationBuilder(args);
builder.Services.AddHostedService<Worker>();

var host = builder.Build();
host.Run();
```

5. In Worker.cs, note that the Worker class inherits from BackgroundService and implements its ExecuteAsync method by looping until a cancellation is requested, logging the current date/time, and then pausing for one second, as shown in the following code:

```
namespace Northwind.Background.Workers
{
  public class Worker : BackgroundService
  {
    private readonly ILogger<Worker> _logger;

    public Worker(ILogger<Worker> logger)
    {
      _logger = logger;
    }

    protected override async Task ExecuteAsync(
      CancellationToken stoppingToken)
    {
      while (!stoppingToken.IsCancellationRequested)
      {
        _logger.LogInformation("Worker running at: {time}",
          DateTimeOffset.Now);

        await Task.Delay(1000, stoppingToken);
      }
    }
  }
}
```

6. Start the project without debugging, note the current time is output once per second, and then press *Ctrl + C* to shut down the worker service, as shown in the following output:

```
info: Northwind.Queue.Worker.Worker[0]
      Worker running at: 06/12/2023 08:25:02 +01:00
info: Microsoft.Hosting.Lifetime[0]
      Application started. Press Ctrl+C to shut down.
info: Microsoft.Hosting.Lifetime[0]
      Hosting environment: Development
info: Microsoft.Hosting.Lifetime[0]
      Content root path: C:\apps-services-net8\Chapter09\Northwind.Queue.
Worker
info: Northwind.Queue.Worker.Worker[0]
      Worker running at: 06/12/2023 08:25:03 +01:00
```

```
info: Northwind.Queue.Worker.Worker[0]
      Worker running at: 06/12/2023 08:25:04 +01:00
info: Northwind.Queue.Worker.Worker[0]
      Worker running at: 06/12/2023 08:25:05 +01:00
info: Microsoft.Hosting.Lifetime[0]
      Application is shutting down...
```

Processing queued message using a worker service

Now, we can do some useful work, like reading messages from a RabbitMQ queue:

1. Rename `Worker.cs` to `QueueWorker.cs` and the `Worker` class to `QueueWorker`.

2. In `Program.cs`, change the hosted service class name from `Worker` to `QueueWorker`, as shown in the following code:

    ```
    builder.Services.AddHostedService<QueueWorker>();
    ```

3. In `QueueWorker.cs`, import namespaces to work with RabbitMQ queues and implement a queue processor, as highlighted in the following code:

    ```
    using Northwind.Queue.Models; // To use ProductQueueMessage.
    using RabbitMQ.Client; // To use ConnectionFactory.
    using RabbitMQ.Client.Events; // To use EventingBasicConsumer.
    using System.Text.Json; // To use JsonSerializer.

    namespace Northwind.Background.Workers;

    public class QueueWorker : BackgroundService
    {
      private readonly ILogger<QueueWorker> _logger;

      // RabbitMQ objects.
      private const string queueNameAndRoutingKey = "product";
      private readonly ConnectionFactory _factory;
      private readonly IConnection _connection;
      private readonly IModel _channel;
      private readonly EventingBasicConsumer _consumer;

      public QueueWorker(ILogger<QueueWorker> logger)
      {
        _logger = logger;

        _factory = new() { HostName = "localhost" };
    ```

```
    _connection = _factory.CreateConnection();
    _channel = _connection.CreateModel();
    _consumer = new(_channel);

    _channel.QueueDeclare(queue: queueNameAndRoutingKey, durable: false,
      exclusive: false, autoDelete: false, arguments: null);

    _consumer = new(_channel);

    _consumer.Received += (model, args) =>
    {
      byte[] body = args.Body.ToArray();

      ProductQueueMessage? message = JsonSerializer
        .Deserialize<ProductQueueMessage>(body);

      if (message is not null)
      {
        _logger.LogInformation($"Received product. Id: {
          message.Product.ProductId}, Name: {message.Product
          .ProductName}, Message: {message.Text}");
      }
      else
      {
        _logger.LogInformation("Received unknown: {0}.",
          args.Body.ToArray());
      }
    };

    // Start consuming as messages arrive in the queue.
    _channel.BasicConsume(queue: queueNameAndRoutingKey,
      autoAck: true, consumer: _consumer);
  }

protected override async Task ExecuteAsync(
  CancellationToken stoppingToken)
{
  while (!stoppingToken.IsCancellationRequested)
  {
    _logger.LogInformation("Worker running at: {time}",
      DateTimeOffset.Now);
```

```
        await Task.Delay(3000, stoppingToken);
      }
    }
  }
```

4. Start the RabbitMQ container, as shown in the following command:

```
docker run -it --rm --name rabbitmq -p 5672:5672 -p 15672:15672
rabbitmq:3.12-management
```

5. Wait for the messages to say it is ready for clients to connect on port 5672, as shown in the following output:

```
2023-06-12 08:50:16.591574+00:00 [info] <0.599.0> Ready to start client
connection listeners
2023-06-12 08:50:16.593090+00:00 [info] <0.744.0> started TCP listener on
[::]:5672
```

6. Leave the command prompt or terminal running.

7. If your database server is not running (for example, because you are hosting it in Docker, a virtual machine, or in the cloud), then make sure to start it.

8. Start the Northwind.WebApi.Service project without debugging so that we can query for products in the Northwind database.

9. Start the Northwind.WebApi.Client.Mvc project without debugging so that we can send messages to the RabbitMQ queue.

10. In the MVC website, click **Send a message**, and then enter a message of apples and a product ID of 1.

11. Repeat for bananas and 2, and cherries and 3.

12. Start the Northwind.Background.Workers project without debugging, and note the three messages are processed from the queue, as shown in the following output:

```
info: Northwind.Background.Workers.QueueWorker[0]
      Queue product is waiting for messages.
info: Northwind.Background.Workers.QueueWorker[0]
      Worker running at: 06/12/2023 09:58:59 +01:00
info: Microsoft.Hosting.Lifetime[0]
      Application started. Press Ctrl+C to shut down.
info: Microsoft.Hosting.Lifetime[0]
      Hosting environment: Development
info: Microsoft.Hosting.Lifetime[0]
      Content root path: C:\apps-services-net8\Chapter09\Northwind.Queue.
Worker
info: Northwind.Background.Workers.QueueWorker[0]
```

```
        Received product. Id: 1, Name: Chai, Message: apples
info: Northwind.Background.Workers.QueueWorker[0]
        Received product. Id: 2, Name: Chang, Message: bananas
info: Northwind.Background.Workers.QueueWorker [0]
        Received product. Id: 3, Name: Aniseed Syrup, Message: cherries
```

Executing code on a timed schedule

Another common use of worker services is to implement timed events. A timer-based background service can use the System.Threading.Timer class that triggers the DoWork method.

Let's add another service to the background worker project:

1. In the Northwind.Background.Workers project, add a new class named TimerWorker.cs.
2. Modify the class, as shown in the following code:

```csharp
namespace Northwind.Background.Workers;

public class TimerWorker : IHostedService, IAsyncDisposable
{
  private readonly ILogger<TimerWorker> _logger;

  private int _executionCount = 0;
  private Timer? _timer;
  private int _seconds = 5;

  public TimerWorker(ILogger<TimerWorker> logger)
  {
    _logger = logger;
  }

  private void DoWork(object? state)
  {
    int count = Interlocked.Increment(ref _executionCount);

    _logger.LogInformation(
        "{0} is working, execution count: {1:#,0}",
        nameof(TimerWorker), count);
  }

  public Task StartAsync(CancellationToken cancellationToken)
  {
    _logger.LogInformation("{0} is running.", nameof(TimerWorker));
```

```
    _timer = new Timer(callback: DoWork, state: null,
      dueTime: TimeSpan.Zero,
      period: TimeSpan.FromSeconds(_seconds));

    return Task.CompletedTask;
  }

  public Task StopAsync(CancellationToken cancellationToken)
  {
    _logger.LogInformation("{0} is stopping.", nameof(TimerWorker));

    _timer?.Change(dueTime: Timeout.Infinite, period: 0);

    return Task.CompletedTask;
  }

  public async ValueTask DisposeAsync()
  {
    if (_timer is IAsyncDisposable asyncTimer)
    {
      await asyncTimer.DisposeAsync();
    }

    _timer = null;
  }
}
```

3. In Program.cs, add a statement to register the timer worker service, as shown in the following code:

```
builder.Services.AddHostedService<TimerWorker>();
```

4. Start the Northwind.Background.Workers project without debugging, and note the initialization of both workers, as shown in the following output:

```
info: Northwind.Background.Workers.QueueWorker[0]
      Worker running at: 06/12/2023 12:58:25 +01:00
info: Northwind.Background.Workers.TimerWorker[0]
      TimerWorker is running.
info: Microsoft.Hosting.Lifetime[0]
      Application started. Press Ctrl+C to shut down.
info: Microsoft.Hosting.Lifetime[0]
      Hosting environment: Development
```

```
info: Microsoft.Hosting.Lifetime[0]
      Content root path: C:\apps-services-net8\Chapter09\Northwind.
Background.Workers
```

5. Leave the background workers running for at least 10 seconds, and note the queue worker writes to the log every second and the timer worker writes to the log every five seconds, as shown in the following output:

```
info: Northwind.Background.Workers.TimerWorker[0]
      TimerWorker is working, execution count: 1
info: Northwind.Background.Workers.QueueWorker[0]
      Worker running at: 06/12/2023 12:58:26 +01:00
info: Northwind.Background.Workers.QueueWorker[0]
      Worker running at: 06/12/2023 12:58:27 +01:00
info: Northwind.Background.Workers.QueueWorker[0]
      Worker running at: 06/12/2023 12:58:28 +01:00
info: Northwind.Background.Workers.QueueWorker[0]
      Worker running at: 06/12/2023 12:58:29 +01:00
info: Northwind.Background.Workers.TimerWorker[0]
      TimerWorker is working, execution count: 2
```

6. Press *Ctrl* + *C* to shut down the background workers, and note the clean shutdown of the timer worker, as shown in the following output:

```
info: Microsoft.Hosting.Lifetime[0]
      Application is shutting down...
info: Northwind.Background.Workers.TimerWorker[0]
      TimerWorker is stopping.
```

If we wanted to use the timer background service to have more flexibility, instead of running it at a regular interval like five seconds, we could have it run a scheduled task check every second, and only if a task has reached its scheduled time does it then run that task. We need somewhere to define tasks and when they are scheduled to run. Although you can build this infrastructure yourself, it is easier to use a third-party library like **Hangfire**.

Building a website to host Hangfire

Hangfire is open source and free for commercial use. It supports the following patterns of use:

- **Fire-and-forget:** Jobs that are executed once and started immediately.
- **Delayed:** Jobs that are executed once but at a date and time in the future.
- **Recurring:** Jobs that are executed repeatedly at a regular CRON schedule.
- **Continuation:** Jobs that are executed on completion of a parent job.
- **Batches:** Jobs that are transactional. These are only available in the paid version.

Hangfire has persistent storage and can be configured to use:

- SQL Server
- Redis
- In-memory
- Community-developed storage

Let's set up an empty ASP.NET Core project to host Hangfire:

1. Use your preferred code editor to create a new Web API controller-based project, as defined in the following list:

   - Project template: **ASP.NET Core Empty** / web
   - Solution file and folder: Chapter09
   - Project file and folder: Northwind.Background.Hangfire
   - **Configure for HTTPS**: Selected.
   - **Enable Docker**: Cleared.
   - **Do not use top-level statements**: Cleared.

2. In the project file, treat warnings as errors, and add package references to work with Hangfire and persist its data to SQL Server, as shown in the following markup:

   ```
   <ItemGroup>
     <PackageReference Include="Hangfire.Core" Version="1.8.6" />
     <PackageReference Include="Hangfire.SqlServer" Version="1.8.6" />
     <PackageReference Include="Hangfire.AspNetCore" Version="1.8.6" />
     <PackageReference Include="Microsoft.Data.SqlClient" Version="5.1.2" />
   </ItemGroup>
   ```

3. Build the project to restore packages.

4. In the Properties folder, in launchSettings.json, modify the applicationUrl of the profile named https to use port 5095 for https and port 5096 for http, as highlighted in the following configuration:

   ```
   "profiles": {
     ...
     "https": {
       "commandName": "Project",
       "dotnetRunMessages": true,
       "launchBrowser": true,
       "launchUrl": "swagger",
       "applicationUrl": "https://localhost:5095;http://localhost:5096",
       "environmentVariables": {
         "ASPNETCORE_ENVIRONMENT": "Development"
       }
   ```

5. In `appsettings.Development.json`, add an entry to set the Hangfire log level to `Information`, as highlighted in the following JSON:

```
{
  "Logging": {
    "LogLevel": {
      "Default": "Information",
      "Microsoft.AspNetCore": "Warning",
      "Hangfire": "Information"
    }
  }
}
```

6. Create a SQL Server database named `Northwind.HangfireDb`:

   • If you are using Visual Studio 2022, navigate to **View** | **Server Explorer**, right-click **Data Connections**, choose **Create New SQL Server database...**, enter connection information and the database name, and then click **OK**.

   • If you are using Visual Studio Code, navigate to **SQL Server**, right-click and choose **New Query**, enter connection information, and then in the query window, enter the following SQL command and execute it:

   ```
   USE master
   GO
   CREATE DATABASE [Northwind.HangfireDb]
   GO
   ```

7. In `Program.cs`, delete the existing statements, and then add statements to configure Hangfire to use SQL Server and to enable Hangfire Dashboard, as shown in the following code:

   ```
   using Microsoft.Data.SqlClient; // To use SqlConnectionStringBuilder.
   using Hangfire; // To use GlobalConfiguration.

   SqlConnectionStringBuilder connection = new();

   connection.InitialCatalog = "Northwind.HangfireDb";
   connection.MultipleActiveResultSets = true;
   connection.Encrypt = true;
   connection.TrustServerCertificate = true;
   connection.ConnectTimeout = 5; // Default is 30 seconds.
   connection.DataSource = "."; // To use local SQL Server.

   // To use Windows Integrated authentication.
   connection.IntegratedSecurity = true;
   ```

```
/*
// To use SQL Server authentication.
builder.UserID = "sa";
builder.Password = "123456";
builder.PersistSecurityInfo = false;
*/

var builder = WebApplication.CreateBuilder(args);

builder.Services.AddHangfire(config => config
  .SetDataCompatibilityLevel(CompatibilityLevel.Version_180)
  .UseSimpleAssemblyNameTypeSerializer()
  .UseRecommendedSerializerSettings()
  .UseSqlServerStorage(connection.ConnectionString));

builder.Services.AddHangfireServer();

var app = builder.Build();

app.UseHangfireDashboard();

app.MapGet("/", () =>
  "Navigate to /hangfire to see the Hangfire Dashboard.");

app.MapHangfireDashboard();

app.Run();
```

8. Start the `Northwind.Background.Hangfire` project without debugging, and note the messages written to the console, as shown in the following output:

```
info: Hangfire.SqlServer.SqlServerObjectsInstaller[0]
      Start installing Hangfire SQL objects...
info: Hangfire.SqlServer.SqlServerObjectsInstaller[0]
      Hangfire SQL objects installed.
info: Microsoft.Hosting.Lifetime[14]
      Now listening on: https://localhost:5095
info: Microsoft.Hosting.Lifetime[14]
      Now listening on: http://localhost:5096
info: Hangfire.BackgroundJobServer[0]
```

```
      Starting Hangfire Server using job storage: 'SQL Server: .@
Northwind.HangfireDb'
info: Hangfire.BackgroundJobServer[0]
      Using the following options for SQL Server job storage: Queue poll
interval: 00:00:00.
info: Hangfire.BackgroundJobServer[0]
      Using the following options for Hangfire Server:
          Worker count: 20
          Listening queues: 'default'
          Shutdown timeout: 00:00:15
          Schedule polling interval: 00:00:15
info: Microsoft.Hosting.Lifetime[0]
      Application started. Press Ctrl+C to shut down.
info: Microsoft.Hosting.Lifetime[0]
      Hosting environment: Development
info: Microsoft.Hosting.Lifetime[0]
      Content root path: C:\apps-services-net8\Chapter09\Northwind.
Background.Hangfire
info: Hangfire.Server.BackgroundServerProcess[0]
      Server desktop-j1pqhr7:14120:c8ea792b successfully announced in
140.4628 ms
info: Hangfire.Server.BackgroundServerProcess[0]
      Server desktop-j1pqhr7:14120:c8ea792b is starting the
registered dispatchers: ServerWatchdog, ServerJobCancellationWatcher,
ExpirationManager, CountersAggregator, SqlServerHeartbeatProcess, Worker,
DelayedJobScheduler, RecurringJobScheduler...
info: Hangfire.Server.BackgroundServerProcess[0]
      Server desktop-j1pqhr7:14120:c8ea792b all the dispatchers started
```

9. In the browser, note the plain text message, and then in the address bar, append `hangfire`, and note the **Hangfire Dashboard** user interface, as shown in *Figure 9.7*:

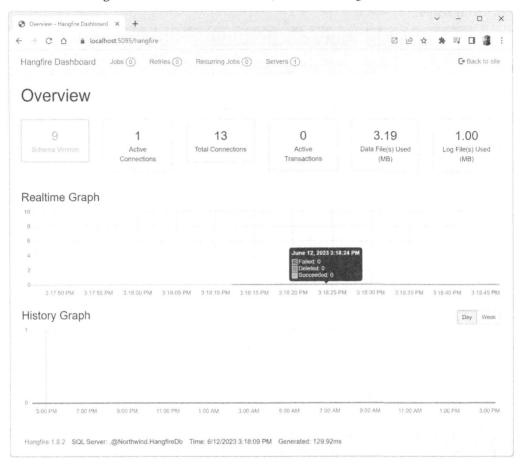

Figure 9.7: Hangfire Dashboard user interface

10. Close the browser window, and at the command prompt or terminal for the Hangfire service, press *Ctrl + C* to cleanly shut down the server, and note the messages, as shown in the following output:

```
info: Microsoft.Hosting.Lifetime[0]
      Application is shutting down...
info: Hangfire.Server.BackgroundServerProcess[0]
      Server desktop-j1pqhr7:14120:c8ea792b caught stopping signal...
info: Hangfire.Server.BackgroundServerProcess[0]
      Server desktop-j1pqhr7:14120:c8ea792b All dispatchers stopped
info: Hangfire.Server.BackgroundServerProcess[0]
      Server desktop-j1pqhr7:14120:c8ea792b successfully reported itself
as stopped in 2.8874 ms
info: Hangfire.Server.BackgroundServerProcess[0]
      Server desktop-j1pqhr7:14120:c8ea792b has been stopped in total
19.6204 ms
```

Scheduling jobs using Hangfire

Next, we will allow a client to schedule a job (in this case, just writing a message to the console a specified number of seconds in the future) by POSTing to the web service:

1. In the `Northwind.Background.Hangfire` project, add a new class file named `WriteMessageJobDetail.cs`.

2. In `WriteMessageJobDetail.cs`, define a class to represent a scheduled job, as shown in the following code:

```
namespace Northwind.Background.Models;

public class WriteMessageJobDetail
{
  public string? Message { get; set; }
  public int Seconds { get; set; }
}
```

3. In the `Northwind.Background.Hangfire` project, add a new class file named `Program.Methods.cs`.

4. In `Program.Methods.cs`, extend the partial `Program` class with a method to write a message to the console in green color, as shown in the following code:

```
using static System.Console;

partial class Program
{
  public static void WriteMessage(string? message)
```

```
    {
      ConsoleColor previousColor = ForegroundColor;
      ForegroundColor = ConsoleColor.Green;
      WriteLine(message);
      ForegroundColor = previousColor;
    }
  }
```

5. In `Program.cs`, import namespaces to work with the job, as shown in the following code:

```
using Northwind.Background.Models; // To use WriteMessageJobDetail.
using Microsoft.AspNetCore.Mvc; // To use [FromBody].
```

6. In `Program.cs`, after the statement to map a GET request, map a POST request to the relative path `/schedulejob`, get the job details from the body of the POST request, and use it to schedule a background job, using Hangfire to run at the specified time in seconds in the future, as shown in the following code:

```
app.MapPost("/schedulejob", ([FromBody] WriteMessageJobDetail job) =>
  {
    BackgroundJob.Schedule(
      methodCall: () => WriteMessage(job.Message),
      enqueueAt: DateTimeOffset.UtcNow +
        TimeSpan.FromSeconds(job.Seconds));
  });
```

7. Start the `Northwind.Background.Hangfire` project without debugging.

8. In the command prompt or terminal, confirm that all the dispatchers started, as shown in the following output:

```
info: Hangfire.Server.BackgroundServerProcess[0]
      Server desktop-j1pqhr7:13916:9f1851b5 all the dispatchers started
```

9. In the browser, navigate to `/hangfire` to view Hangfire Dashboard.

10. In your code editor, in the `HttpRequests` folder, create a file named `hangfire-schedule-job.http`.

11. In `hangfire-schedule-job.http`, add statements to make a POST request to the Hangfire service, as shown in the following code:

```
### Configure a variable for the Hangfire web service base address.
@base_address = https://localhost:5095/

POST {{base_address}}schedulejob
Content-Type: application/json
```

```
{
   "message": "Hangfire is awesome!",
   "seconds": 30
}
```

12. Send the request, and note the successful response, as shown in the following output:

```
HTTP/1.1 200 OK
Content-Length: 0
Connection: close
Date: Mon, 12 Jun 2023 16:04:20 GMT
Server: Kestrel
Alt-Svc: h3=":5095"; ma=86400
```

13. In the browser, in **Hangfire Dashboard**, click **Jobs** in the top menu click **Jobs**, in the left side menu, and then note there is one scheduled job, as shown in *Figure 9.8*:

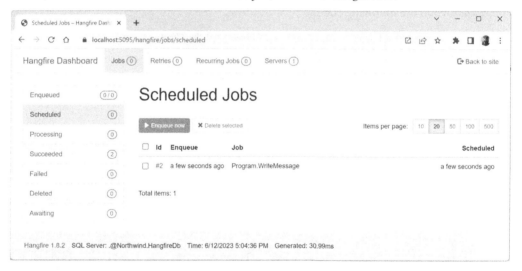

Figure 9.8: Scheduled jobs in Hangfire

14. Wait until 30 seconds have passed, and then in the left -side menu, click **Succeeded**, and note the job has succeeded, as shown in *Figure 9.9*:

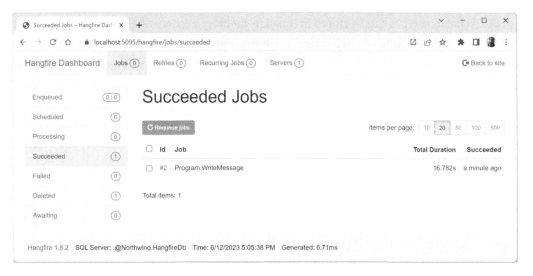

Figure 9.9: Succeeded jobs in Hangfire

15. At the command prompt or terminal, note the message that was written to the console, as shown in the following output:

```
Hangfire is awesome!
```

16. Close the browser and shut down the server.

> **More Information:** You can read more about Hangfire at the following link: `https://www.hangfire.io/`.

Practicing and exploring

Test your knowledge and understanding by answering some questions, getting some hands-on practice, and exploring this chapter's topics with deeper research.

Exercise 9.1 – Test your knowledge

Answer the following questions:

1. How much longer does it take to read 1 MB of data from SSD compared to memory?

2. What is the difference between absolute and sliding expirations?

3. What unit of measurement is used by `Size` for the in-memory cache?

4. You have written the following statement to get information about in-memory caching but `stats` is `null`. What must you do to fix this issue?

```
MemoryCacheStatistics? stats = _memoryCache.GetCurrentStatistics();
```

5. What data types can be stored in (a) an in-memory cache, and (b) a distributed cache?

6. What are the differences between the Retry and Circuit Breaker patterns?

7. When using the RabbitMQ default direct exchange, what must the routing key be for a queue named `product`?

8. What is the difference between a fanout and a topic exchange?

9. What port does RabbitMQ listen on by default?

10. When inheriting from the `BackgroundService` class, what method must you override that is called automatically by the host to run your service?

Exercise 9.2 — Explore topics

Use the links on the following page to learn more details about the topics covered in this chapter:

`https://github.com/markjprice/apps-services-net8/blob/main/docs/book-links.md#chapter-9---caching-queuing-and-resilient-background-services`

Exercise 9.3 — Replace the Distributed Memory Cache with another distributed cache implementation

In this chapter, we used the Distributed Memory Cache implementation to explore how to use a distributed cache.

As an optional exercise, register for an Azure account if you have not already, create an **Azure Cache for Redis** resource, and change your web service project configuration to use it.

In the `Northwind.WebApi.Service`, you will need to reference the Redis package, comment out the previously registered distributed cache implementation, and then call the extension method to register Redis as the distributed cache implementation:

```
// builder.Services.AddDistributedMemoryCache();

builder.Services.AddStackExchangeRedisCache(options =>
{
  options.Configuration = builder.Configuration
    .GetConnectionString("MyRedisConStr");

  options.InstanceName = "SampleInstance";
});
```

Read more at the following links:

*   Azure Cache for Redis: `https://azure.microsoft.com/en-us/products/cache/`.

*   Redis NuGet package: `https://www.nuget.org/packages/Microsoft.Extensions.Caching.StackExchangeRedis`.

*   Redis with .NET: `https://docs.redis.com/latest/rs/references/client_references/client_csharp`.

Exercise 9.4 – Replace Hangfire with Quartz.NET

Quartz.NET is a similar library to Hangfire. Read the official documentation, and then create a project named Northwind.Background.Quartz that implements the same functionality as Northwind. Background.Hangfire:

https://www.quartz-scheduler.net/

Exercise 9.5 – Review the Reliable Web App pattern

The **Reliable Web App (RWA)** pattern is a set of best practices with prescriptive guidance that helps developers successfully migrate an on-premises web project to the cloud. It includes a reference implementation and shows how to make the most of Azure cloud services to modernize mission-critical workloads in a reliable, secure, high-performance, cost-efficient manner using modern design, development, and operational practices:

https://learn.microsoft.com/en-us/azure/architecture/web-apps/guides/reliable-web-app/dotnet/plan-implementation

A collection of videos about the RWA pattern for .NET are at the following link:

https://www.youtube.com/playlist?list=PLI7iePan8aH54gIDJquV61dE3ENyaDi3Q

Summary

In this chapter, you learned:

- About service architecture and how different parts of a system can affect performance.
- How to cache data closer to the action, using in-memory and distributed caching.
- How to control HTTP caching for clients and intermediaries.
- How to implement fault tolerance using Polly.
- How to implement queuing using RabbitMQ.
- How to implement long-running background services using BackgroundService and Hangfire.

In the next chapter, you will learn how to use Azure Functions to implement nano services, aka serverless services.

Learn more on Discord

To join the Discord community for this book – where you can share feedback, ask questions to the author, and learn about new releases – follow the QR code below:

`https://packt.link/apps_and_services_dotnet8`

10

Building Serverless Nanoservices Using Azure Functions

In this chapter, you will be introduced to Azure Functions, which can be configured to only require server-side resources while they execute. They execute when they are triggered by an activity like a message sent to a queue or a file uploaded to Azure Storage, or at a regularly scheduled interval.

This chapter will cover the following topics:

- Understanding Azure Functions
- Building an Azure Functions project
- Responding to timer and resource triggers
- Publishing an Azure Functions project to the cloud
- Cleaning up Azure Functions resources

Understanding Azure Functions

Azure Functions is an event-driven serverless compute platform. You can build and debug locally and later deploy to Microsoft Azure cloud. Azure Functions can be implemented in many languages, not just C# and .NET. It has extensions for Visual Studio 2022 and Visual Studio Code and a command-line tool.

But first, you might be wondering, "How is it possible to have a service without a server?"

Serverless does not literally mean there is no server. What serverless means is a service without a *permanently running server*, and usually that means not running for most of the time or running with low resources and scaling up dynamically when needed. This can save a lot of costs.

For example, organizations often have business functions that only need to run once per hour, once per month, or on an ad hoc basis. Perhaps the organization prints checks (cheques in England) to pay its employees at the end of the month. Those checks might need the salary amounts converted to words to print on the check. A function to convert numbers to words could be implemented as a serverless service.

For another example, with a content management system, editors might upload new images, and those images might need to be processed in various ways, like generating thumbnails and other optimizations. This work can be added to a queue, or an Azure function can be triggered when the file is uploaded to Blob Storage.

Azure Functions can be much more than just a single function. They support complex, stateful, workflows and event-driven solutions using **Durable Functions**.

> I do not cover Durable Functions in this book, so if you are interested, you can learn more about implementing them using C# and .NET at the following link: `https://learn.microsoft.com/en-us/azure/azure-functions/durable/durable-functions-overview?tabs=csharp`.

Azure Functions has a programming model based on triggers and bindings that enable your serverless service to respond to events and connect to other services like data stores.

Azure Functions triggers and bindings

Triggers and **bindings** are key concepts for Azure Functions.

Triggers are what cause a function to execute. Each function must have one, and only one, trigger. The most common triggers are shown in the following list:

- **HTTP:** This trigger responds to an incoming HTTP request, typically a `GET` or `POST`.
- **Azure SQL:** This trigger responds when a change is detected on a SQL table.
- **Cosmos DB:** This trigger uses the Cosmos DB Change Feed to listen for inserts and updates.
- **Timer:** This trigger responds to a scheduled time occurring. It does not retry if a function fails. The function is not called again until the next time on the schedule.
- **SignalR:** This trigger responds to messages sent from Azure SignalR Service.
- **Queue** and **RabbitMQ:** These triggers respond to a message arriving in a queue ready for processing.
- **Blob Storage:** This trigger responds to a new or updated **binary large object (Blob)**.
- **Event Grid** and **Event Hub:** These triggers respond when a predefined event occurs.

Bindings allow functions to have inputs and outputs. Each function can have zero, one, or more bindings. Some common bindings are shown in the following list:

- **Azure SQL:** Read or write to a table in a SQL Server database.
- **Blob Storage:** Read or write to any file stored as a BLOB.
- **Cosmos DB:** Read or write documents to a cloud-scale data store.
- **SignalR:** Receive or make remote method calls.
- **HTTP:** Make an HTTP request and receive the response.
- **Queue** and **RabbitMQ:** Write a message to a queue or read a message from a queue.
- **SendGrid:** Send an email message.

- **Twilio:** Send an SMS message.
- **IoT hub:** Write to an internet-connected device.

 You can see the full list of supported triggers and bindings at the following link: `https://learn.microsoft.com/en-us/azure/azure-functions/functions-triggers-bindings?tabs=csharp#supported-bindings`.

Triggers and bindings are configured differently for different languages. For C# and Java, you decorate methods and parameters with attributes. For the other languages, you configure a file named `function.json`.

NCRONTAB expressions

The **Timer** trigger uses **NCRONTAB expressions** to define the frequency of the timer. The default time zone is **Coordinated Universal Time (UTC)**. This can be overridden but you really should use UTC for the reasons you learned about in *Chapter 7, Handling Dates, Times, and Internationalization.*

If you are hosting in an App Service plan, then you can alternatively use a `TimeSpan`, but I recommend learning NCRONTAB expressions for flexibility.

An NCRONTAB expression consists of five or six parts (if seconds are included):

```
* * * * * *
- - - - - -
| | | | | |
| | | | | +--- day of week (0 - 6) (Sunday=0)
| | | | +----- month (1 - 12)
| | | +------- day of month (1 - 31)
| | +--------- hour (0 - 23)
| +----------- min (0 - 59)
+------------- sec (0 - 59)
```

A star * in the value field above means all legal values, as in parentheses for that column. You can specify ranges using a hyphen, and a step value using /. Here are some examples of how values can be specified in this format:

- 0 means at that value. For example, for hours, at midnight.
- 0,6,12,18 means at those listed values. For example, for hours, at midnight, 6 a.m., 12 noon, and 6 p.m.
- 3-7 means at that inclusive range of values. For example, for hours, at 3 a.m., 4 a.m., 5 a.m., 6 a.m., and 7 a.m.
- 4/3 means a start value of 4 and a step value of 3. For example, for hours, at 4 a.m., 7 a.m., 10 a.m., 1 p.m., 4 p.m., 7 p.m., and 10 p.m.

Table 10.1 shows some more examples:

Expression	Description
`0 5 * * * *`	Once every hour of the day at minute 5 of each hour.
`0 0,10,30,40 * * * *`	Four times an hour – at minutes 0, 10, 30, and 40 during every hour.
`* * */2 * * *`	Every 2 hours.
`0,15 * * * * *`	At 0 and 15 seconds every minute.
`0/15 * * * * *`	At 0, 15, 30, and 45 seconds every minute, aka every 15 seconds.
`0-15 * * * * *`	At 0, 1, 2, 3, and so on up to 15 seconds past each minute, but not 16 to 59 seconds past each minute.
`0 30 9-16 * * *`	Eight times a day – at hours 9:30 A.M, 10:30 A.M, and so on up to 4:30 P.M.
`0 */5 * * * *`	12 times an hour – at second 0 of every 5th minute of every hour.
`0 0 */4 * * *`	6 times a day – at minute 0 of every 4th hour of every day.
`0 30 9 * * *`	9:30 AM every day.
`0 30 9 * * 1-5`	9:30 AM every workday.
`0 30 9 * * Mon-Fri`	9:30 AM every workday.
`0 30 9 * Jan Mon`	9:30 AM every Monday in January.

Table 10.1: Examples of NCRONTAB expressions

Now let's build a simple console app to test your understanding of NCRONTAB expressions:

1. Use your preferred code editor to add a new console app named `NCrontab.Console` to a `Chapter10` solution.

2. In the `NCrontab.Console` project, treat warnings as errors, globally and statically import the `System.Console` class, and add a package reference for `NCrontab.Signed`, as shown in the following markup:

```
<ItemGroup>
  <PackageReference Include="NCrontab.Signed" Version="3.3.3" />
</ItemGroup>
```

 The NCRONTAB library is only for parsing expressions. It is not itself a scheduler. You can learn more about it in the GitHub repository at the following link: `https://github.com/atifaziz/NCrontab`.

3. Build the `NCrontab.Console` project to restore packages.

4. In `Program.cs`, delete the existing statements. Add statements to define a date range for the year 2023, output a summary of NCRONTAB syntax, and construct an NCRONTAB schedule, and then use it to output the next 40 occurrences that would occur in 2023, as shown in the following code:

```
using NCrontab; // To use CrontabSchedule and so on.

DateTime start = new(year: 2023, month: 1, day: 1);
DateTime end = start.AddYears(1);

WriteLine($"Start at:   {start:ddd, dd MMM yyyy HH:mm:ss}");
WriteLine($"End at:     {end:ddd, dd MMM yyyy HH:mm:ss}");
WriteLine();

string sec = "0,30";
string min = "*";
string hour = "*";
string dayOfMonth = "*";
string month = "*";
string dayOfWeek = "*";

string expression = string.Format(
  "{0,-3} {1,-3} {2,-3} {3,-3} {4,-3} {5,-3}",
  sec, min, hour, dayOfMonth, month, dayOfWeek);

WriteLine($"Expression: {expression}");
WriteLine(@"             \ / \ / \ / \ / \ / \ /");
WriteLine($"              -   -   -   -   -   -");
WriteLine($"              |   |   |   |   |   |");
WriteLine($"              |   |   |   |   |   +--- day of week (0 - 6)
(Sunday=0)");
WriteLine($"              |   |   |   |   +------- month (1 - 12)");
WriteLine($"              |   |   |   +----------- day of month (1 -
31)");
WriteLine($"              |   |   +--------------- hour (0 - 23)");
WriteLine($"              |   +------------------- min (0 - 59)");
WriteLine($"              +----------------------- sec (0 - 59)");
WriteLine();

CrontabSchedule schedule = CrontabSchedule.Parse(expression,
  new CrontabSchedule.ParseOptions { IncludingSeconds = true });

IEnumerable<DateTime> occurrences = schedule.GetNextOccurrences(start,
end);

// Output the first 40 occurrences.
```

```
foreach (DateTime occurrence in occurrences.Take(40))
{
  WriteLine($"{occurrence:ddd, dd MMM yyyy HH:mm:ss}");
}
```

Note the following:

- The default potential time span for occurrences is the whole year of 2023.

- The default expression is `0,30 * * * * *`, meaning at 0 and 30 seconds of every minute of every hour of every day of every weekday of every month.

- The formatting for the syntax help assumes each component will be three characters wide because `-3` is used for output formatting. You could write a cleverer algorithm to dynamically adjust the arrows to point to variable width components, but I was lazy. I will leave that as an exercise for you.

- Our expression includes seconds, so when parsing, we must set that as an additional option.

- After defining the schedule, the schedule calls its `GetNextOccurrences` method to return a sequence of all the calculated occurrences.

- The loop only outputs the first 40 occurrences. That should be enough to understand how most expressions work.

5. Start the console app without debugging, and note the occurrences are every 30 seconds, as shown in the following partial output:

```
Start at:   Sun, 01 Jan 2023 00:00:00
End at:     Mon, 01 Jan 2024 00:00:00

Expression: 0,30 *   *   *   *   *
            \ / \ / \ / \ / \ / \ /
             -   -   -   -   -   -
             |   |   |   |   |   |
             |   |   |   |   |   +--- day of week (0 - 6) (Sunday=0)
             |   |   |   |   +------- month (1 - 12)
             |   |   |   +----------- day of month (1 - 31)
             |   |   +--------------- hour (0 - 23)
             |   +------------------- min (0 - 59)
             +----------------------- sec (0 - 59)


Sun, 01 Jan 2023 00:00:30
Sun, 01 Jan 2023 00:01:00
Sun, 01 Jan 2023 00:01:30
...
Sun, 01 Jan 2023 00:19:30
Sun, 01 Jan 2023 00:20:00
```

Note that although the start time is Sun, 01 Jan 2023 00:00:00, that value is excluded from the occurrences because it is not a "next" occurrence.

6. Close the console app.
7. In Program.cs, modify the components of the expression to test some of the examples in the table, or make up your own examples. Try the expression 0 0 */4 * * *, and note it should have the following partial output:

```
Start at:   Sun, 01 Jan 2023 00:00:00
End at:     Mon, 01 Jan 2024 00:00:00

Expression: 0   0   */4 *   *   *
            \ / \ / \ / \ / \ / \ /
             -   -   -   -   -   -
            |   |   |   |   |   |
            |   |   |   |   |   +--- day of week (0 - 6) (Sunday=0)
            |   |   |   |   +------- month (1 - 12)
            |   |   |   +----------- day of month (1 - 31)
            |   |   +--------------- hour (0 - 23)
            |   +------------------- min (0 - 59)
            +----------------------- sec (0 - 59)

Sun, 01 Jan 2023 04:00:00
Sun, 01 Jan 2023 08:00:00
Sun, 01 Jan 2023 12:00:00
Sun, 01 Jan 2023 16:00:00
Sun, 01 Jan 2023 20:00:00
Mon, 02 Jan 2023 00:00:00
Mon, 02 Jan 2023 04:00:00
Mon, 02 Jan 2023 08:00:00
Mon, 02 Jan 2023 12:00:00
Mon, 02 Jan 2023 16:00:00
Mon, 02 Jan 2023 20:00:00
Tue, 03 Jan 2023 00:00:00
...
Sat, 07 Jan 2023 12:00:00
Sat, 07 Jan 2023 16:00:00
```

Note that although the start time is `Sun, 01 Jan 2023 00:00:00`, that value is excluded from the occurrences because it is not a "next" occurrence. So, Sunday only has five occurrences. Monday onward has the expected six occurrences per day.

Azure Functions versions and languages

Azure Functions version 4 of the runtime host is the only version still generally available. All older versions have reached end-of-life.

 Good Practice: Microsoft recommends using v4 for functions in all languages. v1, v2, and v3 are in maintenance mode and should be avoided.

Languages and platforms supported by Azure Functions v4 include:

- **C#, F#:** .NET 8, .NET 7, .NET 6, and .NET Framework 4.8. Note that .NET 6 and .NET 7 (and in future, .NET 9) are only supported in the isolated worker model because they are **Standard-Term Support** (**STS**) releases, or, in the case of .NET 6, they are older LTS releases. .NET 8 is supported in both isolated and in-process worker models because it is a **Long-Term Support** (**LTS**) release.
- **JavaScript:** Node 14, 16, and 18. TypeScript is supported via transpiling (transforming/compiling) to JavaScript.
- **Java** 8, 11, and 17.
- **PowerShell** 7.2.
- **Python** 3.7, 3.8, 3.9, and 3.10.

 More Information: You can review the whole table of languages at the following link: `https://learn.microsoft.com/en-us/azure/azure-functions/functions-versions?tabs=v4&pivots=programming-language-csharp#languages`.

In this book, we will only look at implementing Azure Functions using C# and .NET 8 so that we can use the in-process and isolated worker models and get LTS.

 For advanced uses, you can even register a custom handler that would enable you to use any language you like for the implementation of an Azure function. You can read more about Azure Functions custom handlers at the following link: `https://learn.microsoft.com/en-us/azure/azure-functions/functions-custom-handlers`.

Azure Functions worker models

Azure Functions have two worker models, in-process and isolated, as described in the following list:

- **In-process:** Your function is implemented in a class library that must run in the same process as the host, which means your functions must run on the most recent LTS release of .NET. The latest LTS release is .NET 8. The next LTS release will be .NET 10 in November 2025, but .NET 8 will be the last release that supports in-process hosting. After .NET 8, only the isolated worker model will be supported for all versions.

- **Isolated:** Your function is implemented in a console app that runs in its own process. Your function can therefore execute on any supported .NET version, have full control over its `Main` entry point, and have additional features like invocation middleware. From .NET 9 onward, this will be the only worker model. You can read more about this decision at the following link: `https://techcommunity.microsoft.com/t5/apps-on-azure-blog/net-on-azure-functions-august-2023-roadmap-update/ba-p/3910098`.

 Good Practice: New projects should use the isolated worker model.

Azure Functions hosting plans

After testing locally, you must deploy your Azure Functions project to an Azure hosting plan. There are three Azure Functions plans to choose from, as described in the following list:

- **Consumption:** In this plan, host instances are dynamically added and removed based on activity. This plan is the closest to *serverless*. It scales automatically during periods of high load. The cost is only for compute resources when your functions are running. You can configure a timeout for function execution times to ensure your functions do not run forever.

- **Premium:** This plan supports elastic scaling up and down, perpetually warm instances to avoid cold starts, unlimited execution duration, multicore instance sizes up to four cores, potentially more predictable costs, and high-density app allocation for multiple Azure Functions projects. The cost is based on the number of core seconds and memory allocated across instances. At least one instance must be allocated at all times, so there will always be a minimum monthly cost per active plan, even if it never executes that month.

- **Dedicated:** Executes in the cloud equivalent of a server farm. Hosting is provided by an Azure App Service plan that controls the allocated server resources. Azure App Service plans include Basic, Standard, Premium, and Isolated. This plan can be an especially good choice if you already have an App Service plan used for other projects like ASP.NET Core MVC websites, gRPC, OData, and GraphQL services, and so on. The cost is only for the App Service plan. You can host as many Azure Functions and other web apps in it as you like.

 Warning! Premium and Dedicated plans both run on Azure App Service plans. You must carefully select the correct App Service plan that works with your Azure Functions hosting plan. For example, for Premium, you should choose an Elastic Premium plan like `EP1`. If you choose an App Service plan like `P1V1`, then you are choosing a dedicated plan that will not elastically scale!

You can read more about your choices at the following link: `https://learn.microsoft.`
`com/en-us/azure/azure-functions/functions-scale`.

Azure Storage requirements

Azure Functions requires an Azure Storage account for storing information for some bindings and triggers. These Azure Storage services can also be used by your code for its implementation:

- **Azure Files:** Stores and runs your function app code in a Consumption or Premium plan.
- **Azure Blob Storage:** Stores state for bindings and function keys.
- **Azure Queue Storage:** Used for failure and retry handling by some triggers.
- **Azure Table Storage:** Task hubs in Durable Functions use Blob, Queue, and Table Storage.

Testing locally with Azurite

Azurite is an open-source local environment for testing Azure Functions with its related Blob, Queue, and Table Storage. Azurite is cross-platform on Windows, Linux, and macOS. Azurite supersedes the older Azure Storage Emulator.

To install Azurite:

- For Visual Studio 2022, Azurite is included.
- For Visual Studio Code, search for and install the Azurite extension.
- For JetBrains Rider, install the Azure Toolkit for Rider plugin, which includes Azurite.
- For installation at the command prompt, you must have Node.js version 8 or later installed and then you can enter the following command:

```
npm install -g azurite
```

Once you have locally tested an Azure function, you can switch to an Azure Storage account in the cloud.

 You can learn more about Azurite at the following link: `https://learn.microsoft.com/`
`en-us/azure/storage/common/storage-use-azurite`.

Azure Functions authorization levels

Azure Functions has three authorization levels that control whether an API key is required:

- **Anonymous:** No API key is required.
- **Function:** A function-level key is required.
- **Admin:** The master key is required.

API keys are available through the Azure portal.

Azure Functions support for dependency injection

Dependency injection in Azure Functions is built on the standard .NET dependency injection features, but there are implementation differences depending on your chosen worker model.

To register dependency services, create a class that inherits from the `FunctionsStartup` class and override its `Configure` method. Add the `[FunctionsStartup]` assembly attribute to specify the class name registered for startup. Add services to the `IFunctionsHostBuilder` instance passed to the method. You will do this in a task later in this chapter.

Normally, the class that implements an Azure Functions function is `static` with a `static` method. A `static` class is not instantiated with a constructor. Dependency injection uses constructor injection so that means you must use instance classes for injected services and for your function class implementation. You will see how to do this in the coding task.

Installing Azure Functions Core Tools

Azure Functions Core Tools provides the core runtime and templates for creating functions, which enable local development on Windows, macOS, and Linux using any code editor.

 Azure Functions Core Tools is included in the **Azure development** workload of Visual Studio 2022, so you might already have it installed.

You can install the latest version of **Azure Functions Core Tools** from the following link:

`https://www.npmjs.com/package/azure-functions-core-tools`

The page found at the preceding link has instructions for installing using **Microsoft Software Installer** (**MSI**) and `winget` on Windows, Homebrew on Mac, `npm` on any operating system, and common Linux distributions.

If you are using JetBrains Rider, then install Azure Functions Core Tools via Rider.

Building an Azure Functions project

Now, we can create an Azure Functions project. Although they can be created in the cloud using the Azure portal, developers will have a better experience creating and running them locally first. You can then deploy to the cloud once you have tested your function on your own computer.

Each code editor has a slightly different experience to get started with an Azure Functions project, so let's have a look at each in turn, starting with Visual Studio 2022.

Using Visual Studio 2022

If you prefer to use Visual Studio 2022, here are the steps to create an Azure Functions project:

1. In Visual Studio 2022, create a new project, as defined in the following list:

    - Project template: **Azure Functions**

- Solution file and folder: Chapter10
- Project file and folder: Northwind.AzureFunctions.Service
- **Functions worker: .NET 8.0 Isolated (Long Term Support)**
- **Function: Http trigger**
- **Use Azurite for runtime storage account (AzureWebJobsStorage):** Selected
- **Enable Docker:** Cleared
- **Authorization level: Anonymous**

2. Click **Create**.
3. Configure the startup project for the solution to be the current selection.

Using Visual Studio Code

If you prefer to use Visual Studio Code, here are the steps to create an Azure Functions project:

1. In Visual Studio Code, navigate to **Extensions** and search for Azure Functions (ms-azuretools.vscode-azurefunctions). It has dependencies on two other extensions: Azure Account (ms-vscode.azure-account) and Azure Resources (ms-azuretools.vscode-azureresourcegroups), so those will be installed too. Click the **Install** button to install the extension.
2. Create a folder named Northwind.AzureFunctions.Service. (If you previously created the same project using Visual Studio 2022, then create a new folder named Chapter10-vscode and create this new project folder in there instead.)
3. In Visual Studio Code, open the Northwind.AzureFunctions.Service folder.
4. Navigate to **View | Command Palette**, type azure f, and then in the list of **Azure Functions** commands, click **Azure Functions: Create New Project...**.
5. Select the Northwind.AzureFunctions.Service folder to contain your function project.
6. At the prompts, select the following:

   - Select a language: **C#**
   - Select a .NET runtime: **.NET 8 Isolated LTS**.
   - Select a template for your project's first function: **HTTP trigger**.
   - Provide a function name: NumbersToWordsFunction
   - Provide a namespace: Northwind.AzureFunctions.Service
   - Select the authorization level: **Anonymous**

7. Navigate to **Terminal | New Terminal**.
8. At the command prompt, build the project, as shown in the following command:

```
dotnet build
```

Using the func CLI

If you prefer to use the command line and some other code editor, here are the steps to create and start an Azure Functions project:

1. Create a `Chapter10-cli` folder with a subfolder named `Northwind.AzureFunctions.Service`.

2. In command prompt or terminal, in the `Northwind.AzureFunctions.Service` folder, create a new Azure Functions project using C#, as shown in the following command:

```
func init --csharp
```

3. In command prompt or terminal, in the `Northwind.AzureFunctions.Service` folder, create a new Azure Functions function using `HTTP trigger` that can be called anonymously, as shown in the following command:

```
func new --name NumbersToWordsFunction --template "HTTP trigger"
--authlevel "anonymous"
```

4. Optionally, you can start the function locally, as shown in the following command:

```
func start
```

 If you cannot find `func` at the command prompt or terminal, then try installing the Azure Functions Core Tools using Chocolatey, as described at the following link: `https://community.chocolatey.org/packages/azure-functions-core-tools`.

Reviewing the Azure Functions project

Before we write a function, let's review what makes an Azure Functions project:

1. Open the project file, and note the Azure Functions version and the package references needed to implement an Azure function that responds to HTTP requests, as shown in the following markup:

```
<Project Sdk="Microsoft.NET.Sdk">
  <PropertyGroup>
    <TargetFramework>net8.0</TargetFramework>
    <AzureFunctionsVersion>v4</AzureFunctionsVersion>
    <OutputType>Exe</OutputType>
    <ImplicitUsings>enable</ImplicitUsings>
    <Nullable>enable</Nullable>
  </PropertyGroup>
  <ItemGroup>
    <PackageReference Version="1.19.0"
      Include="Microsoft.Azure.Functions.Worker" />
    <PackageReference Version="3.0.13"
      Include="Microsoft.Azure.Functions.Worker.Extensions.Http" />
    <PackageReference Version="1.14.0"
      Include="Microsoft.Azure.Functions.Worker.Sdk" />
  </ItemGroup>
```

```xml
  <ItemGroup>
    <None Update="host.json">
      <CopyToOutputDirectory>PreserveNewest</CopyToOutputDirectory>
    </None>
    <None Update="local.settings.json">
      <CopyToOutputDirectory>PreserveNewest</CopyToOutputDirectory>
      <CopyToPublishDirectory>Never</CopyToPublishDirectory>
    </None>
  </ItemGroup>
  <ItemGroup>
    <Using Include="System.Threading.ExecutionContext"
           Alias="ExecutionContext" />
  </ItemGroup>
</Project>
```

2. In host.json, note that logging to Application Insights is enabled but excludes Request types, as shown in the following markup:

```json
{
  "version": "2.0",
  "logging": {
    "applicationInsights": {
      "samplingSettings": {
        "isEnabled": true,
        "excludedTypes": "Request"
      },
      "enableLiveMetricsFilters": true
    }
  }
}
```

 Application Insights is Azure's monitoring and logging service. We will not be using it in this chapter.

3. In local.settings.json, confirm that during local development, your project will use local development storage and an isolated worker model, as shown in the following markup:

```json
{
  "IsEncrypted": false,
  "Values": {
    "AzureWebJobsStorage": "UseDevelopmentStorage=true",
```

```
        "FUNCTIONS_WORKER_RUNTIME": "dotnet-isolated"
    }
}
```

4. If the AzureWebJobsStorage setting is blank or missing, which might happen if you are using Visual Studio Code, then add it, set it to UseDevelopmentStorage=true, and then save changes.

 FUNCTIONS_WORKER_RUNTIME is the language being used by your project. dotnet means a .NET class library; dotnet-isolated means a .NET console app. Other values include java, node, powershell, and python.

5. In the Properties folder, in launchSettings.json, note the randomly assigned port number for the web service, as shown in the following configuration:

```
{
    "profiles": {
        "Northwind.AzureFunctions.Service": {
            "commandName": "Project",
            "commandLineArgs": "--port 7274",
            "launchBrowser": false
        }
    }
}
```

6. Change the port number to 5101 and save the changes to the file.

Implementing a simple function

Let's implement the function to convert numbers into words by using the Humanizer package:

1. In the project file, add a package reference for Humanizer, as shown in the following markup:

```
<PackageReference Include="Humanizer" Version="2.14.1" />
```

2. Build the project to restore packages.

    If you are using Visual Studio 2022, in the Northwind.AzureFunctions.Service project, right-click Function1.cs and rename it to NumbersToWordsFunction.cs.

3. In NumbersToWordsFunction.cs, modify the contents to implement an Azure function to convert an amount as a number into words, as shown in the following code:

```
using Humanizer; // To use ToWords extension method.
using Microsoft.Azure.Functions.Worker; // To use [HttpTrigger].
using Microsoft.Azure.Functions.Worker.Http; // To use HttpResponseData.
using Microsoft.Extensions.Logging; // To use ILogger.
```

```csharp
namespace Northwind.AzureFunctions.Service;

public class NumbersToWordsFunction
{
  private readonly ILogger _logger;

  public NumbersToWordsFunction(ILoggerFactory loggerFactory)
  {
    _logger = loggerFactory.CreateLogger<NumbersToWordsFunction>();
  }

  [Function(nameof(NumbersToWordsFunction))]
  public HttpResponseData Run(
    [HttpTrigger(AuthorizationLevel.Anonymous,
      "get", "post", Route = null)] HttpRequestData req)
  {
    _logger.LogInformation("C# HTTP trigger function processed a
request.");

    string? amount = req.Query["amount"];

    HttpResponseData response;

    if (long.TryParse(amount, out long number))
    {
      response = req.CreateResponse(System.Net.HttpStatusCode.OK);
      response.WriteString(number.ToWords());
    }
    else
    {
      response = req.CreateResponse(System.Net.HttpStatusCode.
BadRequest);
      response.WriteString($"Failed to parse: {amount}");
    }

    return response;
  }
}
```

Testing a simple function

Now we can test the function in our local development environment:

1. Start the `Northwind.AzureFunctions.Service` project:

   - If you are using Visual Studio Code, you will need to navigate to the **Run and Debug** pane, make sure that **Attach to .NET Functions** is selected, and then click the **Run** button.

   - On Windows, if you see a **Windows Security Alert** from **Windows Defender Firewall**, then click **Allow access**.

2. Note that **Azure Functions Core Tools** hosts your function, as shown in the following output and in *Figure 10.1*:

```
Azure Functions Core Tools
Core Tools Version:       4.0.5390 Commit hash: N/A  (64-bit)
Function Runtime Version: 4.25.3.21264


[2023-10-01T11:42:05.319Z] Found C:\apps-services-net8\Chapter10\
Northwind.AzureFunctions.Service\Northwind.AzureFunctions.Service.csproj.
Using for user secrets file configuration.


Functions:

        NumbersToWordsFunction: [GET,POST] http://localhost:5101/api/
NumbersToWordsFunction


For detailed output, run func with --verbose flag.
[2023-06-05T11:42:14.265Z] Host lock lease acquired by instance ID '00000
00000000000000000011150C3D'.
```

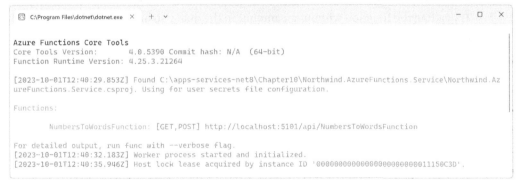

Figure 10.1: Azure Functions Core Tools hosting a function

 It might take a few minutes for the `Host lock lease` message to appear so do not worry if it doesn't show immediately.

3. Select the URL for your function and copy it to the clipboard.

4. Start Chrome.

5. Paste the URL into the address box, append the query string `?amount=123456`, and note the successful response in the browser of **one hundred and twenty-three thousand four hundred and fifty-six**, as shown in *Figure 10.2*:

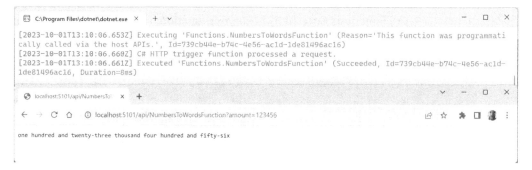

Figure 10.2: A successful call to the Azure function running locally

6. In the command prompt or terminal, note the function was called successfully, as shown in the following output:

```
[2023-101-01T11:32:51.574Z] Executing 'NumbersToWordsFunction'
(Reason='This function was programmatically called via the host APIs.',
Id=234d3122-ff3d-4896-94b3-db3c8b5013d8)
[2023-10-01T11:32:51.603Z] C# HTTP trigger function processed a request.
[2023-10-01T11:32:51.629Z] Executed 'NumbersToWordsFunction' (Succeeded,
Id=234d3122-ff3d-4896-94b3-db3c8b5013d8, Duration=96ms)
```

7. Try calling the function without an amount in the query string, or a non-integer value for the amount like `apples`, and note the function returns a `400` status code indicating a bad request with a custom message, `Failed to parse: apples`.

8. Close Chrome and shut down the web server (or in Visual Studio Code, stop debugging).

Responding to timer and resource triggers

Now that you have seen an Azure Functions function that responds to an HTTP request, let's build some that respond to other types of triggers.

Support for HTTP and timer triggers is built in. Support for other bindings is implemented as extension packages.

Implementing a Timer triggered function

First, we will make a function that runs every hour and requests a page from `amazon.com` for the eighth edition of my book, *C# 12 and .NET 8 – Modern Cross-Platform Development Fundamentals*, so that I can keep track of its Best Sellers Rank in the United States.

The function will need to make HTTP GET requests so we should inject the HTTP client factory. To do that, we will need to add some extra package references and create a special startup class:

1. In the Northwind.AzureFunctions.Service project, add package references for working with Azure Functions extensions and timers, as shown in the following markup:

```
<PackageReference Include="Microsoft.Azure.Functions.Extensions"
                  Version="1.1.0" />
<PackageReference Version="4.2.0"
  Include="Microsoft.Azure.Functions.Worker.Extensions.Timer" />
```

2. Build the Northwind.AzureFunctions.Service project to restore packages.

3. In Program.cs, import namespaces for working with dependency injection and HTTP media headers, as shown in the following code:

```
using Microsoft.Extensions.DependencyInjection; // To use
AddHttpClient().
using System.Net.Http.Headers; // To use MediaTypeWithQualityHeaderValue.
```

4. In Program.cs, add statements to configure a HTTP client factory for making requests to Amazon as if it was the Chrome browser as a dependency service, as shown highlighted in the following code:

```
var host = new HostBuilder()
  .ConfigureFunctionsWorkerDefaults()
  .ConfigureServices(services =>
  {
    services.AddHttpClient(name: "Amazon",
      configureClient: options =>
    {
      options.BaseAddress = new Uri("https://www.amazon.com");

      // Pretend to be Chrome with US English.
      options.DefaultRequestHeaders.Accept.Add(
        new MediaTypeWithQualityHeaderValue("text/html"));
      options.DefaultRequestHeaders.Accept.Add(
        new MediaTypeWithQualityHeaderValue("application/xhtml+xml"));
      options.DefaultRequestHeaders.Accept.Add(
        new MediaTypeWithQualityHeaderValue("application/xml", 0.9));
      options.DefaultRequestHeaders.Accept.Add(
        new MediaTypeWithQualityHeaderValue("image/avif"));
      options.DefaultRequestHeaders.Accept.Add(
        new MediaTypeWithQualityHeaderValue("image/webp"));
      options.DefaultRequestHeaders.Accept.Add(
```

```
            new MediaTypeWithQualityHeaderValue("image/apng"));
        options.DefaultRequestHeaders.Accept.Add(
            new MediaTypeWithQualityHeaderValue("*/*", 0.8));


        options.DefaultRequestHeaders.AcceptLanguage.Add(
            new StringWithQualityHeaderValue("en-US"));
        options.DefaultRequestHeaders.AcceptLanguage.Add(
            new StringWithQualityHeaderValue("en",0.8));


        options.DefaultRequestHeaders.UserAgent.Add(
            new(productName: "Chrome", productVersion: "114.0.5735.91"));
    });
})
  .Build();


host.Run();
```

The Chrome version on June 5, 2023, was `114.0.5735.91`. The major version number usually increments monthly, so in November 2023, it will likely be `119`, and in November 2024, it will likely be `131`.

5. Add a class file named `ScrapeAmazonFunction.cs`.

6. Modify its contents to implement a function that requests the page for the seventh edition of my book on the Amazon website and process the response, which is compressed using GZIP, to extract the book's Best Seller Rank, as shown in the following code:

```
using Microsoft.Azure.Functions.Worker; // To use [Function].
using Microsoft.Extensions.Logging; // To use ILogger.
using System.IO.Compression; // To use GZipStream, CompressionMode.

namespace Northwind.AzureFunctions.Service;

public class ScrapeAmazonFunction
{
  private const string relativePath =
    "12-NET-Cross-Platform-Development-Fundamentals/dp/1837635870/";

  private readonly IHttpClientFactory _clientFactory;
  private readonly ILogger _logger;

  public ScrapeAmazonFunction(IHttpClientFactory clientFactory,
```

```
    ILoggerFactory loggerFactory)
{
  _clientFactory = clientFactory;
  _logger = loggerFactory.CreateLogger<ScrapeAmazonFunction>();
}

[Function(nameof(ScrapeAmazonFunction))]
public async Task Run( // Every hour.
  [TimerTrigger("0 0 * * * *")] TimerInfo timer)
{
  _logger.LogInformation($"C# Timer trigger function executed at {
    DateTime.UtcNow}.");

  _logger.LogInformation(
    $"C# Timer trigger function next three occurrences at: {
      timer.ScheduleStatus?.Next}.");

  HttpClient client = _clientFactory.CreateClient("Amazon");
  HttpResponseMessage response = await client.GetAsync(relativePath);

  _logger.LogInformation(
    $"Request: GET {client.BaseAddress}{relativePath}");

  if (response.IsSuccessStatusCode)
  {
    _logger.LogInformation("Successful HTTP request.");

    // Read the content from a GZIP stream into a string.
    Stream stream = await response.Content.ReadAsStreamAsync();
    GZipStream gzipStream = new(stream, CompressionMode.Decompress);
    StreamReader reader = new(gzipStream);
    string page = reader.ReadToEnd();

    // Extract the Best Sellers Rank.
    int posBsr = page.IndexOf("Best Sellers Rank");
    string bsrSection = page.Substring(posBsr, 45);

    // bsrSection will be something like:
    //    "Best Sellers Rank: </span> #22,258 in Books ("

    // Get the position of the # and the following space.
```

```csharp
          int posHash = bsrSection.IndexOf("#") + 1;
          int posSpaceAfterHash = bsrSection.IndexOf(" ", posHash);

          // Get the BSR number as text.
          string bsr = bsrSection.Substring(
            posHash, posSpaceAfterHash - posHash);

          bsr = bsr.Replace(",", null); // remove commas

          // Parse the text into a number.
          if (int.TryParse(bsr, out int bestSellersRank))
          {
            _logger.LogInformation(
              $"Best Sellers Rank #{bestSellersRank:N0}.");
          }
          else
          {
            _logger.LogError(
              $"Failed to extract BSR number from: {bsrSection}.");
          }
        }
        else
        {
          _logger.LogError("Bad HTTP request.");
        }
      }
    }
```

Testing the Timer triggered function

Information about a function can be retrieved by making an HTTP GET request in the following format:

`http://locahost:5101/admin/functions/<functionname>`

Now we can test the Timer function in our local development environment:

1. Start the `Northwind.AzureFunctions.Service` project:

    *   If you are using Visual Studio Code, you will need to make sure you have the Azurite extension installed and the Azurite services running. Navigate to the **Run and Debug** pane, make sure that **Attach to .NET Functions** is selected, and then click the **Run** button.

2. Note there are now two functions, as shown in the following partial output:

```
Functions:
```

```
        NumbersToWordsFunction: [GET,POST] http://localhost:5101api/
NumbersToWordsFunction


        ScrapeAmazonFunction: timerTrigger


For detailed output, run func with --verbose flag.
```

3. In the HttpRequests folder, add a new file named azurefunctions-scrapeamazon.http.

4. Modify its contents to define a global variable and two requests to the Azure Functions locally hosted service, as shown in the following code:

```
### Configure a variable for the Azure Functions service base address.
@base_address = http://localhost:5101/


### Get information about the NumbersToWordsFunction function.
{{base_address}}admin/functions/NumbersToWordsFunction


### Get information about the ScrapeAmazonFunction function.
{{base_address}}admin/functions/ScrapeAmazonFunction
```

5. Send the first request and note that a JSON document is returned with information about the NumbersToWordsFunction function, as shown in the following response:

```
HTTP/1.1 200 OK
Content-Length: 918
Connection: close
Content-Type: application/json; charset=utf-8
Date: Mon, 05 Jun 2023 13:32:11 GMT
Server: Kestrel


{
  "name": "NumbersToWordsFunction",
  "script_root_path_href": null,
  "script_href": "http://localhost:5101/admin/vfs/bin/Northwind.
AzureFunctions.Service.dll",
  "config_href": null,
  "test_data_href": null,
  "href": "http://localhost:5101/admin/functions/NumbersToWordsFunction",
  "invoke_url_template": "http://localhost:5101/api/
numberstowordsfunction",
  "language": "dotnet-isolated",
  "config": {
    "name": "NumbersToWordsFunction",
```

```json
    "entryPoint": "Northwind.AzureFunctions.Service.
NumbersToWordsFunction.Run",
      "scriptFile": "Northwind.AzureFunctions.Service.dll",
      "language": "dotnet-isolated",
      "functionDirectory": null,
      "bindings": [
        {
          "name": "req",
          "direction": "In",
          "type": "httpTrigger",
          "authLevel": "Anonymous",
          "methods": [
            "get",
            "post"
          ],
          "properties": {}
        },
        {
          "name": "$return",
          "type": "http",
          "direction": "Out"
        }
      ]
    },
    "files": null,
    "test_data": null,
    "isDisabled": false,
    "isDirect": true,
    "isProxy": false
  }
```

6. Send the second request and note that a JSON document is returned with information about the ScrapeAmazonFunction function. The most interesting information for this function is the binding type and schedule, as shown in the following partial response:

```json
  "bindings": [
    {
      "name": "timer",
      "direction": "In",
      "type": "timerTrigger",
      "schedule": "0 0 * * * *",
      "properties": {}
```

```
    }
  ],
```

7. Add a third request that will trigger the timer function manually without having to wait for the hour mark by sending a POST request with an empty JSON document in the body to its admin endpoint, as shown in the following code:

```
### Make a manual request to the Timer function.
POST {{base_address}}admin/functions/ScrapeAmazonFunction
Content-Type: application/json

{}
```

8. Send the third request and note that it was successfully accepted, as shown in the following response:

```
HTTP/1.1 202 Accepted
```

9. Remove the {} in the body of the request, send it again, and note the client error response from which we can deduce that an empty JSON document is required, as shown in the following response:

```
HTTP/1.1 400 Bad Request
```

10. Add the empty JSON document back.

11. At the command prompt or terminal for the Azure Functions service, note that the function was triggered by our call. It outputs the time it was triggered (13:49 p.m.) and the time of its next occurrence in its normal timer schedule (2 p.m.) if I were to leave the service running, as shown in the following output:

```
[2023-10-01T13:49:53.939Z] Executing 'Functions.ScrapeAmazonFunction'
(Reason='This function was programmatically called via the host APIs.',
Id=1df349a1-79c5-4b52-a7f1-d0f8f0d5cd9c)
[2023-10-01T13:49:54.095Z] C# Timer trigger function executed at
01/10/2023 13:49:54.
[2023-10-01T13:49:54.095Z] C# Timer trigger function next occurrence at:
01/10/2023 14:00:00.
[2023-10-01T13:49:54.105Z] Start processing HTTP request GET https://www.
amazon.com/12-NET-Cross-Platform-Development-Fundamentals/dp/1837635870/
[2023-10-01T13:49:54.106Z] Sending HTTP request GET https://www.amazon.
com/12-NET-Cross-Platform-Development-Fundamentals/dp/1837635870/
[2023-10-01T13:49:54.520Z] Received HTTP response after 407.4353ms - OK
[2023-10-01T13:49:54.521Z] End processing HTTP request after 420.1273ms -
OK
[2023-10-01T13:49:56.212Z] Successful HTTP request.
```

```
[2023-10-01T13:49:56.212Z] Request: GET https://www.amazon.com/12-NET-
Cross-Platform-Development-Fundamentals/dp/1837635870/
[2023-10-01T13:49:56.251Z] Best Sellers Rank #384,269.
[2023-10-01T13:49:56.275Z] Executed 'Functions.ScrapeAmazonFunction'
(Succeeded, Id=1df349a1-79c5-4b52-a7f1-d0f8f0d5cd9c, Duration=2362ms)
```

12. Optionally, wait until the hour mark and note that the next occurrence triggers, as shown in the following output:

```
[2023-10-01T14:00:00.023Z] Executing 'Functions.ScrapeAmazonFunction'
(Reason='Timer fired at 2023-10-01T15:00:00.0220351+01:00', Id=aa9f7495-
6066-4b0a-ba81-42582d677321)
[2023-10-01T14:00:00.027Z] C# Timer trigger function executed at
01/10/2023 14:00:00.
[2023-10-01T14:00:00.028Z] Start processing HTTP request GET https://www.
amazon.com/12-NET-Cross-Platform-Development-Fundamentals/dp/1837635870/
[2023-10-01T14:00:00.027Z] C# Timer trigger function next occurrence at:
01/10/2023 15:00:00.
[2023-10-01T14:00:00.028Z] Sending HTTP request GET https://www.amazon.
com/12-NET-Cross-Platform-Development-Fundamentals/dp/1837635870/
[2023-10-01T14:00:00.337Z] Received HTTP response after 305.1877ms - OK
[2023-10-01T14:00:00.339Z] End processing HTTP request after 305.5222ms -
OK
[2023-10-01T14:00:01.899Z] Successful HTTP request.
[2023-10-01T14:00:01.899Z] Request: GET https://www.amazon.com/12-NET-
Cross-Platform-Development-Fundamentals/dp/1837635870/
[2023-10-01T14:00:01.931Z] Best Sellers Rank #387,339.
[2023-10-01T14:00:01.931Z] Executed 'Functions.ScrapeAmazonFunction'
(Succeeded, Id=aa9f7495-6066-4b0a-ba81-42582d677321, Duration=1909ms)
```

13. If I were to stop the service running, wait for more than an hour, and then start the service, it would immediately run the function because it is past due, as shown highlighted in the following output:

```
[2023-10-01T16:19:31.369Z] Trigger Details: UnscheduledInvocationReason:
IsPastDue, OriginalSchedule: 2023-10-01T15:00:00.0000000+01:00
```

14. Shut down the Azure Functions service.

Implementing a function that works with queues and BLOBs

The HTTP-triggered function responded directly to the GET request with plain text. We will now define a similar function to bind to Queue Storage and add a message to a queue to indicate that an image needs to be generated and uploaded to Blob Storage. This can then be printed as a check.

When running the service locally, we want to generate the image of the check BLOB in the local filesystem to make it easier to ensure it is working correctly. We will set a custom environment variable in local settings to detect that condition.

We need a font that looks like handwriting. Google has a useful website where you can search for, preview, and download fonts. The one we will use is Caveat, as shown at the following link:

```
https://fonts.google.com/specimen/Caveat?category=Handwriting&preview.text=one%20
hundred%20and%20twenty%20three%20thousand,%20four%20hundred%20and%20fifty%20six&preview.
text_type=custom#standard-styles
```

Let's go:

1. Download the font at the link above, extract the ZIP file, and copy the files into a folder named `fonts`, as shown in Visual Studio 2022 in *Figure 10.3*:

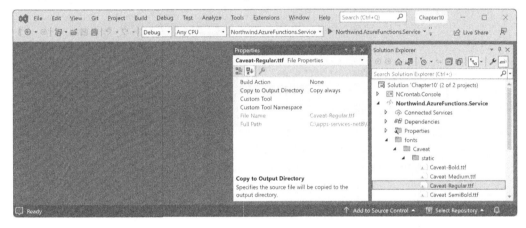

Figure 10.3: The fonts folder with the Caveat font files in Visual Studio 2022

1. Select the `Caveat-Regular.ttf` font file.
2. In **Properties**, set **Copy to Output Directory** to **Copy always**, as shown in *Figure 10.3*. This adds an entry to the project file, as shown highlighted in the following markup:

```
<ItemGroup>
  <None Update="fonts\Caveat\static\Caveat-Regular.ttf">
    <CopyToOutputDirectory>Always</CopyToOutputDirectory>
  </None>
  <None Update="host.json">
    <CopyToOutputDirectory>PreserveNewest</CopyToOutputDirectory>
  </None>
  <None Update="local.settings.json">
    <CopyToOutputDirectory>PreserveNewest</CopyToOutputDirectory>
```

```
    <CopyToPublishDirectory>Never</CopyToPublishDirectory>
  </None>
</ItemGroup>
```

If you are using Visual Studio Code, manually add the preceding entry to the project file.

3. In the `Northwind.AzureFunctions.Service` project, add package references for working with the Azure Queue and Blob Storage extensions and drawing with `ImageSharp`, as shown in the following markup:

```
<PackageReference Version="5.2.0" Include=
  "Microsoft.Azure.Functions.Worker.Extensions.Storage.Queues" />
<PackageReference Version="6.2.0" Include=
  "Microsoft.Azure.Functions.Worker.Extensions.Storage.Blobs" />
<PackageReference Include="SixLabors.ImageSharp" Version="3.0.2" />
<PackageReference Include="SixLabors.ImageSharp.Drawing"
                  Version="2.0.0" />
```

4. Build the project to restore packages.

5. In the `Northwind.AzureFunctions.Service` project, add a new class named `NumbersToChecksFunction.cs`.

6. In `NumbersToChecksFunction.cs`, add statements to register the function with an output binding for Queue Storage so that it can write to a named queue, and when the amount is successfully parsed to return the words to the queue, as shown in the following code:

```
using Humanizer; // To use ToWords extension method.
using Microsoft.Azure.Functions.Worker; // To use [Function] and so on.
using Microsoft.Azure.Functions.Worker.Http; // To use HttpRequestData.
using Microsoft.Extensions.Logging; // To use ILogger.

namespace Northwind.AzureFunctions.Service;

public class NumbersToChecksFunction
{
  private readonly ILogger _logger;

  public NumbersToChecksFunction(ILoggerFactory loggerFactory)
  {
    _logger = loggerFactory.CreateLogger<NumbersToChecksFunction>();
  }

  [Function(nameof(NumbersToChecksFunction))]
  [QueueOutput("checksQueue")] // Return value is written to this queue.
```

```
    public string Run(
      [HttpTrigger(AuthorizationLevel.Anonymous,
        "get", "post", Route = null)] HttpRequestData request)
    {
      _logger.LogInformation("C# HTTP trigger function processed a
request.");

      string? amount = request.Query["amount"];

      if (long.TryParse(amount, out long number))
      {
        return number.ToWords();
      }
      else
      {
        return $"Failed to parse: {amount}";
      }
    }
  }
}
```

7. In `local.settings.json`, add an environment variable named `IS_LOCAL` with a value of true, as shown highlighted in the following configuration:

```
{
  "IsEncrypted": false,
  "Values": {
    "AzureWebJobsStorage": "UseDevelopmentStorage=true",
    "FUNCTIONS_WORKER_RUNTIME": "dotnet-isolated",
    "IS_LOCAL": true
  }
}
```

8. Add a class file named `CheckGeneratorFunction.cs`.

9. Modify its contents, as shown in the following code:

```
using Microsoft.Azure.Functions.Worker; // To use [Function] and so on.
using Microsoft.Extensions.Logging; // To use ILogger.
using SixLabors.Fonts; // To use Font.
using SixLabors.ImageSharp.Drawing; // To use IPath.
using SixLabors.ImageSharp.Drawing.Processing; // To use Brush, Pen.

namespace Northwind.AzureFunctions.Service;
```

```csharp
public class CheckGeneratorFunction
{
  private readonly ILogger _logger;

  public CheckGeneratorFunction(ILoggerFactory loggerFactory)
  {
    _logger = loggerFactory.CreateLogger<NumbersToWordsFunction>();
  }

  [Function(nameof(CheckGeneratorFunction))]
  [BlobOutput("checks-blob-container/check.png")]
  public byte[] Run(
    [QueueTrigger("checksQueue")] string message)
  {
    _logger.LogInformation("C# Queue trigger function executed.");
    _logger.LogInformation($"Body: {message}.");

    // Create a new blank image with a white background.
    using (Image<Rgba32> image = new(width: 1200, height: 600,
      backgroundColor: new Rgba32(r: 255, g: 255, b: 255, a: 100)))
    {
      // Load the font file and create a large font.
      FontCollection collection = new();
      FontFamily family = collection.Add(
        @"fonts\Caveat\static\Caveat-Regular.ttf");

      Font font = family.CreateFont(72);

      string amount = message.Body.ToString();

      DrawingOptions options = new()
      {
        GraphicsOptions = new()
        {
          ColorBlendingMode = PixelColorBlendingMode.Multiply
        }
      };

      // Define some pens and brushes.

      Pen blackPen = Pens.Solid(Color.Black, 2);
```

```
Pen blackThickPen = Pens.Solid(Color.Black, 8);
Pen greenPen = Pens.Solid(Color.Green, 3);
Brush redBrush = Brushes.Solid(Color.Red);
Brush blueBrush = Brushes.Solid(Color.Blue);

// Define some paths and draw them.

IPath border = new RectangularPolygon(
  x: 50, y: 50, width: 1100, height: 500);

image.Mutate(x => x.Draw(options, blackPen, border));

IPath star = new Star(x: 150.0f, y: 150.0f,
  prongs: 5, innerRadii: 20.0f, outerRadii: 30.0f);

image.Mutate(x => x.Fill(options, redBrush, star)
                   .Draw(options, greenPen, star));

IPath line1 = new Polygon(new LinearLineSegment(
  new PointF(x: 100, y: 275), new PointF(x: 1050, y: 275)));

image.Mutate(x => x.Draw(options, blackPen, line1));

IPath line2 = new Polygon(new LinearLineSegment(
  new PointF(x: 100, y: 365), new PointF(x: 1050, y: 365)));

image.Mutate(x => x.Draw(options, blackPen, line2));

RichTextOptions textOptions = new(font)
{
  Origin = new PointF(100, 200),
  WrappingLength = 1000,
  HorizontalAlignment = HorizontalAlignment.Left
};

image.Mutate(x => x.DrawText(
  textOptions, amount, blueBrush, blackPen));

string blobName = $"{DateTime.UtcNow:yyyy-MM-dd-hh-mm-ss}.png";
_logger.LogInformation($"Blob filename: {blobName}.");
```

```
        try
        {
          if (Environment.GetEnvironmentVariable("IS_LOCAL") == "true")
          {
            // Create blob in the local filesystem.

            string folder = $@"{System.Environment.CurrentDirectory}\
    blobs";
            if (!Directory.Exists(folder))
            {
              Directory.CreateDirectory(folder);
            }
            log.LogInformation($"Blobs folder: {folder}");

            string blobPath = $@"{folder}\{blobName}";

            image.SaveAsPng(blobPath);
          }

          // Create BLOB in Blob Storage via a memory stream.

          MemoryStream stream = new();

          image.SaveAsPng(stream);

          stream.Seek(0, SeekOrigin.Begin);

          return stream.ToArray();
        }
        catch (System.Exception ex)
        {
          log.LogError(ex.Message);
        }
        return Array.Empty<byte>();
      }
    }
  }
```

Note the following:

- The `[QueueTrigger("checksQueue")] string message` parameter means the function is triggered by a message being added to the checksQueue and the queued item is automatically passed to the parameter named message.

- We use ImageSharp to create a 1200x600 image of a check.
- We use the current UTC date and time to name the BLOB to avoid duplicates. In a real implementation, you would need something more robust like GUIDs.
- If the IS_LOCAL environment variable is set to true, then we save the image as a PNG to the local filesystem in a blobs subfolder.
- We save the image as a PNG to a memory stream that is then returned as a byte array and uploaded to the BLOB container defined by the [BlobOutput("checks-blob-container/check.png")] attribute.

Testing the function that works with queues and BLOBs

Now we can test the function that works with queues and BLOBs in our local development environment:

1. Start the Northwind.AzureFunctions.Service project:

    If you are using Visual Studio Code, you will need to navigate to the **Run and Debug** pane, make sure that **Attach to .NET Functions** is selected, and then click the **Run** button.

2. Note there are now four functions, as shown in the following partial output:

```
Functions:

        NumbersToChecksFunction: [GET,POST] http://localhost:5101/api/
NumbersToChecksFunction

        NumbersToWordsFunction: [GET,POST] http://localhost:5101/api/
NumbersToWordsFunction

        CheckGeneratorFunction: queueTrigger

        ScrapeAmazonFunction: timerTrigger
```

3. In the HttpRequests folder, add a new file named azurefunctions-numberstochecks.http.
4. Modify its contents, as shown in the following code:

```
### Configure a variable for the Azure Functions base address.
@base_address = http://localhost:5101/

### Trigger the NumbersToChecksFunction function.
GET {{base_address}}api/NumbersToChecksFunction?amount=123456
```

5. Send the request and note that a JSON document is returned with information about the NumbersToWordsFunction function, as shown in the following response:

```
Response time: 2524 ms
```

```
Status code: OK (200)
Transfer-Encoding: chunked
Date: Mon, 05 Jun 2023 13:53:11 GMT
Server: Kestrel


Content-Type: text/plain; charset=utf-8
Content-Length: 64



-------------------------------------------------
Content:
one hundred and twenty-three thousand four hundred and fifty-six
```

6.   At the command prompt or terminal, note the function call was successful and a message was sent to the queue that then triggered the `CheckGeneratorFunction`, as shown in the following output:

```
[2023-06-05T13:53:12.175Z] Executing 'NumbersToWordsFunction'
(Reason='This function was programmatically called via the host APIs.',
Id=b6a49d34-edbf-4c2a-97f2-195f8d06cd13)
[2023-06-05T13:53:12.195Z] C# HTTP trigger function processed a request.
[2023-06-05T13:53:12.262Z] Executed 'NumbersToWordsFunction' (Succeeded,
Id=b6a49d34-edbf-4c2a-97f2-195f8d06cd13, Duration=104ms)
[2023-06-05T13:53:14.302Z] Executing 'CheckGeneratorFunction'
(Reason='New queue message detected on 'checksqueue'.', Id=2697ddc0-46dd-
4c06-b960-fb5a443ec929)
[2023-06-05T13:53:14.305Z] Trigger Details: MessageId: 229e4961-
bfaf-46da-bb17-040ffc2bbf91, DequeueCount: 1, InsertedOn: 2023-06-
05T13:53:12.000+00:00
[2023-06-05T13:53:14.313Z] C# Queue trigger function executed.
[2023-06-05T13:53:14.314Z] MessageId: 229e4961-bfaf-46da-bb17-
040ffc2bbf91.
[2023-06-05T13:53:14.316Z] InsertedOn: 05/06/2023 13:53:12 +00:00.
[2023-06-05T13:53:14.317Z] ExpiresOn: 12/06/2023 13:53:12 +00:00.
[2023-06-05T13:53:14.318Z] Body: one hundred and twenty-three thousand
four hundred and fifty-six.
[2023-06-05T13:53:14.845Z] Blob name: 2023-06-05-01-53-14.png.
[2023-06-05T13:53:14.848Z] Blobs folder: C:\apps-services-net8\Chapter10\
Northwind.AzureFunctions.Service\bin\Debug\net8.0\blobs
[2023-06-05T13:53:15.057Z] Blob sequence number: 0.
[2023-06-05T13:53:15.060Z] Executed 'CheckGeneratorFunction' (Succeeded,
Id=2697ddc0-46dd-4c06-b960-fb5a443ec929, Duration=776ms)
[2023-06-05T13:53:20.979Z] Host lock lease acquired by instance ID '00000
00000000000000000011150C3D'.
```

7. In the `Northwind.AzureFunctions.Service\bin\Debug\net8.0\blobs` folder, note the image created locally in the `blobs` folder, as shown in *Figure 10.4*:

Figure 10.4: The check image generated in the project blobs folder

8. Note the check image, as shown in *Figure 10.5*:

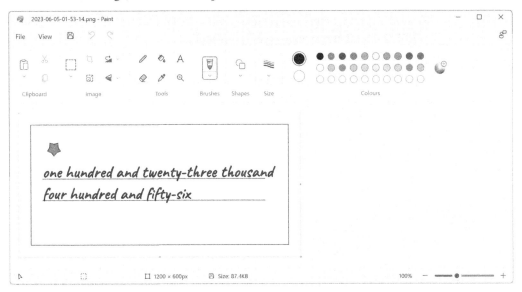

Figure 10.5: The check image opened in Windows Paint

Publishing an Azure Functions project to the cloud

Now, let's create a function app and related resources in an Azure subscription, then deploy your functions to the cloud and run it there.

If you do not already have an Azure account, then you can sign up for a free one at the following link: `https://azure.microsoft.com/en-us/free/`.

Using Visual Studio 2022 to publish

Visual Studio 2022 has a GUI to publish to Azure:

1. In **Solution Explorer**, right-click the `Northwind.AzureFunctions.Service` project and select **Publish**.

2. Select **Azure** and then click **Next**.

3. Select **Azure Function App (Linux)** and click **Next**.

4. Sign in and enter your Azure credentials.

5. Select your subscription; for example, I chose my subscription named **Pay-As-You-Go**.

6. In the **Function Instance** section, click the **+ Create New** button.

7. Complete the dialog box, as shown in *Figure 10.6*:

   - **Name:** This must be globally unique. It suggested a name based on the project name and the current date and time.

   - **Subscription name:** Select your subscription.

   - **Resource group:** Select or create a new resource group to make it easier to delete everything later. I chose `apps-services-book`.

   - **Plan Type: Consumption** (pay for only what you use).

   - **Location:** A data center nearest to you. I chose **UK South**.

   - **Azure Storage:** Create a new account named `northwindazurefunctions` (or something else that is globally unique) in a data center nearest to you and choose **Standard – Locally Redundant Storage** for the account type.

   - **Application Insights: None.**

Figure 10.6: Creating a new Azure function app

8. Click **Create**. This process can take a minute or more.

9. In the **Publish** dialog, click **Finish** and then click **Close**.

10. In the **Publish** window, click the **Publish** button, as shown in *Figure 10.7*:

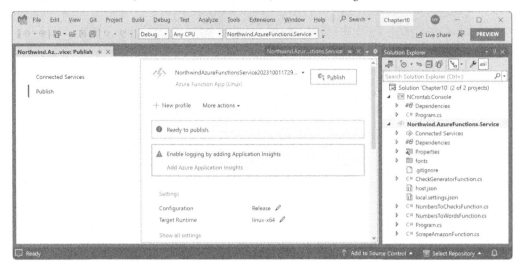

Figure 10.7: An Azure Function App ready to publish using Visual Studio 2022

11. Review the output window, as shown in the following publishing output:

```
Build started...
1>------ Build started: Project: Northwind.AzureFunctions.Service,
Configuration: Release Any CPU ------
1>Northwind.AzureFunctions.Service -> C:\apps-services-net8\Chapter10\
Northwind.AzureFunctions.Service\bin\Release\net8.0\Northwind.
AzureFunctions.Service.dll
2>------ Publish started: Project: Northwind.AzureFunctions.Service,
Configuration: Release Any CPU ------
2>Northwind.AzureFunctions.Service -> C:\apps-services-net8\Chapter10\
Northwind.AzureFunctions.Service\bin\Release\net8.0\Northwind.
AzureFunctions.Service.dll
2>Northwind.AzureFunctions.Service -> C:\apps-services-net8\Chapter10\
Northwind.AzureFunctions.Service\obj\Release\net8.0\PubTmp\Out\
2>Publishing C:\apps-services-net8\Chapter10\Northwind.
AzureFunctions.Service\obj\Release\net8.0\PubTmp\Northwind.
AzureFunctions.Service - 20230605152148071.zip to https://
northwindazurefunctionsservice20230605151137.scm.azurewebsites.net/api/
zipdeploy...
2>Zip Deployment succeeded.
========== Build: 1 succeeded, 0 failed, 0 up-to-date, 0 skipped
==========
```

```
========== Build started at 3:21 PM and took 03:34.100 minutes ==========
========== Publish: 1 succeeded, 0 failed, 0 skipped ==========
========== Publish started at 3:21 PM and took 03:34.100 minutes
==========
Waiting for Function app to be ready...
Function app is ready
```

12. In the **Publish** window, click **Open site** and note your Azure Functions v4 host site is ready.

13. Test the function in your browser by appending the following relative URL to the address box, as shown in *Figure 10.8*:

```
/api/NumbersToWordsFunction?amount=987654321
```

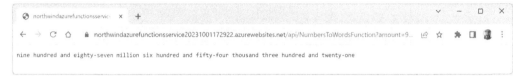

Figure 10.8: Calling the function hosted in the Azure cloud

Using Visual Studio Code to publish

You can learn how to publish using Visual Studio Code at the following link:

```
https://learn.microsoft.com/en-us/azure/azure-functions/functions-develop-vs-
code?tabs=csharp#sign-in-to-azure
```

Now that you've successfully published your Azure Functions project to the cloud, it's important to understand how to manage your resources efficiently. Let's explore how to clean up our Azure Functions resources to avoid unnecessary costs and ensure tidy resource management.

Cleaning up Azure Functions resources

You can use the following steps to delete the function app and its related resources to avoid incurring further costs:

1. In your browser, navigate to `https://portal.azure.com/`.

2. In the Azure portal, in your function app's **Overview** blade, select **Resource Group**.

3. Confirm that it contains only resources that you want to delete; for example, there should be a **Storage account**, a **Function App**, and an **App Service plan**.

4. If you are sure you want to delete all the resources in the group, then click **Delete resource group** and accept any other confirmations. Alternatively, you can delete each resource individually.

Practicing and exploring

Test your knowledge and understanding by answering some questions, getting some hands-on practice, and exploring this chapter's topics with deeper research.

Exercise 10.1 – Test your knowledge

Answer the following questions:

1. What is the difference between the in-process and isolated worker models for Azure Functions?
2. What attribute do you use to cause a function to trigger when a message arrives in a queue?
3. What attribute do you use to make a queue available to send messages to?
4. What schedule does the following NCRONTAB expression define?

   ```
   0 0 */6 * 6 6
   ```

5. How can you configure a dependency service for use in a function?

Exercise 10.2 – Explore topics

Use the links on the following page for more details on the topics covered in this chapter:

https://github.com/markjprice/apps-services-net8/blob/main/docs/book-links.md#chapter-10---building-serverless-nanoservices-using-azure-functions

Summary

In this chapter, you learned:

- Some of the concepts around Azure Functions
- How to build serverless services using Azure Functions
- How to respond to HTTP, Timer, and Queue triggers
- How to bind to Queue and Blob Storage
- How to deploy an Azure Functions project to the cloud

In the next chapter, you will learn about SignalR, a technology for performing real-time communication between client and server.

11

Broadcasting Real-Time Communication Using SignalR

In this chapter, you will be introduced to SignalR, a technology that enables a developer to create a service that can have multiple clients and broadcast messages to all of them or a subset of them live in real time. The canonical example is a group chat app. Other examples include notification systems and dashboards that need instantly up-to-date information like stock prices.

This chapter will cover the following topics:

- Understanding SignalR
- Building a live communication service using SignalR
- Building a web client using the SignalR JavaScript library
- Building a .NET console app client
- Streaming data using SignalR

Understanding SignalR

To understand the problem that SignalR solves, we need to understand what web development is like without it. The foundation of the web is HTTP, which for more than 30 years has been great for building general-purpose websites and services. However, the web was not designed for specialized scenarios that require a web page to be instantaneously updated with new information as it becomes available.

The history of real-time communication on the web

To understand the benefits of SignalR, it helps to know the history of HTTP and how organizations worked to make it better for real-time communication between clients and servers.

In the early days of the Web in the 1990s, browsers had to make a full-page HTTP GET request to the web server to get fresh information to show to the visitor.

In late 1999, Microsoft released Internet Explorer 5 with a component named **XMLHttpRequest** that could make asynchronous HTTP calls in the background. This, alongside **dynamic HTML (DHTML)**, allowed parts of the web page to be updated with fresh data smoothly.

The benefits of this technique were obvious, and soon, all browsers added the same component.

AJAX

Google took maximum advantage of this capability to build clever web applications such as Google Maps and Gmail. A few years later, the technique became popularly known as **Asynchronous JavaScript and XML (AJAX)**.

AJAX still uses HTTP to communicate, however, and that has limitations:

- First, HTTP is a request-response communication protocol, meaning that the server cannot push data to the client. It must wait for the client to make a request.
- Second, HTTP request and response messages have headers with lots of potentially unnecessary overhead.

WebSocket

WebSocket is full-duplex, meaning that either the client or server can initiate communicating new data. WebSocket uses the same TCP connection for the life cycle of the connection. It is also more efficient in the message sizes that it sends because they are minimally framed with 2 bytes.

WebSocket works over HTTP ports 80 and 443 so it is compatible with the HTTP protocol, and the WebSocket handshake uses the HTTP **Upgrade** header to switch from the HTTP protocol to the Web-Socket protocol.

Modern web apps are expected to deliver up-to-date information. Live chat is the canonical example, but there are lots of potential applications, from stock prices to games.

Whenever you need the server to push updates to the web page, you need a web-compatible, real-time communication technology. WebSocket could be used, but it is not supported by all clients. You can check which clients support WebSocket using the web page found at the following link: https://caniuse.com/websockets.

 WebSocket or WebSockets? "The **WebSocket** protocol was standardized by the IETF as RFC 6455 in 2011. The current API specification allowing web applications to use this protocol is known as *WebSockets*." From the Wikipedia page found at the following link: https://en.wikipedia.org/wiki/WebSocket.

Introducing SignalR

ASP.NET Core SignalR is an open-source library that simplifies adding real-time web functionality to apps by being an abstraction over multiple underlying communication technologies, which allows you to add real-time communication capabilities using C# code.

The developer does not need to understand or implement the underlying technology used, and SignalR will automatically switch between underlying technologies depending on what the visitor's web browser supports. For example, SignalR will use WebSocket when it's available and gracefully falls back on other technologies such as AJAX long polling when it isn't, while your application code stays the same.

SignalR is an API for server-to-client **remote procedure calls** (**RPCs**). The RPCs call JavaScript functions on clients from server-side .NET code. SignalR has hubs to define the pipeline and handles the message dispatching automatically using two built-in hub protocols: JSON and a binary one based on MessagePack.

On the server side, SignalR runs everywhere that ASP.NET Core runs: Windows, macOS, or Linux servers. SignalR supports the following client platforms:

- JavaScript clients for current browsers including Chrome, Firefox, Safari, and Edge.
- .NET clients including Blazor, .NET MAUI, and Xamarin for Android and iOS mobile apps.
- Java 8 and later.

Azure SignalR Service

Earlier, I mentioned that it would be good practice to separate the SignalR service hosting project from the web project that uses the JavaScript library to act as a client. This is because a SignalR service potentially needs to handle lots of simultaneous client requests and respond quickly to them all.

Once you separate the SignalR hosting, you can take advantage of **Azure SignalR Service**. This offers global reach and a world-class data center and network, and it scales to millions of connections while meeting SLAs like providing compliance and high security.

 You can learn more about Azure SignalR Service at the following link: `https://learn.microsoft.com/en-us/azure/azure-signalr/signalr-overview`.

Designing method signatures

When designing the method signatures for a SignalR service, it is good practice to define methods with a single message parameter rather than multiple simple type parameters. This good practice is not enforced by the technology with SignalR, so you will have to be disciplined.

For example, instead of passing multiple `string` (or other type) values, define a type with multiple properties to use as the single `Message` parameter, as shown in the following code:

```
// Bad practice: RPC method with multiple parameters.
public void SendMessage(string to, string body)

// Good practice: single parameter using a complex type.
public class Message
{
```

```
    public string To { get; set; }
    public string Body { get; set; }
}
```

```
public void SendMessage(Message message)
```

The reason for this good practice is that it allows future changes like adding a third property for the message `Title`. For the bad practice example, a third `string` parameter named `title` would need to be added and existing clients would get errors because they are not sending the extra `string` value. But using the good practice example will not break the method signature so existing clients can continue to call it as before the change. On the server side, the extra `Title` property will just have a `null` value that can be checked for, and perhaps be set to a default value.

SignalR method parameters are serialized as JSON, so all nested objects are accessible in JavaScript if needed.

Now that we've explored the fundamentals of SignalR and its various aspects like good practices for method signature design, let's walk through how to build a live communication service using SignalR.

Building a live communication service using SignalR

The SignalR *server* library is included in ASP.NET Core, but the JavaScript *client* library is not automatically included in the project. Remember, SignalR supports multiple client types, and a web page using JavaScript is just one of them.

We will use the **Library Manager CLI** to get the client library from **unpkg**, a **content delivery network (CDN)** that can deliver anything found in the Node.js package manager.

Let's add a SignalR server-side hub and client-side JavaScript to an ASP.NET Core MVC project to implement a chat feature that allows visitors to send messages to:

- Everyone currently using the website.
- Dynamically defined groups.
- A single specified user.

 Good Practice: In a production solution, it would be better to host the SignalR hub in a separate web project so that it can be hosted and scaled independently from the rest of the website. Live communication can often put excessive load on a website.

Defining some shared models

First, we will define two shared models that can be used on both the server-side and client-side .NET projects that will work with our chat service:

1. Use your preferred code editor to create a new project, as defined in the following list:

    - Project template: **Class Library** / `classlib`

- Solution file and folder: `Chapter11`
- Project file and folder: `Northwind.Common`

2. In the `Northwind.Common` project, rename the `Class1.cs` file to `UserModel.cs`.

3. Modify its contents to define a model for registering a user's name, unique connection ID, and the groups that they belong to, as shown in the following code:

```
namespace Northwind.Chat.Models;

public class UserModel
{
  public string Name { get; set; } = null!;
  public string ConnectionId { get; set; } = null!;
  public string? Groups { get; set; } // comma-separated list
}
```

> **Good Practice:** In a real-world app, you would want to use a collection of `string` values for the `Groups` property, but this coding task is not about how to provide a web user experience for editing multiple `string` values. We will provide a simple text box instead and focus on learning SignalR.

4. In the `Northwind.Common` project, add a class file named `MessageModel.cs`. Modify its contents to define a message model with properties for whom the message is sent to and who the message was sent from, and the message body, as shown in the following code:

```
namespace Northwind.Chat.Models;

public class MessageModel
{
  public string From { get; set; } = null!;
  public string To { get; set; } = null!;
  public string? Body { get; set; }
}
```

Enabling a server-side SignalR hub

Next, we will enable a SignalR hub on the server side in an ASP.NET Core MVC project:

1. Use your preferred code editor to add a new project, as defined in the following list:

- Project template: **ASP.NET Core Web App (Model-View-Controller)** / mvc
- Solution file and folder: `Chapter11`
- Project file and folder: `Northwind.SignalR.Service.Client.Mvc`
- Authentication type: None.

- • Configure for HTTPS: Selected.
- • Enable Docker: Cleared.
- • Do not use top-level statements: Cleared.

2. In the `Northwind.SignalR.Service.Client.Mvc` project, treat warnings as errors and add a project reference to the `Northwind.Common` project, as shown in the following markup:

```
<ItemGroup>
  <ProjectReference
    Include="..\Northwind.Common\Northwind.Common.csproj" />
</ItemGroup>
```

3. In the `Properties` folder, in `launchSettings.json`, in the `https` profile, modify the `applicationUrl` to use port `5111` for `https` and `5112` for `http`, as shown highlighted in the following configuration:

```
"https": {
  "commandName": "Project",
  "dotnetRunMessages": true,
  "launchBrowser": true,
  "applicationUrl": "https://localhost:5111;http://localhost:5112",
  "environmentVariables": {
    "ASPNETCORE_ENVIRONMENT": "Development"
  }
```

4. In the `Northwind.SignalR.Service.Client.Mvc` project, add a class file named `ChatHub.cs`.
5. In `ChatHub.cs`, modify its contents to inherit from the `Hub` class and implement two methods that can be called by a client, as shown in the following code:

```
using Microsoft.AspNetCore.SignalR; // To use Hub.
using Northwind.Chat.Models; // To use UserModel, MessageModel.

namespace Northwind.SignalR.Service.Hubs;

public class ChatHub : Hub
{
  // A new instance of ChatHub is created to process each method so we
  // must store user names, connection IDs, and groups in a static field.
  private static Dictionary<string, UserModel> Users = new();

  public async Task Register(UserModel newUser)
  {
    UserModel user;
    string action = "registered as a new user";
```

```csharp
// Try to get a stored user with a match on new user.
if (Users.ContainsKey(newUser.Name))
{
  user = Users[newUser.Name];

  // Remove any existing group registrations.
  if (user.Groups is not null)
  {
    foreach (string group in user.Groups.Split(','))
    {
      await Groups.RemoveFromGroupAsync(user.ConnectionId, group);
    }
  }
  user.Groups = newUser.Groups;

  // Connection ID might have changed if the browser
  // refreshed so update it.
  user.ConnectionId = Context.ConnectionId;

  action = "updated your registered user";
}
else
{
  if (string.IsNullOrEmpty(newUser.Name))
  {
    // Assign a GUID for name if they are anonymous.
    newUser.Name = Guid.NewGuid().ToString();
  }
  newUser.ConnectionId = Context.ConnectionId;
  Users.Add(key: newUser.Name, value: newUser);
  user = newUser;
}

if (user.Groups is not null)
{
  // A user does not have to belong to any groups
  // but if they do, register them with the Hub.

  foreach (string group in user.Groups.Split(','))
  {
```

```
        await Groups.AddToGroupAsync(user.ConnectionId, group);
    }
  }


  // Send a message to the registering user informing of success.

  MessageModel message = new()
  {
    From = "SignalR Hub", To = user.Name,
    Body = string.Format(
      "You have successfully {0} with connection ID {1}.",
      arg0: action, arg1: user.ConnectionId)
  };


  IClientProxy proxy = Clients.Client(user.ConnectionId);
  await proxy.SendAsync("ReceiveMessage", message);
}

public async Task SendMessage(MessageModel message)
{
  IClientProxy proxy;

  if (string.IsNullOrEmpty(message.To))
  {
    message.To = "Everyone";
    proxy = Clients.All;
    await proxy.SendAsync("ReceiveMessage", message);
    return;
  }

  // Split To into a list of user and group names.
  string[] userAndGroupList = message.To.Split(',');

  // Each item could be a user or group name.
  foreach (string userOrGroup in userAndGroupList)
  {
    if (Users.ContainsKey(userOrGroup))
    {
      // If the item is in Users then send the message to that user
      // by looking up their connection ID in the dictionary.
      message.To = $"User: {Users[userOrGroup].Name}";
```

```
            proxy = Clients.Client(Users[userOrGroup].ConnectionId);
        }
        else // Assume the item is a group name to send the message to.
        {
            message.To = $"Group: {userOrGroup}";
            proxy = Clients.Group(userOrGroup);
        }
        await proxy.SendAsync("ReceiveMessage", message);
    }
  }
}
```

Note the following:

- ChatHub has a private field to store a list of registered users. It is a dictionary with their name as a unique key.

- ChatHub has two methods that a client can call: Register and SendMessage.

- Register has a single parameter of type UserModel. The user's name, connection ID, and groups are stored in the static dictionary so that the user's name can be used to look up the connection ID later and send messages directly to that one user. After registering a new user or updating the registration of an existing user, a message is sent back to the client informing them of success.

- SendMessage has a single parameter of type MessageModel. The method branches based on the value of the To property. If To does not have a value, it calls the All property to get a proxy that will communicate with every client. If To has a value, the string is split using comma separators into an array. Each item in the array is checked to see if it matches a user in Users. If it matches, it calls the Client method to get a proxy that will communicate just with that one client. If it does not match, the item might be a group, so it calls the Group method to get a proxy that will communicate with just the members of that group. Finally, it sends the message asynchronously using the proxy.

6. In Program.cs, import the namespace for your SignalR hub, as shown in the following code:

```
using Northwind.SignalR.Service.Hubs; // To use ChatHub.
```

7. In the section that configures services, add a statement to add support for SignalR to the services collection, as shown in the following code:

```
builder.Services.AddSignalR();
```

8. In the section that configures the HTTP pipeline, before the call to map controller routes, add a statement to map the relative URL path /chat to your SignalR hub, as shown in the following code:

```
app.MapHub<ChatHub>("/chat");
```

Building a web client using the SignalR JavaScript library

Next, we will add the SignalR client-side JavaScript library so that we can use it on a web page:

1. Open a command prompt or terminal for the `Northwind.SignalR.Service.Client.Mvc` project/folder.

2. Install the Library Manager CLI tool, as shown in the following command:

    ```
    dotnet tool install -g Microsoft.Web.LibraryManager.Cli
    ```

     This tool might already be installed globally. To update it to the latest version, repeat the command but replace `install` with `update`.

3. Enter a command to add the `signalr.js` and `signalr.min.js` libraries to the project from the unpkg source, as shown in the following command:

    ```
    libman install @microsoft/signalr@latest -p unpkg -d wwwroot/js/signalr
    --files dist/browser/signalr.js --files dist/browser/signalr.min.js
    ```

     Never copy long commands from a PDF and paste them directly to the command prompt. Always clean them up in a basic text editor to remove extraneous new lines and so on and then recopy them. To make it easier to enter long command lines, you can copy them from the following link: `https://github.com/markjprice/apps-services-net8/blob/main/docs/command-lines.md`

4. Note the success message, as shown in the following output:

    ```
    wwwroot/js/signalr/dist/browser/signalr.js written to disk
    wwwroot/js/signalr/dist/browser/signalr.min.js written to disk
    Installed library "@microsoft/signalr@latest" to "wwwroot/js/signalr"
    ```

     Visual Studio 2022 also has a GUI for adding client-side JavaScript libraries. To use it, right-click a web project and then navigate to **Add** | **Client Side Libraries**.

Adding a chat page to the MVC website

Next, we will add chat functionality to the home page:

1. In `Views/Home`, in `Index.cshtml`, modify its contents, as shown in the following markup:

```
@using Northwind.Chat.Models
@{
  ViewData["Title"] = "SignalR Chat";
}
<div class="container">
  <h1>@ViewData["Title"]</h1>
  <hr />
  <div class="row">
    <div class="col">
      <h2>Register User</h2>
      <div class="mb-3">
        <label for="myName" class="form-label">My name</label>
        <input type="text" class="form-control"
               id="myName" value="Alice" required />
      </div>
      <div class="mb-3">
        <label for="myGroups" class="form-label">My groups</label>
        <input type="text" class="form-control"
               id="myGroups" value="Sales,IT" />
      </div>
      <div class="mb-3">
        <input type="button" class="form-control"
               id="registerButton" value="Register User" />
      </div>
    </div>
    <div class="col">
      <h2>Send Message</h2>
      <div class="mb-3">
        <label for="from" class="form-label">From</label>
        <input type="text" class="form-control"
               id="from" value="Alice" readonly />
      </div>
      <div class="mb-3">
        <label for="to" class="form-label">To</label>
        <input type="text" class="form-control" id="to" />
      </div>
      <div class="mb-3">
        <label for="body" class="form-label">Body</label>
        <input type="text" class="form-control" id="body" />
      </div>
      <div class="mb-3">
```

```
            <input type="button" class="form-control"
                   id="sendButton" value="Send Message" />
      </div>
    </div>
  </div>
  <div class="row">
    <div class="col">
      <hr />
      <h2>Messages received</h2>
      <ul id="messages"></ul>
    </div>
  </div>
</div>
<script src="~/js/signalr/dist/browser/signalr.js"></script>
<script src="~/js/chat.js"></script>
```

Note the following:

- There are three sections on the page: **Register User**, **Send Message**, and **Messages received**.

- The **Register User** section has two inputs for the visitor's name, a comma-separated list of the groups that they want to be a member of, and a button to click to register.

- The **Send Message** section has three inputs for the name of the user that the message is from, the names of users and groups that the message will be sent to, and the body of the message – and a button to click to send the message.

- The **Messages received** section has a bullet list element that will be dynamically populated with a list item when a message is received.

- There are two script elements for the SignalR JavaScript client-side library and the JavaScript implementation of the chat client.

2. In wwwroot/js, add a new JavaScript file named chat.js and modify its contents, as shown in the following code:

```
"use strict";

var connection = new signalR.HubConnectionBuilder()
  .withUrl("/chat").build();

document.getElementById("registerButton").disabled = true;
document.getElementById("sendButton").disabled = true;

document.getElementById("myName").addEventListener("input",
  function () {
```

```
      document.getElementById("from").value =
        document.getElementById("myName").value;
  }
);

connection.start().then(function () {
  document.getElementById("registerButton").disabled = false;
  document.getElementById("sendButton").disabled = false;
}).catch(function (err) {
  return console.error(err.toString());
});

connection.on("ReceiveMessage", function (received) {
  var li = document.createElement("li");
  document.getElementById("messages").appendChild(li);

  li.textContent =
    // This string must use backticks ` to enable an interpolated
    // string. If you use single quotes ' then it will not work!
    `To ${received.to}, From ${received.from}: ${received.body}`;
});

document.getElementById("registerButton").addEventListener("click",
  function (event) {
    var registermodel = {
      name: document.getElementById("myName").value,
      groups: document.getElementById("myGroups").value
    };
    connection.invoke("Register", registermodel).catch(function (err) {
      return console.error(err.toString());
    });
    event.preventDefault();
  });

document.getElementById("sendButton").addEventListener("click",
  function (event) {
    var messagemodel = {
      from: document.getElementById("from").value,
      to: document.getElementById("to").value,
      body: document.getElementById("body").value
    };
```

```
        connection.invoke("SendMessage", messagemodel).catch(function (err) {
          return console.error(err.toString());
        });
        event.preventDefault();
    });
```

Note the following:

- The script creates a SignalR hub connection builder specifying the relative URL path to the chat hub on the server /chat.
- The script disables the **Register** and **Send** buttons until the connection is successfully established to the server-side hub.
- An input event handler is added to the **My name** text box to keep it synchronized with the **From** text box.
- When the connection gets a ReceiveMessage call from the server-side hub, it adds a list item element to the messages bullet list. The content of the list item contains details of the message like from, to, and body. For the two models that we defined in C#, note that JavaScript uses camelCase compared to C#, which uses PascalCase.

 The message is formatted using a JavaScript interpolated string. This feature requires backticks ` at the start and end of the string value and the use of curly brackets ${} for dynamic placeholders.

- A click event handler is added to the **Register User** button that creates a register model with the user's name and their groups and then invokes the Register method on the server side.
- A click event handler is added to the **Send Message** button that creates a message model with the from, to, and body, and then invokes the SendMessage method on the server side.

Testing the chat feature

Now we are ready to try sending chat messages between multiple website visitors:

1. Start the Northwind.SignalR.Service.Client.Mvc project website using the https profile:

   - If you are using Visual Studio 2022, then select the **https** profile in the toolbar, and then start the Northwind.SignalR.Service.Client.Mvc project without debugging.
   - If you are using Visual Studio Code, then at the command prompt or terminal, enter the following command:

     ```
     dotnet run --launch-profile https
     ```

   - On Windows, if Windows Defender Firewall blocks access, then click **Allow access**.

2. Start Chrome and navigate to **https://localhost:5111/**.

3. Note that Alice is already entered for the name, and Sales,IT is already entered for her groups. Click **Register User**, and note the response back from the **SignalR Chat**, as shown in *Figure 11.1*:

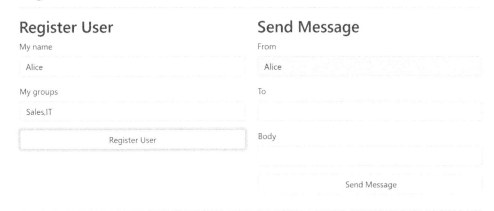

Figure 11.1: Registering a new user in chat

4. Open a new Chrome window or start another browser like Firefox or Edge.

5. Navigate to https://localhost:5111/.

6. Enter Bob for the name, Sales for his groups, and then click **Register User**.

7. Open a new Chrome window or start another browser like Firefox or Edge.

8. Navigate to https://localhost:5111/.

9. Enter Charlie for the name, IT for his groups, and then click **Register User**.

10. Arrange the browser windows so that you can see all three simultaneously.

 A great tool for arranging windows is PowerToys and its FancyZones feature. Learn more at the following link: https://learn.microsoft.com/en-us/windows/powertoys/.

11. In Alice's browser, enter the following:

    • **To:** Sales
    • **Body:** Sell more!

12. Click **Send Message.**

13. Note that Alice and Bob receive the message, as shown in *Figure 11.2*:

Figure 11.2: Alice sends a message to the Sales group

14. In Bob's browser, enter the following:

    • **To:** IT

    • **Body:** Fix more bugs!

15. Click **Send Message**.

16. Note that Alice and Charlie receive the message, as shown in *Figure 11.3*:

Figure 11.3: Bob sends a message to the IT group

17. In Alice's browser, enter the following:

    - **To:** Bob
    - **Body:** Bonjour Bob!

18. Click **Send Message.**

19. Note that only Bob receives the message.

20. In Charlie's browser, enter the following:

    - **To:** Leave it empty.
    - **Body:** Everybody dance now!

21. Click **Send Message.**

22. Note that everyone receives the message, as shown in *Figure 11.4:*

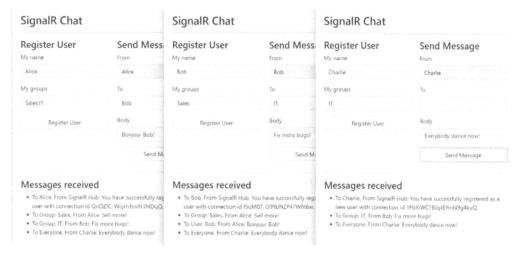

Figure 11.4: Charlie sends a message to everyone

23. In Charlie's browser, enter the following:

    - **To:** HR,Alice
    - **Body:** Is anyone in HR listening?

24. Click **Send Message.**

25. Note that Alice receives the message sent directly to her, but since the HR group does not exist, no one receives the message sent to that group, as shown in *Figure 11.5:*

Figure 11.5: Charlie sends a message to Alice and a group that does not exist

26. Close the browsers and shut down the web server.

Building a .NET console app client

You have just seen a .NET service hosting a SignalR hub, and a JavaScript client exchanging messages with other clients via that SignalR hub. Now, let's create a .NET client for SignalR.

Creating a .NET client for SignalR

We will use a console app, although any .NET project type would need the same package reference and implementation code:

1. Use your preferred code editor to add a new project, as defined in the following list:

   - Project template: **Console Application** / `console`
   - Solution file and folder: `Chapter11`
   - Project file and folder: `Northwind.SignalR.Client.Console`

2. Add a package reference for the ASP.NET Core SignalR client and a project reference for `Northwind.Common`, treat warnings as errors, and globally and statically import the `System.Console` class, as shown in the following markup:

```xml
<ItemGroup>
  <PackageReference Include="Microsoft.AspNetCore.SignalR.Client"
                    Version="8.0.0" />
</ItemGroup>

<ItemGroup>
  <ProjectReference
    Include="..\Northwind.Common\Northwind.Common.csproj" />
</ItemGroup>
```

3. Build the project to restore packages and build referenced projects.

4. In Program.cs, delete the existing statements, import namespaces for working with SignalR as a client and the chat models, and then add statements to prompt the user to enter a username and groups to register with, create a hub connection, and finally, listen for received messages, as shown in the following code:

```csharp
using Microsoft.AspNetCore.SignalR.Client; // To use HubConnection.
using Northwind.Chat.Models; // To use UserModel, MessageModel.

Write("Enter a username (required): ");
string? username = ReadLine();

if (string.IsNullOrEmpty(username))
{
  WriteLine("You must enter a username to register with chat!");
  return;
}

Write("Enter your groups (optional): ");
string? groups = ReadLine();

HubConnection hubConnection = new HubConnectionBuilder()
  .WithUrl("https://localhost:5111/chat")
  .Build();

hubConnection.On<MessageModel>("ReceiveMessage", message =>
{
  WriteLine($"To {message.To}, From {message.From}: {message.Body}");
});

await hubConnection.StartAsync();

WriteLine("Successfully started.");

UserModel registration = new()
{
  Name = username,
  Groups = groups
};

await hubConnection.InvokeAsync("Register", registration);

WriteLine("Successfully registered.");
```

```
WriteLine("Listening... (press ENTER to stop.)");
ReadLine();
```

Testing the .NET console app client

Let's start the SignalR service and call it from the console app:

1. Start the `Northwind.SignalR.Service.Client.Mvc` project website using the `https` profile without debugging.

2. Start Chrome and navigate to `https://localhost:5111/`.

3. Click **Register User**.

4. Start the `Northwind.SignalR.Client.Console` project.

5. Enter your name and the groups: `Sales,Admins`.

6. Arrange the browser and console app windows so that you can see both simultaneously.

7. In Alice's browser, enter the following:

   - **To:** `Sales`

   - **Body:** `Go team!`

8. Click **Send Message**, and note that Alice and you receive the message, as shown in *Figure 11.6*:

Figure 11.6: Alice sends a message to the Sales team including a user in a console app

9. In the console app, press *Enter* to stop it from listening.

10. Close Chrome and shut down the web server.

Streaming data using SignalR

So far, we have seen how SignalR can broadcast structured messages to one or more clients. This works well with data that is relatively small and structured and exists completely at a point in time. But what about data that comes in parts over time?

Streams can be used for these scenarios. SignalR supports both service-to-client (downloading data from a stream) and client-to-service (uploading data to a stream).

To enable download streaming, a hub method must return `IAsyncEnumerable<T>` (only supported by C# 8 or later) or `ChannelReader<T>`.

To enable upload streaming, a hub method must accept a parameter of type `IAsyncEnumerable<T>` (only supported by C# 8 or later) or `ChannelReader<T>`.

Defining a hub for streaming

Let's add some streaming methods to see how they work in action:

1. In the `Northwind.Common` project, add a new file named `StockPrice.cs` and modify its content to define a `record` for stock price data, as shown in the following code:

    ```
    namespace Northwind.SignalR.Streams;

    public record StockPrice(string Stock, double Price);
    ```

2. Build the `Northwind.SignalR.Service.Client.Mvc` project to update its referenced projects.

3. In the `Northwind.SignalR.Service.Client.Mvc` project, add a new class named `StockPriceHub.cs`, and modify its contents to define a hub with two streaming methods, as shown in the following code:

    ```
    using Microsoft.AspNetCore.SignalR; // To use Hub.
    using System.Runtime.CompilerServices; // To use
    [EnumeratorCancellation].
    using Northwind.SignalR.Streams; // To use StockPrice.

    namespace Northwind.SignalR.Service.Hubs;

    public class StockPriceHub : Hub
    {
      public async IAsyncEnumerable<StockPrice> GetStockPriceUpdates(
        string stock,
        [EnumeratorCancellation] CancellationToken cancellationToken)
      {
    ```

```csharp
        double currentPrice = 267.10; // Simulated initial price.

        for (int i = 0; i < 10; i++)
        {
          // Check the cancellation token regularly so that the server will
stop
          // producing items if the client disconnects.
          cancellationToken.ThrowIfCancellationRequested();

          // Increment or decrement the current price by a random amount.
          // The compiler does not need the extra parentheses but it
          // is clearer for humans if you put them in.
          currentPrice += (Random.Shared.NextDouble() * 10.0) - 5.0;

          StockPrice stockPrice = new(stock, currentPrice);

         Console.WriteLine("[{0}] {1} at {2:C}",
           DateTime.UtcNow, stockPrice.Stock, stockPrice.Price);

          yield return stockPrice;

          await Task.Delay(4000, cancellationToken); // milliseconds
        }
      }

      public async Task UploadStocks(IAsyncEnumerable<string> stocks)
      {
        await foreach (string stock in stocks)
        {
          Console.WriteLine($"Receiving {stock} from client...");
        }
      }
    }
```

4. In the `Northwind.SignalR.Service.Client.Mvc` project, in `Program.cs`, register the stock price hub after the statement that registers the chat hub, as shown in the following code:

```csharp
app.MapHub<StockPriceHub>("/stockprice");
```

Creating a .NET console app client for streaming

Now, we can create a simple client to download a stream of data from the SignalR hub and upload a stream of data to the SignalR hub:

1. Use your preferred code editor to add a new project, as defined in the following list:

    • Project template: **Console Application** / console
    • Solution file and folder: Chapter11
    • Project file and folder: Northwind.SignalR.Client.Console.Streams

2. In the Northwind.SignalR.Client.Console.Streams project file, treat warnings as errors, add a package reference for the ASP.NET Core SignalR client, add a project reference to Northwind. Common, and globally and statically import the System.Console class, as shown highlighted in the following markup:

```
<ItemGroup>
  <PackageReference Include="Microsoft.AspNetCore.SignalR.Client"
                    Version="8.0.0" />
</ItemGroup>

<ItemGroup>
  <ProjectReference
    Include="..\Northwind.Common\Northwind.Common.csproj" />
</ItemGroup>
```

3. In the Northwind.SignalR.Client.Console.Streams project, add a new class file named Program.Methods.cs, and modify its content to define static methods in the partial Program class to generate ten random four-letter stock codes asynchronously, as shown in the following code:

```
// Defined in the empty default namespace to merge with the auto-
// generated partial Program class.

partial class Program
{
  static async IAsyncEnumerable<string> GetStocksAsync()
  {
    for (int i = 0; i < 10; i++)
    {
      // Return a random four-letter stock code.
      yield return $"{AtoZ()}{AtoZ()}{AtoZ()}{AtoZ()}";

      await Task.Delay(TimeSpan.FromSeconds(3));
    }
  }

  static string AtoZ()
  {
```

```
        return char.ConvertFromUtf32(Random.Shared.Next(65, 91));
    }
}
```

4. In the Northwind.SignalR.Client.Console.Streams project, in Program.cs, delete the existing statements. Import namespaces for working with SignalR as a client, and then add statements to prompt the user to enter a stock, create a hub connection, listen for received streams of stock prices, and then send an asynchronous stream of stocks to the service, as shown in the following code:

```csharp
using Microsoft.AspNetCore.SignalR.Client; // To use HubConnection.
using Northwind.SignalR.Streams; // To use StockPrice.

Write("Enter a stock (press Enter for MSFT): ");
string? stock = ReadLine();

if (string.IsNullOrEmpty(stock))
{
    stock = "MSFT";
}

HubConnection hubConnection = new HubConnectionBuilder()
    .WithUrl("https://localhost:5111/stockprice")
    .Build();

await hubConnection.StartAsync();

try
{
    CancellationTokenSource cts = new();

    IAsyncEnumerable<StockPrice> stockPrices =
        hubConnection.StreamAsync<StockPrice>(
            "GetStockPriceUpdates", stock, cts.Token);

    await foreach (StockPrice sp in stockPrices)
    {
        WriteLine($"{sp.Stock} is now {sp.Price:C}.");

        Write("Do you want to cancel (y/n)? ");
        ConsoleKey key = ReadKey().Key;
        if (key == ConsoleKey.Y)
```

```
      {
        cts.Cancel();
      }
      WriteLine();
    }
  }
  catch (Exception ex)
  {
    WriteLine($"{ex.GetType()} says {ex.Message}");
  }
  WriteLine();

  WriteLine("Streaming download completed.");

  await hubConnection.SendAsync("UploadStocks", GetStocksAsync());

  WriteLine("Uploading stocks to service... (press ENTER to stop.)");
  ReadLine();

  WriteLine("Ending console app.");
```

Testing the streaming service and client

Finally, we can test the streaming data functionality:

1. Start the `Northwind.SignalR.Service.Client.Mvc` project website using the `https` profile without debugging.

2. Start the `Northwind.SignalR.Client.Console.Streams` console app without debugging.

3. Arrange the console windows for the ASP.NET Core MVC website and the client console app so that you can see both side by side.

4. In the client console app, press *Enter* to use the Microsoft stock code, as shown in the following output:

```
Enter a stock (press Enter for MSFT):
MSFT is now £265.00.
Do you want to cancel (y/n)?
```

5. In the website console window, wait for about ten seconds, and note that several stock prices have been generated in the service but not yet sent to the client, as shown in the following output:

```
info: Microsoft.Hosting.Lifetime[14]
      Now listening on: https://localhost:5131
info: Microsoft.Hosting.Lifetime[14]
```

```
        Now listening on: http://localhost:5132
info: Microsoft.Hosting.Lifetime[0]
        Application started. Press Ctrl+C to shut down.
info: Microsoft.Hosting.Lifetime[0]
        Hosting environment: Development
info: Microsoft.Hosting.Lifetime[0]
        Content root path: C:\apps-services-net7\Chapter13\Northwind.
SignalR.Service.Client.Mvc
[12/09/2022 17:52:26] MSFT at £265.00
[12/09/2022 17:52:30] MSFT at £260.78
[12/09/2022 17:52:34] MSFT at £264.86
[12/09/2022 17:52:38] MSFT at £262.10
```

6. In the client console app, press *n* to receive the next updated price. Keep pressing *n* until the prices have been sent from the service and read by the client, and then press *y*, and note that a cancellation token is received by the SignalR service so it stops, and the client now starts uploading stocks, as shown in the following output:

```
MSFT is now £260.78.
Do you want to cancel (y/n)? n
MSFT is now £264.86.
Do you want to cancel (y/n)? n
MSFT is now £262.10.
Do you want to cancel (y/n)? y
System.Threading.Tasks.TaskCanceledException says A task was canceled.

Streaming download completed.
Uploading stocks to service... (press ENTER to stop.)
```

7. In the website console window, note that the random stock codes are received, as shown in the following output:

```
Receiving PJON from client...
Receiving VWJD from client...
Receiving HMOJ from client...
Receiving QQMQ from client...
```

8. Close both console windows.

Practicing and exploring

Test your knowledge and understanding by answering some questions, getting some hands-on practice, and exploring this chapter's topics with deeper research.

Exercise 11.1 – Test your knowledge

Answer the following questions:

1. What transports does SignalR use, and which is the default?
2. What is a good practice for RPC method signature design?
3. What tool can you use to download the SignalR JavaScript library?
4. What happens if you send a SignalR message to a client with a connection ID that does not exist?
5. What are the benefits of separating a SignalR service from other ASP.NET Core components?

Exercise 11.2 – Explore topics

Use the links on the following page to learn more details about the topics covered in this chapter:

https://github.com/markjprice/apps-services-net8/blob/main/docs/book-links.md#chapter-11---broadcasting-real-time-communication-using-signalr

Summary

In this chapter, you learned about:

- The history of technologies before SignalR.
- The concepts and technologies that underpin SignalR.
- Implementing the chat functionality using SignalR, including building a hub hosted in a website project, and clients using JavaScript and a .NET console app.
- Downloading and uploading streams of data using SignalR.

In the next chapter, you will learn about GraphQL, another standard that enables client control over the data returned from a service.

12

Combining Data Sources Using GraphQL

In this chapter, you will be introduced to GraphQL, a service technology that provides a more modern approach to combining data from various sources and then providing a standard way to query that data.

This chapter will cover the following topics:

- Understanding GraphQL
- Building a service that supports GraphQL
- Defining GraphQL queries for EF Core models
- Building .NET clients for a GraphQL service
- Implementing GraphQL mutations
- Implementing GraphQL subscriptions

Understanding GraphQL

In *Chapter 8, Building and Securing Web Services Using Minimal APIs*, you learned how to define a Web API service by mapping request path endpoints to lambda expressions or methods that return the response. Any parameters and the format of responses are under the control of the service. A client cannot ask for what they exactly need or use more efficient data formats.

If you completed the online-only section, *Exposing Data via the Web Using OData*, then you know that OData has a built-in query language for the client to control what data they want to be returned. However, OData has a rather old-fashioned approach and is tied to the HTTP standard, for example, using query strings in an HTTP request.

If you would prefer to use a more modern and flexible technology to combine and expose your data as a service, then a good alternative is **GraphQL**.

Like OData, GraphQL is a standard for describing your data and then querying it that gives the client control over exactly what they need. It was developed internally by Facebook in 2012 before being open sourced in 2015, and it is now managed by the GraphQL Foundation.

Some of the key benefits of GraphQL over OData are:

- GraphQL does not require HTTP because it is transport-agnostic, so you could use alternative transport protocols like WebSockets or TCP.
- GraphQL has more client libraries for different platforms than OData has.
- GraphQL has a single endpoint, usually simply /graphql.

GraphQL query document format

GraphQL uses its own document format for its queries, which are a bit like JSON, but GraphQL queries do not require commas between field names, as shown in the following query, which requests some fields and related data for the product with an ID of 23:

```
{
  product (productId: 23) {
    productId
    productName
    unitPrice
    supplier {
      companyName
      country
    }
  }
}
```

 The official media type for GraphQL query documents is `application/graphql`.

Requesting fields

The most basic GraphQL query requests one or more fields from a type, for example, requesting three fields for each customer entity, as shown in the following code:

```
# The query keyword is optional. Comments are prefixed with #.
query {
  customer {
    customerId
    companyName
    country
```

```
    }
  }
```

The response is in the JSON format, for example, an array of customer objects, as shown in the following document:

```
{
  "data": [
    {
      "customerId": "ALFKI",
      "companyName": "Alfreds Futterkiste",
      "country": "Germany"
    },
    ...
  ]
}
```

Specifying filters and arguments

With an HTTP or REST-style API, the caller is limited to only passing parameters when the API predefines that. With GraphQL, you can set parameters anywhere in the query, for example, filtering orders by order date and by the country of the customer who made the order, as shown in the following code:

```
query GetOrdersByDateAndCountry {
  order(orderDate: "23/04/1998") {
    orderId
    orderDate
    customer(country: "UK") {
      companyName
      country
    }
  }
}
```

Note that although GraphQL uses camelCase for entity, property, and parameter names, you should use PascalCase for query names.

You might want to pass values for named parameters instead of hardcoding them, as shown in the following code:

```
query GetOrdersByDateAndCountry($country: String, $orderDate: String) {
  order(orderDate: $orderDate) {
    orderId
    orderDate
    customer(country: $country) {
      companyName
```

```
      country
    }
  }
}
```

 You can learn more about the GraphQL query language at the following link: `https://graphql.org/learn/queries/`.

Understanding other GraphQL capabilities

As well as queries, other standard GraphQL features are mutations and subscriptions:

- **Mutations** enable you to create, update, and delete resources.
- **Subscriptions** enable a client to get notified when resources change. They work best with additional communication technologies like WebSockets.

Understanding the ChilliCream GraphQL platform

GraphQL.NET is one of the most popular platforms for implementing GraphQL with .NET. In my opinion, GraphQL.NET requires too much configuration for even the most basic example, and the documentation is frustrating. I have a feeling that, although it is powerful, it implements the GraphQL specification in a one-to-one manner instead of rethinking how a .NET platform could make it easier to get started.

 You can learn about GraphQL.NET at the following link: `https://graphql-dotnet.github.io/`.

For this book, I looked for alternatives, and I found exactly what I was looking for. ChilliCream is a company that has created a whole platform to work with GraphQL:

- **Hot Chocolate** enables you to create GraphQL services for .NET.
- **Strawberry Shake** enables you to create GraphQL clients for .NET.
- **Banana Cake Pop** enables you to run queries and explore a GraphQL endpoint using a Monaco-based GraphQL IDE.
- **Green Donut** enables better performance when loading data.

Unlike some other packages that can be used to add support for GraphQL, ChilliCream packages are designed to be as easy to implement as possible, using conventions and simple POCO classes instead of complex types and special schemas. It works in a similar way to how Microsoft might have built a GraphQL platform for .NET, with sensible defaults and conventions rather than lots of boilerplate code and configuration.

As ChilliCream says on its home page, *"We at ChilliCream build the ultimate GraphQL platform. Most of our code is open-source and will forever remain open-source."*

 The GitHub repository for Hot Chocolate is at the following link: `https://github.com/ChilliCream/hotchocolate`.

Building a service that supports GraphQL

There is no dotnet new project template for GraphQL, so we will use the **ASP.NET Core Empty** project template. Even though GraphQL does not have to be hosted on a web server because it is not tied to HTTP, it is a sensible choice to get started. We will then add a package reference for GraphQL support:

1. Use your preferred code editor to add a new project, as defined in the following list:

   - Project template: **ASP.NET Core Empty** / web
   - Solution file and folder: `Chapter12`
   - Project file and folder: `Northwind.GraphQL.Service`
   - Other Visual Studio 2022 options:

     - **Configure for HTTPS**: Selected
     - **Enable Docker**: Cleared
     - **Do not use top-level statements**: Cleared

2. In the project file, add a package reference for Hot Chocolate hosted in ASP.NET Core, as shown in the following markup:

```
<ItemGroup>
  <PackageReference Include="HotChocolate.AspNetCore" Version="13.5.1" />
</ItemGroup>
```

 Version 13.6.0 was in preview at the time of writing. To use the most recent preview version, you can set it to `13.6-*`. But I recommend that you go to the following link and then reference the latest GA version: `https://www.nuget.org/packages/HotChocolate.AspNetCore/`.

3. In the project file, treat warnings as errors and disable the warning `AD0001`, as highlighted in the following markup:

```
<PropertyGroup>
  <TargetFramework>net8.0</TargetFramework>
  <Nullable>enable</Nullable>
  <ImplicitUsings>enable</ImplicitUsings>
  <TreatWarningsAsErrors>true</TreatWarningsAsErrors>
  <NoWarn>AD0001</NoWarn>
</PropertyGroup>
```

4.   In the `Properties` folder, in `launchSettings.json`, for the `https` profile, modify the `applicationUrl` to use port 5121 for `https` and port 5122 for `http`. Then, add a `launchUrl` of `graphql`, as highlighted in the following configuration:

```
"https": {
  "commandName": "Project",
  "dotnetRunMessages": true,
  "launchBrowser": true,
  "launchUrl": "graphql",
  "applicationUrl": "https://localhost:5121;http://localhost:5122",
  "environmentVariables": {
    "ASPNETCORE_ENVIRONMENT": "Development"
  }
}
```

5.   Build the `Northwind.GraphQL.Service` project.

Defining the GraphQL schema for Hello World

The first task is to define what we want to expose as GraphQL models in the web service.

Let's define a GraphQL query for the most basic `Hello World` example, which will respond with plain text when a request for a greeting is made:

1.   In the `Northwind.GraphQL.Service` project/folder, add a class file named `Query.cs`.

2.   Modify the class to have a method named `GetGreeting` that returns the plain text `"Hello, World!"`, as shown in the following code:

```
namespace Northwind.GraphQL.Service;

public class Query
{
  public string GetGreeting() => "Hello, World!";
}
```

3.   In `Program.cs`, import the namespace where we defined the `Query` class, as shown in the following code:

```
using Northwind.GraphQL.Service; // To use Query.
```

4. In the section to configure services, after the call to `CreateBuilder`, add a statement to add GraphQL server-side support, and add the query type to the collection of registered services, as shown in the following code:

```
builder.Services
  .AddGraphQLServer()
  .AddQueryType<Query>();
```

5. Modify the statement that maps a `GET` request to return a more useful plain text message, as shown in the following code:

```
app.MapGet("/", () => "Navigate to: https://localhost:5121/graphql");
```

6. In the section to configure the HTTP pipeline, before the call to `Run`, add a statement to map GraphQL as an endpoint, as shown in the following code:

```
app.MapGraphQL();
```

7. Start the `Northwind.GraphQL.Service` web project, using the `https` profile without debugging:

    - If you are using Visual Studio 2022, then select the **https** profile, start the project without debugging, and note that the browser starts automatically.
    - If you are using Visual Studio Code, then enter the command `dotnet run --launch-profile https`, start Chrome manually, and navigate to `https://localhost:5121/graphql`.

8. Note the **BananaCakePop** user interface, and then click the **Create Document** button.

9. In the top-right corner, click the **Connection Settings** button, as shown in *Figure 12.1*:

Figure 12.1: A new BananaCakePop document and connection settings button

10. In **Connection Settings**, confirm that the **Schema Endpoint** is correct, and then click **Cancel**, as shown in *Figure 12.2*:

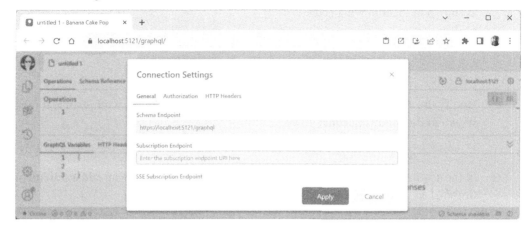

Figure 12.2: Reviewing the BananaCakePop connection settings

11. At the top of the **untitled 1** document, click the **Schema Reference** tab.

12. In the **Schema Reference** tab, note "The Query type is a special type that defines the entry point of every GraphQL query", and it has a field named greeting that returns a String! value. The exclamation mark indicates that the value will *not* be null.

13. Click the **Schema Definition** tab, and note there is only one type defined, the special Query object with its greeting field, which is a non-null String value, as shown in the following code:

```
type Query {
  greeting: String!
}
```

Writing and executing GraphQL queries

Now that we know the schema, we can write and run a query:

1. In **Banana Cake Pop**, in the **untitled 1** document, click the **Operations** tab.

2. On the left-hand side, type an open curly brace, {, and note that a close curly brace, }, is written for you.

3. Type the letter g , and note that the autocomplete shows it recognizes the greeting field, as shown in *Figure 12.3*:

Figure 12.3: Autocomplete for the greeting field

4. Press *Enter* to accept the autocomplete suggestion.

5. Click the **Run** button and note the response, as shown in the following output:

```
{
  "data": {
    "greeting": "Hello, World!"
  }
}
```

6. Close Chrome, and shut down the web server.

Naming GraphQL queries aka operations

The query that we wrote was unnamed. We could also have created it as a named query, as shown in the following code:

```
query QueryNameGoesHere {
  greeting
}
```

Named queries allow clients to identify queries and responses for telemetry purposes, for example, when hosting in Microsoft Azure cloud services and monitoring using Application Insights.

Understanding field conventions

The C# method we created in the Query class was named GetGreeting, but when querying it, we used greeting. The Get prefix on method names that represent fields in GraphQL is optional. Let's see some more examples:

1. In Query.cs, add two more methods without the Get prefix, as highlighted in the following code:

    ```
    namespace Northwind.GraphQL.Service;

    public class Query
    {
      public string GetGreeting() => "Hello, World!";
      public string Farewell() => "Ciao! Ciao!";
      public int RollTheDie() => Random.Shared.Next(1, 7);
    }
    ```

2. Start the Northwind.GraphQL.Service project, using the https profile without debugging.

3. Click the **Schema Definition** tab, and note the updated schema, as shown in the following code:

    ```
    type Query {
      greeting: String!
      farewell: String!
      rollTheDie: Int!
    }
    ```

     C# methods use PascalCase. GraphQL fields use camelCase.

4. Click the **Operations** tab, and modify the query to specify a name and request the rollTheDie field, as shown in the following code:

    ```
    query GetNumber {
      rollTheDie
    }
    ```

5. Click **Run** again multiple times. Note that the responses contain a random number between 1 and 6, and a history of requests and responses is stored for the current browser session, as shown in *Figure 12.4*:

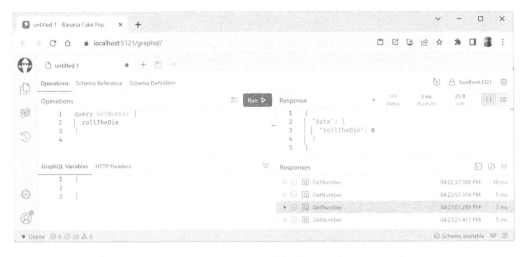

Figure 12.4: Executing a named query and the history of requests and responses

6.   Close Chrome, and shut down the web server.

Defining GraphQL queries for EF Core models

Now that we have a basic GraphQL service operating successfully, let's extend it to enable querying the Northwind database.

Adding support for EF Core

We must add another Hot Chocolate package to allow easy dependency service integration of our EF Core database context with GraphQL query classes:

1.   Add a package reference for Hot Chocolate integration with EF Core and a project reference to the Northwind database context project, as highlighted in the following markup:

```
<ItemGroup>
  <PackageReference Include="HotChocolate.AspNetCore" Version="13.5.1" />
  <PackageReference Include="HotChocolate.Data.EntityFramework"
                    Version="13.5.1" />
</ItemGroup>

<ItemGroup>
  <ProjectReference Include="..\..\Chapter03\Northwind.Common.DataContext
.SqlServer\Northwind.Common.DataContext.SqlServer.csproj" />
</ItemGroup>
```

The path to the project must not have a line break. All Hot Chocolate packages should have the same version number.

2. Build the `Northwind.GraphQLService` project at the command prompt or terminal using `dotnet build`.

 When you reference a project outside of the current solution, you must build the project at least once at the command prompt or terminal before you can use the Visual Studio 2022 **Build** menu to compile it.

3. In `Program.cs`, import the namespace to work with our EF Core model for the Northwind database, as shown in the following code:

```
using Northwind.EntityModels; // To use AddNorthwindContext method.
```

4. Add a statement after the `CreateBuilder` method to register the `Northwind` database context class, and add a statement after adding the GraphQL server support to register the `NorthwindContent` class for dependency injection, as highlighted in the following code:

```
builder.Services.AddNorthwindContext();

builder.Services
  .AddGraphQLServer()
  .RegisterDbContext<NorthwindContext>()
  .AddQueryType<Query>();
```

5. In `Query.cs`, add statements to define an object graph type that has some types of queries to return a list of categories, a single category, products for a category, products with a minimum unit price, and all products, as highlighted in the following code:

```
using Microsoft.EntityFrameworkCore; // To use Include method.
using Northwind.EntityModels; // To use NorthwindContext.

namespace Northwind.GraphQL.Service;

public class Query
{
```

```
    public string GetGreeting() => "Hello, World!";
    public string Farewell() => "Ciao! Ciao!";
    public int RollTheDie() => Random.Shared.Next(1, 7);

  public IQueryable<Category> GetCategories(NorthwindContext db) =>
    db.Categories.Include(c => c.Products);

  public Category? GetCategory(NorthwindContext db, int categoryId)
  {
    Category? category = db.Categories.Find(categoryId);
    if (category == null) return null;
    db.Entry(category).Collection(c => c.Products).Load();
    return category;
  }

  public IQueryable<Product> GetProducts(NorthwindContext db) =>
    db.Products.Include(p => p.Category);

  public IQueryable<Product> GetProductsInCategory(
    NorthwindContext db, int categoryId) =>
      db.Products.Where(p => p.CategoryId == categoryId);

  public IQueryable<Product> GetProductsByUnitPrice(
    NorthwindContext db, decimal minimumUnitPrice) =>
      db.Products.Where(p => p.UnitPrice >= minimumUnitPrice);
}
```

Exploring GraphQL queries with Northwind

Now we can test writing GraphQL queries for the categories and products in the Northwind database:

1. If your database server is not running, for example, because you are hosting it in Docker, a virtual machine, or the cloud, then make sure to start it.

2. Start the Northwind.GraphQL.Service project, using the https profile without debugging.

3. In **Banana Cake Pop**, click the + to open a new tab.

4. Click the **Schema Definition** tab, and note the query and type definitions for `Category`, as partially shown in *Figure 12.5*:

Figure 12.5: Schema for querying the Northwind categories and products using GraphQL

5. Note the full definitions in the following code:

```
type Query {
  greeting: String!
  farewell: String!
  rollTheDie: Int!
  categories: [Category!]!
  category(categoryId: Int!): Category
  products: [Product!]!
  productsInCategory(categoryId: Int!): [Product!]!
  productsByUnitPrice(minimumUnitPrice: Decimal!): [Product!]!
}

type Category {
  categoryId: Int!
  categoryName: String!
  description: String
  picture: [Byte!]
  products: [Product!]!
}

type Product {
  productId: Int!
  productName: String!
  supplierId: Int
```

```
    categoryId: Int
    quantityPerUnit: String
    unitPrice: Decimal
    unitsInStock: Short
    unitsOnOrder: Short
    reorderLevel: Short
    discontinued: Boolean!
    category: Category
    orderDetails: [OrderDetail!]!
    supplier: Supplier
}
```

6. Click the **Operations** tab, and write a named query to request the ID, name, and description fields for all categories, as shown in the following markup:

```
query AllCategories {
  categories {
    categoryId
    categoryName
    description
  }
}
```

7. Click **Run**, and note the response, as shown in *Figure 12.6* and the following partial output:

```
{
  "data": {
    "categories": [
      {
        "categoryId": 1,
        "categoryName": "Beverages",
        "description": "Soft drinks, coffees, teas, beers, and ales"
      },
      {
        "categoryId": 2,
        "categoryName": "Condiments",
        "description": "Sweet and savory sauces, relishes, spreads, and
seasonings"
      },
      ...
```

Figure 12.6: Getting all categories

8. Click the **+** to open a tab for a new document named **untitled 2**, and write a query to request the category with ID 2, including the ID, name, and price of its products, as shown in the following markup:

```
query Condiments {
  category (categoryId: 2) {
    categoryId
    categoryName
    products {
      productId
      productName
      unitPrice

    }
  }
}
```

      Make sure that the **I** in `categoryId` is uppercase.

9. Click **Run**, and note the response, as shown in the following partial output:

```
{
  "data": {
    "category": {
      "categoryId": 2,
      "categoryName": "Condiments",
      "products": [
        {
          "productId": 3,
```

```
      "productName": "Aniseed Syrup",
      "unitPrice": 10
    },
    {
      "productId": 4,
      "productName": "Chef Anton's Cajun Seasoning",
      "unitPrice": 22
    },
    ...
```

10. In the GraphQL web service command prompt or terminal, note the SQL statements executed for this query, as shown in the following output:

```
info: Microsoft.EntityFrameworkCore.Database.Command[20101]
      Executed DbCommand (68ms) [Parameters=[@__p_0='?' (DbType =
Int32)], CommandType='Text', CommandTimeout='30']
      SELECT TOP(1) [c].[CategoryId], [c].[CategoryName], [c].
[Description], [c].[Picture]
      FROM [Categories] AS [c]
      WHERE [c].[CategoryId] = @__p_0
info: Microsoft.EntityFrameworkCore.Database.Command[20101]
      Executed DbCommand (5ms) [Parameters=[@__p_0='?' (DbType = Int32)],
CommandType='Text', CommandTimeout='30']
      SELECT [p].[ProductId], [p].[CategoryId], [p].[Discontinued],
[p].[ProductName], [p].[QuantityPerUnit], [p].[ReorderLevel], [p].
[SupplierId], [p].[UnitPrice], [p].[UnitsInStock], [p].[UnitsOnOrder]
      FROM [Products] AS [p]
      WHERE [p].[CategoryId] = @__p_0
```

 Although the GraphQL query did not need the picture of each category and only needed the ID, name, and unit price, the dynamically-generated queries from EF Core returned all properties.

11. Click the + tab to open a new tab, and write a query to request the ID, name, and units in stock of the products in the category with ID 1, as shown in the following markup:

```
query BeverageProducts {
  productsInCategory (categoryId: 1) {
    productId
    productName
    unitsInStock
  }
}
```

12. Click **Run**, and note the response, as shown in the following partial output:

```
{
  "data": {
    "productsInCategory": [
      {
        "productId": 1,
        "productName": "Chai",
        "unitsInStock": 39
      },
      {
        "productId": 2,
        "productName": "Chang",
        "unitsInStock": 17
      },
      ...
```

13. Click the + tab to open a new tab, and write a query to request the ID, name, and units in stock of products, along with their category names, as shown in the following markup:

```
query ProductsWithCategoryNames {
  products {
    productId
    productName
    category {
      categoryName
    }
    unitsInStock
  }
}
```

14. Click **Run**, and note the response, as shown in the following partial output:

```
{
  "data": {
    "products": [
      {
```

```
        "productId": 1,
        "productName": "Chai",
        "category": {
          "categoryName": "Beverages"
        },
        "unitsInStock": 39
    },
    {
        "productId": 2,
        "productName": "Chang",
        "category": {
          "categoryName": "Beverages"
        },
        "unitsInStock": 17
    },
    ...
```

15. Click the + tab to open a new tab, and write a query to request the ID and name of a category, select the category by specifying its category ID, and include the ID and name for each of its products. The ID of the category will be set using a variable, as shown in the following markup:

```
query CategoryAndItsProducts($id: Int!){
  category(categoryId: $id) {
    categoryId
    categoryName
    products {
      productId
      productName
    }
  }
}
```

16. In the **Variables** section, define a value for the variable, as shown in the following code and in *Figure 12.7*:

```
{
  "id": 1
}
```

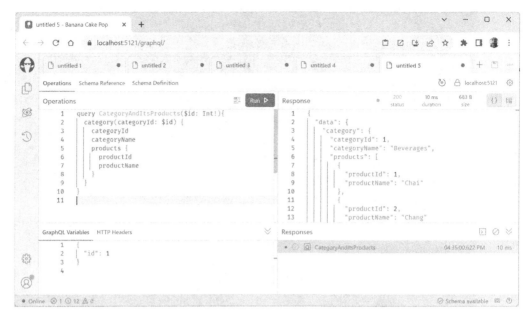

Figure 12.7: Executing a GraphQL query with a variable

17. Click **Run**, and note the response, as shown in the following partial output:

```
{
  "data": {
    "category": {
      "categoryId": 1,
      "categoryName": "Beverages",
      "products": [
        {
          "productId": 1,
          "productName": "Chai"
        },
        {
          "productId": 2,
          "productName": "Chang"
        },
        ...
```

18. Click the + tab to open a new tab, write a query to request the ID and name of a category, select the category by specifying its category ID, and include the ID and name for each of its products. The ID of the category will be set using a variable, as shown in the following markup:

```
query ProductsWithMinimumPrice($unitPrice: Decimal!){
  productsByUnitPrice(minimumUnitPrice: $unitPrice) {
      productId
```

```
            productName
            unitPrice
        }
    }
```

19. In the **Variables** section, define a value for the variable, as shown in the following code:

```
{
    "unitPrice": 100
}
```

20. Click **Run**, and note the response, as shown in the following output:

```
{
  "data": {
    "productsByUnitPrice": [
      {
        "productId": 29,
        "productName": "Thüringer Rostbratwurst",
        "unitPrice": 123.79
      },
      {
        "productId": 38,
        "productName": "Côte de Blaye",
        "unitPrice": 263.5
      }
    ]
  }
}
```

21. Close Chrome, and shut down the web server.

Implementing paging support

When we request products using the GetProducts method (the products query), all 77 products are returned. Let's add paging support:

1. In Query.cs, add statements to define a query to return all products, using paging, and note that its implementation is the same as the query for products without paging, but it is decorated with the [UsePaging] attribute, as shown in the following code:

```
[UsePaging]
public IQueryable<Product> GetProductsWithPaging(NorthwindContext db) =>
    db.Products.Include(p => p.Category);
```

Good Practice: The [UsePaging], [UseFiltering], and [UseSorting] attributes must be decorated onto a query method that returns IQueryable<T>, allowing GraphQL to dynamically configure the LINQ query before executing it against the data store.

2.   Start the Northwind.GraphQL.Service project, using the https profile without debugging.

3.   In **Banana Cake Pop**, click the + to open a new tab.

4.   Click the **Schema Definition** tab, and note the queries named products (without paging) and productsWithPaging, which documents how to use the query to request a page of products, as shown in the following output:

```
products: [Product!]!
productsInCategory(categoryId: Int!): [Product!]!
productsByUnitPrice(minimumUnitPrice: Decimal!): [Product!]!
productsWithPaging(
    """
    Returns the first _n_ elements from the list.
    """
    first: Int

    """
    Returns the elements in the list that come after the specified cursor.
    """
    after: String

    """
    Returns the last _n_ elements from the list.
    """
    last: Int

    """
    Returns the elements in the list that come before the specified cursor.
    """
    before: String
): ProductsWithPagingConnection
```

5.   Click the **Operations** tab, and write a named query to request the first page of 10 products, as shown in the following markup:

```
query FirstTenProducts {
  productsWithPaging(first: 10) {
    pageInfo {
```

```
        hasPreviousPage
        hasNextPage
        startCursor
        endCursor
      }
    nodes {
      productId
      productName
    }
  }
}
}
```

6. Click **Run**, and note the response, including the pageInfo section, which tells us that there is another page of products and the cursor for this page ranges from MA== to OQ==, as shown in the following partial output:

```
{
  "data": {
    "productsWithPaging": {
      "pageInfo": {
        "hasPreviousPage": false,
        "hasNextPage": true,
        "startCursor": "MA==",
        "endCursor": "OQ=="
      },
      "nodes": [
        {
          "productId": 1,
          "productName": "Chai"
        },
...
        {
          "productId": 10,
          "productName": "Ikura"
        }
      ]
    }
  }
}
```

7. Click the + to open a new tab, and write a named query to request the second page of 10 products, by specifying that we want the cursor that starts after 0Q==, as shown in the following markup:

```
query SecondTenProducts {
  productsWithPaging(after: "0Q==") {
    pageInfo {
      hasPreviousPage
      hasNextPage
      startCursor
      endCursor
    }
    nodes {
      productId
      productName
    }
  }
}
```

8. Click **Run**, and note the response, including the pageInfo section, which tells us that there is another page of products and the cursor for this page ranges from MTA= to MTk=, as shown in the following partial output:

```
{
  "data": {
    "productsWithPaging": {
      "pageInfo": {
        "hasPreviousPage": true,
        "hasNextPage": true,
        "startCursor": "MTA=",
        "endCursor": "MTk="
      },
      "nodes": [
        {
          "productId": 11,
          "productName": "Queso Cabrales"
        },
...
        {
          "productId": 20,
          "productName": "Sir Rodney's Marmalade"
        }
      ]
    }
```

```
    }
  }
```

9. Close Chrome, and shut down the web server.

Implementing filtering support

When we explored queries earlier in this chapter, we predefined some queries with parameters, for example, a query that returns all the products in a category by passing a `categoryId` parameter.

However, what if you do not know ahead of time what filtering you want to perform?

Let's add filtering support to our GraphQL queries:

1. In `Program.cs`, add a call to `AddFiltering` after calling `AddGraphQLServer`, as highlighted in the following code:

    ```
    builder.Services
      .AddGraphQLServer()
      .AddFiltering()
      .RegisterDbContext<NorthwindContext>()
      .AddQueryType<Query>();
    ```

2. In `Query.cs`, decorate the `GetProducts` method with the `[UseFiltering]` attribute, as highlighted in the following code:

    ```
    [UseFiltering]
    public IQueryable<Product> GetProducts(NorthwindContext db) =>
      db.Products.Include(p => p.Category);
    ```

3. Start the `Northwind.GraphQL.Service` project, using the `https` profile without debugging.

4. In **Banana Cake Pop**, click the + to open a new tab.

5. Click **Scheme Definition** , and note that the `products` query now accepts a filter input, as shown in the following markup:

    ```
    products(where: ProductFilterInput): [Product!]!
    ```

6. Scroll down the schema definition to find `ProductFilterInput`, and note the filtering options include Boolean operators like and and or, as well as field filters like `IntOperationFilterInput` and `StringOperationFilterInput`, as shown in the following markup:

    ```
    input ProductFilterInput {
      and: [ProductFilterInput!]
      or: [ProductFilterInput!]
      productId: IntOperationFilterInput
      productName: StringOperationFilterInput
      supplierId: IntOperationFilterInput
      categoryId: IntOperationFilterInput
    ```

```
    quantityPerUnit: StringOperationFilterInput
    unitPrice: DecimalOperationFilterInput
    unitsInStock: ShortOperationFilterInput
    unitsOnOrder: ShortOperationFilterInput
    reorderLevel: ShortOperationFilterInput
    discontinued: BooleanOperationFilterInput
    category: CategoryFilterInput
    orderDetails: ListFilterInputTypeOfOrderDetailFilterInput
    supplier: SupplierFilterInput
}
```

7. Scroll down the schema definition to find `IntOperationFilterInput` and `StringOperationFilterInput`, and note the operations you can use with them, like equals (eq), not equals (neq), in an array (in), greater than (gt), `contains`, and `startsWith`, as shown in the following markup:

```
input IntOperationFilterInput {
    eq: Int
    neq: Int
    in: [Int]
    nin: [Int]
    gt: Int
    ngt: Int
    gte: Int
    ngte: Int
    lt: Int
    nlt: Int
    lte: Int
    nlte: Int
}

input StringOperationFilterInput {
    and: [StringOperationFilterInput!]
    or: [StringOperationFilterInput!]
    eq: String
    neq: String
    contains: String
    ncontains: String
    in: [String]
    nin: [String]
    startsWith: String
    nstartsWith: String
```

```
    endsWith: String
    nendsWith: String
}
```

8. Click **Operations**, and then write a named query to request products with more than 120 units in stock, as shown in the following markup:

```
query ProductsWithMoreThan40InStock {
  products(where: { unitsInStock: { gt: 120 } }) {
    productId
    productName
    unitsInStock
  }
}
```

9. Click **Run**, and note the response, as shown in the following output:

```
{
  "data": {
    "products": [
      {
        "productId": 40,
        "productName": "Boston Crab Meat",
        "unitsInStock": 123
      },
      {
        "productId": 75,
        "productName": "Rhönbräu Klosterbier",
        "unitsInStock": 125
      }
    ]
  }
}
```

10. Click the + to open a new tab, click **Operations**, and then write a named query to request products whose names start with Cha, as shown in the following markup:

```
query ProductNamesCha {
  products(where: { productName: { startsWith: "Cha" } }) {
    productId
    productName
  }
}
```

11. Click **Run**, and note the response, as shown in the following output:

```
{
  "data": {
    "products": [
      {
        "productId": 1,
        "productName": "Chai"
      },
      {
        "productId": 2,
        "productName": "Chang"
      },
      {
        "productId": 39,
        "productName": "Chartreuse verte"
      }
    ]
  }
}
```

12. In the GraphQL service command prompt or terminal, note the EF Core-generated SQL filters using parameters, as shown in the following output:

```
info: Microsoft.EntityFrameworkCore.Database.Command[20101]
      Executed DbCommand (2ms) [Parameters=[@__p_0_rewritten='?' (Size =
40)], CommandType='Text', CommandTimeout='30']
      SELECT [p].[ProductId], [p].[CategoryId], [p].[Discontinued],
[p].[ProductName], [p].[QuantityPerUnit], [p].[ReorderLevel], [p].
[SupplierId], [p].[UnitPrice], [p].[UnitsInStock], [p].[UnitsOnOrder],
[c].[CategoryId], [c].[CategoryName], [c].[Description], [c].[Picture]
      FROM [Products] AS [p]
      LEFT JOIN [Categories] AS [c] ON [p].[CategoryId] = [c].
[CategoryId]
      WHERE [p].[ProductName] LIKE @__p_0_rewritten ESCAPE N'\'
```

13. Close Chrome, and shut down the web server.

Implementing sorting support

To enable sorting with a GraphQL service, call the AddSorting method, as highlighted in the following code:

```
builder.Services
  .AddGraphQLServer()
```

```
  .AddFiltering()
  .AddSorting()
  .RegisterDbContext<NorthwindContext>()
  .AddQueryType<Query>();
```

Then, decorate a query method that returns IQueryable<T> with the [UseSorting] attribute, as high-lighted in the following code:

```
[UseFiltering]
[UseSorting]
public IQueryable<Product> GetProducts(NorthwindContext db) =>
  db.Products.Include(p => p.Category);
```

In a query, apply one or more sort orders, as shown in the following code:

```
query ProductsSortedByMostExpensive {
  products(order: [ { unitPrice: DESC } ]) {
    productId
    productName
    unitPrice
  }
}
```

SortEnumType has two values, as shown in the following code:

```
enum SortEnumType {
  ASC
  DESC
}
```

I will leave adding sorting capabilities to your GraphQL service to you.

Building .NET clients for a GraphQL service

Now that we have explored some queries with the **Banana Cake Pop** tool, let's see how a client could call the GraphQL service. Although the **Banana Cake Pop** tool is convenient, it runs in the same domain as the service, so some issues might not become apparent until we create a separate client.

Choosing GraphQL request formats

Most GraphQL services process GET and POST requests in either the application/graphql or application/json media formats. An application/graphql request would only contain a query document. The benefit of using application/json is that as well as the query document, you can specify operations when you have more than one, and define and set variables, as shown in the following code:

```
{
  "query": "...",
```

```
    "operationName": "...",
    "variables": { "variable1": "value1", ... }
}
```

We will use the `application/json` media format so that we can pass variables and their values.

Understanding the GraphQL response format

A GraphQL service should return a JSON document containing the expected data object and maybe some errors in an array, with the following structure:

```
{
  "data": { ... },
  "errors": [ ... ]
}
```

The `errors` array should only be in the document if there are errors.

Using REST Client as a GraphQL client

Before we write code as a client to the GraphQL service, it would be good to test it with your code editor's `.http` file support. This is so that if our .NET client app does not work, we know the problem is in our client code rather than the service:

1. If you are using Visual Studio Code and have not already installed REST Client by Huachao Mao (`humao.rest-client`), then install it now.

2. In your preferred code editor, start the `Northwind.GraphQL.Service` project web service, using the `https` profile without debugging, and leave it running.

3. In your code editor, in the `HttpRequests` folder, create a file named `graphql-queries.http`, and modify its contents to contain a request to get products in the seafood category, as shown in the following code:

    ```
    ### Configure a variable for the GraphQL service base address.
    @base_address = https://localhost:5121/graphql

    ### Get all products in the specified category.
    POST {{base_address}}
    Content-Type: application/json

    {
      "query" : "{productsInCategory(categoryId:8){productId productName
    unitsInStock}}"
    }
    ```

4. Send the query request, and note the response, as shown in *Figure 12.8*:

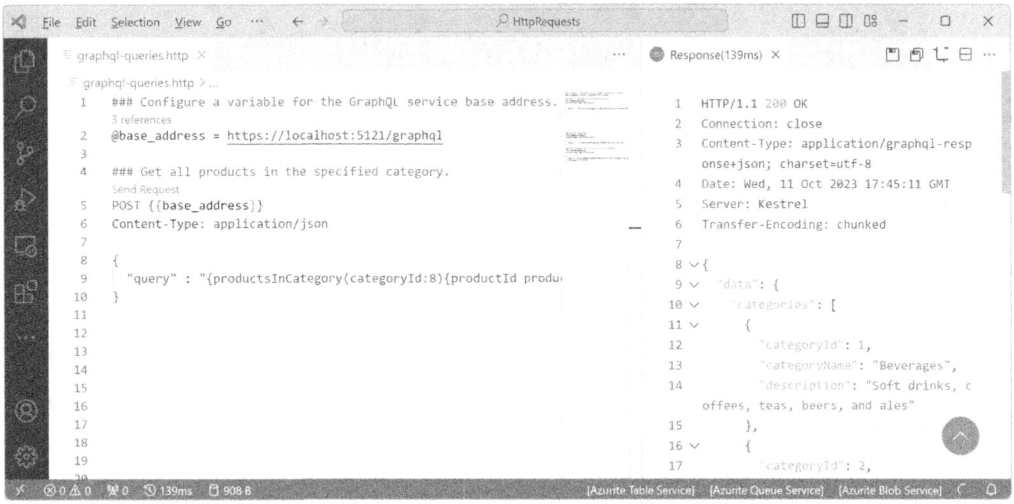

Figure 12.8: Requesting seafood products using REST Client

5. Add a query to make a request to get the ID, name, and description of all categories, as shown in the following code:

```
### Get all categories.
POST {{base_address}}
Content-Type: application/json

{
  "query" : "{categories{categoryId categoryName description}}"
}
```

6. Send the query request, and note the response contains the eight categories in a data property.

7. In the query document, change categoryId to id.

8. Send the query request, and note the response contains an errors array, as shown in the following response:

```
Response time: 60 ms
Status code: BadRequest (400)
Alt-Svc: h3=":5121"; ma=86400
Transfer-Encoding: chunked
Date: Tue, 06 Jun 2023 16:35:18 GMT
Server: Kestrel

Content-Type: application/graphql-response+json; charset=utf-8
Content-Length: 338
```

```json
----------------------------------------------------
Content:
{
  "errors": [
    {
      "message": "The field `id` does not exist on the type `Category`.",
      "locations": [
        {
          "line": 1,
          "column": 13
        }
      ],
      "path": [
        "categories"
      ],
      "extensions": {
        "type": "Category",
        "field": "id",
        "responseName": "id",
        "specifiedBy": "http://spec.graphql.org/October2021/#sec-Field-
Selections-on-Objects-Interfaces-and-Unions-Types"
      }
    }
  ]
}
```

9. In the query document, change id back to categoryId.

10. Add a query to request to get the ID and name of a category specified by a parameter for its ID, along with the ID and name of each of its products, as shown in the following code:

```
### Get a category and its products using a variable.
POST {{base_address}}
Content-Type: application/json

{
  "query": "query categoryAndItsProducts($id: Int!){category(categoryId:
$id){categoryId categoryName products{productId productName}}}",
  "variables": {"id":1}
}
```

11. Send the query request, and note the response contains category 1, Beverages, with its products in a data property.

12. Change the ID to 4, send the request, and note the response contains category 4, Dairy Products, with its products in a data property.

Now that we have done some basic testing of the service and its responses to queries that we want to run, we can build a client to make those queries and process the JSON responses.

Using an ASP.NET Core MVC project as a GraphQL client

We will create a model class to make it easy to deserialize the response:

1. Use your preferred code editor to add a new project, as defined in the following list:

    1. Project template: **ASP.NET Core Web App (Model-View-Controller)** / mvc
    2. Solution file and folder: Chapter12
    3. Project file and folder: Northwind.GraphQL.Client.Mvc
    4. Other Visual Studio 2022 options:

        • **Authentication Type:** None
        • **Configure for HTTPS:** Selected
        • **Enable Docker:** Cleared
        • **Do not use top-level statements:** Cleared

2. In Visual Studio 2022, set the startup project with the current selection.

3. In the Northwind.GraphQL.Client.Mvc project, add a project reference to the Northwind entity models project, as shown in the following markup:

```
<ItemGroup>
  <ProjectReference Include="..\..\Chapter03\Northwind.Common.
EntityModels
.SqlServer\Northwind.Common.EntityModels.SqlServer.csproj" />
</ItemGroup>
```

 The path to the project must not have a line break.

4. Build the Northwind.GraphQL.Client.Mvc project at the command prompt or terminal.

5. In the Properties folder, in launchSettings.json, modify the applicationUrl to use port 5123 for https and port 5124 for http, as highlighted in the following configuration:

```
"https": {
  "commandName": "Project",
  "dotnetRunMessages": true,
  "launchBrowser": true,
  "applicationUrl": "https://localhost:5123;http://localhost:5124",
```

```
    "environmentVariables": {
      "ASPNETCORE_ENVIRONMENT": "Development"
    }
```

6. In the Northwind.GraphQL.Client.Mvc project, in the Models folder, add a new class file named ResponseErrors.cs, as shown in the following code:

```csharp
namespace Northwind.GraphQL.Client.Mvc.Models;

public class ResponseErrors
{
  public Error[]? Errors { get; set; }
}

public class Error
{
  public string Message { get; set; } = null!;
  public Location[] Locations { get; set; } = null!;
  public string[] Path { get; set; } = null!;
}

public class Location
{
  public int Line { get; set; }
  public int Column { get; set; }
}
```

7. In the Models folder, add a new class file named ResponseProducts.cs, as shown in the following code:

```csharp
using Northwind.EntityModels; // To use Product.

namespace Northwind.GraphQL.Client.Mvc.Models;

public class ResponseProducts
{
  public class DataProducts
  {
    public Product[]? ProductsInCategory { get; set; }
  }

  public DataProducts? Data { get; set; }
}
```

8. In the `Models` folder, add a new class file named `ResponseCategories.cs`, as shown in the following code:

    ```
    using Northwind.EntityModels; // To use Category.

    namespace Northwind.GraphQL.Client.Mvc.Models;

    public class ResponseCategories
    {
      public class DataCategories
      {
        public Category[]? Categories { get; set; }
      }

      public DataCategories? Data { get; set; }
    }
    ```

9. In the `Models` folder, add a new class file named `IndexViewModel.cs`, which will have properties to store all the data that we might want to show in the view, as shown in the following code:

    ```
    using Northwind.EntityModels; // To use Product.
    using System.Net; // To use HttpStatusCode.

    namespace Northwind.GraphQL.Client.Mvc.Models;

    public class IndexViewModel
    {
      public HttpStatusCode Code { get; set; }
      public string? RawResponseBody { get; set; }
      public Product[]? Products { get; set; }
      public Category[]? Categories { get; set; }
      public Error[]? Errors { get; set; }
    }
    ```

10. In `Program.cs`, import the namespace to set HTTP headers, as shown in the following code:

    ```
    using System.Net.Http.Headers; // To use MediaTypeWithQualityHeaderValue.
    ```

11. In `Program.cs`, after the `CreateBuilder` method call, add statements to register an HTTP client for the GraphQL service, as shown in the following code:

    ```
    builder.Services.AddHttpClient(name: "Northwind.GraphQL.Service",
      configureClient: options =>
      {
        options.BaseAddress = new Uri("https://localhost:5121/");
    ```

```
    options.DefaultRequestHeaders.Accept.Add(
      new MediaTypeWithQualityHeaderValue(
      "application/json", 1.0));
  });
```

12. In the `Controllers` folder, in `HomeController.cs`, import the namespace to work with text encodings and for the local project models, as shown in the following code:

```
using Northwind.Mvc.GraphQLClient.Models; // To use IndexViewModel.
using System.Text; // To use Encoding.
```

13. Define a field to store the registered HTTP client factory, and set it in the constructor, as shown in the following code:

```
protected readonly IHttpClientFactory _clientFactory;

public HomeController(ILogger<HomeController> logger,
  IHttpClientFactory clientFactory)
{
  _logger = logger;
  _clientFactory = clientFactory;
}
```

14. In the `Index` action method, modify the method to be asynchronous. Then, add statements to call the GraphQL service, and note that the HTTP request is a `POST`, the media type is for an `application/json` document that contains a GraphQL query, and the query requests the ID, name, and number of units in stock for all products in a given category, passed as a parameter named `id`, as shown in the following code:

```
public async Task<IActionResult> Index(string id = "1")
{
  IndexViewModel model = new();

  try
  {
    HttpClient client = _clientFactory.CreateClient(
      name: "Northwind.GraphQL.Service");

    // First, try a simple GET request to service root.

    HttpRequestMessage request = new(
      method: HttpMethod.Get, requestUri: "/");

    HttpResponseMessage response = await client.SendAsync(request);
```

```
      if (!response.IsSuccessStatusCode)
      {
        model.Code = response.StatusCode;
        model.Errors = new[] { new Error { Message =
          "Service is not successfully responding to GET requests." } };
        return View(model);
      }

      // Next, make a request to the GraphQL endpoint.

      request = new(
        method: HttpMethod.Post, requestUri: "graphql");

      request.Content = new StringContent(content: $$$"""
{
  "query": "{productsInCategory(categoryId:{{{id}}}){productId
productName unitsInStock}}"
}
        """,
        encoding: Encoding.UTF8,
        mediaType: "application/json");

      response = await client.SendAsync(request);

      model.Code = response.StatusCode;
      model.RawResponseBody = await response.Content.ReadAsStringAsync();

      if (response.IsSuccessStatusCode)
      {
        model.Products = (await response.Content
          .ReadFromJsonAsync<ResponseProducts>())?.Data?.
ProductsInCategory;
      }
      else
      {
        model.Errors = (await response.Content
          .ReadFromJsonAsync<ResponseErrors>())?.Errors;
      }
    }
    catch (Exception ex)
    {
```

```
  _logger.LogWarning(
    $"Northwind.GraphQL.Service exception: {ex.Message}");

  model.Errors = new[] { new Error { Message = ex.Message } };
}

return View(model);
}
```

Good Practice: To set the content of our request, we will use the C# 11 or later raw interpolated string literal syntax of three-dollar signs and three double quotes. This allows us to embed the id variable using three curly braces, which should not be confused with the two curly braces after unitsInStock, which end the query itself.

15. In the Views/Home folder, in Index.cshtml, delete its existing markup, and then add markup to render the seafood products, as shown in the following markup:

```
@using Northwind.EntityModels
@using Northwind.GraphQL.Client.Mvc.Models @* for VS Code only *@
@model IndexViewModel
@{
  ViewData["Title"] = "Products from GraphQL service";
}
<div class="text-center">
  <h1 class="display-4">@ViewData["Title"]</h1>
  <div class="card card-body">
    <form>
      Enter a category id
      <input name="id" value="1" />
      <input type="submit" />
    </form>
  </div>
  @if (Model.Errors is not null)
  {
    <div class="alert alert-danger" role="alert">
      <table class="table table-striped">
        <thead>
        <tr>
          <td>Message</td>
          <td>Path</td>
          <td>Locations</td>
        </tr>
```

```
            </thead>
            <tbody>
              @foreach (Error error in Model.Errors)
              {
                <tr>
                  <td>@error.Message</td>
                  <td>
                    @if (error.Path is not null)
                    {
                      @foreach (string path in error.Path)
                      {
                        <span class="badge bg-danger">@path</span>
                      }
                    }
                  </td>
                  <td>
                    @if (error.Locations is not null)
                    {
                      @foreach (Location location in error.Locations)
                      {
                        <span class="badge bg-danger">
                          @location.Line, @location.Column
                        </span>
                      }
                    }
                  </td>
                </tr>
              }
            </tbody>
          </table>
        </div>
      }
      @if (Model.Categories is not null)
      {
        <div>
          <p class="alert alert-success" role="alert">
            There are @Model.Categories.Count() products.</p>
          <p>
            @foreach (Category category in Model.Categories)
            {
              <span class="badge bg-dark">
```

```
                @category.CategoryId
                @category.CategoryName
              </span>
            }
          </p>
        </div>
      }
      @if (Model.Products is not null)
      {
        <div>
          <p class="alert alert-success" role="alert">
            There are @Model.Products.Count() products.</p>
          <p>
            @foreach (Product p in Model.Products)
            {
              <span class="badge bg-dark">
                @p.ProductId
                @p.ProductName
                -
                @(p.UnitsInStock is null ? "0" : p.UnitsInStock.Value) in
stock
              </span>
            }
          </p>
        </div>
      }
      <p>
        <a class="btn btn-primary" data-bs-toggle="collapse"
           href="#collapseExample" role="button"
           aria-expanded="false" aria-controls="collapseExample">
          Show/Hide Details
        </a>
      </p>
      <div class="collapse" id="collapseExample">
        <div class="card card-body">
          Status code @((int)Model.Code): @Model.Code
          <hr />
          @Model.RawResponseBody
        </div>
      </div>
    </div>
```

Testing the .NET client

Now, we can test our .NET client:

1. If your database server is not running, for example, because you are hosting it in Docker, a virtual machine, or in the cloud, then make sure to start it.

2. Start the `Northwind.GraphQL.Service` project, using its `https` profile without debugging.

3. Start the `Northwind.GraphQL.Client.Mvc` project, using its `https` profile without debugging.

4. Note that products are successfully retrieved using GraphQL, as shown in *Figure 12.9*:

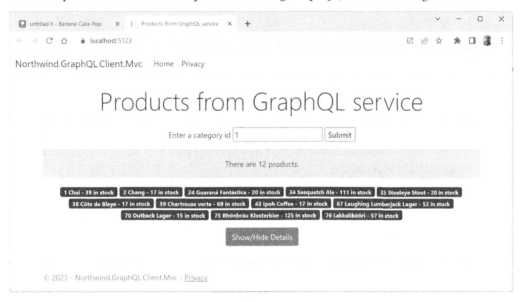

Figure 12.9: Products in the Beverages category from the GraphQL service

5. Enter another category ID that exists, for example, 4.

6. Enter a category ID that is out of range, for example, 13, and note that there are 0 products returned.

7. Close Chrome, and shut down the web server for the `Northwind.GraphQL.Client.Mvc` project.

8. In `HomeController.cs`, modify the query to make a deliberate mistake, like changing `productId` to `productid`.

9. Start the `Northwind.GraphQL.Client.Mvc` project, using the `https` profile without debugging.

10. Click the **Show/Hide Details** button, and note the error message and response details, as shown in the following output:

```
{"errors":[{"message":"The field \u0060productid\u0060
does not exist on the type \u0060Product\u0060.",
 "locations":[{"line":1,"column":35}],
 "path":["productsInCategory"],
 "extensions":{"type":"Product","field":"productid",
 "responseName":"productid",
```

```
"specifiedBy":"http://spec.graphql.org/October2021/
#sec-Field-Selections-on-Objects-Interfaces-and-Unions-Types"}}]}
```

11. Close Chrome, and shut down both web servers.

12. Fix the mistake in the query!

Creating a console app client using Strawberry Shake

Instead of using ordinary HTTP clients, ChilliCream has a GraphQL client library to more easily build .NET clients to GraphQL services.

 More Information: You can learn more about Strawberry Shake at the following link: https://chillicream.com/docs/strawberryshake

Now, let's create another client using Strawberry Shake so that you can see the benefits:

1. Use your preferred code editor to add a new **Console App** / console project, named Northwind. GraphQL.Client.Console.

2. At the command prompt or terminal for the project folder, create a tools manifest file, as shown in the following command:

```
dotnet new tool-manifest
```

3. At the command line or terminal, install the Strawberry Shake tools, as shown in the following command:

```
dotnet tool install StrawberryShake.Tools --local
```

4. Note Strawberry Shake is installed, as shown in the following output:

```
You can invoke the tool from this directory using the following commands:
'dotnet tool run dotnet-graphql' or 'dotnet dotnet-graphql'.
Tool 'strawberryshake.tools' (version '13.5.1') was successfully
installed.
Entry is added to the manifest file C:\apps-services-net8\Chapter12\
Northwind.GraphQL.Client.Console\.config\dotnet-tools.json.
```

5. In the project, treat warnings as errors, add references to NuGet packages for Microsoft extensions for dependency injection, working with HTTP, and Strawberry Shake code generation, and then globally and statically import the Console class, as highlighted in the following markup:

```
<Project Sdk="Microsoft.NET.Sdk">

  <PropertyGroup>
    <OutputType>Exe</OutputType>
```

```xml
    <TargetFramework>net8.0</TargetFramework>
    <ImplicitUsings>enable</ImplicitUsings>
    <Nullable>enable</Nullable>
    <TreatWarningsAsErrors>true</TreatWarningsAsErrors>
  </PropertyGroup>

  <ItemGroup>
    <PackageReference Version="8.0.0"
      Include="Microsoft.Extensions.DependencyInjection" />
    <PackageReference Version="8.0.0"
      Include="Microsoft.Extensions.Http" />
    <PackageReference Version="13.5.1"
      Include="StrawberryShake.Server" />
  </ItemGroup>

  <ItemGroup>
    <Using Include="System.Console" Static="true" />
  </ItemGroup>

</Project>
```

You need to use different Strawberry Shake packages for different types of .NET project. For console apps and ASP.NET Core apps, reference `StrawberryShake.Server`. For Blazor WebAssembly apps, reference `StrawberryShake.Blazor`. For .NET MAUI apps, reference `StrawberryShake.Maui`.

6. Build the `Northwind.GraphQL.Client.Console` project to restore packages.

7. Start the `Northwind.GraphQL.Service` project, using the `https` profile without debugging, and leave it running so that the Strawberry Shake tool can talk to it.

8. In the `Northwind.GraphQL.Client.Console` project, at the command prompt or terminal, add a client for your GraphQL service, as shown in the following command:

```
dotnet graphql init https://localhost:5121/graphql/ -n NorthwindClient
```

9. Note the results, as shown in the following output:

```
Download schema started.
Download schema completed in 189 ms
Client configuration started.
Client configuration completed in 83 ms
```

10. In the `Northwind.GraphQL.Client.Console` project, in the `.graphqlrc.json` file, add an entry to control the C# namespace used during code generation, as highlighted in the following markup:

```
{
  "schema": "schema.graphql",
  "documents": "**/*.graphql",
  "extensions": {
    "strawberryShake": {
      "name": "NorthwindClient",
      "namespace": "Northwind.GraphQL.Client.Console",
      "url": "https://localhost:5111/graphql/",
      "records": {
        "inputs": false,
        "entities": false
      },
      "transportProfiles": [
        {
          "default": "Http",
          "subscription": "WebSocket"
        }
      ]
    }
  }
}
```

11. In the `Northwind.GraphQL.Client.Console` project, add a new file named `seafoodProducts.graphql`, which defines a query to get seafood products, as shown in the following document:

```
query SeafoodProducts {
  productsInCategory(categoryId:8) {
    productId
    productName
    unitsInStock
  }
}
```

  GraphQL queries used by Strawberry Shake must be named.

12. If you are using Visual Studio 2022, it might automatically modify the project file to explicitly remove this file from the build process because it does not recognize it. If it has, then delete or comment out that element, as shown in the following markup:

```
<!-- An element like this will remove the file from the build process.
<ItemGroup>
  <GraphQL Remove="seafoodProducts.graphql" />
</ItemGroup>
-->
```

 Good Practice: There must be at least one `.graphql` file for the Strawberry Shake tool to be able to generate its code automatically. An element like the proceeding one will prevent the Strawberry Shake tool from generating its code, and you will later get compile errors. You should delete or comment out that element.

13. Build the `Northwind.GraphQL.Client.Console` project to make Strawberry Shake process the GraphQL query file and generate proxy classes.

14. Note the `obj\Debug\net8.0\berry` folder that was autogenerated, the file named `NorthwindClient.Client.cs`, and the dozen or so types defined by it, including the `INorthwindClient` interface, as shown in *Figure 12.10*:

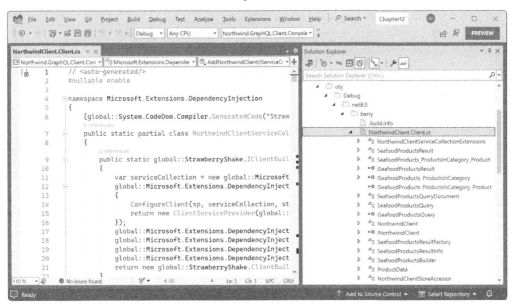

Figure 12.10: The generated class file for the Northwind GraphQL service

15. In `Program.cs`, delete the existing statements. Add statements to create a new service collection, add the autogenerated `NorthwindClient` to it with the correct URL for the service, and then get and use the dependency service to fetch the seafood products, as shown in the following code:

```
using Microsoft.Extensions.DependencyInjection; // To use
ServiceCollection.
using Northwind.GraphQL.Client.Console; // To use INorthwindClient.
using StrawberryShake; // To use EnsureNoErrors extension method.

ServiceCollection serviceCollection = new();

serviceCollection
  .AddNorthwindClient() // Strawberry Shake extension method.
  .ConfigureHttpClient(client =>
    client.BaseAddress = new Uri("https://localhost:5121/graphql"));

IServiceProvider services = serviceCollection.BuildServiceProvider();

INorthwindClient client = services.
GetRequiredService<INorthwindClient>();

var result = await client.SeafoodProducts.ExecuteAsync();
result.EnsureNoErrors();

if (result.Data is null)
{
  WriteLine("No data!");
  return;
}

foreach (var product in result.Data.ProductsInCategory)
{
  WriteLine("{0}: {1}",
    product.ProductId, product.ProductName);
}
```

16. Run the console app and note the results, as shown in the following output:

```
10: Ikura
13: Konbu
18: Carnarvon Tigers
30: Nord-Ost Matjeshering
36: Inlagd Sill
```

```
37: Gravad lax
40: Boston Crab Meat
41: Jack's New England Clam Chowder
45: Rogede sild
46: Spegesild
58: Escargots de Bourgogne
73: Röd Kaviar
```

Implementing GraphQL mutations

Most services need to modify data as well as query it. GraphQL calls these **mutations**. A mutation has three related components:

- The mutation itself, which defines the change that will be made to the graph. It should be named using a verb, a noun, and use camel casing, for example, addProduct.

- The **input** is the input for a mutation, and it should have the same name as the mutation with a suffix of Input, for example, AddProductInput. Although there is only one input, it is an object graph, so it can be as complex as you need.

- The **payload** is the returned document for a mutation, and it should have the same name as the mutation with a suffix of Payload, for example, AddProductPayload. Although there is only one payload, it is an object graph, so it can be as complex as you need.

Adding mutations to the GraphQL service

Let's define mutations for adding, and later, we will define some to update and delete products:

1. In the Northwind.GraphQL.Service project/folder, add a class file named Mutation.cs.

2. In the class file, define a record and two classes to represent the three types needed to perform an addProduct mutation, as shown in the following code:

```
using Northwind.EntityModels; // To use Product.

namespace Northwind.GraphQL.Service;

// Inputs are readonly so we will use a record.
public record AddProductInput(
  string ProductName,
  int? SupplierId,
  int? CategoryId,
  string QuantityPerUnit,
  decimal? UnitPrice,
  short? UnitsInStock,
  short? UnitsOnOrder,
  short? ReorderLevel,
```

```
    bool Discontinued);

public class AddProductPayload
{
  public AddProductPayload(Product product)
  {
    Product = product;
  }


  public Product Product { get; }
}

public class Mutation
{
  public async Task<AddProductPayload> AddProductAsync(
    AddProductInput input, NorthwindContext db)
  {
    // This could be a good place to use a tool like AutoMapper,
    // but we will do the mapping between two objects manually.

    Product product = new()
    {
      ProductName = input.ProductName,
      SupplierId = input.SupplierId,
      CategoryId = input.CategoryId,
      QuantityPerUnit = input.QuantityPerUnit,
      UnitPrice = input.UnitPrice,
      UnitsInStock = input.UnitsInStock,
      UnitsOnOrder = input.UnitsOnOrder,
      ReorderLevel = input.ReorderLevel,
      Discontinued = input.Discontinued
    };

    db.Products.Add(product);

    int affectedRows = await db.SaveChangesAsync();

    // We could use affectedRows to return an error
    // or some other action if it is 0.

    return new AddProductPayload(product);
```

```
    }
  }
```

3. In `Program.cs`, add a call to the `AddMutationType<T>` method to register your `Mutation` class, as highlighted in the following code:

```
builder.Services
  .AddGraphQLServer()
  .AddFiltering()
  .AddSorting()
  .RegisterDbContext<NorthwindContext>()
  .AddQueryType<Query>()
  .AddMutationType<Mutation>();
```

Exploring the add product mutation

Now, we can explore mutations using Banana Cake Pop:

1. Start the `Northwind.GraphQL.Service` project, using the `https` profile without debugging.

2. In **Banana Cake Pop**, click the + to open a new tab.

3. Click the **Schema Definition** tab, and note the mutation type, as partially shown in *Figure 12.11*:

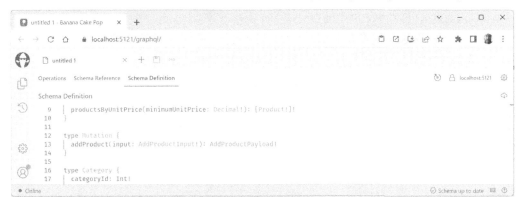

Figure 12.11: Schema to mutate a product using GraphQL

4. Note the full schema definitions for the `addProduct` mutation and its related types, as shown in the following code:

```
type Mutation {
  addProduct(input: AddProductInput!): AddProductPayload!
}

type Product {
  productId: Int!
  productName: String!
  supplierId: Int
```

```
    categoryId: Int
    quantityPerUnit: String
    unitPrice: Decimal
    unitsInStock: Short
    unitsOnOrder: Short
    reorderLevel: Short
    discontinued: Boolean!
    category: Category
    supplier: Supplier
    orderDetails: [OrderDetail!]!
}


...


type AddProductPayload {
    product: Product!
}

input AddProductInput {
    productName: String!
    supplierId: Int
    categoryId: Int
    quantityPerUnit: String!
    unitPrice: Decimal
    unitsInStock: Short
    unitsOnOrder: Short
    reorderLevel: Short
    discontinued: Boolean!
}
```

5. Click the **Operations** tab and, if necessary, create a new blank document, and then enter a mutation to add a new product named `Tasty Burgers`. Then, from the returned product object, just select the ID and name, as shown in the following code:

```
mutation AddProduct {
  addProduct(
    input: {
      productName: "Tasty Burgers"
      supplierId: 1
      categoryId: 2
```

```
          quantityPerUnit: "6 per box"
          unitPrice: 40
          unitsInStock: 0
          unitsOnOrder: 0
          reorderLevel: 0
          discontinued: false
      }
    )
    {
      product {
        productId
        productName
      }
    }
  }
```

6. Click **Run**, and note that the new product has been successfully added and assigned the next sequential number by the SQL Server database, which could be any number over 77, depending on if you have already added some other products, as shown in the following output and in *Figure 12.12*:

```
{
  "data": {
    "addProduct": {
      "product": {
        "productId": 79,
        "productName": "Tasty Burgers",
      }
    }
  }
}
```

 Warning! Please make a note of the ID assigned to the new product you have added. In the next section, you will update this product and then delete it. You cannot delete any of the existing products with IDs between 1 and 77 because they are related to other tables, and doing so would throw a referential integrity exception!

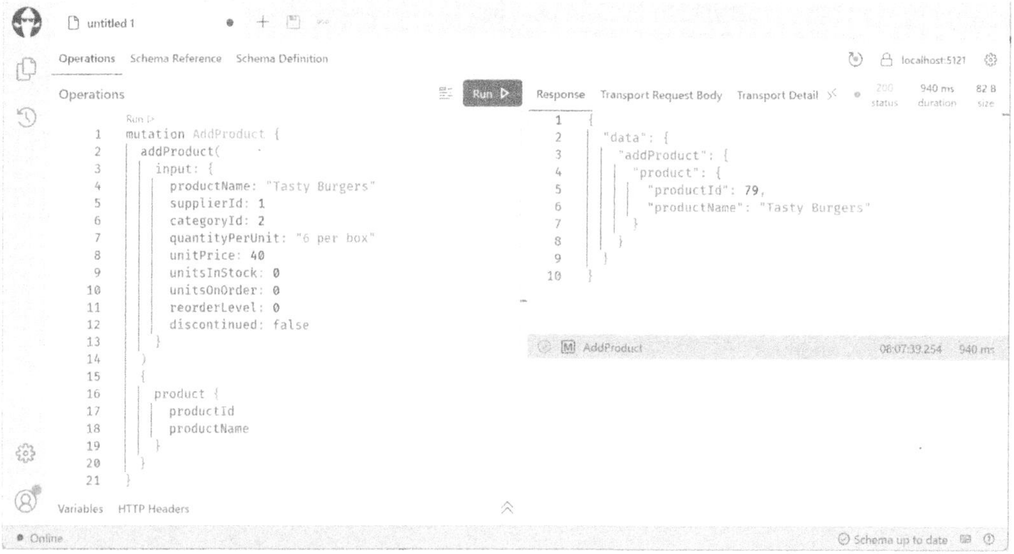

Figure 12.12: Adding a new product using a GraphQL mutation

7.   Close the browser, and shut down the web server.

Implementing updates and deletes as mutations

Next, we will define mutations to update just the unit price for a product, all the "units" fields for a product, and delete a product:

1.   In `Mutation.cs`, define three `record` types to represent the inputs needed to perform two `updateProduct` and one `deleteProduct` mutations, as shown in the following code:

```
public record UpdateProductPriceInput(
    int? ProductId,
    decimal? UnitPrice);

public record UpdateProductUnitsInput(
    int? ProductId,
    short? UnitsInStock,
    short? UnitsOnOrder,
    short? ReorderLevel);

public record DeleteProductInput(
    int? ProductId);
```

2.   In `Mutation.cs`, define two class types to represent the types needed to return the results from an `update` or `delete` mutation, including if the action was successful, as shown in the following code:

```
public class UpdateProductPayload
{
  public UpdateProductPayload(Product? product, bool updated)
  {
    Product = product;
    Success = updated;
  }

  public Product? Product { get; }
  public bool Success { get; }
}

public class DeleteProductPayload
{
  public DeleteProductPayload(bool deleted)
  {
    Success = deleted;
  }

  public bool Success { get; }
}
```

3. In `Mutation.cs`, in the `Mutation` class, define three methods to implement two `updateProduct` and one `deleteProduct` mutations, as shown in the following code:

```
public async Task<UpdateProductPayload> UpdateProductPriceAsync(
  UpdateProductPriceInput input, NorthwindContext db)
{
  Product? product = await db.Products.FindAsync(input.ProductId);

  int affectedRows = 0;

  if (product is not null)
  {
    product.UnitPrice = input.UnitPrice;

    affectedRows = await db.SaveChangesAsync();
  }

  return new UpdateProductPayload(product,
    updated: affectedRows == 1);
}
```

```csharp
public async Task<UpdateProductPayload> UpdateProductUnitsAsync(
  UpdateProductUnitsInput input, NorthwindContext db)
{
  Product? product = await db.Products.FindAsync(input.ProductId);

  int affectedRows = 0;

  if (product is not null)
  {
    product.UnitsInStock = input.UnitsInStock;
    product.UnitsOnOrder = input.UnitsOnOrder;
    product.ReorderLevel = input.ReorderLevel;

    affectedRows = await db.SaveChangesAsync();
  }

  return new UpdateProductPayload(product,
    updated: affectedRows == 1);
}

public async Task<DeleteProductPayload> DeleteProductAsync(
  DeleteProductInput input, NorthwindContext db)
{
  Product? product = await db.Products.FindAsync(input.ProductId);

  int affectedRows = 0;

  if (product is not null)
  {
    db.Products.Remove(product);

    affectedRows = await db.SaveChangesAsync();
  }

  return new DeleteProductPayload(
    deleted: affectedRows == 1);
}
```

4. If your database server is not running, for example, because you are hosting it in Docker, a virtual machine, or in the cloud, then make sure to start it.

5. Start the `Northwind.GraphQL.Service` project, using the `https` profile without debugging.

6. In **Banana Cake Pop**, click the + to open a new tab.

7. Write a named query to request products that you have added, for example, with a `productId` greater than 77, as shown in the following markup:

```
query NewProducts {
  products(where: { productId: { gt: 77 } }) {
    productId
    productName
    unitPrice
    unitsInStock
    unitsOnOrder
    reorderLevel
  }
}
```

8. Click **Run**, and note the response includes the new product you previously added with a unit price of **40**, as shown in the following output:

```
{
  "data": {
    "products": [
      {
        "productId": 79,
        "productName": "Tasty Burgers",
        "unitPrice": 40,
        "unitsInStock": 0,
        "unitsOnOrder": 0,
        "reorderLevel": 0
      }
    ]
  }
}
```

9. Make a note of the `productId` of the product you added. In my case, it is 79.

10. In **Banana Cake Pop**, click the + to open a new tab.

11. Enter a mutation to update the unit price of your new product to 75, and then from the returned product object, just select the ID, name, unit price, and units in stock, as shown in the following code:

```
mutation UpdateProductPrice {
  updateProductPrice(
    input: {
```

```
        productId: 79
        unitPrice: 75
      }
    )
    {
      product {
        productId
        productName
        unitPrice
        unitsInStock
      }
    }
  }
```

12. Click **Run**, and note the response, as shown in the following output:

```
{
  "data": {
    "updateProductPrice": {
      "product": {
        "productId": 79,
        "productName": "Tasty Burgers",
        "unitPrice": 75,
        "unitsInStock": 0
      }
    }
  }
}
```

13. Click the + to open a new tab, enter a mutation to update the units of an existing product, and then from the returned product object just select the ID, name, unit price, and units in stock, as shown in the following code:

```
mutation UpdateProductUnits {
  updateProductUnits(
    input: {
      productId: 79
      unitsInStock: 20
      unitsOnOrder: 0
      reorderLevel: 10
    }
  )
  {
    success
```

```
    }
  }
```

14. Click **Run**, and note the response, as shown in the following output:

```
{
  "data": {
    "updateProductUnits": {
      "success": true
    }
  }
}
```

15. In the query tab to request new products, click **Run**, and note the response, as shown in the following output:

```
{
  "data": {
    "products": [
      {
        "productId": 79,
        "productName": "Tasty Burgers",
        "unitPrice": 75,
        "unitsInStock": 20,
        "unitsOnOrder": 0,
        "reorderLevel": 10
      }
    ]
  }
}
```

16. Click the + to open a new tab, and enter a mutation to delete the product and show if it was successful, as shown in the following code:

```
mutation DeleteProduct {
  deleteProduct(
    input: {
      productId: 79
    }
  )
  {
    success
  }
}
```

Warning! You will not be able to delete products that are referenced in other tables. IDs 1 to 77 will throw a referential integrity exception.

17. Click **Run**, and note the response, as shown in the following output:

```
{
  "data": {
    "deleteProduct": {
      "success": true
    }
  }
}
```

18. Confirm that the product was deleted by re-running the query for new products, and note that you get an empty array, as shown in the following output:

```
{
  "data": {
    "products": []
  }
}
```

19. Close the browser, and shut down the web server.

Implementing GraphQL subscriptions

GraphQL subscriptions, by default, work over WebSockets but can also work over **Server-Sent Events (SSE)**, SignalR, or even gRPC.

Imagine that a client app wants to be notified when a product has its unit price reduced. It would be great if the client could subscribe to an event that gets triggered whenever a unit price is reduced, instead of having to query for changes to the unit prices.

Adding a subscription and topic to the GraphQL service

Let's add this feature to our GraphQL service using subscriptions:

1. Add a new class file named `ProductDiscount.cs`.

2. Modify the contents to define a model to notify a client about a product's unit price reduction, as shown in the following code:

```
namespace Northwind.GraphQL.Service;

public class ProductDiscount
```

```
    {
        public int? ProductId { get; set; }
        public decimal? OriginalUnitPrice { get; set; }
        public decimal? NewUnitPrice { get; set; }
    }
```

3. Add a new class file named `Subscription.cs`.

4. Modify the contents to define a subscription to an event (aka a topic) named `OnProductDiscounted` that a client can subscribe to, as shown in the following code:

```
namespace Northwind.GraphQL.Service;

public class Subscription
{
    [Subscribe]
    [Topic]
    public ProductDiscount OnProductDiscounted(
        [EventMessage] ProductDiscount productDiscount)
            => productDiscount;
}
```

5. In `Mutation.cs`, in the `UpdateProductPriceAsync` method, add statements to send a message over the topic whenever a product has its unit price reduced, as highlighted in the following code:

```
public async Task<UpdateProductPayload> UpdateProductPriceAsync(
    UpdateProductPriceInput input, NorthwindContext db,
    ITopicEventSender eventSender)
{
    Product? product = await db.Products.FindAsync(input.ProductId);

    int affectedRows = 0;

    if (product is not null)
    {
        if (input.UnitPrice < product.UnitPrice)
        {
            // If the product has been discounted,
            // send a message to subscribers.
            ProductDiscount productDiscount = new()
            {
                ProductId = input.ProductId,
                OriginalUnitPrice = product.UnitPrice,
```

```
        NewUnitPrice = input.UnitPrice
    };

    await eventSender.SendAsync(topicName:
        nameof(Subscription.OnProductDiscounted),
        message: productDiscount);
  }

  product.UnitPrice = input.UnitPrice;

  affectedRows = await db.SaveChangesAsync();
}

return new UpdateProductPayload(product,
  updated: affectedRows == 1);
}
```

6. In `Program.cs`, configure the GraphQL service to register the `Subscription` class and to store active subscriptions in-memory, as highlighted in the following code:

```
builder.Services
  .AddGraphQLServer()
  .AddFiltering()
  .AddSorting()
  .AddSubscriptionType<Subscription>()
  .AddInMemorySubscriptions()
  .RegisterDbContext<NorthwindContext>()
  .AddQueryType<Query>()
  .AddMutationType<Mutation>();
```

 As well as in-memory, you can use Redis and other data stores to keep track of active subscriptions.

7. Optionally, after building the app, configure the use of WebSockets, as shown in the following code:

```
app.UseWebSockets(); // For subscriptions.
```

 This is optional because the GraphQL service can fall back to using SSE over `https`.

Exploring subscribing to a topic

Let's subscribe to a topic and see the results:

1. Start the `Northwind.GraphQL.Service` project, using the `https` profile without debugging.

2. In **Banana Cake Pop**, click the **+** to open a new tab.

3. Click the **Schema Reference** tab, click the `Subscription` type, and note the topic named **on-ProductDiscounted**, as shown in *Figure 12.13*:

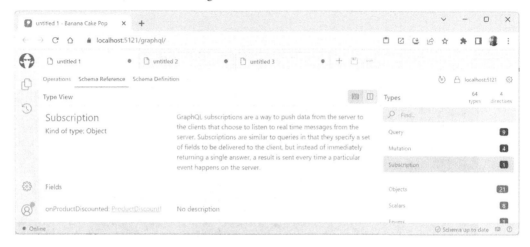

Figure 12.13: A subscription with a topic

4. Click **Operations**, enter a subscription to the topic, and choose all the fields to show in the results, as shown in the following code:

```
subscription {
  onProductDiscounted {
    productId
    originalUnitPrice
    newUnitPrice
  }
}
```

5. Click **Run**, and note that the subscription starts but no results are shown yet.

6. Click the **+** to open a new tab, and enter a mutation to update the unit price of the existing product `1` to `8.99`. Then, from the returned `product` object, select the ID and unit price, and show if the update succeeded, as shown in the following code:

```
mutation UpdateProductPrice {
  updateProductPrice(
    input: {
      productId: 1
      unitPrice: 8.99
```

```
      }
    )
    {
      product {
        productId
        unitPrice
      }
      success
    }
  }
```

7. Click **Run**, and note the response, as shown in the following output:

```
{
  "data": {
    "updateProductPrice": {
      "product": {
        "productId": 1,
        "unitPrice": 8.99
      },
      "success": true
    }
  }
}
```

8. Switch back to the tab with the subscription, and note the response and that the subscription is still active, indicated by the spinners on the tab and the **Cancel** button, as shown in *Figure 12.14*:

Figure 12.14: An active subscription shows a spinner

9. Switch back to the tab with the update mutation, change the unit price to 7.99, and click **Run**. Then, switch back to the tab with the subscription, and note that it receives that update notification too.

10. Switch back to the tab with the update mutation, change the unit price to 9.99, and click **Run**. Then, switch back to the tab with the subscription, and note that it has not been sent any notifications because the unit price was increased, not reduced.

11. Close the browser, and shut down the web server.

Practicing and exploring

Test your knowledge and understanding by answering some questions, getting some hands-on practice, and exploring this chapter's topics with deeper research.

Exercise 12.1 – Test your knowledge

Answer the following questions:

1. What transport protocol does a GraphQL service use?

2. What media type does GraphQL use for its queries?

3. How can you parameterize GraphQL queries?

4. What are the benefits of using Strawberry Shake over a regular HTTP client for GraphQL queries?

5. How might you insert a new product into the Northwind database?

Exercise 12.2 – Explore topics

Use the links on the following page to learn more details about the topics covered in this chapter:

https://github.com/markjprice/apps-services-net8/blob/main/docs/book-links.md#chapter-12---combining-data-sources-using-graphql

Exercise 12.3 – Practice building .NET clients

In `HomeController.cs`, add an action method named `Categories`, and implement it to query the `categories` field with a variable for the `id`. On the page, allow the visitor to submit an `id`, and note the category information and a list of its products.

Summary

In this chapter, you learned about:

- Some of the concepts of GraphQL.
- How to build a `Query` class with fields that represent entities that can be queried.
- How to use the Banana Cake Pop tool to explore a GraphQL service schema.
- How to use the REST Client extension to POST to a GraphQL service.
- How to create a .NET client for a GraphQL service.
- How to implement GraphQL mutations.
- How to implement GraphQL subscriptions.

In the next chapter, you will learn about the gRPC service technology that can be used to implement efficient microservices.

Learn more on Discord

To join the Discord community for this book – where you can share feedback, ask questions to the author, and learn about new releases – follow the QR code below:

`https://packt.link/apps_and_services_dotnet8`

13

Building Efficient Microservices Using gRPC

In this chapter, you will be introduced to gRPC, which enables a developer to build services that can communicate highly efficiently across most platforms.

However, web browsers do not have full support for programmatic access to all features of HTTP/2, which is required by gRPC. This makes gRPC most useful for implementing intermediate tier-to-tier services and microservices because they must perform a lot of communication between multiple microservices to achieve a complete task. Improving the efficiency of that communication is vital to the success of the scalability and performance of microservices.

A modular monolithic, two-tier, client-to-service style service is inherently more efficient because the communication between modules is in-process and there is only one layer of network communication between the whole service and the clients.

Microservice architecture has more tiers, and therefore more layers of network communication between the many microservices. It becomes more important to have highly efficient communication between those layers, and gRPC is designed to be ultra-efficient for network communication, as shown in *Figure 13.1*:

Two-tier modular monolithic service   Multi-tier microservices

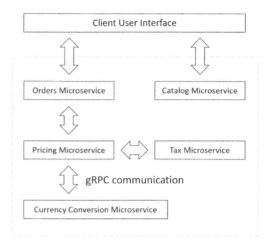

Figure 13.1: Comparing a two-tier modular monolithic service with multi-tier microservices

> **Good Practice:** It has been fashionable in the past decade or so to assume that microservices are best for all scenarios, and so for a new system to immediately be implemented using cool microservices rather than as a traditional monolith. More recently, there has been a pushback against this assumption. The industry seems to be settling on the recommendation to start by implementing a system as a modular monolith. Only later, if necessary, should you break the modules apart into actual microservices. As well as being inherently slower due to the extra network communication between microservices, you also need to consider whether the extra coordination and complexity of deployments and orchestration of microservices is worth it.

This chapter will cover the following topics:

- Understanding gRPC
- Building a gRPC service and client
- Implementing gRPC for an EF Core model
- Taking gRPC further
- Handling dates, times, and decimal numbers
- Implementing interceptors and handling faults
- Implementing gRPC JSON transcoding

Understanding gRPC

gRPC is a modern, open-source, high-performance **Remote Procedure Call** (**RPC**) framework that can run in any environment. An RPC is when one computer calls a procedure in another process or on another computer over a network as if it were calling a local procedure. It is an example of a client-server architecture.

You can learn more about RPCs at the following link: `https://en.wikipedia.org/wiki/Remote_procedure_call`.

How gRPC works

A gRPC service developer defines a service interface for the methods that can be called remotely, including defining the method parameters and return types. The service implements this interface and runs a gRPC server to handle client calls.

On the client, a strongly typed gRPC client provides the same methods as on the server.

Defining gRPC contracts with .proto files

gRPC uses contract-first API development that supports language-agnostic implementations. A **contract** in this case is an agreement that a service will expose a defined list of methods with specified parameters and return types that implement a prescribed behavior. A client that wishes to call the service can be certain that the service will continue to conform to the contract over time. For example, although new methods might be added, existing ones will never change or be removed.

You write the contracts using .proto files that have their own language syntax and then use tools to convert them into various languages like C#. The .proto files are used by both the server and client to exchange messages in the correct format.

Here's an example .proto file using proto3 syntax to define a message request that uses a custom enum:

```
// Setting the syntax must be first non-comment line.
syntax = "proto3"; // proto2 is the default.

/* When this .proto file is used in a .NET project, it will use the
   following C# namespace for the auto-generated code files. */
option csharp_namespace = "Northwind.Grpc.Service";

enum SearchType {
  SEARCHTYPE_UNSPECIFIED = 0;
  SEARCHTYPE_STARTSWITH = 1;
  SEARCHTYPE_CONTAINS = 2;
  SEARCHTYPE_ENDSWITH = 3;
}

message SearchRequest {
  string query = 1; // Fields must have order numbers.
  SearchType search_type = 2;
```

```
    int32 page = 3;
    int32 page_size = 4;
}

message SearchResponse {
  /* Message types can be nested and/or repeated to create the
     equivalent of collections or arrays. */
  repeated SearchResult results = 1;
}

message SearchResult {
  string url = 1;
  string title = 2;
  repeated string authors = 3;
}

service Searcher {
  rpc PerformSearch (SearchRequest) returns (SearchResponse);
}
```

 More Information: The Protobuf style guide recommends using all lowercase with underscores for field names, all uppercase with underscores for enum values, and so on. The C# tooling will automatically convert to .NET styles in the auto-generated types it creates for you. You can read more recommendations at the following link: `https://protobuf.dev/programming-guides/style/`.

Fields must be given a unique number between 1 and 536,870,911. You cannot use the range 19,000 to 19,999 because they are reserved for the Protocol Buffers implementation. These numbers are used instead of the field name during serialization to save space in the binary format.

 Good Practice: Field numbers cannot be changed once you start using a message because they are tightly bound to the very efficient wire format used by gRPC. Changing a field number is the equivalent of deleting and creating a new field. You should also never reuse a field number. You can read about the consequences of misusing field numbers at the following link: `https://protobuf.dev/programming-guides/proto3/#consequences`.

Field data types cannot be null, so all number types default to zero (0). Number and other field data types are shown in *Table 13.1*:

Type	Description
string	Text values. Defaults to an empty string.
bool	Boolean values. Defaults to false.
int32, int64	Variable length encoded 32- and 64-bit integer values. Although they can be used for negative values, it is more efficient to use sint32 or sint64. The C# equivalents to int and long.
sint32, sint64, uint32, uint64	Variable length encoded 32- and 64-bit signed and unsigned integer values. The C# equivalent to int and long, and uint and ulong.
fixed32, fixed64, sfixed32, sfixed64	Always four bytes for 32, or eight bytes for 64. The C# equivalent to uint and ulong, and int and long.
float, double	Floating point real numbers.
bytes	Maximum 2^{32} bytes (4,294,967,296). Use ByteString.CopyFrom(byte[] data) to create a new instance. Use ToByteArray() to get the byte array. Defaults to an empty ByteString value.

Table 13.1: Number and other field data types in Protobuf

More Information: The official guide is found at the following link: https://protobuf. dev/programming-guides/proto3/.

gRPC benefits

gRPC minimizes network usage by using **Protobuf** binary serialization that is not human-readable, unlike JSON or XML used by web services.

gRPC requires HTTP/2, which provides significant performance benefits over earlier versions, like binary framing and compression, and multiplexing of HTTP/2 calls over a single connection.

Binary framing means how the HTTP messages are transferred between the client and server. HTTP/1.x uses newline delimited plaintext. HTTP/2 splits communication into smaller messages (frames) that are encoded in binary format. Multiplexing means combining multiple messages from different sources into a single message to more efficiently use a shared resource like a network transport.

More Information: If you are interested in more details about HTTP/2 and how it makes gRPC more efficient, you can read about it at the following link: https://grpc.io/blog/ grpc-on-http2/.

gRPC limitations

The main limitation of gRPC is that it cannot be used in web browsers because no browser provides the level of control required to support a gRPC client. For example, browsers do not allow a caller to require that HTTP/2 be used.

Another limitation for developers is that due to the binary format of the messages, it is harder to diagnose and monitor issues. Many tools do not understand the format and cannot show messages in a human-readable format.

There is an initiative called **gRPC-Web** that adds an extra proxy layer, and the proxy forwards requests to the gRPC server. However, it only supports a subset of gRPC due to the listed limitations.

Types of gRPC methods

gRPC has four types of method.

The first method is the most common:

- **Unary** methods have structured request and response messages. A unary method completes when the response message is returned. Unary methods should be chosen in all scenarios that do not require a stream.

Streaming methods are used when a large amount of data must be exchanged, and they do so by using a stream of bytes. They have the `stream` keyword prefix for either an input parameter, an output parameter, or both.

The three streaming methods are as follows:

- **Server streaming** methods receive a request message from the client and return a stream. Multiple messages can be returned over the stream. A server streaming call ends when the server side method returns, but the server side method could run until it receives a cancellation token from the client.
- **Client streaming** methods only receive a stream from the client without any message. The server side method processes the stream until it is ready to return a response message. Once the server side method returns its message, the client streaming call is done.
- **Bi-directional streaming** methods only receive a stream from the client without any message and only return data via a second stream. The call is done when the server side method returns. Once a bi-directional streaming method is called, the client and service can send messages to each other at any time.

In this book, we will only look at the details of unary methods. If you would like the next edition to cover streaming methods, please let me know.

Microsoft's gRPC packages

Microsoft has invested in building a set of packages for .NET to work with gRPC and, since May 2021, it is Microsoft's recommended implementation of gRPC for .NET.

Microsoft's gRPC for .NET includes:

- `Grpc.AspNetCore` for hosting a gRPC service in ASP.NET Core.
- `Grpc.Net.Client` for adding gRPC client support to any .NET project by building on `HttpClient`.
- `Grpc.Net.ClientFactory` for adding gRPC client support to any .NET code base by building on `HttpClientFactory`.

 You can learn more at the following link: `https://github.com/grpc/grpc-dotnet`.

Building a gRPC service and client

Let's see an example service and client for sending and receiving simple messages.

Building a Hello World gRPC service

We will start by building the gRPC service using one of the project templates provided as standard:

1. Use your preferred code editor to create a new project, as defined in the following list:

    - Project template: **ASP.NET Core gRPC Service** / `grpc`
    - Solution file and folder: `Chapter13`
    - Project file and folder: `Northwind.Grpc.Service`
    - **Enable Docker:** Cleared.
    - **Do not use top-level statements:** Cleared.
    - **Enable native AOT publish:** Selected.

     Good Practice: Make sure to select **Enable native AOT publish**. With .NET 8 and later, gRPC projects can be **ahead-of-time** (**AOT**) compiled for native platforms. This gives improved performance and a reduced start time, which is important for microservices that are frequently redeployed and spun up and down during scaling.

2. In the `Protos` folder, in `greet.proto`, note that it defines a service named `Greeter` with a method named `SayHello` that exchanges messages named `HelloRequest` and `HelloReply`, as shown in the following code:

    ```
    syntax = "proto3";

    option csharp_namespace = "Northwind.Grpc.Service";

    package greet;

    // The greeting service definition.
    ```

```
service Greeter {
  // Sends a greeting
  rpc SayHello (HelloRequest) returns (HelloReply);
}

// The request message containing the user's name.
message HelloRequest {
  string name = 1;
}

// The response message containing the greetings.
message HelloReply {
  string message = 1;
}
```

 For working with .proto files in Visual Studio Code, you can install the extension **vscode-proto3** (zxh404.vscode-proto3). For Rider, you can install the Protocol Buffers plugin from JetBrains, as shown at the following link: https://plugins.jetbrains.com/plugin/14004-protocol-buffers.

3.   In Northwind.Grpc.Service.csproj, note that this project has native AOT publish enabled, the .proto file is registered for use on the server side, and the package reference for implementing a gRPC service hosted in ASP.NET Core, as shown highlighted in the following markup:

```
<Project Sdk="Microsoft.NET.Sdk.Web">

  <PropertyGroup>
    <TargetFramework>net8.0</TargetFramework>
    <Nullable>enable</Nullable>
    <ImplicitUsings>enable</ImplicitUsings>
    <InvariantGlobalization>true</InvariantGlobalization>
    <PublishAot>true</PublishAot>
  </PropertyGroup>

  <ItemGroup>
    <Protobuf Include="Protos\greet.proto" GrpcServices="Server" />
  </ItemGroup>

  <ItemGroup>
    <PackageReference Include="Grpc.AspNetCore" Version="2.59.0" />
  </ItemGroup>

</Project>
```

For JetBrains Rider, manually add `<PublishAot>true</PublishAot>` if it is missing.

4. Set invariant globalization to `false`, as shown in the following markup:

```
<InvariantGlobalization>false</InvariantGlobalization>
```

5. In the `Services` folder, in `GreeterService.cs`, note that it inherits from a class named `GreeterBase` and it asynchronously implements the `Greeter` service contract by having a `SayHello` method that accepts a `HelloRequest` input parameter and returns a `HelloReply`, as shown in the following code:

```
using Grpc.Core;
using Northwind.Grpc.Service

namespace Northwind.Grpc.Service.Services
{
  public class GreeterService : Greeter.GreeterBase
  {
    private readonly ILogger<GreeterService> _logger;

    public GreeterService(ILogger<GreeterService> logger)
    {
      _logger = logger;
    }

    public override Task<HelloReply> SayHello(
      HelloRequest request, ServerCallContext context)
    {
      return Task.FromResult(new HelloReply
      {
        Message = "Hello " + request.Name
      });
    }
  }
}
```

6. If you are using Visual Studio 2022, in **Solution Explorer**, click **Show All Files**. If you are using JetBrains Rider, then hover over the **Solution** pane and click the eyeball icon.

7. In the obj\Debug\net8.0\Protos folder, note the two class files named Greet.cs and GreetGrpc.cs that are automatically generated from the greet.proto file, as shown in *Figure 13.2*:

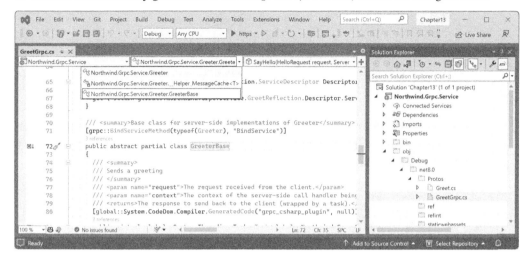

Figure 13.2: The autogenerated class files from a .proto file for a gRPC service

8. In GreetGrpc.cs, note the Greeter.GreeterBase class that the GreeterService class inherited from. You do not need to understand how this base class is implemented, but you should know it is what handles all the details of gRPC's efficient communication.

9. If you are using Visual Studio 2022, in **Solution Explorer**, expand **Dependencies**, expand **Packages**, expand **Grpc.AspNetCore**, and note that it has dependencies on Google's **Google.Protobuf** package, and Microsoft's **Grpc.AspNetCore.Server.ClientFactory** and **Grpc.Tools** packages, as shown in *Figure 13.3*:

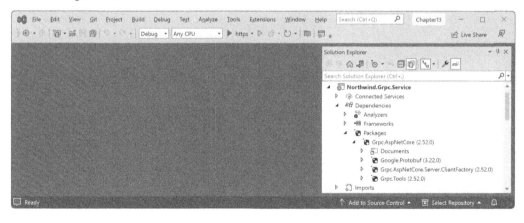

Figure 13.3: The Grpc.AspNetCore package references the Grpc.Tools and Google.Protobuf packages

The Grpc.Tools package generates the C# class files from the registered .proto files, and those class files use types defined in Google's package to implement the serialization to the Protobuf serialization format. The Grpc.AspNetCore.Server.ClientFactory package includes both server side and client-side support for gRPC in a .NET project.

10. In Program.cs, in the section that configures services, note the call to add gRPC to the Services collection, as shown in the following code:

```
builder.Services.AddGrpc();
```

11. In Program.cs, in the section for configuring the HTTP pipeline, note the call to map the Greeter service, as shown in the following code:

```
app.MapGrpcService<GreeterService>();
```

12. In the Properties folder, open launchSettings.json and modify the applicationUrl setting to use port 5131 for https and port 5132 for http, as shown highlighted in the following markup:

```
{
  "$schema": "http://json.schemastore.org/launchsettings.json",
  "profiles": {
    "http": {
      "commandName": "Project",
      "dotnetRunMessages": true,
      "launchBrowser": false,
      "applicationUrl": "http://localhost:5132",
      "environmentVariables": {
        "ASPNETCORE_ENVIRONMENT": "Development"
      }
    },
    "https": {
      "commandName": "Project",
      "dotnetRunMessages": true,
      "launchBrowser": false,
      "applicationUrl": "https://localhost:5131;http://localhost:5132",
      "environmentVariables": {
        "ASPNETCORE_ENVIRONMENT": "Development"
      }
    }
  }
}
```

13. Build the Northwind.Grpc.Service project.

Project file item configuration

Before we continue, let's quickly review common project file item configuration syntax.

Item configuration generated by Visual Studio 2022 commonly uses attributes for the item properties, as shown in the following markup:

```xml
<Protobuf Include="Protos\greet.proto" GrpcServices="Client" />
```

Properties not explicitly set will have their default values.

Item configuration generated by other tools like JetBrains Rider commonly uses child elements for the item properties, as shown in the following markup:

```xml
<Protobuf>
  <Include>Protos\greet.proto</Include>
  <GrpcServices>Client</>
  <Access>Public</Access>
  <ProtoCompile>True</ProtoCompile>
  <CompileOutputs>True</CompileOutputs>
  <OutputDir>obj\Debug\net8.0\</OutputDir>
  <Generator>MSBuild:Compile</Generator>
<Protobuf>
```

They both usually achieve the same ends. The first is more concise and recommended for use.

Building a Hello World gRPC client

We will add an ASP.NET Core MVC website project and then add the gRPC client packages to enable it to call the gRPC service:

1. Use your preferred code editor to add a new project, as defined in the following list:

    *   Project template: **ASP.NET Core Web App (Model-View-Controller)** / mvc
    *   Solution file and folder: Chapter13
    *   Project file and folder: Northwind.Grpc.Client.Mvc
    *   **Authentication type:** None.
    *   **Configure for HTTPS:** Selected.
    *   **Enable Docker:** Cleared.
    *   **Do not use top-level statements:** Cleared.

2. In the Northwind.Grpc.Client.Mvc project, treat warnings as errors, add package references for Microsoft's gRPC client factory and tools, and Google's .NET library for Protocol Buffers, as shown in the following markup:

    ```xml
    <ItemGroup>
      <PackageReference Include="Google.Protobuf" Version="3.24.4" />
      <PackageReference Include="Grpc.Net.ClientFactory" Version="2.57.0" />
    ```

```xml
<PackageReference Include="Grpc.Tools" Version="2.58.0">
  <PrivateAssets>all</PrivateAssets>
  <IncludeAssets>runtime; build; native; contentfiles;
    analyzers; buildtransitive</IncludeAssets>
</PackageReference>
</ItemGroup>
```

Good Practice: The `Grpc.Net.ClientFactory` package references the `Grpc.Net.Client` package that implements client-side support for gRPC in a .NET project, but it does not reference other packages like `Grpc.Tools` or `Google.Protobuf`. We must reference those packages explicitly. The `Grpc.Tools` package is only used during development, so it is marked as `PrivateAssets=all` to ensure that the tools are not published with the production website.

3. In the `Properties` folder, open `launchSettings.json`, and for the `https` profile, modify the `applicationUrl` setting to use ports 5133 for `https` and 5134 for `http`, as shown highlighted in the following partial markup:

```json
"profiles": {
  ...
  "https": {
    "commandName": "Project",
    "dotnetRunMessages": true,
    "launchBrowser": true,
    "applicationUrl": "https://localhost:5133;http://localhost:5134",
    "environmentVariables": {
      "ASPNETCORE_ENVIRONMENT": "Development"
    }
  }
```

4. Copy the `Protos` folder from the `Northwind.Grpc.Service` project/folder to the `Northwind.Grpc.Client.Mvc` project/folder.

In Visual Studio 2022, you can drag and drop to copy. In Visual Studio Code or JetBrains Rider, drag and drop while holding the *Ctrl* or *Cmd* key.

5. In the `Northwind.Grpc.Client.Mvc` project, in the `Protos` folder, in `greet.proto`, modify the namespace to match the namespace for the current project so that the automatically generated classes will be in the same namespace, as shown in the following code:

```
option csharp_namespace = "Northwind.Grpc.Client.Mvc";
```

6. In the `Northwind.Grpc.Client.Mvc` project file, add or modify the item group that registers the `.proto` file to indicate that it is being used on the client side, as shown highlighted in the following markup:

```
<ItemGroup>
  <Protobuf Include="Protos\greet.proto" GrpcServices="Client" />
</ItemGroup>
```

 Visual Studio 2022 will have created the item group for you, but it will set `GrpcServices` to `Server` by default, so you must manually change that to `Client`. For other code editors, you might have to create the whole `<ItemGroup>` manually. JetBrains Rider has more configuration but you can ignore it.

7. Build the `Northwind.Grpc.Client.Mvc` project to ensure that the automatically generated classes are created.

8. In the `Northwind.Grpc.Client.Mvc` project, in the `obj\Debug\net8.0\Protos` folder, in `GreetGrpc.cs`, note the `Greeter.GreeterClient` class, as partially shown in the following code:

```
public static partial class Greeter
{
  ...
  public partial class GreeterClient : grpc::ClientBase<GreeterClient>
  {
```

9. In `Program.cs`, import the namespace for `Greeter.GreeterClient`, as shown in the following code:

```
using Northwind.Grpc.Client.Mvc; // To use Greeter.GreeterClient.
```

10. In `Program.cs`, in the section for configuring services, write a statement to add the `GreeterClient` as a named gRPC client that will be communicating with a service that is listening on port 5131, as shown in the following code:

```
builder.Services.AddGrpcClient<Greeter.GreeterClient>("Greeter",
  options =>
  {
    options.Address = new Uri("https://localhost:5131");
  });
```

11. In the `Models` folder, add a new class named `HomeIndexViewModel.cs`.

12. In `HomeIndexViewModel.cs`, define a class to store a greeting and an error message, as shown in the following code:

```
namespace Northwind.Grpc.Client.Mvc.Models;

public class HomeIndexViewModel
```

```
{
  public string? Greeting { get; set; }
  public string? ErrorMessage { get; set; }
}
```

13. In the `Controllers` folder, in `HomeController.cs`, import the namespace to work with the gRPC client factory, as shown in the following code:

```
using Grpc.Net.ClientFactory; // To use GrpcClientFactory.
```

14. In the `Controller` class, declare a field to store a `Greeter Client` instance and set it by using the client factory in the constructor, as shown highlighted in the following code:

```
public class HomeController : Controller
{
  private readonly ILogger<HomeController> _logger;
  private readonly Greeter.GreeterClient _greeterClient;

  public HomeController(ILogger<HomeController> logger,
    GrpcClientFactory factory)
  {
    _logger = logger;
    _greeterClient = factory.CreateClient<Greeter.
GreeterClient>("Greeter");
  }
```

15. In the `Index` action method, make the method asynchronous, add a `string` parameter named name with a default value of `Henrietta`, and then add statements to use the gRPC client to call the `SayHelloAsync` method, passing a `HelloRequest` object and storing the `HelloReply` response in `ViewData`, while catching any exceptions, as shown highlighted in the following code:

```
public async Task<IActionResult> Index(string name = "Henrietta")
{
  HomeIndexViewModel model = new();

  try
  {
    HelloReply reply = await _greeterClient.SayHelloAsync(
      new HelloRequest { Name = name });

    model.Greeting = "Greeting from gRPC service: " + reply.Message;
  }
  catch (Exception ex)
  {
```

```
    _logger.LogWarning($"Northwind.Grpc.Service is not responding.");

    model.ErrorMessage = ex.Message;
  }

  return View(model);
}
```

16. In `Views/Home`, in `Index.cshtml`, after the **Welcome** heading, remove the existing `<p>` element and then add markup to render a form for the visitor to enter their name, and then if they submit and the gRPC service responds, to output the greeting, as shown highlighted in the following markup:

```
@using Northwind.Grpc.Client.Mvc.Models
@model HomeIndexViewModel
@{
  ViewData["Title"] = "Home Page";
}
<div class="text-center">
  <h1 class="display-4">Welcome</h1>
  <div class="alert alert-secondary">
    <form>
      <input name="name" placeholder="Enter your name" />
      <input type="submit" />
    </form>
  </div>
  @if (Model.Greeting is not null)
  {
    <p class="alert alert-primary">@Model.Greeting</p>
  }
  @if (Model.ErrorMessage is not null)
  {
    <p class="alert alert-danger">@Model.ErrorMessage</p>
  }
</div>
```

If you clean a gRPC project, then you will lose the automatically generated types and see compile errors. To recreate them, simply make any change to a `.proto` file or close and reopen the project/solution.

Testing a gRPC service and client

Now we can start the gRPC service and see if the MVC website can call it successfully:

1. Start the `Northwind.Grpc.Service` project without debugging.

2. Start the `Northwind.Grpc.Client.Mvc` project.

3. If necessary, start a browser and navigate to the home page: `https://localhost:5133/`.

4. Note the greeting on the home page, as shown in *Figure 13.4*:

Figure 13.4: Home page after calling the gRPC service to get a greeting

5. View the command prompt or terminal for the ASP.NET Core MVC project and note the info messages that indicate an HTTP/2 `POST` was processed by the `greet.Greeter/SayHello` endpoint in about 41ms, as shown in the following output:

```
info: System.Net.Http.HttpClient.Greeter.LogicalHandler[100]
      Start processing HTTP request POST https://localhost:5131/greet.
Greeter/SayHello
info: System.Net.Http.HttpClient.Greeter.ClientHandler[100]
      Sending HTTP request POST https://localhost:5131/greet.Greeter/
SayHello
info: System.Net.Http.HttpClient.Greeter.ClientHandler[101]
      Received HTTP response headers after 60.5352ms - 200
info: System.Net.Http.HttpClient.Greeter.LogicalHandler[101]
      End processing HTTP request after 69.1623ms - 200
```

6. Enter and submit your own name on the page.

7. Close the browser and shut down the web servers.

Implementing gRPC for an EF Core model

Now we will add a service for working with the Northwind database to the gRPC project.

Implementing the gRPC service

We will reference the EF Core model that you created in *Chapter 3, Building Entity Models for SQL Server Using EF Core*, then define a contract for the gRPC service using a `.proto` file, and finally implement the service.

We will start with the Shippers table because it is simple. Each shipper only has three properties, an int and two string values, and there are only three records in the table. Let's go:

1. In the Northwind.Grpc.Service project, add a project reference to the Northwind database context project, as shown in the following markup:

```
<ItemGroup>
  <ProjectReference Include="..\..\Chapter03\Northwind.Common.DataContext
.SqlServer\Northwind.Common.DataContext.SqlServer.csproj" />
</ItemGroup>
```

 The Include path must not have a line break.

2. At the command prompt or terminal, build the Northwind.Grpc.Service project, as shown in the following command: dotnet build.

3. In the Northwind.Grpc.Service project, in the Protos folder, add a new file (the item template is named **Protocol Buffer File** in Visual Studio 2022) named shipper.proto, as shown in the following code:

```
syntax = "proto3";

option csharp_namespace = "Northwind.Grpc.Service";

package shipper;

service Shipper {
  rpc GetShipper (ShipperRequest) returns (ShipperReply);
}

message ShipperRequest {
  int32 shipper_id = 1;
}

message ShipperReply {
  int32 shipper_id = 1;
  string company_name = 2;
  string phone = 3;
}
```

4. Open the project file and add an entry to include the `shipper.proto` file, as shown highlighted in the following markup:

```
<ItemGroup>
  <Protobuf Include="Protos\greet.proto" GrpcServices="Server" />
  <Protobuf Include="Protos\shipper.proto" GrpcServices="Server" />
</ItemGroup>
```

5. Build the `Northwind.Grpc.Service` project.

6. In the `Services` folder, add a new class file named `ShipperService.cs`, and modify its contents to define a shipper service that uses the Northwind database context to return shippers, as shown in the following code:

```
using Grpc.Core; // To use ServerCallContext.
using Northwind.EntityModels; // To use NorthwindContext.
using ShipperEntity = Northwind.EntityModels.Shipper;

namespace Northwind.Grpc.Service.Services;

public class ShipperService : Shipper.ShipperBase
{
  private readonly ILogger<ShipperService> _logger;
  private readonly NorthwindContext _db;

  public ShipperService(ILogger<ShipperService> logger,
    NorthwindContext context)
  {
    _logger = logger;
    _db = context;
  }

  public override async Task<ShipperReply?> GetShipper(
    ShipperRequest request, ServerCallContext context)
  {
    ShipperEntity? shipper = await _db.Shippers
      .FindAsync(request.ShipperId);

    return shipper is null ? null : ToShipperReply(shipper);
  }

  // A mapping method to convert from a Shipper in the
  // entity model to a gRPC ShipperReply.
  private ShipperReply ToShipperReply(ShipperEntity shipper)
```

```
      {
        return new ShipperReply
        {
          ShipperId = shipper.ShipperId,
          CompanyName = shipper.CompanyName,
          Phone = shipper.Phone
        };
      }
}
```

> The .proto file generates classes that represent the messages sent to and from a
> gRPC service. We therefore cannot use the entity classes defined for the EF Core
> model. We need a helper method like ToShipperReply that can map an instance of
> an entity class to an instance of the .proto-generated classes like ShipperReply.
> This could be a good use for AutoMapper, although in this case, the mapping is
> simple enough to hand-code.

7. In Program.cs, import the namespace for the Northwind database context, as shown in the
    following code:

    ```
    using Northwind.EntityModels; // To use AddNorthwindContext method.
    ```

8. In the section that configures services, add a call to register the Northwind database context,
    as shown in the following code:

    ```
    builder.Services.AddNorthwindContext();
    ```

9. In the section that configures the HTTP pipeline, after the call to register GreeterService, add
    a statement to register ShipperService, as shown in the following code:

    ```
    app.MapGrpcService<ShipperService>();
    ```

Implementing the gRPC client

Now we can add client capabilities to the Northwind MVC website:

1. Copy the shipper.proto file from the Protos folder in the Northwind.Grpc.Service project
    to the Protos folder in the Northwind.Grpc.Client.Mvc project.

2. In the Northwind.Grpc.Client.Mvc project, in shipper.proto, modify the namespace to
    match the namespace for the current project so that the automatically generated classes will
    be in the same namespace, as shown highlighted in the following code:

    ```
    option csharp_namespace = "Northwind.Grpc.Client.Mvc";
    ```

3. In the `Northwind.Grpc.Client.Mvc` project file, modify or add the entry to register the `.proto` file as being used on the client side, as shown highlighted in the following markup:

```
<ItemGroup>
  <Protobuf Include="Protos\greet.proto" GrpcServices="Client" />
  <Protobuf Include="Protos\shipper.proto" GrpcServices="Client" />
</ItemGroup>
```

 If you are using a code editor like JetBrains Rider that adds extra configuration, I recommend that you simplify the elements as shown in the preceding markup. If you do not, then you might get errors later in this coding task.

4. In the `Northwind.Grpc.Client.Mvc` project file, in `Program.cs`, add a statement to register the `ShipperClient` class to connect to the gRPC service listening on port 5131, as shown in the following code:

```
builder.Services.AddGrpcClient<Shipper.ShipperClient>("Shipper",
  options =>
  {
    options.Address = new Uri("https://localhost:5131");
  });
```

5. In the `Models` folder, in `HomeIndexViewModel.cs`, add a property to store a summary of a shipper, as shown in the following code:

```
public string? ShipperSummary { get; set; }
```

6. In the `Controllers` folder, in `HomeController.cs`, declare a field to store a shipper client instance and set it by using the client factory in the constructor, as shown highlighted in the following code:

```
public class HomeController : Controller
{
  private readonly ILogger<HomeController> _logger;
  private readonly Greeter.GreeterClient _greeterClient;
  private readonly Shipper.ShipperClient _shipperClient;

  public HomeController(ILogger<HomeController> logger,
    GrpcClientFactory factory)
  {
    _logger = logger;
    _greeterClient = factory.CreateClient<Greeter.
GreeterClient>("Greeter");
```

```
    _shipperClient = factory.CreateClient<Shipper.
ShipperClient>("Shipper");
    }
```

7. In `HomeController.cs`, in the `Index` action method, add a parameter named `id` and statements to call the `Shipper` gRPC service to get a shipper with the matching `ShipperId`, as shown highlighted in the following code:

```
public async Task<IActionResult> Index(
    string name = "Henrietta", int id = 1)
{
    HomeIndexViewModel model = new();

    try
    {
        HelloReply reply = await greeterClient.SayHelloAsync(
            new HelloRequest { Name = name });

        model.Greeting = "Greeting from gRPC service: " + reply.Message;

        ShipperReply shipperReply = await _shipperClient.GetShipperAsync(
            new ShipperRequest { ShipperId = id });

        model.ShipperSummary = "Shipper from gRPC service: " +
            $"ID: {shipperReply.ShipperId}, Name: {shipperReply.CompanyName},"
            + $" Phone: {shipperReply.Phone}.";
    }
    catch (Exception ex)
    {
        _logger.LogWarning($"Northwind.Grpc.Service is not responding.");

        model.ErrorMessage = ex.Message;
    }

    return View();
}
```

8. In `Views/Home`, in `Index.cshtml`, add code to render a form for the visitor to enter a shipper ID, and render the shipper details after the greeting, as shown highlighted in the following markup:

```
@using Northwind.Grpc.Client.Mvc.Models
@model HomeIndexViewModel
@{
```

```
    ViewData["Title"] = "Home Page";
}
<div class="text-center">
  <h1 class="display-4">Welcome</h1>
  <div class="alert alert-secondary">
    <form>
      <input name="name" placeholder="Enter your name" />
      <input type="submit" />
    </form>
    <form>
      <input name="id" placeholder="Enter a shipper id" />
      <input type="submit" />
    </form>
  </div>
  @if (Model.Greeting is not null)
  {
    <p class="alert alert-primary">@Model.Greeting</p>
  }
  @if (Model.ErrorMessage is not null)
  {
    <p class="alert alert-danger">@Model.ErrorMessage</p>
  }
  @if (Model.ShipperSummary is not null)
  {
    <p class="alert alert-primary">@Model.ShipperSummary</p>
  }
</div>
```

9. If your database server is not running, for example, because you are hosting it in Docker, a virtual machine, or in the cloud, then make sure to start it.

10. Start the `Northwind.Grpc.Service` project without debugging.

11. Start the `Northwind.Grpc.Client.Mvc` project.

12. If necessary, start a browser and navigate to the MVC website home page: `https://localhost:5133/`.

13. Note that an exception is thrown in the gRPC service because the `GetShipper` method uses EF Core, which is attempting to dynamically compile a LINQ query, and that is not supported with native AOT compilation, as shown in the following partial output:

```
fail: Grpc.AspNetCore.Server.ServerCallHandler[6]
      Error when executing service method 'GetShipper'.
      System.PlatformNotSupportedException: Dynamic code generation is
not supported on this platform.
```

```
        at System.Reflection.Emit.AssemblyBuilder.
ThrowDynamicCodeNotSupported()

...

        at Microsoft.EntityFrameworkCore.Storage.Database.
CompileQuery[TResult](Expression query, Boolean async)

...

        at Northwind.Grpc.Service.Services.ShipperService.
GetShipper(ShipperRequest request, ServerCallContext context) in C:\apps-
services-net8\Chapter13\Northwind.Grpc.Service\Services\ShipperService.
cs:line 22

...
```

14. Close the browser and shut down the web servers.

15. In the project file, comment out the publish AOT option, as shown in the following markup:

```
<!--<PublishAot>true</PublishAot>-->
```

 You might be wondering what the point was of enabling AOT when we created the project and chose to implement parts of the service using EF Core, if we were just going to have to disable AOT later. Two reasons: I want you to see the error so you recognize it if you try to do similar with your own gRPC projects, and we *will* be able to use EF Core in the future with .NET 9 or .NET 10.

16. Start the `Northwind.Grpc.Service` project without debugging.

17. Start the `Northwind.Grpc.Client.Mvc` project.

18. Note the shipper information on the services page, as shown in *Figure 13.5*:

Welcome

Enter your name | Submit
Enter a shipper id | Submit

Greeting from gRPC service: Hello Henrietta

Shipper from gRPC service: ID: 1, Name: Speedy Express, Phone: (503) 555-9831.

Figure 13.5: Home page after calling the gRPC service to get a shipper

19. There are three shippers in the Northwind database with IDs of 1, 2, and 3. Try entering their IDs to ensure they can all be retrieved, and try entering an ID that does not exist, like 4.

20. Close the browser and shut down the web servers.

Taking gRPC further

Now let's look at some more advanced topics like native AOT compilation support, getting metadata, adding deadlines, handling dates, times, and decimal types, adding interceptors, and handling exceptions and transient faults.

Improving a gRPC service with native AOT publish

.NET 8 introduces gRPC support for native AOT. But as you have just seen, it is not (yet) compatible with some parts of .NET like EF Core.

Let's change our gRPC service to use the SQL client instead of EF Core. We will leave most of the EF Core code in the project so you can switch back if you want in the future, for example, if you upgrade to EF Core 9 and it supports native AOT:

1. In the `Northwind.Grpc.Service` project, uncomment out the option to publish AOT and add a package reference for the SQL client, as shown in the following markup:

    ```
    <PackageReference Include="Microsoft.Data.SqlClient" Version="5.1.2" />
    ```

2. In the `Services` folder, in `ShipperService.cs`, import namespaces for working with `SqlClient`, as shown in the following code:

    ```
    using Microsoft.Data.SqlClient; // To use SqlConnection and so on.
    using System.Data; // To use CommandType.
    ```

3. In the `GetShipper` method, comment out the statements to get the shipper from the Northwind data context, and replace it with code to get the shipper using `SqlClient`, as shown highlighted in the following code:

    ```
    public override async Task<ShipperReply?> GetShipper(
      ShipperRequest request, ServerCallContext context)
    {
      // We cannot use EF Core in a native AOT compiled project.
      // ShipperEntity? shipper = await _db.Shippers
      //   .FindAsync(request.ShipperId);

      SqlConnectionStringBuilder builder = new();

      builder.InitialCatalog = "Northwind";
      builder.MultipleActiveResultSets = true;
      builder.Encrypt = true;
      builder.TrustServerCertificate = true;
      builder.ConnectTimeout = 10; // Default is 30 seconds.
      builder.DataSource = "."; // To use local SQL Server.
      builder.IntegratedSecurity = true;
    ```

```
/*
// To use SQL Server Authentication:
builder.UserID = Environment.GetEnvironmentVariable("MY_SQL_USR");
builder.Password = Environment.GetEnvironmentVariable("MY_SQL_PWD");
builder.PersistSecurityInfo = false;
*/

SqlConnection connection = new(builder.ConnectionString);

await connection.OpenAsync();

SqlCommand cmd = connection.CreateCommand();

cmd.CommandType = CommandType.Text;
cmd.CommandText = "SELECT ShipperId, CompanyName, Phone"
  + " FROM Shippers WHERE ShipperId = @id";
cmd.Parameters.AddWithValue("id", request.ShipperId);

SqlDataReader r = await cmd.ExecuteReaderAsync(
  CommandBehavior.SingleRow);

ShipperReply? shipper = null;

// Read the expected single row.
if (await r.ReadAsync())
{
  shipper = new()
  {
    ShipperId = r.GetInt32("ShipperId"),
    CompanyName = r.GetString("CompanyName"),
    Phone = r.GetString("Phone")
  };
}

await r.CloseAsync();

return shipper;
}
```

4. Double-check that you have re-enabled the publish AOT option.

5. In `Program.cs`, we could alter a statement to use the slim builder for the web application, as shown in the following code:

```
// Use the slim builder to reduce the size of the application
// when using the publish AOT project option.
// var builder = WebApplication.CreateSlimBuilder(args);
```

> The `CreateSlimBuilder` method does not include support for HTTPS or HTTP/3, although you can add those back in yourself if you need them. If we switch to the slim builder, then we must also switch from using HTTPS to HTTP to communicate with the gRPC service. In this task, we will continue to use the "full fat" builder so we can continue to use HTTPS.

6. In the `Northwind.Grpc.Service` project file, add an element to emit compiler-generated files, as shown highlighted in the following markup:

```
<PropertyGroup>
  <TargetFramework>net8.0</TargetFramework>
  ...
  <EmitCompilerGeneratedFiles>true</EmitCompilerGeneratedFiles>
</PropertyGroup>
```

7. Build the `Northwind.Grpc.Service` project.

8. If you are using Visual Studio 2022, toggle **Show All Files** in **Solution Explorer**. If you are using JetBrains Rider, hover over and then click the eyeball icon.

9. Expand the `obj\Debug\net8.0\generated` folder, and then note the folders and files that have been created by the source generators for AOT and JSON serialization, as shown in *Figure 13.6*:

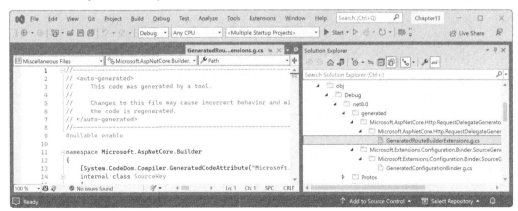

Figure 13.6: Folders and files created by source generators in an AOT gRPC project

10. At the command prompt or terminal, publish the gRPC service using native AOT, as shown in the following command:

```
dotnet publish
```

11. Note the message about generating native code and trim warnings for packages like `Microsoft.Data.SqlClient`, as shown in the following partial output:

```
Generating native code
...
C:\Users\markj\.nuget\packages\microsoft.data.sqlclient\5.1.1\runtimes\
win\lib\net6.0\Microsoft.Data.SqlClient.dll : warning IL2104: Assembly
'Microsoft
.Data.SqlClient' produced trim warnings. For more information see
https://aka.ms/dotnet-illink/libraries [C:\apps-services-net8\Chapter13\
Northwind.Grpc.Service\Northwind.Grpc.Service.csproj]
...
```

12. Start **File Explorer** and open the `bin\Release\net8.0\win-x64\publish` folder and note the EXE file is about 45 MB. This and the `Microsoft.Data.SqlClient.SNI.dll` file are the only files that need to be deployed onto another Windows computer for the web service to work. The `appsettings.json` files are only needed to override configuration if needed. The PDB files are only needed if debugging and, anyway, two of them are only because we left the EF Core code in the project for reference to make it easier to switch back to non-AOT publishing.

13. Open the `bin\Release\net8.0\win-x64\publish` folder at the command prompt or terminal.

14. At the command prompt or terminal, run `Northwind.Grpc.Service.exe` and explicitly specify the URL with the port number to use, as shown in the following command:

```
Northwind.Grpc.Service.exe --urls "https://localhost:5131"
```

 The `launchSettings.json` file is only used by code editors like Visual Studio 2022 so the ports specified there are ignored and not deployed with the service in production.

15. Start the `Northwind.Grpc.Client.Mvc` project.

16. Note the web page shows the shipper with an ID of 1 and that you can search for the other shippers.

17. Close the browser and shut down the web servers.

 More Information: You can learn more about gRPC and native AOT at the following link: https://learn.microsoft.com/en-us/aspnet/core/grpc/native-aot.

Getting request and response metadata

Formally defined request and response messages as part of a contract are not the only mechanisms to pass data between a client and service using gRPC. You can also use metadata sent as headers and trailers. Both are simple dictionaries that are passed along with the messages.

Let's see how you can get metadata about a gRPC call:

1. In the Northwind.Grpc.Client.Mvc project, in the Controllers folder, in HomeController.cs, import the namespace to use the AsyncUnaryCall<T> class, as shown in the following code:

   ```
   using Grpc.Core; // To use AsyncUnaryCall<T>.
   ```

2. In the Index method, comment out the statement that makes the call to the gRPC shipper service. Add statements that get the underlying AsyncUnaryCall<T> object, then use it to get the headers, output them to the log, and then get the response, as shown highlighted in the following code:

   ```
   // ShipperReply shipperReply = await _shipperClient.GetShipperAsync(
   //    new ShipperRequest { ShipperId = id });

   // The same call as above but not awaited.
   AsyncUnaryCall<ShipperReply> shipperCall = _shipperClient.
   GetShipperAsync(
     new ShipperRequest { ShipperId = id });

   Metadata metadata = await shipperCall.ResponseHeadersAsync;

   foreach (Metadata.Entry entry in metadata)
   {
     // Not really critical, just doing this to make it easier to see.
     _logger.LogCritical($"Key: {entry.Key}, Value: {entry.Value}");
   }

   ShipperReply shipperReply = await shipperCall.ResponseAsync;

   ViewData["shipper"] = "Shipper from gRPC service: " +
     $"ID: {shipperReply.ShipperId}, Name: {shipperReply.CompanyName},"
     + $" Phone: {shipperReply.Phone}.";
   ```

3. Start the Northwind.Grpc.Service project without debugging.
4. Start the Northwind.Grpc.Client.Mvc project.
5. If necessary, start a browser and navigate to the home page: https://localhost:5133/.

6. Note the client successfully making POST requests to the gRPC Greeter and Shipper services and the red critical messages outputting the two entries in the gRPC metadata for the call to GetShipper, with keys of date and server, as shown in *Figure 13.7*:

```
C:\apps-services-net8\Chapter13\Northwind.Grpc.Client.Mvc\bin\Debug\net8.0\Northwind.Grpc.Client.Mvc.exe    X    +    ∨        −    □    ×
info: Microsoft.Hosting.Lifetime[0]
      Content root path: C:\apps-services-net8\Chapter13\Northwind.Grpc.Client.Mvc
info: System.Net.Http.HttpClient.Greeter.LogicalHandler[100]
      Start processing HTTP request POST https://localhost:5131/greet.Greeter/SayHello
info: System.Net.Http.HttpClient.Greeter.ClientHandler[100]
      Sending HTTP request POST https://localhost:5131/greet.Greeter/SayHello
info: System.Net.Http.HttpClient.Greeter.ClientHandler[101]
      Received HTTP response headers after 249.2595ms - 200
info: System.Net.Http.HttpClient.Greeter.LogicalHandler[101]
      End processing HTTP request after 261.7622ms - 200
info: System.Net.Http.HttpClient.Shipper.LogicalHandler[100]
      Start processing HTTP request POST https://localhost:5131/shipper.Shipper/GetShipper
info: System.Net.Http.HttpClient.Shipper.ClientHandler[100]
      Sending HTTP request POST https://localhost:5131/shipper.Shipper/GetShipper
info: System.Net.Http.HttpClient.Shipper.ClientHandler[101]
      Received HTTP response headers after 1278.3375ms - 200
info: System.Net.Http.HttpClient.Shipper.LogicalHandler[101]
      End processing HTTP request after 1278.4549ms - 200
crit: Northwind.Grpc.Client.Mvc.Controllers.HomeController[0]
      Key: date, Value: Tue, 13 Jun 2023 13:57:22 GMT
crit: Northwind.Grpc.Client.Mvc.Controllers.HomeController[0]
      Key: server, Value: Kestrel
```

Figure 13.7: Logging metadata from a gRPC call

7. Close the browser and shut down the web servers.

   The trailers equivalent of the ResponseHeadersAsync property is the GetTrailers method. It has a return value of Metadata that contains the dictionary of trailers. Trailers are accessible at the end of a call.

Adding a deadline for higher reliability

Setting a deadline for a gRPC call is recommended practice because it controls the upper limit of how long a gRPC call can run. It prevents gRPC services from potentially consuming too many server resources.

The deadline information is sent to the service, so the service has an opportunity to give up its work once the deadline has passed instead of continuing forever. Even if the server completes its work within the deadline, the client may give up before the response arrives at the client because the deadline has passed due to the overhead of communication.

Let's see an example:

1. In the Northwind.Grpc.Service project, in the Services folder, in ShipperService.cs, in the GetShipper method, add statements to log the deadline and to pause for five seconds, as shown highlighted in the following code:

```
public override async Task<ShipperReply> GetShipper(
    ShipperRequest request, ServerCallContext context)
```

```
{
    _logger.LogCritical($"This request has a deadline of {
      context.Deadline:T}. It is now {DateTime.UtcNow:T}.");

    await Task.Delay(TimeSpan.FromSeconds(5));

    ...
}
```

2. In the `Northwind.Grpc.Service` project, in `appsettings.Development.json`, modify the logging level for ASP.NET Core from the default of `Warning` to `Information`, as shown highlighted in the following configuration:

```
{
  "Logging": {
    "LogLevel": {
      "Default": "Information",
      "Microsoft.AspNetCore": "Information"
    }
  }
}
```

3. In the `Northwind.Grpc.Client.Mvc` project, in the `Controllers` folder, in `HomeController.cs`, in the `Index` method, set a deadline of three seconds when calling the `GetShipperAsync` method, as shown highlighted in the following code:

```
AsyncUnaryCall<ShipperReply> shipperCall = shipperClient.GetShipperAsync(
  new ShipperRequest { ShipperId = id },
  // Deadline must be a UTC DateTime.
  deadline: DateTime.UtcNow.AddSeconds(3));
```

4. In `HomeController.cs`, in the `Index` method, before the existing `catch` block, add a `catch` block for an `RpcException` when the exception's status code matches the code for deadline exceeded, as shown highlighted in the following code:

```
catch (RpcException rpcex) when (rpcex.StatusCode ==
  global::Grpc.Core.StatusCode.DeadlineExceeded)
{
  _logger.LogWarning("Northwind.Grpc.Service deadline exceeded.");

  model.ErrorMessage = rpcex.Message;
}
catch (Exception ex)
{
  _logger.LogWarning($"Northwind.Grpc.Service is not responding.");
```

```
        model.ErrorMessage = ex.Message;
    }
```

5. In the `Northwind.Grpc.Client.Mvc` project, in `appsettings.Development.json`, modify the logging level for ASP.NET Core from the default of `Warning` to `Information`, as shown highlighted in the following configuration:

```
{
  "Logging": {
    "LogLevel": {
      "Default": "Information",
      "Microsoft.AspNetCore": "Information"
    }
  }
}
```

6. Start the `Northwind.Grpc.Service` project without debugging.

7. Start the `Northwind.Grpc.Client.Mvc` project.

8. If necessary, start a browser and navigate to the home page: `https://localhost:5133/`.

9. At the command prompt or terminal for the gRPC service, note the request has a three-second deadline, as shown in the following output:

```
crit: Northwind.Grpc.Service.Services.ShipperService[0]
      This request has a deadline of 14:56:30. It is now 14:56:27.
```

10. In the browser, note that after three seconds, the home page shows a deadline exceeded exception, as shown in *Figure 13.8*:

Figure 13.8: A deadline has been exceeded

11. At the command prompt or terminal for the ASP.NET Core MVC client, note the logs that start at the point where a request is made to the `GetShipper` method on the gRPC service, but the deadline is exceeded, as shown in the following output:

```
info: System.Net.Http.HttpClient.Shipper.LogicalHandler[100]
        Start processing HTTP request POST https://localhost:5131/shipper.
Shipper/GetShipper
info: System.Net.Http.HttpClient.Shipper.ClientHandler[100]
        Sending HTTP request POST https://localhost:5131/shipper.Shipper/
GetShipper
warn: Grpc.Net.Client.Internal.GrpcCall[7]
        gRPC call deadline exceeded.
info: Grpc.Net.Client.Internal.GrpcCall[3]
        Call failed with gRPC error status. Status code:
'DeadlineExceeded', Message: ''.
```

12. Close the browser and shut down the web servers.

13. In `ShipperService.cs`, comment out the statement that causes a five-second delay, as shown in the following code:

```
// await Task.Delay(TimeSpan.FromSeconds(5));
```

 Good Practice: The default is no deadline. Always set a deadline in the client call. In your service implementation, get the deadline and use it to automatically abandon the work if it is exceeded. Pass the cancellation token to any asynchronous calls so that work completes quickly on the server and frees up resources.

Handling dates, times, and decimal numbers

You might have noted that there are no date/time types built into gRPC. To store these values, you must use well-known type extensions, for example, `google.protobuf.Timestamp` (equivalent to `DateTimeOffset`) and `google.protobuf.Duration` (equivalent to `TimeSpan`).

To use them as field types in a message, they must be imported, as shown in the following code:

```
syntax = "proto3";

import "google/protobuf/duration.proto";
import "google/protobuf/timestamp.proto";

message Employee {
  int32 employeeId = 1;
  google.protobuf.Timestamp birth_date = 2;
  google.protobuf.Duration earned_vacation_time = 3;

  ...
}
```

The class generated will not use .NET types directly. Instead, there are intermediate types, as shown in the following code:

```
public class Employee
{
  public int EmployeeId;
  public Timestamp BirthDate;
  public Duration EarnedVacationTime;
}
```

There are conversion methods on the types `FromDateTimeOffset`, `ToDateTimeOffset`, `FromTimeSpan`, and `ToTimeSpan`, as shown in the following code:

```
Employee employee = new()
{
  EmployeeId = 1,
  BirthDate = Timestamp.FromDateTimeOffset(new DateTimeOffset(
    year: 1998, month: 11, day: 30, hour: 0, minute: 0, second: 0,
    offset: TimeSpan.FromHours(-5)),
  EarnedVacationTime = Duration.FromTimeSpan(TimeSpan.FromDays(15))
};

DateTimeOffset when = employee.BirthDate.ToDateTimeOffset();
TimeSpan daysoff = employee.EarnedVacationTime.ToTimeSpan();
```

gRPC also does not natively support `decimal` values. In the future, that support might be added, but for now, you must create a custom message to represent it. If you choose to do this, then keep in mind that developers on other platforms will have to understand your custom format and implement their own handling for it.

Defining a custom decimal type and using date/time types

Let's add gRPC services for working with products (which have a `UnitPrice` property that is a `decimal`) and employees (which have `HireDate` properties that are `DateTime` values):

1. In the `Northwind.Grpc.Service` project, in the `Protos` folder, add a new file named `decimal.proto`, and add statements to define a message format for safely storing a decimal value, as shown in the following code:

    ```
    syntax = "proto3";

    option csharp_namespace = "Northwind.Grpc.Service";

    package decimal;

    // Example: 12345.6789 -> { units = 12345, nanos = 678900000 }
    ```

```
message DecimalValue {

    // To store the whole units part of the amount.
    int64 units = 1;

    // To store the nano units of the amount (10^-9).
    // Must be same sign as units.
    sfixed32 nanos = 2;
}
```

2. Add a new file named `product.proto`, and add statements to define messages and service methods to get one product, all products, or products that cost a minimum price, as shown in the following code:

```
syntax = "proto3";

option csharp_namespace = "Northwind.Grpc.Service";

import "Protos/decimal.proto";

package product;

service Product {
  rpc GetProduct (ProductRequest) returns (ProductReply);
  rpc GetProducts (ProductsRequest) returns (ProductsReply);
  rpc GetProductsMinimumPrice (ProductsMinimumPriceRequest)
      returns (ProductsReply);
}

message ProductRequest {
  int32 product_id = 1;
}

message ProductsRequest {
}

message ProductsMinimumPriceRequest {
  decimal.DecimalValue minimum_price = 1;
}

message ProductReply {
```

```
    int32 product_id = 1;
    string product_name = 2;
    int32 supplier_id = 3;
    int32 category_id = 4;
    string quantity_per_unit = 5;
    decimal.DecimalValue unit_price = 6;
    int32 units_in_stock = 7;
    int32 units_on_order = 8;
    int32 reorder_level = 9;
    bool discontinued = 10;
}

message ProductsReply {
    repeated ProductReply products = 1;
}
```

3. Add a new file named employee.proto, and modify it to define messages and service methods to get one employee or all employees, and note we must import the Google extension for timestamp.proto, as shown in the following code:

```
syntax = "proto3";

option csharp_namespace = "Northwind.Grpc.Service";

import "google/protobuf/duration.proto";
import "google/protobuf/timestamp.proto";

package employee;

service Employee {
  rpc GetEmployee (EmployeeRequest) returns (EmployeeReply);
  rpc GetEmployees (EmployeesRequest) returns (EmployeesReply);
}

message EmployeeRequest {
  int32 employee_id = 1;
}

message EmployeesRequest {
}

message EmployeeReply {
```

```
    int32 employee_id = 1;
    string last_name = 2;
    string first_name = 3;
    string title = 4;
    string title_of_courtesy = 5;
    google.protobuf.Timestamp birth_date = 6;
    google.protobuf.Timestamp hire_date = 7;
    string address = 8;
    string city = 9;
    string region = 10;
    string postal_code = 11;
    string country = 12;
    string home_phone = 13;
    string extension = 14;
    bytes photo = 15;
    string notes = 16;
    int32 reports_to = 17;
    string photo_path = 18;
}

message EmployeesReply {
    repeated EmployeeReply employees = 1;
}
```

4. In the project file, add elements to tell the gRPC tool to process the new .proto files, as shown highlighted in the following markup:

```
<ItemGroup>
  <Protobuf Include="Protos\greet.proto" GrpcServices="Server" />
  <Protobuf Include="Protos\shipper.proto" GrpcServices="Server" />
  <Protobuf Include="Protos\decimal.proto" GrpcServices="Server" />
  <Protobuf Include="Protos\product.proto" GrpcServices="Server" />
  <Protobuf Include="Protos\employee.proto" GrpcServices="Server" />
</ItemGroup>
```

5. Rebuild the project to make sure the gRPC tool has created the C# classes in the obj\Debug\
    net8.0\Protos folder, as shown in *Figure 13.9*:

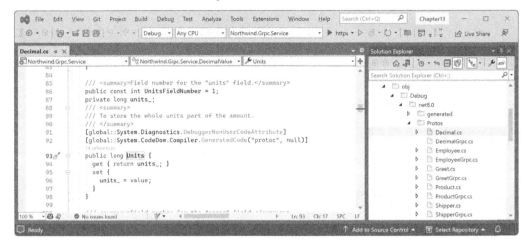

Figure 13.9: gRPC tool-generated classes for a custom decimal type with a Units property

6. In the Northwind.Grpc.Service project, add a new folder named Converters.

7. In the Converters folder, add a new class file named DecimalValue.Converters.cs, and modify
    its contents to extend the partial class created by the gRPC tools with a constructor and a pair
    of operators to convert between our custom DecimalValue type and the built-in .NET decimal
    type, as shown in the following code:

```csharp
namespace Northwind.Grpc.Service;

// This will merge with the DecimalValue type generated by the
// gRPC tools in the obj\Debug\net8.0\Protos\Decimal.cs file.

public partial class DecimalValue
{
  private const decimal NanoFactor = 1_000_000_000;

  public DecimalValue(long units, int nanos)
  {
    Units = units;
    Nanos = nanos;
  }

  public static implicit operator decimal(DecimalValue grpcDecimal)
  {
    return grpcDecimal.Units + (grpcDecimal.Nanos / NanoFactor);
  }
```

```
    public static implicit operator DecimalValue(decimal value)
    {
      long units = decimal.ToInt64(value);
      int nanos = decimal.ToInt32((value - units) * NanoFactor);
      return new DecimalValue(units, nanos);
    }
  }
```

Implementing the product and employee gRPC services

Now we need to implement and register the services:

1. In the `Northwind.Grpc.Service` project, in the `Services` folder, add a new class file named `ProductService.cs` and modify its content to implement the products service. I will leave this as an optional exercise for you, or you can copy the code from the following link: https://github.com/markjprice/apps-services-net8/blob/main/code/Chapter13/Northwind.Grpc.Service/Services/ProductService.cs.

2. In the `Services` folder, add a new class file named `EmployeeService.cs` and modify its content to implement the products service. I will leave this as an optional exercise for you, or you can copy the code from the following link: https://github.com/markjprice/apps-services-net8/blob/main/code/Chapter13/Northwind.Grpc.Service/Services/EmployeeService.cs.

3. In `Program.cs`, register the two new services, as shown in the following code:

    ```
    app.MapGrpcService<ProductService>();
    app.MapGrpcService<EmployeeService>();
    ```

Adding product and employee gRPC clients

Next, we need to add clients to the MVC project to call the two new gRPC services:

1. In the `Northwind.Grpc.Client.Mvc` project, copy the three `.proto` files from the service project to the MVC project `Protos` folder.

2. In the three `.proto` files, modify the namespace, as shown in the following code:

    ```
    option csharp_namespace = "Northwind.Grpc.Client.Mvc";
    ```

3. In the project file, register the three files to create client-side representations, as shown in the following markup:

    ```
    <ItemGroup>
      <Protobuf Include="Protos\greet.proto" GrpcServices="Client" />
      <Protobuf Include="Protos\shipper.proto" GrpcServices="Client" />
      <Protobuf Include="Protos\decimal.proto" GrpcServices="Client" />
      <Protobuf Include="Protos\employee.proto" GrpcServices="Client" />
    ```

```
<Protobuf Include="Protos\product.proto" GrpcServices="Client" />
</ItemGroup>
```

 If you are using a code editor like JetBrains Rider that adds extra configuration, I recommend that you simplify the elements as shown in the preceding markup. If you do not, then you might get errors later in this coding task.

4. Copy the `Converters` folder from the gRPC project to the MVC project.

5. In the `Converters` folder, in `DecimalValue.Converters.cs`, modify the namespace to use the client, as shown in the following code:

```
namespace Northwind.Grpc.Client.Mvc;
```

6. In the `Northwind.Grpc.Client.Mvc` project, in `Program.cs`, add statements to register clients for the two new services, as shown in the following code:

```
builder.Services.AddGrpcClient<Product.ProductClient>("Product",
  options =>
  {
    options.Address = new Uri("https://localhost:5131");
  });

builder.Services.AddGrpcClient<Employee.EmployeeClient>("Employee",
  options =>
  {
    options.Address = new Uri("https://localhost:5131");
  });
```

7. In the `Controllers` folder, in `HomeController.cs`, add two fields for the two new clients and set them in the constructor. (Hint: follow the same pattern as for greeter and shipper.)

8. In `HomeController.cs`, add two action methods for products and employees, as shown in the following code:

```
public async Task<IActionResult> Products(decimal minimumPrice = 0M)
{
  ProductsReply reply = await _productClient.
GetProductsMinimumPriceAsync(
    new ProductsMinimumPriceRequest() { MinimumPrice = minimumPrice });

  return View(reply.Products);
}

public async Task<IActionResult> Employees()
```

```
{
  EmployeesReply reply = await _employeeClient.GetEmployeesAsync(
    new EmployeesRequest());

  return View(reply.Employees);
}
```

9. In the `Views\Shared` folder, in `_Layout.cshtml`, after the menu item for navigating to the home page, add menu items for navigating to products and employees, as shown highlighted in the following markup:

```html
<li class="nav-item">
  <a class="nav-link text-dark" asp-area="" asp-controller="Home" asp-action="Index">Home</a>
</li>
<li class="nav-item">
  <a class="nav-link text-dark" asp-area="" asp-controller="Home" asp-action="Products">Products</a>
</li>
<li class="nav-item">
  <a class="nav-link text-dark" asp-area="" asp-controller="Home" asp-action="Employees">Employees</a>
</li>
```

10. In the `Views\Home` folder, add a new Razor View file named `Products.cshtml`, and modify it to show a table of products, as shown in the following markup:

```razor
@using Google.Protobuf.Collections
@using Northwind.Grpc.Client.Mvc
@model RepeatedField<ProductReply>
@{
  ViewData["Title"] = "Products";
  decimal price = 0;
}
<h1>@ViewData["Title"]</h1>
<table class="table table-primary table-bordered">
  <thead>
    <tr>
      <th>Product ID</th>
      <th>Product Name</th>
      <th>Unit Price</th>
      <th>Units In Stock</th>
      <th>Units On Order</th>
      <th>Reorder Level</th>
```

```
            <th>Discontinued</th>
          </tr>
        </thead>
        <tbody>
          @foreach (ProductReply p in Model)
          {
            <tr>
              <td>@p.ProductId</td>
              <td>@p.ProductName</td>
              @{ price = p.UnitPrice; }
              <td>@price.ToString("C")</td>
              <td>@p.UnitsInStock</td>
              <td>@p.UnitsOnOrder</td>
              <td>@p.ReorderLevel</td>
              <td>@p.Discontinued</td>
            </tr>
          }
        </tbody>
      </table>
```

11. In the Views\Home folder, add a new Razor View file named Employees.cshtml, and modify it
    to show a table of employees, as shown in the following markup:

```
@using Google.Protobuf.Collections
@using Northwind.Grpc.Client.Mvc
@model RepeatedField<EmployeeReply>
@{
  ViewData["Title"] = "Employees";
}
<h1>@ViewData["Title"]</h1>
<table class="table table-primary table-bordered">
  <thead>
    <tr>
      <th>Employee ID</th>
      <th>Full Name</th>
      <th>Job Title</th>
      <th>Address</th>
      <th>Birth Date</th>
      <th>Photo</th>
    </tr>
  </thead>
  <tbody>
```

```
      @foreach (EmployeeReply e in Model)
      {
        <tr>
          <td>@e.EmployeeId</td>
          <td>@e.TitleOfCourtesy @e.FirstName @e.LastName</td>
          <td>@e.Title</td>
          <td>@e.Address<br />@e.City<br />@e.Region<br />
              @e.PostalCode<br />@e.Country</td>
          <td>@e.BirthDate.ToDateTimeOffset().ToString("D")</td>
          <td><img src="data:image/jpg;base64,
            @Convert.ToBase64String(e.Photo.ToByteArray())" />
          </td>
        </tr>
      }
    </tbody>
  </table>
```

Testing decimal, date, and bytes handling

Finally, we can test the specialized type handling we implemented:

1. Start the Northwind.Grpc.Service project without debugging.

2. Start the Northwind.Grpc.Client.Mvc project.

3. On the home page, in the top navigation bar, click **Products**, and note all products are included in the table, as shown in *Figure 13.10*:

Figure 13.10: Products including unit prices that use a custom decimal implementation

4. Enter a minimum price such as 100, click **Filter Products**, and note that only products with a unit price of that amount or more are included in the table.

5. In the top navigation bar, click **Employees,** and note employees and their birth dates and photos are included in the table, as shown in *Figure 13.11*:

Figure 13.11: Employees including birth dates and photos using timestamp and bytes

6. Close the browser and shut down the web servers.

You've now seen how to use gRPC to build several services that work with data. Now let's see some more advanced features of gRPC.

Implementing interceptors and handling faults

gRPC interceptors are a way to perform additional processing during requests and responses and they can be injected at the client or service. They are often used for logging, monitoring, and validation.

Adding a client-side interceptor

Let's add a client-side gRPC interceptor for logging:

1. In the Northwind.Grpc.Client.Mvc project, add a new folder named Interceptors.
2. In the Interceptors folder, add a new class file named ClientLoggingInterceptor.cs, and then add statements to define an interceptor, as shown in the following code:

```
using Grpc.Core.Interceptors; // To use Interceptor and so on.
using Grpc.Core; // To use AsyncUnaryCall<T>.

namespace Northwind.Grpc.Client.Mvc.Interceptors;

public class ClientLoggingInterceptor : Interceptor
{
  private readonly ILogger _logger;
```

```
public ClientLoggingInterceptor(ILoggerFactory loggerFactory)
{
  _logger = loggerFactory.CreateLogger<ClientLoggingInterceptor>();
}

public override AsyncUnaryCall<TResponse>
  AsyncUnaryCall<TRequest, TResponse>(TRequest request,
  ClientInterceptorContext<TRequest, TResponse> context,
  AsyncUnaryCallContinuation<TRequest, TResponse> continuation)
{
  _logger.LogWarning("Starting call. Type: {0}. Method: {1}.",
    context.Method.Type, context.Method.Name);

  return continuation(request, context);
}
}
```

 Interceptors form a pipeline, so in your interceptor, you must call the next interceptor in the pipeline, represented by the continuation delegate, and pass it the
request and context.

3. In the Northwind.Grpc.Client.Mvc project, in Program.cs, before any of the calls to add
    gRPC services, add a call to register the interceptor as a singleton service, as shown in the
    following code:

    ```
    // Register the interceptor before attaching it to a gRPC client.
    builder.Services.AddSingleton<ClientLoggingInterceptor>();
    ```

4. In Program.cs, at the end of the statement to register the product client, add the interceptor,
    as shown highlighted in the following code:

    ```
    builder.Services.AddGrpcClient<Product.ProductClient>("Product",
      options =>
      {
        options.Address = new Uri("https://localhost:5131");
      })
      .AddInterceptor<ClientLoggingInterceptor>();
    ```

 You can attach the logging interceptor to as many clients as you want.

5. Start the `Northwind.Grpc.Service` project without debugging.

6. Start the `Northwind.Grpc.Client.Mvc` project.

7. On the home page, in the top navigation bar, click **Products**.

8. In the MVC website project command prompt or terminal, note the warning, which will be distinct from information messages as it is yellow-on-black by default, as shown in the following output:

```
warn: Northwind.Grpc.Client.Mvc.Interceptors.ClientLoggingInterceptor[0]
      Starting call. Type: Unary. Method: GetProductsMinimumPrice.
```

9. Close the browser and shut down the web servers.

 More Information: You might be thinking, "Interceptors sound a lot like ASP.NET Core middleware!" You can read a useful comparison at the following link: `https://learn.microsoft.com/en-us/aspnet/core/grpc/interceptors#grpc-interceptors-versus-middleware`.

Exception and transient fault handling

gRPC has built-in support to automatically retry failed calls, which is a good way to handle transient faults like temporary network disconnects and down or busy services.

In the client, an `RpcException` could be thrown that includes details of the error.

First, let's add a transient fault to the gRPC service and see how the client handles it:

1. In the `Northwind.Grpc.Service` project, in the `Services` folder, in `GreeterService.cs`, modify the `SayHello` method to wait for one second and then, randomly, one in three times it should work but two in three times throw a service unavailable exception, as shown in the following code:

```
public override async Task<HelloReply> SayHello(
  HelloRequest request, ServerCallContext context)
{
  await Task.Delay(1000);

  if (Random.Shared.Next(1, 4) == 1)
  {
    return new HelloReply
    {
      Message = "Hello " + request.Name
    };
  }
  else
  {
```

```
    throw new RpcException(new Status(StatusCode.Unavailable,
        "Service is temporarily unavailable. Try again later."));
  }
}
```

2. Start the Northwind.Grpc.Service project without debugging.

3. Start the Northwind.Grpc.Client.Mvc project.

4. On the home page, note the exception, as shown in *Figure 13.12*:

Figure 13.12: Service is unavailable exception

5. If you don't get an exception, refresh the page until you do.

6. Close the browser and shut down the web servers.

Now, let's see how to add transient fault handling to the MVC website client:

1. In the Northwind.Grpc.Client.Mvc project, in Program.cs, before adding the greeter client to the services collection, add statements to define a MethodConfig with a retry policy that retries up to five times for status codes indicating an unavailable service, and then after configuring the greeter client address, apply the method config, as shown highlighted in the following code:

```
MethodConfig configForAllMethods = new()
{
  Names = { MethodName.Default },
  RetryPolicy = new RetryPolicy
  {
    MaxAttempts = 5,
    InitialBackoff = TimeSpan.FromSeconds(1),
    MaxBackoff = TimeSpan.FromSeconds(5),
    BackoffMultiplier = 1.5,
    RetryableStatusCodes = { StatusCode.Unavailable }
  }
};

builder.Services.AddGrpcClient<Greeter.GreeterClient>("Greeter",
  options =>
  {
```

```
      options.Address = new Uri("https://localhost:5131");
  })
  .ConfigureChannel(channel =>
  {
    channel.ServiceConfig = new ServiceConfig
    {
      MethodConfigs = { configForAllMethods }
    };
  });
```

2. Start the `Northwind.Grpc.Service` project without debugging.

3. Start the `Northwind.Grpc.Client.Mvc` project.

4. On the home page, note the home page might take a few seconds to appear, but eventually, it will successfully appear with the `Hello Henrietta` message from the gRPC service, and if you review the gRPC service output, it will include multiple attempts to call `SayHello` before finally working, as shown in the following output:

```
info: Microsoft.AspNetCore.Hosting.Diagnostics[1]
      Request starting HTTP/2 POST https://localhost:5131/greet.Greeter/
SayHello - application/grpc -
info: Microsoft.AspNetCore.Routing.EndpointMiddleware[0]
      Executing endpoint 'gRPC - /greet.Greeter/SayHello'
info: Grpc.AspNetCore.Server.ServerCallHandler[7]
      Error status code 'Unavailable' with detail 'Service is temporarily
unavailable. Try again later.' raised.
info: Microsoft.AspNetCore.Routing.EndpointMiddleware[1]
      Executed endpoint 'gRPC - /greet.Greeter/SayHello'
info: Microsoft.AspNetCore.Hosting.Diagnostics[2]
      Request finished HTTP/2 POST https://localhost:5131/greet.Greeter/
SayHello - 200 0 application/grpc 1039.4626ms
info: Microsoft.AspNetCore.Hosting.Diagnostics[1]
      Request starting HTTP/2 POST https://localhost:5131/greet.Greeter/
SayHello - application/grpc -
info: Microsoft.AspNetCore.Routing.EndpointMiddleware[0]
      Executing endpoint 'gRPC - /greet.Greeter/SayHello'
info: Grpc.AspNetCore.Server.ServerCallHandler[7]
      Error status code 'Unavailable' with detail 'Service is temporarily
unavailable. Try again later.' raised.
info: Microsoft.AspNetCore.Routing.EndpointMiddleware[1]
      Executed endpoint 'gRPC - /greet.Greeter/SayHello'
info: Microsoft.AspNetCore.Hosting.Diagnostics[2]
```

```
        Request finished HTTP/2 POST https://localhost:5131/greet.Greeter/
SayHello - 200 0 application/grpc 1008.1375ms
info: Microsoft.AspNetCore.Hosting.Diagnostics[1]
        Request starting HTTP/2 POST https://localhost:5131/greet.Greeter/
SayHello - application/grpc -
info: Microsoft.AspNetCore.Routing.EndpointMiddleware[0]
        Executing endpoint 'gRPC - /greet.Greeter/SayHello'
info: Microsoft.AspNetCore.Routing.EndpointMiddleware[1]
        Executed endpoint 'gRPC - /greet.Greeter/SayHello'
info: Microsoft.AspNetCore.Hosting.Diagnostics[2]
        Request finished HTTP/2 POST https://localhost:5131/greet.Greeter/
SayHello - 200 - application/grpc 1016.4590ms
```

Implementing gRPC JSON transcoding

JSON is the most popular format for services that return data to a browser or mobile device. It would be great if we could create a gRPC service and magically make it callable via non-HTTP/2 using JSON.

Thankfully, there is a solution.

Microsoft has a technology they call **gRPC JSON transcoding**. It is an ASP.NET Core extension that creates HTTP endpoints with JSON for gRPC services, based on Google's HttpRule class for their gRPC transcoding.

 More Information: You can read about Google's HttpRule class at the following link: https://cloud.google.com/dotnet/docs/reference/Google.Api.CommonProtos/latest/Google.Api.HttpRule.

Enabling gRPC JSON transcoding

Let's see how to enable gRPC JSON transcoding in our gRPC service:

1. In the Northwind.Grpc.Service project, add a package reference for gRPC JSON transcoding, as shown highlighted in the following markup:

    ```xml
    <ItemGroup>
      <PackageReference Include="Grpc.AspNetCore" Version="2.59.0" />
      <PackageReference Include="Microsoft.Data.SqlClient" Version="5.1.2" />
      <PackageReference Include="Microsoft.AspNetCore.Grpc.JsonTranscoding"
                        Version="8.0.0" />
    </ItemGroup>
    ```

2. Build the Northwind.Grpc.Service project to restore packages.

3. In `appsettings.json`, modify the `Protocols` option to enable HTTP/1.1 as well as HTTP/2, as shown highlighted in the following markup:

```
{
  "Logging": {
    "LogLevel": {
      "Default": "Information",
      "Microsoft.AspNetCore": "Warning"
    }
  },
  "AllowedHosts": "*",
  "Kestrel": {
    "EndpointDefaults": {
      "Protocols": "Http1AndHttp2"
    }
  }
}
```

 Good Practice: By default, a gRPC project will be configured to only allow HTTP/2 requests. To support clients like `.http` files in your code editor, or Unity, enable both HTTP/1.1 and HTTP/2. Allowing HTTP/1.1 and HTTP/2 on the same port requires TLS for protocol negotiation, which is another good reason to leave HTTPS enabled in a gRPC service and therefore not use `CreateSlimBuilder`.

4. In `Program.cs`, add a call to add JSON transcoding after the call to add gRPC, as shown highlighted in the following code:

```
builder.Services.AddGrpc().AddJsonTranscoding();
```

5. In the `Northwind.Grpc.Service` project/folder, add a folder named `google`.

6. In the google folder, add a folder named `api`.

7. In the api folder, add two `.proto` files named `http.proto` and `annotations.proto`.

8. Copy and paste the raw contents for the two files from the files found at the following link: `https://github.com/dotnet/aspnetcore/tree/main/src/Grpc/JsonTranscoding/test/testassets/Sandbox/google/api`.

9. In the `Protos` folder, in `employee.proto`, import the annotations `.proto` file, and use it to add an option to expose an endpoint to make an HTTP request to the `GetEmployee` method, as shown in the following code:

```
syntax = "proto3";

option csharp_namespace = "Northwind.Grpc.Service";
```

```
import "google/protobuf/duration.proto";
import "google/protobuf/timestamp.proto";
import "google/api/annotations.proto";


package employee;


service Employee {
  rpc GetEmployee (EmployeeRequest) returns (EmployeeReply) {
    option (google.api.http) = {
      get: "/v1/employee/{employee_id}"
    };
  };
  rpc GetEmployees (EmployeesRequest) returns (EmployeesReply);
}
```

Testing gRPC JSON transcoding

Now we can start the gRPC service and call it directly from any browser:

1. Start the `Northwind.Grpc.Service` project.

2. Start any browser, show the developer tools, and click the **Network** tab to start recording network traffic.

3. Navigate to a URL to make a `GET` request that will call the `GetEmployee` method, `https://localhost:5131/v1/employee/1`, and note the JSON response returned by the gRPC service, as shown in *Figure 13.13*:

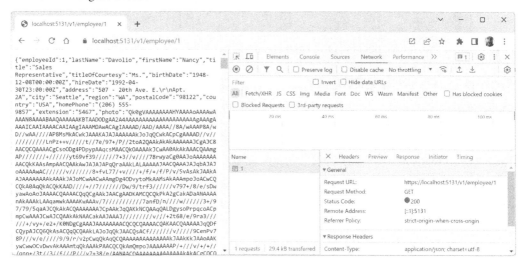

Figure 13.13: Making an HTTP 1.1 GET request to a gRPC service and receiving a response in JSON

4. In your code editor, in the `HttpRequests` folder, create a new file named `grpc-json-transcoding.http`, and add statements to make requests for employees using HTTP/1.1, as shown in the following code:

```
### Configure a variable for the gRPC service base address.
@base_address = https://localhost:5131/

### Get Nancy Davolio.
GET {{base_address}}v1/employee/1

### Get Andrew Fuller Davolio.
GET {{base_address}}v1/employee/2
```

5. Send both requests, confirm the responses are correct, and then review the gRPC service command prompt or terminal to confirm that the requests were made using HTTP/1.1, as shown in the following output:

```
info: Microsoft.AspNetCore.Hosting.Diagnostics[1]
      Request starting HTTP/1.1 GET https://localhost:5131/v1/employee/2
- - -
info: Microsoft.AspNetCore.Routing.EndpointMiddleware[0]
      Executing endpoint 'gRPC - /v1/employee/{employee_id}'
info: Microsoft.AspNetCore.Routing.EndpointMiddleware[1]
      Executed endpoint 'gRPC - /v1/employee/{employee_id}'
info: Microsoft.AspNetCore.Hosting.Diagnostics[2]
      Request finished HTTP/1.1 GET https://localhost:5131/v1/employee/2
- 200 - application/json;+charset=utf-8 7.9328ms
```

6. Close the `.http` file, close the browser, and shut down the web server.

Comparing with gRPC-Web

gRPC-Web is an alternative to gRPC JSON transcoding to allow gRPC services to be called from a browser. gRPC-Web achieves this by executing a gRPC-Web client inside the browser. This has the advantage that the communications between the browser and gRPC service use Protobuf and therefore get all the performance and scalability benefits of true gRPC communication.

As you have seen, gRPC JSON transcoding allows browsers to call gRPC services as if they were HTTP APIs with JSON. The browser needs to know nothing about gRPC. The gRPC service is responsible for converting those HTTP API calls into calls to the actual gRPC service implementation.

To simplify and summarize:

- gRPC JSON transcoding happens on the server side.
- gRPC-Web happens on the client side.

Good Practice: Add gRPC JSON transcoding support to all your gRPC services hosted in ASP.NET Core. This provides the best of both worlds. Clients that cannot use gRPC natively can call the Web API. Clients that can use gRPC natively can call it directly.

Practicing and exploring

Test your knowledge and understanding by answering some questions, getting some hands-on practice, and exploring this chapter's topics with deeper research.

Exercise 13.1 – Test your knowledge

Answer the following questions:

1. What are three benefits of gRPC that make it a good choice for implementing services?
2. How are contracts defined in gRPC?
3. Which of the following .NET types require extensions to be imported: `int`, `double`, or `DateTime`?
4. Why should you set a deadline when calling a gRPC method?
5. What are the benefits of enabling gRPC JSON transcoding to a gRPC service hosted in ASP. NET Core?

Exercise 13.2 – Compare gRPC services with HTTP APIs

Review the article found at the following link:

`https://learn.microsoft.com/en-us/aspnet/core/grpc/comparison`

Exercise 13.3 – Explore topics

Use the links on the following page to learn more details about the topics covered in this chapter:

`https://github.com/markjprice/apps-services-net8/blob/main/docs/book-links.md#chapter-13---building-efficient-microservices-using-grpc`

Summary

In this chapter, you:

- Learned about some concepts of gRPC services, how they work, and their benefits.
- Implemented a simple gRPC service.
- Implemented a gRPC service that uses an EF Core model that cannot yet use AOT publish.
- Implemented a gRPC service that uses `SqlClient` libraries that can use AOT publish and are therefore smaller and faster.
- Learned how to set deadlines and read metadata sent as headers and trailers.

- Implemented a custom `decimal` type and used extended date/time types.
- Implemented a client-side interceptor.
- Extended a gRPC service with support for being called as an HTTP service with JSON, to support clients that cannot work with gRPC natively.

In the next chapter, you will review how to build website user interfaces using ASP.NET Core MVC.

14

Building Web User Interfaces Using ASP.NET Core

This chapter is about building web user interfaces with ASP.NET Core. You will learn about ASP.NET Core MVC views, Razor syntax, HTML and Tag Helpers, internationalizing your website, and how to use Bootstrap for quick user interface prototyping.

This chapter will cover the following topics:

- Setting up an ASP.NET Core MVC website
- Defining web user interfaces with Razor views
- Localizing and globalizing with ASP.NET Core
- Defining web user interfaces with Tag Helpers
- Output caching

Setting up an ASP.NET Core MVC website

The **Model-View-Controller** (**MVC**) design pattern allows a clean separation between technical concerns, as shown in the following list:

- **Models:** Classes that represent the data entities and view models used on the website.
- **Views:** Razor files, that is, `.cshtml` files, that render data in view models into HTML web pages. Blazor uses the `.razor` file extension, but do not confuse them with Razor files!
- **Controllers:** Classes that execute code when an HTTP request arrives at the web server. The controller methods usually create a view model that may contain entity models and pass it to a view to generate an HTTP response to send back to the web browser or other client.

ASP.NET Core has many Razor file types, which can be confusing because they all use the term "Razor", so I will now remind you of them and highlight the important similarities and differences, as shown in *Table 14.1*:

Technology	Special filename	File extension	Directive
Razor Component (for Blazor)		`.razor`	
Razor Component (for Blazor with page routing)		`.razor`	`@page`
Razor Page		`.cshtml`	`@page`
Razor View (for MVC)		`.cshtml`	
Razor Layout	`_{customname}`	`.cshtml`	
Razor View (partial)	`_{customname}`	`.cshtml`	
Razor View Start	`_ViewStart`	`.cshtml`	
Razor View Imports	`_ViewImports`	`.cshtml`	

Table 14.1: Important similarities and differences between Razor files

 Warning! Be careful to use the correct file extension and directive at the top of the file or you will get unexpected behavior.

A Razor View file is technically identical to a Razor Layout or a Razor View (partial). That is why it is so important to follow the convention of prefixing a layout or partial view with an underscore.

What turns a Razor View into a Razor Layout is the name of the Razor file being set as the `Layout` property of another Razor file or the default layout in the `_ViewStart.cshtml` file, as shown in the following code:

```
@{
    Layout = "_LayoutWithAdverts";
}
```

What turns a Razor View into a Razor View (partial) is the Razor View name being used in a `<partial>` component on a page, as shown in the following code:

```
<partial name="_Product" model="product" />
```

 Good Practice: The naming convention for special and shared Razor files like layouts and partial views is to prefix them with an underscore _, for example, `_ViewStart.cshtml`, `_Layout.cshtml`, or `_Product.cshtml` (this might be a partial view for rendering a product).

Creating an ASP.NET Core MVC website

You will use a project template to create an ASP.NET Core MVC website project that has a local database for authenticating and authorizing users.

Visual Studio 2022 defaults to using SQL Server LocalDB for the accounts database.

Visual Studio Code (or more accurately the dotnet CLI tool) uses SQLite by default and you can specify a switch to use SQL Server LocalDB instead.

Let's see it in action:

1. Use your preferred code editor to create an ASP.NET Core MVC website project with authentication accounts stored in a database, as defined in the following list:

    *   Project template: **ASP.NET Core Web App (Model-View-Controller) [C#]** / mvc
    *   Project file and folder: Northwind.Mvc
    *   Solution file and folder: Chapter14
    *   Authentication type: **Individual Accounts** / --auth Individual
    *   Configure for HTTPS: Selected.
    *   Enable Docker: Cleared.
    *   Do not use top-level statements: Cleared.

2. Build the Northwind.Mvc project.

    *   If you created the MVC project using Visual Studio 2022, then the database for authentication and authorization will be stored in SQL Server LocalDB. But the database does not yet exist. At a command prompt or terminal, in the Northwind.Mvc folder, enter the command to run database migrations so that the database used to store credentials for authentication is created, as shown in the following command:

        ```
        dotnet ef database update
        ```

    *   If you created the MVC project using dotnet new, then the database for authentication and authorization will be stored in SQLite and the file has already been created, named app.db.

3. In the root folder for the MVC website project, in the appsettings.json file, note the connection string for the authentication database named DefaultConnection, as shown in the following configuration:

    *   Using SQL Server LocalDB:

        ```
        {
          "ConnectionStrings": {
            "DefaultConnection": "Server=(localdb)\\
        mssqllocaldb;Database=aspnet-Northwind.Mvc-...;Trusted_
        Connection=True;MultipleActiveResultSets=true"
          },
        ```

- Using SQLite:

```
{
  "ConnectionStrings": {
    "DefaultConnection": "DataSource=app.db;Cache=Shared"
  },
```

Exploring the default ASP.NET Core MVC website

Let's review the behavior of the default ASP.NET Core MVC website project template:

1. In the Northwind.Mvc project, expand the Properties folder, open the launchSettings.json file, and for the https profile, for its applicationUrl setting, change the port numbers to 5141 for https and 5142 for http, as shown in the following setting:

    ```
    "applicationUrl": "https://localhost:5141;http://localhost:5142",
    ```

2. Save the changes to the launchSettings.json file.

3. In your preferred code editor or at the command line, start the Northwind.Mvc project with the https profile and using Chrome as the browser:

    - If you are using Visual Studio 2022, then select the https profile as the **Startup Project**, and **Google Chrome** as the **Web Browser**, then start the Northind.Mvc website project without debugging.

    - If you are using Visual Studio Code, then at the command prompt or terminal, enter the following command: dotnet run --launch-profile https. Start Chrome and navigate to: https://localhost:5141/.

    - On Windows, if the **Windows Defender Firewall** displays a **Windows Security Alert** because it "has blocked some features of this app," then click **Allow access**.

4. In Chrome, open **Developer Tools**.

5. Refresh the home page and note the following, as shown in *Figure 14.1*:

    - The top navigation menu with links to **Home**, **Privacy**, **Register**, and **Login**. If the viewport width is 575 pixels or less, then the navigation collapses into a hamburger menu.

    - The title of the website, **Northwind.Mvc**, shown in the header and footer.

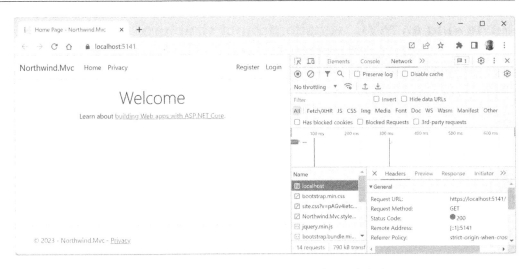

Figure 14.1: The ASP.NET Core MVC project template website home page

Understanding visitor registration

By default, passwords must have at least one non-alphanumeric character, at least one digit (0-9), and at least one uppercase letter (A-Z). I use `Pa$$w0rd` in scenarios like this when I am just exploring.

The MVC project template follows best practices for **double-opt-in** (**DOI**), meaning that after filling in an email address and password to register, an email is sent to the email address, and the visitor must click a link in that email to confirm that they want to register.

We have not yet configured an email provider to send that email, so we must simulate that step:

1. Close the **Developer Tools** pane.
2. In the top navigation menu, click **Register**.
3. Enter an email and password, and then click the **Register** button. (I used `test@example.com` and `Pa$$w0rd`.)
4. Click the link with the text **Click here to confirm your account** and note that you are redirected to a **Confirm email** web page that you could customize.
5. In the top navigation menu, click **Login**, enter your email address and password (note that there is an optional checkbox to remember you, and there are links if the visitor has forgotten their password or they want to register as a new visitor), and then click the **Log in** button.
6. Click your email address in the top navigation menu. This will navigate to an account management page. Note that you can set a phone number, change your email address, change your password, enable two-factor authentication (if you add an authenticator app), and download and delete your personal data. This last feature is good for compliance with legal regulations like the European GDPR.
7. Close Chrome, and then at the command prompt or terminal for the MVC website, press *Ctrl* + *C* to cleanly shut down the web server.

Reviewing an MVC website project structure

In your code editor, in Visual Studio 2022 **Solution Explorer** (toggle on **Show All Files**) or Visual Studio Code **EXPLORER – SOLUTION EXPLORER**, review the structure of an MVC website project, as shown in *Figure 14.2*:

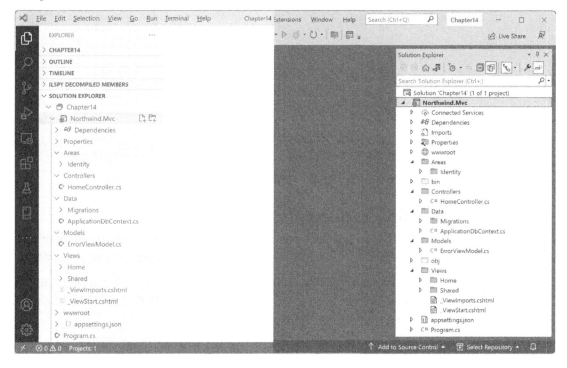

Figure 14.2: VS Code and VS 2022 Solution Explorers for an ASP.NET Core MVC project

We will look in more detail at some of these parts later, but for now, note the following:

- `Areas`: This folder contains nested folders and a file needed to integrate your website project with ASP.NET Core Identity, which is used for authentication.

- `bin`, `obj`: These folders contain temporary files needed during the build process and the compiled assemblies for the project. Solution Explorer for Visual Studio Code + C# Dev Kit does not show hidden folders like these, but you can see them in the folder view (labeled **CHAPTER14** in *Figure 14.2*).

- `Controllers`: This folder contains C# classes that have methods (known as actions) that fetch a model and pass it to a view, for example, `HomeController.cs`.

- `Data`: This folder contains Entity Framework Core migration classes used by the ASP.NET Core Identity system to provide data storage for authentication and authorization, for example, `ApplicationDbContext.cs`.

- `Models`: This folder contains C# classes that represent all the data gathered together by a controller and passed to a view, for example, `ErrorViewModel.cs`.

- **Properties**: This folder contains a configuration file for Kestrel (or IIS or IIS Express on Windows) named launchSettings.json, for launching the website during development. This file is only used on the local development machine and is not deployed to your production website.

- **Views**: This folder contains the .cshtml Razor files that combine HTML and C# code to dynamically generate HTML responses. The _ViewStart.cshtml file sets the default layout and _ViewImports.cshtml imports common namespaces used in all views like Tag Helpers:

  - **Home**: This subfolder contains Razor files for the home and privacy pages.

  - **Shared**: This subfolder contains Razor files for the shared layout, an error page, and two partial views for logging- in and validation scripts.

- **wwwroot**: This folder contains static content used by the website, such as CSS for styling, libraries of JavaScript, JavaScript for this website project, and a favicon.ico file. You also put images and other static file resources like PDF documents in here. The project template includes Bootstrap and jQuery libraries.

- **appsettings.json** and **appsettings.Development.json**: These files contain settings that your website can load at runtime, for example, the database connection string for the ASP.NET Core Identity system and logging levels.

- **Northwind.Mvc.csproj**: This file contains project settings like the use of the Web .NET SDK, an entry for SQLite to ensure that the app.db file is copied to the website's output folder, and a list of NuGet packages that your project requires such as EF Core for your chosen database provider, including:

  - Microsoft.AspNetCore.Diagnostics.EntityFrameworkCore

  - Microsoft.AspNetCore.Identity.EntityFrameworkCore

  - Microsoft.AspNetCore.Identity.UI

  - Microsoft.EntityFrameworkCore.Sqlite or Microsoft.EntityFrameworkCore.SqlServer

  - Microsoft.EntityFrameworkCore.Tools

- **Program.cs**: This file defines an auto-generated Program class that contains the <Main>$ entry point. It builds a pipeline for processing incoming HTTP requests and hosts the website using default options, like configuring the Kestrel web server and loading appsettings. It adds and configures services that your website needs, for example, ASP.NET Core Identity for authentication, SQLite or SQL Server for identity data storage, and so on, and routes for your application.

 If you choose to use SQLite instead of SQL Server for the ASP.NET Core Identity database, then you will also see a file named **app.db**. This is the SQLite database that stores registered visitors.

Referencing an EF Core class library and registering a data context

We will reference the EF Core model that you created in *Chapter 3, Building Entity Models for SQL Server Using EF Core*:

1. In the `Northwind.Mvc.csproj` project file, treat warnings as errors and add a project reference to the Northwind database context project, as shown in the following markup:

```
<ItemGroup>
  <ProjectReference Include="..\..\Chapter03\Northwind.Common.DataContext
.SqlServer\Northwind.Common.DataContext.SqlServer.csproj" />
</ItemGroup>
```

 The `Include` path must not have a line break.

2. At the command prompt or terminal, build the `Northwind.Mvc` project, as shown in the following command: `dotnet build`.

3. In `Program.cs`, import the namespace to use the `AddNorthwindContext` extension method, as shown in the following code:

```
using Northwind.EntityModels; // To use AddNorthwindContext method.
```

4. In the section that adds services to the container, add a statement that registers `NorthwindContext` as a service, as shown in the following code:

```
builder.Services.AddNorthwindContext();
```

Defining web user interfaces with Razor views

Let's review how we can build the user interface of a web page in a modern ASP.NET Core MVC website.

Understanding Razor views

In MVC, the V stands for *view*. The responsibility of a view is to transform a model into HTML or other formats.

There are multiple **view engines** that could be used to do this. The default view engine is called **Razor**, and it uses the @ symbol to indicate server-side code execution.

Let's review the home page view and how it uses a shared layout:

1. In the `Views/Home` folder, open the `Index.cshtml` file and note the block of C# code wrapped in @{ }. This will execute first and can be used to store data that needs to be passed into a shared layout file, like the title of the web page, as shown in the following code:

```
@{
  ViewData["Title"] = "Home Page";
}
```

2. Note the static HTML content in the `<div>` element that uses Bootstrap classes like `text-center` and `display-4` for styling, as shown in the following markup:

```
<div class="text-center">
  <h1 class="display-4">Welcome</h1>
  <p>Learn about <a href="https://learn.microsoft.com/aspnet/
core">building Web apps with ASP.NET Core</a>.</p>
</div>
```

3. In the Views folder, open the `_ViewImports.cshtml` file and note that it imports the namespace for the project and the namespace for the Models folder in the project, and then adds the ASP. NET Core Tag Helpers, which we will learn more about later in this chapter, as shown in the following code:

```
@using Northwind.Mvc
@using Northwind.Mvc.Models
@addTagHelper *, Microsoft.AspNetCore.Mvc.TagHelpers
```

4. In the Views folder, open the `_ViewStart.cshtml` file. It gets executed when the View method is called in a controller class. It is used to set defaults that apply to all views. For example, note that it sets the Layout property of all views to a shared layout file (without its file extension), as shown in the following markup:

```
@{
  Layout = "_Layout";
}
```

 This file is not executed when a partial view is rendered, for example, when you call the `PartialView` method instead of the View method.

5. In the Shared folder, open the `_Layout.cshtml` file.

6. Note that `<title>` is being set from the ViewData dictionary that was set earlier in the Index. cshtml view, as shown in the following markup:

```
<title>@ViewData["Title"] – Northwind.Mvc</title>
```

 The title is shown in the browser tab for the current page or the browser window.

7. Note the rendering of links to support Bootstrap and a site stylesheet, where ~ means the
    wwwroot folder in the project, as shown in the following markup:

    ```
    <link rel="stylesheet"
          href="~/lib/bootstrap/dist/css/bootstrap.min.css" />
    <link rel="stylesheet" href="~/css/site.css" asp-append-version="true" />
    <link rel="stylesheet" href="~/Northwind.Mvc.styles.css"
          asp-append-version="true" />
    ```

8. Note the rendering of a navigation bar in the header, as shown in the following markup:

    ```
    <body>
      <header>
        <nav class="navbar ...">
    ```

9. Note the rendering of a collapsible <div> containing a partial view named _LoginPartial
    for logging in, and hyperlinks to allow users to navigate between pages using ASP.NET Core
    Tag Helpers with attributes like asp-controller and asp-action, as shown in the following
    markup:

    ```
    <div class="navbar-collapse collapse d-sm-inline-flex
                justify-content-between">
      <ul class="navbar-nav flex-grow-1">
        <li class="nav-item">
          <a class="nav-link text-dark" asp-area=""
             asp-controller="Home" asp-action="Index">Home</a>
        </li>
        <li class="nav-item">
          <a class="nav-link text-dark" asp-area=""
             asp-controller="Home" asp-action="Privacy">Privacy</a>
        </li>
      </ul>
      <partial name="_LoginPartial" />
    </div>
    ```

The <a> elements use Tag Helper attributes named asp-controller and asp-
action to specify the controller name and action name that will execute when
the link is clicked on. The asp-area attribute can be used to organize and group
pages within large, complex MVC websites. If you want to navigate to a feature in
a Razor Class Library, then you can also use asp-area to specify the feature name.

10. Note the rendering of the body inside the `<main>` element, as shown in the following markup:

```
<div class="container">
  <main role="main" class="pb-3">
    @RenderBody()
  </main>
</div>
```

 The RenderBody method injects the contents of a specific Razor view for a page like the Index.cshtml file at that point in the shared layout.

11. Note the rendering of `<script>` elements at the bottom of the page so that it does not slow down the display of the page, and that you can add your own script blocks into an optional defined section named Scripts, as shown in the following markup:

```
<script src="~/lib/jquery/dist/jquery.min.js"></script>
<script src="~/lib/bootstrap/dist/js/bootstrap.bundle.min.js">
</script>
<script src="~/js/site.js" asp-append-version="true"></script>
@await RenderSectionAsync("Scripts", required: false)
```

12. In the Shared folder, open the _LoginPartial.cshtml file, and note the if statement, which if the visitor is logged in renders links to their account and to log out, or if they are not logged in, renders links to register or log in.

13. In the Shared folder, open the _ValidationScriptsPartial.cshtml file, and note it contains two script blocks for adding validation to the client-side browser using JavaScript, as shown in the following markup:

```
<script src="~/lib/jquery-validation/dist/jquery.validate.min.js"></
script>
<script src="~/lib/jquery-validation-unobtrusive/jquery.validate.
unobtrusive.min.js"></script>
```

 Good Practice: You need to add this partial view to the Scripts section if you want to enable validation in a Razor View like Index.cshtml, as shown in the following markup:

```
@section Scripts {
  <partial name="_ValidationScriptsPartial" />
}
```

14. In the Shared folder, open the Error.cshtml file, and note it contains markup to render an exception.

Prototyping with Bootstrap

Bootstrap is the world's most popular framework for building responsive, mobile-first websites. It combines CSS stylesheets with JavaScript libraries to implement its functionality.

It is a good choice for prototyping a website user interface, although before going public you might want to hire a web designer to build a custom Bootstrap theme or replace it with a completely custom set of CSS stylesheets to give your website a distinct brand.

Bootstrap is like Marmite. Some developers love it; some hate it.

Good reasons to use Bootstrap include:

- It saves time.
- It is customizable.
- It is open-source.
- It is well documented officially and has lots of answers about it on sites like Stack Overflow.

But implementing Bootstrap without care has the following negatives:

- Your website will look generic.
- Bootstrap themes do not work well with the default views built-in with ASP.NET Core Identity.
- It is heavy compared to a hand-crafted solution.

In the previous edition of this book, I included about five pages reviewing some of the features of Bootstrap that are most used. But Bootstrap is not .NET, and the second edition is already crammed with content, so I have moved the Bootstrap content to an online-only resource section. You can read it at the following link: `https://github.com/markjprice/apps-services-net8/blob/main/docs/ch14-bootstrap.md`.

 Good Practice: As well as defining your own styles, base your styles on a common library, such as Bootstrap, that implements responsive design. However, if you are building a website that needs a distinct identity or brand, make sure you use Bootstrap's theming support. Do not just accept the defaults.

Understanding Razor syntax and expressions

Before we customize the home page view, let's review an example Razor file. The file has an initial Razor code block that instantiates an order with price and quantity and then outputs information about the order on the web page, as shown in the following markup:

```
@{
  Order order = new()
  {
    OrderId = 123,
    Product = "Sushi",
    Price = 8.49M,
    Quantity = 3
```

```
    };
}
```

```
<div>Your order for @order.Quantity of @order.Product has a total cost of $@
order.Price * @order.Quantity</div>
```

The preceding Razor file would result in the following incorrect output:

```
Your order for 3 of Sushi has a total cost of $8.49 * 3
```

Although Razor markup can include the value of any single property using the `@object.property` syntax, you should wrap expressions in parentheses, as shown in the following markup:

```
<div>Your order for @order.Quantity of @order.Product has a total cost of $@
(order.Price * order.Quantity)</div>
```

The preceding Razor expression results in the following correct output:

```
Your order for 3 of Sushi has a total cost of $25.47
```

Understanding HTML Helper methods

When creating a view for ASP.NET Core MVC, you can use the `Html` object and its methods to generate markup. When Microsoft first introduced ASP.NET MVC in 2009, these HTML Helper methods were the way to programmatically render HTML.

Modern ASP.NET Core retains these HTML Helper methods for backward compatibility and provides Tag Helpers, which are usually easier to read and write in most scenarios. But there are notable situations where Tag Helpers cannot be used, like in Razor components.

You will learn about Tag Helpers later in this chapter.

Some useful `Html` object methods include the following:

- `ActionLink`: Use this to generate an anchor `<a>` element that contains a URL path to the specified controller and action. For example, `Html.ActionLink(linkText: "Binding", actionName: "ModelBinding", controllerName: "Home")` would generate `<a href="/home/modelbinding">Binding</a>`.
- `AntiForgeryToken`: Use this inside a `<form>` to insert a `<hidden>` element containing an anti-forgery token that can be validated when the form is submitted.
- `Display` and `DisplayFor`: Use this to generate HTML markup for the expression relative to the current model using a display template. There are built-in display templates for .NET types and custom templates can be created in the `DisplayTemplates` folder. The folder name is case-sensitive on case-sensitive filesystems.
- `DisplayForModel`: Use this to generate HTML markup for an entire model instead of a single expression.

- `Editor` and `EditorFor`: Use this to generate HTML markup for the expression relative to the current model using an editor template. There are built-in editor templates for .NET types that use `<label>` and `<input>` elements, and custom templates can be created in the `EditorTemplates` folder. The folder name is case-sensitive on case-sensitive filesystems.

- `EditorForModel`: Use this to generate HTML markup for an entire model instead of a single expression.

- `Encode`: Use this to safely encode an object or string into HTML. For example, the string value `"<script>"` would be encoded as `"&lt;script&gt;"`. This is not normally necessary since the Razor @ symbol encodes string values by default.

- `Raw`: Use this to render a string value *without* encoding as HTML.

- `PartialAsync` and `RenderPartialAsync`: Use these to generate HTML markup for a partial view. You can optionally pass a model and view data.

Defining a strongly-typed Razor view

To improve the IntelliSense when writing a view, you can define what type the view can expect using an `@model` directive at the top. Let's modify the home page to display a table of orders from the Northwind database:

1. In the `Controllers` folder, in `HomeController.cs`, import the namespace for the Northwind entity models and EF Core features, as shown in the following code:

```
using Northwind.EntityModels; // To use Northwind entity models.
using Microsoft.EntityFrameworkCore; // To use Include method.
```

2. In the controller class, define a field to store the Northwind data context and set it in the constructor, as shown highlighted in the following code:

```
private readonly NorthwindContext _db;

public HomeController(ILogger<HomeController> logger
  , NorthwindContext db)
{
  _logger = logger;
  _db = db;
}
```

3. In the `Index` action method, add statements to create a view model containing all the orders and their related order details, as shown highlighted in the following code:

```
public IActionResult Index()
{
  IEnumerable<Order> model = _db.Orders
    .Include(order => order.Customer)
    .Include(order => order.OrderDetails)
```

```
    .OrderByDescending(order => order.OrderDetails
      .Sum(detail => detail.Quantity * detail.UnitPrice))
    .AsEnumerable();


  return View(model);
}
```

4. In the Views folder, in _ViewImports.cshtml, add a statement to import the EF Core entity models for all Razor views and pages, as shown in the following code:

```
@using Northwind.EntityModels
```

5. In the Views\Home folder, in Index.cshtml, at the top of the file, add a statement to set the model type to use a collection of orders, as shown in the following code:

```
@model IEnumerable<Order>
```

Now, whenever we type Model in this view, our code editor will know the correct type for the model and will provide IntelliSense for it.

While entering code in a view, remember the following:

- Declare the type for the model using @model (with a lowercase m).
- Interact with the instance of the model using @Model (with an uppercase M).

6. In Index.cshtml, in the initial Razor code block, replace the existing content with an HTML table of the orders, as shown in the following markup:

```
@model IEnumerable<Order>
@{
  ViewData["Title"] = "Orders";
}
<div class="text-center">
  <h1 class="display-4">@ViewData["Title"]</h1>
  <table class="table table-bordered table-striped">
    <thead>
      <tr>
        <th>Order ID</th>
        <th>Order Date</th>
        <th>Company Name</th>
        <th>Country</th>
        <th>Item Count</th>
        <th>Order Total</th>
      </tr>
    </thead>
```

```
    <tbody>
      @foreach (Order order in Model)
      {
        <tr>
          <td>@order.OrderId</td>
          <td>@order.OrderDate?.ToString("D")</td>
          <td>@order.Customer?.CompanyName</td>
          <td>@order.Customer?.Country</td>
          <td>@order.OrderDetails.Count()</td>
          <td>@order.OrderDetails.Sum(detail => detail.Quantity * detail.
UnitPrice).ToString("C")</td>
        </tr>
      }
    </tbody>
  </table>
</div>
```

Let's see the result of our customized home page:

7. If your database server is not running, for example, because you are hosting it in Docker, a virtual machine, or in the cloud, then make sure to start it.

8. Start the `Northwind.Mvc` website project without debugging.

9. Note that the home page now shows a table of orders with the highest-value order displayed first, as shown in *Figure 14.3*:

Northwind.Mvc   Home Privacy   Register Login

Orders

Order ID	Order Date	Company Name	Country	Item Count	Order Total
10865	02 February 1998	QUICK-Stop	Germany	2	£17,250.00
11030	17 April 1998	Save-a-lot Markets	USA	4	£16,321.90
10981	27 March 1998	Hanari Carnes	Brazil	1	£15,810.00
10372	04 December 1996	Queen Cozinha	Brazil	4	£12,281.20
10424	23 January 1997	Mère Paillarde	Canada	3	£11,493.20
10817	06 January 1998	Königlich Essen	Germany	4	£11,490.70

Figure 14.3: The updated Northwind MVC website home page

I am running my web server on my local laptop, and its operating system, Windows 11, is configured to use United Kingdom culture for date, time, and currency values. Next, we will see how to localize the web page for the preferred culture of the visitor.

10. Close Chrome and shut down the web server.

Now that you've been reminded of how to build a basic MVC website that displays data, let's look at an important intermediate-level topic that is often overlooked when building websites for the World Wide Web: supporting all the world's languages and cultures.

Localizing and globalizing with ASP.NET Core

In *Chapter 7, Handling Dates, Times, and Internationalization*, you learned about working with dates, times, and time zones, and how to globalize and localize a .NET codebase.

In this section, we will look specifically at how to localize a website that uses ASP.NET Core.

As well as localizing `string` values into languages like French and Spanish using `IStringLocalizer`, you can localize HTML content using `IHtmlLocalizer`, but this should be used with care. Usually, HTML markup should be the same for all locales. For views, you can use `IViewLocalizer`.

Request localization means that the browser can request what culture it prefers in the following ways:

- Add a query string parameter, for example, `?culture=en-US&ui-culture=en-US`.
- Send a cookie with the request, for example, `c=en-US|uic=en-US`.
- Set an HTTP header, for example, `Accept-Language:   en-US,en;q=0.9,fr-FR;q=0.8,fr;q=0.7,en-GB;q=0.6`.

To enable request localization, call the `UseRequestLocalization` method when you configure the HTTP request pipeline in `Program.cs`. This tells ASP.NET Core to look for these requests and to automatically change the current thread that is processing that request (and only that request, no one else's requests) to use the appropriate culture to format data and load resource values.

Let's create some resource files to localize the web user interface into American English, British English, and French, and then globalize the data like dates and currency values:

1. In the `Northwind.Mvc` project, add a new folder named `Resources`. This is the default name for the folder that localizer services look in for `*.resx` resource files.
2. In `Resources`, add a new folder named `Views`.
3. In `Views`, add a new folder named `Home`.

Creating resource files

How you create resource files (`*.resx`) depends on your code editor.

 To save time, you can just copy the `.resx` files from the GitHub repository found in the folder at the following link: `https://github.com/markjprice/apps-services-net8/tree/main/code/Chapter14/Northwind.Mvc/Resources/Views/Home`.

If you are using Visual Studio 2022

You can use a special project item type and editor:

1. In Home, add a file type of **Resources File** named Index.en-US.resx.
2. Use the editor to define names and values, as shown in *Figure 14.4*:

Figure 14.4: Using the Resources File editor to define the localized labels

 JetBrains Rider has its own resource file editor that combines all .resx files in one experience as a grid. Each language has its own column, side-by-side. It's much more useful than having to edit each file individually as in Visual Studio 2022.

3. Close the editor.
4. Copy and paste the file and rename it Index.en-GB.resx.

 Warning! You must not change any of the entries in the **Name** column because these are used to look up localized values for all languages! You can only change the entries in the **Value** or **Comment** columns.

5. In Index.en-GB.resx, modify Orders (USA) to Orders (UK). This is so we can see a difference.
6. Close the editor.
7. Copy and paste the file and rename it as Index.fr-FR.resx.
8. In Index.fr-FR.resx, modify the value column to use French. (See the step-by-step instructions in the next section for Visual Studio Code for the translations.)
9. Copy and paste the file and rename it Index.fr.resx.
10. In Index.fr.resx, modify the last value to be Commandes (Neutral French).

If you are using Visual Studio Code

You will have to edit the file without a special editor:

1. In Home, add a new file named Index.en-US.resx.

2. Modify the contents to contain American English language resources, as shown in the following markup:

```xml
<?xml version="1.0" encoding="utf-8"?>
<root>
  <data name="Company Name" xml:space="preserve">
    <value>Company Name</value>
  </data>
  <data name="Country" xml:space="preserve">
    <value>Country</value>
  </data>
  <data name="Item Count" xml:space="preserve">
    <value>Item Count</value>
  </data>
  <data name="Order Date" xml:space="preserve">
    <value>Order Date</value>
  </data>
  <data name="Order ID" xml:space="preserve">
    <value>Order ID</value>
  </data>
  <data name="Order Total" xml:space="preserve">
    <value>Order Total</value>
  </data>
  <data name="Orders" xml:space="preserve">
    <value>Orders (USA)</value>
  </data>
</root>
```

3. Copy and paste the file and rename it `Index.en-GB.resx`.

4. In `Index.en-GB.resx`, modify `Orders (USA)` to `Orders (UK)`. This is so we can see a difference.

5. Copy and paste the file and rename it `Index.fr-FR.resx`.

6. In `Index.fr-FR.resx`, modify the `value` column to use French:

```xml
<?xml version="1.0" encoding="utf-8"?>
<root>
  <data name="Company Name" xml:space="preserve">
    <value>Nom de l'entreprise</value>
  </data>
  <data name="Country" xml:space="preserve">
    <value>Pays</value>
  </data>
```

```xml
      <data name="Item Count" xml:space="preserve">
        <value>Nombre d'éléments</value>
      </data>
      <data name="Order Date" xml:space="preserve">
        <value>Date de commande</value>
      </data>
      <data name="Order ID" xml:space="preserve">
        <value>Numéro de commande</value>
      </data>
      <data name="Order Total" xml:space="preserve">
        <value>Total de la commande</value>
      </data>
      <data name="Orders" xml:space="preserve">
        <value>Commandes (France)</value>
      </data>
    </root>
```

7. Copy and paste the file and rename it `Index.fr.resx`.

8. In `Index.fr.resx`, modify the last value to be `Commandes (Neutral French)`.

Localizing Razor views with an injected view localizer

Now we can continue with these steps for both code editors:

1. In the `Views/Home` folder, in `Index.cshtml`, import the namespace for working with localization, inject the `IViewLocalizer` service, and make changes to use the labels in the view model, as shown highlighted in the following markup:

```razor
@using Microsoft.AspNetCore.Mvc.Localization
@model IEnumerable<Order>
@inject IViewLocalizer Localizer
@{
  ViewData["Title"] = Localizer["Orders"];
}

<div class="text-center">
  <h1 class="display-4">@ViewData["Title"]</h1>
  <table class="table table-bordered table-striped">
    <thead>
      <tr>
        <th>@Localizer["Order ID"]</th>
        <th>@Localizer["Order Date"]</th>
        <th>@Localizer["Company Name"]</th>
        <th>@Localizer["Country"]</th>
```

```
            <th>@Localizer["Item Count"]</th>
            <th>@Localizer["Order Total"]</th>
         </tr>
      </thead>
```

 Good Practice: The key values like `"Order ID"` are used to look up the localized values. If a value is missing, then it returns the key as a default. It is good practice to therefore use keys that also work as a good fallback, which is why I used US English proper titles with spaces as the keys above and in the `.resx` files.

2. In `Program.cs`, before the call to `AddControllersWithViews`, add a statement to add localization and set the path to find resource files to the `Resources` folder, and after the call to `AddControllersWithViews`, append a call to add view localization, as shown highlighted in the following code:

    ```
    builder.Services.AddLocalization(
      options => options.ResourcesPath = "Resources");

    builder.Services.AddControllersWithViews()
      .AddViewLocalization();
    ```

3. In `Program.cs`, after the call to `Build` the app object, add statements to declare four cultures that we will support: US English, British English, neutral French, and French in France. Then, create a new localization options object and add those cultures as supported for both localization of user interfaces (`UICultures`) and globalization of data values like dates and currency (`Cultures`), as shown in the following code:

    ```
    string[] cultures = { "en-US", "en-GB", "fr", "fr-FR" };

    RequestLocalizationOptions localizationOptions = new();

    // cultures[0] will be "en-US"
    localizationOptions.SetDefaultCulture(cultures[0])

      // Set globalization of data formats like dates and currencies.
      .AddSupportedCultures(cultures)

      // Set localization of user interface text.
      .AddSupportedUICultures(cultures);

    app.UseRequestLocalization(localizationOptions);
    ```

4. Start the `Northwind.Mvc` website project.

5. In Chrome, navigate to **Settings**.

6. In the **Search settings** box, type `lang`, and note you will find the **Preferred languages** section, as shown in *Figure 14.5*:

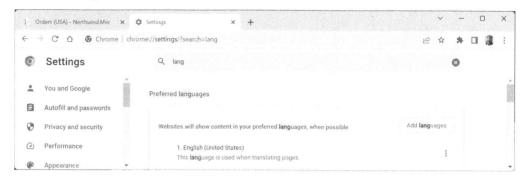

Figure 14.5: Searching Chrome Settings for the Preferred languages section

 Warning! If you are using a localized version of Chrome, in other words, its user interface is in your local language, like French, then you will need to search for the word "language" in your own language. (Although "language" in French is "langue", so entering "lang" will still work. But in Spanish you would need to search for "idioma".)

7. Click **Add languages**, search for `french`, select both **French - francais** and **French (France) – francais (France)**, and then click **Add**.

 Warning! If you are using a localized version of Chrome, then you will need to search for the word "French" in your own language. For example, in Spanish, it would be "Francés," and in Welsh, it would be "Ffrangeg."

8. Add **English (United States)** and **English (United Kingdom)** if you do not have them in the list already.

9. In the dots **...** menu to the right of **French (France)**, click **Move to the top**, and confirm that it is at the top of your list of languages.

10. Close the **Settings** tab.

11. In Chrome, perform a hard reload/refresh (for example, hold down *Ctrl* and click the **Refresh** button), and note the home page now uses localized labels and French formats for dates and currency, as shown in *Figure 14.6*:

Commandes (France)

Numéro de commande	Date de commande	Nom de l'entreprise	Pays	Nombre d'éléments	Total de la commande
10865	lundi 2 février 1998	QUICK-Stop	Germany	2	17 250,00 €
11030	vendredi 17 avril 1998	Save-a-lot Markets	USA	4	16 321,90 €
10981	vendredi 27 mars 1998	Hanari Carnes	Brazil	1	15 810,00 €
10372	mercredi 4 décembre 1996	Queen Cozinha	Brazil	4	12 281,20 €
10424	jeudi 23 janvier 1997	Mère Paillarde	Canada	3	11 493,20 €

Figure 14.6: The Orders table localized and globalized into French in France

12. Repeat the above steps for the other languages, for example, **English (United Kingdom)**.

13. View **Developer Tools**, and note the request headers have been set with British English (en-GB) first, as shown in *Figure 14.7*:

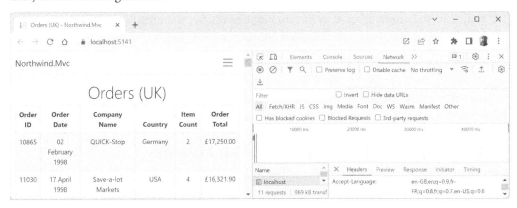

Figure 14.7: Orders localized and globalized into British English due to the Accept-Language: en-GB header

14. Close the browser and shut down the web server.

Understanding the Accept-Language header

You might wonder how the Accept-Language header works:

```
Accept-Language: en-US,en;q=0.9,fr-FR;q=0.8,fr;q=0.7,en-GB;q=0.6
```

The `Accept-Language` header uses commas as separators between culture codes. Each culture code can be neutral (just a language) or specific (language and region), and each can have a **quality value** (q) between 0.0 and 1.0 (default). The preceding `Accept-Language` header example should therefore be read as follows:

- `en-US`: English language in the United States ranked highest at 1.0 (if q not explicitly set).
- `en;q=0.9`: English language anywhere in the world ranked at 0.9.
- `fr-FR;q=0.8`: French language in France ranked at 0.8.
- `fr;q=0.7`: French language anywhere in the world ranked at 0.7.
- `en-GB;q=0.6`: English language in United Kingdom ranked lowest at 0.6.

Defining web user interfaces with Tag Helpers

Tag Helpers make it easier to make HTML elements dynamic. The markup is cleaner and easier to read, edit, and maintain than if you use HTML Helpers.

However, Tag Helpers do not completely replace HTML Helpers because there are some things that can only be achieved with HTML Helpers, like rendering output that contains multiple nested tags. Tag Helpers also cannot be used in Razor components. So, you must learn HTML Helpers and treat Tag Helpers as an optional choice that is better in some scenarios.

Tag Helpers are especially useful for **Front End** (**FE**) developers who primarily work with HTML, CSS, and JavaScript because the FE developer does not have to learn C# syntax. Tag Helpers just use what look like normal HTML attributes on elements. The attribute names and values can also be selected from IntelliSense if your code editor supports that; both Visual Studio 2022 and Visual Studio Code do.

Comparing HTML Helpers and Tag Helpers

For example, to render a linkable hyperlink to a controller action, you could use an HTML Helper method, as shown in the following markup:

```
@Html.ActionLink("View our privacy policy.", "Privacy", "Index")
```

To make it clearer how it works, you could use named parameters, as shown in the following code:

```
@Html.ActionLink(linkText: "View our privacy policy.",
  action: "Privacy", controller: "Index")
```

But using a Tag Helper would be even clearer and cleaner for someone who works more with HTML than C#, as shown in the following markup:

```
<a asp-action="Privacy" asp-controller="Home">View our privacy policy.</a>
```

All three examples above generate the same rendered HTML element, as shown in the following markup:

```
<a href="/home/privacy">View our privacy policy.</a>
```

In the next few sections, we will review some of the more common Tag Helpers:

- Anchor Tag Helper
- Cache Tag Helper
- Environment Tag Helper
- Image Tag Helper
- Forms-related Tag Helpers

Exploring the Anchor Tag Helper

First, we will create three clickable hyperlinks styled as buttons to view the home page with all orders, the orders for a single customer, and the orders in a single country. This will allow us to see the basics of creating links to controllers and actions, as well as passing parameters using a route parameter and arbitrary query string parameters.

Let's explore these examples of the Anchor Tag Helper:

1. In the Views folder, in _ViewImports.cshtml, note the @addTagHelper directive, which adds the ASP.NET Core Tag Helpers, as shown highlighted in the following code:

```
@using Northwind.Mvc
@using Northwind.Mvc.Models
@addTagHelper *, Microsoft.AspNetCore.Mvc.TagHelpers
@using Northwind.EntityModels
```

> You could create your own Tag Helpers and you would have to register them in the same way. But that is beyond the scope of this book. If you want to learn how, you can read the following documentation: https://learn.microsoft.com/en-us/aspnet/core/mvc/views/tag-helpers/authoring.

2. In the Views/Home folder, in Privacy.cshtml, add markup to define a paragraph with clickable hyperlinks styled as buttons using the <a> tag, as shown in the following markup:

```
<p>
  <a asp-controller="Home" asp-action="Index"
    class="btn btn-primary" role="button">Orders</a>

  <a asp-controller="Home"
    class="btn btn-outline-primary" role="button">This Page</a>

  <a asp-controller="Home" asp-action="Index" asp-route-id="ALFKI"
    class="btn btn-outline-primary" role="button">
    Orders for Alfreds Futterkiste</a>
```

```
<a asp-controller="Home" asp-action="Index" asp-route-country="Brazil"
    class="btn btn-outline-primary" role="button">Orders in Brazil</a>
</p>
```

 If you set a controller name without an action name, then it defaults to the current action, in this case, `Privacy`. The `asp-route-{parametername}` attribute can use any arbitrary parameter name. In the code example above, we used `id` and `country`. `id` will map to the route parameter with the same name. `country` is not a route parameter, so it will be passed as a query string.

3. In the `Controllers` folder, in `HomeController.cs`, modify the `Index` action method to define two optional parameters to pass a customer ID and the name of a country, and then modify the LINQ query to use them to filter the orders if they are set, as shown highlighted in the following code:

```
public IActionResult Index(
    string? id = null, string? country = null)
{
    // Start with a simplified initial model.
    IEnumerable<Order> model = db.Orders
        .Include(order => order.Customer)
        .Include(order => order.OrderDetails);

    // Add filtering based on parameters.
    if (id is not null)
    {
        model = model.Where(order => order.Customer?.CustomerId == id);
    }
    else if (country is not null)
    {
        model = model.Where(order => order.Customer?.Country == country);
    }

    // Add ordering and make enumerable.
    model = model
        .OrderByDescending(order => order.OrderDetails
            .Sum(detail => detail.Quantity * detail.UnitPrice))
        .AsEnumerable();

    return View(model);
}
```

4. Start the `Northwind.Mvc` website project.

5. View **Developer Tools** and click the **Elements** tab.

6. On the home page, click **Privacy** to navigate to that page, and note the buttons, including their raw HTML, which shows the `href` attribute paths that were generated by the Anchor Tag Helper, as shown in Figure *14.8*:

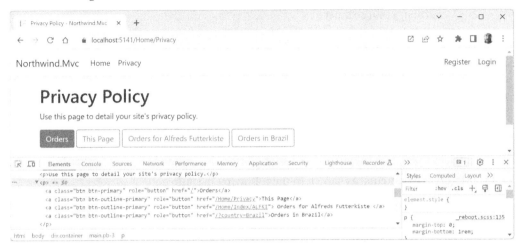

Figure 14.8: Three hyperlinks styled as buttons generated by Anchor Tag Helper

7. Click each button and then come back to the **Privacy Policy** page to make sure they work correctly.

8. Close the browser and shut down the web server.

9. In the `Views/Home` folder, in `Index.cshtml`, at the end of the table of orders, add an anchor tag to indicate the end of the orders table, as shown highlighted in the following markup:

```
</table>
<a id="endOfTable" />
</div>
```

10. In the `Views/Home` folder, in `Privacy.cshtml`, after the existing anchor tags, add another one to link to the anchor with an `id` of `endOfTable` by setting the `asp-fragment` attribute, as shown in the following markup:

```
<a asp-controller="Home" asp-action="Index" asp-fragment="endOfTable"
    class="btn btn-outline-primary">Orders (end of table)</a>
```

11. Modify the second anchor tag to explicitly set the protocol to use `https`, as shown highlighted in the following markup:

```
<a asp-controller="Home" asp-protocol="https"
    class="btn btn-outline-primary">This Page</a>
```

12. In the `Controllers` folder, in `HomeController.cs`, add an action method named `Shipper`. Give it a parameter to receive a shipper entity and then pass it to the view, as shown in the following code:

```
public IActionResult Shipper(Shipper shipper)
{
  return View(shipper);
}
```

 This action method can respond to any method of request, for example, GET or POST. With a GET request, the shipper entity would be passed as query string key-value pairs. With a POST request, the shipper entity would be passed in the body.

13. In the `Views/Home` folder, add an empty Razor view named `Shipper.cshtml`.

14. Modify the contents, as shown in the following markup:

```
@model Shipper
@{
  ViewData["Title"] = "Shippers";
}
<h1>@ViewData["Title"]</h1>
<div>
  <div class="mb-3">
    <label for="shipperIdInput" class="form-label">Shipper Id</label>
    <input type="number" class="form-control" id="shipperIdInput"
           value="@Model.ShipperId">
  </div>
  <div class="mb-3">
    <label for="companyNameInput" class="form-label">Company Name</label>
    <input class="form-control" id="companyNameInput"
           value="@Model.CompanyName">
  </div>
  <div class="mb-3">
    <label for="phoneInput" class="form-label">Phone</label>
    <input class="form-control" id="phoneInput" value="@Model.Phone">
  </div>
</div>
```

15. In the `Views/Home` folder, in `Privacy.cshtml`, at the top of the file, add code and markup to inject the Northwind database context. Then, use it to define a Razor function to create a dictionary with string values for both the key and value populated from the shippers table, as shown highlighted in the following code:

```
@inject NorthwindContext db
@{
    ViewData["Title"] = "Privacy Policy";
}
@functions {
    public async Task<IDictionary<string, string>> GetShipperData()
    {
        // Find the shipper with ID of 1.
        Shipper? shipper = await db.Shippers.FindAsync(1);

        Dictionary<string, string> keyValuePairs = new();

        if (shipper != null)
        {
            keyValuePairs = new()
            {
                { "ShipperId", shipper.ShipperId.ToString() },
                { "CompanyName", shipper.CompanyName },
                { "Phone", shipper.Phone ?? string.Empty }
            };
        }

        return keyValuePairs;
    }
}
```

16. After the existing anchor tags, add another one to pass the dictionary to the current page, as shown in the following markup:

```
<a asp-controller="Home" asp-action="Shipper"
    asp-all-route-data="await GetShipperData()"
    class="btn btn-outline-primary">Shipper</a>
```

 Passing a complex object as a query string like this quickly hits the limit of about 1,000 characters for a URL. To send larger objects, you should use POST instead of GET by using a <form> element instead of an anchor tag <a>.

17. If your database server is not running, for example, because you are hosting it in Docker, a virtual machine, or the cloud, then make sure to start it.

18. Start the Northwind.Mvc website project.

19. View **Developer Tools** and click **Elements**.

20. On the home page, click **Privacy** to navigate to that page and note the buttons, including their raw HTML, which shows the `href` attribute paths that were generated by the Anchor Tag Helper, as shown in Figure *14.9*:

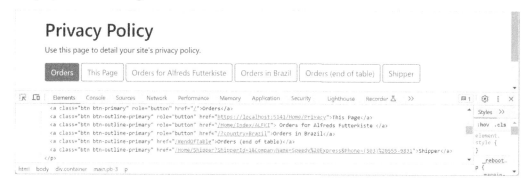

Figure 14.9: Using a fragment and passing a complex object using query string parameters

A side benefit of specifying the protocol is that the generated URL must include the protocol, domain, and any port number, as well as the relative path, so it is a convenient way to get an absolute URL instead of the default relative path URL, as shown in the second link above.

21. Click the **Orders (end of table)** button and note the browser navigates to the home page and then jumps to the end of the orders table.
22. Go back to the **Privacy** page, click the **Shipper** button, and note the shipper details are pre-entered into the shipper form.
23. Close the browser and shut down the web server.

Exploring the Cache Tag Helpers

The Cache and Distributed Cache Tag Helpers improve the performance of your web pages by caching their content using the in-memory or registered distributed cache providers respectively. We covered reading and writing objects to these caches in *Chapter 9, Caching, Queuing, and Resilient Background Services*. Now we will see how to store fragments of HTML for a view in them.

As a reminder, an in-memory cache is best for a single web server or a web server farm with session affinity enabled. Session affinity means that subsequent requests from the same browser are served by the same web server. A distributed cache is best for a web server farm or in a cloud provider like Azure. You can register providers for SQL Server, Redis, or NCache, or create your own custom provider.

Attributes that can be applied to the Cache Tag Helper include:

- enabled: Default value is true. This exists so that you can include the <cache> element in the markup but decide at runtime if it should be enabled or not.
- expires-after: A TimeSpan value to expire after. The default is 00:20:00, meaning 20 minutes.
- expires-on: A DateTimeOffset value to expire at. No default.
- expires-sliding: A TimeSpan value to expire after if the value has not been accessed during that time. This is useful when storing database entities that cost a lot to create and have varied popularity. The popular entities will stay cached if they continue to be accessed. Less popular entities will drop out. No default.
- vary-by-{type}: These attributes allow multiple different cached versions based on differences in an HTTP header value, a user, a route, cookie, or query string value, or a custom value.

Let's see an example of the Cache Tag Helper:

1. In the Views/Home folder, in Index.cshtml, between the heading and the table, add <div> elements to define a Bootstrap row with two columns that show the current UTC date and time twice, once live and then once cached, as shown in the following markup:

```
<div class="row">
  <div class="col">
    <h2>Live</h2>
    <p class="alert alert-info">
    UTC: @DateTime.UtcNow.ToLongDateString() at
        @DateTime.UtcNow.ToLongTimeString()
    </p>
  </div>
  <div class="col">
    <h2>Cached</h2>
    <p class="alert alert-secondary">
      <cache>
        UTC: @DateTime.UtcNow.ToLongDateString() at
            @DateTime.UtcNow.ToLongTimeString()
      </cache>
    </p>
  </div>
</div>
```

2. Start the Northwind.Mvc website project.

3. Refresh the home page several times over several seconds and note the left-hand time is always refreshed to show the live time, and the right-hand time is cached (for 20 minutes by default), as shown in *Figure 14.10*:

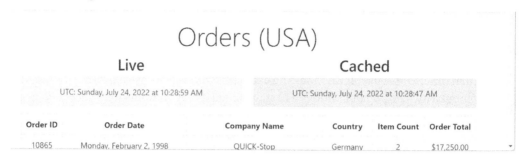

Figure 14.10: Live and cached UTC times

4. Close the browser and shut down the web server.

5. In the `Views/Home` folder, in `Index.cshtml`, modify the `<cache>` element to expire after 10 seconds, as shown highlighted in the following markup:

```
<cache expires-after="@TimeSpan.FromSeconds(10)">
```

6. Start the `Northwind.Mvc` website project.

7. Refresh the home page several times over several seconds and note the left-hand time is always refreshed to show the live time, and the right-hand time is cached for 10 seconds before it then refreshes.

8. Close the browser and shut down the web server.

Exploring the Environment Tag Helper

The Environment Tag Helper renders its content only if the current environment matches one of the values in a comma-separated list of names. This is useful if you want to render some content like instructions to a tester when hosted in a staging environment, or content like customer-specific information that developers and testers do not need to see while hosted in the production environment.

As well as a `names` attribute to set the comma-separated list of environments, you can also use `include` (works the same as `names`) and `exclude` (renders for all environments *except* the ones in the list).

Let's see an example:

1. In the `Views/Home` folder, in `Privacy.cshtml`, inject the dependency service for the web host environment, as shown in the following code:

```
@inject IWebHostEnvironment webhost
```

2. After the heading, add two `<environment>` elements, the first to show output only for developers and testers, and the second to show output only for product visitors, as shown in the following markup:

```
<environment names="Development,Staging">
  <div class="alert alert-warning">
    <h2>Attention developers and testers</h2>
    <p>
      This is a warning that only developers and testers will see.
      Current environment:
      <span class="badge bg-warning">@webhost.EnvironmentName</span>
    </p>
  </div>
</environment>
<environment names="Production">
  <div class="alert alert-info">
    <h2>Welcome, visitor!</h2>
    <p>
      This is information that only a visitor to the production website
      will see. Current environment:
      <span class="badge bg-info">@webhost.EnvironmentName</span>
    </p>
  </div>
</environment>
```

3. Start the Northwind.Mvc website project.

4. Navigate to the **Privacy** page, and note the message for developers and testers, as shown in *Figure 14.11*:

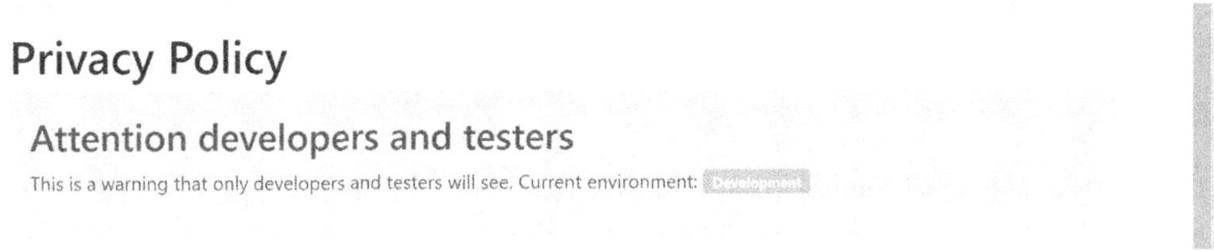

Privacy Policy

Attention developers and testers

This is a warning that only developers and testers will see. Current environment: Development

Figure 14.11: The Privacy page in the Development environment

5. Close the browser and shut down the web server.

6. In the Properties folder, in launchSettings.json, for the https profile, change the environment setting to Production, as shown highlighted in the following JSON:

```
"https": {
  ...
  "environmentVariables": {
    "ASPNETCORE_ENVIRONMENT": "Production"
  }
},
```

7. Start the Northwind.Mvc website project.

8. Navigate to the **Privacy** page, and note the message for public visitors, as shown in *Figure 14.12*:

Figure 14.12: The Privacy page in the Production environment

9. Close the browser and shut down the web server.

10. In the Properties folder, in launchSettings.json, for the https profile, change the environment setting back to Development.

Understanding how cache busting with Tag Helpers works

When asp-append-version is specified with a true value in a <link>, <img>, or <script> element, the Tag Helper for that tag type is invoked.

They work by automatically appending a query string value named v that is generated from a SHA256 hash of the referenced source file, as shown in the following example generated output:

```
<script src="~/js/site.js? v=Kl_dqr9NVtnMdsM2MUg4qthUnWZm5T1fCEimBPWDNgM"></
script>
```

>   You can see this for yourself in the current project because the _Layout.cshtml file has
>   the <script src="~/js/site.js" asp-append-version="true"></script> element.

If even a single byte within the site.js file changes, then its hash value will be different, and therefore if a browser or CDN is caching the script file, then it will bust the cached copy and replace it with the new version.

The src attribute must be set to a static file stored on the local web server, usually in the wwwroot folder, but you can configure additional locations. Remote references are not supported.

Exploring Forms-related Tag Helpers

The Form Tag Helper generates the <form> elements action attribute for an MVC controller action or named route. Like the Anchor Tag Helper, you can pass parameters using the asp-route-<parametername> attribute. It also generates a hidden verification token to prevent cross-site request forgery. You must apply the [ValidateAntiForgeryToken] attribute to the HTTP POST action method to properly use this feature.

The Label and Input Tag Helpers bind labels and inputs to properties on a model. They can then generate the id, name, and for attributes automatically, as well as add validation attributes and messages.

Let's see an example of a form for entering shipper information:

1. In the Views/Home folder, in Shipper.cshtml, duplicate the existing markup that outputs shipper details, wrap it in a <form> element that uses the Form Tag Helper, and modify the <label> and <input> elements to use the Label and Input Tag Helpers, as shown highlighted in the following markup:

```
@model Shipper
@{
  ViewData["Title"] = "Shippers";
}
<h1>@ViewData["Title"]</h1>
<h2>Without Form Tag Helper</h2>
<div>
  <div class="mb-3">
    <label for="shipperIdInput" class="form-label">Shipper ID</label>
    <input type="number" class="form-control" id="shipperIdInput"
           value="@Model.ShipperId">
  </div>
  <div class="mb-3">
    <label for="companyNameInput" class="form-label">Company Name</label>
    <input class="form-control" id="companyNameInput"
           value="@Model.CompanyName">
  </div>
  <div class="mb-3">
    <label for="phoneInput" class="form-label">Phone</label>
    <input class="form-control" id="phoneInput" value="@Model.Phone">
  </div>
</div>
<h2>With Form Tag Helper</h2>
<form asp-controller="Home" asp-action="ProcessShipper"
      class="form-horizontal" role="form">
  <div>
    <div class="mb-3">
      <label asp-for="ShipperId" class="form-label" />
      <input asp-for="ShipperId" class="form-control">
    </div>
    <div class="mb-3">
      <label asp-for="CompanyName" class="form-label" />
      <input asp-for="CompanyName" class="form-control">
```

```
      </div>
      <div class="mb-3">
        <label asp-for="Phone" class="form-label" />
        <input asp-for="Phone" class="form-control">
      </div>
      <div class="mb-3">
        <input type="submit" class="form-control">
      </div>
    </div>
</form>
```

2. In the Controllers folder, in HomeController.cs, add an action method named ProcessShipper.
    Give it a parameter to receive a shipper entity and then return it as a JSON document using the
    Json method, as shown in the following code:

```
[HttpPost]
[ValidateAntiForgeryToken]
public IActionResult ProcessShipper(Shipper shipper)
{
  return Json(shipper);
}
```

3. Start the Northwind.Mvc website project.
4. Navigate to the **Privacy** page, and then click the **Shipper** button.
5. On the **Shipper** page, right-click, select **View page source**, and note the different HTML output
    for the form generated by the Form, Input, and Label Tag Helpers, including a hidden element
    named __RequestVerificationToken, as shown in the following markup:

```
<h2>With Form Tag Helper</h2>
<form class="form-horizontal" role="form" action="/Home/ProcessShipper"
method="post">
  <div>
    <div class="mb-3">
      <label class="form-label" for="ShipperId" />
      <input class="form-control" type="number" data-val="true"
data-val-required="The ShipperId field is required." id="ShipperId"
name="ShipperId" value="1">
    </div>
    <div class="mb-3">
      <label class="form-label" for="CompanyName" />
```

```
        <input class="form-control" type="text" data-val="true" data-val-
    length="The field CompanyName must be a string with a maximum length
    of 40." data-val-length-max="40" data-val-required="The CompanyName
    field is required." id="CompanyName" maxlength="40" name="CompanyName"
    value="Speedy Express">
        </div>
        <div class="mb-3">
            <label class="form-label" for="Phone" />
            <input class="form-control" type="text" data-val="true" data-
    val-length="The field Phone must be a string with a maximum length of
    24." data-val-length-max="24" id="Phone" maxlength="24" name="Phone"
    value="(503) 555-9831">
        </div>
        <div class="mb-3">
            <input type="submit" class="form-control">
        </div>
    </div>
<input name="__RequestVerificationToken" type="hidden"
value="CfDJ8NTt08jabvBCqd1P4J-HCq3X9CDrTPjBphdDdVmG6UT0GFBJk1w7F1OLmNT-jE
GjlGIjfV3kmNUaofOAxlGgiZJwbAR73g-QgFw8oFV_0vjlo45t9dL9E1l1hZzjLXtj8B7y
sDkCYcm8W9zS0T7V3R0" /></form>
```

6. In the form, change the shipper ID and company name, noting that attributes like maxlength="40" prevent a company name longer than 40 characters, and type="number" only allows numbers for the shipper ID.

7. Click the **Submit** button and note the JSON document returned, as shown in the following output:

```
{"shipperId":1,"companyName":"Speedy Express","phone":"(503)
555-9831","orders":[]}
```

8. Close the browser and shut down the web server.

Output caching

In some ways, output caching is like response caching, which we covered in *Chapter 9, Caching, Queuing, and Resilient Background Services*. Output caching can store dynamically generated responses on the server so that they do not have to be regenerated again for another request. This can improve performance. Unlike response caching, output caching does not rely on clients and intermediaries doing what they are told by the HTTP response headers.

Output caching endpoints

Let's see it in action with a really simple example of applying output caching to some endpoints to make sure it is working properly:

1. In the `Northwind.Mvc` project, in `Program.cs`, after the call to `AddNorthwindContext`, add a statement to add the output cache middleware and override the default expiration timespan to make it only 10 seconds, as shown in the following code:

```
builder.Services.AddOutputCache(options =>
{
  options.DefaultExpirationTimeSpan = TimeSpan.FromSeconds(10);
});
```

 Good Practice: The default expiration time span is one minute. Think carefully about what the duration should be.

2. In `Program.cs`, before the call to map controller routes, add a statement to use output cache, as shown in the following code:

```
app.UseOutputCache();
```

3. In `Program.cs`, after the call to map Razor Pages, add statements to create two simple endpoints that respond with plain text, one that is not cached and one that uses the output cache, as shown in the following code:

```
app.MapGet("/notcached", () => DateTime.Now.ToString());
app.MapGet("/cached", () => DateTime.Now.ToString()).CacheOutput();
```

4. In `appsettings.Development.json`, add a log level of `Information` for the output caching middleware, as shown highlighted in the following configuration:

```
{
  "Logging": {
    "LogLevel": {
      "Default": "Information",
      "Microsoft.AspNetCore": "Warning",
      "Microsoft.AspNetCore.OutputCaching": "Information"
    }
  }
}
```

5. Start the `Northwind.Mvc` website project and arrange the browser window and command prompt or terminal window so that you can see both.

6. In the browser, navigate to `https://localhost:5141/notcached`, and note nothing is written to the command prompt or terminal.

7. In the browser, click the **Refresh** button several times and note that the time is always updated because it is not served from the output cache.

8. In the browser, navigate to `https://localhost:5141/cached`, and note that messages are written to the command prompt or terminal to tell you that you have made a request for a cached resource but it does not have anything in the output cache so it has now cached the output, as shown in the following output:

```
info: Microsoft.AspNetCore.OutputCaching.OutputCacheMiddleware[7]
      No cached response available for this request.
info: Microsoft.AspNetCore.OutputCaching.OutputCacheMiddleware[9]
      The response has been cached.
```

9. In the browser, click the **Refresh** button several times and note that the time is not updated, and an output caching message tells you that the value was served from the cache, as shown in the following output:

```
info: Microsoft.AspNetCore.OutputCaching.OutputCacheMiddleware[5]
      Serving response from cache.
```

10. Continue refreshing until 10 seconds have passed and note that messages are written to the command line or terminal to tell you that the cached output has been updated.

11. Close the browser and shut down the web server.

Output caching MVC views

Now let's see how we can output cache an MVC view:

1. In `Program.cs`, at the end of the call to map controllers, add a call to the `CacheOutput` method, as shown highlighted in the following code:

```
app.MapControllerRoute(
    name: "default",
    pattern: "{controller=Home}/{action=Index}/{id?}")
  .CacheOutput();
```

2. Start the `Northwind.Mvc` website project and arrange the browser window and command prompt or terminal window so that you can see both.

3. At the command prompt or terminal, note that the home page with its table of orders is not in the output cache, so SQL commands are executed to get the data, and then once the Razor view generates the page, it is stored in the cache, as shown highlighted in the following output:

```
info: Microsoft.Hosting.Lifetime[14]
      Now listening on: https://localhost:5141
info: Microsoft.Hosting.Lifetime[14]
```

```
           Now listening on: http://localhost:5142
info: Microsoft.Hosting.Lifetime[0]
           Application started. Press Ctrl+C to shut down.
info: Microsoft.Hosting.Lifetime[0]
           Hosting environment: Development
info: Microsoft.Hosting.Lifetime[0]
           Content root path: C:\apps-services-net8\Chapter14\Northwind.Mvc
info: Microsoft.AspNetCore.OutputCaching.OutputCacheMiddleware[7]
           No cached response available for this request.
dbug: 6/16/2023 10:40:15.252 RelationalEventId.CommandExecuting[20100]
(Microsoft.EntityFrameworkCore.Database.Command)
           Executing DbCommand [Parameters=[], CommandType='Text',
CommandTimeout='30']
           SELECT [o].[OrderId], [o].[CustomerId], [o].[EmployeeId], [o].
[Freight], [o].[OrderDate], [o].[RequiredDate], [o].[ShipAddress], [o].
[ShipCity], [o].[ShipCountry], [o].[ShipName], [o].[ShipPostalCode],
[o].[ShipRegion], [o].[ShipVia], [o].[ShippedDate], [c].[CustomerId],
[c].[Address], [c].[City], [c].[CompanyName], [c].[ContactName], [c].
[ContactTitle], [c].[Country], [c].[Fax], [c].[Phone], [c].[PostalCode],
[c].[Region], [o0].[OrderId], [o0].[ProductId], [o0].[Discount], [o0].
[Quantity], [o0].[UnitPrice]
           FROM [Orders] AS [o]
           LEFT JOIN [Customers] AS [c] ON [o].[CustomerId] = [c].[CustomerId]
           LEFT JOIN [Order Details] AS [o0] ON [o].[OrderId] = [o0].[OrderId]
           ORDER BY [o].[OrderId], [c].[CustomerId], [o0].[OrderId]
info: Microsoft.EntityFrameworkCore.Database.Command[20101]
           Executed DbCommand (32ms) [Parameters=[], CommandType='Text',
CommandTimeout='30']
           SELECT [o].[OrderId], [o].[CustomerId], [o].[EmployeeId], [o].
[Freight], [o].[OrderDate], [o].[RequiredDate], [o].[ShipAddress], [o].
[ShipCity], [o].[ShipCountry], [o].[ShipName], [o].[ShipPostalCode],
[o].[ShipRegion], [o].[ShipVia], [o].[ShippedDate], [c].[CustomerId],
[c].[Address], [c].[City], [c].[CompanyName], [c].[ContactName], [c].
[ContactTitle], [c].[Country], [c].[Fax], [c].[Phone], [c].[PostalCode],
[c].[Region], [o0].[OrderId], [o0].[ProductId], [o0].[Discount], [o0].
[Quantity], [o0].[UnitPrice]
           FROM [Orders] AS [o]
           LEFT JOIN [Customers] AS [c] ON [o].[CustomerId] = [c].[CustomerId]
           LEFT JOIN [Order Details] AS [o0] ON [o].[OrderId] = [o0].[OrderId]
           ORDER BY [o].[OrderId], [c].[CustomerId], [o0].[OrderId]
info: Microsoft.AspNetCore.OutputCaching.OutputCacheMiddleware[8]
           The response has been cached.
```

4. On the home page, note the current time, and then refresh the page and note that the whole page, including the time and orders table, is served from the output cache, as shown in the following output:

```
info: Microsoft.AspNetCore.OutputCaching.OutputCacheMiddleware[5]
      Serving response from cache.
```

5. Keep refreshing until 10 seconds have passed and note that the page is then regenerated from the database and the current time is shown.

6. Close the browser and shut down the web server.

There are many other ways to vary the cached results for output caching and the ASP.NET Core team intends to add more capabilities in the future.

Practicing and exploring

Test your knowledge and understanding by answering some questions, getting some hands-on practice, and exploring this chapter's topics with deeper research.

Exercise 14.1 – Test your knowledge

Answer the following questions:

1. What is the advantage of declaring a strongly typed Razor view and how do you do it?
2. How do you enable Tag Helpers in a view?
3. What are the pros and cons of HTML Helper methods compared to Tag Helpers?
4. How can a browser request a preferred language for localization?
5. How do you localize text in a view?
6. What is the prefix for attributes recognized by Tag Helpers?
7. How can you pass a complex object as a query string parameter?
8. How can you control how long the contents of the <cache> element are cached for?
9. What is the <environment> element used for?
10. How does cache busting with Tag Helpers work?

Exercise 14.2 – Practice building user interfaces with Boostrap

Create a new ASP.NET Core MVC project named Ch14Ex02_ExploringBootstrap. Add views that implement the following Bootstrap features:

- Accordion: https://getbootstrap.com/docs/5.3/components/accordion/.
- Cards: https://getbootstrap.com/docs/5.3/components/card/.
- Carousel: https://getbootstrap.com/docs/5.3/components/carousel/.
- NavBar: https://getbootstrap.com/docs/5.3/components/navbar/.
- Popovers: https://getbootstrap.com/docs/5.3/components/popovers/.
- Toast: https://getbootstrap.com/docs/5.3/components/toasts/.

- Tooltips: `https://getbootstrap.com/docs/5.3/components/tooltips/`.

Exercise 14.3 – Explore topics

Use the links on the following page to learn more about the topics covered in this chapter:

`https://github.com/markjprice/apps-services-net8/blob/main/docs/book-links.md#chapter-14---building-web-user-interfaces-using-aspnet-core`

Summary

In this chapter, you learned how to build user interfaces using ASP.NET Core MVC. You learned about:

- ASP.NET Core Razor views and Razor syntax
- Some common Bootstrap styles
- Localizing and globalizing an ASP.NET Core website
- HTML Helpers and Tag Helpers
- Output caching endpoints and views

In the next chapter, you will learn how to build web user interface components using Blazor.

15

Building Web Components Using Blazor

This chapter is about building web components using Blazor. These can be rich and interactive user interfaces that render as HTML and CSS to provide cross-platform browser support.

There are many advantages to using .NET for client-side web development. You can write 99% of your code using C# instead of JavaScript and interop with JavaScript modules for the other 1%. You can share business logic between the server and the client. Blazor implements .NET Standard as well as the latest .NET 8 libraries, so you can use the extensive older .NET libraries, both from Microsoft and third parties.

In the previous edition of this book, this chapter covered **Blazor WebAssembly**, a hosting model where the entire Blazor app and the .NET runtime were downloaded to the browser and executed there. One of the problems with Blazor WebAssembly is a slow initial startup experience for the visitor because a lot needs to be downloaded and executed on the client.

Many .NET developers were frustrated with having to choose between different technologies to build web apps, because none of them are perfect and all have pros and cons.

In this edition of the book, this chapter covers the new unified Blazor Full Stack model introduced with .NET 8. This enables you to mix the best of all worlds in a single project, including the following:

- Blazor components that execute on the client-side using WebAssembly. This replaces what is possible with a Blazor WebAssembly project.
- Blazor components that execute on the server-side and communicate live with the **Document Object Model** (DOM) in the browser, using SignalR to perform updates. This replaces what is possible with a Blazor Server project.
- Blazor components that provide **static server rendering** (SSR) and return an HTTP response, with static content that does not interact live with the server. This replaces what is possible with Razor Pages or Razor Views used in traditional ASP.NET Core websites.
- Blazor components that provide server-side streaming so that some content is shown to the visitor as soon as possible, while the rest streams to the browser in the background. This is a brand-new feature.

- A future release will enable Blazor to execute in any .NET process, like a console app, so that it can be used as a **static site generator** (**SSG**).

This chapter will cover the following topics:

- Understanding Blazor
- Building Blazor components
- Building a Blazor data component
- Implementing caching using local storage

Understanding Blazor

Blazor is Microsoft's framework for web component development built on .NET.

Blazor hosting models

Blazor has multiple hosting models to choose from:

- **Blazor Server:** All the components execute on the web server and user interface updates are sent to the browser using SignalR. The nature of Blazor Server provides some key benefits, including complete .NET API support, direct access to all server-side resources like databases, fast initial load time, and your code is protected because it never leaves the server. This hosting model was introduced with .NET Core 3.0 in November 2019.

- **Blazor WebAssembly:** All the components execute in the web browser like other **single page application** (**SPA**) frameworks, for example, React and Angular. Your .NET assemblies and the .NET runtime are downloaded to the browser and cached for future use. The nature of Blazor WebAssembly provides some key benefits, including the ability to run the app offline when not connected to the network, to host the app on a static website or serve it from a **content delivery network** (**CDN**), and to offload processing to the client, which increases scalability. This hosting model was introduced as an extension to .NET Core 3.1 in May 2020 and was built-in with .NET 5 in November 2020.

- **Blazor Hybrid/.NET MAUI Blazor App:** All the components execute in a local web view hosted in a native client app. The app can be built using .NET MAUI if the app needs to be cross-plat-form, or using Windows Presentation Foundation or Windows Forms if you are only targeting Windows. The main benefit of Blazor Hybrid compared to the first two hosting models is access to native client capabilities that can provide a better user experience. This hosting model was introduced with .NET 7 in November 2022.

- **Blazor Full Stack:** Components can execute on the server and generate static markup, but each individual component can be switched to any of the following: streaming rendering, interactive server-side with live updates of the COM using SignalR, or interactive client-side with WebAssembly. This new hosting model was formerly known as Blazor United during .NET 8 previews. It was introduced as Blazor Full Stack with .NET 8 in November 2023. In future versions, I expect it to be simply known as Blazor.

Good Practice: For new projects, **Blazor Web App** should be your choice of project template. If you need a pure SPA project that can be hosted on Azure Static Web Apps or a CDN, then **Blazor WebAssembly Standalone App** will be your best choice because Blazor Web App requires a web server. For static websites, Blazor WebAssembly is still the right solution rather than the new Blazor Full Stack.

Instead of multiple *hosting models*, Blazor Full Stack has multiple equivalent *rendering modes*. The Blazor Server project template that hosted and executed its code on the server-side is now replaced by the *interactive server rendering mode*. The Blazor WebAssembly project templates that could be hosted even on a static website and execute their code on the client-side can now be replaced by the *interactive WebAssembly rendering mode*.

Blazor supports the latest version of all four major web browsers – Chrome, Firefox, Edge, and Safari, on mobile and desktop platforms. Blazor Hybrid supports the latest web view components on the three major platforms – Chrome on Android, Safari on iOS and macOS, and Edge WebView2 on Windows.

More Information: The official Blazor documentation has a useful table to help you choose between the hosting models. You can find it at the following link: `https://learn.microsoft.com/en-us/aspnet/core/blazor/hosting-models#which-blazor-hosting-model-should-i-choose`.

Blazor components

Blazor is all about **components**. A component is a part of a web app, like a button, a grid, a form for gathering input from the visitor, or even a whole page. Components can be reused and nested to build more complex components.

A Blazor component usually consists of a Razor file with the file extension `.razor`. Like Razor views in ASP.NET Core MVC or Razor Pages, Razor files used by Blazor components easily mix HTML and C# code. As well as the HTML elements that make up the user interface parts, and the CSS used to style them, the Razor file also has a code block to implement event handling, properties, and other statements to provide the functionality of the component.

For example, a Blazor component named `ProgressBar.razor` could implement a progress bar using Bootstrap. It might define parameters for a minimum, maximum, and the current value of the progress bar, and have Boolean parameters to enable animation style and show the current value as text, as shown in the following markup:

```
<div class="progress">
  <div class="progress-bar progress-bar-striped bg-info
              @(IsAnimated ? " progress-bar-animated" : "")"
       role="progressbar" aria-label="@LabelText" style="width: @Value%"
       aria-valuenow="@Value" aria-valuemin="@Minimum" aria-valuemax="@
Maximum">
    @(ShowValue ? Value + "%" : "")
```

```
      </div>
    </div>

    @code {
      [Parameter]
      public int Value { get; set; } = 0;

      [Parameter]
      public int Minimum { get; set; } = 0;

      [Parameter]
      public int Maximum { get; set; } = 100;

      [Parameter]
      public bool IsAnimated { get; set; } = false;

      [Parameter]
      public bool ShowValue { get; set; } = false;

      [Parameter]
      public string? LabelText { get; set; } = "Progress bar";
    }
```

To embed an instance of the component on a page, you use the component name as if it were an HTML element and set its parameters using HTML attributes, as shown in the following markup:

```
<ProgressBar Value="25" IsAnimated="true" ShowValue="true"
             LabelText="Progress of database deletion" />
```

Blazor routing to page components

The Router component in the App.razor file enables routing to components, as shown in the following markup:

```
<Router AppAssembly="@typeof(Program).Assembly">
  <Found Context="routeData">
    <RouteView RouteData="@routeData"
               DefaultLayout="@typeof(Layout.MainLayout)" />
    <FocusOnNavigate RouteData="@routeData" Selector="h1" />
  </Found>
</Router>
```

The Router component scans the assembly specifically in its AppAssembly parameter for components decorated with the [Route] attribute, registering their URL paths.

If a route match is found, then the context of the request is stored in a variable named routeData and passed to the matching Razor file. The default layout is set to use a class defined in the file named MainLayout.razor.

The FocusOnNavigate component has a Selector property that must be set to a valid CSS selector. This could be a tag selector like the default h1, or a more specific CSS selector that uses a CSS class or an ID. The setting is common across all components in your app, so you will need to set one that works across all your components. In the Razor file, the focus is set to the first <h1> element. If the Razor file contains a form, then you might want to set the first form input element like a text box to have the focus.

For example, in a typical ASP.NET Core MVC project, an MVC controller could be decorated with the [Route] attribute, as shown in the following code:

```
[Route("customers")]
public class CustomersController
{
```

An HTTP GET request to the relative path /customers would be matched to the route.

To create an equivalent routable page component, add the @page directive to the top of a component's .razor file, as shown in the following markup:

```
@page "customers"
```

A page component can have multiple @page directives to register multiple routes.

If you were to write code that uses reflection to find the component class generated for you from the Razor markup file, then you would discover that it is decorated with the [Route] attribute due to the @page directive.

At runtime, the page component is merged with any specific layout that you have specified, just like an MVC view or Razor Page would be. By default, Blazor project templates define a file named MainLayout. razor as the layout for page components.

Good Practice: By convention, put routable page Blazor components in the Components\ Pages folder and non-page components in the Components folder.

How to pass route parameters

Blazor routes can include case-insensitive named parameters, and your code can most easily access the passed values by binding the parameter to a property in the code block, using the [Parameter] attribute, as shown in the following markup:

```
@page "/employees/{country}"

<div>Country parameter as the value: @Country</div>

@code {
  [Parameter]
  public string Country { get; set; }
}
```

The recommended way to handle a parameter that should have a default value when it is missing is to suffix the parameter in the route with ?, using the null coalescing operator in the OnParametersSet method, as shown highlighted in the following markup:

```
@page "/employees/{country?}"

<div>Country parameter as the value: @Country</div>

@code {
  [Parameter]
  public string? Country { get; set; }

  protected override void OnParametersSet()
  {
    // if the automatically set property is null
    // set its value to USA
    Country = Country ?? "USA";
  }
}
```

Setting parameters from a query string

You can also set component properties using parameters from a query string, as shown in the following code:

```
[Parameter]
[SupplyParameterFromQuery(Name = "country")]
public string? Country { get; set; }
```

Route constraints for parameters

Route constraints validate that the data type is correct for a passed parameter. If a potential request with a parameter value violates the constraint, then a match for that route is not made, and other routes will be evaluated instead. If no routes match, then a 404 status code is returned.

If you do not set constraints, then any value is acceptable as a route match, but a data type conversion exception may result when the value is converted into the C# method's expected data type. Some route constraint examples are shown in *Table 15.1*:

Constraint example	Description
{isanimated:bool}	The IsAnimated property must be set to a valid Boolean value, for example, TRUE or true.
{hiredate:datetime}	The HireDate property must be a valid date/time value.
{price:decimal}	The UnitPrice property must be a valid decimal value.
{shipweight:double}	The ShipWeight property must be a valid double value.
{shipwidth:float}	The ShipWidth property must be a valid float value.
{orderid:guid}	The OrderId property must be a valid Guid value.
{categoryid:int}	The CategoryId property must be a valid int value.
{nanoseconds:long}	The Nanoseconds property must be a valid long value.

Table 15.1: Route constraint examples

 Good Practice: Route constraints assume invariant culture, so your URLs must not be localized. For example, always use invariant culture formats to pass date and time parameter values.

Base component classes

The OnParametersSet method is defined by the base class that components inherit from by default, named ComponentBase, as shown in the following code:

```
using Microsoft.AspNetCore.Components;

public abstract class ComponentBase : IComponent, IHandleAfterRender,
IHandleEvent
{
  // members not shown
}
```

`ComponentBase` has some useful methods that you can call and override, as shown in *Table 15.2*:

Method(s)	Description
InvokeAsync	Call this method to execute a function on the associated renderer's synchronization context. This avoids the requirement to write thread-synchronizing code when accessing shared resources. Multiple threads are not allowed to access the rendering process at the same time. The use of `InvokeAsync` means that only one thread will access components at any given moment, which eliminates the need to write thread-locking and synchronization code for shared state.
OnAfterRender, OnAfterRenderAsync	Override these methods to invoke code each time the component has been rendered.
OnInitialized, OnInitializedAsync	Override these methods to invoke code after the component has received its initial parameters from its parent in the render tree.
OnParametersSet, OnParametersSetAsync	Override these methods to invoke code after the component has received parameters and the values have been assigned to properties.
ShouldRender	Override this method to indicate if the component should render.
StateHasChanged	Call this method to cause the component to re-render.

Table 15.2: Useful methods of ComponentBase

Blazor layouts

Blazor components can have shared layouts in a similar way to MVC views and Razor Pages. You would create a `.razor` component file and make it explicitly inherit from `LayoutComponentBase`, as shown in the following markup:

```
@inherits LayoutComponentBase

<div>
  ...
  @Body
  ...
</div>
```

The base class has a property named `Body` that you can render in the markup at the correct place within the layout.

You can set a default layout for components in the `App.razor` file and its `Router` component. To explicitly set a layout for a component, use the `@layout` directive, as shown in the following markup:

```
@page "/employees"

@layout AlternativeLayout
```

```
<div>
  ...
</div>
```

How to navigate Blazor routes to page components

Microsoft provides a dependency service named `NavigationManager` that understands Blazor routing and the `NavLink` component. The `NavigateTo` method is used to go to the specified URL.

In HTML, you use the `<a>` element to define navigation links, as shown in the following markup:

```
<a href="/employees">Employees</a>
```

In Blazor, use the `<NavLink>` component, as shown in the following markup:

```
<NavLink href="/employees">Employees</NavLink>
```

The `NavLink` component is better than an anchor element because it automatically sets its class to `active` if its `href` is a match on the current location URL. If your CSS uses a different class name, then you can set the class name in the `NavLink.ActiveClass` property.

By default, in the matching algorithm, the `href` is a path *prefix*, so if `NavLink` has an `href` of `/employees`, as shown in the preceding code example, then it would match all the following paths and set them all to have the `active` class style:

```
/employees
/employees/USA
/employees/UK/London
```

To ensure that the matching algorithm only performs matches on *all* of the text in the path, (in other words, there is only a match when the whole complete text matches and not when just part of the path matches), then set the `Match` parameter to `NavLinkMatch.All`, as shown in the following code:

```
<NavLink href="/employees" Match="NavLinkMatch.All">Employees</NavLink>
```

If you set other attributes such as `target`, they are passed through to the underlying `<a>` element that is generated.

CSS and JavaScript isolation

Blazor components often need to provide their own CSS to apply styling or JavaScript for activities that cannot be performed purely in C#, like access to browser APIs. To ensure this does not conflict with site-level CSS and JavaScript, Blazor supports CSS and JavaScript isolation.

If you have a component named `Home.razor`, simply create a CSS file named `Home.razor.css`. The styles defined within this file will override any other styles in the project for this component, but not for the rest of the website.

For JavaScript isolation, you do not use a naming convention in the same way as with CSS. Instead, Blazor enables JavaScript isolation using JavaScript modules, imported using the JavaScript interop feature of Blazor, as you will see later in this chapter.

 You can read more about JavaScript isolation at the following link: `https://learn.` `microsoft.com/en-us/aspnet/core/blazor/javascript-interoperability/call-` `javascript-from-dotnet#javascript-isolation-in-javascript-modules`.

Building Blazor components

With ASP.NET Core 8, Blazor introduced a new project template to start a project that supports the most flexible hosting model and all rendering modes. It provides a basic template to run, and a `Weather` component, which shows a table with five rows of random temperatures that uses streaming rendering.

Reviewing the new Blazor project template

First, we will create a Blazor Web App project and review its important parts:

1. Use your preferred code editor to create a new project and solution, using the Blazor Web App project template, as defined in the following list:

    • Project template: **Blazor Web App** / `blazor --interactivity None`
    • Project file and folder: `Northwind.Blazor`
    • Solution file and folder: `Chapter15`
    • **Authentication type:** None
    • **Configure for HTTPS:** Selected
    • **Interactive render mode:** None
    • **Interactivity location:** Per page/component
    • **Include sample pages:** Selected
    • **Do not use top-level statements:** Cleared

 If you are using Visual Studio Code or JetBrains Rider, then enter the following command at the command prompt or terminal in the `Chapter15` folder: `dotnet` `new blazor --interactivity None -o Northwind.Blazor`.

 Good Practice: We have not selected the options to use interactive WebAssembly or server components so that we can build up your knowledge about how Blazor works step by step. In real-world projects, you are likely to want to select these options from the start. We have also selected sample pages, which you would likely want to clear in a real-world project.

2. Build the `Northwind.Blazor` project.

3. In `Northwind.Blazor.csproj`, note that it is identical to an ASP.NET Core project that uses the Web SDK and targets .NET 8.

4. In the `Northwind.Blazor` project, in `Program.cs`, note that the statements enable the ASP.NET Core service collection and HTTP pipeline, with Blazor-specific statements to add Razor components and then use them, as shown highlighted in the following code:

```
using Northwind.Blazor.Components;

var builder = WebApplication.CreateBuilder(args);

// Add services to the container.
builder.Services.AddRazorComponents();

var app = builder.Build();

// Configure the HTTP request pipeline.
if (!app.Environment.IsDevelopment())
{
  app.UseExceptionHandler("/Error", createScopeForErrors: true);
  // The default HSTS value is 30 days. You may want to change this for
production scenarios, see https://aka.ms/aspnetcore-hsts.
  app.UseHsts();
}

app.UseHttpsRedirection();

app.UseStaticFiles();
app.UseAntiforgery();

app.MapRazorComponents<App>();

app.Run();
```

5. In the `Northwind.Blazor` project, expand the `Properties` folder, open the `launchSettings.json` file, and for the `applicationUrl` setting of the `https` profile, change the port numbers to `5151` for `https` and `5152` for `http`, as shown in the following setting:

```
"applicationUrl": "https://localhost:5151;http://localhost:5152",
```

6. Save the changes to the `launchSettings.json` file.

7. In the `Northwind.Blazor` project, in the `Components` folder, open `App.razor`, as shown in the following markup:

```
<!DOCTYPE html>
<html lang="en">

<head>
  <meta charset="utf-8" />
  <meta name="viewport" content="width=device-width, initial-scale=1.0" />
  <base href="/" />
  <link rel="stylesheet" href="bootstrap/bootstrap.min.css" />
  <link rel="stylesheet" href="app.css" />
  <link rel="stylesheet" href="Northwind.Blazor.styles.css" />
  <link rel="icon" type="image/png" href="favicon.png" />
  <HeadOutlet />
</head>

<body>

  <Routes />
  <script src="_framework/blazor.web.js"></script>
</body>
</html>
```

Note the following:

- A `<HeadOutlet />` Blazor component to inject additional content into the `<head>` section. This is one of the built-in components available in all Blazor projects.

- A `<Routes />` Blazor component to define the custom routes in this project. This component can be completely customized by the developer because it is part of the current project, in a file named `Routes.razor`.

- A script block for `blazor.web.js` that manages communication back to the server for Blazor's dynamic features, like downloading WebAssembly components in the background and later switching from server-side to client-side component execution.

8. In the `Components` folder, in `Routes.razor`, note that a `<Router>` enables routing for all Blazor components found in the current assembly, and that if a matching route is found, then `RouteView` is executed, which sets the default layout for the component to `MainLayout` and passes any route data parameters to the component. For that component, the first `<h1>` element in it will get the focus, as shown in the following code:

```
<Router AppAssembly="@typeof(Program).Assembly">
  <Found Context="routeData">
```

```
    <RouteView RouteData="@routeData"
               DefaultLayout="@typeof(Layout.MainLayout)" />
    <FocusOnNavigate RouteData="@routeData" Selector="h1" />
  </Found>
</Router>
```

9. In the Components folder, in _Imports.razor, note that this file imports some useful name-spaces for use in all your custom Blazor components.

10. In the Components\Layout folder, note that MainLayout.razor defines <div> for a sidebar, containing a navigation menu that is implemented by the NavMenu.razor component file in this project, and HTML5 elements like <main> and <article> for the content, as shown in the following markup:

```
@inherits LayoutComponentBase

<div class="page">
  <div class="sidebar">
    <NavMenu />
  </div>

  <main>
    <div class="top-row px-4">
      <a href="https://learn.microsoft.com/aspnet/core/"
         target="_blank">About</a>
    </div>

    <article class="content px-4">
        @Body
    </article>
  </main>
</div>
```

11. In the Components\Layout folder, open NavMenu.razor, as shown in the following markup:

```
<div class="top-row ps-3 navbar navbar-dark">
  <div class="container-fluid">
    <a class="navbar-brand" href="">Northwind.Blazor</a>
  </div>
</div>

<input type="checkbox" title="Navigation menu" class="navbar-toggler" />

<div class="nav-scrollable"
```

```
      onclick="document.querySelector('.navbar-toggler').click()">
    <nav class="flex-column">
      <div class="nav-item px-3">
        <NavLink class="nav-link" href="" Match="NavLinkMatch.All">
          <span class="bi bi-house-door-fill-nav-menu" aria-
hidden="true"></span> Home
        </NavLink>
      </div>

      <div class="nav-item px-3">
        <NavLink class="nav-link" href="weather">
          <span class="bi bi-list-nested-nav-menu" aria-hidden="true">
          </span> Weather
        </NavLink>
      </div>
    </nav>
  </div>
```

Note the following:

- The `NavMenu` component does not have a `@page` directive because it does not use a shared layout or render as a page.
- It uses Bootstrap to provide a menu of choices that responsively adapts to the width of the viewport. It will collapse into a hamburger menu when there is not enough horizontal space, and then the visitor can toggle the navigation on and off.
- There are currently two menu items: **Home** and **Weather**. We will add more throughout this chapter.

12. In the `Components\Pages` folder, in `Home.razor`, note the `@page` directive that configures a route for the root path to go to this page component, and then change the heading from `world` to `Blazor Full Stack`, as shown highlighted in the following markup:

```
@page "/"

<PageTitle>Home</PageTitle>

<h1>Hello, Blazor Full Stack!</h1>

Welcome to your new app.
```

13. Start the `Northwind.Blazor` project, using its `https` profile without debugging:

- If you are using Visual Studio 2022, then in **Solution Explorer**, select the `Northwind.Blazor` project to make it active. In the Visual Studio 2022 toolbar, select the `https` profile as the **Startup Project**, and **Google Chrome** as the **Web Browser**.

- If you are using Visual Studio Code, then at the command line or terminal, enter the following command:

```
dotnet run --launch-profile https
```

14. In Chrome, note the left-side navigation and the home page component, as shown in *Figure 15.1*:

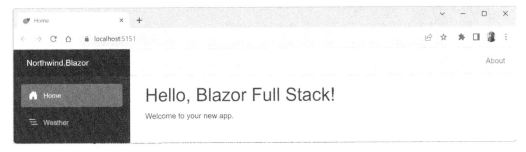

Figure 15.1: A simple web page implemented as a Blazor page component

15. Finally, close the browser and shut down the web server.

Using Bootstrap icons

The older Blazor project templates included all the Bootstrap icons. In the new project template, only three icons are defined using **Scalable Vector Graphics (SVG)**. Let's see how the team defined those icons, and then add some more for our own use:

1. In the Components\Layout folder, in the CSS stylesheet file named NavMenu.razor.css, find the text bi-house, and note the three icons defined using SVG, as partially shown in the following code:

```
.bi-house-door-fill-nav-menu {
    background-image: url("data:image/svg+xml,...");
}

.bi-plus-square-fill-nav-menu {
    background-image: url("data:image/svg+xml,...");
}

.bi-list-nested-nav-menu {
    background-image: url("data:image/svg+xml,...");
}
```

2. In your favorite browser, navigate to: https://icon-sets.iconify.design/bi/, and note that **Bootstrap Icons** have an MIT license and contain more than 2,000 icons.

3. In the **Search Bootstrap Icons** box, enter globe, and note that six globe icons are found.

4. Click the first globe, scroll down the page, and click the **SVG as data: URI** button. Note that you could copy and paste the definition of this icon for use in the CSS stylesheet, but you do not need to because I have already created a CSS file for you to use, with five icons defined for you to use in your Blazor project.

5. In your favorite browser, navigate to: `https://github.com/markjprice/apps-services-net8/blob/main/code/Chapter15/Northwind.Blazor/wwwroot/icons.css`, download the file, and save it in your own project in its `wwwroot` folder.

6. In the `Components` folder, in the `App.razor` component, in the `<head>`, add a `<link>` element to reference the `icons.css` stylesheet, as shown in the following markup:

    ```
    <link rel="stylesheet" href="icons.css" />
    ```

7. Save and close the file.

Referencing an EF Core class library and registering a data context

We will reference the EF Core model that you created in *Chapter 3, Building Entity Models for SQL Server Using EF Core*:

1. In the `Northwind.Blazor.csproj` project file, treat warnings as errors, and add a project reference to the Northwind database context project, as shown in the following markup:

    ```
    <ItemGroup>
      <ProjectReference Include="..\..\Chapter03\Northwind.Common.DataContext
    .SqlServer\Northwind.Common.DataContext.SqlServer.csproj" />
    </ItemGroup>
    ```

     The `Include` path must not have a line break.

2. At the command prompt or terminal, build the `Northwind.Blazor` project using the dotnet `build` command.

3. In the `Components` folder, in `_Imports.razor`, import the namspaces to use asynchronous methods with EF Core and to with the Northwind entity models, as shown in the following code:

    ```
    @using Microsoft.EntityFrameworkCore @* To use ToListAsync method. *@
    @using Northwind.EntityModels @* To use NorthwindContext and so on. *@
    ```

Importing the namespaces here means we do not have to import them at the top of .razor files. The _Imports.razor file only applies to .razor files. If you use code-behind .cs files to implement component code, then they must have namespaces imported separately, or use global usings to implicitly import the namespace. Note the statement to statically import the render mode type: @using static Microsoft.AspNetCore.Components.Web.RenderMode.

4. In Program.cs, import the namespace to use the AddNorthwindContext extension method, as shown in the following code:

```
using Northwind.EntityModels; // To use AddNorthwindContext method.
```

5. In the section that adds services to the container, add a statement that registers NorthwindContext as a service, as shown in the following code:

```
builder.Services.AddNorthwindContext();
```

Building a static server rendered component for data

Next, we will add a component that can do the same job as a Razor Page or Razor View in a traditional ASP.NET Core website. It will not have any interactivity that requires the component to execute on the server or client.

It will allow the visitor to see a table of products from the Northwind database:

1. In the Components\Pages folder, add a new file named Products.razor. In Visual Studio 2022, the project item template is named **Razor Component**. In JetBrains Rider, the project item template is named **Blazor Component**.

Good Practice: Component filenames must start with an uppercase letter, or you will have compile errors!

2. In Products.razor, set the route to /products, inject a Northwind data context, define a table to render products, and write a code block to get the products when the page has initialized, as shown in the following markup:

```
@page "/products"
@inject NorthwindContext db
<h1>Products</h1>
<table class="table">
  <thead>
    <tr>
      <th>Product ID</th>
      <th>Product Name</th>
```

```
        <th>Unit Price</th>
      </tr>
    </thead>
    <tbody>
      @if ((products is null) || (products.Count == 0))
      {
        <tr><td colspan="4">No products found.</td></tr>
      }
      else
      {
        @foreach (Product p in products)
        {
          <tr>
            <td>@p.ProductId</td>
            <td>@p.ProductName</td>
            <td>@(p.UnitPrice.HasValue ?
              p.UnitPrice.Value.ToString("C") : "n/a")</td>
          </tr>
        }
      }
    </tbody>
  </table>

  @code {
    private List<Product>? products;

    protected override async Task OnInitializedAsync()
    {
      products = await db.Products.ToListAsync();
    }
  }
```

3. In the Components\Layout folder, in NavMenu.razor, after the menu item to navigate to the home page, add a menu item to navigate to the products page, as shown in the following markup:

```
<div class="nav-item px-3">
  <NavLink class="nav-link" href="products">
    <span class="bi bi-globe" aria-hidden="true"></span> Products
  </NavLink>
</div>
```

4. If your database server is not running, (for example, because you are hosting it in Docker, a virtual machine, or the cloud), then make sure to start it.

5. Start the Northwind.Blazor project, using its https profile without debugging.

6. In the left-side navigation, click **Products**, and note the table of products.

7. Close the browser and shut down the web server.

Building a component with server interactivity

Next, we will add a component that requires some interactivity, so we will enable Blazer with SignalR to dynamically update the browser DOM live at runtime:

1. In the Components folder, add a new file named Counter.razor.

2. In Counter.razor, define a label to render the current value of the counter number, and a button to increment it, and a code block to store the current counter value with a click event handler, to increment the number, as shown in the following markup:

```
<h3>Counter: @CounterValue</h3>
<button id="buttonIncrement" @onclick="IncrementCounter"
  class="btn btn-outline-primary">Increment</button>

@code {
  public int CounterValue { get; set; } = 0;

  public void IncrementCounter()
  {
    CounterValue++;
  }
}
```

 Note that this component will not act as a page, so we do not decorate it with the @page directive or define a route to the component. It will only be used embedded in some other component.

3. In the Components\Pages folder, in Home.razor, at the bottom of the page, render the counter component, as shown in the following markup:

```
<Counter />
```

4. Start the Northwind.Blazor project, using its https profile without debugging.

5. On the home page, click the button, and note that nothing happens. When you create a project using the Blazor Web App template with the --interactivity None switch or the **Interactive render mode** set to **None**, no component interactivity is enabled in a Blazor Web App project.

6. Close the browser and shut down the web server.

7. In Program.cs, at the end of the statement that adds Razor components, add a call to a method to add interactive server components, as shown highlighted in the following code:

```
builder.Services.AddRazorComponents()
  .AddInteractiveServerComponents();
```

8. In `Program.cs`, at the end of the statement that maps Razor components, add a call to a method to add interactive server render mode, as shown highlighted in the following code:

```
app.MapRazorComponents<App>()
    .AddInteractiveServerRenderMode();
```

9. In the `Components` folder, in `Counter.razor`, at the top of the file, add a directive to set render mode to interactive server, as shown in the following markup:

```
@rendermode InteractiveServer
```

10. Start the `Northwind.Blazor` project, using its `https` profile without debugging.

11. In **Developer Tools**, click the **Console** tab, and note the `blazor.web.js` files establishes a WebSocket connection, as shown in the following output:

```
[2023-10-20T11:25:52.498Z] Information: Normalizing '_blazor' to
'https://localhost:5151/_blazor'.
[2023-10-20T11:25:52.675Z] Information: WebSocket connected to wss://
localhost:5151/_blazor?id=j6Fc0Mbay_jWkZTWfIqs_w.
```

12. In **Developer Tools**, click the **Network** tab, click **WS** to filter by WebSockets, and refresh the home page.

13. On the home page, click the **Increment** button, note the counter increments, note the _**blazor?id=...** request, select the request for **_blazor?id=...**, and click the **Initiator** tab, and note that the initiator was the `blazor.web.js` file that is added to all pages by the `App.razor` file, as shown in *Figure 15.2*:

Figure 15.2: Blazor.web.js requests to SignalR on the server to update the DOM for live interactivity

14. Close the browser and shut down the web server.

Building a Blazor progress bar component

In this section, we will build a component to provide a progress bar. It will use Bootstrap classes to set a stripped light blue color, with options to animate the bar and show the current value of the progress as a percentage:

1. In the `Northwind.Blazor` project, in the `Components` folder, add a new file named `ProgressBar.razor`.

2. In `ProgressBar.razor`, add statements to render `<div>` elements that use Bootstrap classes to define a progress bar with bindable parameters, setting various properties, as shown in the following markup:

```razor
@rendermode InteractiveServer
<div class="progress">
  <div class="progress-bar progress-bar-striped bg-info
              @(IsAnimated ? " progress-bar-animated" : "")"
       role="progressbar" aria-label="@LabelText"
       style="width: @Value%" aria-valuenow="@Value"
       aria-valuemin="@Minimum" aria-valuemax="@Maximum">
    @(ShowValue ? Value + "%" : "")
  </div>
</div>

@code {
  [Parameter]
  public int Value { get; set; } = 0;

  [Parameter]
  public int Minimum { get; set; } = 0;

  [Parameter]
  public int Maximum { get; set; } = 100;

  [Parameter]
  public bool IsAnimated { get; set; } = false;

  [Parameter]
  public bool ShowValue { get; set; } = false;

  [Parameter]
  public string? LabelText { get; set; } = "Progress bar";
}
```

3. In the `Components\Pages` folder, in `Home.razor`, at the bottom of the file, add statements to define a Bootstrap row with two equal columns, and add a `<ProgressBar>` component set to 25%, as shown in the following markup:

```
<div class="row">
  <div class="col">
    <div class="alert alert-info">
      <h4>Progress of database deletion</h4>
      <ProgressBar Value="25" IsAnimated="true" ShowValue="true"
                   LabelText="Progress of database deletion" />
    </div>
  </div>
  <div class="col">
    More components coming soon.
  </div>
</div>
```

4. Start the `Northind.Blazor` project, using its `https` profile without debugging.

5. Note the progress bar that shows the progress of the (simulated!) database deletion.

6. Close the browser and shut down the web server.

Building a Blazor dialog box component

In this section, we will build a component to provide a popup dialog box for interaction with the website visitor. It will use Bootstrap classes to define a button that, when clicked, shows a dialog box with two buttons with configurable labels.

By default, the Blazor Web App project template uses a local copy of Bootstrap 5.1 but only the CSS part. We will need to add a script tag to add the JavaScript parts of Bootstrap. We may as well upgrade to the latest version of Bootstrap and use the CDN version too.

 You can find the latest CDN links at the following link: `https://getbootstrap.com/docs/5.3/getting-started/introduction/#cdn-links`.

The component will also define two event callbacks that can be handled by the parent to customize what code executes when the two buttons are clicked.

1. In `App.razor`, comment out the `<link>` to the local CSS file and add a reference to the latest CDN version, as shown highlighted in the following markup:

```
@*<link rel="stylesheet" href="bootstrap/bootstrap.min.css" />*@
<link rel="stylesheet" href="https://cdn.jsdelivr.net/npm/
bootstrap@5.3.2/dist/css/bootstrap.min.css" integrity="sha384-T3
c6CoIi6uLrA9TneNEoa7RxnatzjcDSCmG1MXxSR1GAsXEV/Dwwykc2MPK8M2HN"
crossorigin="anonymous">
```

2. In `App.razor`, after the `<script>` tag for Blazor, add a `<script>` to the latest CDN version, and suppress error RZ/BL9992, as shown in the following markup:

```
<script src="https://cdn.jsdelivr.net/npm/bootstrap@5.3.2/dist/js/
bootstrap.bundle.min.js" integrity="sha384-C6RzsynM9kWDrMNeT87bh95OGNyZ
PhcTNXj1NW7RuBCsyN/o0jlpcV8Qyq46cDfL" crossorigin="anonymous" suppress-
error="BL9992"></script>
```

 We suppress the error BL9992 (also referred to as RZ9992), which warns that, "Script tags should not be placed inside components because they cannot be updated dynamically." For more information, see `https://aka.ms/AAe3qu3`.

3. In the `Northwind.Blazor` project, in the `Components` folder, add a new file named `DialogBox.razor`.

4. In `DialogBox.razor`, add statements to render `<div>` elements that use Bootstrap classes to define a button and modal dialog box with bindable parameters, setting various properties, as shown in the following markup:

```
@rendermode InteractiveServer
<!-- Button to show the dialog box. -->
<button type="button" class="btn btn-primary"
        data-bs-toggle="modal" data-bs-target="#dialogBox">
  @DialogTitle
</button>
<!-- Dialog box to popup. -->
<div class="modal fade" id="dialogBox"
     data-bs-backdrop="static" data-bs-keyboard="false" tabindex="-1"
     aria-labelledby="dialogBoxLabel" aria-hidden="true">
  <div class="modal-dialog">
    <div class="modal-content">
      <div class="modal-header">
        <h5 class="modal-title" id="dialogBoxLabel">@DialogTitle</h5>
        <button type="button" class="btn-close"
                data-bs-dismiss="modal" aria-label="Close"></button>
      </div>
      <div class="modal-body">
        @ChildContent
      </div>
      <div class="modal-footer">
        <button type="button" class="btn btn-primary"
                @onclick="OnClickPrimary">
            @PrimaryButtonText
```

```
        </button>
        <button type="button" class="btn btn-secondary"
                data-bs-dismiss="modal" @onclick="OnClickSecondary">
            @SecondaryButtonText
        </button>
      </div>
    </div>
  </div>
</div>
@code {
  [Parameter]
  public string? DialogTitle { get; set; }

  // ChildContent is a special name that is set automatically by any
  // markup content within the component begin and end elements.
  [Parameter]
  public RenderFragment? ChildContent { get; set; }

  [Parameter]
  public string? PrimaryButtonText { get; set; } = "OK";

  [Parameter]
  public EventCallback<MouseEventArgs> OnClickPrimary { get; set; }

  [Parameter]
  public string? SecondaryButtonText { get; set; } = "Cancel";

  [Parameter]
  public EventCallback<MouseEventArgs> OnClickSecondary { get; set; }
}
```

 Note that the two buttons have default text values of OK and Cancel, and they both have event callback parameters that will have information about the mouse pointer passed as event arguments. Also, note the button with class="btn-close" that visually appears as the **X** button in the top-right corner to close the dialog.

5. In the Components\Pages folder, in Home.razor, at the top of the file, add statements to set render mode as the interactive server, as shown in the following markup:

    ```
    @rendermode InteractiveServer
    ```

6. In the Components\Pages folder, in Home.razor, near the bottom of the file, replace the text More components coming soon with statements to add a <DialogBox> component that sets the two button labels to Yes and No, and then at the bottom of the file, add a Razor code block to define event handlers for the two click events that output which button was clicked and the current position of the mouse pointer, as shown highlighted in the following markup:

    ```
    <div class="col">
      <DialogBox DialogTitle="Delete Database"
                 PrimaryButtonText="Yes" OnClickPrimary="Yes_Click"
                 SecondaryButtonText="No" OnClickSecondary="No_Click">
        Are you sure you want to delete the entire database? Really?
      </DialogBox>
    </div>
    </div>

    @code {
      private void Yes_Click(MouseEventArgs e)
      {
        Console.WriteLine("User clicked 'Primary' button at ({0}, {1}).",
          arg0: e.ClientX, arg1: e.ClientY);
      }

      private void No_Click(MouseEventArgs e)
      {
        Console.WriteLine("User clicked 'Secondary' button at ({0}, {1}).",
          arg0: e.ClientX, arg1: e.ClientY);
      }
    }
    ```

     Any content between the <DialogBox> and </DialogBox> elements is automatically set as the ChildContent property.

7. Start the Northwind.Blazor project, using its https profile without debugging.

8. Click the **Delete Database** button, and note the modal dialog box that pops up, as shown in *Figure 15.3*:

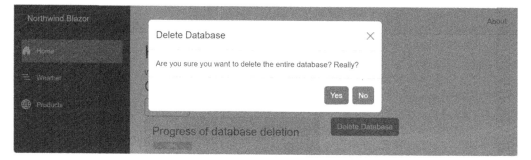

Figure 15.3: A pop-up modal dialog box that a Blazor component built using Bootstrap

9. Arrange the command prompt or terminal and the browser window so that you can see both.

10. In the **Delete Database** dialog box, click the **Yes** button and **No** button a few times (clicking the **No** button or the **x** button will close the dialog, so click the **Delete Database** button again to reshow the dialog box), and note the messages written to the console, as shown in *Figure 15.4*:

```
User clicked 'Primary' button at (682, 188).
User clicked 'Secondary' button at (738, 183).
User clicked 'Primary' button at (685, 182).
User clicked 'Primary' button at (688, 194).
User clicked 'Secondary' button at (755, 182).
```

Figure 15.4: The dialog box component writing to the server console

 JavaScript in the client displays the Bootstrap dialog box. Clicks on the buttons trigger the SignalR connection over WebSockets to execute the component event handling code, executing on the server.

11. Close the browser, and shut down the web server.

 You can read more about the supported event arguments at the following link: https://learn.microsoft.com/en-us/aspnet/core/blazor/components/event-handling#event-arguments.

Building a Blazor alert component

In this section, we will build a component to provide alerts to show messages to the website visitor. It will use Bootstrap classes to define a colorful area for the message, which can be dismissed. The message, title, icon, and color theme can be configured:

1. In the `Northwind.Blazor` project, in the `Components` folder, add a new file named the `Bootstrap.Constants.cs` file.

2. In `Bootstrap.Constants.cs`, add statements to define some static classes with `string` constant values for common Bootstrap color themes and icons, as shown in the following code:

```
namespace Northwind.Blazor.Components;

public static class BootstrapColors
{
  public const string Primary = "primary";
  public const string Secondary = "secondary";
  public const string Danger = "danger";
  public const string Warning = "warning";
  public const string Success = "success";
  public const string Info = "info";
}

public static class BootstrapIcons
{
  public const string Globe = "bi bi-globe";
  public const string GlobeEmea = "bi bi-globe-europe-africa";
  public const string Pencil = "bi bi-pencil";
  public const string Trash = "bi bi-trash";
  public const string PlusSquare = "bi bi-plus-square";
  public const string InfoCircle = "bi bi-info-circle";
  public const string ExclamationTriangleFill =
    "bi bi-exclamation-triangle-fill";
}
```

3. In the `Components` folder, add a new file named `Alert.razor`.

4. In `Alert.razor`, add statements to render `<div>` elements that use Bootstrap classes to define a `<div>` with bindable parameters, setting various properties, as shown in the following markup:

```
@rendermode InteractiveServer
<div class="alert alert-@ColorTheme d-flex align-items-center
    @(IsDismissable ? " alert-dismissible fade show" : "")"
role="alert">
  <div>
    <h4 class="alert-heading"><span class="@Icon" aria-hidden="true">
      </span> @Title</h4>
    @Message
```

```
    @if (IsDismissable)
    {
      <button type="button" class="btn-close"
              data-bs-dismiss="alert" aria-label="Close"></button>
    }
  </div>
</div>

@code {
  [Parameter]
  public bool IsDismissable { get; set; } = true;

  [Parameter]
  public string ColorTheme { get; set; } = BootstrapColors.Primary;

  [Parameter]
  public string Icon { get; set; } = BootstrapIcons.InfoCircle;

  [Parameter]
  public string? Title { get; set; }

  [Parameter]
  public string? Message { get; set; }
}
```

5. In the `Components\Pages` folder, in `Home.razor`, add an `Alert` element below the `<DialogBox>` element, as shown in the following markup:

```
<Alert IsDismissable="true"
       Icon="@(BootstrapIcons.ExclamationTriangleFill)"
       ColorTheme="@(BootstrapColors.Warning)"
       Title="Warning"
       Message="Deleting the database cannot be undone." />
```

6. Start the `Northwind.Blazor` project, using its `https` profile without debugging.

7. On the home page, note the warning alert, as shown in *Figure 15.5*:

Figure 15.5: The alert component with a dismiss button

8. Click the close button to dismiss the warning.

9. Close the browser, and shut down the web server.

Building a Blazor data component

In this section, we will build a component that will list, create, and edit employees in the Northwind database.

We will build it over several steps:

1. Make a Blazor component that renders the name of an employee, set as a parameter.

2. Make it work as a routable page as well as a component.

3. Build and call an ASP.NET Core Minimal APIs web service.

4. Call the web service in the component.

Making the component

We will add the new component to the existing Blazor project:

1. In the `Northwind.Blazor` project, in the `Components\Pages` folder, add a new file named `Employees.razor`.

2. Add statements to output a heading for the `Employees` component and define a code block, defining a property to store the name of a country, as shown highlighted in the following markup:

```
@rendermode InteractiveServer
<h1>Employees @(string.IsNullOrWhiteSpace(Country)
    ? "Worldwide" : "in " + Country)</h1>

@code {
```

```
    [Parameter]
    public string? Country { get; set; }
}
```

3. In the Components\Pages folder, in Home.razor, after the welcome message, instantiate the Employees component twice: once setting USA as the Country parameter, and once without setting the country, as shown highlighted in the following markup:

```
<h1>Hello, Blazor Full Stack!</h1>
Welcome to your new app.
<Employees Country="USA" />
<Employees />
```

4. Start the Northwind.Blazor project, using its https profile without debugging.

5. Start Chrome, navigate to https://localhost:5151/, and note the Employees components, as shown in *Figure 15.6*:

Figure 15.6: The Employees component, with the Country parameter set to USA and without parameters set

6. Close the browser, and shut down the web server.

Making the component a routable page component

It is simple to turn this component into a routable page component with a route parameter for the country:

1. In the Components\Pages folder, in the Home.razor component, remove the two <Employee> elements because we will now use them as pages.

2. In the Components\Pages folder, in the Employees.razor component, add a statement at the top of the file to register /employees as its route, with an optional country route parameter, as shown highlighted in the following markup:

```
@rendermode InteractiveServer
@page "/employees/{country?}"
```

3. In the Components\Layout folder, in NavMenu.razor, add list item elements after **Products** to navigate to show employees worldwide and in the USA or UK, as shown in the following markup:

```
<div class="nav-item px-3">
  <NavLink class="nav-link" href="employees" Match="NavLinkMatch.All">
```

```
    <span class="bi bi-globe" aria-hidden="true"></span> Worldwide
  </NavLink>
</div>

<div class="nav-item px-3">
  <NavLink class="nav-link" href="employees/USA">
    <span class="bi bi-people" aria-hidden="true"></span> Employees in
USA
  </NavLink>
</div>

<div class="nav-item px-3">
  <NavLink class="nav-link" href="employees/UK">
    <span class="bi bi-person" aria-hidden="true"></span> Employees in UK
  </NavLink>
</div>
```

4. Start the `Northwind.Blazor` project, using its `https` profile without debugging.

5. Start Chrome and navigate to `https://localhost:5151/`.

6. In the left navigation menu, click **Employees in USA**. Note that the country name is correctly passed to the page component and that the component uses the same shared layout as the other page components, like `Home.razor`. Also note the URL: `https://localhost:5151/employees/USA`.

7. Close Chrome, and shut down the web server.

Getting entities into a component by building a web service

Now that you have seen the minimum implementation of an entity component, we can add the functionality to get entities from the server. In this case, we will use the Northwind database context to get employees from the database and expose it as an ASP.NET Core Minimal APIs web service:

1. Use your preferred code editor to add a project to the `Chapter15` solution, as defined in the following list:

   - Project template: **ASP.NET Core Web API** / webapi
   - Solution file and folder: Chapter15
   - Project file and folder: Northwind.MinimalApi.Service
   - **Authentication type:** None
   - **Configure for HTTPS:** Selected
   - **Enable Docker:** Cleared
   - **Enable OpenAPI support:** Selected
   - **Do not use top-level statements:** Cleared
   - **Use controllers:** Cleared

2. Add a project reference to the Northwind database context project for SQL Server that you
    created in *Chapter 3, Building Entity Models for SQL Server Using EF Core*, as shown in the fol-
    lowing markup:

```
<ItemGroup>
  <ProjectReference Include="..\..\Chapter03\Northwind.Common.DataContext
.SqlServer\Northwind.Common.DataContext.SqlServer.csproj" />
</ItemGroup>
```

 The path cannot have a line break. If you did not complete the task of creating
the class libraries in *Chapter 3*, then download the solution projects from the
GitHub repository.

3. In the project file, change invariant globalization to `false`, and treat warnings as errors, as
    shown in the following markup:

```
<Project Sdk="Microsoft.NET.Sdk.Web">

  <PropertyGroup>
    <TargetFramework>net8.0</TargetFramework>
    <Nullable>enable</Nullable>
    <ImplicitUsings>enable</ImplicitUsings>
    <InvariantGlobalization>false</InvariantGlobalization>
    <TreatWarningsAsErrors>true</TreatWarningsAsErrors>
  </PropertyGroup>
```

4. At the command prompt or terminal, build the `Northwind.MinimalApi.Service` project to
    make sure the entity model class library projects outside the current solution are properly
    compiled, as shown in the following command:

```
dotnet build
```

5. In the `Properties` folder, in `launchSettings.json`, modify the `applicationUrl` of the profile
    named `https` to use port 5153 and `http` to use port 5154, as shown highlighted in the following
    configuration:

```
"profiles": {
  ...
  "https": {
    "commandName": "Project",
    "dotnetRunMessages": true,
    "launchBrowser": true,
    "launchUrl": "swagger",
    "applicationUrl": "https://localhost:5153;http://localhost:5154",
```

```
      "environmentVariables": {
        "ASPNETCORE_ENVIRONMENT": "Development"
      }
```

6. In `Program.cs`, import namespaces to work with Minimal APIs attributes, registering the North-wind database context extension method, and serialize JSON, as shown in the following code:

```
using Microsoft.AspNetCore.Mvc; // To use [FromServices].
using Northwind.EntityModels; // To use AddNorthwindContext.
using System.Text.Json.Serialization; // To use ReferenceHandler.

// Define an alias for the JsonOptions class.
using HttpJsonOptions = Microsoft.AspNetCore.Http.Json.JsonOptions;
```

7. In `Program.cs`, at the end of the section to configure services, before the call to `Build`, add a statement to configure the Northwind database context and the registered dependency service for JSON options, setting its reference handler to preserve references, so that the reference between an employee and their manager does not cause a runtime exception due to circular references, as shown in the following code:

```
builder.Services.AddNorthwindContext();

builder.Services.Configure<HttpJsonOptions>(options =>
{
  // If we do not preserve references then when the JSON serializer
  // encounters a circular reference it will throw an exception.
  Options.SerializerOptions.ReferenceHandler = ReferenceHandler.Preserve;
});
```

 Be careful to configure `Microsoft.AspNetCore.Http.Json.JsonOptions` and not `Microsoft.AspNetCore.Mvc.JsonOptions`! I have created an alias to make this explicit, since we need to import the `Microsoft.AspNetCore.Mvc` namespace of other types.

8. In `Program.cs`, before the call to the `app.Run()` method, add statements to define some end-points to `GET` and `POST` employees, as shown in the following code:

```
app.MapGet("api/employees", (
  [FromServices] NorthwindContext db) =>
    Results.Json(db.Employees))
  .WithName("GetEmployees")
  .Produces<Employee[]>(StatusCodes.Status200OK);

app.MapGet("api/employees/{id:int}", (
```

```
  [FromServices] NorthwindContext db,
  [FromRoute] int id) =>
  {
    Employee? Employee = db.Employees.Find(id);
    if (employee == null)
    {
      return Results.NotFound();
    }
    else
    {
      return Results.Json(employee);
    }
  })
  .WithName("GetEmployeesById")
  .Produces<Employee>(StatusCodes.Status200OK)
  .Produces(StatusCodes.Status404NotFound);

app.MapGet("api/employees/{country}", (
  [FromServices] NorthwindContext db,
  [FromRoute] string country) =>
    Results.Json(db.Employees.Where(employee =>
    employee.Country == country)))
  .WithName("GetEmployeesByCountry")
  .Produces<Employee[]>(StatusCodes.Status200OK);

app.MapPost("api/employees", async ([FromBody] Employee employee,
  [FromServices] NorthwindContext db) =>
  {
    db.Employees.Add(employee);
    await db.SaveChangesAsync();
    return Results.Created($"api/employees/{employee.EmployeeId}",
employee);
  })
  .Produces<Employee>(StatusCodes.Status201Created);
```

9. Optionally, delete the statements to set up the weather endpoint.

 Due to the {id:int} constraint, a GET request to a path like api/employees/3 will map to the GetEmployeesById endpoint, and a GET request to a path like api/employess/USA will map to the GetEmployeesByCountry endpoint. When POST-ing to the api/employees endpoint, the response includes a URL to the newly created employee with its database-assigned ID.

Getting entities into a component by calling the web service

Now, we can add the functionality to the entity component to call the web service:

1. In the `Northwind.Blazor` project, in its project file, add a package reference for QuickGrid, as shown in the following markup:

   ```
   <ItemGroup>
     <PackageReference Include=
       "Microsoft.AspNetCore.Components.QuickGrid" Version="8.0.0" />
   </ItemGroup>
   ```

2. Build the project to restore packages.

3. In `Program.cs`, import the namespace to work with HTTP headers, as shown in the following code:

   ```
   using System.Net.Http.Headers; // To use MediaTypeWithQualityHeaderValue.
   ```

4. In the `Northwind.Blazor` project, in `Program.cs`, before the call to the `builder.Build()`, add statements to configure an HTTP client factory to call the web service, as shown in the following code:

   ```
   builder.Services.AddHttpClient(name: "Northwind.Blazor.Service",
     configureClient: options =>
     {
       options.BaseAddress = new("https://localhost:5153/");
       options.DefaultRequestHeaders.Accept.Add(
         new MediaTypeWithQualityHeaderValue(
           "application/json", 1.0));
     });
   ```

5. In the `Components` folder, in `_Imports.razor`, import the namespaces to work with QuickGrid and serialize JSON, ensuring that the Blazor components we build do not need to import the namespaces individually, as shown in the following markup:

   ```
   @using Microsoft.AspNetCore.Components.QuickGrid
   @using System.Text.Json @* To use JsonSerializerOptions. *@
   @using System.Text.Json.Serialization @* To use ReferenceHandler. *@
   ```

6. In the `Components\Pages` folder, in `Employees.razor`, add statements to inject the HTTP client factory, and then use it to output a grid of either all employees or employees in the specific country, as shown highlighted in the following code:

   ```
   @rendermode InteractiveServer
   @page "/employees/{country?}"
   @inject IHttpClientFactory httpClientFactory
   <h1>
   ```

```
   Employees @(string.IsNullOrWhiteSpace(Country) ? "Worldwide" : "in " +
Country)
</h1>


<QuickGrid Items="@employees" Class="table table-striped table-bordered">
  <PropertyColumn Property="@(emp => emp.EmployeeId)"
                  Title="ID" />
  <PropertyColumn Property="@(emp => emp.FirstName)" />
  <PropertyColumn Property="@(emp => emp.LastName)" />
  <PropertyColumn Property="@(emp => emp.City)" />
  <PropertyColumn Property="@(emp => emp.Country)" />
  <PropertyColumn Property="@(emp => emp.HireDate)"
                  Format="yyyy-MM-dd" />
</QuickGrid>


@code {
  [Parameter]
  public string? Country { get; set; }

  // QuickGrid works best if it binds to an IQueryable<T> sequence.
  private IQueryable<Employee>? employees;

  protected override async Task OnParametersSetAsync()
  {
    Employee[]? employeesArray = null;

    // Employee entity has circular reference to itself so
    // we must control how references are handled.
    JsonSerializerOptions jsonOptions = new()
    {
        ReferenceHandler = ReferenceHandler.Preserve,
        PropertyNameCaseInsensitive = true
    };

    HttpClient client = httpClientFactory.CreateClient(
      "Northwind.Blazor.Service");
```

```
    string path = "api/employees";

    try
    {
      employeesArray = (await client.GetFromJsonAsync<Employee[]?>(
        path, jsonOptions));
    }
    catch (Exception ex)
    {
      Console.WriteLine($"{ex.GetType()}: {ex.Message}");
    }

    if (employeesArray is not null)
    {
      employees = employeesArray.AsQueryable();

      if (!string.IsNullOrWhiteSpace(Country))
      {
        employees = employees.Where(emp => emp.Country == Country);
      }
    }
  }
}
```

 Although the web service has an endpoint that allows you to return only employees in a specified country, later we will add caching for employees, so in this implementation we will request all employees and use client-side filtering for the bound data grid.

7. If your database server is not running, (for example, because you are hosting it in Docker, a virtual machine, or in the cloud), then make sure to start it.

8. Start the Northwind.MinimalApi.Service project, using its https profile without debugging.

9. Start the Northwind.Blazor project, using its https profile without debugging.

10. Start Chrome, and navigate to https://localhost:5151/.

11. In the left navigation menu, click **Employees in USA**, and note that the grid of employees loads from the web service and renders in the web page, as shown in *Figure 15.7*:

Figure 15.7: The grid of employees in the USA

12. In the left navigation menu, click **Employees in UK**, and note that the grid of employees is filtered to only show employees in the UK.

13. Close Chrome, and shut down the web server.

Practicing and exploring

Test your knowledge and understanding by answering some questions, getting some hands-on practice, and exploring this chapter's topics with deeper research.

Exercise 15.1 – Test your knowledge

Answer the following questions:

1. What is the benefit of the new Blazor Full Stack hosting model in .NET 8 compared to the legacy hosting models like Blazor Server?

2. Does Blazor WebAssembly support all features of the latest .NET APIs?

3. What is the file extension for Blazor components?

4. How do you set the default layout for all Blazor page components?

5. How do you register a route for a Blazor page component?

6. When would you set the `Match` property of a `<NavLink>` component to `NavLinkMatch.All`?

7. You have imported a custom namespace in the `_Imports.razor` file, but when you try to use a class in that namespace in a code-behind file for the Blazor component, the class is not found. Why? How can you fix the issue?

8. What must you do to a property in a component class to have it set to a query string parameter automatically?

9. What is QuickGrid?

10. How can a Blazor component access browser features like local storage?

Exercise 15.2 – Practice building Blazor components

Create a Blazor component named Carousel that wraps the Bootstrap classes to work with carousels as a component, and then use it to show the eight categories in the Northwind database, including images.

> You can learn about the Bootstrap carousel at the following link: https://getbootstrap. com/docs/5.3/components/carousel/.

Exercise 15.3 – Practice building an IndexedDB interop service

Browser local and session storage its okay for storing small amounts of data, but if you need a more robust and capable storage in the browser, then you can use the IndexedDB API.

Create a Blazor service named IndexedDbService, with a JavaScript module for interop, with the IndexedDB API, and then use it to cache the employees.

> You can learn more about the methods of the window.indexedDB object at the following link: https://developer.mozilla.org/en-US/docs/Web/API/IndexedDB_API.

Exercise 15.4 – Explore topics

Use the links on the following page to learn more details about the topics covered in this chapter:

https://github.com/markjprice/apps-services-net8/blob/main/docs/book-links.md#chapter-15---building-web-components-using-blazor

Exercise 15.5 – Explore Blazor WebAssembly topics

To read more about topics related specifically to Blazor WebAssembly projects, I have written an online-only section, found at the following link: https://github.com/markjprice/apps-services-net8/blob/main/docs/ch15-blazor-webassembly.md.

Exercise 15.6 – Explore Progressive Web Apps with Blazor

To read more about topics related specifically to Blazor PWA support, I have written an online-only section, found at the following link: https://github.com/markjprice/apps-services-net8/blob/main/docs/ch15-blazor-pwa.md.

Exercise 15.7 – Leveraging Open Source Blazor Component Libraries

To learn how to use some common Blazor open-source components, I have written an online-only section, found at the following link: `https://github.com/markjprice/apps-services-net8/blob/main/docs/ch15-blazor-libraries.md`.

Summary

In this chapter, you learned:

- About some important concepts surrounding Blazor, like hosting models, components, routing, and how to pass parameters.
- How to build Blazor components with settable parameters, child content, and custom events.
- How to build Blazor components that get data from a web service.

In the next chapter, you will learn how to build cross-platform apps for mobile and desktop devices, using .NET MAUI.

Learn more on Discord

To join the Discord community for this book – where you can share feedback, ask questions to the author, and learn about new releases – follow the QR code below:

`https://packt.link/apps_and_services_dotnet8`

16

Building Mobile and Desktop Apps Using .NET MAUI

This chapter is about learning how to make **graphical user interface (GUI)** apps by building a cross-platform mobile and desktop app for iOS and Android, macOS Catalyst, and Windows using **.NET MAUI (Multi-platform App UI)**. According to the MAUI team, there are no breaking API changes between .NET 7 and .NET 8. They focused primarily on fixing bugs and improving performance.

You will see how **eXtensible Application Markup Language (XAML)** makes it easy to define the **user interface (UI)** for a graphical app. XAML is pronounced "zamel."

Cross-platform GUI development cannot be learned in only a hundred or so pages, but I want to introduce you to some of what is possible. Think of this .NET MAUI chapter and the additional online-only sections as an introduction that will give you a taste to inspire you, and then you can learn more from a book dedicated to mobile or desktop development.

The app will allow the listing and management of customers in the Northwind database. The mobile app that you create will call an ASP.NET Core Minimal APIs web service. We will start building it in this chapter and then continue building the app in the online-only section, *Implementing Model-View-View-Model for .NET MAUI*, which you will find in the exercises at the end of this chapter.

A Windows computer with Visual Studio 2022 version 17.8 or later, or any operating system with Visual Studio Code and the dotnet CLI or JetBrains Rider, can be used to create a .NET MAUI project. But you will need a computer with Windows to compile WinUI 3 apps, and you will need a computer with macOS and Xcode to compile for macOS Catalyst and iOS.

In this chapter, we will cover the following topics:

- Understanding XAML
- Understanding .NET MAUI
- Building mobile and desktop apps using .NET MAUI
- Using shared resources
- Using data binding

Understanding XAML

Let's start by looking at the markup language used by .NET MAUI.

In 2006, Microsoft released **Windows Presentation Foundation (WPF)**, which was the first technology to use XAML. Silverlight, for web and mobile apps, quickly followed, but it is no longer supported by Microsoft. WPF is still used today to create Windows desktop applications; for example, Visual Studio 2022 is partially built using WPF.

XAML can be used to build parts of the following apps:

- **.NET MAUI apps** for mobile and desktop devices, including Android, iOS, Windows, and macOS. It is an evolution of a technology named **Xamarin.Forms**.
- **WinUI 3 apps** for Windows 10 and 11.
- **Universal Windows Platform (UWP) apps** for Windows 10 and 11, Xbox, Mixed Reality, and Meta Quest VR headsets.
- **WPF apps** for Windows desktop, including Windows 7 and later.
- **Avalonia** and **Uno Platform apps** using cross-platform third-party technologies.

Simplifying code using XAML

XAML simplifies C# code, especially when building a UI.

Imagine that you need two or more pink buttons laid out horizontally to create a toolbar, which execute a method for their implementation when clicked.

In C#, you might write the following code:

```
HorizontalStackPanel toolbar = new();

Button newButton = new();
newButton.Content = "New";
newButton.Background = new SolidColorBrush(Colors.Pink);
newButton.Clicked += NewButton_Clicked;
toolbar.Children.Add(newButton);

Button openButton = new();
openButton.Content = "Open";
openButton.Background = new SolidColorBrush(Colors.Pink);
openButton.Clicked += OpenButton_Clicked;
toolbar.Children.Add(openButton);
```

In XAML, this could be simplified to the following lines of code. When this XAML is processed, the equivalent properties are set, and methods are called to achieve the same goal as the preceding C# code:

```
<HorizontalStackPanel x:Name="toolbar">
  <Button x:Name="newButton" Background="Pink"
          Clicked="NewButton_Clicked">New</Button>
  <Button x:Name="openButton" Background="Pink"
          Clicked="OpenButton_Clicked">Open</Button>
</StackPanel>
```

You can think of XAML as an alternative and easier way of declaring and instantiating .NET types, especially when defining a UI and the resources that it uses.

XAML allows resources like brushes, styles, and themes to be declared at different levels, like a UI element or a page, or globally for the application to enable resource sharing.

XAML allows data binding between UI elements or between UI elements and objects and collections.

If you choose to use XAML to define your UI and related resources at compile time, then the code-behind file must call the InitializeComponent method in the page constructor, as shown highlighted in the following code:

```
public partial class MainPage : ContentPage
{
  public MainPage()
  {
    InitializeComponent(); // Process the XAML markup.
  }

  private void NewButton_Clicked(object sender, EventArgs e)
  {
    ...
  }

  private void OpenButton_Clicked(object sender, EventArgs e)
  {
    ...
  }
}
```

Calling the InitializeComponent method tells the page to read its XAML, create the controls defined in it, and set their properties and event handlers.

.NET MAUI namespaces

.NET MAUI has several important namespaces where its types are defined, as shown in *Table 16.1*:

Namespace	Description
`Microsoft.Maui`	Utility types like `FlowDirection`, `IButton`, `IImage`, and `Thickness`.
`Microsoft.Maui.Controls`	Common controls, pages, and related types like `Application`, `Brush`, `Button`, `CheckBox`, `ContentPage`, `Image`, and `VerticalStackPanel`.
`Microsoft.Maui.Graphics`	Types for graphics like `Color`, `Font`, `ImageFormat`, `PathBuilder`, `Point`, and `Size`.

Table 16.1: Important MAUI namespaces

To import a namespace using XAML, in the root element you add `xmlns` attributes. One namespace is imported as the default, and others must be named using a prefix.

For example, .NET MAUI types are imported by default, so the element names do not need a prefix; general XAML syntax is imported using the x prefix for doing common things like naming a control or the class name that the XAML will be compiled as. Your project types are often imported using the `local` prefix, as shown in the following markup:

```xml
<?xml version="1.0" encoding="utf-8" ?>
<ContentPage xmlns="http://schemas.microsoft.com/dotnet/2021/maui"
             xmlns:x="http://schemas.microsoft.com/winfx/2009/xaml"
             xmlns:local="clr-namespace:MyMauiApp.Controls"
             x:Class="MyMauiApp.MainPage"
             ...>

  <Button x:Name="NewFileButton" ...>New File</Button>
  <local:CustomerList x:Name="CustomerList" ... />
  ...
</ContentPage>
```

In the example above, the project is named `MyMauiApp` and its controls like the `CustomerList` control are defined in a namespace named `MyMauiApp.Controls`. This namespace has been registered with the prefix `local`, so when an instance of the `CustomerList` control is needed, it is declared using `<local:CustomerList>`.

You can import as many namespaces with different prefixes as you need.

Type converters

Type converters convert XAML attribute values that must be set as `string` values into other types. For example, the following button has its `Background` property set to the `string` value "Pink":

```xml
<Button x:Name="newButton" Background="Pink" ...
```

This is converted into a `SolidColorBrush` instance using a type converter, as shown in the following equivalent code:

```
newButton.Background = new SolidColorBrush(Colors.Pink);
```

There are many type converters provided by .NET MAUI and you can create and register your own. These are especially useful for custom data visualizations.

Choosing between .NET MAUI controls

There are lots of predefined controls that you can choose from for common UI scenarios. .NET MAUI (and most dialects of XAML) support these controls, as shown in *Table 16.2*:

Controls	Description
Button, ImageButton, MenuItem, ToolbarItem	Executing actions
CheckBox, RadioButton, Switch	Choosing options
DatePicker, TimePicker	Choosing dates and times
CollectionView, ListView, Picker, TableView	Choosing items from lists and tables
CarouselView, IndicatorView	Scrolling animated views that show one item at a time
AbsoluteLayout, BindableLayout, FlexLayout, Grid, HorizontalStackLayout, StackLayout, VerticalStackLayout	Layout containers that affect their children in different ways
Border, BoxView, Frame, ScrollView	Visual elements
Ellipse, Line, Path, Polygon, Polyline, Rectangle, RoundRectangle	Graphical elements
ActivityIndicator, Label, ProgressBar, RefreshView	Displaying read-only text and other read-only displays
Editor, Entry	Editing text
GraphicsView, Image	Embedding images, videos, and audio files
Slider, Stepper	Selecting within ranges of numbers
SearchBar	Adding a search feature
BlazorWebView, WebView	Embedding Blazor and web components
ContentView	Building custom controls

Table 16.2: MAUI user interface controls

.NET MAUI defines its controls in the `Microsoft.Maui.Controls` namespace. It has some specialized controls too:

- `Application`: Represents a cross-platform graphical application. It sets the root page, manages windows, themes, and resources, and provides app-level events like `PageAppearing`, `ModalPushing`, and `RequestedThemeChanged`. It also has methods that you can override to hook into app events like `OnStart`, `OnSleep`, `OnResume`, and `CleanUp`.
- `Shell`: A `Page` control that provides UI features that most applications require, like flyout or tab bar navigation, navigation tracking and management, and navigation events.

 Most .NET MAUI controls derive from `View`. One of the most important characteristics of a `View`-derived type is that they can be nested. This allows you to build complex custom user interfaces.

Markup extensions

To support some advanced features, XAML uses markup extensions. Some of the most important enable element and data binding and the reuse of resources, as shown in the following list:

- `{Binding}` links an element to a value from another element or a data source.
- `{OnPlatform}` sets properties to different values depending on the current platform.
- `{StaticResource}` and `{DynamicResource}` link an element to a shared resource.
- `{AppThemeBinding}` links an element to a shared resource defined in a theme.

.NET MAUI provides the `OnPlatform` markup extension to allow you to set different markup depending on the platform. For example, iPhone X and later introduced the notch that takes up extra space at the top of the phone display. We could add extra padding to an app that applies to all devices, but it would be better if we could add that extra padding only to iOS, as shown in the following markup:

```
<VerticalStackLayout>
  <VerticalStackLayout.Padding>
    <OnPlatform x:TypeArguments="Thickness">
      <On Platform="iOS" Value="30,60,30,30" />
      <On Platform="Android" Value="30" />
      <On Platform="WinUI" Value="30" />
    </OnPlatform>
  </VerticalStackLayout.Padding>
```

There is a simplified syntax too, as shown in the following markup:

```
<VerticalStackLayout Padding"{OnPlatform iOS='30,60,30,30', Default='30'}">
```

Understanding .NET MAUI

To create a mobile app that only needs to run on iPhones, you might choose to build it with either the Objective-C or Swift language and the UIkit libraries using the Xcode development tool.

To create a mobile app that only needs to run on Android phones, you might choose to build it with either the Java or Kotlin language and the Android SDK libraries using the Android Studio development tool.

But what if you need to create a mobile app that can run on iPhones *and* Android phones? And what if you only want to create that mobile app once using a programming language and development platform that you are already familiar with? And what if you realized that with a bit more coding effort to adapt the UI to desktop-size devices, you could target macOS and Windows desktops too?

.NET MAUI enables developers to build cross-platform mobile apps for Apple iOS (iPhone), iPadOS, macOS using Catalyst, Windows using WinUI 3, and Google Android using C# and .NET, which are then compiled to native APIs and executed on native phone and desktop platforms.

Business logic layer code can be written once and shared between all platforms. UI interactions and APIs are different on various mobile and desktop platforms, so the UI layer is sometimes custom for each platform.

Like WPF and UWP apps, .NET MAUI uses XAML to define the UI once for all platforms using abstractions of platform-specific UI components. Applications built with .NET MAUI draw the UI using native platform widgets, so the app's look and feel fits naturally with the target mobile platform.

A user experience built using .NET MAUI will not perfectly fit a specific platform in the same way that one custom built with native tools for that platform would, but for mobile and desktop apps that will not have millions of users, it is good enough. With some effort, you can build beautiful apps, as illustrated by the Microsoft challenge that you can read about at the following link:

`https://devblogs.microsoft.com/dotnet/announcing-dotnet-maui-beautiful-ui-challenge/`

.NET MAUI and Xamarin support

Major versions of .NET MAUI ship with .NET starting with .NET 7 but as an optional workload. This means that .NET MAUI does not follow the same **Short Term Support (STS)/Long Term Support (LTS)** as the main .NET platform. Every version of .NET MAUI only has 18 months of support, so .NET MAUI effectively is always an STS release, and this includes the .NET MAUI version that ships as a workload with .NET 8.

.NET MAUI has dependencies on other OSes like iOS and macOS so it gets complicated. Major versions of iOS usually release in September, and major versions of iPadOS and macOS often release later in October or November. This does not give the .NET MAUI team much time to make sure their platform works well with those operating systems before a major version of .NET is released in early November.

Warning! Xamarin reaches its **end-of-life (EOL)** on May 1, 2024 so any Xamarin and Xamarin.Forms projects should migrate to .NET MAUI or an alternative like Avalonia or Uno before then.

Development tools for mobile first, cloud first

Mobile apps are often supported by services in the cloud.

Satya Nadella, CEO of Microsoft, famously said the following:

> *To me, when we say mobile first, it's not the mobility of the device, it's actually the mobility of the individual experience. [...] The only way you are going to be able to orchestrate the mobility of these applications and data is through the cloud.*

When installing Visual Studio 2022, you must select the **.NET Multi-platform App UI development** workload, which is in the **Desktop & Mobile** section, as shown in *Figure 16.1*:

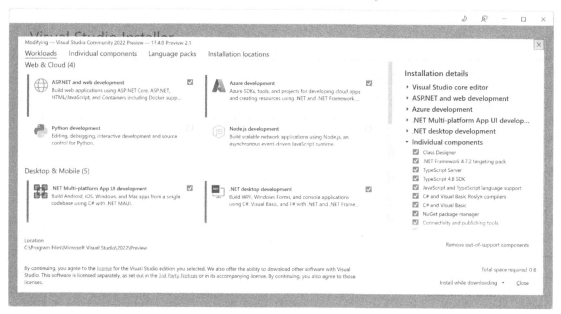

Figure 16.1: Selecting the .NET MAUI workload for Visual Studio 2022

Installing .NET MAUI workloads manually

Installing Visual Studio 2022 should install the required .NET MAUI workloads if you selected them. If not, then you can make sure that the workloads are installed manually.

To see which workloads are currently installed, enter the following command:

```
dotnet workload list
```

The currently installed workloads will appear in a table, as shown in the following output:

```
Installed Workload Ids      Manifest Version      Installation Source
-----------------------------------------------------------------------
maui-maccatalyst            6.0.486/6.0.400       SDK 7.0.100
```

To see which workloads are available to install, enter the following command:

```
dotnet workload search
```

The currently available workloads will appear in a table, as shown in the following output:

```
Workload ID                  Description
------------------------------------------------------------------------------
-----
android                      .NET SDK Workload for building Android
applications.
ios                          .NET SDK Workload for building iOS applications.
maccatalyst                  .NET SDK Workload for building MacCatalyst
applications.
macos                        .NET SDK Workload for building macOS applications.
maui                         .NET MAUI SDK for all platforms
maui-android                 .NET MAUI SDK for Android
maui-desktop                 .NET MAUI SDK for Desktop
maui-ios                     .NET MAUI SDK for iOS
maui-maccatalyst             .NET MAUI SDK for Mac Catalyst
maui-mobile                  .NET MAUI SDK for Mobile
maui-tizen                   .NET MAUI SDK for Tizen
maui-windows                 .NET MAUI SDK for Windows
tvos                         .NET SDK Workload for building tvOS applications.
wasi-experimental            workloads/wasi-experimental/description
wasm-experimental            workloads/wasm-experimental/description
wasm-experimental-net7       .NET WebAssembly experimental tooling for net7.0
wasm-tools                   .NET WebAssembly build tools
wasm-tools-net6              .NET WebAssembly build tools for net6.0
wasm-tools-net7              .NET WebAssembly build tools for net7.0
```

To install the .NET MAUI workloads for all platforms, enter the following command at the command line or terminal:

```
dotnet workload install maui
```

To update all existing workload installations, enter the following command:

```
dotnet workload update
```

To add missing workload installations required for a project, in the folder containing the project file, enter the following command:

```
dotnet workload restore <projectname>
```

Over time you are likely to install multiple versions of workloads related to different versions of .NET SDKs. Before .NET 8, developers tried to manually delete workload folders, which can cause problems. Introduced with .NET 8 is a new feature to remove leftover and unneeded workloads, as shown in the following command:

```
dotnet workload clean
```

 More Information: If you want to use Visual Studio 2022 to create an iOS mobile app or a macOS Catalyst desktop app, then you can connect over a network to a **Mac build host.** Instructions can be found at the following link: https://learn.microsoft.com/en-us/dotnet/maui/ios/pair-to-mac.

.NET MAUI user interface component categories

.NET MAUI includes some common controls for building user interfaces. They can be divided into four categories:

- **Pages** represent cross-platform application screens, for example, Shell, ContentPage, NavigationPage, FlyoutPage, and TabbedPage.
- **Layouts** represent the structure of a combination of other UI components, for example, Grid, StackLayout, and FlexLayout.
- **Views** represent a single user interface component, for example, CarouselView, CollectionView, Label, Entry, Editor, and Button.
- **Cells** represent a single item in a list or table view, for example, TextCell, ImageCell, SwitchCell, and EntryCell.

Shell control

The Shell control is designed to simplify app development by providing standardized navigation and search capabilities. In your project, you would create a class that inherits from the Shell control class. Your derived class defines components like a TabBar, which contains Tab items, FlyoutItem instances, and ShellContent, which contain the ContentPage instances for each page. A TabBar should be used when there are only up to about four or five pages to navigate between. FlyoutItem navigation should be used when there are more items because they can be presented as a vertical scrollable list. You can use both, with the TabBar showing a subset of items. The Shell will keep them synchronized.

Flyout navigation is when a list of items flies out (or slides) from the left side of a mobile device's screen or desktop app's main window. The user invokes it by tapping on a "hamburger" icon with three horizontal lines stacked on top of each other. When the user taps a flyout item, its page is instantiated when needed, as the user navigates around the UI.

The top bar automatically shows a **Back** button when needed to allow the user to navigate back to a previous page.

ListView control

The ListView control is used for long lists of data-bound values of the same type. It can have headers and footers and its list items can be grouped.

It has cells to contain each list item. There are two built-in cell types: text and image. Developers can define custom cell types.

Cells can have context actions that appear when the cell is swiped on an iPhone, long-pressed on Android, or right-clicked on a desktop OS. A context action that is destructive can be shown in red, as shown in the following markup:

```
<TextCell Text="{Binding CompanyName}" Detail="{Binding Location}">
  <TextCell.ContextActions>
    <MenuItem Clicked="Customer_Phoned" Text="Phone" />
    <MenuItem Clicked="Customer_Deleted" Text="Delete" IsDestructive="True" />
  </TextCell.ContextActions>
</TextCell>
```

Entry and Editor controls

The Entry and Editor controls are used for editing text values and are often data-bound to an entity model property, as shown in the following markup:

```
<Editor Text="{Binding CompanyName, Mode=TwoWay}" />
```

 Good Practice: Use Entry for a single line of text. Use Editor for multiple lines of text.

.NET MAUI handlers

In .NET MAUI, XAML controls are defined in the Microsoft.Maui.Controls namespace. Components called **handlers** map these common controls to native controls on each platform. On iOS, a handler will map a .NET MAUI Button to an iOS-native UIButton defined by UIkit. On macOS, Button is mapped to NSButton defined by AppKit. On Android, Button is mapped to an Android-native AppCompatButton.

Handlers have a NativeView property that exposes the underlying native control. This allows you to work with platform-specific features like properties, methods, and events, and customize all instances of a native control.

Writing platform-specific code

If you need to write code statements that only execute for a specific platform like Android, then you can use compiler directives.

For example, by default, `Entry` controls on Android show an underline character. If you want to hide the underline, you could write some Android-specific code to get the handler for the `Entry` control, use its `NativeView` property to access the underlying native control, and then set the property that controls that feature to `false`, as shown in the following code:

```
#if __ANDROID__
  Handlers.EntryHandler.EntryMapper[nameof(IEntry.BackgroundColor)] = (h, v) =>
  {
    (h.NativeView as global::Android.Views.Entry).UnderlineVisible = false;
  };
#endif
```

Predefined compiler constants include the following:

*   `__ANDROID__`
*   `__IOS__`
*   `WINDOWS`

The compiler `#if` statement syntax is slightly different from the C# `if` statement syntax, as shown in the following code:

```
#if __IOS__
  // iOS-specific statements
#elif __ANDROID__
  // Android-specific statements
#elif WINDOWS
  // Windows-specific statements
#endif
```

Now that you have been introduced to some of the important concepts around MAUI apps, and you've set up the additional components needed for MAUI, let's get practical and build a MAUI project.

Building mobile and desktop apps using .NET MAUI

We will build a mobile and desktop app for managing customers in Northwind.

> **Good Practice:** If you have a Mac and you have never run Xcode on it, then run it now until you see the *Start* window. This will ensure that all its required components are installed and registered. If you do not do this, then you might get errors with your projects later.

Creating a virtual Android device for local app testing

To target Android, you must install at least one Android SDK. A default installation of Visual Studio 2022 with the mobile development workload already includes one Android SDK, but it is often an older version designed to support as many Android devices as possible.

To use the latest features of .NET MAUI, you must configure a more recent Android virtual device:

1. In Windows, start **Visual Studio 2022**. If you see the modal dialog box **Welcome Experience**, then click **Continue without code**.

2. Navigate to **Tools | Android | Android Device Manager**. If you are prompted by **User Account Control** to allow this app to make changes to your device, click **Yes**.

3. In the **Android Device Manager**, click the **+ New** button to create a new device.

4. In the dialog box, make the following choices, as shown in *Figure 16.2*:

   - **Base Device: Pixel 5**
   - **Processor: x86_64**
   - **OS: Android 13.0 – API 33**
   - **Google APIs:** Selected
   - **Google Play Store:** Cleared

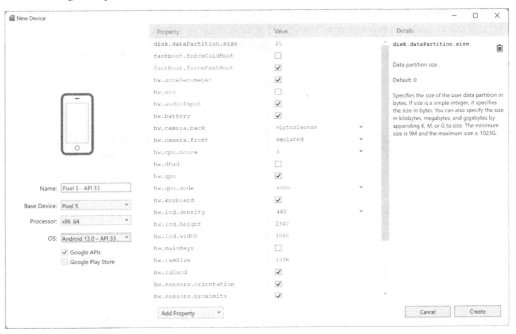

Figure 16.2: Selecting the hardware and OS for a virtual Android device

5. Click **Create**.

6. Accept any license agreements.

7. Wait for any required downloads.

8. In **Android Device Manager,** in the list of devices, in the row for the device that you just created, click **Start.**

9. Be patient! It can take a few minutes for the emulator to start.

10. When the Android device has finished starting, click the Chrome browser and test that it has access to the network by navigating to `https://www.bbc.co.uk/news`.

11. Close the emulator.

12. Close **Android Device Manager.**

13. Restart Visual Studio 2022 to ensure that it is aware of the new emulator.

Enabling Windows developer mode

To create apps for Windows, you must enable developer mode:

1. Navigate to **Start | Settings | Privacy & security | For developers,** and then switch on **Developer Mode.** (You can also search for "developers".)

2. Accept the warning about how it "**could expose your device and personal data to security risk or harm your devicee."**

3. Close the **Settings** app.

Creating a .NET MAUI project

We will now create a project for a cross-platform mobile and desktop app:

1. In Visual Studio 2022, add a new project, as defined in the following list:

    •   Project template: **.NET MAUI App** / maui

         You can select **C#** for the language and **MAUI** for the project type to filter and show only the appropriate project templates.

    •   Project file and folder: `Northwind.Maui.Client`
    •   Solution file and folder: `Chapter16`

2. On Windows, if you see a Windows security alert that **Windows Defender Firewall has blocked some features of Broker on all public and private networks,** then select **Private networks** and clear **Public networks,** and then click the **Allow access** button.

3. In the project file, note the element that targets iOS, Android, and Mac Catalyst, and the element to enable Windows targeting if the operating system is Windows, as well as the elements that set the project to be a single MAUI project, as shown highlighted in the following partial markup:

```
<Project Sdk="Microsoft.NET.Sdk">

  <PropertyGroup>
    <TargetFrameworks>net8.0-ios;net8.0-android;net8.0-maccatalyst</
TargetFrameworks>
    <TargetFrameworks Condition="$([MSBuild]::IsOSPlatform('windows'))">$
(TargetFrameworks);net8.0-windows10.0.19041.0</TargetFrameworks>

    ...

    <OutputType>Exe</OutputType>
    <RootNamespace>Northwind.Maui.Client</RootNamespace>
    <UseMaui>true</UseMaui>
    <SingleProject>true</SingleProject>
```

 If you see the error Error NU1012 Platform version is not present for one or more target frameworks, even though they have specified a platform: net8.0-ios, net8.0-maccatalyst, then at the command prompt or terminal, in the project folder, restore workloads for the project, as shown in the following command:

```
dotnet workload restore
```

4. To the right of the **Run** button in the toolbar, set **Framework** to **net8.0-android**, and select the **Pixel 5 - API 33 (Android 13.0 - API 33)** emulator image that you previously created, as shown in *Figure 16.3*:

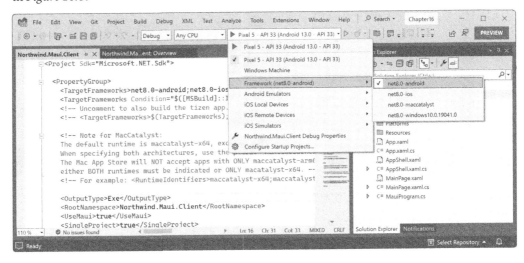

Figure 16.3: Selecting an Android device as the target for startup

5. Click the **Run** button in the toolbar and wait for the device emulator to start the Android operating system, and then deploy and launch your mobile app. This can take more than five minutes, especially the first time that you build a new MAUI project. Keep an eye on the Visual Studio 2022 status bar, as shown in *Figure 16.4*:

Figure 16.4: Status bar shows progress of the .NET MAUI app deployment

 If you're doing this for the first time, there might be another Google license agreement to confirm.

6. In the .NET MAUI app, click the **Click me** button to increment the counter three times, as shown in *Figure 16.5*:

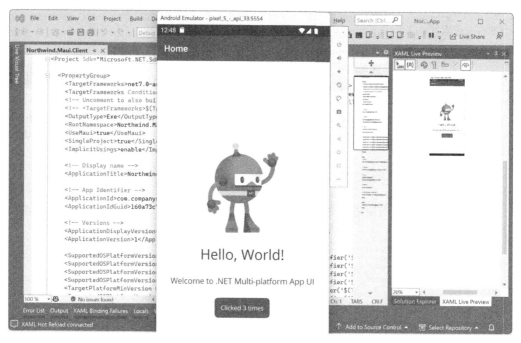

Figure 16.5: Incrementing the counter three times in the .NET MAUI app on Android

7. Close the Android device emulator. You do not need to power down the emulator.

8. To the right of the **Run** button in the toolbar, set **Framework** to **net8.0-windows10.0.19041.0**.

9. Make sure that the **Debug** configuration is selected and then click the solid green triangle **Start** button labeled **Windows Machine**. You might see a warning about missing packages that should be installed on the first run. Just click the **start** button a second time and they should now be installed and it will work.

10. After a few moments, note that the Windows app displays with the same **Click me** button and counter functionality as shown in *Figure 16.6*:

Figure 16.6: The same .NET MAUI app on Windows

11. Close the Windows app.

> **Good Practice:** You should test your .NET MAUI app on all the potential devices that it will need to run on. In this chapter, even if I do not explicitly tell you to do so, I recommend that you try the app by running it on your emulated Android device and on Windows after each task to add a new feature. That way, you will have at least seen how it looks on a mobile device with a primarily tall and thin portrait size, and on a desktop device with a larger landscape size. If you are using a Mac, then I recommend that you test it in the iOS Simulator, Android Emulator, and as a Mac Catalyst desktop app.

Adding shell navigation and more content pages

Now, let's review the existing structure of the .NET MAUI app and then add some new pages and navigation to the project:

1. In the `Northwind.Maui.Client` project, in `MauiProgram.cs`, note that the `builder` object calls `UseMauiApp` and specifies `App` as its generic type, as shown highlighted in the following code:

```
using Microsoft.Extensions.Logging;

namespace Northwind.Maui.Client;

public static class MauiProgram
```

```
{
  public static MauiApp CreateMauiApp()
  {
    var builder = MauiApp.CreateBuilder();
    builder
      .UseMauiApp<App>()
        .ConfigureFonts(fonts =>
        {
          fonts.AddFont("OpenSans-Regular.ttf", "OpenSansRegular");
          fonts.AddFont("OpenSans-Semibold.ttf", "OpenSansSemibold");
        });

#if DEBUG
    builder.Logging.AddDebug();
#endif

    return builder.Build();
  }
}
```

2. In **Solution Explorer**, expand `App.xaml`, open `App.xaml.cs`, and note the `MainPage` property of the `App` is set to an instance of `AppShell`, as shown highlighted in the following code:

```
namespace Northwind.Maui.Client;

public partial class App : Application
{
  public App()
  {
    InitializeComponent();

    MainPage = new AppShell();
  }
}
```

3. In `AppShell.xaml`, note that the shell disables flyout mode and only has a single content page named `MainPage`, as shown highlighted in the following code:

```
<?xml version="1.0" encoding="UTF-8" ?>
<Shell
  x:Class="Northwind.Maui.Client.AppShell"
  xmlns="http://schemas.microsoft.com/dotnet/2021/maui"
  xmlns:x="http://schemas.microsoft.com/winfx/2009/xaml"
```

```
  xmlns:local="clr-namespace:Northwind.Maui.Client"
  Shell.FlyoutBehavior="Disabled"
  Title="Northwind.Maui.Client">

  <ShellContent
    Title="Home"
    ContentTemplate="{DataTemplate local:MainPage}"
    Route="MainPage" />

</Shell>
```

 A shell with only one content page does not show any navigation. You must have at least two shell content items.

4. In the Resources folder, in the Images folder, add images for some icons that we will use for flyout items in the navigation we are about to add.

 You can download the images from the GitHub repository at the following link: https://github.com/markjprice/apps-services-net8/tree/main/code/ Chapter16/Northwind.Maui.Client/Resources/Images.

5. In AppShell.xaml, enable flyout mode, set the background to a pale blue color, add an icon for the MainPage content, add a flyout header, and then add some flyout items with more shell content, as shown highlighted in the following markup:

```
<?xml version="1.0" encoding="UTF-8" ?>
<Shell
  x:Class="Northwind.Maui.Client.AppShell"
  xmlns="http://schemas.microsoft.com/dotnet/2021/maui"
  xmlns:x="http://schemas.microsoft.com/winfx/2009/xaml"
  xmlns:local="clr-namespace:Northwind.Maui.Client"
  Shell.FlyoutBehavior="Flyout"
  Title="Northwind.Maui.Client"
  FlyoutBackgroundColor="AliceBlue">

  <Shell.FlyoutHeader>
    <HorizontalStackLayout Spacing="10" HorizontalOptions="Start">
      <Image Source="wind_face_3d.png"
              WidthRequest="80" HeightRequest="80" />
      <Label Text="Northwind" FontFamily="OpenSansSemibold"
```

```
                FontSize="32" VerticalOptions="Center" />
    </HorizontalStackLayout>
  </Shell.FlyoutHeader>

  <ShellContent Title="Home"
    Icon="file_cabinet_3d.png"
    ContentTemplate="{DataTemplate local:MainPage}"
    Route="MainPage" />

  <ShellContent Title="Categories"
    Icon="delivery_truck_3d.png"
    ContentTemplate="{DataTemplate local:CategoriesPage}"
    Route="Categories" />

  <ShellContent Title="Products"
    Icon="cityscape_3d.png"
    ContentTemplate="{DataTemplate local:ProductsPage}"
    Route="Products" />

  <ShellContent Title="Customers"
    Icon="card_index_3d.png"
    ContentTemplate="{DataTemplate local:CustomersPage}"
    Route="Customers" />

  <ShellContent Title="Employees"
    Icon="identification_card_3d.png"
    ContentTemplate="{DataTemplate local:EmployeesPage}"
    Route="Employees" />

  <ShellContent Title="Settings"
    Icon="gear_3d.png"
    ContentTemplate="{DataTemplate local:SettingsPage}"
    Route="Settings" />

</Shell>
```

You will see warnings on some of the ContentTemplate lines about missing pages because we have not created them yet. AliceBlue looks good in light mode, but if your operating system uses dark mode, then you might prefer an alternative color like #75858a.

6. In Visual Studio 2022, right-click the `Northwind.Maui.Client` project folder, choose **Add | New Item...** or press *Ctrl + Shift + A*, select **.NET MAUI** in the template types tree, select **.NET MAUI ContentPage (XAML)**, enter the name `SettingsPage`, and click **Add**.

 Visual Studio Code and JetBrains Rider do not have project item templates for MAUI. You can create this item using the CLI, as shown in the following command:

```
dotnet new maui-page-xaml --name SettingsPage.xaml
```

7. Repeat the previous step to add content pages named:

    •   `CategoriesPage`

    •   `CustomersPage`

    •   `CustomerDetailPage`

    •   `EmployeesPage`

    •   `ProductsPage`

8. In **Solution Explorer**, double-click on the `CategoriesPage.xaml` file to open it for editing. Note that Visual Studio 2022 does not yet have a graphical design view for XAML.

9. In the `<ContentPage>` element, change the `Title` to `Categories`, and in the `<Label>` element, change the `Text` to `Categories`, as shown highlighted in the following markup:

```xml
<?xml version="1.0" encoding="utf-8" ?>
<ContentPage xmlns="http://schemas.microsoft.com/dotnet/2021/maui"
             xmlns:x="http://schemas.microsoft.com/winfx/2009/xaml"
             x:Class="Northwind.Maui.Client.CategoriesPage"
             Title="Categories">
    <VerticalStackLayout>
        <Label
            Text="Categories"
            VerticalOptions="Center"
            HorizontalOptions="Center" />
    </VerticalStackLayout>
</ContentPage>
```

10. Navigate to **View | Toolbox** or press *Ctrl + W, X*. Note that the toolbox has sections for **Controls, Layouts, Cells,** and **General**. If you are using a code editor without a toolbox, you can just type the markup instead of using the toolbox.

11. At the top of the toolbox is a search box. Enter the letter b, and then note that the list of controls is filtered to show controls like **Button, ProgressBar,** and **AbsoluteLayout**.

12. Drag and drop the **Button** control from the toolbox into the XAML markup after the existing `<Label>` control, before the closing element of the `VerticalStackLayout`, and change its `Text` property to `Hello!`, as shown in the following markup:

```
<Button Text="Hello!" />
```

13. Set the startup to **Windows Machine** and then start the `Northwind.Maui.Client` project with debugging. Note that the Visual Studio status bar shows us that **XAML Hot Reload** is connected.

14. In the top-left corner of the app, click the flyout menu (the "hamburger" icon), and note the header and the images used for the icons in the flyout items, as shown in *Figure 16.7*:

Figure 16.7: A flyout with image icons

15. In the flyout menu, click **Categories**, and note that the text on the button says **Hello!** and that it stretches across the width of the app window.

16. Leave the app running, and then in Visual Studio 2022, change the `Text` property to `Click Me`, add an attribute to set the `WidthRequest` property to `100`, and note that the **XAML Hot Reload** feature automatically reflects the changes in the app itself, as shown in *Figure 16.8*:

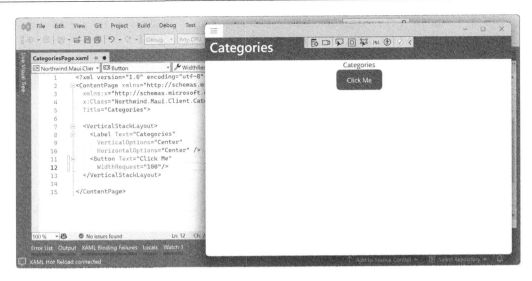

Figure 16.8: XAML Hot Reload automatically updating changes in the XAML in the live app

17. Close the app.

18. Modify the Button element to give it the name of ClickMeButton and a new event handler for its Clicked event, as shown in *Figure 16.9*:

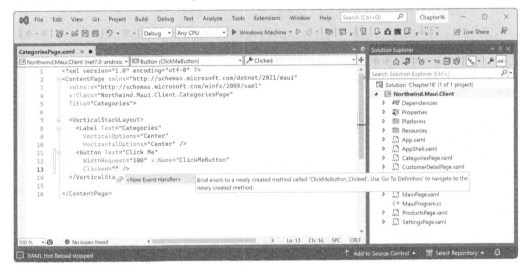

Figure 16.9: Adding an event handler to a control

19. Right-click the event handler name and select **Go To Definition** or press *F12*.

20. Add a statement to the event handler method that sets the content of the button to the current time, as shown highlighted in the following code:

```
private void ClickMeButton_Click(object sender, EventArgs e)
{
  ClickMeButton.Text = DateTime.Now.ToString("hh:mm:ss");
}
```

21. Start the `Northwind.Maui.Client` project on at least one mobile device and one desktop device.

 Good Practice: When deploying to an Android emulator or an iOS simulator, the old version of the app could still be running. Make sure to wait for the deployment of the new version of your app before interacting with it. You can keep an eye on the Visual Studio status bar to track the deployment progress or just wait until you see the message **XAML Hot Reload connected**.

22. Navigate to **Categories**, click the button, and note that its text label changes to the current time.
23. Close the app.

Implementing more content pages

Now, let's implement some of the new pages:

1. In `EmployeesPage.xaml`, change the `Title` to `Employees` and add markup to define the UI for a simple calculator, as shown highlighted in the following markup:

```xml
<?xml version="1.0" encoding="utf-8" ?>
<ContentPage xmlns="http://schemas.microsoft.com/dotnet/2021/maui"
             xmlns:x="http://schemas.microsoft.com/winfx/2009/xaml"
             x:Class="Northwind.Maui.Client.EmployeesPage"
             Title="Employees">

  <VerticalStackLayout>

    <Grid Background="DarkGray" Margin="10"
          Padding="5" x:Name="GridCalculator"
          ColumnDefinitions="Auto,Auto,Auto,Auto"
          RowDefinitions="Auto,Auto,Auto,Auto">
      <Button Grid.Row="0" Grid.Column="0" Text="X" />
      <Button Grid.Row="0" Grid.Column="1" Text="/" />
      <Button Grid.Row="0" Grid.Column="2" Text="+" />
      <Button Grid.Row="0" Grid.Column="3" Text="-" />
      <Button Grid.Row="1" Grid.Column="0" Text="7" />
      <Button Grid.Row="1" Grid.Column="1" Text="8" />
      <Button Grid.Row="1" Grid.Column="2" Text="9" />
```

```
    <Button Grid.Row="1" Grid.Column="3" Text="0" />
    <Button Grid.Row="2" Grid.Column="0" Text="4" />
    <Button Grid.Row="2" Grid.Column="1" Text="5" />
    <Button Grid.Row="2" Grid.Column="2" Text="6" />
    <Button Grid.Row="2" Grid.Column="3" Text="." />
    <Button Grid.Row="3" Grid.Column="0" Text="1" />
    <Button Grid.Row="3" Grid.Column="1" Text="2" />
    <Button Grid.Row="3" Grid.Column="2" Text="3" />
    <Button Grid.Row="3" Grid.Column="3" Text="=" />
  </Grid>
  <Label x:Name="Output" FontSize="24"
         VerticalOptions="Center"
         HorizontalOptions="Start" />

</VerticalStackLayout>
</ContentPage>
```

2. Add an event handler for the page's Loaded event, as shown highlighted in the following markup:

```
Title="Employees"
Loaded="ContentPage_Loaded">
```

3. In EmployeesPage.xaml.cs, add statements to resize each button in the grid and hook up an event handler for the Clicked event, as shown in the following code:

```
private void ContentPage_Loaded(object sender, EventArgs e)
{
  foreach (Button button in GridCalculator.Children.OfType<Button>())
  {
    button.FontSize = 24;
    button.WidthRequest = 54;
    button.HeightRequest = 54;
    button.Clicked += Button_Clicked;
  }
}
```

4. Add a Button_Clicked method, with statements to handle the clicked button by concatenating the text of the button to the output label, as shown in the following code:

```
private void Button_Clicked(object sender, EventArgs e)
{
  string operationChars = "+-/X=";

  Button button = (Button)sender;
```

```
    if (operationChars.Contains(button.Text))
    {
      Output.Text = string.Empty;
    }
    else
    {
      Output.Text += button.Text;
    }
}
```

This is not a proper implementation for a calculator because the operations have not been implemented. It just simulates one for now because we are focusing on how to build UIs with .NET MAUI. You can Google how to implement a simple calculator as an optional exercise.

5.   Start the Northwind.Maui.Client project with at least one desktop and one mobile device.

6.   Navigate to **Employees**, click some of the buttons, and note that the label updates to show what is clicked, as shown on an emulated Android device in *Figure 16.10*:

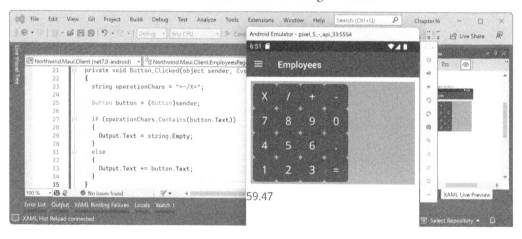

Figure 16.10: A simulated calculator on an emulated Android

7.   Close the app.

By now, we have built a few simple UIs using XAML and MAUI. Next, let's see some techniques to improve apps, like defining and sharing resources.

Using shared resources

When building graphical UIs, you will often want to use a resource, such as a brush to paint the background of controls or an instance of a class to perform custom conversions. Resources can be defined at the following levels and shared with everything at that level or lower:

- Application
- Page
- Control

Defining resources to share across an app

A good place to define shared resources is at the app level, so let's see how to do that:

1. In the Resources folder, in the Styles folder, add a new **.NET MAUI Resource Dictionary (XAML)** project item named Northwind.xaml.

     Visual Studio Code and JetBrains Rider do not have project item templates for MAUI. You can create this item using the CLI, as shown in the following command:

    ```
    dotnet new maui-dict-xaml --name Northwind.xaml
    ```

2. Add markup inside the existing ResourceDictionary element to define a linear gradient brush with a key of Rainbow, as shown highlighted in the following markup:

    ```xml
    <?xml version="1.0" encoding="utf-8" ?>
    <ResourceDictionary xmlns="http://schemas.microsoft.com/dotnet/2021/maui"
                xmlns:x="http://schemas.microsoft.com/winfx/2009/xaml"
                x:Class="Northwind.Maui.Client.Resources.Styles.Northwind">

      <LinearGradientBrush x:Key="Rainbow">
        <GradientStop Color="Red" Offset="0" />
        <GradientStop Color="Orange" Offset="0.1" />
        <GradientStop Color="Yellow" Offset="0.3" />
        <GradientStop Color="Green" Offset="0.5" />
        <GradientStop Color="Blue" Offset="0.7" />
        <GradientStop Color="Indigo" Offset="0.9" />
        <GradientStop Color="Violet" Offset="1" />
      </LinearGradientBrush>

    </ResourceDictionary>
    ```

3. In App.xaml, add an entry to the merged resource dictionaries to reference the resource file in the Styles folder named Northwind.xaml, as shown highlighted in the following markup:

    ```xml
    <?xml version = "1.0" encoding = "UTF-8" ?>
    <Application xmlns="http://schemas.microsoft.com/dotnet/2021/maui"
                xmlns:x="http://schemas.microsoft.com/winfx/2009/xaml"
                xmlns:local="clr-namespace:Northwind.Maui.Client"
                x:Class="Northwind.Maui.Client.App">
    ```

```
<Application.Resources>
  <ResourceDictionary>
    <ResourceDictionary.MergedDictionaries>
      <ResourceDictionary Source="Resources/Styles/Colors.xaml" />
      <ResourceDictionary Source="Resources/Styles/Styles.xaml" />
      <ResourceDictionary Source="Resources/Styles/Northwind.xaml" />
    </ResourceDictionary.MergedDictionaries>
  </ResourceDictionary>
</Application.Resources>
</Application>
```

Referencing shared resources

Now we can reference the shared resource:

1. In `CategoriesPage.xaml`, modify the `ContentPage` to set its background to the brush resource with the key of `Rainbow`, as shown highlighted in the following markup:

    ```
    <ContentPage xmlns="http://schemas.microsoft.com/dotnet/2021/maui"
                 xmlns:x="http://schemas.microsoft.com/winfx/2009/xaml"
                 x:Class="Northwind.Maui.Client.CategoriesPage"
                 Background="{StaticResource Rainbow}"
                 Title="Categories">
    ```

     `StaticResource` means the resource is read once when the app first starts. If the resource changes after that, any elements that reference it will not be updated.

2. Start the `Northwind.Maui.Client` project with debugging.

3. Navigate to **Categories** and note that the background of the page is a rainbow.

4. Close the app.

Changing shared resources dynamically

Now we can implement a settings page to allow the user to change between light mode, dark mode, or system mode used in the UI at runtime:

1. In the `Resources` folder, in the `Styles` folder, add a new **.NET MAUI Resource Dictionary (XAML)** project item named `LightDarkModeColors.xaml`.

2. Add markup inside the existing `ResourceDictionary` element to define sets of suitable colors for light and dark mode, as shown in the following markup:

    ```
    <?xml version="1.0" encoding="utf-8" ?>
    <ResourceDictionary xmlns="http://schemas.microsoft.com/dotnet/2021/maui"
    ```

```xml
      xmlns:x="http://schemas.microsoft.com/winfx/2009/xaml"
      x:Class="Northwind.Maui.Client.Resources.Styles.LightDarkModeColors">

  <Color x:Key="LightPageBackgroundColor">White</Color>
  <Color x:Key="LightNavigationBarColor">AliceBlue</Color>
  <Color x:Key="LightPrimaryColor">WhiteSmoke</Color>
  <Color x:Key="LightSecondaryColor">Black</Color>
  <Color x:Key="LightPrimaryTextColor">Black</Color>
  <Color x:Key="LightSecondaryTextColor">White</Color>
  <Color x:Key="LightTertiaryTextColor">Gray</Color>

  <Color x:Key="DarkPageBackgroundColor">Black</Color>
  <Color x:Key="DarkNavigationBarColor">Teal</Color>
  <Color x:Key="DarkPrimaryColor">Teal</Color>
  <Color x:Key="DarkSecondaryColor">White</Color>
  <Color x:Key="DarkPrimaryTextColor">White</Color>
  <Color x:Key="DarkSecondaryTextColor">White</Color>
  <Color x:Key="DarkTertiaryTextColor">WhiteSmoke</Color>

</ResourceDictionary>
```

3. In the `Resources` folder, in the `Styles` folder, add a new **.NET MAUI Resource Dictionary (XAML)** project item named `DarkModeTheme.xaml`.

4. Add markup inside the existing `ResourceDictionary` element to define styles to use in dark mode, as shown in the following markup:

```xml
<?xml version="1.0" encoding="utf-8" ?>
<ResourceDictionary xmlns="http://schemas.microsoft.com/dotnet/2021/maui"
    xmlns:x="http://schemas.microsoft.com/winfx/2009/xaml"
    x:Class="Northwind.Maui.Client.Resources.Styles.DarkModeTheme">

  <Style TargetType="Shell">
    <Setter Property="FlyoutBackgroundColor"
            Value="{StaticResource DarkNavigationBarColor}" />
  </Style>

  <Style TargetType="ContentPage">
    <Setter Property="BackgroundColor"
            Value="{StaticResource DarkPageBackgroundColor}" />
  </Style>

  <Style TargetType="Button">
```

```xml
            <Setter Property="BackgroundColor"
                   Value="{StaticResource DarkPrimaryColor}" />
            <Setter Property="TextColor"
                   Value="{StaticResource DarkSecondaryColor}" />
            <Setter Property="HeightRequest" Value="45" />
            <Setter Property="WidthRequest" Value="190" />
            <Setter Property="CornerRadius" Value="18" />
        </Style>

    </ResourceDictionary>
```

5. In the `Resources` folder, in the `Styles` folder, add a new **.NET MAUI Resource Dictionary (XAML)** project item named `LightModeTheme.xaml`.

6. Add markup inside the existing `ResourceDictionary` element to define styles to use in light mode, as shown in the following markup:

```xml
<?xml version="1.0" encoding="utf-8" ?>
<ResourceDictionary xmlns="http://schemas.microsoft.com/dotnet/2021/maui"
    xmlns:x="http://schemas.microsoft.com/winfx/2009/xaml"
    x:Class="Northwind.Maui.Client.Resources.Styles.LightModeTheme">

    <Style TargetType="Shell">
      <Setter Property="FlyoutBackgroundColor"
             Value="{StaticResource LightNavigationBarColor}" />
    </Style>

    <Style TargetType="ContentPage">
      <Setter Property="BackgroundColor"
             Value="{StaticResource LightPageBackgroundColor}" />
    </Style>

    <Style TargetType="Button">
      <Setter Property="BackgroundColor"
             Value="{StaticResource LightPrimaryColor}" />
      <Setter Property="TextColor"
             Value="{StaticResource LightSecondaryColor}" />
      <Setter Property="HeightRequest" Value="45" />
      <Setter Property="WidthRequest" Value="190" />
      <Setter Property="CornerRadius" Value="18" />
    </Style>

    </ResourceDictionary>
```

7. In the Resources folder, in the Styles folder, add a new **.NET MAUI Resource Dictionary (XAML)** project item named SystemModeTheme.xaml.

8. Add markup inside the existing ResourceDictionary element to define styles to use with light and dark mode depending on how the operating system has had its option set, as shown in the following markup:

```xml
<?xml version="1.0" encoding="utf-8" ?>
<ResourceDictionary xmlns="http://schemas.microsoft.com/dotnet/2021/maui"
  xmlns:x="http://schemas.microsoft.com/winfx/2009/xaml"
  x:Class="Northwind.Maui.Client.Resources.Styles.SystemModeTheme">

  <Style TargetType="Shell">
    <Setter Property="FlyoutBackgroundColor"
            Value="{AppThemeBinding Light={StaticResource
LightNavigationBarColor}, Dark={StaticResource DarkNavigationBarColor}}"
/>
  </Style>

  <Style TargetType="ContentPage">
    <Setter Property="BackgroundColor"
            Value="{AppThemeBinding Light={StaticResource
LightPageBackgroundColor}, Dark={StaticResource
DarkPageBackgroundColor}}" />
  </Style>

  <Style TargetType="Button">
    <Setter Property="BackgroundColor"
            Value="{AppThemeBinding Light={StaticResource
LightPrimaryColor}, Dark={StaticResource DarkPrimaryColor}}" />
    <Setter Property="TextColor"
            Value="{AppThemeBinding Light={StaticResource
LightSecondaryColor}, Dark={StaticResource DarkSecondaryColor}}" />
    <Setter Property="HeightRequest" Value="45" />
    <Setter Property="WidthRequest" Value="190" />
    <Setter Property="CornerRadius" Value="18" />
  </Style>

</ResourceDictionary>
```

Note the use of the AppThemeBinding extension to dynamically bind to two pre-defined special filters, Light and Dark. These are bound to system modes.

9. In `App.xaml`, add the light and dark mode colors and system theme resources, as shown highlighted in the following markup:

```xml
<ResourceDictionary.MergedDictionaries>
  <ResourceDictionary Source="Resources/Styles/Colors.xaml" />
  <ResourceDictionary Source="Resources/Styles/Styles.xaml" />
  <ResourceDictionary Source="Resources/Styles/Northwind.xaml" />
  <ResourceDictionary Source="Resources/Styles/LightDarkModeColors.xaml"
/>
  <ResourceDictionary Source="Resources/Styles/SystemModeTheme.xaml" />
</ResourceDictionary.MergedDictionaries>
```

> **Good Practice:** The `SystemModeTheme.xaml` resources file references colors defined in the `LightDarkModelColors.xaml` file, so the order is important.

10. In the project, create a folder named `Controls`.

11. In the `Controls` folder, add a class file named `ThemeEnum.cs`, and define an enum type with three values: `System`, `Light`, and `Dark`, for selecting themes, as shown in the following code:

```csharp
namespace Northwind.Maui.Client.Controls;

public enum Theme
{
  System,
  Light,
  Dark
}
```

12. In the `Controls` folder, add a class file named `EnumPicker.cs`, and define a class that inherits from the `Picker` control that can be bound to any enum type and show a dropdown list of its values, as shown in the following code:

```csharp
using System.Reflection; // To use GetTypeInfo method.

namespace Northwind.Maui.Client.Controls;

public class EnumPicker : Picker
{
  public Type EnumType
  {
    set => SetValue(EnumTypeProperty, value);
    get => (Type)GetValue(EnumTypeProperty);
```

```
    }

    public static readonly BindableProperty EnumTypeProperty =
      BindableProperty.Create(
        propertyName: nameof(EnumType),
        returnType: typeof(Type),
        declaringType: typeof(EnumPicker),
        propertyChanged: (bindable, oldValue, newValue) =>
      {
        EnumPicker picker = (EnumPicker)bindable;

        if (oldValue != null)
        {
          picker.ItemsSource = null;
        }

        if (newValue != null)
        {
          if (!((Type)newValue).GetTypeInfo().IsEnum)
            throw new ArgumentException(
              "EnumPicker: EnumType property must be enumeration type");

          picker.ItemsSource = Enum.GetValues((Type)newValue);
        }
      });
    }
```

13. In `SettingsPage.xaml`, import a local namespace for using our custom `EnumPicker` control, an `ios` namespace for adding a special property that only applies to iOS apps, change the `Title` to `Settings`, and create an instance of `EnumPicker` for selecting a theme, as shown highlighted in the following markup:

```xml
<?xml version="1.0" encoding="utf-8" ?>
<ContentPage xmlns="http://schemas.microsoft.com/dotnet/2021/maui"
             xmlns:x="http://schemas.microsoft.com/winfx/2009/xaml"
             xmlns:local="clr-namespace:Northwind.Maui.Client.Controls"
             xmlns:ios="clr-namespace:Microsoft.Maui.Controls.
PlatformConfiguration.iOSSpecific;assembly=Microsoft.Maui.Controls"
             x:Class="Northwind.Maui.Client.SettingsPage"
             Title="Settings">

  <VerticalStackLayout HorizontalOptions="Center">
```

```
        <local:EnumPicker ios:Picker.UpdateMode="WhenFinished"
                          EnumType="{x:Type local:Theme}"
                          Title="Select Theme"
                          SelectedIndexChanged="ThemePicker_SelectionChanged"
                          Loaded="ThemePicker_Loaded"
                          x:Name="ThemePicker" />
    </VerticalStackLayout>
</ContentPage>
```

14. In SettingsPage.xaml.cs, add statements to handle the events for the picker, as shown highlighted in the following code:

```
using Northwind.Maui.Client.Controls; // To use enum Theme.
using Northwind.Maui.Client.Resources.Styles; // To use DarkModeTheme.

namespace Northwind.Maui.Client;

public partial class SettingsPage : ContentPage
{
  public SettingsPage()
  {
    InitializeComponent();
  }

  private void ThemePicker_SelectionChanged(object sender, EventArgs e)
  {
    Picker picker = sender as Picker;
    Theme theme = (Theme)picker.SelectedItem;

    ICollection<ResourceDictionary> resources =
      Application.Current.Resources.MergedDictionaries;

    if (resources is not null)
    {
      resources.Clear();
```

```
    resources.Add(new Resources.Styles.Northwind());
    resources.Add(new LightDarkModeColors());


    ResourceDictionary themeResource = theme switch
    {
      Theme.Dark  => new DarkModeTheme(),
      Theme.Light => new LightModeTheme(),
      _           => new SystemModeTheme()
    };


    resources.Add(themeResource);
  }
}


private void ThemePicker_Loaded(object sender, EventArgs e)
{
  ThemePicker.SelectedItem = Theme.System;
}
}
```

15. Start the `Northwind.Maui.Client` project with at least one desktop and mobile device.

16. Note that the colors and shape of the button on the home page are in light mode, as shown on a **Window** machine in *Figure 16.11*:

Figure 16.11: Light mode button on Windows

17. Leave the app running, start the Windows **Settings** app, navigate to **Personalization | Colors,** and in the **Choose your mode** section, select **Dark,** as shown in *Figure 16.12:*

Figure 16.12: Switching the system color mode in Windows Settings

18. Leave **Settings** open, switch back to the app, and note that it has dynamically switched to dark mode colors, as shown in *Figure 16.13:*

Figure 16.13: Dark mode in our app

19. Close the app.

20. In **Settings,** switch back to **Light** mode.

Good Practice: A resource can be an instance of any object. To share it within an application, define it in the `App.xaml` file and give it a unique key. To set an element's property with a resource once when the app first starts, use `{StaticResource key}`. To set an element's property with a resource whenever the resource value changes during the lifetime of the app, use `{DynamicResource key}`. To load a resource using code, use the `TryGetValue` method of the `Resources` property. If you treat the `Resources` property as a dictionary and use array-style syntax, like `Resources[key]`, it will only find resources defined directly in the dictionary, not in any merged dictionaries.

Resources can be defined and stored inside any element of XAML, not just at the app level. For example, if a resource is only needed on `MainPage`, then it can be defined there. You can also dynamically load XAML files at runtime.

More Information: You can read more about .NET MAUI resource dictionaries at the following link: `https://learn.microsoft.com/en-us/dotnet/maui/fundamentals/resource-dictionaries`. In particular, note the section about resource lookup behavior.

Using data binding

When building graphical UIs, you will often want to bind a property of one control to another, or to some data.

Binding to elements

The simplest type of binding is between two elements. One element acts as a source for a value and the other elements acts as the target.

Let's take the following steps:

1. In `CategoriesPage.xaml`, under the existing button in the vertical stack layout, add a label for instructions, another label to show the current degree of rotation, a slider for selecting a rotation, and a rainbow square to rotate, as shown highlighted in the following markup:

```
<?xml version="1.0" encoding="utf-8" ?>
<ContentPage xmlns="http://schemas.microsoft.com/dotnet/2021/maui"
             xmlns:x="http://schemas.microsoft.com/winfx/2009/xaml"
             x:Class="Northwind.Maui.Client.CategoriesPage"
             Background="{StaticResource Rainbow}"
             Title="Categories">

  <VerticalStackLayout>

    <Button Text="Click Me" WidthRequest="100"
            x:Name="ClickMeButton"
```

```
              Clicked="ClickMeButton_Clicked" />

    <Label Margin="10">
      Use the slider to rotate the square:
    </Label>

    <Label BindingContext="{x:Reference Name=SliderRotation}"
           Text="{Binding Path=Value, StringFormat='{0:N0} degrees'}"
           FontSize="30" HorizontalTextAlignment="Center" />

    <Slider Value="0" Minimum="0" Maximum="180"
            x:Name="SliderRotation" Margin="10,0" />

    <Rectangle HeightRequest="200" WidthRequest="200"
               Fill="{StaticResource Rainbow}"
               BindingContext="{x:Reference Name=SliderRotation}"
               Rotation="{Binding Path=Value}" />

  </VerticalStackLayout>

</ContentPage>
```

 Note that the text of the label and the angle of the rotation of the rectangle are both bound to the slider's value using a binding context and the {Binding} markup extension.

2. Start the Northwind.Maui.Client project.
3. Navigate to the **Categories** page.

4. Click and pull the slider to change the rotation of the rainbow square, as shown in *Figure 16.14*:

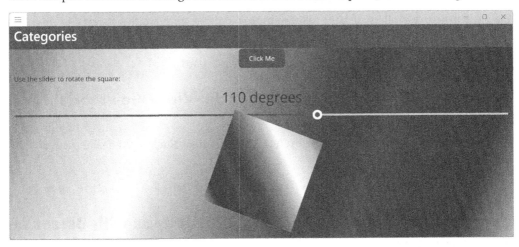

Figure 16.14: A slider data bound to a label and the rotation of a rectangle on Windows

5. Close the app.

Practicing and exploring

Test your knowledge and understanding by answering some questions, getting some hands-on practice, and exploring this chapter's topics with more in-depth research.

Exercise 16.1 – Test your knowledge

Answer the following questions:

1. What are the four categories of .NET MAUI UI components, and what do they represent?
2. What is the benefit of the `Shell` component and what kinds of UI does it implement?
3. How can you enable a user to perform an action on a cell in a list view?
4. When would you use an `Entry` instead of an `Editor`?
5. What is the effect of setting `IsDestructive` to `true` for a menu item in a cell's context actions?
6. You have defined a `Shell` with a content page, but no navigation is shown. Why might this be?
7. What is the difference between `Margin` and `Padding` for an element like a `Button`?
8. How are event handlers attached to an object using XAML?
9. What do XAML styles do?
10. Where can you define resources?

Exercise 16.2 – Explore topics

Use the links on the following page to learn more detail about the topics covered in this chapter:

```
https://github.com/markjprice/apps-services-net8/blob/main/docs/book-links.md#chapter-
16---building-mobile-and-desktop-apps-using-net-maui
```

Exercise 16.3 – Implementing Model-View-ViewModel for .NET MAUI

In this online-only section, you will learn how to implement the MVVM design pattern with a .NET MAUI app:

```
https://github.com/markjprice/apps-services-net8/blob/main/docs/ch16-mvvm.md
```

Exercise 16.4 – Integrating .NET MAUI apps with Blazor and native platforms

In this online-only section, you will learn how to integrate a .NET MAUI app with native mobile features:

```
https://github.com/markjprice/apps-services-net8/blob/main/docs/ch16-maui-blazor.md
```

Summary

In this chapter, you learned:

- How to build a cross-platform mobile and desktop app using .NET MAUI.
- How to define shared resources and reference them.
- How to use data binding with common controls.

In the *Epilogue*, you will learn how to continue your learning journey with apps and services for .NET.

Epilogue

I wanted this book to be different from the others on the market. I hope that you found it to be a brisk, fun read, packed with practical, hands-on walkthroughs of each subject.

This epilogue contains the following short sections:

- Cloud-native development using .NET Aspire
- Introducing the Survey Project Challenge
- Third edition coming in December 2025
- Next steps on your C# and .NET learning journey
- Good luck!

Cloud-native development using .NET Aspire

In this book you have seen lots of technologies that are used to build cloud-native applications, like gRPC for efficient communication between services, caching of various types, and fault tolerance using Polly.

As you implement more and more of these technologies, managing your development environment gets harder and harder. Connection strings, secret keys, port numbers, rate limiting, and caching configurations: if any are wrong, things break, or work in unexpected ways, and it can be hard to identify and then fix the issue.

At .NET Conf 2023 on November 14, 2023, the .NET team announced a new product: **.NET Aspire**. It is currently available in preview and the team plan to release version 1.0 in the spring of 2024.

 If you want to try out the preview, then when installing Visual Studio 2022 version 17.9 Preview 1 or later, make sure to select **.NET Aspire SDK (Preview)** under the **Individual components** tab.

As stated in the official announcement blog article, .NET Aspire "is an opinionated stack for building resilient, observable, and configurable cloud-native applications with .NET."

It provides the following:

- **Aspire components:** Based on existing mature technologies like Redis and OpenTelemetry, but wrapped in Aspire-specific packages that provide quick and easy configuration, Aspire components provide standardized functionality including service discovery, telemetry, resilience, and health checks.

- **Aspire Starter and Empty project templates:** These will get you started with a working solution to try out Aspire features. The starter solution includes several projects: a Blazor app front-end for a dashboard to monitor all the services and apps you build, a back-end web API, a shared project for setting defaults that will apply to all projects, and an Aspire host to manage everything.

- **Aspire Orchestration:** This provides features to run and connect complex multi-project applications and their dependencies. Custom extension methods are written for you to configure all the components in your projects following best practices, but you can change them if you have special requirements.

If you want to learn more about .NET Aspire, you can read the documentation at the following link:

```
https://learn.microsoft.com/en-us/dotnet/aspire/
```

I plan to write a chapter about .NET Aspire in the third book of my .NET 8 trilogy, *Tools and Skills for .NET 8 Pros*, which we plan to publish in the first half of 2024.

Introducing the Survey Project Challenge

To help us learn all the different technologies that .NET developers need to know these days, it would be great to attempt to implement a project that needs a mix of technologies and skills. It should be as real as possible, be cool, fun, and practical, and have already been implemented by others with public products that we can be inspired by.

The Survey Project Challenge is an optional complete project with a common set of problems that will give you a real-world set of projects to build. You can read more about it at the following link:

```
https://github.com/markjprice/apps-services-net8/blob/main/docs/ch17-survey-project.md
```

Third edition coming in December 2025

I have already started work on identifying areas for improvement for the next edition, which we plan to publish about a month after the **general availability** (GA) release of .NET 10 in November 2025. While I do not expect major new features at the level of the unification of the Blazor hosting models, I do expect .NET 9 and .NET 10 to make worthwhile improvements to all aspects of .NET.

If you have suggestions for topics that you would like to see covered or expanded upon, or you spot mistakes that need fixing in the text or code, then please find me on the Discord channel for this book for a live interaction or let me know the details via the GitHub repository for this book, found at the following link:

```
https://github.com/markjprice/apps-services-net8
```

Next steps on your C# and .NET learning journey

There is never enough space in a book written for print to include everything one might want. For subjects that you want to learn more about, I hope that the notes, good practice tips, and links in the GitHub repository point you in the right direction:

```
https://github.com/markjprice/apps-services-net8/blob/main/docs/book-links.md
```

Companion books to continue your learning journey

Soon, I will have written a trilogy of books to continue your learning journey with .NET 8. The two other books act as companions to this book:

1. The first book covers the fundamentals of C#, .NET, ASP.NET Core, and Blazor for web development.

2. The second book (the one you're reading now) covers more specialized libraries, services, and graphical user interfaces for websites and desktop and mobile apps with Blazor and .NET MAUI.

3. The third book covers important tools and skills you should learn to become a well-rounded professional .NET developer. These include design patterns and solution architecture, debugging, memory analysis, all the important types of testing, from unit to performance and web and mobile, and then hosting and deployment topics like Docker and Azure Pipelines. Finally, it looks at how to prepare for an interview to get the .NET developer job that you want.

A summary of the .NET 8 trilogy and their most important topics is shown in *Figure 17.1*:

- **C# language**, including new C# 12 features, object-oriented programming, debugging, and unit testing.
- **.NET libraries**, including numbers, text, regular expressions, collections, file I/O, and data with EF Core and SQLite.
- **Websites and web services** with ASP.NET Core and Blazor.

- **More libraries**: Internationalization, multitasking, and third-party packages.
- **More data**: SQL Server and Cosmos DB.
- **More services**: Minimal APIs, caching, queuing, GraphQL, gRPC, SignalR, and Azure Functions.
- **More user interfaces**: ASP.NET Core MVC, Blazor, and .NET MAUI.

- **Tools**: IDEs, debugging, memory analysis, and AI assistants.
- **Testing**: Unit, integration, performance, system, and web, including DI and IoC.
- **Design**: Patterns and architecture.
- **Deploy**: Continuous Integration/ Deployment, and Azure hosting.
- **Career**: Interview preparation.

Figure 17.1: Companion books for learning C# and .NET

Tools and Skills for .NET 8 Pros is scheduled to be published in the first half of 2024. Look out for it in your favorite bookstore to complete your .NET 8 trilogy.

To see a list of all the books that I have published with Packt, you can use the following link:

```
https://subscription.packtpub.com/search?query=mark+j.+price
```

Other books to take your learning further

If you are looking for other books from my publisher that cover related subjects, there are many to choose from, as shown in *Figure 17.2*:

Figure 17.2: Packt books to take your apps and services with .NET learning further

Good luck!

I wish you the best of luck with all your .NET projects!

Share your thoughts

Now you've finished *Apps and Services with .NET 8 - Second Edition*, we'd love to hear your thoughts! Scan the QR code below to go straight to the Amazon review page for this book and share your feedback or leave a review on the site that you purchased it from.

https://packt.link/r/1-837-63713-X

Your review is important to us and the tech community and will help us make sure we're delivering excellent quality content.

Index

Download a free PDF copy of this book

Thanks for purchasing this book!

Do you like to read on the go but are unable to carry your print books everywhere? Is your eBook purchase not compatible with the device of your choice?

Don't worry, now with every Packt book you get a DRM-free PDF version of that book at no cost.

Read anywhere, any place, on any device. Search, copy, and paste code from your favorite technical books directly into your application.

The perks don't stop there, you can get exclusive access to discounts, newsletters, and great free content in your inbox daily

Follow these simple steps to get the benefits:

1. Scan the QR code or visit the link below

https://packt.link/free-ebook/9781837637133

2. Submit your proof of purchase
3. That's it! We'll send your free PDF and other benefits to your email directly